New Trends in Long-Life Road Infrastructures: Materials and Structures

New Trends in Long-Life Road Infrastructures: Materials and Structures

Guest Editors

**Jue Li
Junhui Zhang
Junfeng Gao
Junhui Peng
Wensheng Wang**

Basel • Beijing • Wuhan • Barcelona • Belgrade • Novi Sad • Cluj • Manchester

Guest Editors

Jue Li
College of Traffic & Transportation
Chongqing Jiaotong University
Chongqing
China

Junhui Zhang
School of Traffic & Transportation Engineering
Changsha University of Science & Technology
Changsha
China

Junfeng Gao
College of Materials Science and Engineering
Chongqing Jiaotong University
Chongqing
China

Junhui Peng
School of Traffic & Transportation Engineering
Changsha University of Science & Technology
Changsha
China

Wensheng Wang
College of Transportation
Jilin University
Changchun
China

Editorial Office
MDPI AG
Grosspeteranlage 5
4052 Basel, Switzerland

This is a reprint of the Special Issue, published open access by the journal *Applied Sciences* (ISSN 2076-3417), freely accessible at: https://www.mdpi.com/journal/applsci/special_issues/7B2P310BO6.

For citation purposes, cite each article independently as indicated on the article page online and as indicated below:

Lastname, A.A.; Lastname, B.B. Article Title. *Journal Name* **Year**, *Volume Number*, Page Range.

ISBN 978-3-7258-2987-3 (Hbk)
ISBN 978-3-7258-2988-0 (PDF)
https://doi.org/10.3390/books978-3-7258-2988-0

© 2025 by the authors. Articles in this book are Open Access and distributed under the Creative Commons Attribution (CC BY) license. The book as a whole is distributed by MDPI under the terms and conditions of the Creative Commons Attribution-NonCommercial-NoDerivs (CC BY-NC-ND) license (https://creativecommons.org/licenses/by-nc-nd/4.0/).

Contents

Jue Li, Junhui Zhang, Junfeng Gao, Junhui Peng and Wensheng Wang
New Trends in Long-Life Road Infrastructures: Materials and Structures
Reprinted from: *Appl. Sci.* 2024, *14*, 7984, https://doi.org/10.3390/app14177984 1

Xiaobo Du, Hongwei Lin, Mutian Sun, Wenchang Liu and Hongchao Zhang
Field Compaction Characteristics of Ultra-Thin Porous Friction Course Based on Laboratory Simulation
Reprinted from: *Appl. Sci.* 2024, *14*, 5489, https://doi.org/10.3390/app14135489 7

Yihua Nie, Qing Liu, Zhiheng Xiang, Shixiong Zhong and Xinyao Huang
Performance and Modification Mechanism of Recycled Glass Fiber of Wind Turbine Blades and SBS Composite-Modified Asphalt
Reprinted from: *Appl. Sci.* 2023, *13*, 6335, https://doi.org/10.3390/app13106335 23

Jiawang Zhou, Kui Hu, Junfeng Gao, Yujing Chen, Qilin Yang and Xiaotong Du
Study on the Properties and Mechanism of Recycled Aggregate/Asphalt Interface Modified by Silane Coupling Agent
Reprinted from: *Appl. Sci.* 2023, *13*, 10343, https://doi.org/10.3390/app131810343 41

Minghao Mu, Chaochao Liu and Zhengnan Liu
Laboratory Investigation of the Composite Influence of Rock Asphalt and Montmorillonite on the Performance of Bio-Asphalt
Reprinted from: *Appl. Sci.* 2023, *13*, 5174, https://doi.org/10.3390/app13085174 61

Shuyao Yang, Zhigang Zhou and Kai Li
Experimental Study on the Cracking Resistance of Asphalt Mixture with Different Degrees of Aging
Reprinted from: *Appl. Sci.* 2023, *13*, 8578, https://doi.org/10.3390/app13158578 81

Zhengnan Liu, Rui Zhang, Tian Lan, Yu Zhou and Chao Huang
Laboratory Test and Constitutive Model for Quantifying the Anisotropic Swelling Behavior of Expansive Soils
Reprinted from: *Appl. Sci.* 2024, *14*, 2255, https://doi.org/10.3390/app14062255 107

Ziying Huang, Sen Cai, Rongfen Hu, Jianfeng Wang, Mingjie Jiang and Jian Gong
Investigation of the Effect of Relative Density on the Dynamic Modulus and Damping Ratio for Coarse Grained Soil
Reprinted from: *Appl. Sci.* 2024, *14*, 6847, https://doi.org/10.3390/app14156847 126

Wei Wang, Wei Hu and Shunkai Liu
An Investigation of Particle Motion and Energy Dissipation Mechanisms in Soil–Rock Mixtures with Varying Mixing Degrees under Vibratory Compaction
Reprinted from: *Appl. Sci.* 2023, *13*, 11359, https://doi.org/10.3390/app132011359 136

Zong-Tang Zhang, Yan-Hao Wang, Wen-Hua Gao, Wei Hu and Shun-Kai Liu
Permanent Deformation and Its Unified Model of Coal Gangue Subgrade Filler under Traffic Cyclic Loading
Reprinted from: *Appl. Sci.* 2023, *13*, 4128, https://doi.org/10.3390/app13074128 152

Jinli Zhang, Hai Li, Junhui Peng and Zhe Zhang
Effects of Lime Content on Road Performance of Low Liquid Limit Clay
Reprinted from: *Appl. Sci.* 2023, *13*, 8377, https://doi.org/10.3390/app13148377 168

Zhijie Chen, Maohui Li and Lei Guan
Safety and Effect of Fly Ash Content on Mechanical Properties and Microstructure of Green Low-Carbon Concrete
Reprinted from: *Appl. Sci.* **2024**, *14*, 2796, https://doi.org/10.3390/app14072796 . . . . **181**

Ming Lei, Jin Chang, Jianqing Jiang and Rui Zhang
Discussing the Negative Pressure Distribution Mode in Vacuum-Preloaded Soft Foundation Drainage Structures: A Numerical Study
Reprinted from: *Appl. Sci.* **2023**, *13*, 6297, https://doi.org/10.3390/app13106297 . . . . **194**

Fengbing Zhao, Bo Liang, Ningyu Zhao and Bolin Jiang
Shaking Table Testing and Numerical Study on Aseismic Measures of Twin-Tube Tunnel Crossing Fault Zone with Extra-Large Section
Reprinted from: *Appl. Sci.* **2024**, *14*, 2391, https://doi.org/10.3390/app14062391 . . . . **208**

Weijian Jiang, Wen Yi, Lei Zhou
Fibre-Microbial Curing Tests and Slope Stability Analysis
Reprinted from: *Appl. Sci.* **2023**, *13*, 7051, https://doi.org/10.3390/app13127051 . . . . **231**

Zhigang Ma and Xuefeng Li
Experiments on the State Boundary Surface of Aeolian Sand for Road Building in the Tengger Desert
Reprinted from: *Appl. Sci.* **2023**, *13*, 879, https://doi.org/10.3390/app13020879 . . . . **246**

Ying Xu, Xixin Shi and Yongsheng Yao
Performance Assessment of Existing Asphalt Pavement in China's Highway Reconstruction and Expansion Project Based on Coupling Weighting Method and Cloud Model Theory
Reprinted from: *Appl. Sci.* **2024**, *14*, 5789, https://doi.org/10.3390/app14135789 . . . . **260**

Hui Wei, Yunyao Liu, Jue Li, Lihao Liu and Honglin Liu
Reliability Investigation of Pavement Performance Evaluation Based on Blind-Number Theory: A Confidence Model
Reprinted from: *Appl. Sci.* **2023**, *13*, 8794, https://doi.org/10.3390/app13158794 . . . . **276**

Laura N. Mazzoni, Kamilla Vasconcelos, Orlando Albarracín, Liedi Bernucci and Guilherme Linhares
Field Data Analysis of Pavement Marking Retroreflectivity and Its Relationship with Paint and Glass Bead Characteristics
Reprinted from: *Appl. Sci.* **2024**, *14*, 4205, https://doi.org/10.3390/app14104205 . . . . **290**

Weiwei Wang, Wen Xiang, Cheng Li, Songli Qiu, Yujin Wang, Xuhao Wang, et al.
A Case Study of Pavement Foundation Support and Drainage Evaluations of Damaged Urban Cement Concrete Roads
Reprinted from: *Appl. Sci.* **2024**, *14*, 1791, https://doi.org/10.3390/app14051791 . . . . **307**

Chao Han, Jiuda Huang, Xu Yang, Lili Chen and Tao Chen
Long-Term Maintenance Planning Method of Rural Roads under Limited Budget: A Case Study of Road Network
Reprinted from: *Appl. Sci.* **2023**, *13*, 12661, https://doi.org/10.3390/app132312661 . . . . **324**

Jue Li, Wenwei Bi, Yongsheng Yao and Zhengnan Liu
State-of-the-Art Review of Utilization of Microbial-Induced Calcite Precipitation for Improving Moisture-Dependent Properties of Unsaturated Soils
Reprinted from: *Appl. Sci.* **2023**, *13*, 2502, https://doi.org/10.3390/app13042502 . . . . **342**

Editorial

New Trends in Long-Life Road Infrastructures: Materials and Structures

Jue Li [1,*], Junhui Zhang [2], Junfeng Gao [3], Junhui Peng [2,*] and Wensheng Wang [4]

1. College of Traffic & Transportation, Chongqing Jiaotong University, Chongqing 400074, China
2. School of Traffic & Transportation Engineering, Changsha University of Science & Technology, Changsha 410114, China; zjhseu@csust.edu.cn
3. College of Materials Science and Engineering, Chongqing Jiaotong University, Chongqing 400074, China; jfgao@cqjtu.edu.cn
4. College of Transportation, Jilin University, Changchun 130022, China; wangws@jlu.edu.cn
* Correspondence: lijue1207@cqjtu.edu.cn (J.L.); pjh@csust.edu.cn (J.P.)

1. Introduction

The development of long-life road infrastructure has become a pressing global priority, fueled by escalating demands stemming from rapid urbanization, escalating environmental concerns, and the critical necessity for sustainable, environmentally friendly transportation alternatives [1]. With global and ongoing rapid urbanization, current road networks are encountering increasing difficulty in adapting to rising traffic volumes and changing mobility needs. Concurrently, the urgent need to tackle climate change and lower the environmental impact of transportation infrastructure has underscored the importance of constructing environmentally sustainable and resilient road networks [2].

Conventional road designs and methods often fall short of meeting these evolving demands, as they tend to focus on immediate concerns and do not sufficiently prioritize enduring performance and resilience. For instance, the typical design lifespan of road pavements is often restricted to 15–20 years in China, significantly below the benchmarks established by its economic development [3]. This disparity between the existing capacities and emerging demands has instigated a coordinated endeavor to transform the materials, structures, and technologies utilized in the creation and upkeep of road infrastructure.

The quest for long-life road infrastructures has driven researchers and practitioners worldwide to explore innovative approaches that can enhance the performance, serviceability, and sustainability of road systems. The key areas include the development of advanced eco-friendly materials with superior durability [4], the design of resilient structural systems capable of withstanding escalating demands [5], and the integration of cutting-edge numerical and intelligent technologies to optimize the performance and life-cycle management of road networks [6].

In the materials domain, significant advancements have been made in the development of novel cementitious, asphalt, and composite materials that can offer improved strength, flexibility, and resistance to the environmental degradation of road infrastructures [7]. The incorporation of supplementary cementitious materials, such as fly ash and slag, has demonstrated the potential to enhance the sustainability and long-term durability of concrete-based road infrastructures [8]. Similarly, the utilization of modified asphalt binders and renewable aggregates has shown promise in improving the performance and service life of flexible pavement systems [9,10].

Alongside materials innovation, researchers have also dedicated effort to the enhancement of structural design and analysis capabilities. The integration of advanced numerical modeling techniques, including finite element analysis and discrete element modeling, has enabled a deeper understanding of the complex behavior of road structures under various loading and environmental conditions. This, in turn, has facilitated the development of

Citation: Li, J.; Zhang, J.; Gao, J.; Peng, J.; Wang, W. New Trends in Long-Life Road Infrastructures: Materials and Structures. *Appl. Sci.* **2024**, *14*, 7984. https://doi.org/10.3390/app14177984

Received: 5 August 2024
Revised: 27 August 2024
Accepted: 5 September 2024
Published: 6 September 2024

Copyright: © 2024 by the authors. Licensee MDPI, Basel, Switzerland. This article is an open access article distributed under the terms and conditions of the Creative Commons Attribution (CC BY) license (https://creativecommons.org/licenses/by/4.0/).

optimized structural designs that can withstand the demands of increased traffic, climate change, and natural hazards better.

In summary, the convergence of these technological innovations, combined with a holistic emphasis on sustainability and life-cycle performance, has set the stage for a new era in road infrastructure development. This book, titled *New Trends in Long-Life Road Infrastructures: Materials and Structures*, aims to showcase the latest research and advancements in this critical field, providing a platform for the dissemination of cutting-edge knowledge and the exploration of transformative solutions. By advancing our understanding of material behavior, structural performance, and life-cycle management strategies, these research findings can inform the design, construction, and maintenance of more durable, eco-friendly, and adaptable road infrastructures.

2. An Overview of Published Articles

From the Special Issue on "New Trends in Long-Life Road Infrastructures: Materials and Structures", this book features a diverse collection of 20 state-of-the-art research contributions and 1 comprehensive review article. The articles collected in this book span a wide range of topics, including material characterization, structural behavior, performance assessment, and maintenance planning, all aimed at advancing the state of the art in long-life road infrastructure design and construction.

Contribution 1 investigated the field compaction properties of ultra-thin, porous friction course (UPFC) mixtures designed using the Marshall compaction method. Through laboratory simulation and virtual compaction tests, the researchers revealed significant differences between the laboratory and field compaction characteristics of UPFC, highlighting the need for more appropriate design methods to ensure adequate field performance.

Contribution 2 investigated the effects of modification with glass fiber recycled from wind turbine blades on SBS-modified asphalt and their mechanisms. This study evaluated the performance of the GF-WTB/SBS composite-modified asphalt and explored the underlying modification mechanisms.

Contribution 3 investigated the use of a silane coupling agent to enhance the adhesion properties between recycled concrete aggregates (RCAs) and asphalt. The researchers examined the macroscopic properties, interfacial microstructure, and nanoscale interactions to elucidate the mechanism by which the silane coupling agent improved the RCA/asphalt interface, contributing to the development of sustainable asphalt mixtures.

Contribution 4 explored the use of a composite modifier of rock asphalt and montmorillonite to improve the rutting resistance and anti-aging performance of bio-asphalt. This study determined the optimum content of the components and evaluated the rheological properties and anti-aging performance of the modified bio-asphalt.

Contribution 5 investigated the effect of thermo-oxidative aging and the test temperature on the cracking resistance of asphalt mixtures. The researchers analyzed the stress–strain curves and evaluation indexes of asphalt mixtures with different aging degrees and at test temperatures.

Contribution 6 explored the anisotropic swelling characteristics of expansive soils. The researchers developed a nonlinear elastic constitutive model that incorporated the directionally dependent swelling behavior, providing practical tools for assessing the pressures exerted by expansive soils more comprehensively and guiding their utilization and design.

Contribution 7 presents an extensive examination of the dynamic elastic modulus and damping ratio of coarse-grained soils under varying relative densities. The researchers conducted dynamic triaxial tests to reveal the complex relationships between these critical dynamic parameters and the relative density of the soil, providing valuable insights for geotechnical engineering applications.

Contribution 8 explored the effect of mixing homogeneity on the compaction of soil–rock mixtures using the discrete element method. Analysis of the particle motion and energy dissipation mechanisms revealed the critical role of rolling slip energy dissipation in promoting compaction, offering insights for improving the compaction of heterogeneous granular materials.

Contribution 9 investigated the permanent deformation of coal gangue subgrade filler under cyclic loading. This study examined the effects of the confining pressure, grading, and compaction degree on permanent deformation and proposed a unified calculation model for the permanent deformation of coal gangue subgrade filler.

Contribution 10 examined the influence of lime content on the road performance of low liquid limit clay. This study used a limit water content test, a compaction test, and the California bearing ratio test to evaluate the improvements in the basic properties of the subgrade soil after adding lime.

Contribution 11 investigated the use of high volumes of fly ash in the development of high-performance, low-carbon concrete. Through compressive strength, flexural strength, and microscopic tests, the researchers demonstrated the beneficial effects of fly ash on the mechanical properties and microstructure of the concrete, contributing to the promotion of green and sustainable construction materials.

Contribution 12 aimed to clarify the negative pressure distribution in drainage structures of soft foundations reinforced by vacuum preloading. This study established numerical models to analyze the consolidation process of the soft foundation and the distribution of negative pressure in the drainage structure.

Contribution 13 focused on enhancing the seismic resilience of tunnels crossing active fault zones. The researchers conducted large-scale shake table tests and numerical simulations to analyze the seismic responses of a twin-tube tunnel and evaluate the effectiveness of various mitigation measures, such as rock grouting and shock absorption layers, in reducing the amplified seismic demands caused by fault zones.

Contribution 14 explored the effect of combining fiber reinforcement and microbial curing technologies to enhance the deformation resistance and toughness of the soil. This study analyzed the effects of basalt fibers on the strength and toughness of microbial consolidated soil and the stability of the reinforced slope.

Contribution 15 used critical state soil mechanics to study the mechanical properties of Aeolian sand, a special road-building material in desert areas. This study conducted a series of triaxial compression tests to obtain the three-dimensional state boundary surface of the Aeolian sand and provided a basis for constitutive modeling and a reference for road construction in desert areas.

Contribution 16 developed a novel normal cloud framework for a holistic evaluation of the performance of existing asphalt pavements. The researchers integrated a comprehensive weighted indicator system and a cloud model approach to address the fuzziness and randomness inherent in pavement condition data, offering a more sensitive and accurate assessment tool for highway reconstruction and expansion projects.

Contribution 17 introduced a novel approach that employed blind number theory to evaluate the reliability of pavement performance test data. The proposed method aimed to enhance the representativeness of the Pavement Quality Index (PQI) and was demonstrated using detection data on highway asphalt pavements.

Contribution 18 explored the influence of the properties of paint and glass beads on the retroreflectivity performance of pavement markings. By analyzing field data from three test sites, the researchers developed a statistical model that identified the key characteristics with the greatest impact on the retroreflectivity of pavement markings, offering valuable insights for their improved durability and safety.

Contribution 19 investigated the causes of accelerated damage to urban cement concrete pavements. Through field evaluations, including visual inspections, ground-penetrating radar surveys, and permeability tests, the researchers identified the critical roles of an inadequate subgrade bearing capacity and poor drainage conditions in the premature deterioration of urban concrete roads, offering insights for improved pavement foundation design and maintenance.

Contribution 20 focused on the challenges in maintaining and managing rural road networks in China under limited budgets. The researchers proposed an evaluation framework, performance prediction models, and an optimization method for developing cost-effective long-term maintenance strategies for rural roads, providing a theoretical basis for the scientific management of these critical transportation assets.

In Contribution 21, this review discussed the microscopic mechanisms of microbial-induced calcite precipitation (MICP) and its effects on the mechanical properties of unsaturated soils, highlighting the influence of MICP on the moisture-dependent properties of unsaturated soils.

3. Conclusions

The collection of articles presented in this book showcases the latest advancements in the research on long-life road infrastructures, covering a wide range of topics, from materials and structures to performance evaluation and modeling.

The research on evaluating the performance of pavements using blind number theory and confidence models demonstrates an innovative approach to quantifying the reliability of pavement data, which can aid in more accurate and representative assessments of overall pavement quality. Studies on the cracking resistance and aging behavior of asphalt mixtures provide important insights into the durability of road surfaces under various environmental conditions.

Investigations into the use of alternative materials, such as low liquid limit clay stabilized with lime and glass fiber recycled from wind turbine blades, highlight the potential for sustainable and cost-effective solutions in road infrastructure construction. Techniques like fiber–microbial curing and the utilization of coal gangue as subgrade filler also show promise in enhancing the mechanical properties and long-term performance of road structures.

Fundamental research on the mechanical behaviors of specialized geotechnical materials, including Aeolian sand in desert environments and the moisture-dependent properties of unsaturated soils, contributes to a better understanding of the unique challenges faced in different geographical and geological settings. The models proposed and the experimental findings obtained in these studies can inform the design and construction of long-life road infrastructures.

Overall, the articles in this Special Issue demonstrate the multidisciplinary nature of the research in the field of long-life road infrastructures, encompassing advances in materials science, geotechnical engineering, and innovative evaluation and modeling techniques. The knowledge and insights gained from these studies will undoubtedly contribute to the development of more sustainable, durable, and efficient road systems that can withstand the demands of modern transportation networks.

Author Contributions: Conceptualization, J.L., J.Z., J.G., J.P. and W.W.; formal analysis, J.Z.; writing—original draft preparation, J.L. and J.G.; writing—review and editing, J.P. and W.W.; project administration, J.L.; funding acquisition, J.L. and J.G. All authors have read and agreed to the published version of the manuscript.

Funding: This research was funded by the Scientific and Technological Research Program of Chongqing Municipal Education Commission, grant number KJQN20230074, and the Natural Science Foundation of Chongqing, grant numbers CSTB2024NSCQ-MSX1177, CSTB2022NSCQ-MSX0851; the Henan Province Science and Key Technologies Research and Development Program Project, grant number 232102241009.

Acknowledgments: Thanks to all the authors and peer reviewers for their valuable contributions to this Special Issue titled "New Trends in Long-Life Road Infrastructures: Materials and Structures". We would also like to express our gratitude to all the staff and people involved in this Special Issue.

Conflicts of Interest: The authors declare no conflicts of interest.

List of Contributions

1. Du, X.; Lin, H.; Sun, M.; Liu, W.; Zhang, H. Field Compaction Characteristics of Ultra-Thin Porous Friction Course Based on Laboratory Simulation. *Appl. Sci.* **2024**, *14*, 5489.
2. Nie, Y.; Liu, Q.; Xiang, Z.; Zhong, S.; Huang, X. Performance and Modification Mechanism of Recycled Glass Fiber of Wind Turbine Blades and SBS Composite-Modified Asphalt. *Appl. Sci.* **2023**, *13*, 6335.
3. Zhou, J.; Hu, K.; Gao, J.; Chen, Y.; Yang, Q.; Du, X. Study on the Properties and Mechanism of Recycled Aggregate/Asphalt Interface Modified by Silane Coupling Agent. *Appl. Sci.* **2023**, *13*, 10343.
4. Mu, M.; Liu, C.; Liu, Z. Laboratory Investigation of the Composite Influence of Rock Asphalt and Montmorillonite on the Performance of Bio-Asphalt. *Appl. Sci.* **2023**, *13*, 5174.
5. Yang, S.; Zhou, Z.; Li, K. Experimental Study on the Cracking Resistance of Asphalt Mixture with Different Degrees of Aging. *Appl. Sci.* **2023**, *13*, 8578.
6. Liu, Z.; Zhang, R.; Lan, T.; Zhou, Y.; Huang, C. Laboratory Test and Constitutive Model for Quantifying the Anisotropic Swelling Behavior of Expansive Soils. *Appl. Sci.* **2024**, *14*, 2255.
7. Huang, Z.; Cai, S.; Hu, R.; Wang, J.; Jiang, M.; Gong, J. Investigation of the Effect of Relative Density on the Dynamic Modulus and Damping Ratio for Coarse Grained Soil. *Appl. Sci.* **2024**, *14*, 6847.
8. Wang, W.; Hu, W.; Liu, S. An Investigation of Particle Motion and Energy Dissipation Mechanisms in Soil–Rock Mixtures with Varying Mixing Degrees under Vibratory Compaction. *Appl. Sci.* **2023**, *13*, 11359.
9. Zhang, Z.-T.; Wang, Y.-H.; Gao, W.-H.; Hu, W.; Liu, S.-K. Permanent Deformation and Its Unified Model of Coal Gangue Subgrade Filler under Traffic Cyclic Loading. *Appl. Sci.* **2023**, *13*, 4128.
10. Zhang, J.; Li, H.; Peng, J.; Zhang, Z. Effects of Lime Content on Road Performance of Low Liquid Limit Clay. *Appl. Sci.* **2023**, *13*, 8377.
11. Chen, Z.; Li, M.; Guan, L. Safety and Effect of Fly Ash Content on Mechanical Properties and Microstructure of Green Low-Carbon Concrete. *Appl. Sci.* **2024**, *14*, 2796.
12. Lei, M.; Chang, J.; Jiang, J.; Zhang, R. Discussing the Negative Pressure Distribution Mode in Vacuum-Preloaded Soft Foundation Drainage Structures: A Numerical Study. *Appl. Sci.* **2023**, *13*, 6297.
13. Zhao, F.; Liang, B.; Zhao, N.; Jiang, B. Shaking Table Testing and Numerical Study on Aseismic Measures of Twin-Tube Tunnel Crossing Fault Zone with Extra-Large Section. *Appl. Sci.* **2024**, *14*, 2391.
14. Jiang, W.; Yi, W.; Zhou, L. Fibre-Microbial Curing Tests and Slope Stability Analysis. *Appl. Sci.* **2023**, *13*, 7051.
15. Ma, Z.; Li, X. Experiments on the State Boundary Surface of Aeolian Sand for Road Building in the Tengger Desert. *Appl. Sci.* **2023**, *13*, 879.
16. Xu, Y.; Shi, X.; Yao, Y. Performance Assessment of Existing Asphalt Pavement in China's Highway Reconstruction and Expansion Project Based on Coupling Weighting Method and Cloud Model Theory. *Appl. Sci.* **2024**, *14*, 5789.
17. Wei, H.; Liu, Y.; Li, J.; Liu, L.; Liu, H. Reliability Investigation of Pavement Performance Evaluation Based on Blind-Number Theory: A Confidence Model. *Appl. Sci.* **2023**, *13*, 8794.
18. Mazzoni, L.N.; Vasconcelos, K.; Albarracín, O.; Bernucci, L.; Linhares, G. Field Data Analysis of Pavement Marking Retroreflectivity and Its Relationship with Paint and Glass Bead Characteristics. *Appl. Sci.* **2024**, *14*, 4205.
19. Wang, W.; Xiang, W.; Li, C.; Qiu, S.; Wang, Y.; Wang, X.; Bu, S.; Bian, Q. A Case Study of Pavement Foundation Support and Drainage Evaluations of Damaged Urban Cement Concrete Roads. *Appl. Sci.* **2024**, *14*, 1791.

20. Han, C.; Huang, J.; Yang, X.; Chen, L.; Chen, T. Long-Term Maintenance Planning Method of Rural Roads under Limited Budget: A Case Study of Road Network. *Appl. Sci.* **2023**, *13*, 12661.
21. Li, J.; Bi, W.; Yao, Y.; Liu, Z. State-of-the-Art Review of Utilization of Microbial-Induced Calcite Precipitation for Improving Moisture-Dependent Properties of Unsaturated Soils. *Appl. Sci.* **2023**, *13*, 2502.

References

1. Salehi, S.; Arashpour, M.; Kodikara, J.; Guppy, R. Sustainable pavement construction: A systematic literature review of environmental and economic analysis of recycled materials. *J. Clean. Prod.* **2021**, *313*, 127936. [CrossRef]
2. Blaauw, S.A.; Maina, J.W.; Mturi, G.A.; Visser, A.T. Flexible pavement performance and life cycle assessment incorporating climate change impacts. *Transp. Res. Part D Transp. Environ.* **2022**, *104*, 103203. [CrossRef]
3. Wang, L.; Wei, J.; Wu, W.; Zhang, X.; Xu, X.; Yan, X. Technical development and long-term performance observations of long-life asphalt pavement: A case study of Shandong Province. *J. Road Eng.* **2022**, *2*, 369–389. [CrossRef]
4. da Rocha, C.G.; Saldanha, R.B.; de Araújo, M.T.; Consoli, N.C. Social and environmental assessments of eco-friendly pavement alternatives. *Constr. Build. Mater.* **2022**, *325*, 126736. [CrossRef]
5. Deng, Y.; Luo, X.; Zhang, Y.; Cai, S.; Huang, K.; Shi, X.; Lytton, R.L. Determination of flexible pavement deterioration conditions using Long-Term Pavement Performance database and artificial intelligence-based finite element model updating. *Struct. Control Health Monit.* **2021**, *28*, e2671. [CrossRef]
6. Naseri, H.; Fani, A.; Golroo, A. Toward equity in large-scale network-level pavement maintenance and rehabilitation scheduling using water cycle and genetic algorithms. *Int. J. Pavement Eng.* **2022**, *23*, 1095–1107. [CrossRef]
7. Office, J.E.; Chen, J.; Dan, H.; Ding, Y.; Gao, Y.; Guo, M.; Guo, S.; Han, B.; Hong, B.; Hou, Y. New innovations in pavement materials and engineering: A review on pavement engineering research 2021. *J. Traffic Transp. Eng. (Engl. Ed.)* **2021**, *8*, 815–999.
8. Wang, Y.; Jia, J.; Cao, Q.; Gao, X. Effect of calcium formate on the compressive strength, and hydration process of cement composite containing fly ash and slag. *J. Build. Eng.* **2022**, *50*, 104133. [CrossRef]
9. Xie, T.; He, Z.; Yu, H.; Ma, Y.; Shi, C.; Zhang, C.; Ge, J.; Dai, W. Evaluation of styrene butadiene rubber asphalt modification mechanism and adhesion effect based on molecular simulation. *Fuel* **2024**, *364*, 131023. [CrossRef]
10. Li, J.; Qin, Y.; Zhang, J.; Zhang, A.; Zhang, X. Compaction and Shear Characteristics of Recycled Construction & Demolition Aggregates in Subgrade: Exploring Particle Breakage and Shape Effects. *J. Clean. Prod.* **2024**, *465*, 142776.

Disclaimer/Publisher's Note: The statements, opinions and data contained in all publications are solely those of the individual author(s) and contributor(s) and not of MDPI and/or the editor(s). MDPI and/or the editor(s) disclaim responsibility for any injury to people or property resulting from any ideas, methods, instructions or products referred to in the content.

Article

Field Compaction Characteristics of Ultra-Thin Porous Friction Course Based on Laboratory Simulation

Xiaobo Du [1], Hongwei Lin [2,3,*], Mutian Sun [3], Wenchang Liu [3,4] and Hongchao Zhang [3]

1. Postdoctoral Station of Mechanical Engineering, Tongji University, Shanghai 201804, China
2. Guangzhou Baiyun International Airport Co., Ltd., Guangzhou 510470, China
3. Key Laboratory of Road and Traffic Engineering of Ministry of Education, Tongji University, Shanghai 201804, China
4. Shanghai Fengxian Construction Development Group Co., Ltd., Shanghai 201499, China
* Correspondence: 2010750@tongji.edu.cn

Abstract: As a preventive maintenance treatment, the ultra-thin porous friction course (UPFC) has been widely recognized and used in road maintenance because of its excellent performance and cost effectiveness. The Marshall compaction method (MCM) has been adopted to design UPFC mixtures worldwide, particularly in China. However, there are few studies concerning the field compaction properties of MCM-designed UPFCs. The laboratory test results of this study from simulating on-site compaction showed that all UPFC specimens with thicknesses of less than 20 mm barely achieved the target compaction thickness, and all UPFC specimens with different thicknesses failed to meet the air void (AV) requirements of UPFC mixes designed using the MCM. According to the results of a virtual compaction test, and using the discrete element method, the strong force chains were strengthened as the UPFC thickness decreased inside the specimen, making it difficult to evenly diffuse and transfer inside the specimen and resulting in insufficient compaction of the UPFC. Furthermore, it was demonstrated that the MCM-designed UPFC specimens showed significant differences in the AV distributions along the vertical and lateral directions from those of the UPFC specimens that simulated field compaction. The UPFCs designed using the MCM had a poor correlation with field compaction.

Keywords: air void distribution; discrete element method; field compaction characteristics; ultra-thin porous friction course; X-ray computed tomography; compaction method

1. Introduction

Ultra-thin porous friction courses (UPFCs) are currently one of the most widely used maintenance preventive measures. As a typical open-grade friction course (OGFC) mixture, UPFC mainly contains fine aggregates and asphalt, which are applied to maintain the performance of road surfaces [1]. It has been demonstrated that UPFC technology is beneficial for the noise reduction and skidding resistance of road surfaces and enhances the traffic safety of drivers [2,3]. Owing to its excellent technical performance and cost effectiveness, it is currently widely used as a surface layer over highway pavements in Europe, the United States, Asia, and other regions and countries.

The full life-cycle cost of UPFCs has been comprehensively evaluated, demonstrating that they have significant economic and social benefits compared to other maintenance techniques [4–6]. To date, the materials, road performance, and engineering applications of UPFCs have been extensively studied. Son et al. developed a 4.75 mm ultra-thin SMA friction course and assessed the performance and engineering benefits of its wear process under laboratory and field conditions [7]. A high-toughness UPFC was proposed by Yu et al. according to the climatic characteristics of South China, and it has been used in more than 100 cases of road maintenance engineering owing to its excellent noise reduction, anti-skidding properties, and durability [8]. In addition, a low-carbon and sustainable cold-mixed ultra-thin asphalt overlay was proposed [9]. Another study recommended a porous ultra-thin overlay (PUTO) technology [10], and its service performance was evaluated [11]. The compaction characteristics of UPFCs have also been the focus of researchers. It is well known that compared to ordinary asphalt layers, the thickness of a UPFC is only 1–2 cm, resulting in different compaction requirements, temperature, and other conditions in the process of construction [12]. Owing to its minimal thickness, heat is easily lost, leading to a rapid temperature drop rate during the paving process, which has an adverse effect on compaction [13]. Insufficient compaction leads to air void (AV) content in the UPFC over the design range, which impairs the moisture sensitivity, fatigue life, and road performance at different temperatures of the UPFC, making it prone to aggregate peeling, loosening, and other problems [14]. Luo et al. studied the field compaction parameters of a UPFC using laboratory compaction tests based on the energy equivalent principle [13]. Similarly, a study by Suresha et al. investigated the influence of Marshall compaction efforts on the compaction characteristics of UPFCs [15]. It was found that the target mineral gradation and the traffic level are key factors in selecting the suitable compaction efforts of a UPFC mix. Norhidayah et al. focused on the AV characteristics in PUTO using X-ray CT technology [16]. The aggregate size and compaction thickness of the UPFC mix affected the particle flow during the compaction process, thereby affecting the AV characteristics and determining the compaction effect. Similarly, Alvarez et al. investigated the influence of densification on the road performance of UPFC mixes [17]. Density control of the UPFC during construction is suggested to ensure a balance between mix durability and functionality. Furthermore, the internal AV structures were analyzed between laboratory samples and UPFC field cores and it was found that significant differences existed [18]. According to ground-penetrating radar data, Wang et al. studied the thickness and density in the field compaction process of UPFCs and proposed a corresponding prediction algorithm [19]. The current research on the compaction characteristics of UPFCs has made some progress, but further studies are still needed to describe the differences in the compaction characteristics between the field and indoor compaction of UPFCs more accurately to achieve better simulations of field cores with laboratory specimens.

One of the most used design methods for UPFCs is the Marshall compaction method (MCM), particularly in China. Many studies have proven that there is a poor correlation between field cores and MCM-designed asphalt mixtures with ordinary thickness [20–22]. Laboratory UPFC specimens molded via the MCM are 2.5 to 6 times thicker than the actual paving thickness of the UPFCs. The difference in thickness inevitably leads to different compaction characteristics of the UPFC, which have different effects on its volume parameters. If a MCM-designed UPFC cannot reflect the actual compaction condition, the performance evaluation of the UPFC will deviate significantly from that of the actual pavement. Therefore, it cannot contribute to accurate guidance for the application of thin-layer overlays [23,24]. Currently, no studies have used field compaction tests to verify MCM-designed UPFC mixes. There may also be a poor relationship between the MCM-designed UPFC specimens and the field core samples. Considering that the paving thickness of a UPFC is only 1–2 cm, more research on the correlation assessment of the compaction characteristics between on-site compaction and the MCM is required.

The development of nondestructive technologies, especially image analysis and X-ray CT, has enabled road workers to thoroughly study the internal structure inside asphalt mixes over the past two decades. The relative properties can be obtained involving the distribution, orientation, contact, and AV distribution of the aggregates using X-ray CT technology [25]. The AV distributions of the specimens with different gradations molded by Superpave gyratory compaction (SGC) were obtained using X-ray CT to analyze the compaction characteristics [26,27]. In addition, relevant research on the meso-mechanical response of asphalt mixes during the compaction process has made significant progress owing to the continuous progress in the discrete element method (DEM). It has been demonstrated that the SGC test simulated via the DEM was consistent with the laboratory test [28]. Moreover, the DEM was used to explore the effects of force chain evolution and aggregates in the compaction process [29]. There is no doubt that research progress on the application of CT technology and DEM in asphalt mixtures provides a powerful means and experience for exploring the current compaction characteristics of UPFCs.

Therefore, this study explores the field compaction mechanism of a UPFC designed using an MCM. Owing to the lack of field core samples, SGC and rolling-wheel compaction (RWC) methods were used to form laboratory specimens with the same thickness as the paving thinness of a UPFC, with the aim to simulate on-site compaction conditions. Accordingly, the compaction characteristics and mesoscopic force of the UPFC during the compaction process were studied. The research results are significant for improving the road performance of UPFCs.

2. Experimental Design

2.1. Experimental Objective

This study aimed to explore the field compaction properties of MCM-designed UPFC mixes based on laboratory simulations of the SGC and RWC methods. To achieve this objective, the AV characteristics and compaction mechanism of the UPFC were analyzed using X-ray CT and DEM according to the following tasks:

- To analyze the compaction characteristics of the MCM-designed UPFC mixes with different thicknesses, the SGC method was used to simulate field compaction.
- The compaction mechanism of the UPFCs with different thicknesses was analyzed using the DEM.
- To analyze the relationship between the AV characteristics of the MCM-designed laboratory specimens and the simulated field cores molded using the SGC and RWC methods, we evaluated the rationality of the UPFC mixes designed using the MCM.

2.2. Raw Materials and Mix Design

A kind of styrene–butadiene–styrene (SBS) high-viscosity asphalt was selected [30], with a dosage of 6% by weight of mineral aggregates. Limestone aggregates of 0–3 mm and basalt aggregates of 3–5 mm were adopted, and the ore powder was made of limestone. Basalt fiber accounted for 0.3% by weight of the mixture. The technical indexes of all materials met the requirements of the Chinese technical specifications for construction of highway asphalt pavements (JTG F40-2004) [31]. OGFC mixes with a maximum nominal particle size of 4.75 mm (OGFC-5) were adopted to prepare the UPFC, hereinafter referred to as OGFC-5 UPFC. Tables 1 and 2 present the OGFC-5 gradations and the mix designs, respectively.

Table 1. The mineral gradation of OGFC-5 mixtures.

Sieve size (mm)	9.5	4.75	2.36	1.18	0.6	0.3	0.15	0.075
Passing rate (%)	100.0	92.1	16.1	11.7	9.8	7.9	7.2	5.0

Table 2. The results of OGFC-5 mix design.

Mix Design Method	Target Size of Specimen (mm)		OAC (%)	Target AV Ratio (%)	Measured AV Ratio (%)
	Diameter	Height			
Marshall	101.6	63.5	6.0	18.0	17.9

Note: OAC represents optimal asphalt content.

2.3. Methodology and Testing

2.3.1. Compaction Characteristics of OGFC-5 UPFC with Different Thicknesses

Khan et al. demonstrated that an internal rotation angle of 1.25° in the SGC method best reflected the compaction characteristics of the field cores [20]. In addition, the Stratagem Highway Researching Plan (SHRP) recommended an internal rotation angle of

1.16° and a compaction pressure of 600 kPa in the SGC method, which better represents the field compaction. Therefore, to simulate the compaction characteristics of the UPFC with the actual paving thickness, OGFC-5 specimens with different thicknesses were formed using the SGC method, and the compaction height changes in the OGFC-5 specimens under different compaction parameters were analyzed. Considering that the actual paving thickness of the OGFC-5 UPFC in a paving process is as thin as 1 cm, the target compaction heights were selected as 15, 20, 25, 40, and 63.5 mm, respectively. Table 3 lists the SGC parameters. Notably, the mixed masses of the SGC specimens under different test conditions were calculated according to the equivalent volumes of the Marshall specimens to ensure the same density of the mixtures.

Table 3. Compaction parameters.

Compaction Parameters	The Value of Compaction Parameters							
Target height (mm)	15	15	15	15	20	25	40	63.5
Target Radius (mm)	100	100	100	150	100	100	100	100
Vertical pressure (kPa)	600	600	800	600	600	600	600	600
Angle of internal gyration (°)	1.15	1.72	1.15	1.15	1.15	1.15	1.15	1.15
Specimen ID	S100/15	S100/15-1	S100/15-2	S150/15	S100/20	S100/25	S100/40	S100/63.5

2.3.2. Compaction Mechanism of OGFC-5 UPFC with Different Thicknesses

The DEM was used to simulate the SGC test to explore the compaction mechanism of the OGFC-5 mixture with different compaction thicknesses [32–34]. The displacement and force chain transmission of the DEM model were recorded at certain gyratory compaction times. Table 1 presents the OGFC-5 gradations used in the DEM simulations. To enhance the computing speed, the generated particles were greater than 2.36 mm. The Burgers model was used as the contact model, and its parameter values are listed in Table 4 [33,34]. As shown in Figure 1, the heights of the DEM model were 20, 40, and 63.5 mm, respectively. The model set an initial AV content of 35.0%, an angle of 1.15°, compaction pressure of 600 kPa, and a compaction time of 1 h between the loading wall and plane.

Table 4. The model parameters.

Model Parameters			Value
Kelvin model	Spring	shear stiffness (Pa·m)	5.1×10^7
		Normal stiffness (Pa·m)	5.1×10^7
	Dashpot	Normal stiffness (Pa·m·s)	3.6×10^6
		shear stiffness (Pa·m·s)	3.6×10^6
Maxwell model	Spring	shear stiffness (Pa·m)	4.3×10^9
		Normal stiffness (Pa·m)	4.3×10^9
	Dashpot	Normal stiffness (Pa·m·s)	1.8×10^9
		shear stiffness (Pa·m·s)	1.8×10^9

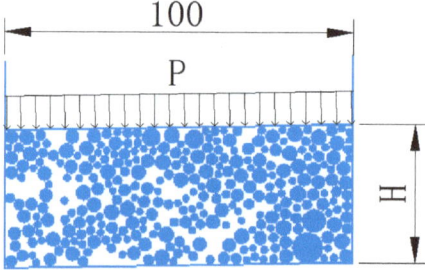

Figure 1. DEM model of SGC method.

2.3.3. AV Characterization of OGFC-5 UPFC Based on CT Scanning

The OGFC-5 mixture possesses an AV content of 18–25%. Internal AV characteristics (such as the AV content and size) are critical for noise reduction and drainage improvement. In view of this, 15 mm OGFC-5 specimens were formed using the SGC and RWC methods to simulate the field core samples of the UPFCs. Similar to the SGC specimen, the mix masses of the RWC specimen were calculated according to the equivalent volume of the Marshall specimens. The roller-forming equipment used was an Italian control pavement roller, as shown in Figure 2. A 400 mm × 300 mm × 15 mm (length, width, height, respectively) cuboid specimen was fabricated using a height control procedure, and core samples were drilled to obtain cylindrical specimens. The samples are listed in Table 5. According to the OFGC-5 UPFC mix design results using the MCM, 15 mm UPFC specimens formed via SGC and RWC that simulate the field compaction were not compacted to the target AV content and height, which indicated that the MCM-designed UPFC mixes did not conform to the field compaction.

Figure 2. Controls pavement roller.

Table 5. Summary of different test specimens.

Specimen ID	Molding Method	Target Specimen Size (Diameter × Height)	Measured Specimen Size (Diameter × Height)	Target AV Ratio (%)	Measured AV Ratio (%)
M100/63.5	Marshall	101.6 mm × 63.5 mm	101.6 mm × 63.0 mm		17.9
S100/15	SGC	100 mm × 15 mm	100 mm × 16.7 mm	18	27.2
S150/15	SGC	150 mm × 15 mm	150 mm × 16.8 mm		26.5
R100/15	RWC	100 mm × 15 mm	100 mm × 17.0 mm		27.4

In the experiment, the PrecisionIICT for industrial use produced by YXLON was used to scan the samples, and pictures were obtained every 0.1 mm along the height of the samples, as shown in Figure 3. These obtained pictures were automatically handled by a macro, and then Image-Pro Plus software (IPP 6.0.0.260) was applied to obtain the AV characteristics. According to the study conducted by Masad et al. [35], the average AV contents of the single and total images were determined using Equations (1) and (2), respectively. In addition, because the AV diameter largely depends on the packing degree of the granular skeleton inside the UPFC samples, the average AV diameter should be analyzed [36]. Therefore, the AV size decreased with increasing packing and particle contact. Equation (3) was adopted to calculate the average AV radius of the i-th image. Furthermore, the horizontal variability in the AV ratios and the mean AV diameter in the cross sections of different radii (Figure 4) were investigated to obtain the horizontal AV distribution of the Marshall specimens and simulated field cores.

$$AV_i = \frac{A_{vi}}{A_i} \tag{1}$$

$$AV_s = \frac{\sum_{i=1}^{n} AV_i}{N} \tag{2}$$

$$d_i = 2\sqrt{\frac{A_{vi}}{\pi n}} \tag{3}$$

where A_i, A_{vi}, AV_i, d_i, and n are the cross-sectional area, AV area, AV ratio, AV mean diameter, and AV number of the i-th image, respectively. The AV_s and N correspond to the AV rate and total number of CT images of the test specimen, respectively.

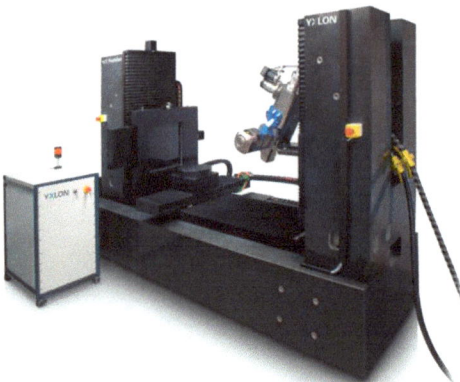

Figure 3. CT scanning.

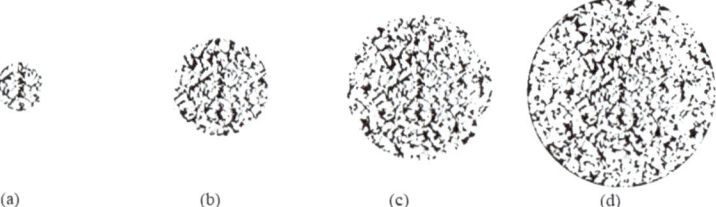

Figure 4. Different radius cross sections used in analysis on horizontal AV variability: (**a**) 1/4 radius; (**b**) 1/2 radius; (**c**) 3/4 radius; (**d**) full radius.

3. Results and Discussion

3.1. Compaction Properties of OGFC-5 UPFC with Different Thickness

According to the compaction parameters in Table 3, different OGFC-5 UPFC samples were prepared to monitor the compaction process. The simulated field compaction results for the OGFC-5 UPFC under different compaction parameters are presented in Table 6 and Figure 5. The curve of the specimen height with respect to the gyratory number is shown in Figure 5a. According to Equation (4), linear regression analysis was performed on the specimen height and gyratory number, as shown in Figure 5b. The results of the linear regression analysis are presented in Table 7.

$$\ln H(N) = a - k \ln(N) \tag{4}$$

where a and k correspond to the fitting parameters, and N and $H(N)$ represent the gyratory number and height at gyratory number of N, respectively. The parameters a and k reflect the initial density and difficulty of the compaction process, respectively. The larger the a and k values, the easier it is for the specimen to be compacted to the target height [37].

Table 6. The compaction results of different SGC compaction parameters.

Specimen ID	S100/15	S100/15-1	S100/15-2	S150/15	S100/20	S100/25	S100/40	S100/63.5
Gyratory number	200	200	200	200	200	128	80	32
Height	16.7	16.7	16.5	16.8	21.7	25.2	40.2	63.4
AV ratio	27.2%	27.3%	27.3%	26.5%	24.4%	18.6%	18.3%	19.1%

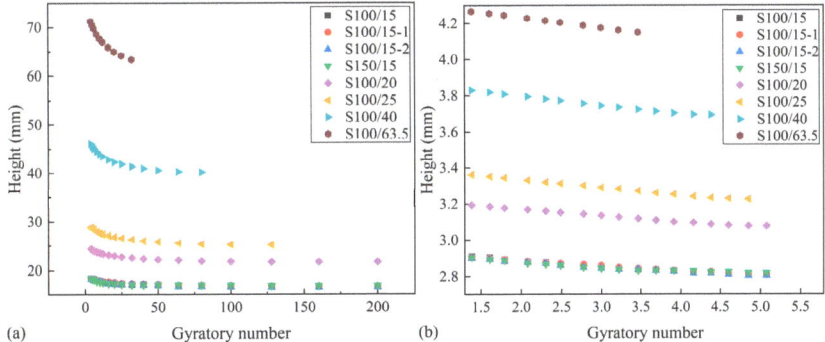

Figure 5. Compaction curves: (**a**) common coordinates; (**b**) semi-logarithmic coordinates.

Table 7. The results of linear-regression analysis.

Specimen ID	S100/15	S100/15-1	S100/15-2	S150/15	S100/20	S100/25	S100/40	S100/63.5
k	0.030	0.027	0.028	0.023	0.035	0.041	0.048	0.058
a	2.949	2.942	2.936	2.925	3.241	3.418	3.894	4.348
R^2	0.978	0.990	0.983	0.903	0.996	0.995	0.992	0.999

As shown in Table 6, 5 test specimens, S100/15, S100/15-1, S100/15-2, S150/15, and S100/20, were insufficiently compacted and did not achieve the target compaction thickness after 200 gyratory numbers. In addition, the AV contents of the five specimens were 27.2%, 27.3%, 27.3%, 26.5%, and 25.4%, respectively, which were much higher than the design AV requirement of 18% for UPFC mixes designed using the MCM.

According to Table 7, for the 15 mm UPFC specimen, the a and k values of all 15 mm × 100 mm (height and diameter, respectively) test samples showed little difference, and increasing the vertical pressure and the internal gyration angle had little effect on the compaction height. The S150/15 specimen had the smallest k value, indicating that the S150/15 specimen was the most difficult to compact to 15 mm. In this regard, the increased radius of the specimen made the compaction pressure more dispersed and increased the difficulty of compaction of the UPFC specimen. In addition, a decrease in the compaction thickness decreased the values of parameters a and k. The initial compaction density of the UPFC specimen decreased, which resulted in compaction difficulties. At the same time,

Figure 5a exhibits that the smaller the compaction thickness, the more gyratory numbers were required. This could be because the pressure inside the specimen was non-uniform as the target compaction height decreased. The aggregates in one or several regions were stabilized and bore the main pressure, whereas the other unstabilized regions received less force, and it was difficult for the particles to move, rotate, and be sufficiently compacted.

3.2. Compaction Mechanism of OGFC-5 UPFC with Different Thickness

3.2.1. Displacement and Stress of Loading Wall

Figure 6 shows the displacement curve of the loading wall with respect to the loading time. Remarkably, there was an initial displacement at the time of formal loading because the wall needed to be preloaded before loading. Figure 6 shows the time it took for the SGC model displacement curves of different compaction thicknesses to reach the stable stage ranked 63.5 mm, 40, and 20 mm in descending order.

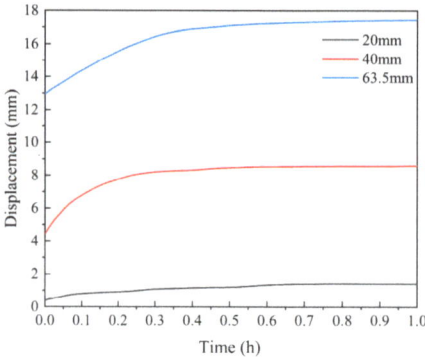

Figure 6. Displacement–time curves of loading wall.

The stress curve of the loading wall with respect to time is shown in Figure 7. The wall continued to move downward at a stress below 600 kPa, indicating that the model was still not fully compacted. The compaction tends to stabilize when the stress is maintained at approximately 600 kPa [38]. As shown in Figure 7, the stress of the 20 mm model was stable and fluctuated around 600 kPa at the earliest. Subsequently, the 40 mm and 63.5 mm models reached a stable stage.

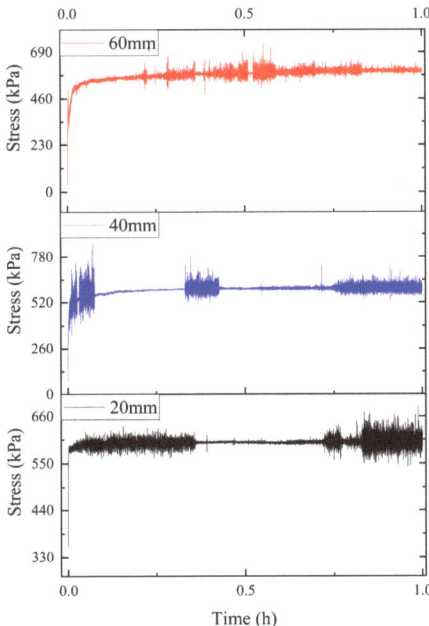

Figure 7. Stress–time curves of loading wall.

A conclusion drawn from Figures 6 and 7 is that the 20 mm UPFC model was the first to reach a steady state. On the one hand, this may be because the 20 mm model is the easiest to compact fully, and it enters the stable state first. However, this may be because the 20 mm model could not be fully compacted, leading to a stable state in advance. Therefore, further analysis of the displacement of the loading wall is required to determine its specific cause. Aggregate crushing can affect the degree of interlocking between aggregate particles and the filling effect of asphalt. However, it should be noted that the DEM model does not take into account the effects of aggregate fragmentation and morphology, which may lead to misjudgment of the compaction process, thereby affecting the stability and durability evaluation of the UPFCs. Crushed aggregates require different compaction energies to achieve optimal compactness. Meanwhile, aggregate crushing affects the volume change and compaction curve of UPFCs. Although the DEM model does not consider the aggregate fragmentation and morphology, which may lead to a certain deviation between the time–displacement curve and the actual compaction, the simulation results can basically explain the above-mentioned laboratory test results, that is, when the UPFC target compaction thickness is too small, no matter what compaction parameters are used, the UPFC sample cannot meet the compaction requirements.

The final displacements of all models with different heights were obtained, representing the compacted thickness of the model. The definition index D_H is the compacted thickness per unit height of the model, which reflects the difficulty of compaction at different heights. The D_H value was equal to the displacement of the loaded wall divided by the height of the model. The calculated D_H values are listed in Table 8. The DH values ranked as D20, D40, and D63.5 in ascending order. This indicates that as the molding height decreased, the model became more difficult to compact. This result explains why a model displacement of 20 mm reached a stable state the earliest, which is consistent with the compaction data in Section 3.1.

Table 8. The DH values.

UPFC Height/mm	20	40	63.5
Displacement of loading wall/mm	1.42	8.61	17.46
D_H	0.07	0.22	0.27

3.2.2. Micromechanical Response

Figure 8 presents the direction results of the normal contact force of the particles after loading for 1 h. The contact normal forces of the different models were distributed in all directions, and there were no distribution concentrations in any specific direction. Remarkably, the contact normal force of the 20 mm model exhibited a sudden increase in several directions. This phenomenon was also found in the 40 mm model, while the increment of the contact normal force was relatively small in comparison to that of the 20 mm model. As for the 63.5 mm model, the force values were relatively uniform in each interval. The maximum contact normal force values of the 20 mm and 40 mm models were 8 times and 2.67 times that of the 63.5 mm model, respectively. The smaller the molding height, the greater the force value observed.

The force chain and contact force were further studied to analyze the load transmission in the model. Figures 9 and 10 show the simulation results of the contact force and force chain, respectively. The colors of the particles in Figure 9 indicate the magnitude of the contact force. A phenomenon occurred where the contact forces of some particles were much stronger than that of other particles. The maximum force value increased with a decrease in model height, and the particle size showed a random trend in the force concentration region, indicating that the concentrated force region was independent of the particle size.

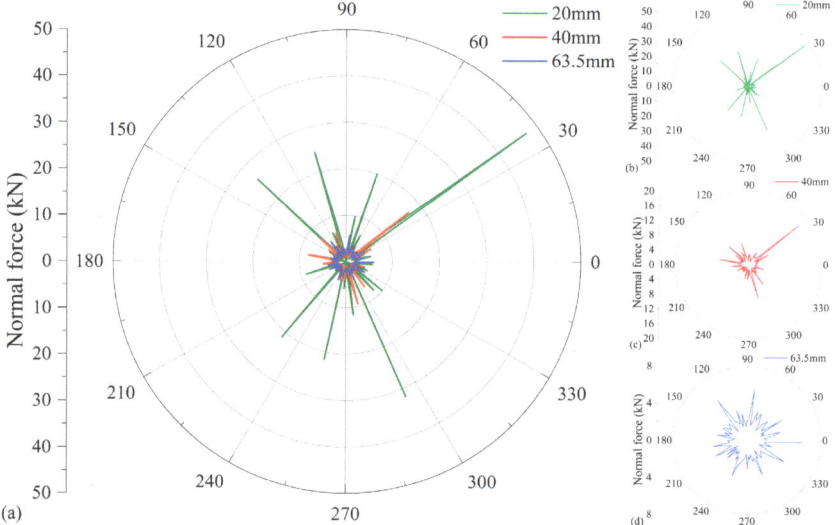

Figure 8. Direction distribution of contact normal force of different thickness UPFC model: (**a**) general drawing; (**b**) 20 mm; (**c**) 40 mm; (**d**) 60 mm.

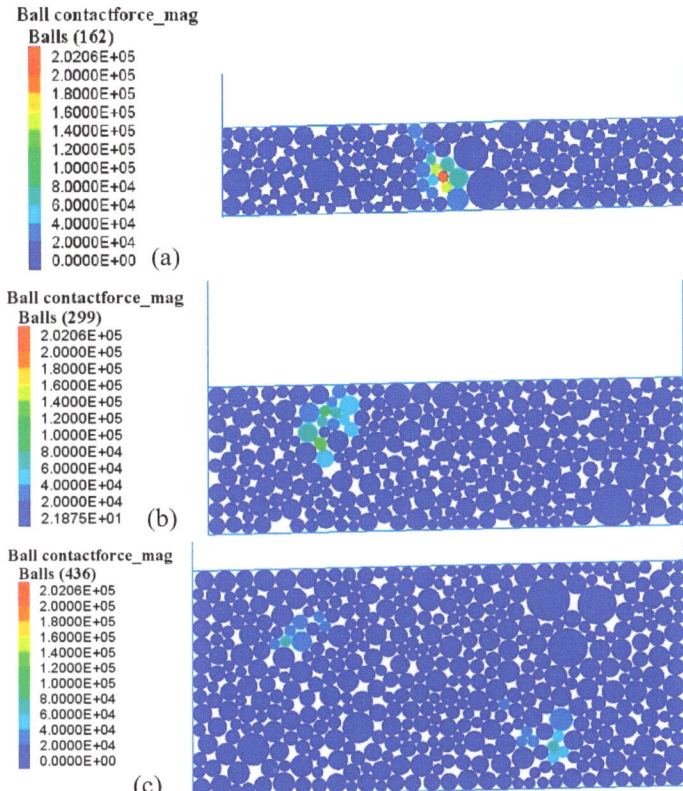

Figure 9. Contact force distribution of different thickness UPFC models: (**a**) 20 mm; (**b**) 40 mm; (**c**) 60 mm.

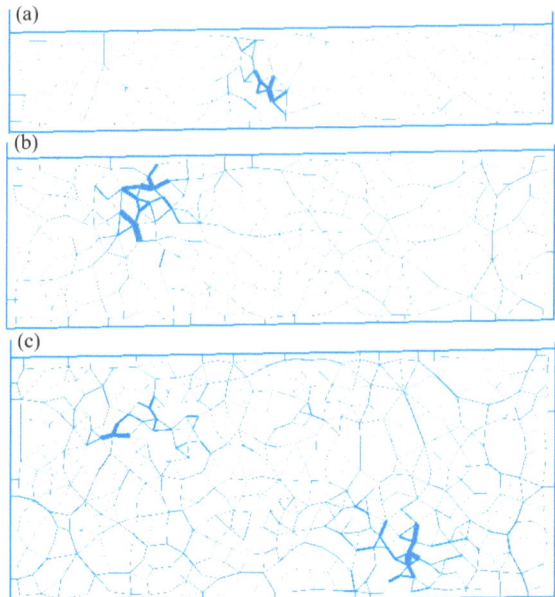

Figure 10. Force chain distribution of different thickness UPFC models: (**a**) 20 mm; (**b**) 40 mm; (**c**) 60 mm.

A schematic of the force chain clearly reflects the load transmission in the model. The thickness of the force chain in Figure 10 indicates the magnitude of the contact force. It can be found that the 63.5 mm model had more uniform thickness in the force chain, while the 20 mm model had less force in other areas owing to the existence of a strong chain area. With a decrease in height, the force chain became more significant, resulting in a load that is more difficult to fully diffuse and transfer inside the model [39]. Particles in the weak force chain region could not move and rotate sufficiently, making the model more difficult to compact. In conclusion, the target height of the UPFC specimen designed by the MCM method was 63.5mm, which varied from the actual UPFC paving thickness, making it difficult to achieve the specified on-site compaction degree. Therefore, it is possible to consider reducing the target height of the UPFC to make the MCM design more in line with construction.

3.3. AV Characterization of OGFC-5 UPFC Based on CT Scanning
3.3.1. Vertical Distribution

The vertical distributions of the AV content and coefficient of variation (COV) are shown in Figure 11. The vertical distribution of the AV diameter is shown in Figure 12. As shown in Figures 11a and 12, the curves of the AV content and AV diameter are in a "bathtub" shape along the vertical direction. The AV content was homogeneous and stable in the middle part, whereas those in the bottom and top parts were much larger than the average AV content. In addition, except for the Marshall specimen, the AV content of the other simulated field cores exceeded the design range. The overall AV content and diameter of the MCM-designed UPFC samples was smaller than those of the simulated field cores. The results show that the MCM-designed UPFC did not correspond well with the field construction situation. Obviously, in order to achieve the AV content of the Marshall-designed UPFC during the on-site construction process, it is necessary to increase the compaction tonnage, which will inevitably lead to an increase in the aggregate crushing. Crushed aggregates further embed and fill voids, resulting in a decrease in porosity. However, this will have an adverse impact on the performance of the UPFC.

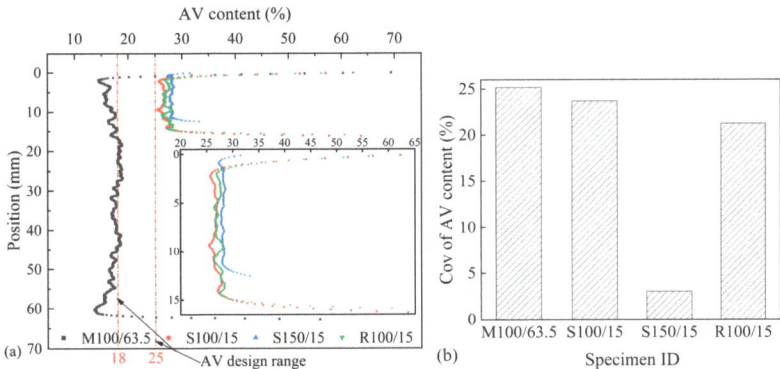

Figure 11. The vertical distribution: (**a**) mean AV content; (**b**) vertical variability.

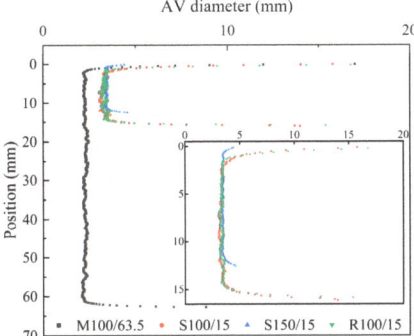

Figure 12. The vertical distribution of AV diameter.

As shown in Figure 11b, the COV of the Marshall specimen was the largest among all test samples. This is because the SGC and RWC methods exert a kneading effect during the compaction process, such that the aggregates can be fully moved and arranged, thereby producing a relatively homogeneous internal structure. However, because the Marshall compaction method relies mainly on vertical impact, the homogeneity of the internal structure of the sample was relatively poor. The COV of the S150/15 specimen was the smallest, indicating that increasing the compaction area improved vertical uniformity [18,40]. In addition, the COV values of the 15 mm specimens were all smaller than those of the 63.5 mm specimen, indicating that a small compaction thickness was conducive to uniform compaction. The reason that the 15 mm UPFC specimen could not reach the target height was not compaction. According to Figures 10 and 12, a concentrated force region existed, resulting in insufficient movement and packing between the aggregates when the compaction thickness of the UPFC was small. Thus, the AV size between the aggregates was large, and the thin UPFC specimen could not be compacted to the target thickness.

3.3.2. Horizontal Distribution

The horizontal distributions of the AV content and COV are presented in Figure 13. The AV content of the 63.5 mm Marshall specimen was the most uniform and stable in the horizontal direction, while that of the other 15 mm simulated field cores exhibited a wave shape along the horizontal distribution. In addition, Figure 13b shows that the COV of all the specimens showed a wavy trend along the radial direction. Remarkably, the S150/15 specimen had the smallest COV, which conforms to the conclusion drawn from Figure 11b. Overall, the horizontal distributions of the AV between the MCM-designed UPFC and the simulated field cores were quite different. It was also proven that the MCM-designed UPFC mixes did not accurately reflect the field construction of the UPFC.

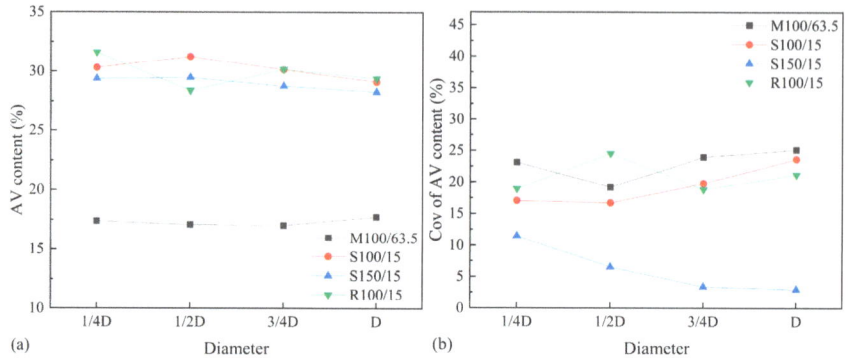

Figure 13. The horizontal distribution: (**a**) mean AV content; (**b**) horizontal variability.

4. Conclusions

The compaction characteristics of an OGFC-5 UPFC specimen designed using the MCM and simulated field cores were studied at multiple scales using laboratory compaction tests, DEM, and X-ray CT techniques. On the basis of the results, some conclusions were drawn, as follows:

(1) The compaction-test data demonstrate that the simulated field specimens with thicknesses of 15 and 20 mm barely achieved the target compaction thicknesses. All the UPFC specimens of different thicknesses failed to meet the AV requirements of the UPFC mixes designed via the MCM.

(2) As the compaction thickness decreased, the values of parameters a and k also decreased. The initial compaction density of the UPFC specimen decreased, which resulted in compaction difficulties.

(3) According to the results of the SGC test based on the DEM, the smaller the height of the virtual specimen, the earlier its displacement and stress reached a stable state. Moreover, as the model decreased in height, the D_H value; that is, the compacted thickness per unit height of the model, decreased, and the model was more difficult to compact.

(4) DEM models with different thicknesses exhibited several force concentration regions. Compared to that of the 63.5 mm model, the maximum contact normal force of the 20 mm and 40 mm models increased by 266% and 800%, respectively. The decrease in the UPFC thickness strengthened the strong force chain in quantity and strength inside the specimen, resulting in difficulty in evenly diffusing and transferring pressure inside the specimen.

(5) Based on the results of the UPFC specimens obtained using CT scanning, a small compaction thickness was conducive to uniform compaction. The AV distributions of the Marshall specimens were quite different in the vertical and horizontal directions from those of the UPFC specimens that simulated the field compaction. The MCM-designed UPFCs showed poor consistency with the field compaction.

(6) According to the investigation results, the MCM-designed UPFC is not in compliance with on-site construction. In order to better align with actual construction and ensure the performance of the UPFC, potential paths to improve UPFC designs from the perspective of mixture design include reducing the height of the MCM design specimens and changing the UPFC design methods.

These research results provide feasible references for achieving more durable UPFCs. However, this study did not take into account the influence of some factors, such as mineral gradation and aggregate characteristics, and it lacked on-site experimental validation. Future research will focus on the above aspects, particularly regarding the effects of aggregate morphology and crushing on the compaction behavior of UPFCs.

Author Contributions: Conceptualization, X.D.; methodology, X.D. and H.L.; validation, M.S.; formal analysis, X.D., H.L. and W.L.; investigation, X.D., H.L., M.S. and W.L.; data curation, X.D., H.L., M.S. and W.L.; writing—original draft preparation, H.L.; writing—review and editing, X.D. and H.L.; supervision, H.Z. All authors have read and agreed to the published version of the manuscript.

Funding: This research received no external funding.

Institutional Review Board Statement: Not applicable.

Informed Consent Statement: Not applicable.

Data Availability Statement: The data presented in this study are available on request from the corresponding author. The data are not publicly available due to the commercial privacy.

Conflicts of Interest: Author Hongwei Lin was employed by Guangzhou Baiyun International Airport Co., Ltd. Author Wenchang Liu was employed by Shanghai Fengxian Construction Development Group Co., Ltd. The remaining authors declare that the research was conducted in the absence of any commercial or financial relationships that could be construed as a potential conflict of interest.

References

1. Suresha, S.N.; George, V.; Ravi Shankar, A.U. Effect of aggregate gradations on properties of porous friction course mixes. *Mater. Struct.* **2009**, *43*, 789–801. [CrossRef]
2. Kandhal, P.S.; Mallick, R.B. *Open Graded Friction Course: State of the Practice*; Transportation Research Board, National Research Council: Washington, DC, USA, 1998.
3. Chen, J.-S.; Yang, C.H. Porous asphalt concrete: A review of design, construction, performance and maintenance. *Int. J. Pavement Res. Technol.* **2021**, *13*, 601–612. [CrossRef]
4. Im, S.; You, T.; Kim, Y.-R.; Nsengiyumva, G.; Rea, R.; Haghshenas, H. Evaluation of Thin-Lift Overlay Pavement Preservation Practice: Mixture Testing, Pavement Performance, and Lifecycle Cost Analysis. *J. Transp. Eng. Part B Pavements* **2018**, *144*, 04018037. [CrossRef]
5. Alvarez, A.E.; Martin, A.E.; Estakhri, C. A review of mix design and evaluation research for permeable friction course mixtures. *Constr. Build. Mater.* **2011**, *25*, 1159–1166. [CrossRef]
6. Wu, W.; Jiang, W.; Xiao, J.; Yuan, D.; Wang, T.; Ling, X. Investigation of LAS-based fatigue evaluation methods for high-viscosity modified asphalt binders with high-content polymers. *Constr. Build. Mater.* **2024**, *422*, 135810. [CrossRef]
7. Son, S.; Al-Qadi, I.L.; Zehr, T. 4.75 mm SMA Performance and Cost-Effectiveness for Asphalt Thin Overlays. *Int. J. Pavement Eng.* **2015**, *17*, 799–809. [CrossRef]
8. Yu, J.; Chen, F.; Deng, W.; Ma, Y.; Yu, H. Design and performance of high-toughness ultra-thin friction course in south China. *Constr. Build. Mater.* **2020**, *246*, 118508. [CrossRef]
9. Yu, J.; Yang, N.; Chen, F.; Chen, Y.; Lin, Z.; Yu, H. Design of Cold-Mixed High-Toughness Ultra-Thin Asphalt Layer towards Sustainable Pavement Construction. *Buildings* **2021**, *11*, 619. [CrossRef]
10. Liu, Z.; Wang, X.; Luo, S.; Yang, X.; Li, Q. Asphalt mixture design for porous ultra-thin overlay. *Constr. Build. Mater.* **2019**, *217*, 251–264. [CrossRef]
11. Liu, Z.; Luo, S.; Quan, X.; Wei, X.; Yang, X.; Li, Q. Laboratory evaluation of performance of porous ultra-thin overlay. *Constr. Build. Mater.* **2019**, *204*, 28–40. [CrossRef]
12. Ding, L.; Wang, X.; Zhang, K.; Zhang, M.; Yang, J.; Chen, Z. Durability evaluation of easy compaction and high-durability ultra-thin overlay. *Constr. Build. Mater.* **2021**, *302*, 124407. [CrossRef]
13. Tian, J.; Luo, S.; Liu, Z.; Yang, X.; Lu, Q. Determination of Construction Parameters of Porous Ultra-Thin Overlays Based on Laboratory Compaction Studies. *Materials* **2020**, *13*, 4496. [CrossRef] [PubMed]
14. Hunter, A.E.; McGreavy, L.; Airey, G.D. Effect of compaction mode on the mechanical performance and variability of asphalt mixtures. *J. Transp. Eng.* **2009**, *135*, 839–851. [CrossRef]
15. Suresha, S.N.; Varghese, G.; Shankar, A.U.R. Characterization of porous friction course mixes for different Marshall compaction efforts. *Constr. Build. Mater.* **2009**, *23*, 2887–2893. [CrossRef]
16. Norhidayah, A.H.; Mahmud, M.Z.H.; Ramadhansyah, P.J. Air Void Characterisation in Porous Asphalt Using X-Ray Computed Tomography. *Adv. Mater. Res.* **2014**, *911*, 443–448. [CrossRef]
17. Alvarez, A.E.; Martin, A.E.; Estakhri, C. Effects of densification on permeable friction course mixtures. *J. Test. Eval.* **2009**, *37*, 11–20. [CrossRef]
18. Alvarez, A.E.; Martin, A.E.; Estakhri, C. Internal structure of compacted permeable friction course mixtures. *Constr. Build. Mater.* **2010**, *24*, 1027–1035. [CrossRef]
19. Wang, S.; Zhao, S.; Al-Qadi, I.L. Real-Time Density and Thickness Estimation of Thin Asphalt Pavement Overlay During Compaction Using Ground Penetrating Radar Data. *Surv. Geophys.* **2019**, *41*, 431–445. [CrossRef]
20. Khan, Z.A.; Wahab, H.I.A.-A.; Asi, I.; Ramadhan, R. Comparative study of asphalt concrete laboratory compaction methods to simulate field compaction. *Constr. Build. Mater. B* **1998**, *12*, 373–384. [CrossRef]

21. Liu, P.; Xu, H.; Wang, D.; Wang, C.; Schulze, C.; Oeser, M. Comparison of mechanical responses of asphalt mixtures manufactured by different compaction methods. *Constr. Build. Mater.* **2018**, *162*, 765–780. [CrossRef]
22. Ji, X.; Han, B.; Hu, J.; Li, S.; Xiong, Y.; Sun, E. Application of the discrete element method and CT scanning to investigate the compaction characteristics of the soil–rock mixture in the subgrade. *Road Mater. Pavement Des.* **2020**, *23*, 397–413. [CrossRef]
23. Li, Y.; Jiang, W.; Shan, J.; Li, P.; Lu, R.; Lou, B. Characteristics of void distribution and aggregate degradation of asphalt mixture specimens compacted using field and laboratory methods. *Constr. Build. Mater.* **2021**, *270*, 121488. [CrossRef]
24. Hekmatfar, A.; Shah, A.; Huber, G.; McDaniel, R.; Haddock, J.E. Modifying laboratory mixture design to improve field compaction. *Road Mater. Pavement Des.* **2015**, *16*, 149–167. [CrossRef]
25. Masad, E.; Muhunthan, B.; Shashidhar, N.; Harman, T. Internal Structure Characterization of Asphalt Concrete Using Image Analysis. *J. Comput. Civil Eng.* **1999**, *13*, 88–95. [CrossRef]
26. Zhang, C.; Wang, H.; You, Z.; Yang, X. Compaction characteristics of asphalt mixture with different gradation type through Superpave Gyratory Compaction and X-ray CT Scanning. *Constr. Build. Mater.* **2016**, *129*, 243–255. [CrossRef]
27. Arambula, E.; Masad, E.; Martin, A.E. Influence of Air Void Distribution on the Moisture—Susceptibility of Asphalt Mixes. *J. Mater. Civil Eng.* **2007**, *13*, 655–664. [CrossRef]
28. Chen, J.; Huang, B.; Chen, F.; Shu, X. Application of discrete element method to Superpave gyratory compaction. *Road Mater. Pavement Des.* **2012**, *13*, 480–500. [CrossRef]
29. Wang, S.; Miao, Y.; Wang, L. Investigation of the force evolution in aggregate blend compaction process and the effect of elongated and flat particles using DEM. *Constr. Build. Mater.* **2020**, *258*, 119674. [CrossRef]
30. Wu, W.; Cavalli, M.C.; Jiang, W.; Kringos, N. Differing perspectives on the use of high-content SBS polymer-modified bitumen. *Constr. Build. Mater.* **2024**, *411*, 134433. [CrossRef]
31. *JTG F40-2004*; Technical Standards of the Chinese Technical Specifications for Construction of Highway Asphalt Pavements. National Standards of the People's Republic of China: Beijing, China, 2004.
32. Lu, X.; Chen, T.; Chen, Z.; Liu, W.; Lin, H. Optimization gradation of permeable asphalt mixture PAC-16. *China Meas. Test* **2024**, *50*, 60–67.
33. Lin, H.; Du, X.; Zhong, C.; Wu, P.; Liu, W.; Sun, M.; Zhang, H. Distribution Properties of Internal Air Voids in Ultrathin Asphalt Friction Course. *J. Wuhan Univ. Technol. Mater. Sci. Ed.* **2023**, *38*, 538–546. [CrossRef]
34. Du, X.; Gao, L.; Rao, F.; Lin, H.; Zhang, H.; Sun, M.; Xu, X. Damage Mechanism of Ultra-thin Asphalt Overlay (UTAO) based on Discrete Element Method. *J. Wuhan Univ. Technol. Mater. Sci. Ed.* **2024**, *39*, 473–486. [CrossRef]
35. Masad, E.; Arambula, E.; Ketcham, R.; Abbas, A.; Martin, A.E. Nondestructive measurements of moisture transport in asphalt mixtures. *Asph. Paving Technol.-Proc.* **2007**, *76*, 919.
36. Watson, D.E.; Masad, E.; Ann Moore, K.; Williams, K.; Cooley, L.A., Jr. Verification of voids in coarse aggregate testing: Determining stone-on-stone contact of hot-mix asphalt mixtures. *Transp. Res. Record* **2004**, *1891*, 182–190. [CrossRef]
37. Bi, Y.; Huang, J.; Pei, J.; Zhang, J.; Guo, F.; Li, R. Compaction characteristics assessment of Hot-Mix asphalt mixture using Superpave gyratory compaction and Stribeck curve method. *Constr. Build. Mater.* **2021**, *285*, 122874. [CrossRef]
38. Ren, J.; Yin, C. Investigating mechanical characteristics of aggregate structure for road materials. *Int. J. Pavement Eng.* **2020**, *23*, 372–386. [CrossRef]
39. Liu, G.; Han, D.; Zhao, Y.; Zhang, J. Effects of asphalt mixture structure types on force chains characteristics based on computational granular mechanics. *Int. J. Pavement Eng.* **2020**, *23*, 1008–1024. [CrossRef]
40. Muraya, P.M. Homogeneous test specimens from gyratory compaction. *Int. J. Pavement Eng.* **2007**, *8*, 225–235. [CrossRef]

Disclaimer/Publisher's Note: The statements, opinions and data contained in all publications are solely those of the individual author(s) and contributor(s) and not of MDPI and/or the editor(s). MDPI and/or the editor(s) disclaim responsibility for any injury to people or property resulting from any ideas, methods, instructions or products referred to in the content.

Article

Performance and Modification Mechanism of Recycled Glass Fiber of Wind Turbine Blades and SBS Composite-Modified Asphalt

Yihua Nie *, Qing Liu, Zhiheng Xiang *, Shixiong Zhong and Xinyao Huang

School of Civil Engineering, Hunan University of Science and Technology, Xiangtan 411201, China; 15111103989@163.com (Q.L.); zsxnow@163.com (S.Z.); 15292276921@163.com (X.H.)
* Correspondence: nieyihua@hnust.edu.cn (Y.N.); mkl-jdx@163.com (Z.X.)

Abstract: Efficient disposal of composite materials recycled from wind turbine blades (WTB) at end-of-life needs to be solved urgently. To investigate the modification effects and mechanism on SBS-modified asphalt of the recycled glass fiber (GF) from WTB, GF-WTB/SBS composite-modified asphalt was prepared. Dynamic shear rheometer (DSR) and bending beam rheometer (BBR) were adopted to evaluate its performance. FTIR, SEM, EDS, and AFM methods were used to assess coupling agent pretreatment effects on GF-WTB and observe the modification mechanism. The macroscopic tests show that reasonable addition of GF-WTB effectively raises the high-temperature performance and low-temperature crack resistance evaluation index k-value of SBS-modified asphalt, and the optimal content is 2 wt% GF-WTB with 4 wt% SBS. FTIR, SEM, and EDS tests show GF-WTB can be successfully grafted by UP152 coupling agent and show that adhesion of the GF-WTB to the SBS-modified asphalt can be improved. AFM observation shows SBS and GF-WTB have good compatibility, improving the asphalt elasticity and toughness. This study provides a feasible solution for environmentally friendly regeneration of the composite materials from WTB and contributes to the development of the secondary modifier of SBS-modified asphalt.

Keywords: composite-modified asphalt; recycled glass fiber; wind turbine blades; silane coupling agent; SBS-modified asphalt

1. Introduction

Wind power can offer clean and renewable energy with a low environmental impact and an increasing number of wind farms are built around the globe. The service life of a wind turbine blade (WTB) is typically 20–25 years [1]. However, many blades are coming out-of-service prior to that due to increasing power. The wind turbine industry is expected to store millions of tons of waste composite wind blades in the coming years [2–4]. These structures are mainly manufactured with glass fiber (with some use of carbon fiber) embedded in thermoset matrix materials such as epoxy, unsaturated polyester resin, or vinyl ester resins [5]. Waste disposal of fiber-reinforced polymer (FRP) composite materials from wind turbine blades at end-of-life, a majority of which are handled by landfills or incineration, is a problem that needs to be solved.

Due to the cross-linked structure after curing of the thermoset matrix materials, the thermoset composite cannot be melted and molded for the second time, meaning that the reinforced materials in thermoset composite are difficult to be recycled. Recycling technologies developed for thermoset composite materials mainly contain mechanical recycling, thermal recycling, and chemical recycling [6–8]. The latter two technologies are in the laboratory stage and currently have no practical application. Mechanical recycling is a simple physical process, which can partly recycle the reinforced materials in thermoset composite. Based on comparative analysis, the mechanical recycling seems to be the best choice at present. The mechanically recycled materials obtained by breaking up the waste into particles or milling into fine powder are mainly used as fillers, reinforcement or raw materials for cement, concrete, etc. One of the most extensive research studies was carried out on Portland cement concrete in which mechanically recycled glass fiber-reinforced polymer (GFRP) waste was incorporated either as reinforcement, aggregate, or filler replacement [9,10]. Asokan et al. [11] assessed that GFRP waste substitution of fine aggregates in concrete could save approximately 15% of the fine aggregate cost. Presently, mechanical recycling has been applied in the waste composite recycling of WTB. Ribeiro et al. [12] reused the mechanically recycled GFRP pultrusion wastes from wind blades as aggregate and filler replacement for concrete–polymer composite materials. Schmidl and Hinrichs [13] mechanically recycled GFRP composites from blades which were used in cement production.

Rich studies have been carried out on various pristine fibers such as polymer fibers, lignin fibers, mineral fibers, glass fibers (GF), etc. in the application of asphalt pavement materials [14]. Many results indicate that the incorporation of fiber can significantly improve the high-temperature performance of asphalt. There are some applications of recycled fibers from waste fiber materials or thermoplastic materials such as waste plastic bottles added to asphalt pavement materials. However, few researchers reported the asphalt pavement engineering applications of recycled fibers from waste thermoset composites in wind energy, automotive, aerospace, construction industries, etc. Compared to the recycled fibers from waste fiber materials, the mechanically recycled glass fibers from wind turbine blades are of smaller size and blended with resin residues. By applying the recycled fibers from waste tires and waste plastic bottles or new polyester fiber to asphalt mixture, Liu [15] found that the high-temperature stability, water stability, and anti-fatigue properties were improved compared with ordinary asphalt mixtures; however, the effect was relatively insignificant compared with the new polyester fiber. Dehghan and Modarres [16] evaluated the effect of recycled polyethylene terephthalate (PET) fibers from waste plastic bottles on the fatigue properties of hot asphalt mix. Qilin Yang et al. [17] found recycled glass fiber chips from GFRP composite of waste airplane cabins blended into the 70/100 penetration bitumen improved high-temperature performance of the bitumen, water resistance, and low-temperature crack resistance of the bitumen mixture.

To summarize, mechanically recycled GF from WTB is viable and promising in the modification of the asphalt pavement materials and provides a new environmentally friendly recycling method for the waste WTB. Though mechanical recycling is relatively simple, the structure of the fiber may be damaged and the mechanical properties may be reduced in the recovery process. Considering the crushing, screening, and surface treatment process, the recycled GF from GFRP composites of WTB is the secondary modifier of SBS-modified asphalt in this study. Modifying the glass fiber prior to adding to SBS-modified asphalt can further improve the stability of composite-modified asphalt. These modification methods mainly include physical modification, surface chemical grafting, and surface chemical etching [18–24]. In this study, the surface chemical grafting by silane coupling agent was chosen as the surface treatment process. The objective of this study is to investigate the pretreated GF-WTB modification effects and mechanism on SBS-modified asphalt by macroscopic high- and low-temperature tests and microscopic observation, providing an effective regeneration solution for GFRP from waste WTB.

2. Materials and Experiments

2.1. Raw Materials and Sample Preparation

2.1.1. Matrix Asphalt and Raw GFRP Composites

The virgin asphalt binder in this study was AH-70 (60–80 penetration) from Petro-China Company Limited (Beijing, China). The raw glass fiber-reinforced polymer (GFRP) composites were obtained from the decommissioned wind turbine blade (WTB) at end-life, as seen in Figure 1a, which was crushed into small pieces using Los Angeles Abrasion Value machines by the Hunan Chuangyi Industrial Material Company (Xiangtan, China), as seen in Figure 1b.

Figure 1. Raw GFRP composites from wind turbine blade at end-of-life: (**a**) wind turbine blade at end-of-life; (**b**) recycled GFRP.

2.1.2. Grading of GFRP Pieces

Using the vibrating screen machine (ZBSX-89), the raw GFRP pieces were screened and recycles with different diameters were mechanically separated. GF components were mainly distributed in the following several diameter particles: A (<0.075 mm), B (0.15–0.075 mm), C (0.3–0.15 mm), as seen in Figure 2. Among the three particle types, particle C is of the best degree of uniformity and relatively large size, which was selected as the original modifier in the following study.

Figure 2. Three types of GF particles obtained after grading of GFRP pieces: (**a**) <0.075 mm; (**b**) 0.15–0.075 mm; (**c**) 0.3–0.15 mm.

2.1.3. GF Particles Heat- and Humidity-Resistance Check and Surface Treatment

According to current Chinese specification [25], under conditions of 210 °C and 1 h, the weight damage rate of the sample must be not more than 6% and the sample should not exhibit combustion. GF particles were placed in a beaker and heated in an oven at 210 °C for 1 h to measure the weight damage rate. With a mean damage rate of 3.2% from two measurements and no combustion, it was determined that the GF was resistant to high temperature and met the relative requirement for asphalt modification. For a humidity-resistance check, GF particles were prepared in a beaker with moderate deionized water and placed in a curing box at about 20 °C and 90% relative humidity to observe its shape and color changes and record quality change after 5 days. With no obvious change of color, no dispersed trend of the fiber clump, and a 1% (less than 5%) water absorption rate, it was determined that the GF was resistant to humidity and met the relative requirement for asphalt modification [25].

The GF particles surface treatment process was as follows. Firstly, the GF particles were dried at 230 °C for 1 h and after cooling they were then soaked in acetone for 1 h to remove the surface impurities. Three types of silane coupling agents (UP152, KH550, and KH792) were chosen for comparison. Silane coupling agent, ethanol, and water (at a volume ratio of 5:85:10) were stirred fully and the blend was placed for 10 min until hydrolysis. The GF particles were immersed in quantitative coupling agent solution for 1 h and was then taken out to be dried and ready for use.

2.1.4. Preparation of GF-WTB/SBS-Modified Asphalt

Quantitative asphalt AH-70 was heated at 145 °C for 0.5 h to reach the flow state and evaporate water and then subsequently added with SBS (based on the weight of the matrix asphalt, 2, 3, 4, 5% SBS) and the blend was shear emulsified under 2000 rpm for 20 min at 160–170 °C.

Silane coupling agent modified GF-WTB was added to the prepared SBS-modified asphalt sample (based on the weight of the matrix asphalt, 0, 1, 2, 4% GF-WTB) and the GF-WTB was kept warm and swelled for 10 min at 160 °C. Then, the GF-WTB incorporated SBS-modified asphalt was evenly dispersed under 4000 rpm for 40 min at 140 °C and finally was developed for 10 min at 150 °C. The sample naming was shown in the following example. If the SBS modifier dosage was 2% and the GF-WTB dosage was 1%, the GF-WTB/SBS composite-modified asphalt sample was marked as SBS2 + WTB1. Figure 3 shows the preparation flowchart of the GF-WTB/SBS composite-modified asphalt.

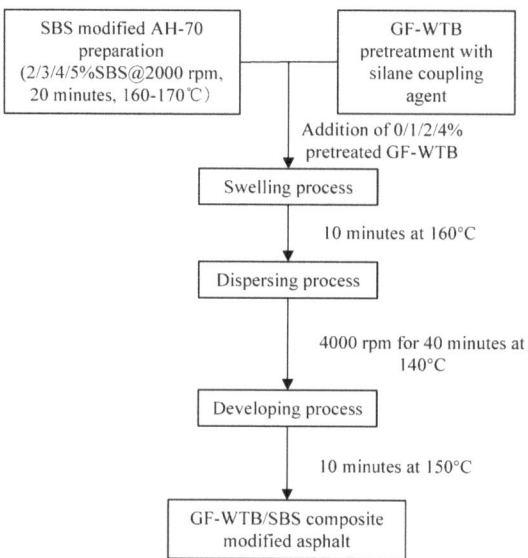

Figure 3. Flowchart of GF-WTB/SBS composite-modified asphalt preparation.

2.2. Rotational Viscosity

According to the standard test methods of asphalt for highway engineering [26], the rotational viscosity of the GF-WTB/SBS composite-modified asphalt was tested using a Brookfield viscometer (model NDJ-1F, Shanghai Changji Geological Instrument Co., Ltd, Shanghai, China) at 135 °C.

2.3. Dynamic Shear Rheometer (DSR) Test

The DSR test was used to characterize viscous and elastic behavior of the GF-WTB/SBS composite-modified asphalt at medium to high temperatures. The DSR model used in the test was DHR-3, adopting the sinusoidal strain control mode. The gap and the diameter for the test were 1 mm and 25 mm, respectively. The angular velocity was 10 rad/s, the control strain was 12%, the range of the scanning temperature was 40–76 °C, and the heating rate was 2 °C/min. For each experimental run using the DSR test, two replicate specimens were measured to avoid the wrong operation or a sample preparation deviation.

2.4. Bending Beam Rheometer (BBR) Test

The BBR test provided a measurement of low-temperature stiffness and relaxation properties of the GF-WTB/SBS composite-modified asphalt. In order to obtain the test results in a relatively short time, according to the time-temperature equivalence principle [27], SHRP researchers increased the test temperature by 10 °C, and the same creep stiffness S-value and the stiffness change rate m-value were obtained when the sample was loaded for 60 s. According to the specification AASHTO T313-2012 [28], the heated sample was poured into BBR mold and after cooling and demolding the asphalt beam was placed in the BBR bath at test temperature for 60 min. In this study, test temperatures of -12 °C, -18 °C, and -24 °C were set and all stiffnesses and m-values were the mean of three measurements.

2.5. Fourier Transform Infrared Spectroscopy (FTIR) Test

Infrared spectral analysis is one of the most widely used methods in the study of chemical structure of polymers. In this study, by comparing with the unpretreated GF particles and observing the changes in the absorption peaks of the main functional groups, characteristics of the functional groups in silane coupling agent pretreated GF particles were expected to be obtained and the surface treatment process of GF particles was expected to be further understood based on chemical changes. The FTIR (Thermo Scientific Nicolet 6700, Waltham, MA, USA) parameters were revolution 4 cm^{-1} with a scan number of 32 times. The sample was blended with potassium bromide (KBr) with ratio of about 1:10, grinded fully, and finally tableted to thin circularity chip. Immediately, the prepared circular specimen was put into FTIR and scanned by infrared light. To avoid the wrong operation or a sample preparation deviation, for each experimental run using the FTIR test, two parallel specimens were measured.

2.6. Scanning Electron Microscope (SEM) Observation and Energy Dispersive Spectrometer (EDS) Analysis

SEM (Zeiss sigma 300) photographs were obtained to observe the surface morphology changes of silane coupling agent pretreated GF particles compared to the unpretreated GF particles. The SEM accelerating voltage was 15 kV and the imaging probe was SE2. The sample was scattered on the conductive glue stuck on the sample stage, sprayed with a thin layer of gold, and then put into the SEM for observation. Combined with the surface morphology observation, the elements distribution on the silane coupling agent pretreated GF particle sample surface was obtained by using the scanning function of the EDS equipped on the SEM.

2.7. Atomic Force Microscope (AFM)

AFM was used to examine the morphology of the matrix asphalt, SBS-modified asphalt, and GF-WTB/SBS composite-modified asphalt at the nanoscale. The asphalt sample was heated and dropped onto the microscope slide to shape the thin film. After cooling down, the AFM specimen was tested by Bruker Dimension ICON in tapping mode.

3. Results and Discussion

The basic technical properties of the virgin asphalt binder AH-70 are listed in Table 1.

Table 1. Technical properties of AH-70.

Technical Index	Specification Requirement	Test Result	Experimental Method [26]
Penetration@25 °C, 100 g, 5 s (0.1 mm)	60~80	60.3	T0604
Penetration index (PI)	-1.5~1.0	-0.5	T0604
Ductility@15 °C, 5 cm/min (cm)	$\geq$100	>120	T0605
Softening point (°C)	$\geq$45	47	T0606

Table 1. *Cont.*

	Technical Index	Specification Requirement	Test Result	Experimental Method [26]
	Rotational viscosity@135 °C (Pa·s)	-	0.571	T0625
	Mass change (%)	≤±0.8	0.1	T0610
RTFOT residue	Residual penetration ratio (%)	≥61	65	T0604
	Residual ductility @15 °C (cm)	≥15	21.8	T0605

3.1. Rotational Viscosity

The effect of GF-WTB content on the rotational viscosity of a certain content (2, 3, 4, or 5 wt%) SBS-modified binders is shown in Figure 4. Figure 4 is the average of the measurement results. Three specimens of each asphalt were measured to ensure reliable test results. The maximum coefficient of variation (CV) of each asphalt sample group in the rotational viscosity test was 3.5%. As seen in Figure 4, the rotational viscosity values of a certain content SBS-modified binders increase with the GF-WTB content. The values of the 5 wt% SBS-modified binder ranged from 3.5 Pa·s for 0 wt% GF-WTB content to 3.9 Pa·s for 4 wt% content, which are both larger than 3.0 Pa·s, which is the maximum allowable value in SHRP specification considering mixing performance. Therefore, the 5 wt% SBS-modified binder was only used for the trend evaluation in the following analysis. In the figure, the maximum rotational viscosity increasing rate 17% appeared in the 4 wt% SBS-modified binder from 2.3 Pa·s for 1 wt% GF-WTB content to 2.7 Pa·s for 2 wt% content. The rotational viscosity test results will be helpful to further research for GF-WTB/SBS composite-modified asphalt mixture pavement performance.

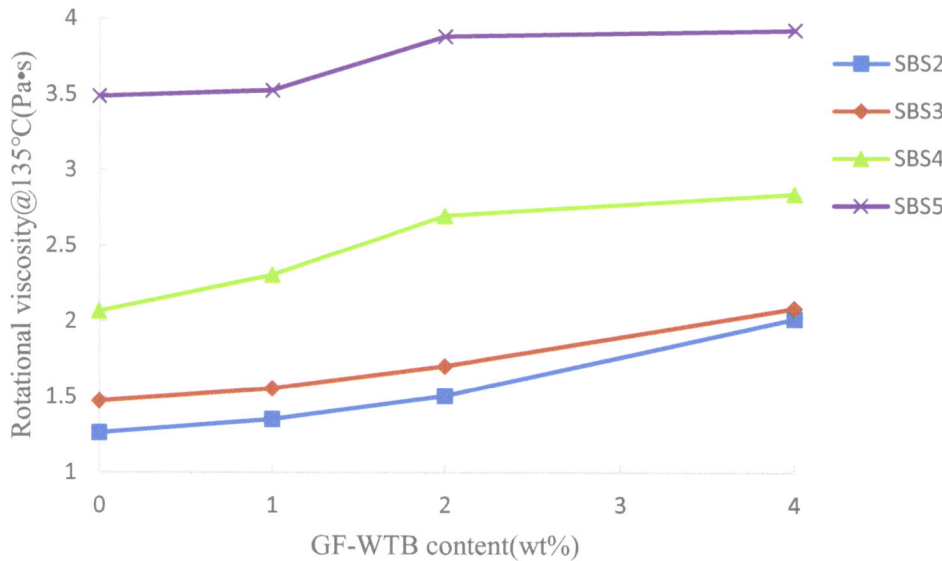

Figure 4. Effect of GF-WTB content on rotational viscosity under certain SBS dosage.

3.2. Dynamic Rheological Properties and Temperature Sensitivity

The complex shear modulus G^* can be considered the binder sample's total resistance to deformation when repeatedly sheared. The log G^* values of the 2, 3, 4, or 5 wt% SBS-modified binders with different GF-WTB contents vs. temperatures from 40 °C to 76 °C are shown in Figure 5. Figure 5 shows that the log G^* values lineally decrease with the increase in temperature for all the asphalt samples. For the same SBS content, the log G^* value at the end temperature 76 °C increases obviously with the GF-WTB content. In addition, the sensitivity of log G* to temperature, i.e., the regression coefficient (regression line slope), decreases with the increase in GF-WTB dosage under certain SBS content. The DSR test result analysis indicates that the addition of silane coupling agent modified GF-WTB reduces G* temperature sensitivity of the SBS-modified asphalt and the increase in the G* value of binder will transmit to the increase in the stiffness of respective asphalt mixture.

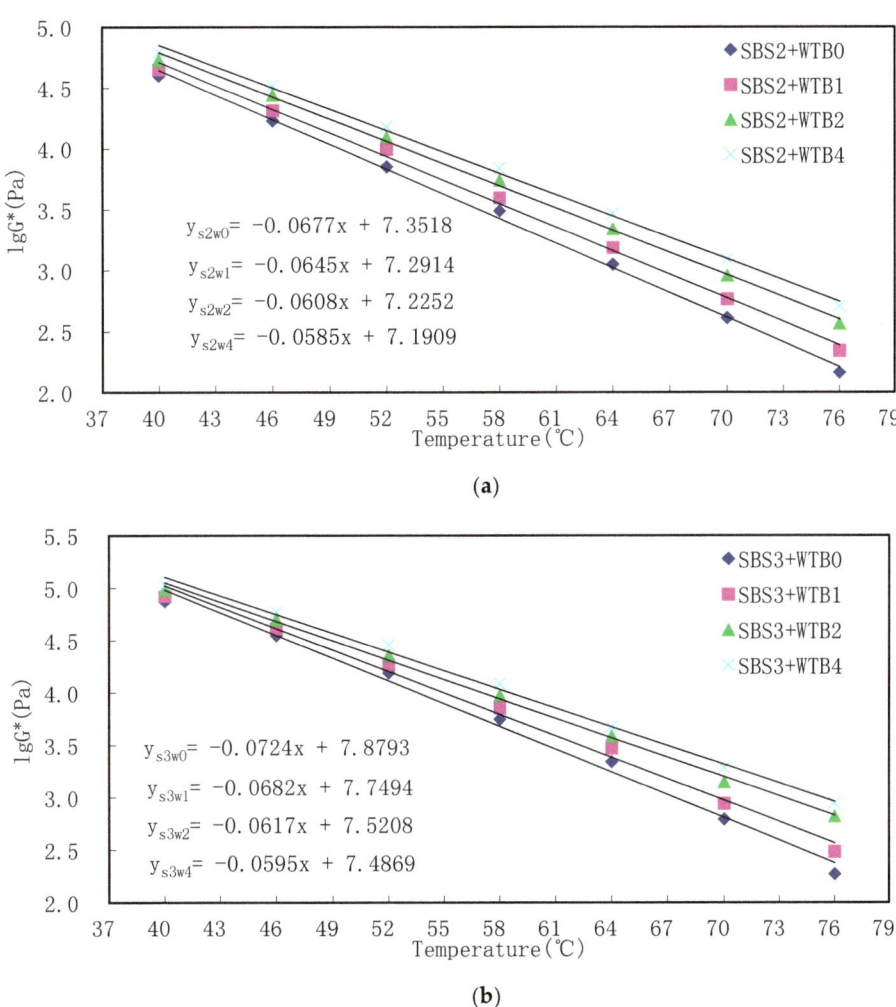

Figure 5. *Cont.*

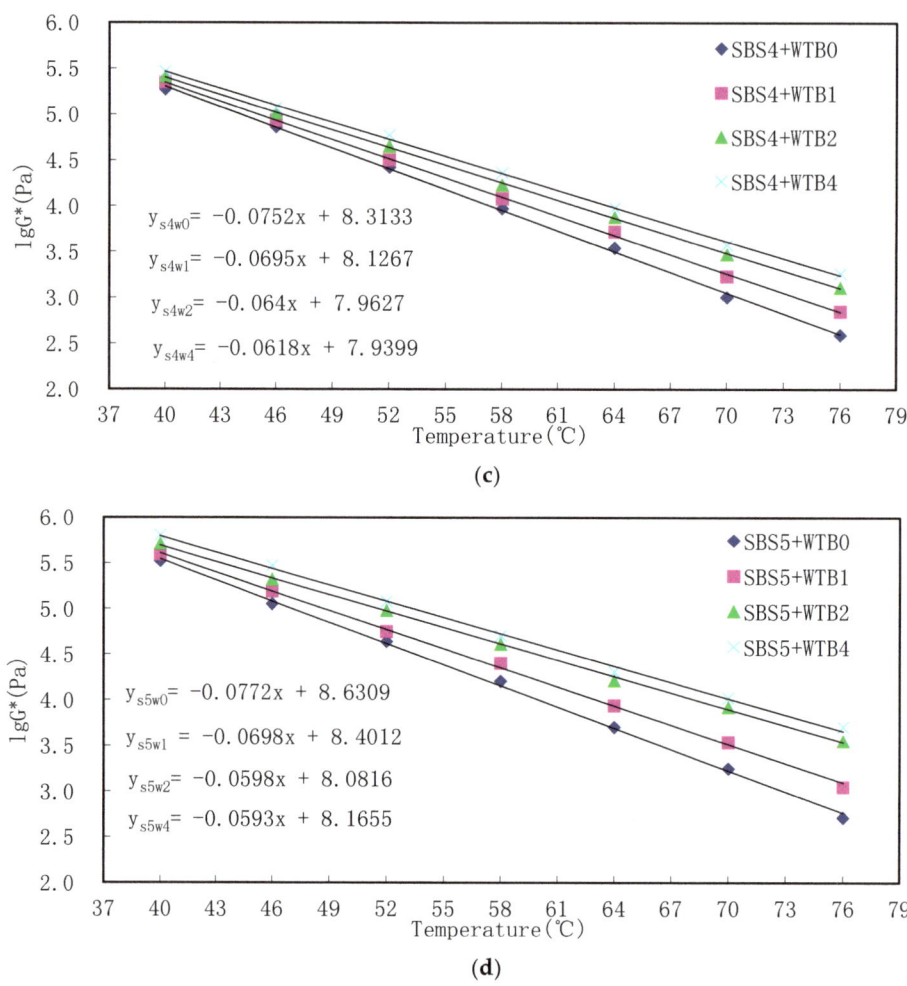

Figure 5. The logarithm of the complex shear modulus of GF-WTB/SBS composite-modified asphalt: (**a**) SBS2 + WTBx; (**b**) SBS3 + WTBx; (**c**) SBS4 + WTBx; (**d**) SBS5 + WTBx.

Under the same G* value, the smaller the phase angle δ, which means the large elastic component and the small viscous one, the stronger the anti-rutting ability of the asphalt material. Under high-temperature conditions, the larger G*/sin δ indicates that G* is larger and δ is smaller [29]. Therefore, the rutting factor G*/sin δ is used to represent the anti-rutting ability in the SHRP specification. The G*/sin δ values of the 2, 3, 4, or 5 wt% SBS-modified binders with different GF-WTB contents vs. high temperatures 64–76 °C are shown in Figure 6. The Figure 6 shows that the G*/sin δ values decrease with the increase in high temperature for all the asphalt samples. Evidently, the rutting factor increases with the SBS dosage. The horizonal line in Figure 6 represents the minimum G*/sin δ value 1.0 kPa for the unaged binder in the performance-graded DSR specifications. Under the same SBS content, the addition of silane coupling agent modified GF-WTB improves the high-temperature performance grade, e.g., for 4 wt% SBS-modified asphalt, incorporation of 2 or 4 wt% GF-WTB elevates the high-temperature PG from 70 °C to 76 °C. The DSR test results show that GF-WTB/SBS composite-modified binders are of better resistance to deformation, anti-rutting ability, and temperature-insensitivity. Among the composite-modified binders with 2, 3, 4 wt% SBS, in comprehensively considering the high-temperature PG, temperature sensitivity, and GF-WTB dosage, SBS4 + WTB2 is the optimal one.

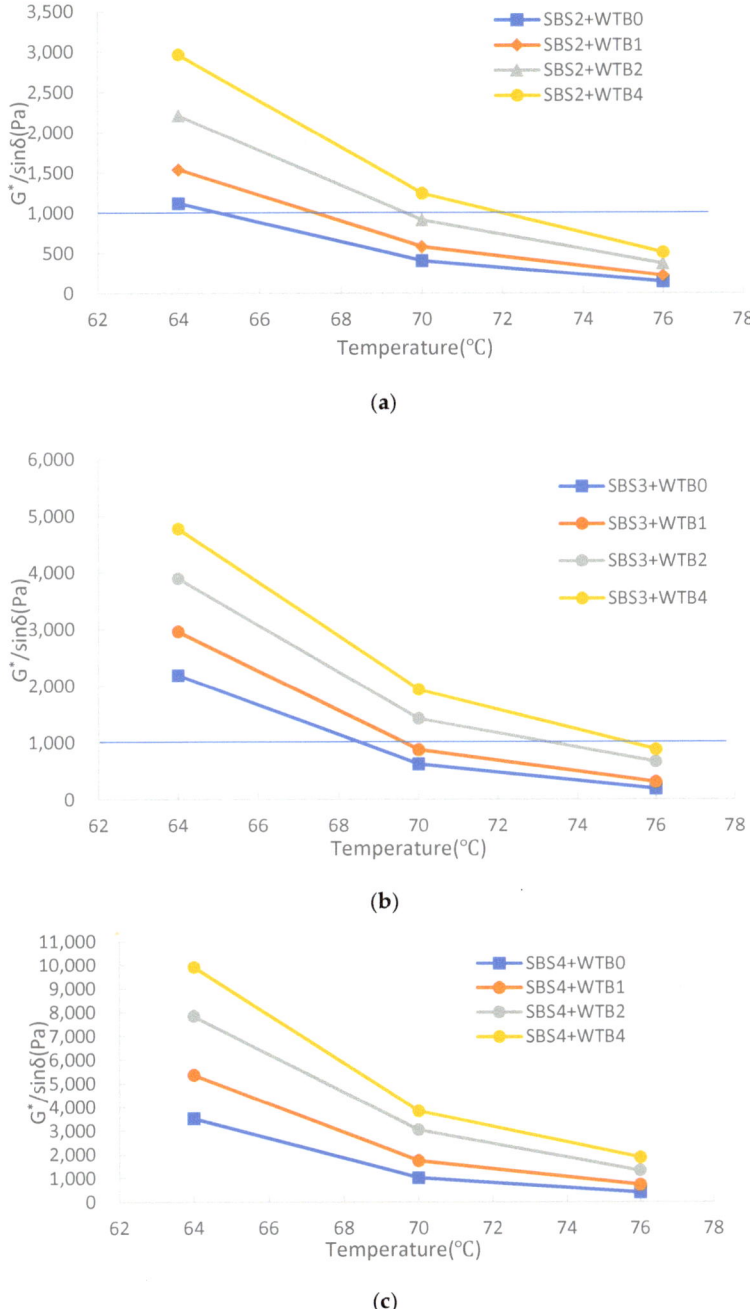

Figure 6. *Cont.*

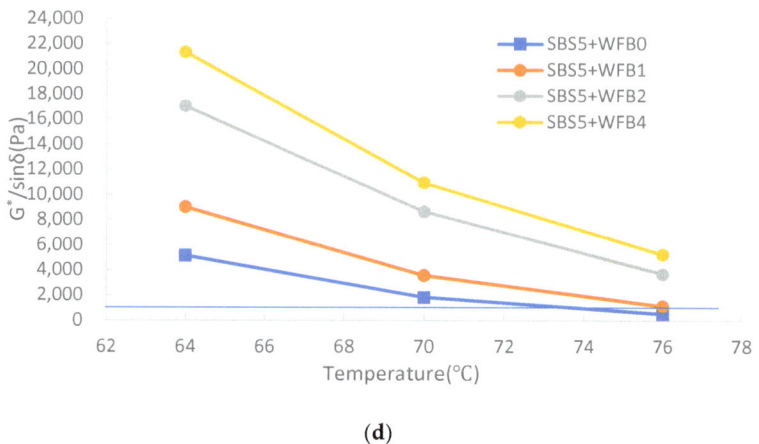

(**d**)

Figure 6. The rutting factor and high-temperature PG of GF-WTB/SBS composite-modified asphalt: (**a**) SBS2 + WTBx; (**b**) SBS3 + WTBx; (**c**) SBS4 + WTBx; (**d**) SBS5 + WTBx.

3.3. Low-Temperature Properties

In this study, BBR test temperatures of −12 °C, −18 °C, and −24 °C were set and S-values and m-values of all GF-WTB/SBS composite-modified binders are in Tables 2 and 3. Tables 2 and 3 present the average of the measurement results. Three BBR specimens of each asphalt were measured to ensure reliable test results. The maximum coefficient of variation of each asphalt sample group in the BBR test was 5.0%. Table 2 shows under −12 °C and 60 s loading conditions, with S-values and m-values of four SBS2 + WTB binders and four SBS3 + WTB binders all satisfying S ≤ 300 MPa and m ≥ 0.3 SHRP specification demands, respectively, and meeting performance-grade PG-22. In addition, for SBS3 + WTB1 and SBS3 + WTB4, the performance grades also reached PG-28 demand. Table 3 shows four SBS4 + WTB binders and four SBS5 + WTB binders that can meet performance-grade PG-34.

Table 2. BBR test results of SBS2 + WTBx and SBS3 + WTBx.

Temp (°C)	Index of BBR Test	Code of the Asphalt Binder							
		SBS2 + WTB0	SBS2 + WTB1	SBS2 + WTB2	SBS2 + WTB4	SBS3 + WTB0	SBS3 + WTB1	SBS3 + WTB2	SBS3 + WTB4
−12	S (MPa)	175	142	160	121	121	112	106	115
	m	0.352	0.315	0.385	0.309	0.312	0.306	0.294	0.321
	k ($\times 10^{-4}$ MPa^{-1})	20.11	22.18	24.06	25.54	25.79	27.32	27.74	27.91
−18	S (MPa)	368	303	208	209	187	198	171	167
	m	0.312	0.307	0.252	0.261	0.279	0.301	0.292	0.305
	k ($\times 10^{-4}$ MPa^{-1})	8.48	10.13	12.12	12.49	14.92	15.20	17.07	18.26
−24	S (MPa)	661	615	594	375	391	340	302	281
	m	0.240	0.257	0.250	0.259	0.273	0.265	0.290	0.295
	k ($\times 10^{-4}$ MPa^{-1})	3.63	4.18	4.21	6.91	6.98	7.79	9.60	10.50
Performance grade		PG-22	PG-22	PG-22	PG-22	PG-22	PG-28	PG-22	PG-28

Table 3. BBR test results of SBS4 + WTBx and SBS5 + WTBx.

Temp (°C)	Index of BBR Test	Code of the Asphalt Binder							
		SBS4 + WTB0	SBS4 + WTB1	SBS4 + WTB2	SBS4 + WTB4	SBS5 + WTB0	SBS5 + WTB1	SBS5 + WTB2	SBS5 + WTB4
−12	S (MPa)	116	107	106	103	96	93	91	89
	m	0.343	0.323	0.342	0.347	0.339	0.341	0.346	0.344
	k (×10^{-4} MPa^{-1})	29.57	30.19	32.26	33.69	35.31	36.67	38.02	38.65
−18	S (MPa)	145	140	132	128	119	115	111	108
	m	0.312	0.317	0.330	0.338	0.332	0.337	0.342	0.339
	k (×10^{-4} MPa^{-1})	21.52	22.64	25.00	26.41	27.90	29.30	30.81	31.39
−24	S (MPa)	263	256	231	246	220	223	184	186
	m	0.306	0.311	0.302	0.331	0.325	0.333	0.301	0.313
	k (×10^{-4} MPa^{-1})	11.63	12.15	13.07	13.46	14.77	14.93	16.36	16.83
	Performance grade	PG-34	PG-34	PG-34	PG-34	PG-34	PG-34	PG-34	PG-34

Relative research shows that when the low-temperature grade of PG classification is set every 6 °C, although different asphalts under the same PG low-temperature grade have the same classification standard, the difference in low-temperature performance between them cannot be reflected [30,31]. Based on the S and m indexes, a new low-temperature evaluation index k = m/S is proposed by combining the two together; that is, the creep rate of asphalt under the unit creep stiffness. It can be seen from the representation that the larger the k index, meaning small creep stiffness and large stiffness change rate, the better the low-temperature crack resistance of asphalt. The index k-values under −12 °C, −18 °C, or −24 °C vs. GF-WTB contents of certain SBS dosage-modified asphalt are shown in Figure 7 and the k-values data are in Tables 2 and 3. Figure 7 shows that k-values decrease with the test temperature decreasing for all the asphalt samples and k-value increases evidently with the SBS dosage increasing. Under the same SBS dosage, GF-WTB content elevates the k-value and the low-temperature crack resistance of SBS-modified asphalt. For SBS4 + WTB composite-modified binders under −12 °C, −18 °C, or −24 °C, from 0 to 4 wt% GF-WTB k-value increases by 13.9%, 22.7%, 15.7%, respectively, from 1 to 2 wt% GF-WTB by 6.9%, 10.4%, 7.5%, respectively, and from 2 to 4 wt% GF-WTB only by 4.4%, 5.6%, 3%, respectively. In comprehensively considering the k-value increasing rate and GF-WTB dosage, SBS4 + WTB2 is the optimal combination.

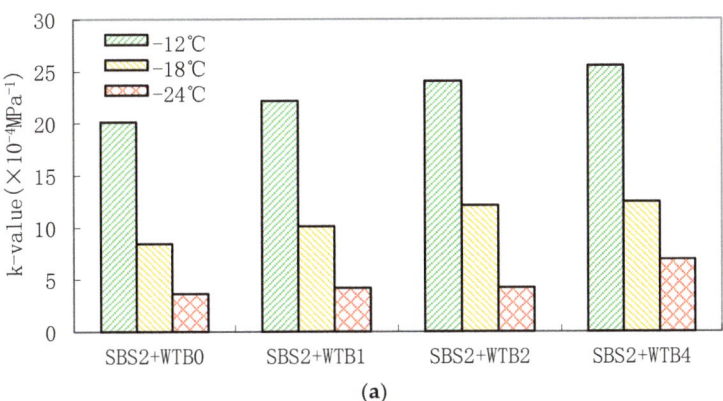

Figure 7. *Cont.*

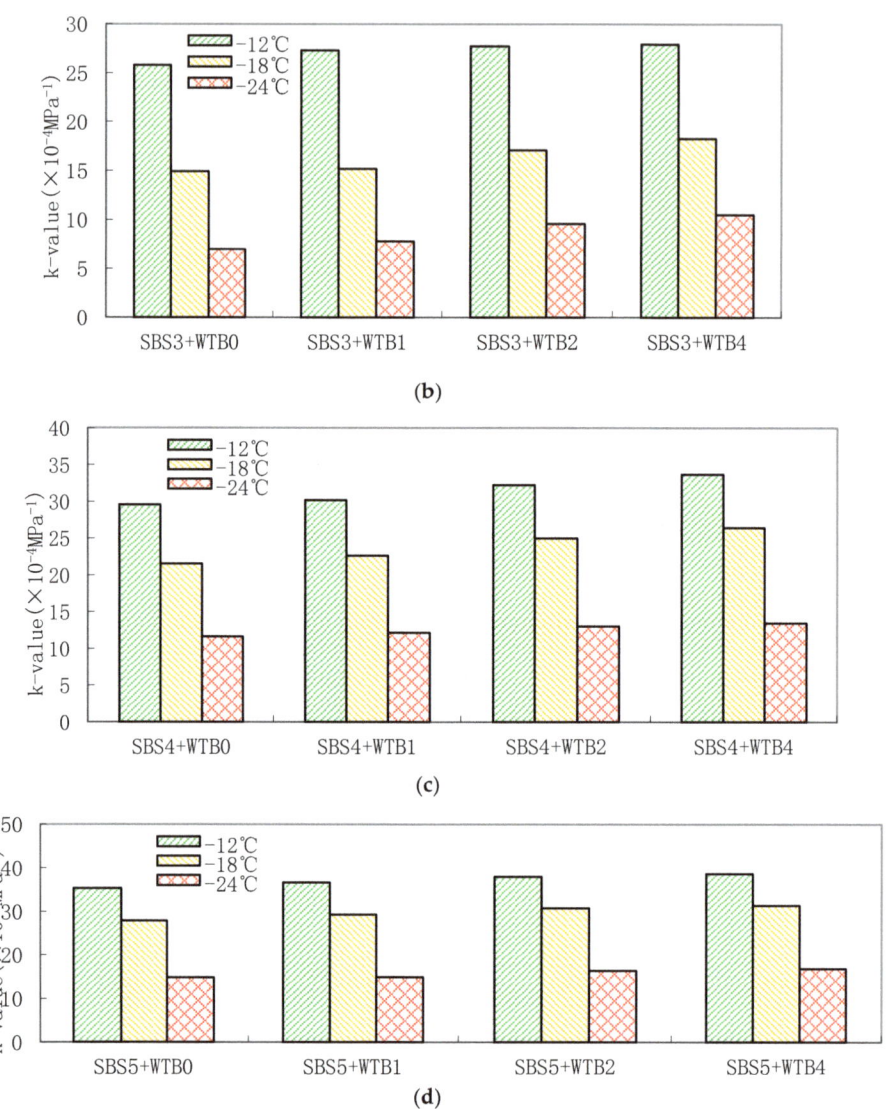

Figure 7. Effect of GF-WTB content on BBR k-value under certain SBS dosage and temperature: (**a**) SBS2 + WTBx; (**b**) SBS3 + WTBx; (**c**) SBS4 + WTBx; (**d**) SBS5 + WTBx.

3.4. Fourier Transform Infrared Spectroscopy (FTIR) Test

The silane coupling agent UP152 used in the study with the chemical name vinyltriacetoxysilane and the molecular formula $C_8H_{12}O_6Si$ was produced by the Nanjing Upchemical company. The chemical reaction mechanism between GF-WTB and UP152 is shown in Figure 8. The UP152 Si functional groups acetoxyl -OAc hydrolyze and generate silanol Si-OH, which are unsteady and generate Si-O-Si in further polycondensation, and the carbon functional group vinyl $CH_2=HC-$ in UP152 can react with some organic functional groups in asphalt materials. Therefore, the UP152 can couple the inorganic glass fiber recycled from WTB with the organic asphalt materials.

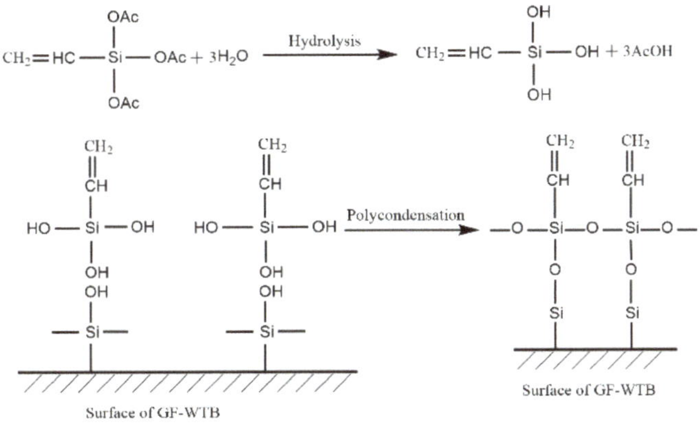

Figure 8. Chemical reaction mechanism between GF-WTB and UP152.

The FTIR spectrograms of the untreated GF-WTB and UP152-modified GF-WTB are in Figure 9. Absorption peaks at 2929 and 2872 cm^{-1} for the original GF-WTB respectively represent C-H stretching of CH_2 and CH in aliphatic of the polyester resin curing agent residues, corresponding to 2954 and 2842 cm^{-1} for the modified GF-WTB [32]. The original GF-WTB and the UP152-modified GF-WTB show the band corresponding to the C=O stretching of the polyester resin curing agent residues respectively at 1728 cm^{-1} and 1720 cm^{-1} [33]. The new absorption peaks at 1635 and 1454 cm^{-1} for UP152-modified GF-WTB respectively characterize the carbon functional group vinyl C=C stretching and the vinyl CH_2 scissor bending vibration. Absorption peaks at 1091, 699, and 479 cm^{-1} for the modified GF-WTB characterize the antisymmetric stretching, symmetric stretching, and bending vibration of Si-O-Si, with the corresponding bands 1073, 699, and 477 cm^{-1} for the original GF-WTB. The three absorption peaks all show the same trend; that is, the absorption peak of UP152-modified GF-WTB is stronger than that of original one. It shows that the chemical reaction between the coupling agent and the glass fiber surface produces new Si-O-Si bonds. The analysis of the FTIR results shows that the silicon coupling agent UP152 was successfully grafted to the surface of the recycled glass fiber from WTB.

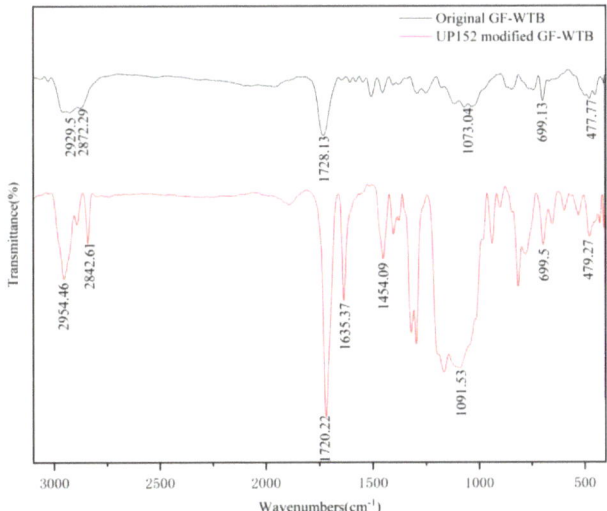

Figure 9. FTIR spectrograms of untreated GF-WTB and UP152-modified GF-WTB.

3.5. Scanning Electron Microscope (SEM) Observation and Energy Dispersive Spectrometer (EDS) Analysis

The SEM photographs of the untreated GF-WTB and UP152-modified GF-WTB are shown in Figure 10. It can be seen from the figure that the surface of the original GF-WTB is smooth without any rough groove structure except for some resin curing agent residues scattered on it. After the modification of UP152, the surface of the fiber is covered with a rough graft layer of silane coupling agent and the fiber diameter also increases, indicating that the graft layer of the coupling agent UP152 has a certain thickness. Figure 11 shows the corresponding EDS element spectrum by spot scanning, and relative contents of elements are listed in Tables 4 and 5. Tables 4 and 5 show that after UP152 modification, the C element on the surface of GF-WTB increases significantly, Si and O contents decrease, and Ca element decreases significantly, indicating that the coupling agent UP152 was successfully grafted.

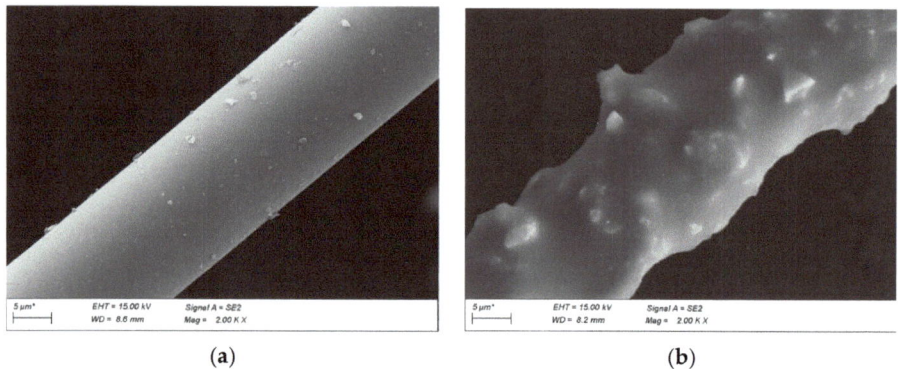

Figure 10. SEM photographs of the GF-WTB: (**a**) untreated; (**b**) UP152-modified.

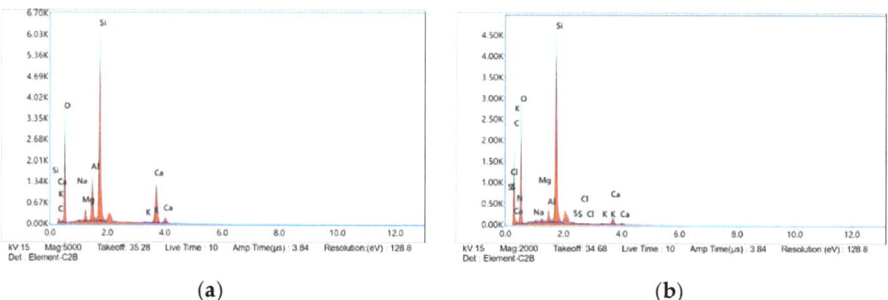

Figure 11. EDS element spectrum of the GF-WTB: (**a**) untreated; (**b**) UP152-modified.

Table 4. Element content of untreated GF-WTB.

Element	Series	Weight %	Atomic %	Error %
C	K	0.36	0.67	20.36
O	K	38.94	54.84	9.30
Na	K	0.45	0.44	14.88
Mg	K	2.08	1.92	7.38
Al	K	7.61	6.36	4.74
Si	K	30.53	24.50	3.72
K	K	0.36	0.21	17.17
Ca	K	19.67	11.06	3.19

Table 5. Element content of UP152-modified GF-WTB.

Element	Series	Weight %	Atomic %	Error %
C	K	33.31	45.25	10.20
N	K	2.27	2.65	20.96
O	K	34.26	34.94	9.54
Na	K	0.66	0.47	17.17
Mg	K	0.71	0.48	12.25
Al	K	1.82	1.10	6.57
Si	K	23.20	13.48	3.05
S	K	0.86	0.44	14.94
Cl	K	0.11	0.05	23.64
K	K	0.28	0.12	13.49
Ca	K	2.52	1.03	7.85

According to the FTIR, SEM, and EDS analysis of the UP152-modified GF-WTB, the coupling agent grafted fiber surface becomes thicker and rougher and introduces a vinyl functional group, which improves the adhesion of the grafted GF-WTB to the SBS-modified asphalt.

3.6. Atomic Force Microscope (AFM)

Figure 12a–c show the AFM three-dimensional images of the matrix asphalt, SBS-modified asphalt (with 4 wt% SBS), and GF-WTB/SBS composite-modified asphalt (with 4 wt% SBS and 2 wt% GF-WTB), respectively. In Figure 12, the dark areas are pits and the bright areas are bumps. It can be seen from Figure 12a that the microscopic morphology of the matrix asphalt surface is relatively uniform. The surface is distributed with alternating dark and pale areas, which are close to bee-shaped structure. Research shows that these bee-shaped structures are the clustering of the asphaltene micelles not completely dispersed in the dispersion medium [34]. It can be seen from Figure 12b that the surface of SBS-modified asphalt presents a network structure, which is formed by the SBS block copolymer crosslink and swelling by absorbing light components in asphalt. This network structure can effectively change the elasticity, plasticity, and ductility of asphalt, thereby improving the high- and low-temperature performance of asphalt.

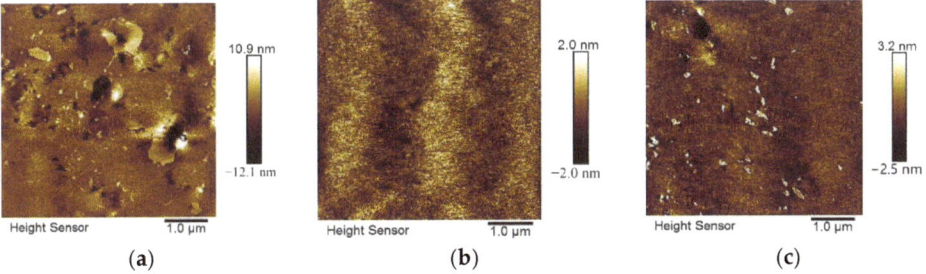

Figure 12. AFM of: (**a**) matrix asphalt; (**b**) SBS-modified asphalt; (**c**) GF-WTB/SBS composite-modified asphalt.

From Figure 12c, the convex GF-WTB particles (white areas) can be clearly seen in the SBS-modified asphalt network structure, and the two modifiers have good compatibility. During preparation, the GF-WTB/SBS composite-modified asphalt was stirred and developed at a high temperature. Swelling, adsorption of the asphalt light components, and reaction between some organic functional groups in asphalt and the vinyl functional group on grafted GF-WTB particles surface occurred. Then, the GF-WTB agents were evenly dispersed in the SBS-modified asphalt in the form of particles and chains, and the

GF-WTB/SBS composite-modified asphalt obtained better toughness and low-temperature crack resistance.

4. Conclusions

In this study, composite-modified asphalt composed of silane coupling agent pre-treated recycled GF from WTB and SBS-modified asphalt was investigated in terms of modification effects and mechanism. The following conclusions can be drawn from this research:

(1) The recycled GF particles from WTB are of good heat- and humidity-resistance performance and in regular asphalt performance tests the rotational viscosity of SBS-modified binders evidently increases with the GF-WTB addition dosage under certain SBS content. In the high-temperature rheology performance DSR test, GF-WTB/SBS composite-modified binders presented better resistance to deformation, anti-rutting ability, and temperature-insensitivity.

(2) In the low-temperature BBR test, for 4 wt% SBS content GF-WTB/SBS composite-modified binders under $-24\ °C$, low-temperature crack resistance evaluation index k-value increased by 15.7% from 0 to 4 wt% GF-WTB dosage. Addition of GF-WTB can elevate the low-temperature crack resistance of SBS-modified asphalt.

(3) In comprehensively considering the high-temperature PG, high-temperature sensitivity, k-value increasing rate, and GF-WTB dosage, 4 wt% SBS content with 2 wt% GF-WTB as a secondary modifier is the optimal combination.

(4) FTIR, SEM, and EDS microscopic tests analysis shows that the GF-WTB successfully grafted by UP152 coupling agent is of thicker and rougher surface and a vinyl functional group was introduced, improving the adhesion of the GF-WTB to the SBS-modified asphalt. Silane coupling agent modification pretreatment for GF-WTB is one important and indispensable step for GF-WTB/SBS composite-modified binder preparation.

(5) AFM observation found that SBS and GF-WTB exist in GF-WTB/SBS composite-modified asphalt in their own specific structural forms and the two modifiers have good compatibility. This compound form can better absorb asphalt light components, improve the elasticity and toughness of asphalt, and then improve high- and low-temperature properties of asphalt.

The good asphalt properties will transmit to the pavement performance in each respective asphalt mixture. GF-WTB/SBS composite-modified asphalt anti-aging performance and its mixture pavement performance will be further researched.

Author Contributions: Conceptualization, Y.N. and Q.L.; methodology, Z.X.; software, Q.L. and S.Z.; validation, X.H.; formal analysis, Q.L. and Z.X.; investigation, S.Z. and X.H.; resources, Y.N.; data curation, Y.N.; writing—original draft preparation, Q.L., Z.X. and S.Z; writing—review and editing, Y.N., Q.L. and X.H.; visualization, Z.X.; supervision, Y.N.; project administration, Y.N.; funding acquisition, Y.N. All authors have read and agreed to the published version of the manuscript.

Funding: This research was funded by the Hunan Provincial Natural Science Foundation of China, grant number 2022JJ30259.

Institutional Review Board Statement: Not applicable.

Informed Consent Statement: Not applicable.

Data Availability Statement: The data used to support the findings of this study are available from the corresponding authors upon reasonable request.

Conflicts of Interest: The authors declare no conflict of interest.

References

1. Beauson, J.; Laurent, A.; Rudolph, D.P.; Jensen, J.P. The complex end-of-life of wind turbine blades: A review of the European context. *Renew. Sust. Energy Rev.* **2022**, *155*, 111847. [CrossRef]
2. Liu, P.; Barlow, C.Y. Wind turbine blade waste in 2050. *Waste Manag.* **2017**, *62*, 229–240. [CrossRef] [PubMed]
3. Chen, J.L.; Wang, J.H.; Ni, A.Q. Recycling and reuse of composite materials for wind turbine blades: An overview. *J. Reinf. Plast. Comp.* **2019**, *12*, 567–577. [CrossRef]
4. Alshannaq, A.A.; Bank, L.C.; Scott, D.W.; Gentry, R. A decommissioned wind blade as a second-life construction material for a transmission pole. *Constr. Mater.* **2021**, *1*, 95–104. [CrossRef]
5. Mishnaevsky, L.; Branner, K.; Petersen, H.N.; Beauson, J.; McGugan, M.; Sørensen, B.F. Materials for wind turbine blades: An overview. *Materials* **2017**, *10*, 1285. [CrossRef]
6. Beauson, J.; Lilholt, H.; Brondsted, P. Recycling solid residues recovered from glass fibre-reinforced composites-a review applied to wind turbine blade materials. *J. Reinf. Plast. Comp.* **2014**, *33*, 1542–1556. [CrossRef]
7. Pickering, S.J. Recycling technologies for thermoset composites–current status. *Comp. A* **2006**, *37*, 1206–1215. [CrossRef]
8. Pimenta, S.; Pinho, S.T. Recycling carbon fibre reinforced polymers for structural applications: Technology review and market outlook. *Waste Manag.* **2011**, *31*, 378–392. [CrossRef]
9. Meira-Castro, A.C.; Carvalho, J.P.; Ribeiro, M.C.S.; Meixedo, J.P.; Silva, F.J.G.; Fiúza, A.; Dinis, M.L. An integrated recycling approach for GFRP pultrusion wastes: Recycling and reuse assessment into new composite materials using Fuzzy Boolean Nets. *J. Clean. Prod.* **2014**, *66*, 420–430. [CrossRef]
10. Paulsen, E.B.; Enevoldsen, P.A. Multidisciplinary review of recycling methods for end-of-life wind turbine blades. *Energies* **2021**, *14*, 4247. [CrossRef]
11. Asokan, P.; Osmani, M.; Price, A.D.F. Assessing the recycling potential of glass fibre reinforced plastic waste in concrete and cement composites. *J. Clean. Prod.* **2009**, *17*, 821–829. [CrossRef]
12. Ribeiro, M.C.S.; Meira-Castro, A.C.; Silva, F.G.; Santos, J.; Meixedo, J.P.; Fiúza, A.; Dinis, M.L.; Alvim, M.R. Re-use assessment of thermoset composite wastes as aggregate and filler replacement for concrete-polymer composite materials: A case study regarding GFRP pultrusion wastes. *Resour. Conserv. Recycl.* **2015**, *104*, 417–426. [CrossRef]
13. Schmidl, E.; Hinrichs, S. Geocycle provides sustainable recycling of rotor blades in cement plant. *DEWI Mag.* **2010**, *36*, 6–14.
14. Zhu, H.Z.; Tan, Q.Q.; Yang, X.S.; Fan, S.P.; Zhao, H.D. Research status and prospect of fiber modified asphalt mixture performance. *Sci. Technol. Eng.* **2022**, *22*, 2573–2584.
15. Liu, H. Study on the Evaluation of Performance of the Regenerated Fiber Reinforced Asphalt Pavements. Master's Thesis, Beijing Jiaotong University, Beijing, China, 2011.
16. Dehghan, Z.; Modarres, A. Evaluating the fatigue properties of hot mix asphalt reinforced by recycled PET fibers using 4-point bending test. *Constr. Build. Mater.* **2017**, *139*, 384–393. [CrossRef]
17. Yang, Q.L.; Hong, B.; Lin, J.; Wang, D.W.; Zhong, J.; Oeser, M. Study on the reinforcement effect and the underlying mechanisms of a bitumen reinforced with recycled glass fiber chips. *J. Clean. Prod.* **2019**, *251*, 119768. [CrossRef]
18. Zhang, Y.; Huang, Y.; Liu, L.; Wu, L.N. Surface modification of aramid fiber with γ-ray radiation for improving interfacial bonding strength with epoxy resin. *J. Appl. Polym. Sci.* **2007**, *106*, 2251–2262. [CrossRef]
19. Gao, J.; Dai, Y.Y.; Wang, X.; Huang, J.Y.; Yao, J.; Yang, J.; Liu, X.Y. Effects of different fluorination routes on aramid fiber surface structures and interlaminar shear strength of its composites. *Appl. Surf. Sci.* **2013**, *270*, 627–633. [CrossRef]
20. Kim, J.G.; Choi, I.; Lee, D.G.; Seo, I.S. Flame and silane treatments for improving the adhesive bonding characteristics of aramid/epoxy composites. *Compos. Struct.* **2011**, *93*, 2696–2705. [CrossRef]
21. Ai, T.; Wang, R.; Zhou, W. Effect of grafting alkoxysilane on the surface properties of Kevlar fiber. *Polym. Composite.* **2007**, *28*, 412–416. [CrossRef]
22. Liu, J.L.; Xie, X.F.; Li, L.F. Experimental study on mechanical properties and durability of grafted nano-SiO_2 modified rice straw fiber reinforced concrete. *Constr. Build. Mater.* **2022**, *347*, 128575. [CrossRef]
23. Lei, L.L.; Wang, Q.; Xu, S.S.; Wang, N.; Zheng, X. Fabrication of superhydrophobic concrete used in marine environment with anti-corrosion and stable mechanical properties. *Constr. Build. Mater.* **2020**, *251*, 118946. [CrossRef]
24. Wang, X.P.; Hong, L.; Wu, H.J.; Liu, H.L.; Jia, D.M. Grafting waste rubber powder and its application in asphalt. *Constr. Build. Mater.* **2021**, *271*, 121881. [CrossRef]
25. JT/T 533-2020; Fiber for Asphalt Pavements. China Communications Press: Beijing, China, 2020.
26. JTG E20-2011; Standard Test Methods of Bitumen and Bituminous Mixtures for Highway Engineering. China Communications Press: Beijing, China, 2011.
27. Premkumar, L.; Chehab, G.; Solaimanian, M. Evaluation of low-temperature properties of asphalt binders and mixtures. *Transport. Res. Rec.* **2013**, *2370*, 102–108. [CrossRef]
28. AASHTO T313-12; Standard Method of Test for Determining the Flexural Creep Stiffness of ASPHALT binder Using the Bending Beam Rheometer (BBR). AASHTO: Washington, DC, USA, 2016.
29. Azarhoosh, A.; Koohmishi, M. Investigation of the rutting potential of asphalt binder and mixture modified by styrene-ethylene/propylene-styrene nanocomposite. *Constr. Build. Mater.* **2020**, *255*, 119363. [CrossRef]
30. Xu, J.Q.; Yang, E.H.; Wang, S.F.; Li, S.J. Study on low temperature performance evaluation indicator of sasobit warm mix asphalt. *J. Highw. Transp. Res. Dev.* **2020**, *37*, 8–14.

31. Tan, Y.Q.; Fu, Y.K.; Ji, L.; Zhang, L. Low-temperature evaluation index of rubber asphalt. *J. Harbin Inst. Technol.* **2016**, *48*, 66–70.
32. Nie, Y.H.; Sun, S.H.; Ou, Y.J.; Zhou, C.Y.; Mao, K.L. Experimental investigation on asphalt binders ageing behavior and rejuvenating feasibility in multicycle repeated ageing and recycling. *Adv. Mater. Sci. Eng.* **2018**, *2018*, 5129260. [CrossRef]
33. Nie, Y.H.; Gao, W.J.; Zhou, C.Y.; Yu, P.H.; Song, X.J. Evaluation of ageing behaviors of asphalt binders using FTIR tests. *Int. J. Pavement Res. Technol.* **2021**, *14*, 615–624. [CrossRef]
34. Loeber, L.; Sutton, O.; Morel, J.; Muller, G. New direct observations of asphalts and asphalt binder by scanning electron microscopy and atomic force microscopy. *J. Microsc.* **1996**, *182*, 32–39. [CrossRef]

Disclaimer/Publisher's Note: The statements, opinions and data contained in all publications are solely those of the individual author(s) and contributor(s) and not of MDPI and/or the editor(s). MDPI and/or the editor(s) disclaim responsibility for any injury to people or property resulting from any ideas, methods, instructions or products referred to in the content.

Article

Study on the Properties and Mechanism of Recycled Aggregate/Asphalt Interface Modified by Silane Coupling Agent

Jiawang Zhou [1], Kui Hu [1,*], Junfeng Gao [2,*], Yujing Chen [1], Qilin Yang [3] and Xiaotong Du [1]

Citation: Zhou, J.; Hu, K.; Gao, J.; Chen, Y.; Yang, Q.; Du, X. Study on the Properties and Mechanism of Recycled Aggregate/Asphalt Interface Modified by Silane Coupling Agent. *Appl. Sci.* 2023, 13, 10343. https://doi.org/10.3390/app131810343

Academic Editor: Luís Picado Santos

Received: 7 August 2023
Revised: 8 September 2023
Accepted: 13 September 2023
Published: 15 September 2023

Copyright: © 2023 by the authors. Licensee MDPI, Basel, Switzerland. This article is an open access article distributed under the terms and conditions of the Creative Commons Attribution (CC BY) license (https://creativecommons.org/licenses/by/4.0/).

[1] College of Civil Engineering and Architecture, Henan University of Technology, Zhengzhou 450001, China; zjw0172@163.com (J.Z.); yujingchen@haut.edu.cn (Y.C.); duxiaotong0601@163.com (X.D.)
[2] College of Materials Science and Engineering, Chongqing Jiaotong University, Chongqing 400074, China
[3] School of Transportation Science and Engineering, Harbin Institute of Technology, Harbin 150090, China; qilin.yang@hit.edu.cn
* Correspondence: mailhukui@haut.edu.cn (K.H.); jfgao@cqjtu.edu.cn (J.G.)

Abstract: The use of recycled concrete aggregates (RCA) instead of natural aggregates in hot-mix asphalt mixtures is one of the ways to achieve energy savings and reduce carbon emissions in road engineering. However, the cement mortar on the surface of RCA adversely affects the adhesion properties between asphalt and aggregates, leading to a reduction in the performance characteristics of asphalt mixtures. In this study, a silane coupling agent (SCA) was employed to improve the adhesion properties of the RCA/asphalt interface. The enhancement mechanism of SCA on the RCA/asphalt interface was investigated from multiple perspectives, including macroscopic properties, interfacial microstructure, and nanoscale interfacial interactions. Firstly, the adhesion behavior and tensile strength of the interface between RCA and asphalt were determined through a boiling water test and direct tensile test, both before and after SCA modification. Secondly, scanning electron microscopy (SEM) was employed to observe the surface microstructure of RCA and the microstructure of the RCA/asphalt interface. Finally, the main component of mortar, calcium silicate hydrate (C-S-H), was taken as the research subject of investigation to examine the hydrogen bonding, interaction energy, and interface transition zone of the C-S-H/asphalt interface system using the molecular dynamics methodology. The results demonstrate a two-level enhancement in the adhesion performance of the interface at the macroscopic scale following SCA modification. The interface tensile strength increased by 72.2% and 119.7% under dry and wet conditions, respectively. At the microscopic scale, it was observed that the surface pores of RCA were repaired after SCA modification, resulting in a more tightly bonded interface between the RCA and asphalt. At the nanoscale, SCA modification reduces the hydrophilicity of the C-S-H surface, increases the interaction energy and water resistance of the C-S-H/asphalt interface, and enhances the weak interface transition zone between C-S-H and asphalt. This study provides a theoretical basis for using SCA to enhance the bond strength of the RCA/asphalt interface and lays the foundation for the application of RCA asphalt mixtures on highways.

Keywords: silane coupling agent; recycled concrete aggregates; RCA/asphalt interface; interface reinforcement mechanism; molecular dynamic

1. Introduction

The amount of construction trash produced each year has increased significantly as a result of the fast urbanization and infrastructural development. However, the utilization rate of solid waste during construction is still very low [1–4]. On the other hand, mining natural aggregates can lead to irreversible ecological damage in mountainous areas, while the processing and transportation processes result in high carbon emissions, highlighting the increasingly prominent environmental and social issues [5–7]. In the context of global efforts to promote energy conservation and emission reduction, the transformation of resource utilization in the construction industry, which involves replacing natural sand and stone with construction solid waste, emerges as the path for the industry to achieve carbon reduction goals and upgrade development [8–10]. With the continuous improvement of construction solid waste particle-size crushing and component-sorting technology, a large amount of uniformly shaped, clean, and high-purity recycled concrete aggregate (RCA) can be obtained, and the cost of using RCA is lower than that of natural aggregates [11–14]. Therefore, the application of RCA in asphalt pavement has significant environmental value and economic benefits [15].

The primary distinction between RCA and natural aggregates is that the surface absorbs a lot of cement mortar [16,17]. According to studies, the main factor that contributes to the inadequate adhesion of asphalt and aggregates is the existence of cement mortar on the surface of RCA [18,19]. The calcium silicate hydrate (C-S-H) in the cement mortar accounts for approximately 60–70% of the hydration products, and it is the principal component and strength source of cement hydration products [20]. However, the chemical bonding between C-S-H and asphalt is weak, which can easily lead to inadequate bond strength between the mortar and asphalt. On the other hand, the mortar pores and microcracks on the surface of RCA are plentiful, and water adsorbed by capillary action is difficult to discharge under natural conditions. Because asphalt is hydrophobic, the existence of water might cause damage to the RCA/asphalt interface [21]. Therefore, in order to add the amount of RCA blending and improve the performance of hot-mix asphalt mixtures, it is necessary to address the problem of inadequate chemical bonding between RCA and asphalt, as well as water damage to the interface.

For enhancing the basic properties of materials, many scholars have chosen different modification methods [22–26]. The addition of anti-spalling chemicals into asphalt mixtures is an efficient technique to boost binding strength and improve resistance to water damage at the asphalt/aggregate interface [27–29]. At the moment, the most popular anti-spalling agent is silane coupling agent (SCA), which is widely applied to enhance the interface binding strength of organic and inorganic materials [30]. This is due mainly to the fact that its organic functional groups and hydrolyzed groups can be chemically linked with organic and inorganic materials, respectively, which helps to improve the interfacial binding strength of organic and inorganic interface materials [31]. Due to the unique nature of SCA, its application in asphalt mixtures has attracted extensive attention from researchers. Li et al. [32] investigated the effect of SCA (KH550) on the adhesion properties between acidic aggregates and asphalt. They found that SCA can act as a molecular bridge to enhance the bond strength between asphalt and acidic aggregates. Ye et al. [33] conducted an analysis on the water stability of SCA-modified asphalt with aggregates, comparing it to SBS-modified asphalt and rock-modified asphalt. The study revealed that SCA-modified asphalt exhibited superior water stability when combined with aggregates. Ran et al. [34] modified oil sludge pyrolysis residue with SCA and found that the surface of the oil sludge pyrolysis residue became rough after treatment with KH550, forming strong physical and chemical adsorption between the oil sludge pyrolysis residue and asphalt.

Currently, most research on the interface between RCA/asphalt is conducted at a macroscopic level. However, the interaction between RCA and asphalt is a complex process that is easily influenced by interactions between different molecular groups. With current experimental techniques, it is still very difficult to understand the impact of SCA modification on the interaction for the RCA/asphalt interface [35]. It is now possible to know how SCA modification affects the interaction between RCA and the asphalt interface, as molecular dynamics simulation techniques have been widely used to investigate the interaction between asphalt and aggregates. Previous studies have used molecular dynamics simulations to establish molecular models of asphalt, aggregates, and C-S-H and have studied their interactions [36,37]. Sun et al. [38] explored the impact of interface water on the structure of asphalt and the interaction energy of the asphalt/aggregate interface and discovered that the existence of interface water altered the nanostructure of the asphalt and diminished the interaction energy of the interface.

Luo et al. [39] revealed that the anisotropy of aggregate surfaces significantly affects the interaction energy with asphalt and the water stability of the interface. Zhai et al. [40] investigated the effect of asphalt aging on the damage behavior of the asphalt/aggregate interface and found that asphalt aging reduced the thermodynamic properties of asphalt, such as surface free energy and cohesive energy. However, it also enhanced the adhesion strength between the asphalt/aggregate interface.

The above study primarily describes the influence of SCA modification on the interfacial performances through experimental methods. It also investigates the interaction relationship between the asphalt and aggregate using molecular dynamics. However, the influence of SCA modification on the interfacial performances and interaction relationship between RCA and asphalt has not yet been resolved. Therefore, the objective of this study is to explore the multi-scale enhancement mechanism of SCA modification on the interface between RCA and asphalt. First, at the macro-scale, the adhesion behavior and tensile strength of the interface between RCA and asphalt were determined before and after SCA modification using a boiling water test and direct tensile test. Second, on a micro-scale, the impact of SCA modification on the microstructure of the RCA/asphalt interface was observed through scanning electron microscopy. Finally, at the nanoscale, the main component of mortar, C-S-H, was taken as the research object to analyze the hydrogen bonding, interaction energy, and interface transition zone of the C-S-H/asphalt interface system using the molecular dynamics method.

2. Materials and Methods

2.1. Main Materials

This study utilized samples of RCA1 and RCA2 in different experimental tests. RCA1 is a cubic sample measuring $30 \times 30 \times 30$ mm, cut from a discarded cement column. It is used to measure the interfacial bond strength in direct tensile tests. RCA2 is obtained by crushing and sieving discarded concrete blocks to obtain samples with dimensions of 13.2–19 mm. It is used in boiling water tests to determine the adhesion properties for the RCA/asphalt interface. The RCA1 and RCA2 samples in this experiment needed to be cleaned and dried before the experiment to avoid the impact of surface pollutants on the experimental results. In addition, SCA (KH-550)-modified RCA was selected to enhance the interface properties. The physical parameters of KH-550 are shown in Table 1. The No. 70 base asphalt was chosen to evaluate the interfacial behavior between RCA and asphalt. The physical parameters of the base asphalt are presented in Table 2. All abbreviations in this paper are shown in Table 3.

Table 1. Physical parameters of KH-550 coupling agent.

Physical Parameters	Units	Value	Test Standard
Boiling point	°C	73.6	ASTM D1078-11 [41]
Density	g/cm^3	48.0	ASTM D4052 [42]
Refractive index ND25	—	102.2	ASTM D542-14 [43]

Table 2. Physical parameters of No. 70 asphalt binder.

Physical Parameters	Units	Value	Test Standard
Penetration (25 °C, 100 g, 5 s)	0.1 mm	73.6	ASTM D5-06 [44]
Softening point	°C	48.0	ASTM D36-06 [45]
Ductility (15 °C, 5 cm/min)	cm	102.2	ASTM D113-07 [46]

Table 3. All prefixes in this paper.

Prefix	Full Name
RCA	Recycled concrete aggregate
RCA1	Discarded cement column (30 × 30 × 30 mm)
RCA2	Recycled concrete aggregate (13.2–19 mm)
C-S-H	Calcium silicate hydrate
SCA	Silane coupling agent
SEM	Scanning electron microscopy
SARA	Saturates, aromatics, resins, and asphaltenes

2.2. Treatment Methods and Reaction Mechanisms

In this study, deionized water and ethanol were chosen as solvents for the hydrolysis reaction of SCA. In addition, to determine the optimal concentration of SCA, conductivity was chosen as a measure to assess the effect of concentration on the degree of SCA hydrolysis. This is because the conductivity of SCA and deionized water is very low, while the conductivity of the hydrolysis products of SCA is high. In addition, in the solution proportioning, there is no effect on the conductivity of the system because ethanol always makes up 50% of the total solution volume in the solution proportion. Therefore, the degree of hydrolysis of the SCA can be confirmed through conductivity measurements. As shown in Figure 1, the conductivity increased significantly when the SCA concentration was increased from 2% to 5%. However, as the SCA concentration continued to increase, the conductivity did not increase; instead, it showed a decreasing trend. The results indicate that the hydrolysis of SCA is highest when the concentration of SCA is 5%. Therefore, the optimal ratio of the SCA mixture solution is SCA:deionized water:ethanol = 5:45:50.

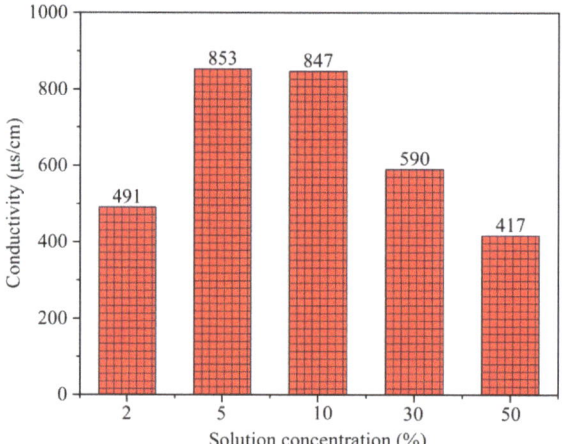

Figure 1. Conductivity of SCA mixed solutions at various concentrations.

The RCA treatment method and modification mechanism are shown in Figure 2. First, the SCA mixed solution (SCA:distilled:ethanol = 5:45:50) was stirred at 60 °C for 30 min to promote the hydrolysis reaction of SCA. Then, the RCA was immersed in an SCA mixture for 30 min to ensure a sufficient reaction between the SCA and RCA. Finally, the RCA was dried at a high temperature of 160 °C for 60 min to undergo a dehydration condensation reaction. During the entire process, the methoxy group ($-OCH_3$) in the molecular structure of SCA (KH550) can hydrolyze into the alkoxy group ($-SiOH$) of silanol in a mix of ethanol and water. Then, under high temperature conditions, the alkoxy group undergoes a dehydration condensation reaction with the hydroxyl group on the RCA surface to form Si-O-Si bonds [47].

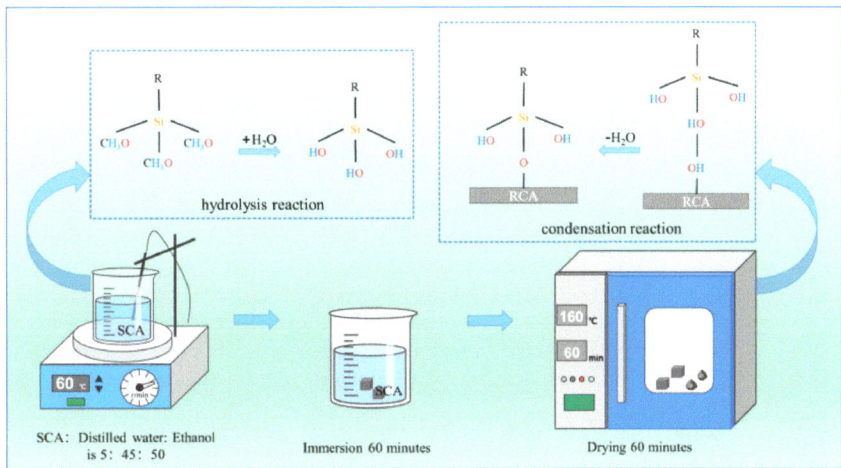

Figure 2. RCA treatment method and modification mechanism.

2.3. Experimental Testing Methods

2.3.1. Boiling Water Test

The boiling water test is a commonly used method to test the adhesion performance of asphalt to aggregate surfaces and evaluate the aggregate's resistance to water stripping. According to ASTM D36-25 [48] and the Chinese boiling test, the specific steps of the experiment are as follows. First, tie the RCA with wire and place it in a 105 °C drying oven to dry. Then, immerse the dried RCA in asphalt at 140 °C for 45 s, remove it, and cool it at room temperature for 15 min. Finally, immerse it in boiling water for 3 min, remove it, and observe the degree of asphalt film peeling on the surface of the RCA to evaluate its adhesion grade according to Table 4.

Table 4. Grade of adhesion of RCA to asphalt.

The Degree of Asphalt Film Spalling on the Surface of RCA after Boiling Water Test	Adhesion Grade
The asphalt film is not damaged and there is no peeling.	5
The thickness of the RCA surface asphalt film is uneven, with a peeling area percentage of less than 10%.	4
The asphalt film is generally retained on the surface of the RCA, with a peeling area percentage of less than 10%.	3
The asphalt film is partially retained on the surface of the RCA, with a peeling area percentage greater than 30%.	2
The surface asphalt film of the RCA has mostly peeled off, allowing the asphalt to float on the water's surface.	1

2.3.2. Direct Tensile Test

The direct tensile test is a crucial method for determining the interface characteristic parameters of asphalt mixtures. This test can be used to assess the fracture performance of the asphalt mixtures. In this study, the direct tensile test was used to examine the influence of SCA modification on the bonding strength of the interface in RCA asphalt mixtures. To prepare the samples, RCA and asphalt were placed in an oven at 170 °C for approximately 30 min. Then, 1.2 g of melted asphalt was dropped onto the RCA surface and evenly spread. Another RCA was then pressed on top. Considering that water penetration into the RCA/asphalt interface may cause damage, the samples were divided into two groups. The first group was tested directly, while the second group was submerged in water for 24 h before testing. Before the experiment, the RCA was secured to the tensile device using epoxy resin adhesive. The loading rate of the tensile test equipment (CTM6001) was set at 0.5 mm/min. The adhesion rate of asphalt on the RCA surface was determined by conducting a black and white image binarization analysis on the side of the RCA surface with less asphalt adhesion after stretching. Three sets of experiments were conducted for each experimental condition, and the average value of the three sets of experiments was calculated. If the ratio of the average value to the maximum or minimum value exceeds 10%, the investigation should be repeated.

2.3.3. SEM

This study utilizes SEM (Hitachi-S3400N) to observe the surface microstructure of RCA and the interface microstructure of RCA/asphalt. For the surface microstructure of RCA, RCA2 samples can be directly observed. For the RCA/asphalt interface microstructure, the intact RCA/asphalt interface was selected for observation after crushing the RCA1 samples. Then, the powder impurities generated at the interface were cleaned with anhydrous ethanol and observed after drying at room temperature (18–25 °C).

3. Simulation Methods
3.1. Computational Models
3.1.1. Asphalt Model

Asphalt is a residual petroleum mixture composed of hydrocarbons, sulfur and nitrogen compounds, and their non-metallic derivatives. These molecules have significant differences in polarity and molecular weight, making it difficult to represent their composition with a single molecule. In order to understand the molecular structure of asphalt, Jennings et al. constructed an average molecular structure based on the nuclear magnetic resonance (NMR) spectra of eight asphalt samples from the Strategic Highway Research Program (SHRP) in the United States. However, these structures cannot reflect the interactions between asphalt components. Subsequently, the asphalt system was divided into four components: saturates, aromatics, resins, and asphaltenes (SARA) using the standard test method (ASTM D4124-09 [49]). Through continuous improvement, Li and Greenfield constructed three 12-component asphalt models (AAA-1, AAK-1, and AAM-1) based on the SARA components. Therefore, in this study, the AAA-1 asphalt 12-component model was selected as a representative of the matrix asphalt for research. Figure 3 shows the molecular structure of the 12-component asphalt model. Figure 4 shows the model parameters of the 12-component asphalt model.

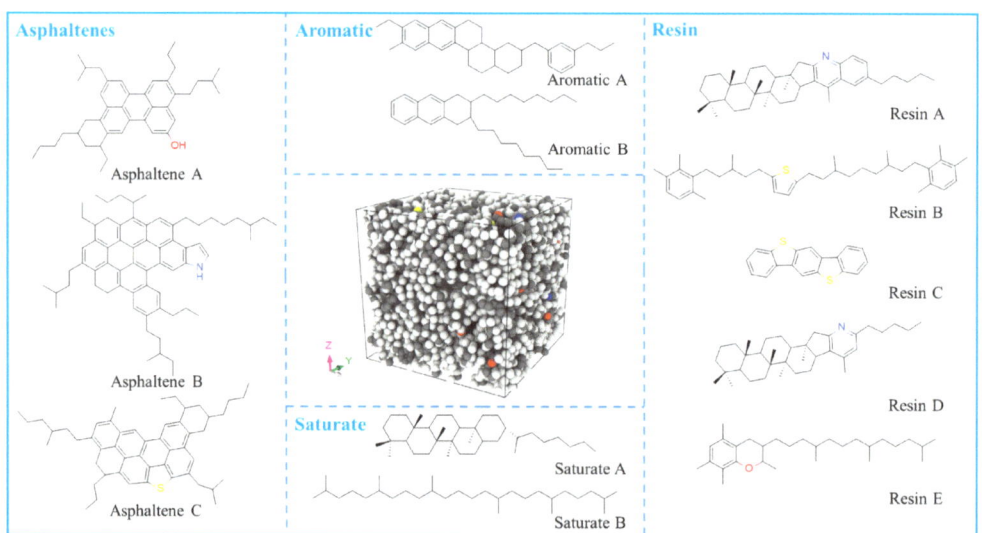

Figure 3. Asphalt 12-component model.

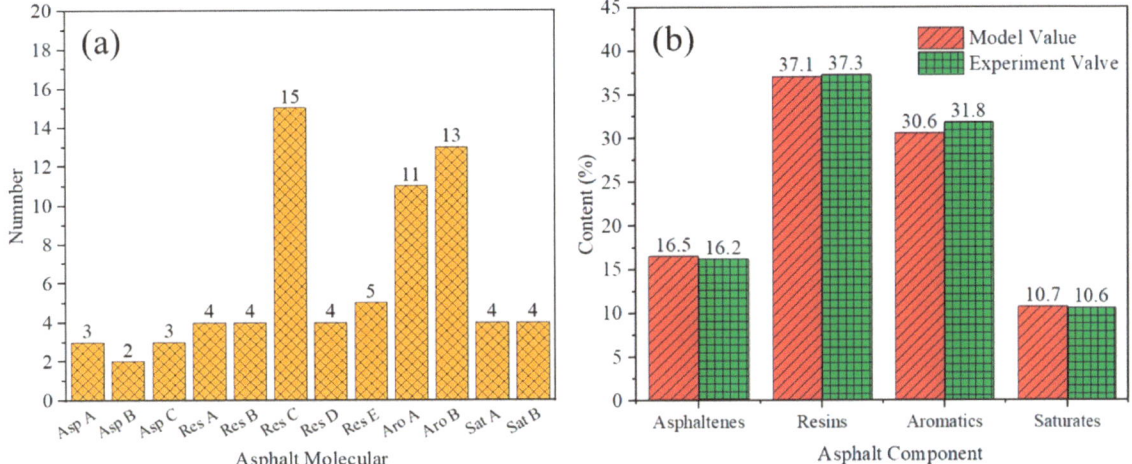

Figure 4. Asphalt 12-component model parameters: (**a**) the number of molecules; (**b**) the mass fraction of asphalt component.

In this study, the density and glass transition temperature (Tg) of the asphalt model were computed to verify the accuracy of the model. In this case, the density of asphalt was calculated using the isobaric–isothermal ensemble (NPT) at 1 atm pressure. As shown in Figure 5a, when the simulation time is greater than 30 ps, the density curve of the asphalt model tends to stabilize, so we calculated the average density of the asphalt model from 50 to 100 ps. From the analysis of the asphalt density curve, it can be concluded that the density of asphalt after equilibrium at 298 K is 1.02 g/cm^3. The experimental density value of SHRP AAA-1 asphalt is 1.01–1.04 g/cm^3, which is consistent with the density of the asphalt model.

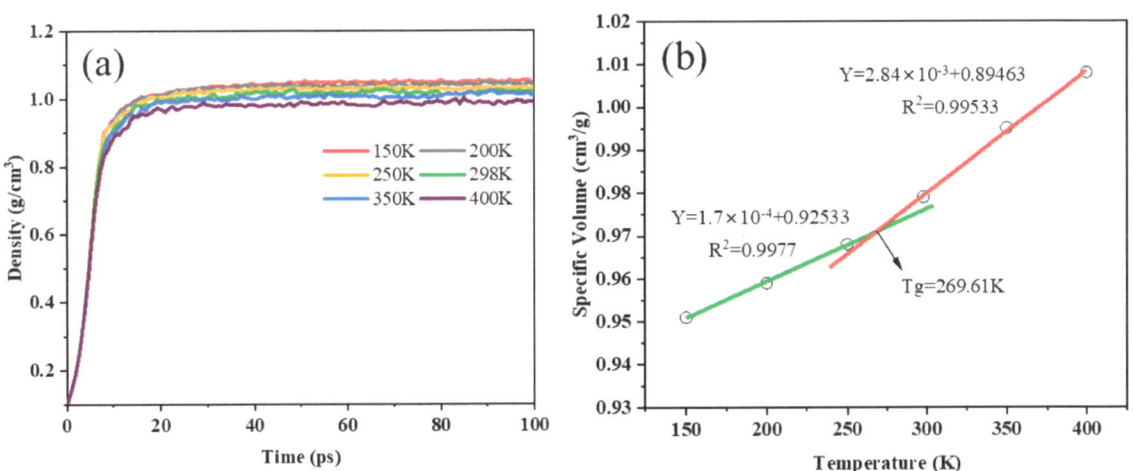

Figure 5. Physical properties of asphalt model: (**a**) density of asphalt; (**b**) glass transition temperature of asphalt.

After obtaining the asphalt density at different temperatures, the curve of asphalt specific volume (reciprocal of density) versus temperature was plotted, and linear regression analysis was performed. As shown in Figure 5b, the Tg of the asphalt is the intersection point of the two fitted lines. The Tg of the asphalt is lower than 273.15 K (0 °C), being at

269.61 K, which is consistent with previous research results [50–52]. Therefore, it can be considered that the asphalt model is reasonable.

3.1.2. SCA/C-S-H Model

For cement mortar adhered to RCA surfaces, C-S-H accounts for about 60–70% of the hydration products and is the main component and strength source of the hydration products [53,54]. In this study, a C-S-H model was established based on the method proposed by Pellenq et al., as shown in Figure 6. The specific steps are as follows: (1) Tobermorite 11 was used as the initial model. After removing the water molecules of the initial model, a $4 \times 3 \times 1$ supercell simulation was performed, and the monoclinic structure was changed to an orthorhombic one (Figure 6a); (2) To get the silicate chains to satisfy Q1 = 11.63%, Q2 = 67.44%, Q3 = 20.93%, and Ca/Si = 1.67, some SiO_2 groups and Si_2O_5 groups were randomly removed from the silicate chains (Figure 6b); (3) The adsorption of water molecules to saturation was achieved using the grand canonical Monte Carlo (GCMC) method (Figure 6c); (4) To achieve equilibrium of model, the relaxation was continued under the NPT system (Figure 7d). Finally, the dimensions of the C-S-H model are 22.32 Å × 22.17 Å × 22.77 Å. The density (2.45 g/cm^3) of the constructed model is close to the results obtained from previous simulations or experiments, indicating that the model is reasonably valid [55,56].

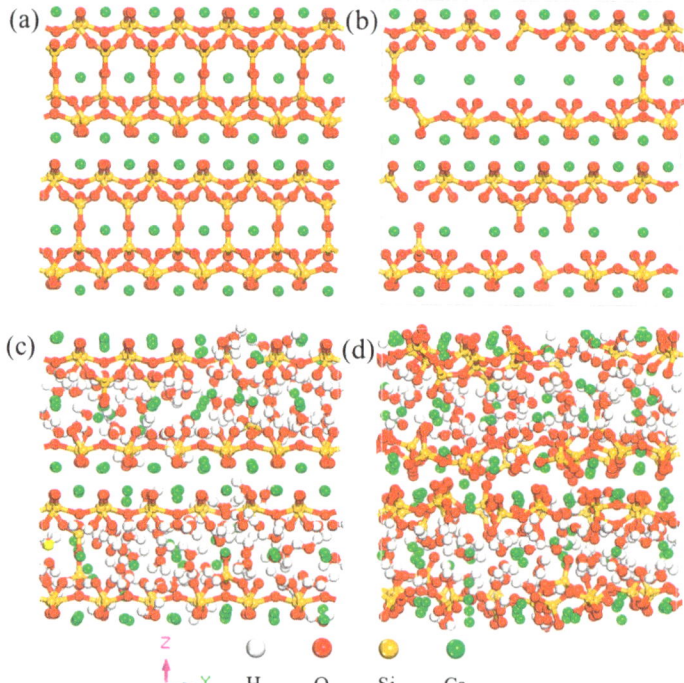

Figure 6. The construction of the C-S-H model (**a**) Orthogonal transformed model; (**b**) Remove some SiO_2 groups and dimer structures; (**c**) Absorb water molecules through the GCMC simulation; (**d**) Relax the model until equilibrium.

Figure 7 illustrates the establishment of the SCA/C-S-H model. Firstly, the C-S-H model $2 \times 2 \times 1$ supercell simulation was performed. Then, based on the SCA and cement mortar binding mechanism, the hydrolysis products of SCA were connected to the non-bridging oxygen atoms of the C-S-H matrix through Si-O-Si chemical bonding. The dimensions of the SCA/C-S-H model are 44.64 Å × 44.34 Å × 24.86 Å.

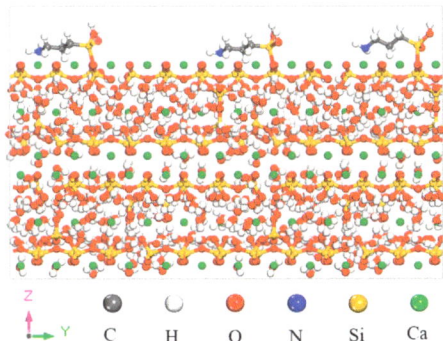

Figure 7. The SCA/C-S-H model.

3.1.3. C-S-H/Asphalt Interface Models

In this study, all simulations were performed using the Materials Studio 2020 software, and the COMPASS force field was selected to investigate the interaction mechanism of the C-S-H/asphalt interface. Taking the unmodified C-S-H model as an example, the asphalt/C-S-H interface model is shown in Figure 8a. For the placement of C-S-H and asphalt in the same simulation box, the dimensions of the C-S-H and asphalt models need to match in the x and y directions. Therefore, the asphalt model was first created with dimensions of 44.64 Å × 44.34 Å × 27.35 Å in the x, y, and z directions and subjected to 50,000 steps of geometry optimization. Next, the C-S-H model was expanded to a 2 × 2 × 1 supercell with lattice parameters: a = 44.64 Å, b = 44.34 Å, and c = 22.17 Å. Then, the C-S-H/asphalt interface model was established, and a 30 Å vacuum layer was added above the asphalt layer to eliminate periodic boundary effects. As shown in Figure 8b, based on the C-S-H/asphalt interface model, the influence of water on the interface bonding was studied by inserting a 2 Å water layer between the C-S-H and asphalt layers. Finally, each interface model was relaxed for 500 ps under the canonical (NVT) ensemble, and the interface properties were analyzed using the trajectory from the last 100 ps.

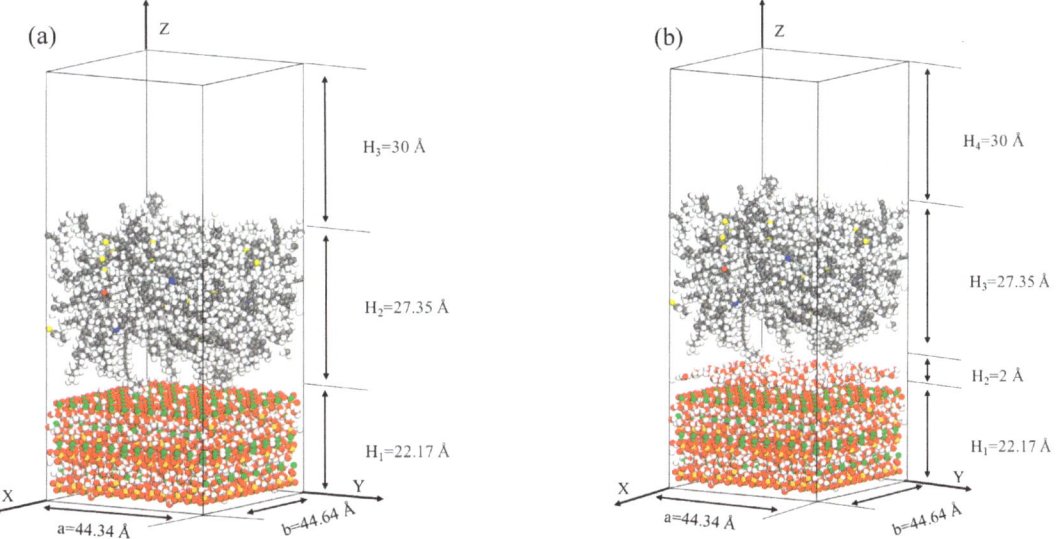

Figure 8. Interface models: (**a**) C-S-H/asphalt interface model; (**b**) C-S-H/water/asphalt interface model.

3.2. Simulation Calculations

3.2.1. Hydrogen Bond

Hydrogen bonding is a type of intermolecular interaction force formed between a hydrogen atom and an atom with a higher electronegativity, such as F, O, or N [57,58]. In this study, hydrogen bonding indirectly characterizes the interaction between the C-S-H surface and water molecules. The conditions for hydrogen bonding formation are as follows: (1) The distance between the hydrogen atom and the acceptor atom is less than 2.5 Å; (2) The donor-hydrogen-acceptor angle is less than 90°. The molecules providing the hydrogen atom and accepting the hydrogen atom are defined as the donor and acceptor, respectively.

3.2.2. Interaction Energy

The interaction energy can reflect the repulsive force and gravity of the C-S-H to the asphalt molecule [38,59]. From the molecular level, its main components include a covalent bond, van der Waals force, electrostatic electron, hydrogen bond, and so on. Here, the interaction energy can be calculated according to Equation (1).

$$E_{Asp-C-S-H} = E_{total} - (E_{Asp} + E_{C-S-H}) \tag{1}$$

where $E_{Asp-C-S-H}$ is the interaction energy between asphalt and $C-S-H$; E_{total} is the total potential energy of the entire interface system; E_{Asp} is the potential energy of asphalt; and E_{C-S-H} is the potential energy of $C-S-H$.

3.2.3. Relative Concentration

The interface transition zone refers to the region where different materials meet. In the C-S-H/asphalt system, the thickness of this zone is indicative of the extent to which asphalt is adsorbed onto the C-S-H surface. This research aims to determine the thickness of the interface transition zone by examining the relative concentration of asphalt and C-S-H in the Z direction. Furthermore, the study also investigates the impact of interface water on the nanostructure of asphalt by analyzing the relative concentration changes of the asphalt SARA components in the Z direction. At the same time, combined with the difference in the content of SARA components in the Z direction, the effect of interfacial moisture on the structure of the asphalt interface is discussed.

4. Results and Discussions

4.1. Boiling Water Test

The peeling condition of the asphalt film on the RCA surface before and after the boiling water test is shown in Figure 9. The results show that there is a significant difference in asphalt film stripping on the surface of RCA before and after SCA modification. Specifically, when the RCA is not modified by SCA, it can be observed that a large area of the asphalt film on the RCA surface peels off after the boiling water test, and the adhesion level is below grade 3 as shown in Table 4. This is because the surface of the aggregate absorbs a considerable amount of cement mortar, and there are massive pores on the surface. When a large number of pores exists on the surface of RCA, it will cause structural defects at the interface between the RCA and asphalt. During the boiling water experiment, the high temperature causes the gas inside the pores of the RCA to expand. This expansion leads to the destruction of the interface between the RCA and the asphalt, resulting in further shedding of the asphalt on the aggregate surface. This results in poor adhesion between asphalt and RCA and a weak interface transition zone. When RCA was modified by SCA, the asphalt film on the surface of RCA remained relatively intact after the boiling water experiment, and no apparent bubbles were observed in the boiling water experiment. According to Table 4, it can be concluded that the adhesion grade of the RCA asphalt mixture reached grade 5. This indicates that the SCA modification improves the interface properties of the RCA asphalt mixture.

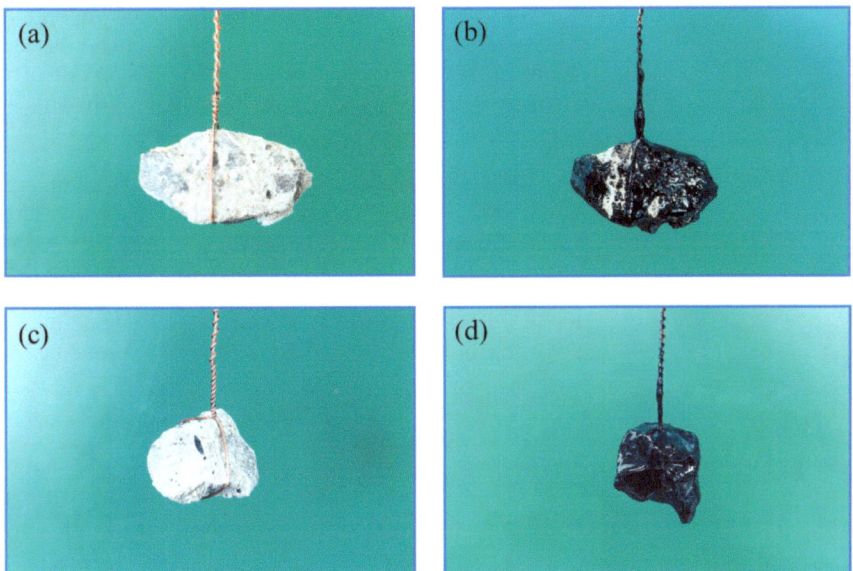

Figure 9. Boiling water test: (**a**) unmodified RCA before the test; (**b**) unmodified RCA after the test; (**c**) SCA-modified RCA before the test; (**d**) SCA-modified RCA after the test.

4.2. Direct Tensile Strength Test

The tensile strength of the interface between the RCA and asphalt is shown in Figure 10. The results indicate that the interface tensile strength significantly increases after SCA modification under both dry and wet conditions. Under dry conditions, the interface tensile strength between RCA and asphalt without SCA modification is 97 kPa. After SCA modification, the interface tensile strength increases by 72.2%. Under wet conditions, the interface tensile strength without SCA modification decreases by 56%. After SCA modification, the interface tensile strength increases by 119.7%.

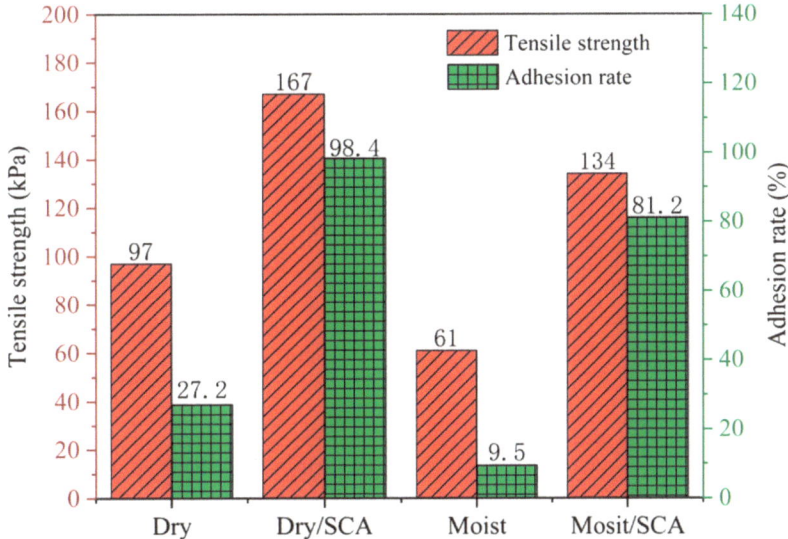

Figure 10. The tensile strength of the interface and adhesion rate of asphalt on RCA surface.

The influence of SCA modification on the interface failure types was analyzed by the interface failure forms shown in Figure 11 and the corresponding adhesion rates in Figure 10. The results showed that the adhesion rate of asphalt on the surface of RCA increased after SCA modification, changing the form of interface failure. In the unmodified RCA, the main type of interface failure was adhesion failure between the asphalt and RCA, with an adhesion rate of approximately 27.2%. However, after SCA modification, the type of interface failure was mostly cohesive failure, and the adhesion rate increased significantly to 98.4%. This is because when the adhesive force of the RCA/asphalt interface is greater than the cohesive force of asphalt itself, the asphalt undergoes cohesive failure. This indicates that SCA modification reinforces the adhesive strength of the interface, making the adhesive force more significant than the cohesive force of asphalt itself. At the same time, SCA modification also showed good performance under wet conditions, increasing the adhesion rate from 9.5% in the unmodified state to 81.2%.

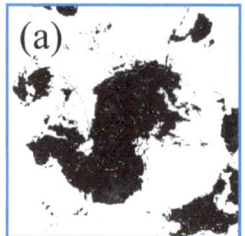 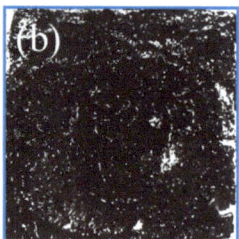 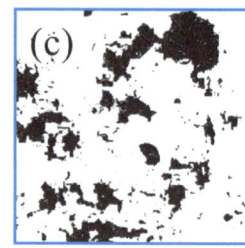 

Figure 11. The fracture surface of RCA after binarization: (**a**) no modification under dry conditions; (**b**) SCA modification under dry conditions; (**c**) no modification under moist conditions; (**d**) SCA modification under moist conditions.

4.3. Microstructure Analysis

The surface microstructure of the RCA is shown in Figure 12. The results indicate that the surface porosity of the RCA is repaired after SCA modification, resulting in a tighter bond between the RCA and the interface. In terms of the surface microstructure of the RCA, without SCA modification, there are a large number of mortar pores on the RCA surface, which is the main reason for the high water absorption and poor adhesion performance of the RCA to asphalt. After SCA modification, the mortar pores of the RCA surface are significantly reduced. The reason for the reduction in surface pores of the RCA is that SCA first undergoes hydrolysis to form silanol, which then undergoes a condensation reaction with the hydroxyl groups on the cement mortar surface, resulting in the coverage of the cement mortar surface with alkyl-terminated siloxane, forming chemical adsorption.

The interface microstructure of the RCA/asphalt is shown in Figure 13. In terms of the interface structure between the RCA and asphalt, without SCA modification, the presence of a large number of pores on the RCA surface leads to defects in the RCA/asphalt interface structure. After SCA modification, the bond between the RCA and asphalt interface becomes denser. This is mainly because one end of the hydrolysis product of SCA is tightly adsorbed on the RCA surface, while the organic functional groups extend into the asphalt, tightly connecting the RCA and the asphalt. It acts as a "molecular bridge" between the RCA and asphalt interface, tightly connecting the RCA and asphalt together and improving the interface properties between the asphalt and RCA.

4.4. Hydrogen Bonding Analysis

In this study, we primarily calculated the number of hydrogen bonds formed between interfacial water and the C-S-H surface to investigate the effect of SCA alteration on the hydrophilicity of the C-S-H surface. As shown in Figure 14, the hydrogen bonds at the interface mainly form between water molecules and the silicate chains, as well as between water molecules and SCA.

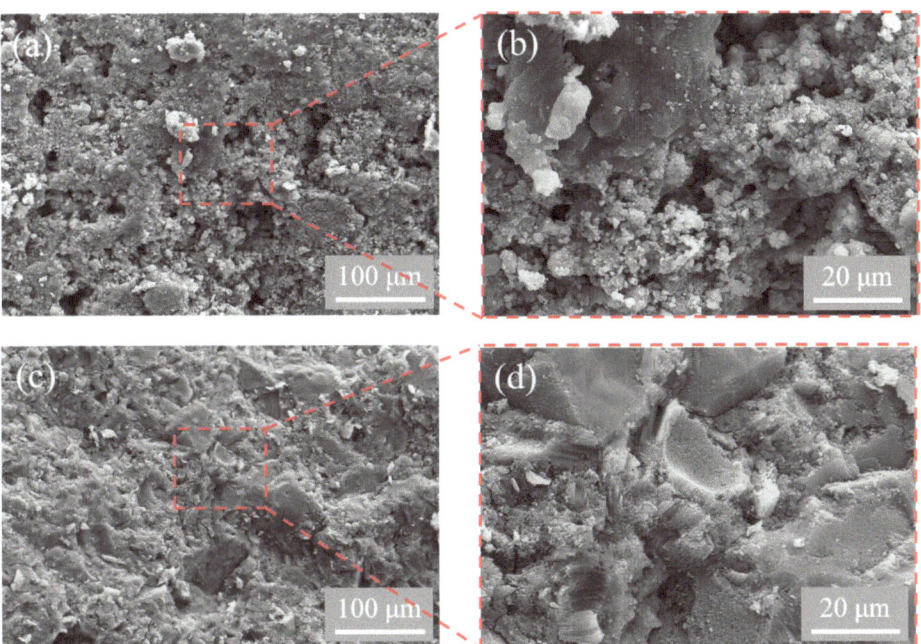

Figure 12. The surface microstructure of the RCA: (**a**,**b**) no modification; (**c**,**d**) SCA modification.

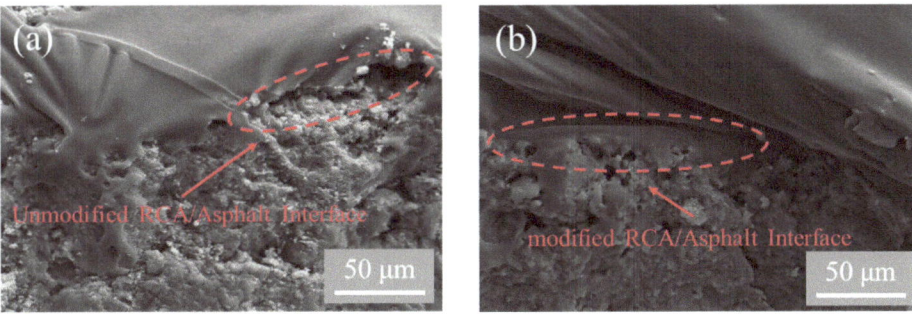

Figure 13. The interface microstructure of the RCA/asphalt: (**a**) no modification; (**b**) SCA modification.

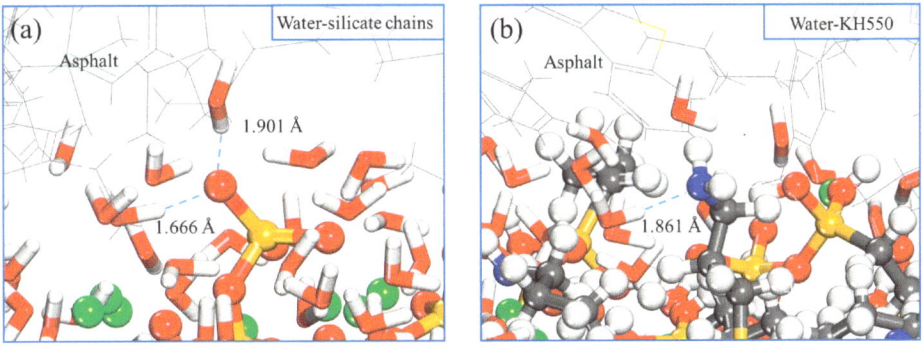

Figure 14. Type of hydrogen bond: (**a**) water-silicate chains; (**b**) water-SCA (KH550).

The number of hydrogen bonds formed between C-S-H and interfacial water is shown in Figure 15. The results indicate that there are fewer hydrogen bonds between C-S-H and interfacial water after SCA modification. Specifically, unmodified C-S-H forms 213 hydrogen bonds with interfacial water. The more hydrogen bonds form between C-S-H and interfacial water, the stronger the hydrophilicity of the C-S-H surface. Due to the hydrophobic nature of asphalt, stronger hydrophilicity of the C-S-H surface leads to weaker adhesion between asphalt and the C-S-H. After SCA modification, the number of hydrogen bonds at the C-S-H interface decreases by 19.7%, indicating a decrease in the hydrophilicity of the C-S-H surface after SCA modification, thereby enhancing the interaction at the asphalt/C-S-H interface. This is mainly because the C-S-H surface is composed of silicate chains and calcium ions, which have strong hydrophilicity. After SCA modification, the distance between interfacial water and the C-S-H surface is increased, thereby reducing the formation of hydrogen bonds and decreasing the hydrophilicity of the C-S-H surface. Compared to the previous SCA-modified SiO_2 interface, the SCA modification can be very effective in reducing the hydrophilicity of both SiO_2 and C-S-H surfaces, thus improving the effect of water molecules on the aggregate/interface [60]. The results show that SCA modification has a positive effect on enhancing the water damage resistance of the aggregate/asphalt interface.

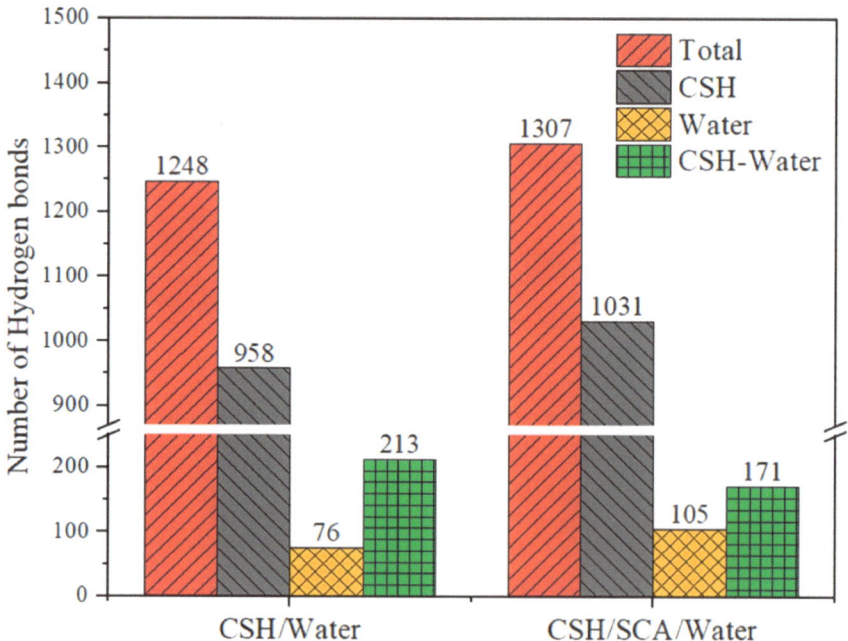

Figure 15. The number of hydrogen bonds for C-S-H/water interface.

4.5. Interaction Energy Analysis

The interaction energy between C-S-H and asphalt is shown in Figure 16. The results indicate that SCA modification can increase the interaction energy of the interface under both dry and wet conditions. Under dry conditions, the interface interaction energy of the SCA modification increased by 32.1%. This increase is attributed to the ability of SCA modification to alleviate the harmful effects of Ca ions and water molecules on the C-S-H surface, thereby improving the interaction energy of the interface. Under wet conditions, the interaction energy of the interface decreased by 47.15%. This is primarily due to the fact that the interaction energy of the interface is mainly governed by van der Waals forces, and the presence of water at the interface increases the distance between the asphalt and

C-S-H interface, resulting in a 48.2% reduction in van der Waals forces. Consequently, the interaction energy of the interface decreases. In comparison, the SCA modification under wet conditions showed a 63.9% increase in interaction energy compared to the unmodified interface. This indicates that SCA modification can effectively enhance the water resistance of the interface. This is because SCA modification reduces the hydrophilicity of the C-S-H interface, diminishing the impact of water molecules on the interface performance and consequently increasing the interaction energy at the asphalt and C-S-H interface.

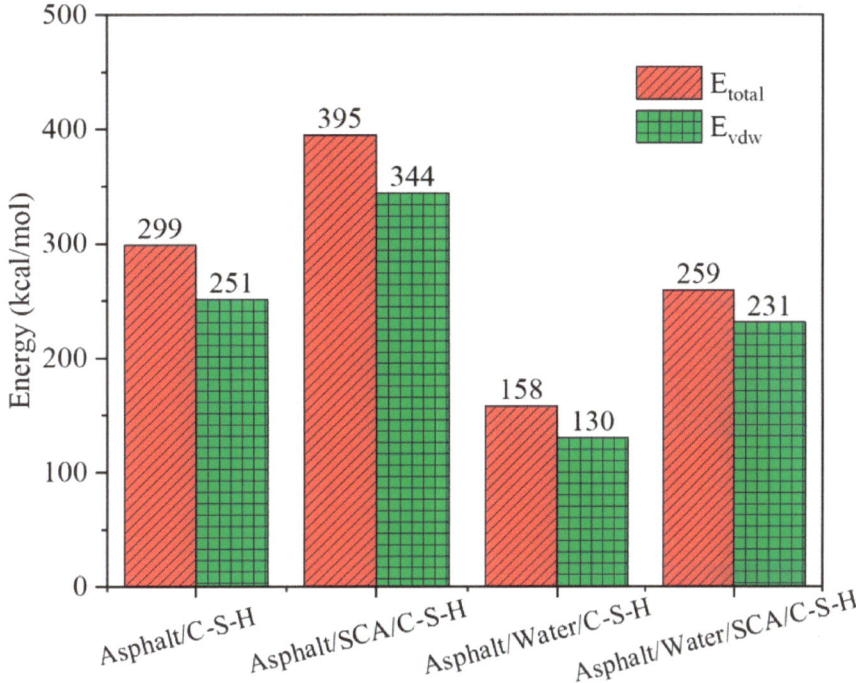

Figure 16. Interaction energy for C-S-H/asphalt interface.

4.6. Interface Transition Zone Analysis

The thickness of the interface transition zone and interface structure for the C-S-H/asphalt interface are shown in Figure 17. It can be seen that SCA modification has an important impact on the transition zone thickness and interface structure. For the unmodified interface, the thickness of the transition zone is 5.04 Å. This may be due to the diffusion of water molecules in C-S-H into the area near the surface of the asphalt, where the water molecules overlap with the asphalt molecules. After SCA modification, the thickness of the transition zone increased from 5.04 Å to 11.2 Å, indicating that SCA modification enhanced the attraction of the C-S-H surface to asphalt. Moreover, two distribution patterns of SCA molecular chains on the C-S-H surface can be observed at the interface structure between C-S-H and asphalt: one is parallel to the C-S-H surface, and the other is inserted into the asphalt layer. The insertion of SCA molecular chains into the asphalt layer is strongly entangled with asphalt molecules, thereby enhancing the weak interface transition zone between C-S-H and asphalt.

The influence of interface water on the asphalt nanostructure is shown in Figure 18. The results indicate that SCA modification reduces the effect of water on the relative concentration of SARA components at the interface. For the unmodified interface, interface water causes a varying degree of decrease in the relative concentration of asphalt SARA components within 0–7 Å. This is why the interaction energy between asphalt and C-S-H decreases when interface water exists. Within the distance of 7–15 Å, the relative concentration of asphaltene, aromatics, and resins increases, indicating that the addition of water molecules causes the asphalt components at the interface to aggregate towards the center, also demonstrating the hydrophobicity of asphalt. After SCA modification, the relative concentration of resins and aromatics at the interface within 0–5 Å remains basically unchanged, while the concentration of saturates slightly increases. It is worth noting that the relative concentration of asphaltene increases at 4–8 Å and forms a peak. This indicates that after SCA modification, the interface structure of SARA components can remain relatively stable even under the action of water, thereby increasing the resistance to water damage between C-S-H and asphalt.

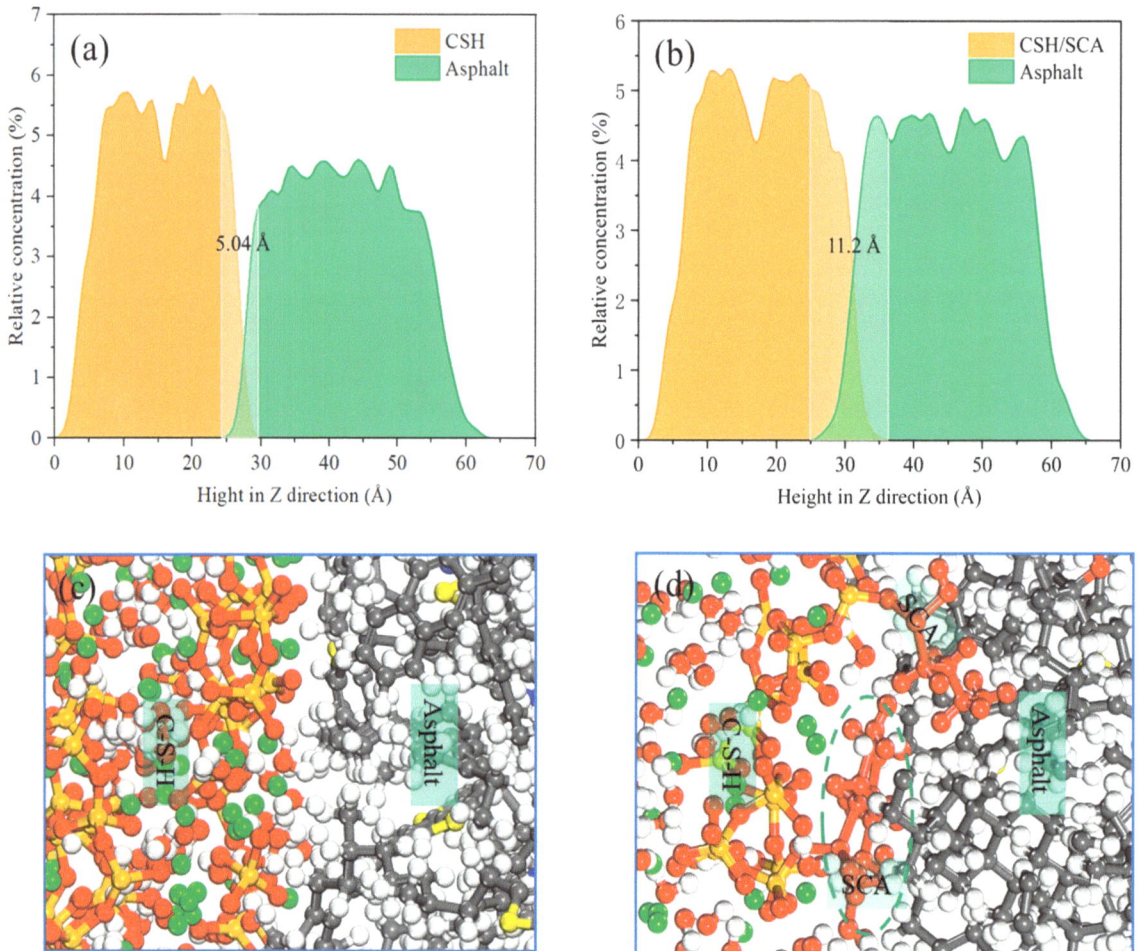

Figure 17. Interface transition zone thickness and interface structure for C-S-H/asphalt interfaces: (**a**) C-S-H/asphalt interface zone thickness; (**b**) C-S-H/SCA/asphalt interface transition zone thickness; (**c**) C-S-H/asphalt interface structure; (**d**) C-S-H/SCA/asphalt interface structure.

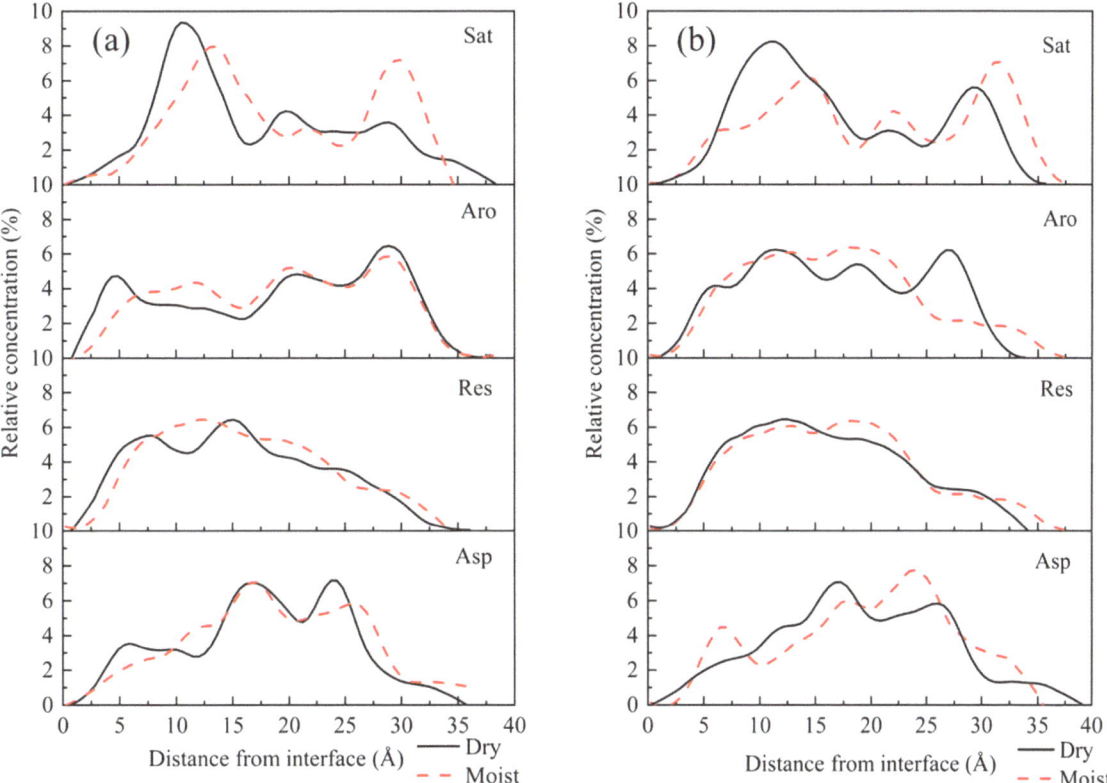

Figure 18. The concentration profiles of SARA components: (**a**) C-S-H/water/asphalt model; (**b**) C-S-H/SCA/water/asphalt model.

5. Conclusions

Based on macroscopic experiments, microscopic structure observation, and molecular dynamics simulation, this study examined the enhancement effect of SCA modification on the interface performance of RCA and asphalt before and after modification and investigates its underlying mechanism for enhancement. The following findings were made.

The results of the boiling water experiment and direct tensile experiment indicate that SCA modification significantly improves the interface behavior between RCA and asphalt. The bond between SCA-modified RCA and asphalt is enhanced by two grades, and the tensile strength goes up by 72.2% in dry conditions and 119.7% in wet conditions.

The observation results of SEM show that SCA modification effectively improves the interface structure defects between RCA and asphalt. Before SCA modification, there are numerous pores on the surface of RCA, resulting in structural defects between the RCA and asphalt interface. After SCA modification, a dense film is formed on the surface of the RCA, effectively filling the pores of the RCA surface mortar and creating a more compact bond at the RCA/asphalt interface.

The results of the molecular dynamics simulations indicate that SCA modification reduces the number of hydrogen bonds formed between C-S-H and water molecules, thereby decreasing the hydrophilicity of the C-S-H surface. SCA modification also improves the interaction energy and water resistance of C-S-H with asphalt. Additionally, SCA molecules can penetrate the asphalt layer to create a dense interfacial transition zone between C-S-H and asphalt. This makes the two substances work better together and reduces the effect of water on the nanoscale structure of the asphalt interface.

The study findings help us understand the mechanisms of interfacial interactions between asphalt and modified aggregate surfaces and develop more effective interface modifications. In addition, it lays the foundation for the application of RCA/asphalt mixtures on road surfaces and for improving the road performance of asphalt mixtures. Future research can consider the influence of SCA modification on the interactions between different interfaces, such as SIO_2/asphalt, $CaCO_3$/asphalt, etc. The interaction mechanism of SCA modification on RCA/asphalt interface is explained from a more comprehensive perspective.

Author Contributions: Conceptualization, K.H.; methodology, J.Z.; software, J.Z.; validation, J.Z.; formal analysis, J.Z.; investigation, J.Z.; resources, J.Z.; data curation, J.Z.; writing—original draft preparation, J.Z. and X.D.; writing—review and editing, J.Z. and Y.C.; visualization, J.Z.; supervision, K.H. and Q.Y.; project administration, K.H. and J.G.; funding acquisition, K.H. All authors have read and agreed to the published version of the manuscript.

Funding: This work was financially supported by the Fundamental Research Fund of Natural Science Foundation of China (No. 52208434), the Central Public Welfare Research Institute (No. 2020-9049), Natural Science Foundation of Henan Province (No. 222300420142), Postdoctoral Fund of Henan Province; Science and Technology Project of Henan Province (No. 192102310229), China Postdoctoral Science Foundation (No. 2022M711079), and Young backbone teachers plan of Henan University of Technology (No. 21420156).

Institutional Review Board Statement: Not applicable.

Informed Consent Statement: Not applicable.

Data Availability Statement: All data from this study are presented in the paper.

Conflicts of Interest: The authors declare no conflict of interest.

References

1. Xiao, J.; Shen, J.; Gao, Q.; Wu, Y. Reuse of construction spoil in China: Current status and future opportunities. *J. Clean. Prod.* **2020**, *290*, 125742. [CrossRef]
2. Piccinali, A.; Diotti, A.; Plizzari, G.; Plizzari, G. Impact of recycled aggregate on the mechanical and environmental properties of concrete: A review. *Materials* **2022**, *15*, 1818. [CrossRef]
3. Ulucan, M.; Alyamac, K.E. A holistic assessment of the use of emerging recycled concrete aggregates after a destructive earthquake: Mechanical, economic and environmental. *Waste. Manag.* **2022**, *146*, 53–65. [CrossRef]
4. Chen, X.; Yang, Y.; Zhang, C.; Hu, R.; Zhang, H.Y.; Li, B.X.; Zhao, Q.L. Valorization of construction waste materials for pavements of sponge cities: A review. *Constr. Build. Mater.* **2022**, *356*, 129247. [CrossRef]
5. Pal, S.; Mandal, I. Impacts of stone mining and crushing on environmental health in Dwarka river basin. *Geocarto Int.* **2021**, *36*, 392–420. [CrossRef]
6. Hua, C.X.; Liu, C.Y.; Chen, J.G.; Yang, C.X.; Chen, L.Y. Promoting construction and demolition waste recycling by using incentive policies in China. *Environ. Sci. Pollut. R.* **2022**, *29*, 53844–53859. [CrossRef]
7. Molla, A.S.; Tang, P.T.; Sher, W.; Bekele, D.N. Chemicals of concern in construction and demolition waste fine residues: A systematic literature review. *J. Environ. Manag.* **2021**, *299*, 113654. [CrossRef]
8. Liu, H.B.; Liu, H.B.; Quan, H.Z.; Xu, X.L.; Wang, Q.Y.; Ni, S.Y. Assessment on the Properties of Biomass-Aggregate Geopolymer Concrete. *Appl. Sci.* **2022**, *12*, 3561. [CrossRef]
9. Mistri, A.; Dhami, N.; Bhattacharyya, S.K.; Barai, S.V.; Mukherjee, A.; Biswas, W.K. Environmental implications of the use of bio-cement treated recycled aggregate in concrete. *Resour. Conserv. Recycl.* **2021**, *167*, 105436. [CrossRef]
10. Ni, S.Y.; Liu, H.B.; Li, Q.Y.; Quan, H.Z.; Gheibi, M.; Fathollahi-Fard, A.M.; Tian, G.D. Assessment of the engineering properties, carbon dioxide emission and economic of biomass recycled aggregate concrete: A novel approach for building green concretes. *J. Clean. Prod.* **2022**, *365*, 132780. [CrossRef]
11. Wang, R.J.; Yu, N.N.; Li, Y. Methods for improving the microstructure of recycled concrete aggregate: A review. *Constr. Build. Mater.* **2020**, *242*, 118164. [CrossRef]
12. Martinez-Lage, I.; Vazquez-Burgo, P.; Vazquez-Burgo, P. Sustainability evaluation of concretes with mixed recycled aggregate based on holistic approach: Technical, economic and environmental analysis. *Waste. Manag.* **2020**, *101*, 9–19. [CrossRef] [PubMed]
13. Colangelo, F.; Petrillo, A.; Farina, I. Comparative environmental evaluation of recycled aggregates from construction and demolition wastes in Italy. *Sci. Total Environ.* **2021**, *798*, 149250. [CrossRef] [PubMed]
14. Mostert, C.; Sameer, H.; Glanz, D.; Bringezu, S. Climate and resource footprint assessment and visualization of recycled concrete for circular economy. *Resour. Conserv. Recycl.* **2021**, *174*, 105767. [CrossRef]

15. Gedik, A. A review on the evaluation of the potential utilization of construction and demolition waste in hot mix asphalt pavements. *Resour. Conserv. Recycl.* **2020**, *161*, 104956. [CrossRef]
16. Liu, C.; Liu, H.W.; Xiao, J.Z.; Bai, G.L. Effect of old mortar pore structure on relative humidity response of recycled aggregate concrete. *Constr. Build. Mater.* **2020**, *247*, 118600. [CrossRef]
17. Jang, H.; Kim, J.; Kim, J. Effect of aggregate size on recycled aggregate concrete under equivalent mortar volume mix design. *Appl. Sci.* **2021**, *11*, 11274. [CrossRef]
18. Huang, Q.B.; Qian, Z.D.; Hu, J.; Zheng, D.; Chen, L.L.; Zhang, M.; Yu, J.Z. Investigation on the properties of aggregate-mastic interfacial transition zones (ITZs) in asphalt mixture containing recycled concrete aggregate. *Constr. Build. Mater.* **2021**, *269*, 121257. [CrossRef]
19. Ji, J.; Li, P.F.; Chen, M.; Zhang, R.; Zhou, W.J.; You, Z.P. Review on the fatigue properties of recycled asphalt concrete containing construction and demolition wastes. *J. Clean. Prod.* **2021**, *327*, 129478. [CrossRef]
20. Liu, S.J.; Cui, S.P.; Guo, H.X.; Wang, Y.L.; Zheng, Y. Adsorption of lead ion from wastewater using non-crystal hydrated calcium silicate gel. *Materials* **2021**, *14*, 842. [CrossRef]
21. Prasad, D.; Singh, B.; Suman, S.K. Utilization of recycled concrete aggregate in bituminous mixtures: A comprehensive review. *Constr. Build. Mater.* **2022**, *326*, 126859. [CrossRef]
22. Foti, D.; Cavallo, D. Mechanical behavior of concretes made with non-conventional organic origin calcareous aggregates. *Constr. Build. Mater.* **2018**, *179*, 100–106. [CrossRef]
23. Spairani, Y.; Cisternino, A.; Foti, D.; Lerna, M.; Ivorra, S. Study of the behavior of structural materials treated with bioconsolidant. *Materials* **2021**, *14*, 5369. [CrossRef] [PubMed]
24. Lerna, M.; Foti, D.; Petrella, A.; Sabbà, M.F.; Mansour, S. Effect of the chemical and mechanical recycling of PET on the thermal and mechanical response of mortars and premixed screeds. *Materials* **2023**, *16*, 3155. [CrossRef] [PubMed]
25. Lerna, M.; Caballero-Jorna, M.; Roig-Flores, M.; Foti, D.; Serna, P. Influence of recycled materials on the mechanical properties of macro synthetic fiber-reinforced concrete. In Proceedings of the FIB International Congress, Oslo, Norway, 12–16 June 2022.
26. Gunka, V.; Demchuk, Y.; Sidun, I.; Miroshnichenko, D.; Nyakuma, B.B.; Pyshyev, S. Application of phenol-cresol-formaldehyde resin as an adhesion promoter for bitumen and asphalt concrete. *Road Mater. Pavement Des.* **2021**, *22*, 2906–2918. [CrossRef]
27. Wang, X.; Zhang, C.S.; Wu, Q.S.; Zhu, H.J.; Liu, Y. Thermal properties of metakaolin-based geopolymer modified by the silane coupling agent. *Mater. Chem. Phys.* **2021**, *267*, 124655. [CrossRef]
28. Liu, J.M.; Ju, B.Y.; Yin, Q.; Xie, W.; Xiao, H.Y.; Dong, S.L. Properties of Concrete Prepared with silane coupling agent impregnated coral aggregate and coral concrete. *Materials* **2021**, *14*, 6454. [CrossRef]
29. Luo, X.Y.; Wei, Y.H.; Ma, L.L.; Tian, W.; Zhu, C.Y. Effect of corrosive aging environments on the flexural properties of silane-coupling-agent-modified basalt-fiber-reinforced composites. *Materials* **2023**, *16*, 1543. [CrossRef]
30. Aziz, T.; Ullah, A.; Fan, H.; Jamil, M.I.; Khan, F.U.; Ullah, R.; Iqbal, M.; Ali, A.; Ullah, B. Recent Progress in Silane Coupling Agent with Its Emerging Applications. *J. Polym. Environ.* **2021**, *29*, 3427–3443. [CrossRef]
31. Feng, Y.; Wang, W.J.; Wang, S.Q.; Niu, Z.J.; Li, L.Y. Multi-scale analysis of mechanical properties of KH-560 coupling agent modified PVA fiber-rubber concrete. *Compos. Interface* **2023**, *30*, 983–1010. [CrossRef]
32. Li, Y.L.; Li, Y.Z.; Li, Y.; Liu, Z.Z.; Wen, L.F.; Zhang, Y.Z.; Zhou, H. Effect of silane coupling agent on improving adhesive property between acidic aggregate and hydraulic asphalt. *J. Mater. Civil Eng.* **2021**, *33*, 04021172. [CrossRef]
33. Ye, Y.L.; Hao, Y.; Zhuang, C.Y.; Shu, S.Q.; Lv, F.L. Evaluation on improvement effect of different anti-stripping agents on pavement performance of granite-asphalt mixture. *Materials* **2022**, *15*, 915. [CrossRef] [PubMed]
34. Ran, W.P.; Zhu, H.L.; Shen, X.Z.; Zhang, Y. Rheological properties of asphalt mortar with silane coupling agent modified oil sludge pyrolysis residue. *Constr. Build. Mater.* **2022**, *329*, 127057. [CrossRef]
35. Guo, F.C.; Pei, J.Z.; Zhang, J.P.; Xue, B.; Sun, G.Q. Study on the adhesion property between asphalt binder and aggregate: A state-of-the-art review. *Constr. Build. Mater.* **2020**, *256*, 119474. [CrossRef]
36. Hou, D.S.; Yang, Q.R.; Jin, Z.Q.; Wang, P.; Wang, M.H.; Wang, X.P.; Zhang, Y. Enhancing interfacial bonding between epoxy and CSH using graphene oxide: An atomistic investigation. *Appl. Surf. Sci.* **2021**, *568*, 150896. [CrossRef]
37. Yu, C.H.; Hu, K.; Yang, Q.L.; Chen, Y.J. Multi-scale observation of oxidative aging on the enhancement of high-temperature property of SBS-modified asphalt. *Constr. Build. Mater.* **2021**, *313*, 125478. [CrossRef]
38. Sun, W.; Wang, H. Moisture effect on nanostructure and adhesion energy of asphalt on aggregate surface: A molecular dynamics study. *Appl. Surf. Sci.* **2020**, *510*, 145435. [CrossRef]
39. Luo, L.; Chu, L.J.; Fwa, T.F. Molecular dynamics analysis of moisture effect on asphalt-aggregate adhesion considering anisotropic mineral surfaces. *Appl. Surf. Sci.* **2020**, *527*, 146830. [CrossRef]
40. Zhai, M.; Li, J.L.; Wang, R.R.; Yue, J.C.; Wang, X.F. Revealing mechanisms of aging and moisture on thermodynamic properties and failure patterns of asphalt-aggregate interface from the molecular Scale. *J. Mater. Civil Eng.* **2023**, *35*, 04022486. [CrossRef]
41. *ASTM D1078-11*; Standard Test Method for Distillation Range of Volatile Organic Liquids. ASTM International: West Conshohocken, PA, USA, 2019.
42. *ASTM D4052*; Standard Test Method for Density, Relative Density, and API Gravity of Liquids by Digital Density Meter. ASTM International: West Conshohocken, PA, USA, 2022.
43. *ASTM D542-14*; Standard Test Method for Index of Refraction of Transparent Organic Plastics. ASTM International: West Conshohocken, PA, USA, 2014.

44. *ASTM D5-06*; Standard Test Method for Penetration of Bituminous Materials. ASTM International: West Conshohocken, PA, USA, 2017.
45. *ASTM D36-06*; Standard Test Method for Softening Point of Bitumen (Ring-and-Ball Apparatus). ASTM International: West Conshohocken, PA, USA, 2010.
46. *ASTM D113-07*; Standard Test Method for Ductility of Bituminous Materials. ASTM International: West Conshohocken, PA, USA, 2018.
47. Liu, T.J.; Wei, H.N.; Zhou, A.; Zou, D.J.; Jian, H.S. Multiscale investigation on tensile properties of ultra-high performance concrete with silane coupling agent modified steel fibers. *Cem. Concr. Compos.* **2020**, *111*, 103638. [CrossRef]
48. *ASTM D36-25*; Standard Practice for Effect of Water on Bituminous-Coated Aggregate Using Boiling Water. ASTM International: West Conshohocken, PA, USA, 2012.
49. *ASTM D4124-09*; Standard Test Method for Separation of Asphalt into Four Fractions. ASTM International: West Conshohocken, PA, USA, 2018.
50. Hu, K.; Yu, C.H.; Chen, Y.J.; Li, W.; Wang, D.D.; Zhang, W.G. Multiscale mechanisms of asphalt performance enhancement by crumbed waste tire rubber: Insight from molecular dynamics simulation. *J. Mol. Model.* **2021**, *27*, 170–184. [CrossRef] [PubMed]
51. Hu, K.; Yu, C.H.; Yang, Q.L.; Li, Z.W.; Zhang, W.G.; Zhang, T.L.; Feng, Y. Mechanistic study of graphene reinforcement of rheological performance of recycled polyethylene modified asphalt: A new observation from molecular dynamics simulation. *Constr. Build. Mater.* **2022**, *320*, 126263. [CrossRef]
52. Yu, C.H.; Yang, Q.L. Investigation of the interfacial interaction of carbon nanomaterials with asphalt matrix: Insights from molecular simulations. *Mol. Simul.* **2023**, *49*, 208–222. [CrossRef]
53. Qin, D.J.; Feng, Y.; Li, L.J. Molecular dynamics study on improvement effect of polyethylene terephthalate on adhesive properties of asphalt and cement-based composite interface. *Mol. Simul.* **2023**, *49*, 1293–1302. [CrossRef]
54. Jiang, F.X.; Yang, Q.R.; Wang, Y.T.; Wang, P.; Hou, D.S.; Jin, Z.Q. Insights on the adhesive properties and debonding mechanism of CFRP/concrete interface under sulfate environment: From experiments to molecular dynamics. *Constr. Build. Mater.* **2021**, *269*, 121247. [CrossRef]
55. Feng, Y.; Li, Y.; Zhao, C.; Qin, D.J.; Wang, C.; Wang, P.Y. Nano-$CaCO_3$ enhances PVA fiber-matrix interfacial properties: An experimental and molecular dynamics study. *Mol. Simul.* **2022**, *48*, 1378–1392. [CrossRef]
56. Hou, D.S.; Yang, Q.R.; Wang, P.; Jin, Z.Q.; Wang, M.H.; Zhang, Y.; Wang, X.P. Unraveling disadhesion mechanism of epoxy/CSH interface under aggressive conditions. *Cem. Concr. Compos.* **2021**, *146*, 106489. [CrossRef]
57. Luo, Q.; Li, Y.Y.; Zhang, Z.; Peng, X.J.; Geng, G.Q. Influence of substrate moisture on the interfacial bonding between calcium silicate hydrate and epoxy. *Constr. Build. Mater.* **2022**, *320*, 126252. [CrossRef]
58. Luo, Q.; Zhang, X.Y.; Li, Y.Y.; Zhang, Z.; Geng, G.Q. Interfacial degradation of calcium silicate hydrate and epoxy under a hygrothermal environment: An experimental and molecular model study. *J. Phys. Chem. C* **2023**, *127*, 1607–1621. [CrossRef]
59. Cui, W.T.; Huang, W.K.; Hu, B.; Xie, J.W.; Xiao, Z.C.; Cai, X.; Wu, K.H. Investigation of the Effects of Adsorbed Water on Adhesion Energy and Nanostructure of Asphalt and Aggregate Surfaces Based on Molecular Dynamics Simulation. *Polymers* **2020**, *12*, 2339. [CrossRef]
60. Cui, B.Y.; Wang, H. Molecular interaction of Asphalt-Aggregate interface modified by silane coupling agents at dry and wet conditions. *Appl. Surf. Sci.* **2022**, *275*, 151365. [CrossRef]

Disclaimer/Publisher's Note: The statements, opinions and data contained in all publications are solely those of the individual author(s) and contributor(s) and not of MDPI and/or the editor(s). MDPI and/or the editor(s) disclaim responsibility for any injury to people or property resulting from any ideas, methods, instructions or products referred to in the content.

Article

Laboratory Investigation of the Composite Influence of Rock Asphalt and Montmorillonite on the Performance of Bio-Asphalt

Minghao Mu [1], Chaochao Liu [2,*] and Zhengnan Liu [2]

1. Shandong Hi-Speed Group Innovation Research Institute, Jinan 250098, China; sdgsmmh@126.com
2. National Engineering Laboratory of Highway Maintenance Technology, Changsha University of Science & Technology, Changsha 410004, China; liuzhengnan@126.com
* Correspondence: lcc@csust.edu.cn; Tel.: +86-152-0089-4449

Abstract: To improve the rutting resistance and anti-aging performance of bio-asphalt, the composite modifier of rock asphalt and montmorillonite is used to modify the bio-asphalt. The optimum content of each component was determined by orthogonal tests based on the results from penetration, softening point, ductility and viscosity tests. The rheological properties and anti-aging performance of rock asphalt and montmorillonite composite-modified bio-asphalt (RAMB) with the optimum content were evaluated as compared to those of matrix asphalt (MA), untreated/treated bio-asphalt (UBA/TBA) and rock asphalt-/montmorillonite-modified bio-asphalt (RMB/MMB). The test results illustrated that the optimum content of each component in the rock asphalt/montmorillonite composite-modified bio-asphalt—as determined by orthogonal experimental design and penetration, softening point, ductility and viscosity tests—was 7% bio-oil treated by thermostatic water bath, 5% rock asphalt and 30% montmorillonite. The high-temperature performance, low-temperature performance and anti-aging performance of RAMB were studied by comparison to those of matrix asphalt, UBA, TBA, RMB and MMB. Additionally, the composite modification mechanism was studied by Fourier transform infrared spectroscopy (FTIR). The results suggested that the high-temperature of TBA was obviously improved compared with UBA. The reason, as seen from infrared spectrum tests, was that the amount of ester compounds decreased after water bath treatment. The light components and soluble substances in bio-oil decreased. Compared to UBA, the unrecoverable creep compliance (J_{nr}) of RAMB decreased by 66.6% and the recovery rate (R) increased by 75.9% at 0.1 KPa. The stiffness modulus (S) of RAMB was 0.87 times that of matrix asphalt and the creep rate (m) was 1.03 times that of base asphalt. Compared to single-modified asphalt, the high- and low-temperature performance of RAMB was good. Meanwhile, the complex modulus aging index (CMAI) and stiffness modulus aging index (SAI) of RAMB were lower than all other asphalt studied, while the phase angle aging index (PAAI) and creep rate aging index (mAI) of RAMB were the largest. The results of infrared spectroscopy also suggest that the mixing of rock asphalt, montmorillonite, bio-oil and matrix asphalt is a physical blending process. During the process, no functional groups are formed. Pretreatment and addition of rock asphalt and montmorillonite can improve high-temperature performance, low-temperature performance and anti-aging performance of the bio-asphalt.

Keywords: bio-asphalt; composite modification; rheological performance; anti-aging; modification mechanism

Citation: Mu, M.; Liu, C.; Liu, Z. Laboratory Investigation of the Composite Influence of Rock Asphalt and Montmorillonite on the Performance of Bio-Asphalt. *Appl. Sci.* **2023**, *13*, 5174. https://doi.org/10.3390/app13085174

Academic Editor: Arcady Dyskin

Received: 9 March 2023
Revised: 17 April 2023
Accepted: 18 April 2023
Published: 21 April 2023

Copyright: © 2023 by the authors. Licensee MDPI, Basel, Switzerland. This article is an open access article distributed under the terms and conditions of the Creative Commons Attribution (CC BY) license (https://creativecommons.org/licenses/by/4.0/).

1. Introduction

The development of road networks plays an important role in the national economy. Petroleum asphalt is rapidly consumed with the quick development of road networks. There is a desperate shortage of petroleum asphalt. To ensure good road performance, the development of economically- and environmentally-friendly alternative materials is highly significant. Bio-asphalt is considered the alternative material with the most potential.

However, the high-temperature performance and anti-aging performance of existing bio-asphalt are seriously insufficient.

According to research findings, bio-oil can replace a portion of petroleum asphalt [1]. The production cost of bio-asphalt is about 3/10~2/5 of that of petroleum asphalt. Bio-asphalt shows reasonable economic and environmental performance [2]. Road workers have performed plenty of tests on the preparation technology, chemical composition, modification mechanism, physicochemical properties and road performance of waste cooking oil bio-asphalt [3–6]. Waste cooking oil contains high amounts of water and volatile substances. This limits the incorporation of waste cooking oil into bio-asphalt. Compared to petroleum asphalt, bio-oil contains hundreds of oxygenated compounds. Its moisture content and oxygen content are higher. Therefore, bio-oil is unstable and the aging rate of bio-oil accelerates with increasing temperature [7,8]. Wang et al. found that the presence of moisture and volatile substances may lead to delamination of bio-oil. Thus, the bio-oil was distilled at 110 °C before being added to asphalt [9]. Zhang et al. treated bio-oil with distilled water at 50 °C, which can remove polar light components in bio-oil [10]. Yang et al. removed water from bio-oil before addition to petroleum asphalt [11]. The mixture's physical properties were tested, such as pH value and water content. Ruikun et al. removed the water in the waste cooking oil [12]. Waste cooking oil- and pre-desulfurization rubber powder-modified asphalt were obtained. The results of Maharaj et al. showed that the anti-fatigue of the mixture was improved with the introduction of waste cooking oil [13]. The bio-asphalt mixture has good low-temperature performance and water stability. Conversely, high-temperature performance and anti-aging performance are poor [4,14,15].

To improve the high-temperature performance of bio-asphalt, Yang et al. added 4% polyethylene and found that the rutting resistance was improved [16]. Sun et al. added SBS to bio-asphalt to improve the high-temperature performance. They found that the activation energy of SBS-modified asphalt was reduced by adding bio-oil. SBS-modified asphalt containing bio-oil had a low viscosity value. Bio-oil can lower the high-temperature rutting resistance [17]. The nitrogen and asphaltene content were much higher in rock asphalt compared to matrix asphalt. As such, rock asphalt-modified asphalt showed good high-temperature performance. Lv et al. found that the high-temperature performance of matrix asphalt was improved by rock asphalt because asphaltenes and gums were increased [18–20]. Menglan et al. prepared composite-modified asphalt by adding European rock asphalt and castor oil bio-asphalt. The addition of composite modifier was in the range of 20–30%. The high-temperature and anti-aging properties of asphalt were upgraded by adding composite modifier. The low-temperature properties and temperature sensitivity of asphalt were also improved. Different performance requirements can be met by adjusting the upper and lower limits of the content. Rock asphalt played a significant role as a high temperature modifier [21]. Yu et al. carried out X-ray diffraction and found that montmorillonite-modified asphalt could form an intercalated structure, while organic montmorillonite-modified asphalt could form an exfoliated structure. This improved the thermal oxidation aging resistance and ultraviolet aging resistance of asphalt [22]. Fen Ye and Vargas performed dynamic shear rheological tests (DSR). Organic montmorillonite-modified asphalt showed better anti-aging performance and high-temperature performance [23,24]. The temperature sensitivity was reduced. Lu compared the effects of nano-montmorillonite and naphthenic oil on SBS-modified asphalt. They found that nano-montmorillonite reduced the low-temperature performance and high-temperature viscosity [25]. To improve the viscosity and high-temperature stability of bio-asphalt, Siqing Liu [26] added hard asphalt particles, C5 petroleum resin, organic montmorillonite and styrene–butadiene rubber to bio-asphalt. According to research findings, the modified bio-asphalt with the best modifier ratio was still soft (penetration was 123 (0.1 mm)). The high-temperature performance was not ideal. The addition of crosslinking agent, anti-aging agent and dispersant improved the high-temperature stability, anti-aging performance and storage stability of the asphalt. Nevertheless, this is difficult to use in engineering applications due to the complex preparation process and many kinds of modified substances and additives. Therefore, further work is needed to improve the high-temperature performance and anti-aging performance of bio-asphalt.

Therefore, this paper employed pretreatment measures. Organic montmorillonite and rock asphalt were selected to modify bio-asphalt. Organic montmorillonite can form stripping structure and improve the anti-aging performance of asphalt. Asphaltene and colloid content in asphalt were increased and the high-temperature performance of asphalt was improved because of the addition of rock asphalt. The rheological properties and anti-aging of modified asphalt were analyzed. The mechanism of composite modification was revealed by FTIR. This provided a basis for improving the performance of waste cooking oil bio-asphalt. A technology roadmap was established, as shown in Figure 1.

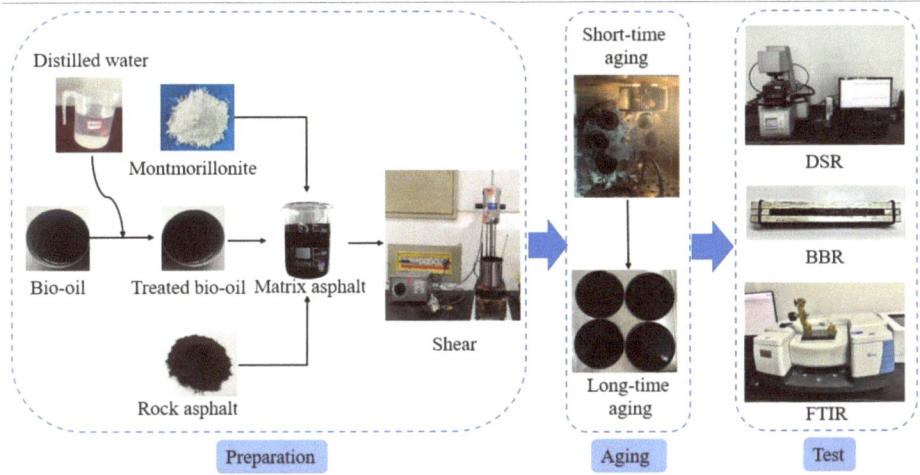

Figure 1. Test flow chart.

2. Materials and Methods

2.1. Materials

2.1.1. Asphalt

No.70 matrix asphalt was used in this paper. The basic performance was measured by "Standard Test Methods of Asphalt and Bituminous Mixtures for Highway Engineering, JTG E20-2011" [27]. The experimental results are listed in Table 1. According to the "Technical Specifications for Construction of Highway Asphalt Pavement, JTG F40-2004" [28], all indicators of No.70 asphalt are within the range of specification requirements.

Table 1. Basic properties of asphalt.

Project		Unit	Demand	Result	Test Method
Penetration (25 °C, 100 g, 5 s)		0.1 mm	60~80	67.6	T 0604-2011
Ductility (10 °C, 5 cm/min)		cm	≥10	13.5	T 0605-2011
Softening point (ring and ball method)		°C	≥46	48.5	T 0606-2011
Penetration index		—	−1.5~+1.0	−0.78	T 0604-2011
Density		g/cm^3	Measured	1.027	T 0603-2011
60 °C Dynamic viscosity		Pa·s	≥180	272	T 0620-2000
Flash point		°C	≥260	294	T 0611-2011
After RTFOT	Mass change rate	%	±0.8	−0.083	T 0610-2011
	Residual penetration ratio	%	≥61	81	T 0604-2011
	Residual ductility (10 °C)	cm	≥6	7	T 0605-2011

2.1.2. Bio-Oil

The bio-oil came from waste cooking oil. It was a by-product obtained in the production of biodiesel. The basic properties are shown in Table 2. Compared to the values in Table 1, the density and viscosity are less than the matrix asphalt and the acid value is larger.

Table 2. Basic properties of bio-oil.

Project	Unit	Index	Test Method
Density	g/mL	0.92~0.95	GB/T 2540
Water content	%	≤0.3	SH/T 0264
60 °C Dynamic viscosity	Pa·s	0.126	GB/T 265
Acid value	mg KOH/g	30~60	SH/T 264

2.1.3. Buton Rock Asphalt

Buton rock asphalt was used, which contains 24.8% asphalt, 74.9% ash and some impurities. After being ground and passed through a 0.15 mm standard sieve, the rock asphalt particles could be used as modifiers. Table 3 lists some indexes of rock asphalt.

Table 3. Technical indexes of rock asphalt.

Project	Unit	Demand	Result	Test Method
Trichloroethylene Solubility	%	≥18	26.65	T0607
Density	g/cm^3	≤1.9	1.71	T0603
Heating loss	%	≤2.0	0.27	T0608
Flash point	°C	≥230	318	T0611

2.1.4. Montmorillonite

Montmorillonite is a good asphalt modifier to improve aging resistance. The montmorillonite in this paper was purchased from China Zhejiang Feng Hong clay chemical plant. The montmorillonite was modified with organic quaternary ammonium salt. As a cationic surfactant, organic quaternary ammonium salt reduced the surface energy of montmorillonite by exchanging interlayer cations of montmorillonite. Thus, the dispersion of organic nano-montmorillonite in asphalt was significantly improved compared to montmorillonite without organic treatment. In addition, organic nano-montmorillonite also has the advantages of large layer spacing, good dispersion and large cation exchange capacity. Some performance indexes of montmorillonite are summarized in Table 4.

Table 4. Basic performance of OMMT.

Project	Unit	Result	Test Method
Density	g·cm^{-3}	1.02	ASTM D854-14
Granularity	Mesh	5000	GB/T 2922
Coefficient of expansion	/	0.05	GB/T 50123-2019
Hardness	/	1.02	-
Montmorillonite content	%	>99	GB/T 17188-2016
Specific surface area	m^2·g^{-1}	750	-
Diameter thickness ratio	/	200	-

2.1.5. Preparation of Rock Asphalt and Montmorillonite Composite-Modified Bio-Asphalt (RAMB)

The distilled water and bio-oil were mixed in a mass ratio of 1:1 and placed in a bath at 50 °C for 10 min. The upper bio-oil was then taken out. Figure 2 shows the bio-oil before and after treatment. The matrix asphalt was heated at 135 °C for 1 h in an oven. When it reached the molten state, the asphalt was taken out and then quickly heated and insulated on the electric furnace. The high-speed shear instrument was turned on and set to a speed of 1000 r/min. Next, 7% bio-oil (mass ratio of bio-oil to matrix asphalt) was added and the rotation speed was adjusted to 3000 r/min; the asphalt was sheared at 150~160 °C for 30 min. At this point, bio-asphalt preparation was complete. Next, 30% montmorillonite (mass ratio of montmorillonite to the matrix asphalt and bio-oil) was added and the mixture was sheared for 60 min. A small amount of 5% of the rock asphalt (mass ratio of rock asphalt to the matrix asphalt and bio-oil) was added after passing through a 0.15 mm standard sieve. This was poured into the asphalt several times and mixed manually while adding. After all rock asphalt was added, this was sheared for 30 min. Rock asphalt swelled and developed with volume expansion. When the rock asphalt particles were dissolved and the surface of the modified asphalt presented a mirror effect, the preparation of RAMB was finished.

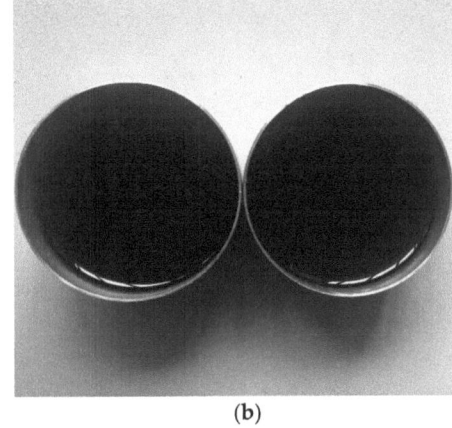

Figure 2. Pretreatment of bio-oil. (**a**) Mixing of water and oil; (**b**) Bio-oil before and after treatment.

2.1.6. Proportion Optimization of RAMB

The orthogonal design method of four factors at three different levels was used to determine the mass ratio of water and bio-oil in RAMB and the optimal content of each material. The influence of bio-oil content, the mass ratio of water and bio-oil and the content of rock asphalt and montmorillonite on penetration, ductility, softening point and rotational viscosity of asphalt was considered. Three levels were set for each factor, as shown in Table 5. According to the orthogonal design table of L9(34) (as shown in Table 6), nine asphalts with different content combinations were prepared and tested.

Table 5. Factors and levels.

Level	Factor			
	Mass Ratio of Water and Bio-Oil	Content of Bio-Oil (%)	Content of Rock Asphalt (%)	Content of Montmorillonite (%)
1	1:1	5	20	3
2	2:1	7	30	5
3	3:1	9	40	7

Table 6. Combinations of orthogonal test L9(34).

Number	Mass Ratio of Water and Bio-Oil	Content of Bio-Oil (%)	Content of Rock Asphalt (%)	Content of Montmorillonite (%)	Orthogonal Combinations
1	1:1	5	20	3	$A_1B_1C_1D_1$
2	1:1	7	30	5	$A_1B_2C_2D_2$
3	1:1	9	40	7	$A_1B_3C_3D_3$
4	2:1	5	30	7	$A_2B_1C_2D_3$
5	2:1	7	40	3	$A_2B_2C_3D_1$
6	2:1	9	20	5	$A_2B_3C_1D_2$
7	3:1	5	40	5	$A_3B_1C_3D_2$
8	3:1	7	20	7	$A_3B_2C_1D_3$
9	3:1	9	30	3	$A_3B_3C_2D_1$

Table 7 lists the orthogonal test results. The penetration of the matrix asphalt was 67.6 (0.1 mm) and the softening point was 48.5 °C in this paper. The penetration values of No.6, No.8 and No.9 were far larger than matrix asphalt. Additionally, the softening point was slightly lower than that of matrix asphalt. This indicates that the high-temperature performance of these three combinations was poor. Improving the high-temperature performance of bio-asphalt was the main purpose of this paper but these three combinations could not meet the requirements. After these three combinations were eliminated, the remaining six combinations were selected by Technique for Order Preference by Similarity to Ideal Solution (TOPSIS) in multi-objective decision-making. The decision matrix was a 6 × 4 matrix [29,30].

Table 7. Basic properties of orthogonal test.

Combinations	Penetration (0.1 mm)	Softening Point (°C)	Ductility at 10 °C (mm)	Rotational Viscosity at 135 °C (Pa·s)
1	59.47	52.2	116.5	0.690
2	63.77	50.6	152.8	0.805
3	62.4	51.3	101.3	0.965
4	52.63	52.7	95.5	0.955
5	62.83	53.3	99.5	0.940
6	95.9	47.6	304.2	0.640
7	57.23	51.4	132.1	0.935
8	81.1	48.3	183.2	0.755
9	83.67	47.8	288.8	0.715

Table 8 lists the ranking results of TOPSIS. According to the table, the second combination was a suitable preparation method for RAMB. In this method, the mass ratio of water and bio-oil was 1:1, the content of bio-oil was 7%, the content of rock asphalt was 30% and the content of montmorillonite was 5%. Note: Di^+ presents the distance between each combination and positive ideal solution; Di^- presents the distance between each combination and negative ideal solution; CI presents approaching index.

Table 8. Results of TOPSIS.

Combination	Di^+	Di^-	CI	Sort
1	0.105575933	0.044310354	0.29562647	4
2	0.08704551	0.047591609	0.353480599	1
3	0.114158233	0.03963836	0.257732365	5
4	0.115642707	0.058291842	0.335136648	3
5	0.115200269	0.039523716	0.255446599	6
7	0.058596286	0.115635936	0.352389578	2

2.2. Methods

To prove the performance of RAMB, six asphalts were prepared, including matrix asphalt, untreated bio-asphalt, treated bio-asphalt, rock asphalt-modified bio-asphalt, montmorillonite-modified bio-asphalt and RAMB. When carrying out different tests, parallel samples of each asphalt were prepared. The repeatability error value according to the specification requirements were determined, to ensure the reliability of the experiment. By comparing a series of experimental indicators, the road performance of RAMB was analyzed. Specific tests and indicators are described as follows.

2.2.1. Dynamic Shear Rheological Test (DSR)

Frequency Scanning Test (FS)

The dynamic shear rheological test is one of the most important tests in the American Strategic Highway Research Program (SHRP). This test shears asphalt using the reciprocating motion of oscillating plates parallel to fixed plates. Wheel movement on a road surface is simulated at 55 miles per hour. Due to the viscoelastic properties of asphalt, strain (stress) delayed response occurs under the action of shear stress (strain). The basic principle of the dynamic shear rheometer is shown in Figure 3.

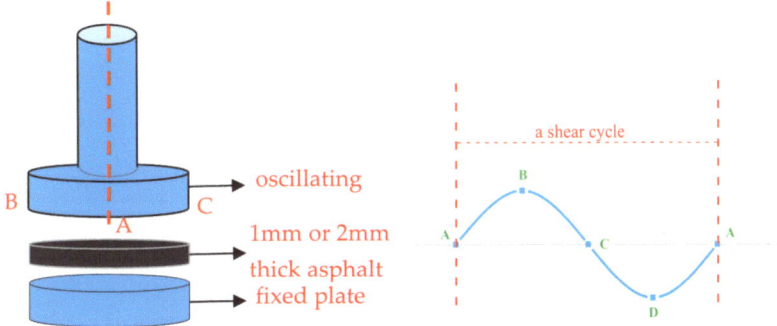

Figure 3. Drawing of dynamic shear rheometer.

The frequency scanning test of unaged asphalt was carried out. The changes in high-temperature rheological parameters of asphalt at different frequencies were revealed. The test temperature was 58 °C. The frequency range was 0~100 Hz. The measurement was carried out from high frequency to low frequency and 31 data points were recorded. The temperature scanning test of unaged, short-term aging and long-term aging asphalt were used to evaluate the anti-aging properties of asphalt. The test angular frequency was 10 rad/s (that is, a constant frequency of 1.59 Hz). There were four temperatures which ranged from 46 °C to 60 °C, with every 6 °C as a temperature interval. A 25 mm oscillating plate was used for the unaged and short-term aging asphalt. The gap between the two parallel plates was 1 mm. The parallel plate was replaced with an 8 mm oscillating plate for the long-term aging asphalt. The gap between the two parallel plates was 2 mm. The differences were used because the long-term aging asphalt was harder than the unaged and short-term aging asphalt. The angle phase (δ) and complex modulus (G^*) of asphalt were obtained and the rutting factor was calculated.

Multiple Stress Creep Recovery Test (MSCR)

MSCR test of the short-term aging asphalt was carried out at 58 °C. The asphalt was subjected to 30 creep recovery cycles at two constant stress levels of 0.1 KPa and 3.2 KPa. The creep occurred for 1 s and the recovery process lasted for 9 s. According to

Equations (1)–(3), the R and J$_{nr}$ values of asphalt at 0.1 KPa and 3.2 KPa were calculated. The elastic recovery ability and high-temperature rutting resistance of asphalt were evaluated.

$$J_{nr}(0.1) = \frac{\varepsilon_r - \varepsilon_0}{0.1} \tag{1}$$

$$J_{nr}(3.2) = \frac{\varepsilon_r - \varepsilon_0}{3.2} \tag{2}$$

$$R = \frac{(\varepsilon_1 - \varepsilon_{10}) \times 100}{\varepsilon_1} \tag{3}$$

2.2.2. Bending Beam Rheological Test (BBR)

The S and m values of asphalt were measured by BBR test, as shown in Figure 4. These two low-temperature rheological indexes are closely related to the low-temperature performance of asphalt. SHRP states that the S value of asphalt should not exceed 300 MPa and the m value of asphalt should not be less than 0.3. BBR tests of the unaged asphalt, short-term aging asphalt and long-term aging asphalt were carried out. The low-temperature performance of asphalt and the effect of aging on the low-temperature performance of asphalt were revealed. An asphalt specimen with a size of 127 mm × 12 mm × 6.35 mm was formed in a cuboid mold without cover. Then, the constant load of 980 mN ± 50 mN was continuously applied to the simply supported beam at −18 °C for 240 s. The deformation and load of specimens were recorded at 8.0 s, 15.0 s, 30.0 s, 60.0 s, 120.0 s and 240.0 s. The S and m values at 60.0 s were acquired as evaluation indexes of the bending beam rheometer test.

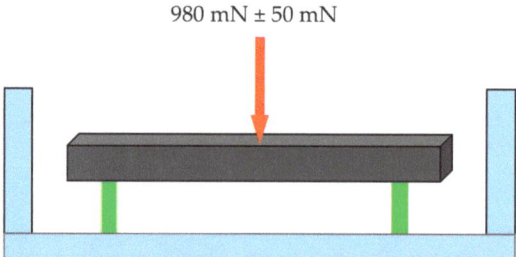

Figure 4. Schematic figure of the bending beam rheometer.

2.2.3. Aging of Asphalt

Asphalt ages under high-temperature and it oxidizes during preparation and mixing with aggregate. Laboratories usually use film oven or rotating thin film oven test under standard conditions to simulate the process of aging. In this study, asphalt underwent short-term aging by the rotating thin film oven test. The asphalt after short-term aging was used for further long-term aging and conducted mechanism tests. Each aging bottle was filled with 35 ± 0.5 g asphalt. A group of 8 aging bottles was placed on the annular supports of the rotating thin film oven. The asphalt was aged for 85 min at 163 °C.

Pressure Aging Vessel-accelerated asphalt aging test (PAV) is a method to simulate the long-term aging of asphalt during service. In this method, asphalt aged by rotating thin film oven was separately divided into PAV sample plates. The quantity of short-term aging asphalt in each sample plate was 50 ± 0.5 g, to form about 3.2 mm-thick asphalt film. Then, the plate was kept at 100 °C and 2.1 MPa for 20 h to accelerate the aging process in a constant-temperature and constant-pressure vessel.

2.2.4. Fourier Transform Infrared Spectroscopy Test (FTIR)

To obtain information about functional groups, FTIR was carried out. The effects of the pretreatment of distilled water and the addition of rock asphalt and montmorillonite on the chemical composition of bio-oil were studied. The infrared spectroscope was Thermo Scientific Nicolet iS50 FT-IR. Solid asphalt and solid powder modifiers (rock asphalt and montmorillonite) were directly measured at room temperature without sample preparation. For solid asphalt, such as the liquid bio-oil at room temperature in this study, the method of sample preparation was with potassium bromide pellets. The infrared spectral curve was collected for liquid asphalt. Because potassium bromide had no absorption peak in the infrared band, it showed a blank spectrum. The spectral curve of the sample shows that the band range is 4000–500 cm^{-1} and the number of scans is 32 [27].

3. Results

3.1. Rheological Properties

3.1.1. High-Temperature Rheological Properties

FS

FS tests were carried out at different frequencies by oscillatory shear strain. They revealed the effect of loading frequency on the viscoelastic properties of RAMB. Figure 5 lists the G* and δ values of six asphalts at different frequencies.

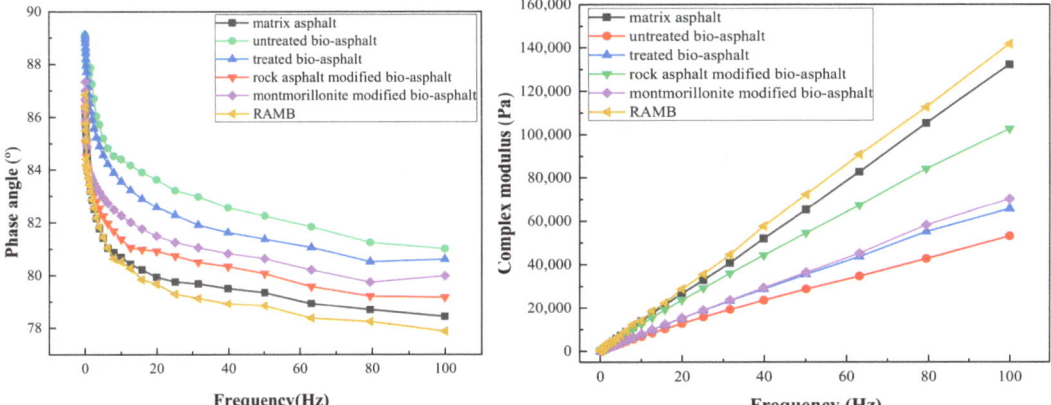

Figure 5. Graph of the G* and δ values of six asphalts at 58 °C.

The composite shear modulus, G*, characterizes the resistance value of the asphalt material during repeated deformation in shear. δ represents the hysteresis of the stress relative to the stress. G* and δ together represent the viscoelastic properties of the asphalt: the larger the δ value, the closer the asphalt is to a viscous body, while the smaller the δ value, the closer the asphalt is to an elastomer, meaning the asphalt is more resistant to deformation at high temperatures. The G* value of the six asphalts gradually increased and the δ value decreased with the increase in frequency. Compared to matrix asphalt, the G* value of bio-asphalt was significantly reduced and the δ value improved. The lack of high-temperature performance can be attributed to bio-oil containing lots of free fatty acids. Free fatty acids are introduced when bio-oil replaces part of the matrix asphalt. This is one of the reasons for the poor rutting resistance of bio-asphalt [31]. Compared to the G* value and δ values of untreated bio-asphalt, treated bio-asphalt, rock asphalt-modified bio-asphalt and montmorillonite-modified bio-asphalt, pretreatment, rock asphalt and montmorillonite improved the G* value of bio-asphalt. The δ value of bio-asphalt was also reduced. The modification effect of rock asphalt was most obvious. The G* value of RAMB was greater than the matrix asphalt. The δ value was lower than the matrix asphalt. Thus, pretreatment, rock asphalt and montmorillonite comprehensively increase the elastic component, the G* value and the high-temperature rutting of bio-asphalt. G* values are sorted as follows: RAMB > matrix asphalt > rock asphalt-modified bio-asphalt > montmorillonite-modified bio-asphalt > treated bio-asphalt > untreated bio-asphalt.

MSCR

The shear strain of the six asphalts is shown in Figure 6. The strain of asphalt under 0.1 KPa was small and the difference between different asphalts was also small. However, the strain of asphalt sharply increased under 3.2 KPa. The growth rate showed a significant difference. The untreated bio-asphalt exhibited a large deformation under the action of load. The shear strain increased rapidly with the repeated loading. The pretreatment and single modifier reduced the shear strain of bio-asphalt, but the effect was not as good as that of rock asphalt–montmorillonite materials composite-modified bio-asphalt.

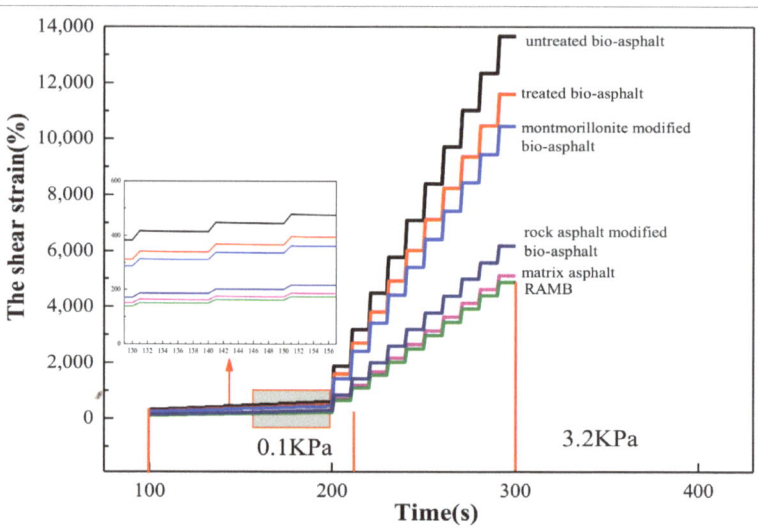

Figure 6. Shear strain figure of six asphalts at 58 °C.

J_{nr} can reflect the permanent deformation resistance of asphalt: the smaller the value, the higher the deformation resistance of the asphalt at high temperatures. R can represent the elastic component of the asphalt: the larger the value, the more elastic the asphalt. J_{nr} and R values of six asphalts at 0.1 KPa and 3.2 KPa are shown in Figures 7 and 8. Shown here, bio-asphalt had the lowest R value and the highest J_{nr} value among the six asphalts. Bio-asphalt had a large shear deformation under the action of stress. The plastic deformation was the main part, with only a small portion of elastic deformation. The R value of montmorillonite-modified bio-asphalt, treated bio-asphalt and untreated bio-asphalt became negative under 3.2 KPa because the high-temperature performance of the three kinds of asphalt at 58 °C was insufficient in the nonlinear viscoelastic range. The order of R values of the 6 groups of asphalt samples was RAMB > MA > RMB > MMB > TBA > UBA. The RAMB had the minimum J_{nr} value and the maximum R value. Compared to the untreated bio-asphalt, the J_{nr} value decreased by 66.6% and the R value increased by 75.9% under 0.1 KPa. The improvement effect of the three measures on the high-temperature rutting resistance is significant. This is consistent with the above frequency scanning results.

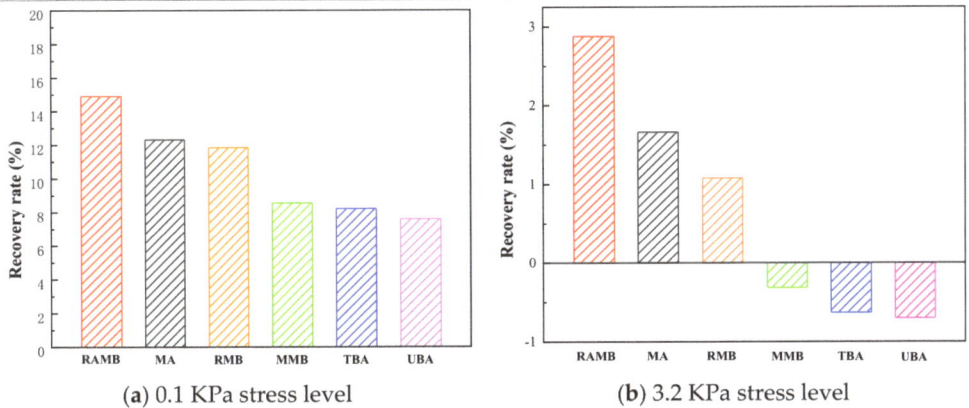

Figure 7. R value of different asphalts.

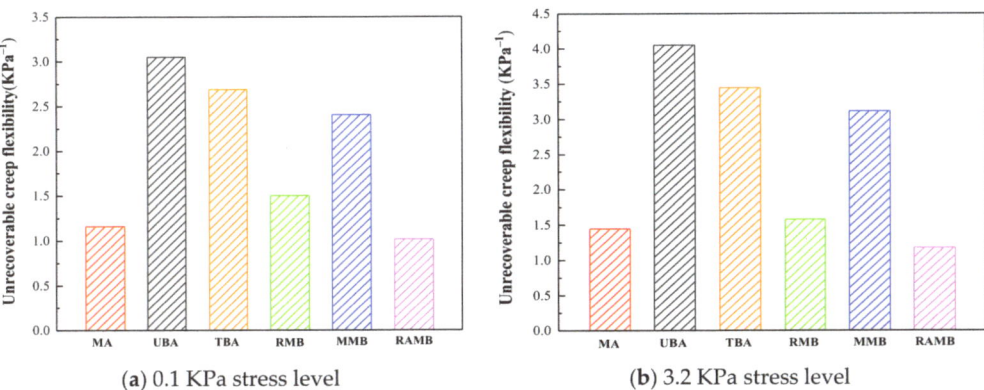

Figure 8. J$_{nr}$ value of different asphalts.

3.1.2. Low-Temperature Rheological Test

S value reflects the resistance of asphalt binder to load, while m value reflects the rate of change in asphalt stiffness with time. Specifications require S < 300 MPa and m > 0.3; additionally, a smaller S value and a larger m value lead to better low-temperature rheological properties. The S and m values of the six unaged asphalts at −18 °C are shown in Figure 9. As shown in Figure 9, untreated bio-asphalt had the lowest S value and the largest m value among the six asphalts. The low-temperature performance was good. The bio-asphalt had satisfactory performance in terms of low-temperature deformation resistance because of the significant softening effect of bio-oil. The low-temperature performance of RAMB was lower than that of bio-asphalt, but the S value was less than 300 MPa at −18 °C and them value was greater than 0.3. The requirements of SHRP for low-temperature performance of asphalt binder were met. The S value was 0.87 times that of matrix asphalt and the m value was 1.03 times that of matrix asphalt. Its low-temperature rheology energy was better than matrix asphalt.

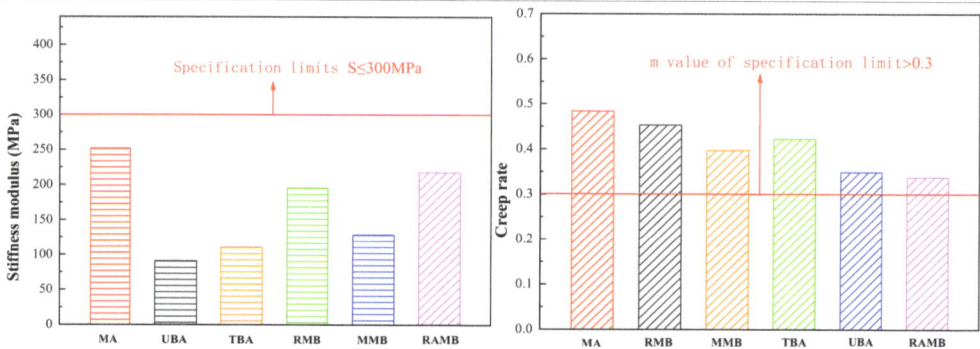

Figure 9. S and m of six asphalts at −18 °C.

3.2. Anti-Aging Performance

3.2.1. Anti-Aging Performance of RAMB Based on High-Temperature Rheological Performance

The dynamic shear rheological test was performed on the short-term and long-term aging of asphalt and the δ and G* values were obtained to calculate the aging index. The rutting indexes for the six asphalts were measured at different temperatures and three aging states (no aging, short-term aging and long-term aging), as shown in Figure 10. The G* value of three of the aging asphalts decreased and the δ value increased as the temperature increased. The high temperature increases the mobility of the asphalt and reduces the anti-deforming capability. The G* value of all asphalts increased and the δ value gradually decreased with aging at constant temperature. The physical hardening effect caused by aging favors the anti-deforming capability of asphalt. The rutting indexes of matrix asphalt, rock asphalt-modified bio-asphalt and RAMB met the requirements. RAMB had the highest G* value and the lowest δ value. The rutting index of the original asphalt was 2.60 times that of the untreated bio-asphalt and 1.12 times that of the matrix asphalt at 64 °C. The rutting index of the short-term aging asphalt at 64 °C was 2.36 times that of the untreated bio-asphalt and 1.11 times that of the matrix asphalt.

The aging resistance of asphalt was evaluated by calculating CMAI and PAAI using Equations (4) and (5). With smaller CMAI, larger PAAI indicates better aging resistance.

$$\text{CMAI} = \frac{\text{Complex modulus of short or long term aging asphalt}}{\text{Complex modulus of original asphalt}} \quad (4)$$

$$\text{PAAI} = \frac{\text{Phase angle of short or long term aging asphalt}}{\text{Phase angle of original asphalt}} \quad (5)$$

The changes in CMAI and PAAI after short- and long-term aging of the six asphalts are shown in Figures 11 and 12. As seen from Figures 11 and 12, untreated bio-asphalt had the largest CMAI and the smallest PAAI in the range of 46 °C to 64 °C. This indicates that untreated bio-asphalt has poor aging resistance and the high-temperature rheological properties are greatly affected by aging because there are many light components in bio-asphalt. The volatilization of light components leads to the change in high-temperature performance of asphalt. The CMAI and PAAI of treated bio-asphalt were improved, compared to untreated bio-asphalt. The pretreatment of distilled water reduced the introduction of light components in matrix asphalt by removing the light components in bio-oil. Thus, the volatilization of light components in bio-asphalt was reduced during the aging. The addition of rock asphalt and montmorillonite reduced the CMAI and increased the PAAI of bio-asphalt. The performance of rock asphalt demonstrated little change under the influence of aging, meaning it can bear rutting deformation under high temperature by serving as the hard particles in bio-asphalt. Montmorillonite within the layered structure reduces the volatilization of light components. Stability of asphalt components is maintained. This prevents oxygen incorporation and reduces the oxidation of asphalt components. The changes in bio-asphalt in terms of chemical composition are reduced. Therefore, the high-temperature rheological properties of treated bio-asphalt, rock asphalt-modified bio-asphalt and montmorillonite-modified bio-asphalt change little under the influence of aging. The CMAI of RAMB is less than that of other asphalts. The PAAI is greater than other asphalts. Its anti-aging properties are better. Bio-asphalt has good anti-aging performance with pretreatment, rock asphalt and montmorillonite.

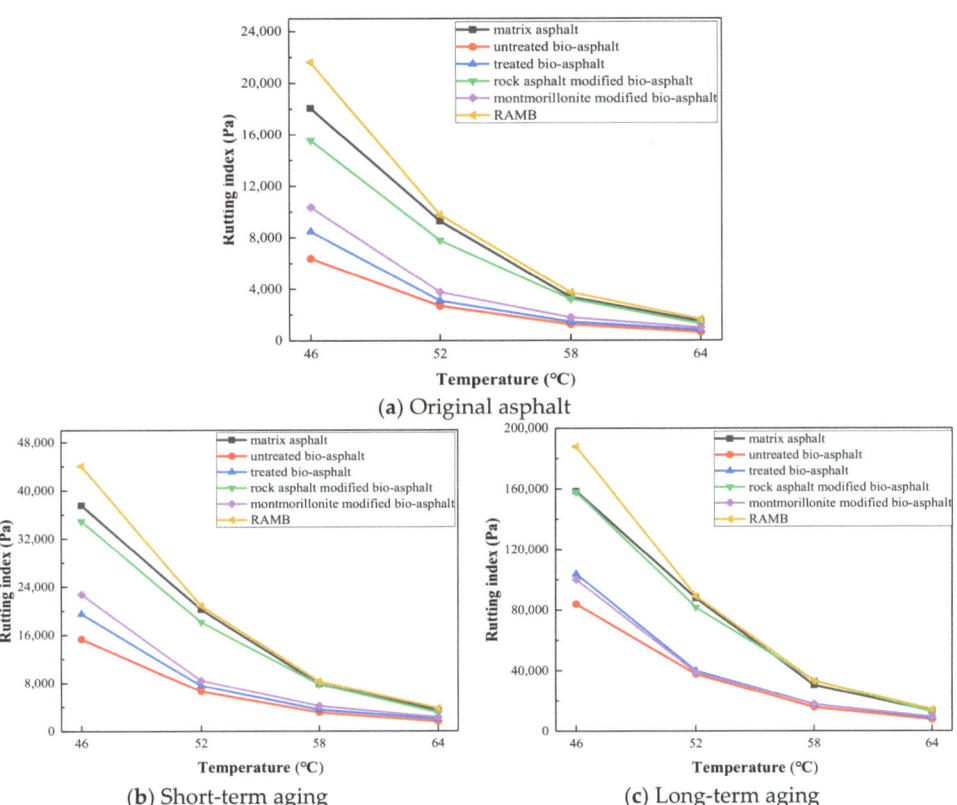

Figure 10. Rutting indexes of six asphalts.

3.2.2. Anti-Aging Performance of RAMB Based on Low-Temperature Rheological Performance

The low-temperature bending beam tests of unaged and aged asphalt were carried out to compare the changes in S and m values. The S value of each asphalt increased after the aging treatment of the original asphalt, as shown in Figure 13. The polymerization reaction occurred inside the asphalt under the influence of aging and the low-molecular weight aromatic phenol was polymerized into high-molecular weight asphaltene. The aging of the asphalt made it physically brittle. Therefore, the aging was more damaging than it was for the original asphalt at low temperature. The m of long-term aging asphalt was greater than that of short-term aging asphalt, while the m of short-term aging asphalt was greater than that of original asphalt. The decrease in the rate of m was accelerated with the increase in aging. On the other hand, the S value of matrix asphalt after short-term aging exceeded 300 MPa and the m value was less than 0.3. The S and m value of rock asphalt-modified bio-asphalt and RAMB after short-term aging met the requirements. This shows that the low-temperature performance of the two asphalts after mixing and paving is better than that of matrix asphalt. Conversely, the S and m values after long-term aging exceeded the standard value. The two asphalts were damaged at low temperature after a period of service, but the time to show damage for these two asphalts was longer than that of matrix asphalt at low temperature under the same service conditions. The low-temperature rheological indexes of the other three asphalts under three aging conditions all met the specification requirements. The stress relaxation ability was good after aging and the deterioration via cracking was slow.

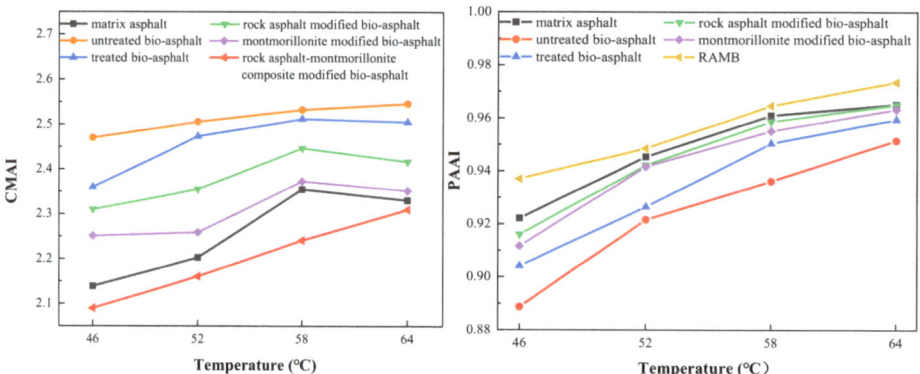

Figure 11. CMAI and PAAI of short-term aging of six asphalts.

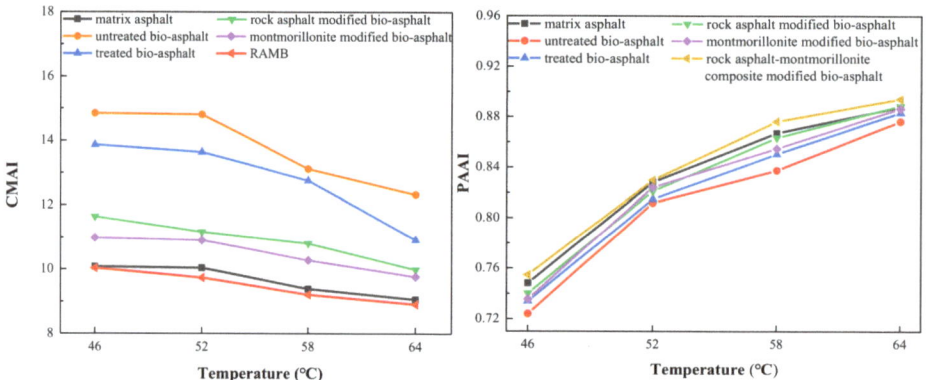

Figure 12. CMAI and PAAI of long-term aging of six asphalts.

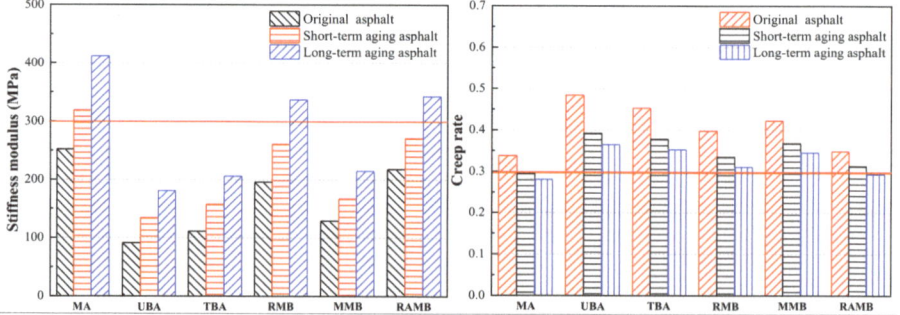

Figure 13. The S and m values of six asphalts in different aging states.

According to Equations (6) and (7), the SAI and mAI were calculated. When SAI is small and mAI is large, that asphalt has strong low-temperature aging resistance. The calculation results of the SAI and mAI are illustrated in Figures 14 and 15. According to Figures 14 and 15, the SAI value of untreated bio-asphalt was the largest among the six asphalts and the mAI value was the smallest. This shows that the deterioration of low-temperature properties was the most serious under the influence of aging. The SAI value was reduced and the mAI value was increased after distilled water treatment. The SAI value of rock asphalt-modified bio-asphalt, montmorillonite-modified bio-asphalt and matrix asphalt showed less differentiation. The anti-aging performance of bio-asphalt was only slightly improved by the addition of rock asphalt. The improvement effect of montmorillonite was obvious, but was not as pronounced as the matrix asphalt. Compared to the matrix asphalt, the SAI value of RAMB was smaller and the mAI value was larger. The SAI value of RAMB after short-term aging was 0.98 times that of matrix asphalt and the SAI value after long-term aging was 0.96 times that of matrix asphalt, while the mAI value after short-term aging was 1.03 times that of matrix asphalt and the mAI value after long-term aging was 1.01 times that of matrix asphalt. RAMB has good anti-aging performance.

$$\text{SAI} = \frac{\text{Stiffness modulus of short or long term aging asphalt}}{\text{Stiffness modulus of original asphalt}} \quad (6)$$

$$\text{mAI} = \frac{\text{Creep rate of short or long term aging asphalt}}{\text{Creep rate of original asphalt}} \quad (7)$$

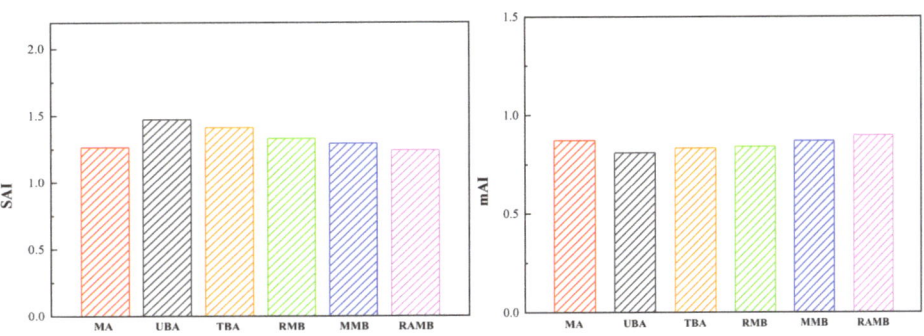

Figure 14. Short-term aging SAI and mAI for six asphalts.

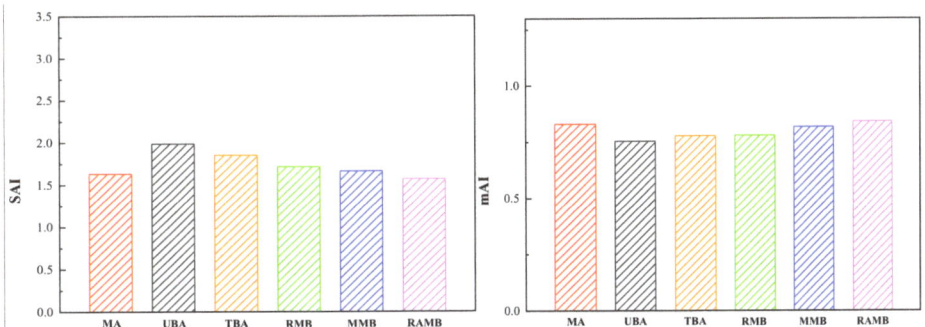

Figure 15. SAI and mAI of six asphalts after long-term aging.

3.3. FTIR

The infrared spectroscopy of untreated bio-oil was coincident with that of treated bio-oil, shown in Figure 16, but the intensity values of some characteristic peaks were different. The intensity of characteristic peaks represents the content of functional groups in asphalt. The peak intensity of two bio-oils were observed at 2923.88 cm^{-1}, 2853.37 cm^{-1}, 1743.18 cm^{-1}, 1463.41 cm^{-1}, 1377.09 cm^{-1}, 1162.01 cm^{-1} and 967.08 cm^{-1}. The peak intensity of treated bio-oils was smaller than that of untreated bio-oils [32]. The peak corresponding to 967.08 cm^{-1} is out-of-plane deformation of C-H bond. The peak corresponding to 1162.01 cm^{-1} is stretching vibration of ester group O=C-O. The peak corresponding to 1377.09 cm^{-1} is in-plane bending vibration of methyl C-H bond. The peak corresponding to 1463.41 cm^{-1} is the in-plane bending vibration of methyl and methylene C-H. The peak corresponding to 1743.18 cm^{-1} is the stretching vibration of ester O-C=O. The peak corresponding to 2923.88 cm^{-1} is the stretching vibration of methylene CH$_2$. The peak corresponding to 2853.37 cm^{-1} is stretching vibration of methyl CH$_3$ [33]. The peaks corresponding to 1162 cm^{-1} and 1743 cm^{-1} indicate that the bio-oil contained ester compounds [16,34]. Ester compounds are volatile substances with low boiling points and strong volatility when heated. The peak intensity of the treated bio-oil was weakened at 1162 cm^{-1} and 1743 cm^{-1}. The volatile substance content of bio-oil was decreased after treatment with distilled water.

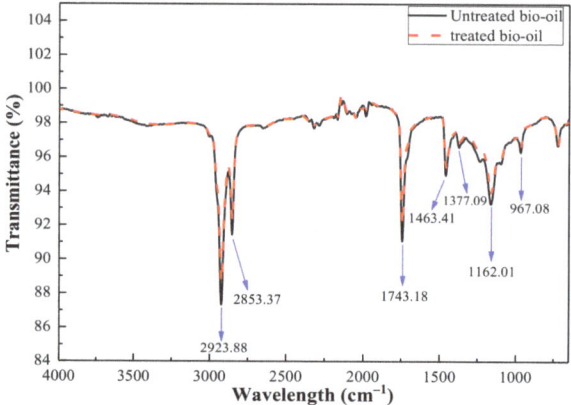

Figure 16. Infrared spectroscopy of untreated and treated bio-oil.

As shown in Figure 17, there were three differences in light absorption in the mid-infrared region between bio-asphalt and matrix asphalt, namely, 1744.54 cm^{-1}, 1159 cm^{-1} and 966.2 cm^{-1}. The stretching vibration of ester group O-C=O corresponds to 1744.54 cm^{-1}. The peak at 1159.83 cm^{-1} corresponds to the stretching vibration of ester group O=C-O. The peak at 966.20 cm^{-1} corresponds to the out-of-plane deformation of trans-carbon–carbon double C-H bond. The three peaks existed in the spectroscopy of bio-oil. Therefore, the three peaks of bio-asphalt were all from bio-oil. The mixing of bio-oil and matrix asphalt is a physical blend system.

As shown in Figures 18–20, the infrared spectroscopy of treated bio-asphalt was consistent with the rock asphalt-modified asphalt, but the absorption peak of bio-asphalt was very weak at 873.41 cm^{-1}, while rock asphalt-modified bio-asphalt showed obvious an absorption peak—the carboxyl C-H in CO_3^{2-} of rock asphalt [35]. When montmorillonite was added to bio-asphalt, there was a strong and wide absorption peak at 1085.08 cm^{-1}—the Si-O-Si antisymmetric stretching vibration bond [36,37]. Other absorption peaks did not change. The new peak of bio-asphalt came from montmorillonite. The incorporation of montmorillonite did not react with bio-asphalt to generate new functional groups. When the rock asphalt and montmorillonite were added into the bio-asphalt, the infrared spectroscopy of the bio-asphalt had two changes. From the above analysis, the emergence of these two peaks is due to the strong vibration of the two peaks in the rock asphalt and montmorillonite. Thus, the preparation process of rock asphalt, montmorillonite and bio-asphalt is also a physical blending process.

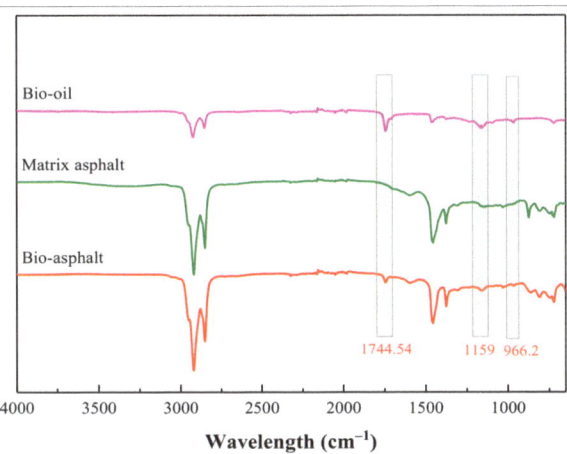

Figure 17. Infrared spectroscopy of bio-oil, matrix asphalt and bio-asphalt.

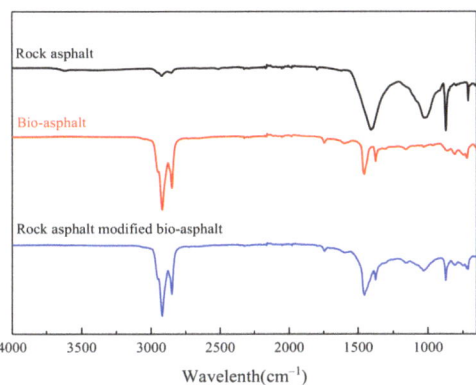

Figure 18. Infrared spectroscopy of rock asphalt, bio-asphalt and rock asphalt-modified bio-asphalt.

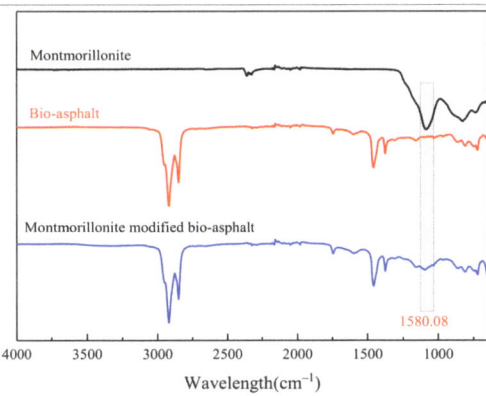

Figure 19. Infrared spectroscopy of montmorillonite, bio-asphalt and montmorillonite-modified bio-asphalt.

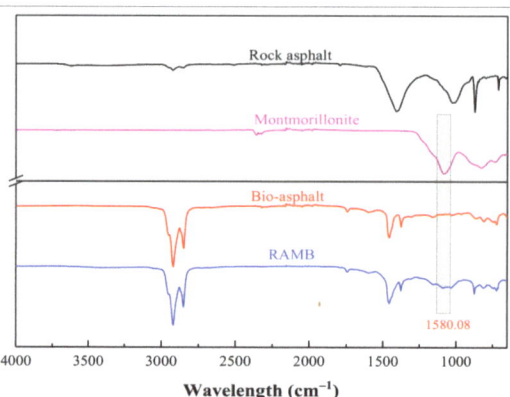

Figure 20. Infrared spectroscopy of rock asphalt, montmorillonite, bio-asphalt and RAMB.

4. Conclusions

To improve the high-temperature performance and anti-aging performance of bio-asphalt, this paper proposed a preparation method for RAMB. The DSR test, BBR test, anti-aging performance test and FTIR test were carried out. From the research, the primary conclusions are as follows:

(1) Through the method in the paper, the high-temperature performance of bio-asphalt is significantly improved. The low-temperature cracking resistance can meet the requirements of SHRP for low-temperature performance of asphalt binder.
(2) The anti-aging performance of RAMB is much better than that of bio-asphalt. The distilled water treatment removes some light components in bio-oil and the addition of rock asphalt and montmorillonite increases the absorption peaks of two functional groups, C-H and Si-O-Si, respectively.
(3) Based on the results of FTIR, the mixing of rock asphalt, montmorillonite and bio-asphalt is a physical blending system. The modification effect and road performance of this mixture still need further experimental research.

Author Contributions: M.M.: Methodology, Conceptualization, Writing—original draft preparation, Validation, Visualization, Formal analysis. C.L.: Conceptualization, Resources, Data curation, Writing—reviewing and editing, Funding acquisition, Project administration. Z.L.: Software, Validation, Investigation, Formal analysis. All authors have read and agreed to the published version of the manuscript.

Funding: This work was supported by the National Natural Science Foundation of China (52208420). Science and technology project of Guangxi Zhuang Autonomous Region (2020AB42007). The Natural Science Foundation of Hunan province of China (2022JJ40484). Open Fund of National Engineering Research Center of Highway Maintenance Technology (Changsha University of Science & Technology) (kfj210108). Technological innovation projects of enterprises in Wuhan (2020020602012145).

Institutional Review Board Statement: Not applicable.

Informed Consent Statement: Not applicable.

Data Availability Statement: Data available on request due to restrictions e.g., privacy or ethical.

Acknowledgments: This work was supported by the National Natural Science Foundation of China (52078063).

Conflicts of Interest: The authors declare no conflict of interest.

References

1. Wang, H.; Ma, Z.; Chen, X.; Mohd Hasan, M.R. Preparation process of bio-oil and bio-asphalt, their performance, and the application of bio-asphalt: A comprehensive review. *J. Traffic Transp. Eng. (Engl. Ed.)* **2020**, *7*, 137–151. [CrossRef]
2. Ren, K.; Liu, C.; Wu, Z.; An, H.; Qu, J.; Zhang, H.; Lv, S. Laboratory investigation on performance of waste-oil cutback asphalt as prime coat on cement stabilized macadam base. *Constr. Build. Mater.* **2023**, *365*, 129965. [CrossRef]
3. Barzegari, S.; Solaimanian, M. Rheological behavior of bio-asphalts and effect of rejuvenators. *Constr. Build. Mater.* **2020**, *251*, 118137. [CrossRef]
4. Liu, J.; Lv, S.; Peng, X.; Yang, S. Improvements on performance of bio-asphalt modified by castor oil-based polyurethane: An efficient approach for bio-oil utilization. *Constr. Build. Mater.* **2021**, *305*, 124784. [CrossRef]
5. Lv, S.; Yuan, J.; Peng, X.; Borges Cabrera, M.; Guo, S.; Luo, X.; Gao, J. Performance and optimization of bio-oil/Buton rock asphalt composite modified asphalt. *Constr. Build. Mater.* **2020**, *264*, 120235. [CrossRef]
6. Zahoor, M.; Nizamuddin, S.; Madapusi, S.; Giustozzi, F. Sustainable asphalt rejuvenation using waste cooking oil: A comprehensive review. *J. Clean. Prod.* **2021**, *278*, 123304. [CrossRef]
7. Peralta, J.; Raouf, M.A.; Tang, S.; Williams, R.C. *Bio-Renewable Asphalt Modifiers and Asphalt Substitutes*; Springer: Berlin/Heidelberg, Germany, 2012; pp. 89–115.
8. Sun, Z.; Yi, J.; Huang, Y.; Feng, D.; Guo, C. Properties of asphalt binder modified by bio-oil derived from waste cooking oil. *Constr. Build. Mater.* **2016**, *102*, 496–504. [CrossRef]
9. Su, N.; Xiao, F.; Wang, J.; Cong, L.; Amirkhanian, S. Productions and applications of bio-asphalts–A review. *Constr. Build. Mater.* **2018**, *183*, 578–591. [CrossRef]
10. Zhang, R.; Wang, H.; You, Z.; Jiang, X.; Yang, X. Optimization of bio-asphalt using bio-oil and distilled water. *J. Clean. Prod.* **2017**, *165*, 281–289. [CrossRef]
11. Yang, X.; Mills-Beale, J.; You, Z. Chemical characterization and oxidative aging of bio-asphalt and its compatibility with petroleum asphalt. *J. Clean. Prod.* **2017**, *142*, 1837–1847. [CrossRef]
12. Dong, R.; Liang, W.; Tang, N.; Zhao, M. Study on the components and viscoelasticity of asphalt modified by rubber powder pre-desulfurization of waste edible oil. *China J. Hhighway Transp.* **2019**, *32*, 226–234.
13. Maharaj, R.; Ramjattan-Harry, V.; Mohamed, N. Rutting and Fatigue Cracking Resistance of Waste Cooking Oil Modified Trinidad Asphaltic Materials. *Sci. World J.* **2015**, *2015*, 385013. [CrossRef]
14. Guarin, A.; Khan, A.; Butt, A.A.; Birgisson, B.; Kringos, N. An extensive laboratory investigation of the use of bio-oil modified bitumen in road construction. *Constr. Build. Mater.* **2016**, *106*, 133–139. [CrossRef]
15. Junfeng, G.; Hainian, W.; Zhanping, Y.; Xi, C.; Xin, J. Evaluation of high temperature performance of bio-asphalt based on MSCR test. *J. South China Univ. Technol. (Nat. Sci. Ed.)* **2017**, *45*, 24–30.
16. Yang, X.; You, Z.; Dai, Q.; Mills-Beale, J. Mechanical performance of asphalt mixtures modified by bio-oils derived from waste wood resources. *Constr. Build. Mater.* **2014**, *51*, 424–431. [CrossRef]
17. Sun, Z.; Yi, J.; Chen, Z.; Xie, S.; Xu, M.; Feng, D. Chemical and rheological properties of polymer modified bitumen incorporating bio-oil derived from waste cooking oil. *Mater. Struct.* **2019**, *52*, 106. [CrossRef]
18. Lv, S.; Fan, X.; Yao, H.; You, L.; You, Z.; Fan, G. Analysis of performance and mechanism of Buton rock asphalt modified asphalt. *J. Appl. Polym. Sci.* **2019**, *136*, 46903. [CrossRef]
19. Lv, S.; Peng, X.; Liu, C.; Qu, F.; Zhu, X.; Tian, W.; Zheng, J. Aging resistance evaluation of asphalt modified by Buton-rock asphalt and bio-oil based on the rheological and microscopic characteristics. *J. Clean. Prod.* **2020**, *257*, 120589. [CrossRef]
20. Li, J.; Zhang, J.H.; Yang, X.R.; Zhang, A.S.; Yu, M. Monte Carlo Simulations of Deformation Behaviour of Unbound Granular Materials Based on a Real Aggregate Library. *Int. J. Pavement Eng.* **2023**, *24*, 2165650. [CrossRef]
21. Zeng, M.; Zhu, W.; Xia, Y.; Li, J. Performance of Bio-asphalt and Rock Asphalt Composite Modified Asphalt. *J. Hunan Univ. Nat. Sci.* **2019**, *46*, 124–131. [CrossRef]
22. Yu, J.; Zeng, X.; Wu, S.; Wang, L.; Liu, G. Preparation and properties of montmorillonite modified asphalts. *Mater. Sci. Eng. A* **2007**, *447*, 233–238. [CrossRef]
23. Vargas, M.A.; Moreno, L.; Montiel, R.; Manero, O.; Vázquez, H. Effects of montmorillonite (Mt) and two different organo-Mt additives on the performance of asphalt. *Appl. Clay Sci.* **2017**, *139*, 20–27. [CrossRef]
24. Ye, F.; Yin, W.; Lu, H.; Dong, Y. Property improvement of Nano-Montmorillonite/SBS modified asphalt binder by naphthenic oil. *Constr. Build. Mater.* **2020**, *243*, 118200. [CrossRef]
25. Lu, H.; Ye, F.; Yuan, J.; Yin, W. Properties comparison and mechanism analysis of naphthenic oil/SBS and nano-MMT/SBS modified asphalt. *Constr. Build. Mater.* **2018**, *187*, 1147–1157. [CrossRef]
26. Liu, S. Preparation and Characterization of Waste Edible Oil-Based Bio-Asphalt. Master's Thesis, Wuhan University of Technology, Wuhan, China, 2018.
27. *JTG E20-2011*; Test Specification for Asphalt and Asphalt Mixture of Highway, Engineering; Transport Industry, Standard. Institute of Highway Science, M.o.T: Beijing, China, 2011; p. 373P.; A374.
28. *JTG F40-2004*; Technical Specification for Construction of Highway Asphalt Pavement. Institute of Highway Science, M.o.T: Beijing, China, 2004; p. 196P.; A194.
29. Sheng, Y.; Wu, Y.; Yan, Y.; Jia, H.; Qiao, Y.; Underwood, B.S.; Niu, D.; Kim, Y.R. Development of environmentally friendly flame retardant to achieve low flammability for asphalt binder used in tunnel pavements. *J. Clean. Prod.* **2020**, *257*, 120487. [CrossRef]

30. Zhang, Y. Research and Application of Multi-Objective Decision Making under Uncertainty Method. Master's Thesis, Yangtze University, Jingzhou, China, 2018.
31. Azahar, W.N.A.W.; Jaya, R.P.; Hainin, M.R.; Bujang, M.; Ngadi, N. Chemical modification of waste cooking oil to improve the physical and rheological properties of asphalt binder. *Constr. Build. Mater.* **2011**, *126*, 218–226. [CrossRef]
32. Liu, C.; Zhao, B.; Xue, Y.; He, Y.; Ding, S.; Wen, Y.; Lv, S. Synchronous method and mechanism of asphalt-aggregate separation and regeneration of reclaimed asphalt pavement. *Constr. Build. Mater.* **2023**, *378*, 131127. [CrossRef]
33. Hallizza, A.; Rehan, K.M. Implementition of Waste Cooking Oil as Rap Rejuvenator. *Proc. East. Asia Soc. Transp. Studies* **2011**, *8*, 267. [CrossRef]
34. Puetuen, E.; Puetuen, A.E.; Apaydin, E. Rice straw as a bio-oil source via pyrolysis and steam pyrolysis. *Energy* **2004**, *29*, 2171–2180. [CrossRef]
35. Jing, H.; Guopeng, F.; Minjia, Z. Partial performance and economic benefit analysis of Budunyan asphalt modified asphalt. *Pet. Asph.* **2019**, *33*, 55–59, 66.
36. Bee, S.-L.; Abdullah, M.A.A.; Mamat, M.; Bee, S.-T.; Sin, L.T.; Hui, D.; Rahmat, A.R. Characterization of silylated modified clay nanoparticles and its functionality in PMMA. *Compos. Part B Eng.* **2017**, *110*, 83–95. [CrossRef]
37. Mishra, A.K.; Allauddin, S.; Narayan, R.; Aminabhavi, T.M.; Raju, K.V.S.N. Characterization of surface-modified montmorillonite nanocomposites. *Ceram. Int.* **2012**, *38*, 929–934. [CrossRef]

Disclaimer/Publisher's Note: The statements, opinions and data contained in all publications are solely those of the individual author(s) and contributor(s) and not of MDPI and/or the editor(s). MDPI and/or the editor(s) disclaim responsibility for any injury to people or property resulting from any ideas, methods, instructions or products referred to in the content.

Article

Experimental Study on the Cracking Resistance of Asphalt Mixture with Different Degrees of Aging

Shuyao Yang *, Zhigang Zhou and Kai Li

Key Laboratory of Road Structure and Material Ministry of Communication, Changsha University of Science and Technology, 960, 2nd Section, Wanjiali South Rd., Tianxin District, Changsha 410114, China; zhou_zgcs@163.com (Z.Z.); likai_cs@163.com (K.L.)
* Correspondence: ysy@stu.csust.edu.cn; Tel.: +86-151-1137-0374

Abstract: The cracking resistance of asphalt mixture is a non-negligible issue. However, the cracking resistance evolution law, motivated by two factors (thermos-oxidative aging degree and test temperature), is not yet well understood. The aim of this investigation is to gain more insight into the effect of thermos-oxidative aging and test temperature on the cracking resistance of asphalt mixture. Asphalt mixture (AC-13) and stone mastic asphalt mixture (SMA-13) were selected and exposed to different thermo-oxidative aging degrees (unaging (UA); short-term thermo-oxidative aging (STOA); long-term thermo-oxidative aging for 2/5/8 days (LTOA2d/LTOA5d/LTOA8d)). A direct tension test at different test temperatures (10 °C, 20 °C, 30 °C, 40 °C) was adopted to obtain their stress–strain curves and evaluation indexes (tensile strength, ultimate strain, pre-peak strain energy density, and post-peak strain energy density). The comprehensive index-cracking resistance index (CRI) was established by the entropy weight method combined with the technique to order preference by similarity to ideal solution (TOPSIS) method and the corresponding aging coefficient was determined. The results showed that STOA can increase the aging coefficient of asphalt mixture, thereby boosting the cracking resistance. Additionally, the effect can be weakened by elevations in the test temperature. Meanwhile, LTOA can decrease the aging coefficient and thereby weaken the cracking resistance. This effect becomes more prominent with elevations in the test temperature. SMA-13 possesses a superior cracking resistance to AC-13, with a gap in CRI value of 3–69%, regardless of the aging degree and test temperature. A good relationship exists between the aging coefficient and the two factors (aging degree and test temperature).

Keywords: cracking resistance; thermo-oxidative aging; entropy weight TOPSIS; comprehensive cracking resistance index; aging coefficient

1. Introduction

Cracking is one of the most common hazards in asphalt pavement, associated with the cracking resistance of the main constituent of asphalt–pavement mixture. Aging occurs throughout the life cycle of asphalt pavement. During mixing, pavement rolling, and service, the asphalt mixture itself is inevitably exposed to complex environmental factors (such as oxygen, a high ambient temperature, light, and water), which can cause changes in the cracking resistance of asphalt mixture to a certain extent, and thereby change the durability of asphalt pavement [1,2]. Generally speaking, aging can be classified into thermo-oxidative aging, light-oxidative aging, and water aging, of which thermo-oxidative aging is the most common. Therefore, it is important to study the cracking resistance of asphalt mixture considering thermo-oxidative aging, and much research has been conducted on this issue. Song et al. [3] demonstrated the existence of aging during the transportation procedure using a direct tension test at low temperatures, and the results revealed that cracking resistance at low temperatures worsened with transportation time. Yan et al. [4] and Zhu et al. [5] investigated the cracking resistance of AC13 in STOA and conditions through a disk-shaped compact tension (DCT) test (−12°C). The results show that STOA can accelerate the cracking propagation regardless of the increased effect on the tensile strength. Song et al. [6] conducted a trabecular bending beam test (0 °C, −10 °C, −20 °C) on a warm mixed asphalt mixture to investigate aging degree variation and discovered that cracking resistance at low temperatures deteriorated more severely in LTOA than STOA. This accordingly emphasized the need for research on asphalt mixtures under LTOA conditions. Bonaquist et al. [7], Chen et al. [8], Wang et al. [9], and Wu [10] examined the effects of different degrees of aging (LTOA and STOA) on cracking resistance by semi-circular bending (SCB) test (15 °C, 20 °C and 25 °C). They all concluded that the cracking process can be sped up with the increase in aging degree. Islam et al. [11] studied the effect of aging duration on the indirect tensile strength of AC at 20 °C and highlighted that tensile strength increased with the extension of LTOA duration, but first increased and then decreased with the extension of STOA duration. Similarly, Radeef et al. [12] adopted an indirect tension (IDT) test (25 °C) to study the rubberized asphalt mixture under LTOA and STOA conditions. They found that STOA can enhance the cracking resistance and LTOA can degrade it in reverse.

Moreover, some researchers took test temperature into consideration, as well as the degree of aging. Omranian et al. [13] used the SCB test (10 °C, 20 °C and 30 °C) to evaluate the cracking resistance of treated AC-14 exposed to different STOA durations. The results showed that mixtures exposed to longer aging durations were more prone to cracking at lower test temperatures and that the regulation is reversed at high temperatures. Ye [14] evaluated the cracking resistance of AC-13 treated with different degrees of aging (UA, STOA, LTOA) by the application of the SCB test (0 °C, −5 °C, −10 °C, −20 °C). It was found that the mixture was more susceptible to cracking when treated by deeper degrees of aging at the discussed test temperature region. Wang et al. [15] compared the significance of LTOA and test temperature on the cracking resistance of AC-13 under unaging and LTOA conditions using the SCB test (−20 °C. −10 °C. 0 °C. 25 °C). It was concluded that cracking resistance was more remarkably affected by test temperature than LTOA. Hamedi et al. [16] studied the impact of short-term aging on the cracking resistance of asphalt mixture using the SCB test (−10 °C to −22 °C). It was demonstrated that the short-term aging asphalt mixture exhibited a superior cracking resistance to that of the mixture under unaging conditions at a lower test temperature, which was captured by the elevation in the surface free energy of the asphalt binder caused by aging.

As described in the above literature, a majority of the current experimental research on cracking resistance that considers different degrees of aging is limited to low or medium temperatures. However, cracking can also occur at high temperatures [17]. Therefore, it is necessary to test cracking resistance at high temperatures. Even so, it is worth noting the cracking resistance of asphalt mixture considering a high temperature (30 °C) was only reported in one study [13]. As the highest temperatures can reach about 40 °C in most parts of southern China, it seems that the highest test temperature should be set at 40 °C instead.

Furthermore, as asphalt mixture is a kind of multi-phase composite material, its overall mechanical properties are bound to be associated with its internal structure, such as its gradation. On this basis, a few studies have been launched to probe the effect of gradation on the cracking resistance of asphalt mixture. Li et al. [18] employed the SCB test at different test temperatures below 0 °C on both continuous gradation and gap gradation asphalt mixtures (AC-16, SMA-16, AC-20). Additionally, test results were more influenced by gradation than test temperature. Yin et al. [19] conducted an indirect tension low-temperature creep test (0 °C, 10 °C, and −20 °C) on AC-20 with different gradations (coarse, medium, and fine). It was revealed that medium gradation showed the best cracking resistance at 0 °C, medium gradation at −10 °C, and coarse gradation at −20 °C.

There are five main types of indoor evaluation method for the cracking resistance of asphalt mixture: semi-circular bending test, indirect tension test, trabecular bending test, disk shaped compact tension test [20,21] and direct tension test. Among them, the direct tension test is simpler regarding the specimen preparation as well as loading mode, more direct regarding the stress–strain data acquisition and better regarding the reflection of actual stress state of the asphalt mixture. Therefore, it is more suitable to be employed than the other four test methods [22–24]. As mentioned in the literature review, however, only the direct tension test was reported [3].

In terms of evaluation indexes, tensile strength, peak deformation, and modulus are most widely used. Nevertheless, Wang et al. [25] believed that conflicting conclusions could be drawn based on the three indexes mentioned above, and a single tensile strength index and failure strain sometimes cannot fully reflect the cracking resistance of the asphalt mixture. Based on this situation, Yang et al. [26] evaluated the cracking resistance by calculating the strain energy density. The result showed that the cracking resistance decay rate of the asphalt mixture prepared by the oven heating method was equivalent to that prepared by the delayed mixing method. Furthermore, Zheng [27] revealed that it is difficult to judge the cracking resistance of asphalt mixture using only the fracture energy index and established a more comprehensive evaluation index by determining the weight of each index through the analytic hierarchy process (AHP). However, the weight definition is susceptible to the decision-makers' preference for the AHP method, leading to less convincing evaluation results. In contrast, the entropy weight TOPSIS method, a combination of the entropy weight method and TOPSIS method, cannot only avoid the influence of human subjectivity on the evaluation results but also has the advantages of less information loss and flexible computation, meaning that it is widely used in economic, management and other scientific fields, but is less applied in the pavement engineering material field [28–30].

Therefore, in this paper, SMA-13 and AC-13 were selected as they are commonly used in road engineering. Additionally, monotonic tensile tests were conducted on these two asphalt mixtures with different thermo-oxidative aging degrees at different test temperatures. The change rule of commonly used indexes (tensile strength, ultimate strain, and pre-peak and post-peak strain energy density) was obtained with different aging degrees, test temperatures, and mixture gradations. Finally, the comprehensive cracking resistance index (CRI) was established by the entropy weight TOPSIS method to evaluate the cracking resistance of asphalt mixture with different thermo-oxidative aging degrees.

2. Materials and Test Protocol

2.1. Materials

The styrene-butadiene-styrene (SBS)-modified asphalt was used and purchased from Shell (Xingyue) Co., Ltd., located in Foshan City, Guangdong Province, China. Its fundamental performance parameters were tested. The results are shown in Table 1. The diabase, limestone, and limestone powder were selected for the coarse aggregate, fine aggregate, and filler, respectively, sourced from a test section of the highway in Foshan City, Guangdong Province, China. Their fundamental performance parameters were tested. The results are summarized in Table 2. Furthermore, the aggregate gradation of AC-13 and SMA-13 is presented in Table 3.

Table 1. Basic performance parameters test results of SBS-modified asphalt.

Performance Parameters	Unit	Test Result	Method
Density	g/cm^3	1.051	ASTM D70-17a
Penetration (25 °C, 100 g, 5 s)	0.1 mm	44.1	ASTM D5-13
Ductility (5 °C, 5 cm/min)	cm	25.8	ASTM D113-17b
Softening point	°C	93.6	ASTM D36-14
Flash point	°C	>230	ASTM D92-12b
Mass loss of residue after TFOT (Thin-film oven test)	%	0.4	ASTM D6-11
Penetration ratio of residue after TFOT (25 °C)	%	72.5	ASTM D5-13
Ductility of residue after TFOT (5 °C, 5 cm/min)	cm	21	ASTM D113-17b

Table 2. Basic performance parameters test results of coarse aggregate, fine aggregate and filler.

Performance Parameters	Unit	Coarse Aggregate	Fine Aggregate	Filler	Method
Los Angeles abrasion	%	10.9			ASTM C131-14
Flat and elongated particles	%	1.4			ASTM D4791-19
Fine aggregate angularity	%		38		AASHTO T304-17
Specific gravity	g/cm³	2.762			ASTM C127-15
Specific gravity	g/cm³		2.73		ASTM C128-15
Specific gravity	g/cm³			2.704	ASTM D854-14

Table 3. Mineral aggregate gradation.

Sieve Size/mm	Passing Percentage/%	
	AC-13	SMA-13
16	100	100
13.2	95	90
9.5	76.5	50
4.75	53	20
2.36	37	15
1.18	26.5	14
0.6	19	12
0.3	13.5	10
0.15	10	9
0.075	6	8

2.2. Specimen Preparation

Compared with existing compaction methods, the wheel-rolling method was selected for the compact asphalt mixture plate specimen (300 mm × 300 mm × 50 mm) by virtue its better field simulation [31]. Then, each plate specimen was cut into a beam specimen (250 mm × 50 mm × 50 mm) by a rock-cutting machine.

The Strategic Highway Research Program (SHRP) proposed oven-heating, delayed mixing, and microwave-heating methods to simulate the thermos-oxidative aging of asphalt mixture. Among them, the oven-heating method is the most effective and common one. Therefore, this method was used in this study.

(1) STOA: put the mixed loose asphalt mixture in the oven with a temperature controlled at 135 °C for 4 h and stir hourly; then, mold the specimen according to the chapter mentioned above.

(2) LTOA: based on STOA, the beam specimen should be placed in the oven with temperature controlled at 85 °C for the intended number of days (2, 5 and 8 days).

2.3. Monotonic Direct Tension Test

The monotonic direct tension test was conducted by the material test systems (MTS) 810 machine imported from MTS Company located in Eden Prairie, MN, USA. For each specimen, each of the two ends was bonded with a round steel loading plate by steel glue. Then, after at least 3 days, specimens were moved into a temperature-controlled cabinet at the corresponding target test temperature for 4 h. Subsequently, specimens were shifted out and clamped onto the loading platform to be tested at a loading rate of 5 mm/min [32]. Pretension was performed at the beginning of each test to prevent eccentric phenomena from occurring during the test process. All the test results were acquired through the built-in computer system at a sampling frequency of 10 Hz. The relative indexes were calculated according to the following equations.

$$\sigma_{max} = \frac{F_{max}}{bd} \quad (1)$$

$$\varepsilon_{max} = \frac{\varepsilon_{1max} + \varepsilon_{2max}}{2} \tag{2}$$

$$\omega_{pre} = \int_0^{\varepsilon_{max}} \sigma d\varepsilon \tag{3}$$

$$\omega_{post} = \int_{\varepsilon_{max}}^{\varepsilon_{\sigma=\frac{1}{2}\sigma_{max}}} \sigma d\varepsilon \tag{4}$$

where σ_{max} denotes the tensile strength (MPa); F_{max} denotes peak loading value (N); b and d denote the width and the height of the specimen, respectively (mm); ε_{max} denotes the ultimate strain (10^{-6}) ε_{1max}, ε_{2max} denote the strain value of extensometers corresponding to the loading value, respectively (10^{-6}); ω_{pre} denotes the pre-peak strain energy density (MJ/m^3); ω_{post} denotes the post-peak strain energy density (MJ/m^3); $\varepsilon_{\sigma=\frac{1}{2}\sigma_{max}}$ denotes the strain at which the corresponding stress drops to half of the tensile strength (10^{-6}); σ denotes stress in the tension process (MPa); ε denotes strain in the tension process (10^{-6}).

2.4. Entropy Weight-TOPSIS Method

The idea of the entropy weight TOPSIS method is to use the entropy weight method to determine the weight of each index and then use the TOPSIS method to calculate the value of the comprehensive indexes. The specific steps are described below.

2.4.1. Establish the Initial Evaluation Matrix

There were 40 evaluation objects and 3 evaluation indexes in this study. The initial evaluation matrix $A = (a_{ij})_{m \times n}$ (m = 40; n = 3) is depicted in the following equation:

$$A = \begin{bmatrix} a_{11} & a_{12} & \cdots & a_{1n} \\ a_{21} & a_{22} & \cdots & a_{2n} \\ \vdots & \vdots & \vdots & \vdots \\ a_{m1} & a_{m2} & \cdots & a_{mn} \end{bmatrix} \tag{5}$$

where a_{ij} denotes the jth evaluation index value of the ith evaluation object.

2.4.2. Standardize the Initial Evaluation Matrix

In view of the different dimensions among the three kinds of indexes, the standardized evaluation matrix $B = (b_{ij})_{m \times n}$ is expressed as follows:

$$b_{ij} = \frac{a_{ij} - \min_j}{\max_j - \min_j} \tag{6}$$

where b_{ij} denotes the jth evaluation index value of the ith evaluation object after standardization; $\min_j$ denotes the minimum value of the jth evaluation index; $\max_j$ denotes the maximum value of the jth evaluation index.

2.4.3. Calculate Entropy Weight of Each Index

The entropy and entropy weight of each index can be calculated according to the following equations:

$$e_j = -\frac{1}{\ln m} \sum_{i=1}^{m} \frac{b_{ij}}{\sum_{i=1}^{m} b_{ij}} \ln \frac{b_{ij}}{\sum_{i=1}^{m} b_{ij}} \tag{7}$$

$$w_j = \frac{1 - e_j}{\sum_{j=1}^{n} e_j} \tag{8}$$

where e_j denotes the entropy of each evaluation index and w_j denotes the entropy weight of each evaluation index.

2.4.4. Establish Weighted Standardization Evaluation Matrix

The weighted standardization evaluation matrix $C = (c_{ij})_{m \times n}$ is established according to the following equation:

$$c_{ij} = b_{ij} \times w_j \tag{9}$$

where c_{ij} denotes the jth evaluation index value of the ith evaluation object after being weighted.

2.4.5. Determine the Ideal Solution and Calculate the Euclidean Distance

The positive and negative ideal solution can be defined as follows:

$$c^+ = [\max(c_{ij})] = [c_1^+ \quad c_2^+ \quad \ldots \quad c_n^+] \tag{10}$$

$$c^- = [\min(c_{ij})] = [c_1^- \quad c_2^- \quad \ldots \quad c_n^-] \tag{11}$$

The Euclidean distance between the evaluation object and the positive and negative ideal solution can be measured as follows.

$$S_i^+ = \sqrt{\sum_{j=1}^n \left(c_{ij} - c_j^+\right)^2} \tag{12}$$

$$S_i^- = \sqrt{\sum_{j=1}^n \left(c_{ij} - c_j^-\right)^2} \tag{13}$$

where c^+ and c^- denote the positive and negative ideal solution, respectively; S_i^+ and S_i^- denote the Euclidean distance between the evaluation object and the positive and negative ideal solution for each evaluation object.

2.4.6. Calculate the Closeness of Each Evaluation Object to the Ideal Solution

The closeness of each of each evaluation object to the ideal solution can finally be defined as follows and can be regarded as the CRI value of each evaluation object.

$$CRI = E_i = \frac{S_i^-}{S_i^+ + S_i^-} \tag{14}$$

where E_i denotes the closeness of each evaluation object to the ideal solution.

3. Results and Discussion

3.1. Stress–Strain Plot

Figures 1–4 show the stress–strain curves in the direct tension test process for AC-13 and SMA-13 with different aging degrees at 10 °C, 20 °C, 30 °C, 40 °C, respectively.

As shown in Figures 1–4, the overall shape of these plots can all be divided into three similar stages and the plot of AC13-UA in Figure 3 is taken as an example for the illustration. (1) Elastic stage: the plot in the initial loading phase is approximately a straight line, and the stress linearly increases with the increase in strain. (2) Strain-hardening stage: with the elevation of strain, the plot begins to deviate from the straight line in the former stage and to stretch as an approximate arc. With the elevation of strain, stress continues to nonlinearly climb to a peak value with a speed slower than that in the former stage. (3) Strain-softening stage: with the continuous elevation of strain, stress shows a remarkable downward trend as soon as stress reaches over the peak value.

For both AC-13 and SMA-13, the stress–strain plots exhibit similar a change with the increase in degree of aging at the same test temperature. The plots of AC13-UA, AC13-STOA, AC13-LTOA2d, AC13-LTOA5d and AC13-LTOA8d in Figure 1 are as shown in Figure: With the increase in aging degree, each plot shifts upward and is left as a whole. Particularly, the slope of the straight line in the elastic stage becomes steeper, which means that the elevation of the degree of aging can increase the rigidity of the asphalt mixture.

The arc length and the radius of curvature of the hardening stage curve decrease. At the same time, the downward trend of the strain-softening stage becomes sharper.

For both AC-13 and SMA-13, the stress–strain plots present a few changes with the elevation of test temperature under the same degree of aging. The plots of SMA13-UA in Figures 1–4 are used as an example. Each entity generally tends to shift downward and to the right. Specifically, the slope of the elastic stage decreases, which indicates that the rigidity of the asphalt mixture can be weakened with the increase in test temperature. The deviation of the strain-hardening stage curve from the former straight line tends to be more pronounced. Furthermore, the downward trend of the strain-softening stage curve becomes gentler.

There are also differences between stress–strain curves of AC-13 and SMA-13 when the same aging degree and test temperature are considered. The plots of AC13-LTOA2d and SMA13-LTOA2d in Figure 4 are taken as an example. The coverage height of the plot of SMA-13 is lower than that of AC-13. However, the coverage width of the plot of SMA-13 is remarkably greater than that of AC-13, which causes the whole plot of SMA-13 to be plumper.

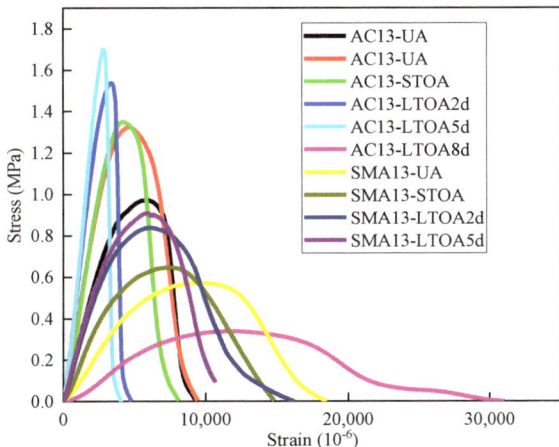

Figure 1. Stress–strain plots of AC-13 and SMA-13 under different aging degrees, plotted at 10 °C.

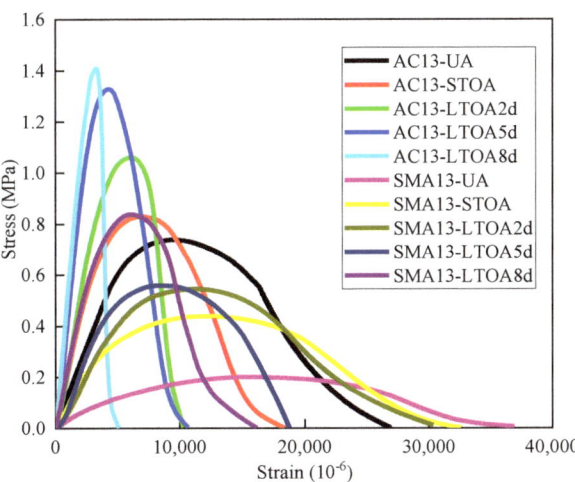

Figure 2. Stress–strain plots of AC-13 and SMA-13 under different aging degrees, plotted at 20 °C.

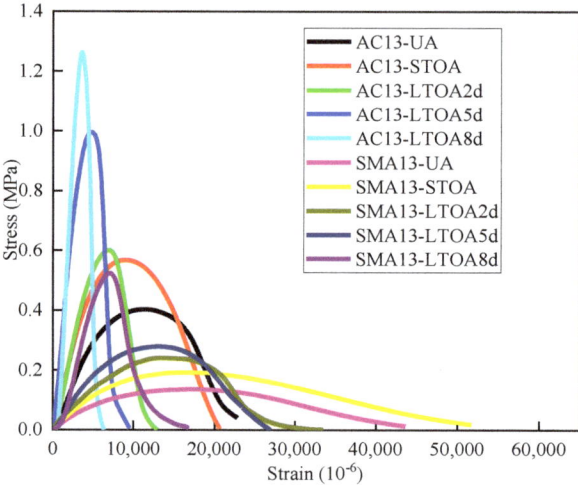

Figure 3. Stress–strain plots of AC-13 and SMA-13 under different aging degrees, plotted at 30 °C.

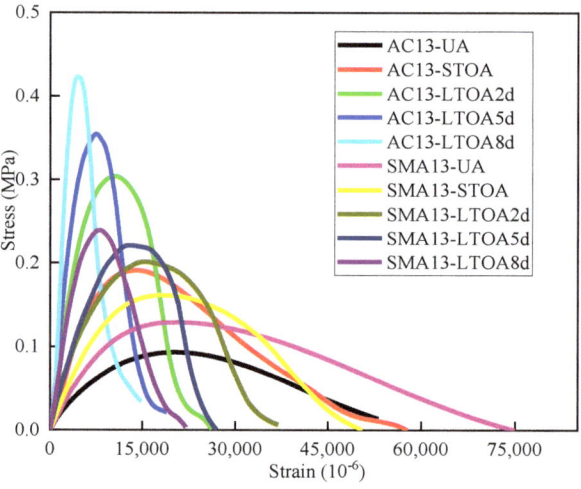

Figure 4. Stress–strain plots of AC-13 and SMA-13 under different aging degrees, plotted at 40 °C.

3.2. Tensile Strength

Table 4 and Figures 5 and 6 present the tensile strength results versus test temperature for AC-13 and SMA-13 under different degrees of aging. As shown in Figures 5 and 6, the tensile strength of both SMA-13 and AC-13 gradually increases with the increase in aging degree when test temperature remains the same. This phenomenon can be explained as follows: under a thermo-oxidative aging environment, light components can be transformed into asphaltene by the chemical reaction between the hydrocarbon (derivatives) in asphalt and oxygen, which undoubtedly increases the number of polar molecules in bitumen. A high temperature can also enhance the polarity of aggregate molecules [33]. It is worth mentioning that the adhesion between asphalt and aggregate is generated by the linkage of polar molecules. Therefore, it follows that the adhesion between bitumen and aggregate can be strengthened and the load-bearing capacity of the asphalt mixture can be enhanced after thermo oxidative aging.

Table 4. Tensile strength at different test temperatures of AC-13 and SMA-13 under different aging degrees.

Gradation	Test Temperature (°C)	Specimen Number	UA			STOA			LTOA2d			LTOA5d			LTOA8d		
			Sample Value (MPa)	Average Value (MPa)	Standard Deviation	Sample Value (MPa)	Average Value (MPa)	Standard Deviation	Sample Value (MPa)	Average Value (MPa)	Standard Deviation	Sample Value (MPa)	Average Value (MPa)	Standard Deviation	Sample Value (MPa)	Average Value (MPa)	Standard Deviation
AC-13	10	1	0.84	0.90	0.040	1.10	1.10	0.013	1.21	1.20	0.004	1.35	1.31	0.031	1.42	1.40	0.051
		2	0.90			1.10			1.21			1.29			1.40		
		3	0.93			1.09			1.20			1.30			1.49		
		4	0.93			1.12			1.20			1.28			1.37		
	20	1	0.71	0.69	0.018	0.72	0.73	0.025	0.92	0.92	0.006	1.15	1.12	0.034	1.16	1.16	0.013
		2	0.70			0.74			0.91			1.11			1.18		
		3	0.66			0.70			0.91			1.14			1.15		
		4	0.68			0.76			0.92			1.07			1.15		
	30	1	0.62	0.58	0.027	0.60	0.60	0.030	0.69	0.69	0.015	0.76	0.77	0.021	0.81	0.80	0.017
		2	0.57			0.56			0.68			0.78			0.81		
		3	0.57			0.62			0.71			0.79			0.78		
		4	0.57			0.63			0.67			0.74			0.81		
	40	1	0.11	0.13	0.027	0.29	0.27	0.028	0.33	0.34	0.015	0.35	0.35	0.002	0.40	0.43	0.041
		2	0.12			0.30			0.36			0.35			0.44		
		3	0.13			0.25			0.32			0.35			0.39		
		4	0.17			0.24			0.34			0.36			0.48		
SMA-13	10	1	0.53	0.55	0.035	0.68	0.69	0.020	0.83	0.78	0.038	0.96	0.90	0.055	1.20	1.22	0.062
		2	0.54			0.68			0.77			0.84			1.26		
		3	0.53			0.66			0.76			0.87			1.28		
		4	0.60			0.71			0.74			0.93			1.14		
	20	1	0.34	0.35	0.014	0.48	0.50	0.019	0.54	0.55	0.009	0.72	0.71	0.022	0.89	0.88	0.057
		2	0.34			0.51			0.56			0.72			0.94		
		3	0.35			0.49			0.54			0.71			0.86		
		4	0.37			0.53			0.54			0.68			0.81		
	30	1	0.15	0.16	0.005	0.35	0.35	0.026	0.52	0.49	0.021	0.53	0.55	0.021	0.61	0.60	0.012
		2	0.16			0.36			0.47			0.54			0.58		
		3	0.16			0.38			0.48			0.58			0.60		
		4	0.15			0.32			0.50			0.56			0.61		
	40	1	0.12	0.10	0.015	0.19	0.23	0.040	0.26	0.25	0.009	0.29	0.31	0.036	0.37	0.40	0.019
		2	0.10			0.22			0.25			0.26			0.40		
		3	0.10			0.22			0.24			0.34			0.39		
		4	0.08			0.29			0.25			0.34			0.42		

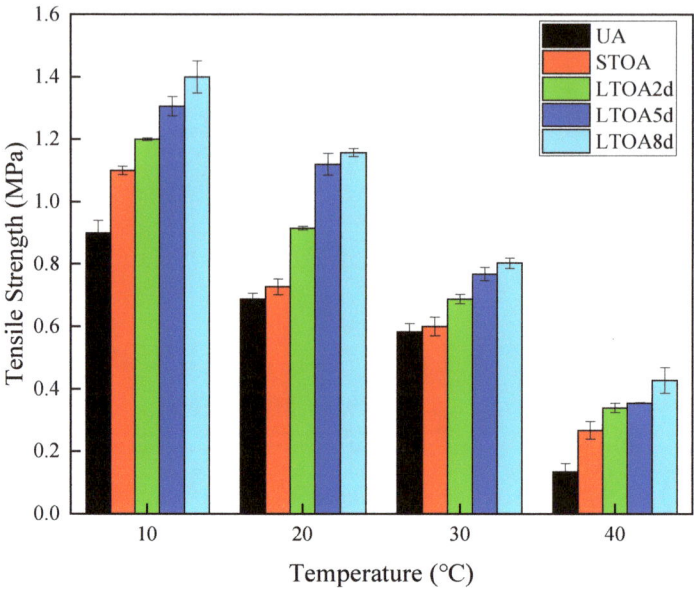

Figure 5. Tensile strength versus test temperature for AC-13 under different degrees of aging.

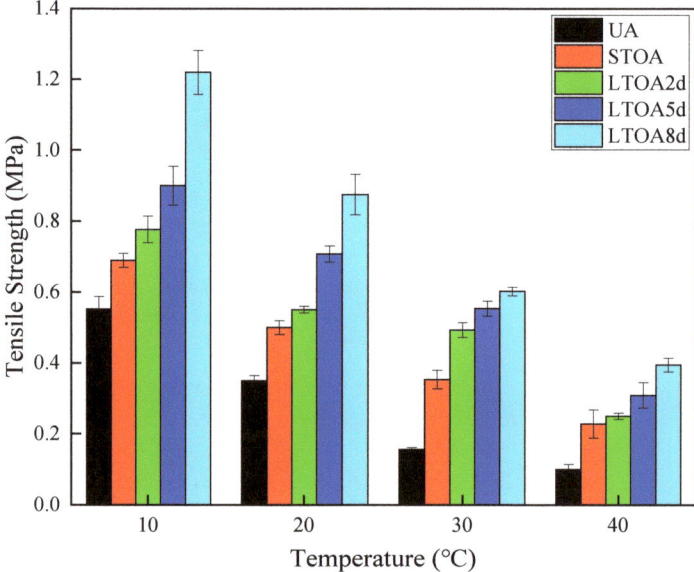

Figure 6. Tensile strength versus test temperature for SMA-13 under different degrees of aging.

For AC-13, the increase trend of the tensile strength becomes weaker with the overall elevation of aging degree. At 10 °C and 30 °C, STOA presents the most obvious increasing effect on tensile strength, with a growth gradient of 22% (10 °C) and 99% (40 °C). With the increase in aging degree, the growth gradient drops to 10% (10 °C) and 55% (40 °C). Comparatively, there are fluctuations in AC-13 at 20 °C and 30 °C, which means that the LTOA2d condition presents the most obvious increasing effect on tensile strength by a growth gradient of 29% (20 °C) and 15% (30 °C). Similarly, the growth gradient drops to 6% for the LTOA8d condition. At 10 °C and 20 °C, the elevation effect of aging degree on tensile strength of SMA-13 fluctuates, but it is worth noting that the LTOA8d condition exhibits the most remarkable elevation effect by a growth gradient of 20% (10 °C) and 13% (20 °C). At 30 °C and 40 °C, while the STOA condition presents the most obvious increasing effect on the tensile strength of SMA-13 by a growth gradient of 20% (30 °C) and 13% (40 °C). The growth gradient declines with the increase in aging degree at 30 °C; however, it fluctuates at 40 °C.

With the elevation in test temperature, the tensile strength at each degree of aging shows a decreasing trend for both AC-13 and SMA-13. The cause of the phenomenon may be illustrated as follows: the increase in test temperature can intensify the periodic thermal movement of macromolecules inside the asphalt mixture, thus enlarging the distance between the macromolecules, weakening the mutual attraction between the macromolecules, and eventually reducing the load required to destroy the structure of the asphalt mixture [34]. For AC-13 under LTOA2d, LTOA5d and LTOA8d conditions, tensile strength decreases approximately linearly, with an average decline rate of 24% with every increase of 10 °C. Comparatively, for AC-13 under STOA conditions, tensile strength decreases unsteadily by 12% (from 10 °C to 20 °C), 30% (from 20 °C to 30 °C) and 21% (from 30 °C to 40 °C). When it comes to AC-13 under UA conditions, tensile strength decreases by an average decline rate of 18% with every increase of 10 °C when temperature is in the range of from 10 °C to 30 °C; however, a sharp drop in tensile strength by 50% appears when temperature goes up from 30 °C to 40 °C. Similarly, for SMA-13 under UA, STOA, LTOA5d and LTOA8d conditions, tensile strength steadily decreases with an average decline rate of 36% (UA and STOA), 22% (LTOA5d and LTOA8d) with every increase of 10 °C. When it comes to SMA-13 under LTOA2d conditions, volatility occurs in the tensile strength descent trend by 29% (from 10 °C to 20 °C), 7% (from 20 °C to 30 °C) and 31% (from 30 °C to 40 °C).

Additionally, it is easy to see that the tensile strength of AC-13 is higher than that of SMA-13 when the aging degree and test temperature remain the same and the value of the gap can be up to 2.8 times as high (UA, 30 °C). This may be attributed to the following causes: the higher admixture of AC-13 aggregate renders a thicker asphalt mortar film, which has a correspondingly stronger ability to grip the aggregate than SMA-13. In addition, the higher distribution uniformity of air voids in AC-13 means that it performs better regarding the overall structural uniformity of the mixture, thus endowing AC-13 with a higher tensile strength at the macroscopic level [35,36]. Furthermore, the gap between the tensile strength of AC-13 and SMA-13 is narrowed by the elevation of aging degree and test temperature.

3.3. Ultimate Strain

Table 5 and Figures 7 and 8 display the ultimate strain results versus test temperature for AC-13 and SMA-13 under different degrees of aging. As shown in Figures 7 and 8, the ultimate strain of both SMA-13 and AC-13 gradually descends with the increase in aging degree at the same test temperature. The reason for this phenomenon may be that during thermos-oxidative aging, long-term exposure to a high temperature increases the kinetic energy of light molecules in asphalt and further widens the diffusion rate gap between light and heavy molecules, thus weakening the intermolecular attraction and reducing the stability of asphalt mortar or even the overall structure of the asphalt mixture [37].

Table 5. Ultimate strain at different test temperatures of AC-13 and SMA-13 under different degrees of aging.

Gradation	Temperature (°C)	Specimen Number	UA Sample Value (10^{-6})	UA Average Value (10^{-6})	UA Standard Deviation	STOA Sample Value (10^{-6})	STOA Average Value (10^{-6})	STOA Standard Deviation	LTOA2d Sample Value (10^{-6})	LTOA2d Average Value (10^{-6})	LTOA2d Standard Deviation	LTOA5d Sample Value (10^{-6})	LTOA5d Average Value (10^{-6})	LTOA5d Standard Deviation	LTOA8d Sample Value (10^{-6})	LTOA8d Average Value (10^{-6})	LTOA8d Standard Deviation
AC-13	10	1	6587	6740	151.43	5335	5400	165.07	3172	3600	407.14	1534	1604	85.92	1503	1400	96.82
		2	6651			5337			4148			1688			1304		
		3	6797			5645			3485			1668			1332		
		4	6925			5284			3995			1526			1461		
	20	1	9310	9620	414.83	7895	7837	212.89	5585	5460	248.89	3148	3070	109.06	1719	2003	272.33
		2	9328			7714			5554			3126			1859		
		3	9644			8110			5088			3097			2095		
		4	10,198			7629			5613			2909			2339		
	30	1	10,037	10,505	657.86	9101	8974	155.44	5844	5814	46.14	3341	3560	288.88	3280	3098	219.75
		2	10,195			8778			5859			3331			2888		
		3	10,310			9097			5794			3941			3295		
		4	11,477			8920			5759			3627			2928		
	40	1	15,108	15,875	1172.51	9480	9578	85.35	8710	8885	204.57	6845	6484	352.42	3853	3951	123.69
		2	16,978			9533			8731			6104			3904		
		3	16,770			9654			9142			6273			3915		
		4	14,643			9645			8957			6714			4132		
SMA-13	10	1	11,807	12,000	342.71	11,723	11,515	173.98	7997	7840	146.21	6226	6210	102.64	5259	5009	201.56
		2	12,431			11,330			7917			6263			4943		
		3	11,656			11,583			7668			6061			5056		
		4	12,106			11,423			7778			6289			4779		
	20	1	17,722	17,075	455.24	16,081	15,730	471.07	13,181	12,135	861.21	10,439	9130	951.75	6711	6401	329.60
		2	17,025			15,035			11,831			9214			6548		
		3	16,882			15,913			11,146			8318			5945		
		4	16,671			15,891			12,382			8549			6400		
	30	1	17,905	17,943	159.40	17,012	17,007	175.60	13,624	13,476	689.62	11,896	12,324	360.91	6494	6800	338.53
		2	18,114			17,152			14,354			12,677			7006		
		3	18,011			17,106			13,195			12,562			6532		
		4	17,741			16,759			12,731			12,162			7168		
	40	1	18,299	18,703	405.98	17,881	17,543	245.39	14,445	14,610	422.88	12,757	12,961	312.65	7536	7377	303.22
		2	18,684			17,297			14,116			12,633			7466		
		3	18,567			17,469			14,785			13,264			6927		
		4	19,262			17,525			15,094			13,190			7578		

92

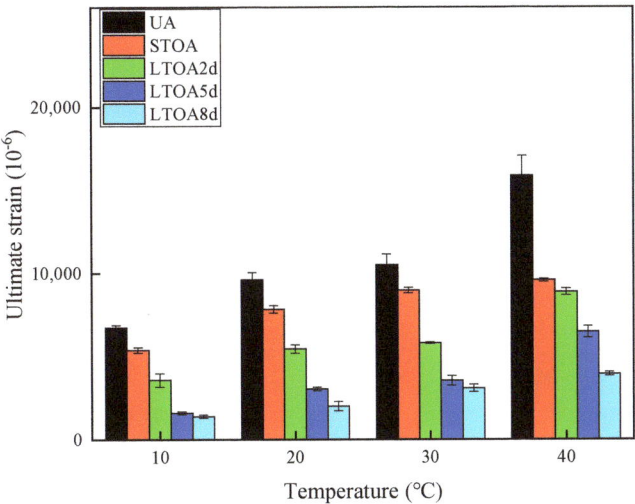

Figure 7. Ultimate strain versus test temperature for AC-13 under different degrees of aging.

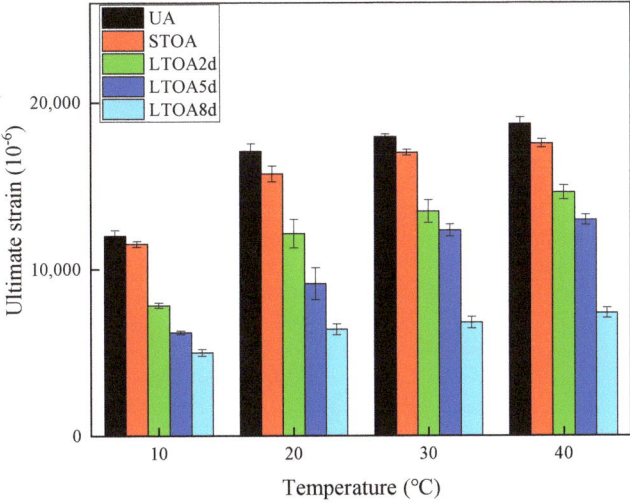

Figure 8. Ultimate strain versus test temperature for SMA-13 under different degrees of aging.

For AC-13, the ultimate strain of the mixture undergoing STOA, LTOA2d, LTOA5d, and LTOA8d is 19–40%, 43–46%, 59–76%, and 75–80% lower than that of the unaging mixture, respectively. For SMA-13, the ultimate strain of the mixture undergoing STOA, LTOA2d, LTOA5d, and LTOA8d decreases by 4–12%, 21–35%, 31–48%, and 58–64%, respectively, compared with that of the unaging mixture. Additionally, the attenuation effect of aging on the ultimate strain of AC-13 is significantly greater than that of SMA-13. For AC-13 at 10 °C, 20 °C and 40 °C, the ultimate strain decreases linearly when aging degree is confined to LTOA2d conditions by a decrease gradient of 23% (10 °C), 31% (20 °C) and 22% (30 °C). When the degree of aging continuously deepens, the ultimate decrease recedes. It is worth noting that the decrease gradient drops to only 3% (10 °C), 4% (20 °C) and 16% (30 °C) when the degree of aging reaches LTOA8d. When the test temperature is 40 °C, AC-13 treated by STOA conditions shows a dramatic drop in ultimate strain, by 40%. Then, the ultimate strain exhibits an approximate linear descent trend with a decrease gradient of

16%. For SMA-13 at 10 °C and 20 °C, the ultimate strain decreases slightly, by 3% (10 °C) and 8% (20 °C), under STOA conditions, and when aging degree reaches LTOA2d, there is a sharper descent with a decrease gradient of 23% (10 °C) and 21% (20 °C). However, when the degree of aging further decreases, the descent of the ultimate strain slows down and becomes steadier, with a decrease gradient of 9% (10 °C) and 17% (20 °C). For SMA-13 at 30 °C and 40 °C, the descent of the ultimate strain exhibits slight fluctuations, with an average decrease gradient of 5% (STOA), 18% (LTOA2d), 8% (LTOA5d) and 30% (LTOA8d).

With the elevation of test temperature, the ultimate strain under each aging degree shows an increasing trend for both AC-13 and SMA-13. The cause of this phenomenon may be explained as follows: the Brownian motion in asphalt molecules becomes more active, and free volume between molecules increases under the impact of rising temperature, which reduces the viscous flow of asphalt mortar and the eventual enhancement in ultimate strain [38]. For AC-13 under STOA and LTOA8d conditions, the ultimate strain grows nearly proportionally by an average increase rate of 26% (STOA) and 61% (LTOA8d) with every increase of 10 °C. Comparatively, for AC-13, under the other aging conditions, ultimate strain increases unsteadily. However, when test temperature climbs from 30 °C to 40 °C, the sharpest variation in ultimate strain can be seen, with an average increase rate of 80% (UA), 85% (LTOA2d) and 182% (LTOA5d). For SMA-13, the increasing tendency of the ultimate strain is weakened with the elevation of test temperature. For SMA-13 under LTOA5d conditions, ultimate strain steadily increases, with an average increase rate of 50% with every rise of 10 °C, when the discussed test temperature is in the range of from 10 °C to 30 °C. When test temperature increases from 30 °C to 40 °C, the average increase rate drops to only 10%. At the same time, for SMA-13 under the other four aging conditions, ultimate strain lifts by 42% (UA), and only 37% (STOA), 55% (LTOA2d) and 28% (LTOA8d), with the elevation of test temperature from 10 °C to 20 °C. With further elevations in test temperature, the ultimate increasing tendency becomes flat, with an average increase rate of 7% (UA), 8% (STOA), 16% (LTOA2d), 10% (LTOA8d).

Moreover, it is apparent that the ultimate strain of SMA-13 is higher than that of AC-13. This can be explained by the following causes: one is that the contact action between coarse aggregates is more prominent in SMA-13 than AC-13. Furthermore, the lignin fiber in SMA-13 can fully contact and fuse with asphalt to form a wet surface under its large surface area and excellent bitumen-absorbing property, which strengthens the viscosity of the bitumen film wrapped around the aggregate [39,40]. The combined action of the above two aspects can better restrain the sliding between aggregates and then improve the overall deformation of the mixture to a certain extent. In addition, the gap between the ultimate strain of AC-13 and SMA-13 is narrowed with the elevation of test temperature. Furthermore, whatever the test temperature, the largest gap between the ultimate strain of AC-13 and SMA-13 exists under LTOA5d conditions by 3 times (10 °C), 2 times (20 °C), 2.5 times (30 °C) and 1.1 times (40 °C).

3.4. Pre-Peak Strain Energy Density

Table 6 and Figures 9 and 10 show the pre-peak strain energy density results versus test temperature for AC-13 and SMA-13 under different degrees of aging. As shown in Figures 9 and 10, at the same test temperature, the strain energy density of AC-13 and SMA-13 both increase after short-term aging and gradually decay as the aging degree deepens into long-term aging. The reason for this phenomenon may be as follows: after thermo-oxidative aging, the content of the carbonyl group, carbonyl group, sulfoxide group, and aromatic group increases to some degree. During short-term aging, the content of the former two groups, which are beneficial for boosting the association between molecules, jumps with a greater degree so that the toughness of the overall structure of the asphalt mixture is enhanced, and more energy is required for cracking [41]. In comparison, the growth of the aromatic group, which has a high rigidity, dominates in the long-term aging process. The results may reduce the toughness of the overall structure of the asphalt mixture and the energy required for cracking under external loads. Specifically, for AC-13, the pre-peak strain energy density under short-term aging ascends by 2% (10 °C), 14% (20 °C), 17% (30 °C) and 35% (40 °C). When the degree of aging extends to LTOA2d, there is a descent in the pre-peak strain energy density by 10% (10 °C and 40 °C), 16% (20 °C) and 19% (30 °C). However, when the degree of aging extends further, the tendency to decrease slows down and becomes steadier, with a decrease rate of 11% (10 °C), 13% (20 °C and 30 °C) and 20% (40 °C). Likewise, for SMA-13, the pre-peak strain energy density under short-term aging ascends by 35% (10 °C), 60% (20 °C) and 39% (30 °C) and 62% (40 °C). When the degree of aging extends to LTOA2d, there is a violent descent in the pre-peak strain energy density, by 11% (10 °C and 20 °C) 21% (30 °C) and 34% (40 °C). With the continuous deepening of the degree of aging, the decrease trend becomes steadier by a decrease rate of only 8.5%.

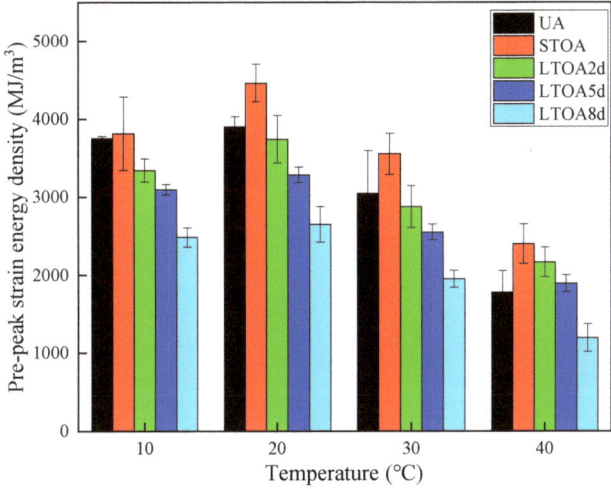

Figure 9. Pre-peak strain energy density versus test temperature for AC-13 under different degrees of aging.

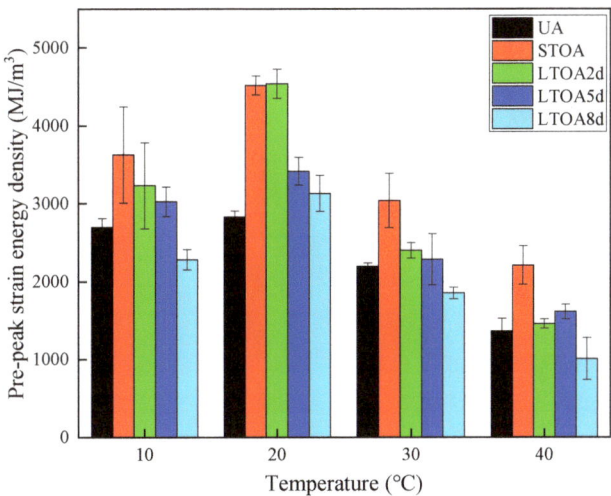

Figure 10. Pre-peak strain energy density versus test temperature for SMA-13 under different degrees of aging.

Table 6. Pre-peak strain energy density at different test temperatures of AC-13 and SMA-13 under different degrees of aging.

Gradation	Test Temperature (°C)	Specimen Number	UA Sample Value (MJ/m³)	UA Average Value (MJ/m³)	UA Standard Deviation	STOA Sample Value (MJ/m³)	STOA Average Value (MJ/m³)	STOA Standard Deviation	LTOA2d Sample Value (MJ/m³)	LTOA2d Average Value (MJ/m³)	LTOA2d Standard Deviation	LTOA5d Sample Value (MJ/m³)	LTOA5d Average Value (MJ/m³)	LTOA5d Standard Deviation	LTOA8d Sample Value (MJ/m³)	LTOA8d Average Value (MJ/m³)	LTOA8d Standard Deviation
AC-13	10	1	3775	3753	28	3675	3816	470	3342	3346	149	3059	3095	66	2640	2484	125
		2	3774			4084			3555			3184			2526		
		3	3748			3222			3276			3034			2364		
		4	3715			4282			3211			3102			2406		
	20	1	3879	3901	131	4410	4463	240	3404	3744	303	3140	3288	99	2463	2649	227
		2	4088			4556			3670			3349			2740		
		3	3855			4160			4137			3330			2928		
		4	3782			4727			3764			3333			2465		
	30	1	3475	3046	552	3791	3555	262	3194	2875	268	2603	2550	100	1841	1953	110
		2	3432			3185			2900			2473			2087		
		3	2286			3578			2539			2665			1890		
		4	2990			3667			2866			2459			1994		
	40	1	2179	1779	279	2671	2400	252	2440	2167	188	1859	1893	110	1065	1194	178
		2	1629			2445			2009			1825			1041		
		3	1754			2422			2110			2056			1423		
		4	1554			2061			2109			1832			1247		
SMA-13	10	1	2566	2697	116	3248	3625	618	2487	3231	552	3277	3026	189	2161	2282	128
		2	2654			3164			3154			3058			2297		
		3	2728			4425			3541			2918			2215		
		4	2839			4061			3742			2830			2455		
	20	1	2739	2830	76	4666	4517	121	4382	4192	203	3364	3414	175	2834	3131	230
		2	2820			4565			3961			3355			3387		
		3	2743			4410			4083			3268			3198		
		4	2900			4427			4342			3669			3105		
	30	1	2204	2196	44	3331	3040	348	2405	2400	100	2223	2287	325	1768	1890	76
		2	2254			2882			2383			1977			1932		
		3	2173			2624			2284			2203			1807		
		4	2153			3323			2528			2745			1893		
	40	1	1247	1363	163	2121	2210	247	1425	1458	61	1500	1611	96	1173	1009	271
		2	1286			2436			1390			1605			1298		
		3	1315			2381			1521			1605			724		
		4	1604			1901			1495			1734			841		

For asphalt mixtures with the same aging duration, the pre-peak strain energy density of AC-13 and SMA-13 slightly increases as the test temperature rises from 10 °C to 20 °C, while it descends as the test temperature continues to rise to 40 °C. The reason for this phenomenon may be that the increase in temperature can increase the amplitude of molecular motion, and thus cause a corresponding increase in the heat energy, which activates the rotation of the segment around the main chain axis and exhibits a crimped and stretched conformation [26]. Thus, more energy is required to fracture the overall macrostructure of the asphalt mixture. Furthermore, asphalt mixture exhibits a leather state in the temperature range of 20–40 °C, in which there is a mutual slide between molecules, and the slip becomes more intense with the increase in temperature [33]. Therefore, the energy required to break the interaction between molecular chains eventually drops. As the test temperature rises from 10 °C to 20 °C, the pre-strain energy density of AC-13 grows slightly by 4% (UA), 17% (STOA), 12% (LTOA2d), 6% (LTOA5d) and 3% (LTOA8d). When the test temperature continues to rise, the pre-strain energy density is nearly proportional, with an average decrease rate of 27% (UA), 23% (STOA), 21% (LTOA2d and LTOA5d) and 27% (LTOA8d) with every increase of 10 °C. Analogously, the pre-strain energy density of AC-13 grows slightly by 4% (UA), 17% (STOA), 12% (LTOA2d), 7% (LTOA5d) and 3% (LTOA8d). Analogously, for SMA-13, the pre-strain energy density slightly increases by 5% (UA), 25% (STOA), 20% (LTOA2d), 13% (LTOA5d) and 37% (LTOA8d) when the test temperature rises from 10 °C to 20 °C. Furthermore, it descends nearly linearly, with an average decrease rate of 26% (UA, STOA and LTOA5d) and 33% (LTOA2d and LTOA8d) with every increase of 10 °C.

Furthermore, when test temperature is 10 °C, 30 °C and 40 °C, the pre-peak strain energy density of AC-13 is higher than that of SMA-13 and the gap reaches about 37% on average. However, the pre-peak strain energy density of AC-13 is lower than that of SMA-13 under both short-term and long-term aging conditions when the test temperature is 20 °C.

3.5. Post-Peak Strain Energy Density

Table 7 and Figures 11 and 12 illustrate post-peak strain energy density results for AC-13 and SMA-13, respectively. Similar to the pre-peak strain energy density, as shown in Figures 11 and 12, at the same test temperature, the post-peak strain energy density of AC-13 and SMA-13 both increases under short-term aging and gradually decrease as the degree of aging moves toward long-term aging. Concretely, for AC-13, the post-peak strain energy density under short-term aging ascends by 53% (1 °C), 42% (20 °C) and 53% (30 °C) and 63% (40 °C). When the degree of aging extends to LTOA2d, there is a violent drop in the post-peak strain energy density by 36% (10 °C, 20 °C and 40 °C) and 31% (20 °C). However, when the degree of aging deepens further, there is a tendency to decrease more flatly, with a decrease rate of 14% (10 °C and 30 °C), 11% (20 °C) and 12% (40 °C). In the same way, for SMA-13, the post-peak strain energy density under short-term aging ascends by 29% (10 °C), 25% (20 °C and 30 °C) and 34% (40 °C). When degree of aging extends to LTOA2d, there is a dramatic drop in the post-peak strain energy density by 20% (10 °C), 31% (20 °C) and 38% (30 °C and 40 °C). With the continuous deepening of the degree of aging, the descent trend becomes steadier, with a decrease rate of 6% 10 °C), 3% (20 °C), 10% (30 °C) and 13% (40 °C).

Table 7. Post-peak strain energy density at different test temperatures of AC-13 and SMA-13 under different degrees of aging.

Gradation	Test Temperature (°C)	Specimen Number	UA Sample Value (MJ/m³)	UA Average Value (MJ/m³)	UA Standard Deviation	STOA Sample Value (MJ/m³)	STOA Average Value (MJ/m³)	STOA Standard Deviation	LTOA2d Sample Value (MJ/m³)	LTOA2d Average Value (MJ/m³)	LTOA2d Standard Deviation	LTOA5d Sample Value (MJ/m³)	LTOA5d Average Value (MJ/m³)	LTOA5d Standard Deviation	LTOA8d Sample Value (MJ/m³)	LTOA8d Average Value (MJ/m³)	LTOA8d Standard Deviation
AC-13	10	1	2022	1953	98	2876	2990	323	2376	1907	422	1373	1349	188	1284	1067	173
		2	1833			2962			1678			1091			914		
		3	2043			2681			2127			1393			943		
		4	1914			3441			1446			1540			1127		
	20	1	2651	2763	155	4044	3912	185	2369	2687	256	2310	2009	337	1647	1753	91
		2	2748			3638			2832			2283			1780		
		3	2986			3969			2494			1651			1723		
		4	2667			3997			2895			1792			1862		
	30	1	2000	1867	119	3095	2854	219	1892	1831	98	1216	1383	153	1021	1000	253
		2	1860			2977			1800			1293			1326		
		3	1712			2626			1707			1486			938		
		4	1896			2717			1924			1536			715		
	40	1	1625	1534	92	2474	2507	202	1656	1567	146	1434	1285	137	914	947	116
		2	1497			2253			1430			1291			943		
		3	1593			2740			1457			1311			1104		
		4	1422			2560			1726			1103			828		
SMA-13	10	1	2591	2336	274	3263	3031	239	2610	2423	152	2137	2154	111	2274	2077	180
		2	2534			2697			2454			2003			2161		
		3	2204			3094			2384			2230			2013		
		4	2015			3069			2244			2246			1859		
	20	1	3580	3500	310	3930	4361	590	3051	3027	574	2917	2905	49	2948	2800	192
		2	3688			4326			2653			2833			2561		
		3	3690			3983			2575			2924			2964		
		4	3041			5206			3829			2944			2727		
	30	1	2710	2699	122	3178	3380	213	2223	2134	430	1973	2005	92	1377	1487	134
		2	2539			3671			1902			1900			1536		
		3	2713			3393			2698			2031			1655		
		4	2834			3278			1714			2116			1380		
	40	1	2486	2506	32	3304	3353	102	1999	2039	199	1653	1695	207	1235	1199	154
		2	2545			3387			2098			1998			1001		
		3	2520			3477			2268			1542			1187		
		4	2473			3243			1791			1567			1372		

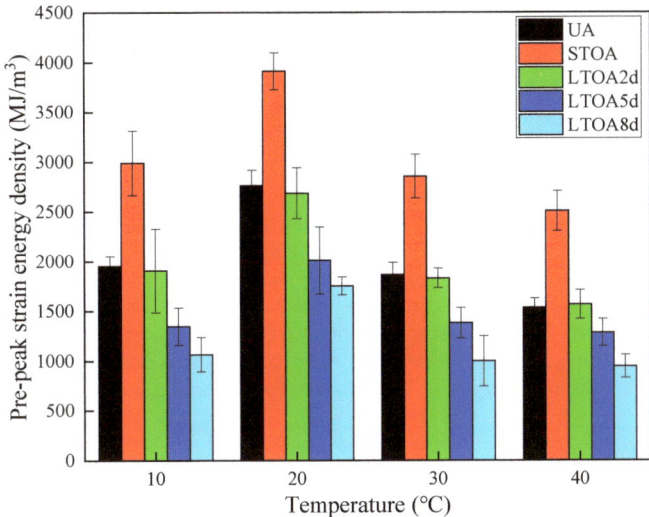

Figure 11. Post-peak strain energy density versus test temperature for AC-13 under different degrees of aging.

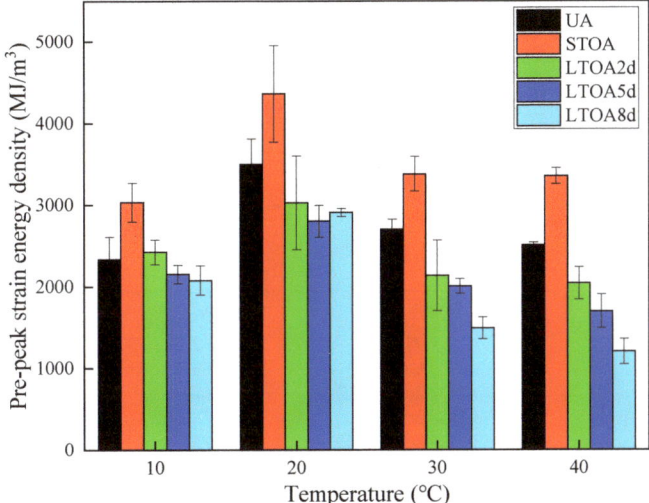

Figure 12. Post-peak strain energy density versus test temperature for SMA-13 under different degrees of aging.

Moreover, when the aging degree remains the same, as the test temperature increases from 10 °C to 20 °C, the post-strain energy density of AC-13 grows slightly, by 41% (UA and LTOA2d), 31% (STOA), 49% (LTOA5d), 64% (LTOA8d). When the test temperature reaches t30 °C, the post-strain energy density drops dramatically, with a decrease rate of 32% (UA, LTOA2d and LTOA5d), 27% (STOA) and 43% (LTOA8d). Comparatively, the descent trend of the post-strain energy density becomes stable, with a decrease rate of 12% (UA and LTOA2d), 17% (STOA) and 22% (LTOA5d LTOA8d). Ulteriorly, the post-strain energy density of SMA-13 grows slightly, by 50% (UA), 44% (STOA), 25% (LTOA2d) and 35% (LTOA8d), as the test temperature climbs from 10 °C to 20 °C. Furthermore, when the test temperature reaches 30 °C, a sudden drop appears in the post-strain energy density of

SMA-13, with a decrease rate of 23% (UA and STOA), 30% (LTOA2d and LTOA5d) and 47% (LTOA8d). Furthermore, when test temperature rises from 30 °C to 40 °C, it also decreases more steadily, with a decrease rate of 6% (UA) 2% (STOA), 4% (LTOA2d), 11% (LTOA5d and LTOA8d).

When the aging degree and test temperature both remain the same, the post-peak strain energy density of SMA-13 is higher than that of AC-13, and the value of the gap can reach up to 95% (LTOA8d, 10 °C). The causes of the phenomenon can be explained as follows: There are more coarse aggregates in SMA-13, which provides it with a better skeleton action between coarse aggregates than AC-13. Additionally, a favorable skeleton action can produce a certain hoop effect on asphalt mortar and hinder asphalt mortar from peeling from aggregates [35]. Furthermore, due to the addition of fiber with a superior tensile performance, the fiber in SMA-13 acts as a reinforcement to the effective transfer of stress when exposed to an external load, thus delaying cracking propagation [42]. Therefore, more energy is needed to destroy the structure of SMA-13.

3.6. Analysis of CRI and Aging Coefficient

Previous analyses have shown that different conclusions may be drawn when different indicators are used to evaluate the cracking resistance of the asphalt mixture. In order to make up for the defects in single-indicator evaluation, the above four indicators are combined to propose a comprehensive indicator. Table 8 shows the weight of each indicator, calculated by the entropy weight method, and Table 9 shows the calculation results of the entropy weight TOPSIS method.

Table 8. Calculation results of entropy weight of four direct tension test indexes.

Index	Entropy	Entropy Weight
Tensile strength	0.942	0.259
Ultimate strain	0.936	0.286
Pre-peak strain energy density	0.958	0.187
Post-peak strain energy density	0.940	0.268

Table 9. Calculation results of CRI for AC-13 and SMA-13.

Item	S_i^+	S_i^-	CRI
SMA13-UA (10 °C)	0.162751	0.108509	0.458683
SMA13-STOA (10 °C)	0.155920	0.116939	0.567867
SMA13-LTOA2d (10 °C)	0.167548	0.102847	0.456206
SMA13-LTOA5d (10 °C)	0.173033	0.100674	0.447181
SMA13-LTOA8d (10 °C)	0.176295	0.100589	0.438167
AC13-UA (10 °C)	0.186440	0.093445	0.447045
AC13-STOA (10 °C)	0.166225	0.129966	0.538652
AC13-LTOA2d (10 °C)	0.175259	0.129923	0.438717
AC13-LTOA5d (10 °C)	0.192069	0.144165	0.412537
AC13-LTOA8d (10 °C)	0.209025	0.154525	0.402688
SMA13-UA (20 °C)	0.136039	0.160869	0.587750
SMA13-STOA (20 °C)	0.128158	0.177350	0.686738
SMA13-LTOA2d (20 °C)	0.130483	0.162080	0.575787
SMA13-LTOA5d (20 °C)	0.153985	0.126742	0.502843
SMA13-LTOA8d (20 °C)	0.172785	0.108632	0.487106
AC13-UA (20 °C)	0.159100	0.110554	0.521773
AC13-STOA (20 °C)	0.152127	0.148879	0.602039
AC13-LTOA2d (20 °C)	0.155233	0.136729	0.500042
AC13-LTOA5d (20 °C)	0.178280	0.127625	0.440272
AC13-LTOA8d (20 °C)	0.189027	0.131564	0.393792
SMA13-UA (30 °C)	0.161795	0.162015	0.491779

Table 9. *Cont.*

Item	S_i^+	S_i^-	CRI
SMA13-STOA (30 °C)	0.141363	0.168257	0.567763
SMA13-LTOA2d (30 °C)	0.162611	0.115018	0.444624
SMA13-LTOA5d (30 °C)	0.177390	0.100384	0.410339
SMA13-LTOA8d (30 °C)	0.213595	0.053093	0.272547
AC13-UA (30 °C)	0.175088	0.097908	0.414888
AC13-STOA (30 °C)	0.146474	0.127872	0.474235
AC13-LTOA2d (30 °C)	0.191802	0.077588	0.322393
AC13-LTOA5d (30 °C)	0.204788	0.083801	0.278172
AC13-LTOA8d (30 °C)	0.216290	0.087031	0.265904
SMA13-UA (40 °C)	0.175162	0.173909	0.478719
SMA13-STOA (40 °C)	0.161526	0.168348	0.545364
SMA13-LTOA2d (40 °C)	0.182497	0.122690	0.419226
SMA13-LTOA5d (40 °C)	0.191950	0.103701	0.355926
SMA13-LTOA8d (40 °C)	0.226150	0.048751	0.197862
AC13-UA (40 °C)	0.191654	0.153199	0.386046
AC13-STOA (40 °C)	0.171434	0.116590	0.399729
AC13-LTOA2d (40 °C)	0.184130	0.095429	0.296814
AC13-LTOA5d (40 °C)	0.207889	0.060709	0.211021
AC13-LTOA8d (40 °C)	0.241313	0.031141	0.143421

As shown in Table 8, the CRI of SMA-13 is larger than that of AC-13, suggesting that the former has superior cracking resistance to the latter. The main reason for this is that ultimate strain and post-peak strain energy density are given greater weight among the four indexes, as shown in Table 8. Furthermore, the CRI of AC-13 and SMA-13 under STOA conditions increases by 4–20% and 14–24%, respectively, compared with the unaging condition. The results show that STOA improves the cracking resistance of both AC-13 and SMA-13. In addition, the benefit is weakened with the increase in the test temperature. In contrast, the CRI under LTOA conditions is lower than that under unaging conditions for both AC-13 and SMA13, suggesting that long-term aging weakens their cracking resistance. Furthermore, this weakening effect becomes more pronounced as the test temperature increases.

Figures 13 and 14 depict the aging coefficient results versus test temperature for AC-13 and SMA-13 under different degrees of aging. The aging coefficient is defined as the ratio of CRI under aging conditions compared to that under unaging conditions, which can eliminate the impact of CRI under unaging conditions. Figures 13 and 14 illustrate the aging coefficient versus test temperature for AC-13 and SMA-13, respectively. As shown in Figures 13 and 14, the aging coefficient of SMA-13 is higher than that of AC-13 by 1.4–36% when aging degree and test temperature remain the same, which means that SMA-13 is superior to AC-13 in terms of aging resistance. In addition, for both AC-13 and SMA-13, the aging coefficient under STOA condition is above 1, which demonstrates that STOA can have an increasing effect on the cracking resistance of AC-13 and SMA-13. For AC-13, the aging coefficient increases by 20%, 15%, 13%, 4%, respectively, at 10 °C, 20 °C, 30 °C and 40 °C; for SMA-13, this increases by 24%, 17%, 16%, 14%, respectively, at 10 °C, 20 °C, 30 °C and 40 °C. It is apparent that the increase amplitude of the aging coefficient of SMA-13 is bigger than that of AC-13, which demonstrates that the gaining effect of STOA is more prominent on SMA-13. Furthermore, it is not difficult to determine that the gaining effect can be lowered with the elevation of test temperature.

Under LTOA conditions, the aging coefficient is below 1, and the aging coefficient decreases with the deepening of the degree of aging. This shows that LTOA conditions can have a weakening effect on the cracking resistance, and the weakening effect becomes increasingly prominent with the deepening of aging degree. For AC-13, the aging coefficient decreases by 2–23% (LTOA2d), 7–45% (LTOA5d), 10–63% (LTOA8d). For SMA-13, the aging coefficient decreases by 1–12% (LTOA2d), 2–25% (LTOA5d), 4–59% (LTOA8d). Additionally, the decrease amplitude of the aging coefficient of SMA-13 is smaller than that of AC-13, which indicates that the weakening effect of LTOA is more prominent on AC-13. Similarly, it is not difficult to find that the gaining effect can be lowered by the elevation of test temperature.

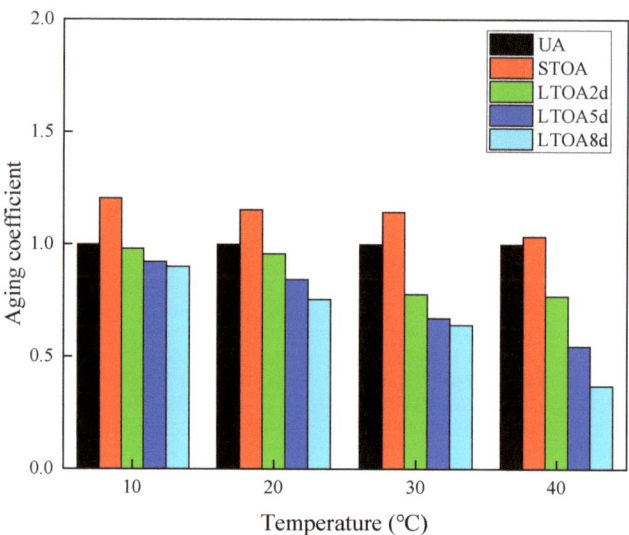

Figure 13. Aging coefficient versus test temperature for AC-13 under different degrees of aging.

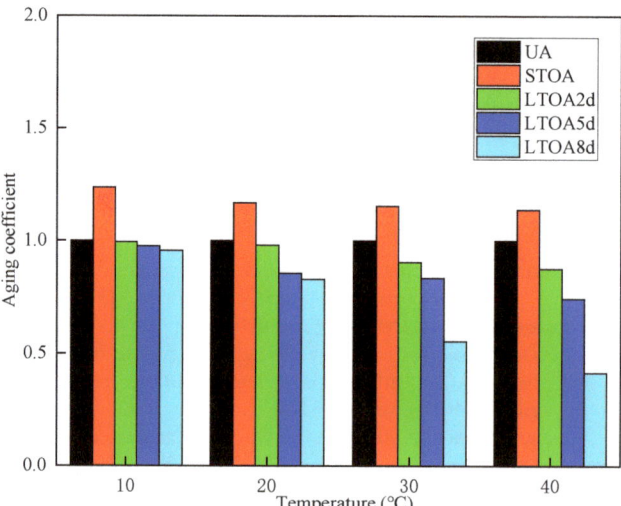

Figure 14. Aging coefficient versus test temperature for SMA-13 under different degrees of aging.

Meanwhile, a non-linear surface fitting method was applied to better describe the relationship between the aging coefficient and long-term aging duration and test temperature. Figure 15 and Table 10 depict the corresponding fitting result. The correlation coefficient of the fitting result of AC-13 and SMA-13 is 0.95 and 0.94, respectively, which reveals that the formula that is used can describe the relationship between the aging coefficient and the long-term aging duration and test temperature, where c denotes aging coefficient, d denotes long-term aging duration, and T denotes test temperature.

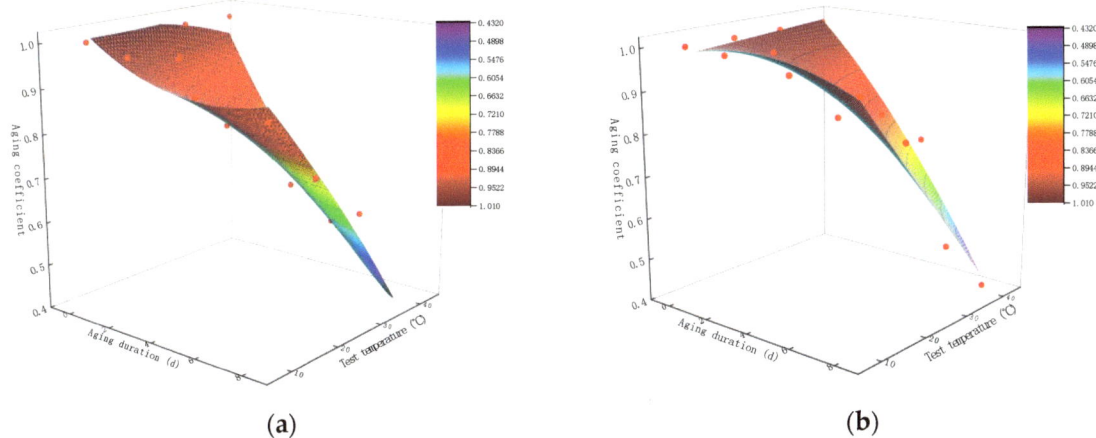

(a) (b)

Figure 15. Non-linear surface fitting graph: (**a**) AC-13; (**b**) SMA-13.

Table 10. Non-linear surface fitting result.

Item	Fitting Formula	R^2
AC-13	$c = 0.999 - 0.017d + 0.003T + 0.003d^2 - 9.590 \times 10^{-5}T^2 - 0.002dT$	0.95
SMA-13	$c = 0.976 + 0.038d + 7.414 \times 10^{-4}T - 0.003 + 4.200 \times 10^{-7}T^2 - 0.002dT$	0.94

In conclusion, SMA-13 is superior to AC-13 regarding the cracking resistance when considering different aging degrees and test temperatures. However, in practical engineering, economic cost is a necessary factor to be considered, so a brief cost analysis is given in Table 11. Table 11 shows that the annual expenses are 16.5 RMB·m^{-2} for AC-13 pavement; however, they are 11.4 RMB·m^{-2} on SMA-13. Apparently, the application of SMA-13 can save costs by 44% when compared with AC-13.

Table 11. Cost calculation of AC-13 and SMA-13 [43].

	Item	Material Name	
		AC-13	SMA-13
Initial cost/RMB·m^{-2}	Height/cm	4	4
	unit cost/RMB·cm^{-1}·m^{-2}	10	12
	Total initial cost/RMB·m^{-2}	40	48
Maintenance cost/RMB·m^{-2}	Paving times	3	2
	paving cost/RMB·m^{-2}	120	96
	Extra maintenance cost/RMB·m^{-2}	100	100
	Total maintenance cost/RMB·m^{-2}	220	196
Residue value/RMB·m^{-2}		13	16
Total cost/RMB·m^{-2}		247	228
Annual Total cost/RMB·m^{-2}		16.5	11.4

4. Conclusions

A direct tension test was conducted on two kinds of asphalt mixture (AC-13 and SMA-13) with five degrees of aging (UA, STOA, LTOA2d, LTOA5d and LTOA8d) at different test temperatures (10 °C, 20 °C, 30 °C, 40 °C). The objective is to comprehensively investigate the effect of aging degree/test temperature/gradation on the cracking resistance of the asphalt mixture. The main findings of this paper are as follows:

1. For both AC-13 and SMA-13, the tensile strength gradually ascends as the degree of aging progresses further, but descends as test temperature rises. Additionally, AC-13 has a higer tensile strength than SMA-13. The ultimate strain increases as the degree of aging degree progresses further, but decreases as the test temperature increases. SMA-13 can produce a higher ultimate strain compared with AC-13.
2. For both AC-13 and SMA-13, the pre-peak strain energy density increases as the degree of aging progresses further, but goes down as the test temperature increases. SMA-13 can produce a higher ultimate strain than AC-13. STOA conditions can boost the pre-peak and post-peak strain energy density, while LTOA conditions can reduce them. Additionally, the pre-peak and post-peak strain energy density both exhibit a tendency to increase first and then decrease, with their maximum occurring at 20 °C. Moreover, the superiority of SMA-13 lies in the post-peak strain energy density rather than the pre-peak strain energy density.
3. In the discussed region of aging degree and test temperature, SMA-13 has a higher CRI and aging coefficient value than AC-13 by 3–69%; this means that SMA-13 is endowed with a better cracking resistance whether it is under aging conditions or not.
4. STOA can enlarge the aging coefficient of the asphalt mixture, which means that STOA can increase cracking resistance even under aging conditions. Additionally, this positive effect can be weakened by an elevation in test temperature. LTOA can lower the aging coefficient, which indicates that LTOA can weaken the cracking resistance and the lowering effect can be boosted by elevations in the test temperature
5. The relationship between aging coefficient and the two factors (aging degree and test temperature) can be reflected by the functional expression of the non-linear surface (R^2 = 0.95 for AC-13 and R^2 = 0.94 for SMA-13).

Author Contributions: Conceptualization, S.Y.; data curation, S.Y. and K.L.; formal analysis, S.Y.; funding acquisition, Z.Z.; investigation, S.Y.; methodology, S.Y.; resources, K.L.; supervision, Z.Z.; validation, K.L.; writing—original draft, S.Y.; writing—review and editing, S.Y. and K.L. All authors have read and agreed to the published version of the manuscript.

Funding: This research was funded by Science and Technology Planning Project of Transportation of Guangdong Province, grant number 1912-0002.

Institutional Review Board Statement: Not applicable.

Informed Consent Statement: Not applicable.

Data Availability Statement: Data sharing not applicable.

Conflicts of Interest: The authors declare no conflict of interest.

References

1. Abouelsaad, A.; White, G. The combined effect of ultraviolet irradiation and temperature on hot mix asphalt mixture aging. *Sustainability* **2022**, *14*, 5942. [CrossRef]
2. Hu, H.W.; Vizzari, D.; Zha, X.D.; Roberts, R. Solar pavements: A critical review. *Renew Sustain. Energy Rev.* **2021**, *152*, 111712. [CrossRef]
3. Song, J.C.; Fu, S. Analysis of aging behavior of drainage asphalt mixture in transportation. *J. Highw. Transp. Res. Dev.* **2019**, *15*, 93–96. (In Chinese)
4. Yan, K.W.; Su, X.; Zhu, Y.F.; Si, C.D. Analysis of low temperature cracking resistance of asphalt mixture and simulation of fracture process. *J. Guangxi. Univ.* **2021**, *46*, 89. (In Chinese)
5. Zhu, Y.; Zhang, J.; Si, C.; Yan, T.; Li, Y. Laboratory Evaluation on Performance of Recycled Asphalt Binder and Mixtures under Short-Term Aging Conditions. *Sustainability* **2021**, *13*, 3404. [CrossRef]
6. Song, Y.; Liu, H.; Ding, N. The low temperature performance of warm mix asphat mixture considering aging. *J. Comp. Mater.* **2018**, *35*, 441–450. (In Chinese) [CrossRef]
7. Bonaquist, R.; Paye, B.; Johnson, C. Application of Intermediate temperature semi-circular bending (SCB) test results to design mixtures with improved load associated cracking resistance. *Road Mater. Pavement Des.* **2016**, *18*, 2–29. [CrossRef]

8. Chen, Q.; Ling, T.; He, L. Study on influence factors of asphalt mixture cracking resistance based on SCB test. *Highw. Traffic Tech.* **2018**, *34*, 37–41. (In Chinese) [CrossRef]
9. Wang, L.; Shan, M.; Li, C. The cracking characteristics of the polymer-modified asphalt mixture before and after aging based on the digital image correlation technology. *Constr. Build. Mater.* **2020**, *260*, 119802. [CrossRef]
10. Wu, B.; Wu, X.; Xiao, P.; Chen, C.; Xia, J.; Lou, K. Evaluation of the Long-Term Performances of SMA-13 Containing Different Fibers. *Appl. Sci.* **2021**, *11*, 5145. [CrossRef]
11. Islam, M.R.; Hossain, M.I.; Tarefder, R.A. A Study of Asphalt aging using indirect tensile strength test. *Constr. Build. Mater.* **2015**, *95*, 218–223. [CrossRef]
12. Radeef, H.R.; Abdul, N.; Razin, A. Effect of aging and moisture damage on the cracking resistance of rubberized asphalt mixture. *Mater. Today Proc.* **2021**, *42*, 2853–2858. [CrossRef]
13. Omranian, S.R.; Hamzah, M.O.; Valentin, J.; Hasan, M.R.M. Determination of optimal mix from the standpoint of short term aging based on asphalt mixture fracture properties using response surface method. *Constr. Build. Mater.* **2018**, *179*, 35–48. [CrossRef]
14. Ye, S. Crack Resistance of Aged Asphalt Mixture at Low Temperatrue Based on SCB Test. Master's Thesis, Anhui University of Science and Technology, Huainan, China, 2022. (In Chinese) [CrossRef]
15. Wang, J.; Qin, Y.; Zeng, W. Crack resistance of plant mixed reclaimed SBS modified asphalt mixture. *J. Chang'an Univ.* **2019**, *39*, 27–34+51. (In Chinese) [CrossRef]
16. Hamedi, G.H.; Saedi, D.; Ghahremani, H. Effect of short-term aging on low-temperature cracking in asphalt mixtures using mechanical and thermodynamic methods. *J. Mater. Civil. Eng.* **2020**, *13*, 04020288. [CrossRef]
17. Arabzadeh, A.; Staver, M.D.; Podolsky, J.H.; Williams, R.C.; Hohmann, A.D.; Cochran, E.W. At the frontline for mitigating the undesired effects of recycled asphalt: An alternative bio oil-based modification approach. *Constr. Build. Mater.* **2021**, *310*, 125253. [CrossRef]
18. Li, P.; Wu, Z.; Ma, K.; Zhang, Y. Study on low temperature crack resistancec of asphalt mixture based on SCB test. *J. Wuhan. Uni. Tech.* **2015**, *39*, 238–241. (In Chinese)
19. Yin, H.; Gao, S. The low temperature crack resistancec of asphalt mixture evaluated by indirect tension test. *J. Func. Mater.* **2021**, *52*, 9126–9130. (In Chinese)
20. Zhang, R.H.; Huang, J.D.; Zheng, W. Evaluation of the significance of different mix design variables on asphalt mixtures cracking performance measured by laboratory performance tests. *Constr. Build. Mater.* **2022**, *350*, 128693. [CrossRef]
21. Ashani, S.S.; Varamini, S.; Elwardany, M.D.; Tighe, S. investigation of low-temperature cracking resistance of asphalt mixtures by conducting disc-shaped compact tension (DCT) and semi-circular bend (SCB) tests. *Constr. Build. Mater.* **2022**, *359*, 129275. [CrossRef]
22. Stewart, C.M.; Oputa, C.W.; Garcia, E. Effect of specimen thickness on the fracture resistance of hot mix asphalt in the disk-shaped compact tension (DCT) configuration. *Constr. Build. Mater.* **2018**, *160*, 487–496. [CrossRef]
23. Phan, T.M.; Nguyen, S.N.; Seo, C.B.; Park, D.W. Effect of treated fibers on performance of asphalt mixture. *Constr. Build. Mater.* **2021**, *274*, 122051. [CrossRef]
24. Li, X.; Gibson, N.; Youtcheff, J. Evaluation of asphalt mixture cracking performance using the monotonic direct tension test in the AMPT. *Road Mater. Pavement Des.* **2017**, *18*, 447–466. [CrossRef]
25. Wang, D.; Guo, D.T.; Chang, H.; Yao, H.X.; Wang, T. Research on the Performance of regenerant modified cold recycled mixture with asphalt emulsions. *Sustainability* **2021**, *13*, 7284. [CrossRef]
26. Yang, T.; Chen, S.Y.; Pan, Y.Y.; Zhao, Y.L. Investigation of the accuracy of fracture energy in evaluating the low-temperature cracking performance of asphalt mixture. *J. Mater. Civ. Eng.* **2022**, *34*, 04022201. [CrossRef]
27. Zheng, D. Research on Key Parameters and Viscoelastic Analysis of Semi-Circular Bending Fracture Test of Asphalt Mixture at Low Temperature. Master's Thesis, Southeast University, Nanjing, China, 2020.
28. Liu, Z.; Li, S.; Wang, Y. Characteristics of asphalt modified by waste engine oil/polyphosphoric acid: Conventional, high-temperature rheological, and mechanism properties. *J. Clean. Prod.* **2022**, *330*, 129844. [CrossRef]
29. Idem, Z.G.; Bura, A. Developing a harvest plan by considering the effects of skidding techniques on forest soil using a hybrid topsis-entropy method. *For. Sci.* **2022**, *68*, 312–324.
30. Fan, A. Evaluation and countermeasures of future medical and pension security problems in shenzhen based on entropy weight and TOPSIS. *Adv. Appl. Math.* **2021**, *10*, 603–616. (In Chinese) [CrossRef]
31. Chang, J.; Li, J.; Hu, H.W.; Qian, J.F.; Yu, M. Numerical investigation of aggregate segregation of superpave gyratory compaction and its influence on mechanical properties of asphalt mixtures. *J. Mater. Civ. Eng.* **2023**, *35*, 04022453. [CrossRef]
32. Wei, H.; Zhang, H.; Li, J.; Zheng, J.; Ren, J. Effect of loading rate on failure characteristics of asphalt mixtures using acoustic emission technique. *Constr. Build. Mater.* **2023**, *364*, 129835. [CrossRef]
33. Li, J.; Zhang, J.H.; Yang, X.R.; Zhang, A.S.; Yu, M. Monte carlo simulations of deformation behaviour of unbound granular materials based on a real aggregate library. *Int. J. Pavement. Eng.* **2023**, *24*, 2165650. [CrossRef]
34. Li, G.N.; Gu, Z.J.; Tan, Y.Q.; Xing, C.; Zhang, J.J.; Zhang, C. Research on the phase structure of styrene-butadiene-styrene modified asphalt based on molecular dynamics. *Constr. Build. Mater.* **2022**, *326*, 126933. [CrossRef]
35. Liu, G.Q.; Han, D.D.; Zhu, C.Z.; Wang, F.F. Asphalt-mixture force chains length distribution and skeleton composition investigation based on computational granular mechanics. *J. Mater. Civ. Eng.* **2021**, *33*, 04021033. [CrossRef]

36. Zhao, Y.J.; Zhang, Y.; Jiang, J.W. Application and Improvement of discrete finite-element method for mesoscale fracture analysis of asphalt mixtures. *J. Transp. Eng. Part B Pavements* **2021**, *147*, 04021001. [CrossRef]
37. Yang, Y.; Wang, Y.X.; Cao, J.; Xu, Z.G.; Li, Y.L.; Liu, Y.H. Reactive molecular dynamic investigation of the oxidative aging impact on asphalt. *Constr. Build. Mater.* **2021**, *279*, 121298. [CrossRef]
38. Yu, C.H.; Hu, K.; Yang, Q.L.; Chen, C.J. Multi–scale observation of oxidative aging on the enhancement of high–temperature property of SBS–modified asphalt. *Constr. Build. Mater.* **2021**, *313*, 125478. [CrossRef]
39. Yue, Y.C.; Abdelsalam, M.; Khater, A.; Mohamed, G. A comparative life cycle assessment of asphalt mixtures modified with a novel composite of diatomite powder and lignin fiber. *Constr. Build. Mater.* **2022**, *323*, 126608. [CrossRef]
40. Xia, Y. Comprehensive Study about Effect of Basalt Fiber, Gradation, Nominal Maximum Aggregate Size and Asphalt on the Anti-Cracking Ability of Asphalt Mixtures. *Appl. Sci.* **2021**, *11*, 2289. [CrossRef]
41. Zhou, Y.; Chen, J.D.; Zhang, K.; Guan, Q.H.; Guo, H.M.; Xu, P.; Wang, J. Study on aging performance of modified asphalt binders based on characteristic peaks and molecular weights. *Constr. Build. Mater.* **2019**, *225*, 1077–1085. [CrossRef]
42. Wu, B.W.; Meng, W.J.; Xia, J.; Xiao, P. Influence of basalt fibers on the crack resistance of asphalt mixtures and mechanism analysis. *Materials* **2022**, *15*, 744. [CrossRef]
43. Ren, Y.; Zheng, Y. The comprehensive benefit analysis of economic SMA based on the whole life cycle theory. *Highway* **2015**, *60*, 201–206.

Disclaimer/Publisher's Note: The statements, opinions and data contained in all publications are solely those of the individual author(s) and contributor(s) and not of MDPI and/or the editor(s). MDPI and/or the editor(s) disclaim responsibility for any injury to people or property resulting from any ideas, methods, instructions or products referred to in the content.

Article

Laboratory Test and Constitutive Model for Quantifying the Anisotropic Swelling Behavior of Expansive Soils

Zhengnan Liu [1,2], Rui Zhang [1,3,4,*], Tian Lan [3,5], Yu Zhou [1] and Chao Huang [6]

1. School of Traffic and Transport Engineering, Changsha University of Science & Technology, Changsha 410114, China; lzn@csust.edu.cn (Z.L.); zy@stu.csust.edu.cn (Y.Z.)
2. Hunan Communications Research Institute Co., Ltd., Changsha 410015, China
3. National Key Laboratory of Green and Long-Life Road Engineering in Extreme Environment (Changsha), Changsha University of Science & Technology, Changsha 410114, China; lantian@hnust.edu.cn
4. Engineering Research Center of Catastrophic Prophylaxis and Treatment of Road & Traffic Safety of Ministry of Education, Changsha University of Science & Technology, Changsha 410114, China
5. School of Civil Engineering, Hunan University of Science and Technology, Xiangtan 411201, China
6. School of Civil Engineering, Central South University, Changsha 410075, China; huangchao-22@csu.edu.cn
* Correspondence: zr@csust.edu.cn

Abstract: Expansive soils exhibit directionally dependent swelling that traditional isotropic models fail to capture. This study investigates the anisotropic swelling characteristics of expansive soil with a medium swelling potential through the use of modified oedometric testing. Vertical swelling strains can reach up to 1.71 times that of the horizontal movements, confirming intrinsic anisotropy. A nonlinear elastic constitutive model incorporates vertical and horizontal elastic moduli with respect to matric suction to characterize anisotropy. Three elastic parameters were determined through the experiments, and predictive equations were developed to estimate the unsaturated moduli. The constitutive model and predictive techniques provide practical tools to better assess expansive soil pressures considering anisotropy, offering guidelines for utilization and design. The outcomes advance understanding of these soils' directionally dependent behavior and stress–strain–suction response.

Keywords: road engineering; constitutive model; swelling test; expansive soil; support structure

1. Introduction

Expansive soils are problematic soils that cause significant damage to infrastructure due to their shrinkage and swelling behavior influenced by changes in moisture content [1]. These soils contain high percentages of clay minerals such as smectite that have the capacity to absorb water into their crystalline structure [2]. Approximately 26 provinces in China contain expansive soils, posing major challenges for transportation and construction projects [3,4].

Expansive soils traditionally excavated from construction sites have been treated as construction and demolition waste and replaced with more engineered fill materials [5]. However, this practice is unsustainable and results in higher costs and environmental impacts from spoil disposal [6]. Recently, there has been a shift towards directly reusing expansive soils as pavement subgrades or engineered fill soils where feasible [7–9]. While this approach offers economic and sustainability benefits, it necessitates a deeper understanding of the mechanical behavior and earth pressure development characteristics of expansive soils, particularly under unsaturated conditions.

When expansive soils absorb moisture, either from rainfall infiltration or rising groundwater levels, they undergo significant volumetric expansion, commonly known as swelling. This process creates vertical swelling pressures that can damage shallow foundations and raise structures from their supporting soils. Additionally, it exerts lateral pressures against

retaining walls, basements, and other structures, leading to structural cracking and failures if not adequately considered in their design [10]. Conversely, during dry periods, expansive soils shrink, contributing to differential settlement issues [11]. Therefore, there is a need to evaluate the swelling behavior of expansive soil and accurately estimate the earth pressure exerted by expansive soil against retaining structures, which is crucial for analyzing slope stability and designing retaining structures in expansive soil areas.

Previous research has primarily focused on characterizing the swelling behavior and stress–strain response of expansive soils through laboratory testing and constitutive modeling. Various empirical and mechanistic models have been developed to describe the volume change phenomena of expansive clays, capture hydromechanical coupling behavior, and enable numerical analysis and design applications [12–14]. For instance, Fredlund's model [15] is popular due to its simplicity, as it relates stress and strain conditions to net stress and matric suction states. The highlights are also focused on the acquisition and prediction of the elastic modulus [16,17]. However, many traditional models assume that expansive soils exhibit isotropic mechanical properties despite evidence that anisotropy is intrinsic to their fabric and swelling at the microstructural scale. The directional arrangement of clay minerals is known to influence the development and magnitude of swelling strains and pressures.

Recent studies have observed distinct anisotropic characteristics between vertical and horizontal swelling of intact expansive soil specimens [18–20]. From the microstructure analysis, flaky clay particles within expansive soils are inclined to orient horizontally after compaction; this preferred orientation phenomenon becomes more apparent with an increase in static pressure, consequently leading to significant differences in swelling behavior [21]. Several researchers have developed experimental methods for determining lateral swelling pressure by modifying traditional oedometer and hydraulic triaxial apparatus [22–26]. By using the modified oedometer apparatus, researchers have consistently found that measured lateral pressures exceed those in the vertical direction under inundation conditions. Additionally, the ratio of swelling pressure in the vertical and lateral directions varies with the surcharge, moisture, and density of the soil specimens [27,28]. This inherent material anisotropy is not fully considered in common isotropic constitutive formulations. Simplified elastic analysis of earth pressures acting on retaining walls may produce non-conservative estimates if true directional deformation behavior is not properly characterized.

The objective of this paper was to experimentally investigate the anisotropic swelling properties of problem expansive soil from southern China and develop a model that can reliably predict lateral earth pressures during wetting based on laboratory-calibrated parameters. A modified unsaturated consolidation testing method was devised to isolate vertical and horizontal swelling responses under controlled stress states. The test results were then used to determine the parameters for a proposed anisotropic elastic model featuring separate elastic moduli for the vertical and horizontal directions. Simple normalization techniques were applied to extend the model for use under varying degrees of saturation. Finally, the model was validated through a comparison of the estimated and measured lateral pressure development curves from consolidation testing. The proposed approach aims to advance practical analysis and design involving expansive soils considering directionally dependent swelling behavior.

2. Materials and Methods

2.1. Materials

The expansive soil used in this study was collected from a site (23°48′11″ N, 106°43′11″ E) along the Longlin–Baise Expressway in Baise, Guangxi Zhuang Autonomous Region, China. Index property tests were conducted to characterize the soil, and the results are shown in Table 1. Atterberg limits testing resulted in a liquid limit of 56.3% and a plastic limit of 21.4%, corresponding to a plasticity index of 34.9%. Particle size analysis revealed that the soil contained 47.9% clay-sized particles (<0.002 mm). X-ray diffraction analysis quantified the mineralogy as being 16.6% smectite, 22% illite, 24% kaolinite, and 1% chlorite.

Table 1. Index properties of the testing soil.

Description	w_L (%)	I_P	G_s	Sand (%)	Silt (%)	Clay (%)	USCS	MDUW (kN/m^3)	OMC (%)
Expansive soil	56.3	34.9	2.75	0	52.1	47.9	CH	17.2	17.9

Note: w_L: liquid limit; I_P: plasticity index; G_s: specific gravity; USCS: unified soil classification system; MDUW: maximum dry unit weight; and OMC: optimum moisture content.

Standard Proctor compaction tests were carried out following the requirement of American Society for Testing Materials (ASTM) [29] to determine the maximum dry unit weight (MDUW) and optimum moisture content (OMC) of the soil. Three specimens were compacted and tested at varying moisture levels, resulting in an MDUW of 17.2 kN/m^3 at an OMC of 17.9%. Free swell index tests indicated that the soil exhibited medium swelling potential according to Highway Engineering Geological Investigation (JTG C20-2011) [30].

2.2. Testing Method

A modified oedometer testing method was developed to capture the directionally dependent swelling behavior of the expansive soil. An automated unsaturated consolidation (UC) apparatus was constructed, incorporating controlled vertical load, lateral confinement, matric suction, and real-time displacement and pressure monitoring capabilities. The apparatus is illustrated in Figure 1.

The apparatus comprised several integrated subsystems within a rigid reaction frame. At the base, a consolidated drained pressure chamber housed a high air-entry value ceramic disk (HAEV disk), which was designed to apply and measure the air and water pressures independently. Digital pressure transducers integrated in the air and water pump with ±1 kPa accuracy can regulate the air (0–500 kPa) and water (0–50 kPa) pressures, and a pressure transducer with ±1 kPa accuracy was equipped on the loading rod connected to the reaction frame to control the vertical load (0–500 kPa) applied through the reaction frame and the vertical movement of the pressure chamber. Extensive drainage lines and outlet valves facilitated the saturation of the disk and equipment using a Mariotte bottle, as well as water delivery and bubble flushing. A pressure regulator maintained a low upward gradient (<50 kPa) to remove bubbles and ensure the full saturation of the HAEV disk. The saturated HAEV disk then acted as an air–water interface, transmitting pore–water stresses to the specimen above. During testing, the water pressure always remains constant at 40 kPa to accelerate the saturation of the HAEV disk and ensure an unobstructed water supply path. After the vertical load (σ_v), air pressure (u_a), and water pressure (u_w) were all applied in the pressure chamber, and the soil specimen was ready to be inundated under the given net normal stress ($\sigma_v - u_a$) and matric suction ($u_a - u_w$). The linear variable displacement transducer (LVDT) for measuring axial strains was mounted on the loading rod and bracketed to the top of the pressure chamber, enabling precise measurements of the axial strains to a precision of 1×10^{-3} mm. Fine threaded rods connected the components and provided adjustability. Signals from the transducers interfaced with a data acquisition system, recording the pressures, vertical displacement, air pressures, and water pressures. Considering the fact that the permeability of expansive soil is extremely small, which results in quite a long period of time to achieve suction equilibrium, the frequency of the recording was set to 5 min intervals. The benchmark for the determination of suction equilibrium was also set as the changes in the readings for lateral pressure and vertical displacement were <1 kPa and 0.010 mm, respectively.

A significant innovation was the integration of a "retractable ring" device for the lateral confinement of the soil specimens during testing. As depicted in Figure 2, it consisted of a stainless steel ring with a 61.8 mm inner diameter and 30 mm height, housing a miniature pressure transducer (0–1000 kPa, ±1 kPa accuracy), thin acrylic spacer, and a curved plate.

An adjustable tightening mechanism joined the halves of the ring, enabling it to close down in discrete steps to maintain the laterally confined state. After assembling, the retractable ring, which contained the loading piston, porous stone, specimen, and lateral miniature pressure transducer component, was positioned above the HAEV disk in the pressure chamber, as shown in Figure 1.

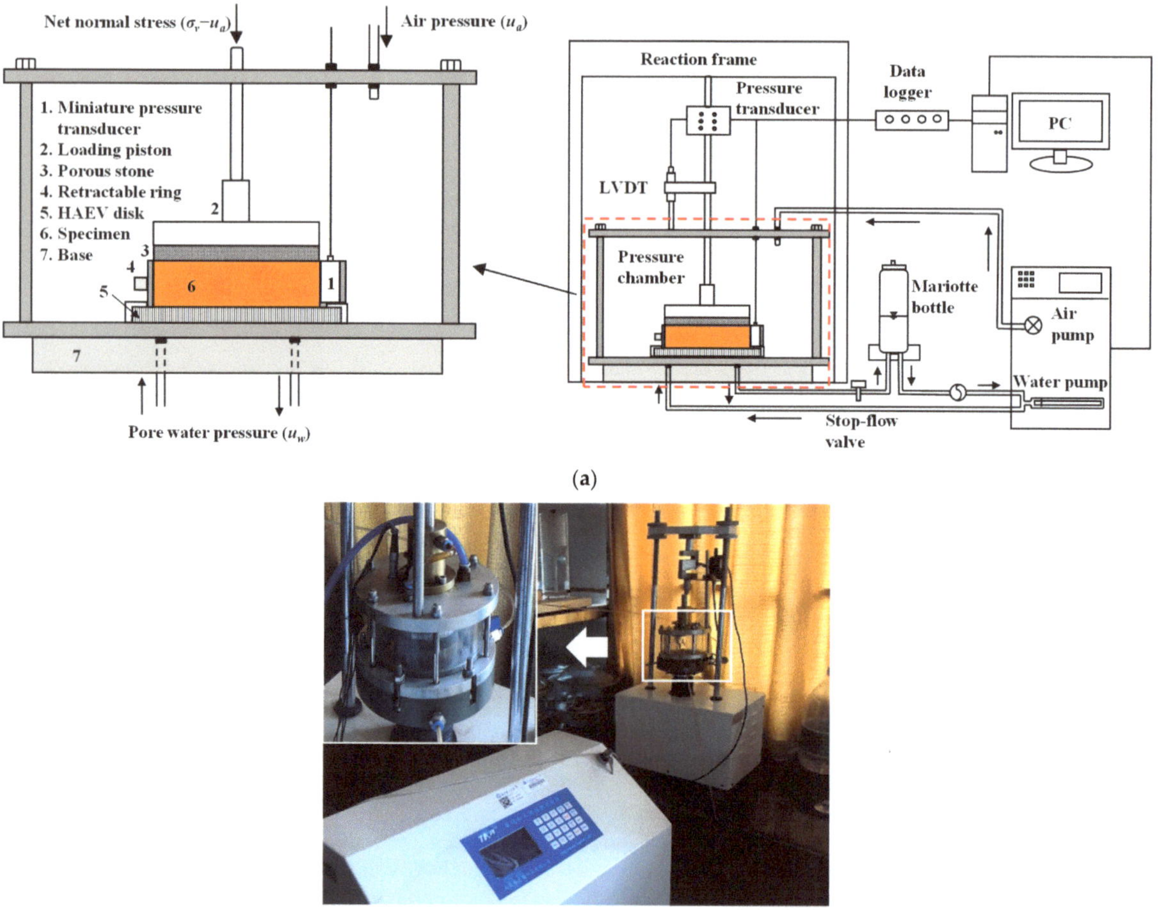

Figure 1. A (**a**) schematic view and (**b**) photo of the modified UC oedometer.

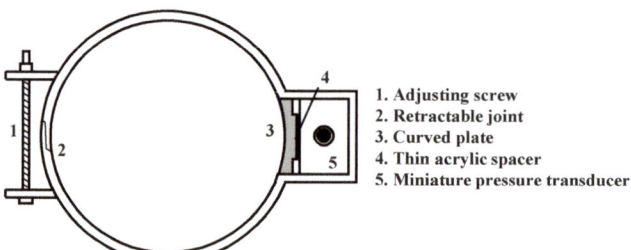

Figure 2. Schematic view of the retractable ring.

Extensive trials were conducted to calibrate the transducer readings and establish an optimal ring closure protocol. As depicted in Figure 3, the lateral pressure generated during the expansion of the specimen can be simulated by a controlled vertical load. Therefore, the calibration process started with a customized "T"-shaped loading frame, as shown in Figure 3a, which can be connected to the threaded loading head of the force gauge through a threaded hole in its upper part. The pressure would be gradually applied to the loading frame by the force gauge and transmitted through the curved plate and thin acrylic spacer to the miniature pressure transducer. The deformation is then monitored by two displacement gauges placed on both sides of the loading frame. Finally, the real-time readings of deformations and pressures are entered into the software interface (Ver 1.0) via displacement and pressure data loggers, respectively. It was observed that maintaining lateral stresses 2–3 kPa higher than the bulk stress state ensured reliable contact while minimizing boundary effects.

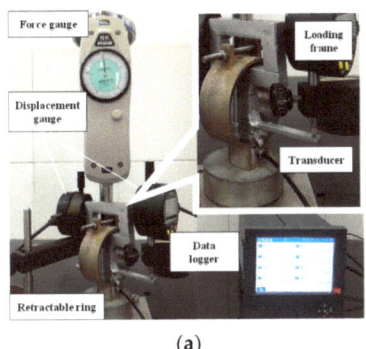
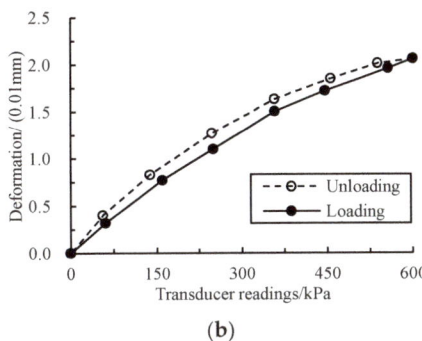

(a)   (b)

Figure 3. Calibration of the retractable ring for the (**a**) process and (**b**) result.

In addition, as shown in Figure 3b, the maximum deformation obtained was 0.021 mm when the miniature pressure transducer reached the full scale of 600 kPa for the force gauge. Based on a specimen diameter of 61.8 mm, it can be calculated that the maximum radial strain is 0.032%, which is less than the requirement of the ASTM standard [31], which states that the maximum radial change in the ring should not be greater than the original diameter of 0.04% to achieve the K_0 condition. In addition, the influence of air pressure on the miniature pressure transducer was also considered. In the subsequent laboratory tests, the maximum value of the applied matric suction was set to 200 kPa; therefore, in the calibration process, the water pressure applied by the pump was always kept constant at 40 kPa, and the air pressure applied by the air pump ranged from 40 to 240 kPa to ensure that the formation of matric suction was in the range of 0–200 kPa. The results show that the readings of the miniature pressure transducer remained unchanged whether the air pressure was reduced from 240 kPa to 0 or increased from 0 to 240 kPa, which indicates that the effect of air pressure on the miniature pressure transducer in this study could be negligible.

Considering the disturbance and loss of moisture content during the transportation of the soil samples retrieved from the field, the specimens prepared in this way can no longer reflect the actual situation in the field. Therefore, remodeled soil samples were used in this study, and the pre-specimens were prepared in the manner of layered static compaction to approximate the layering phenomenon produced via the deposition of the original samples in the field. Specimen preparation involved drying, grinding, and sieving before compacting the samples under predetermined conditions. The expansive soil samples from the field were first dried in the oven at 105 °C, then ground to powder and passed through a sieve with a diameter of 2 mm. Subsequently, the samples were stored in a sealed plastic bag in the shade for at least 24 h. In addition, the expansive soils should be passed through the 2 mm sieve once more before specimen preparation since expansive soil easily clots after being mixed with distilled water.

The specimens were all prepared at an initial moisture content of 18.0% and a dry unit weight of 16.0 kN/m^3. Specimen homogenization entailed the static compaction of the prepared wet soil within a custom cube mold at each 10 mm layer. The compacted "pre-specimens" were extruded and vertically cut or rotated 90° prior to sampling for oedometer vertical swelling (OVS) or horizontal swelling (OHS) tests, respectively. As depicted in Figure 4, the modified preparation approach orientates clay mineral flakes differently to reflect field conditions.

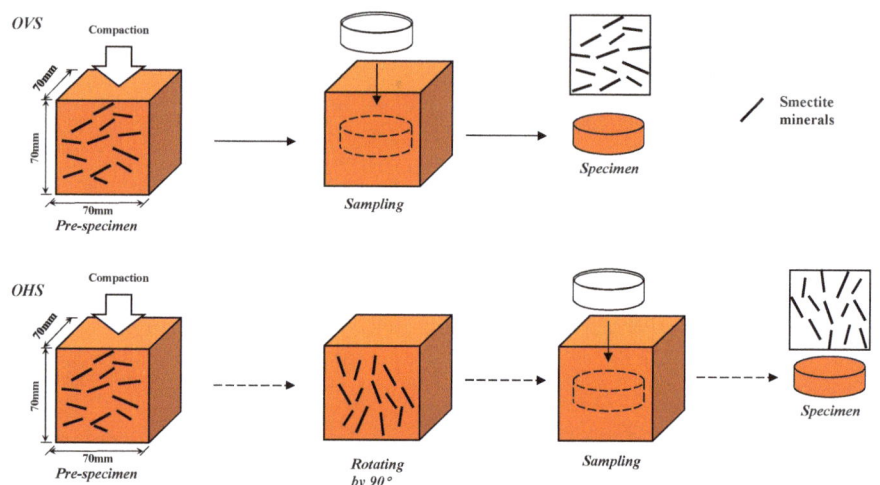

Figure 4. Schematic view of specimen preparation.

For the OHS tests, the pre-specimens were initially rotated 90° prior to coring. This modification oriented the platy clay structure differently to induce intrinsic anisotropy. The extracted specimens were then carefully positioned within the retractable ring for confinement during testing. Trimming and greasing of sample surfaces were carried out to minimize the effects of side friction.

A consistent test procedure was followed for all series under varying net normal stress conditions (Table 2). The initial matric suction of the specimens was measured as 500 kPa using the filter paper method before being gradually reduced in staged equilibrium steps. Vertical swelling displacements, lateral confining pressures, and equilibrium times were recorded, with pressure transducers monitoring net stresses.

Table 2. Summary of testing program conditions.

Type	Test ID	Dry Unit Weight (kN/m^3)	Moisture Content (%)	Net Normal Stress $\sigma_v - u_a$ (kPa)	Matric Suction $u_a - u_w$ (kPa)
OVS	OVS-0			0	
	OVS-12.5			12.5	
	OVS-25			25	
	OVS-50			50	
	OVS-100	16.0	18.0	100	200→100→50→20→10→5→0
OHS	OHS-0			0	
	OHS-12.5			12.5	
	OHS-25			25	
	OHS-50			50	
	OHS-100			100	

Each test series was conducted under constant net normal stress and followed the same decreasing matric suction path. For instance, OHS-12.5 denoted an OHS test series conducted with a net normal stress of 12.5 kPa, and 50→20 indicated that the controlled matric suction decreased from 50 kPa to 20 kPa. Furthermore, the compressed vertical strain of the specimen manifested once a certain net normal stress was applied, leading to the complete alteration of the initial volume and dry unit weight of the tested specimen. Therefore, the matric suction level of 500 kPa was not included, and the matric suction was initiated at 200 kPa.

Upon the completion of swelling under a given suction, the stresses were adjusted to maintain net stress while further lowering suction. The tests were terminated once specimens were fully saturated. This testing program generated a robust anisotropic stress–strain–suction dataset for characterizing soil behavior and developing constitutive models.

3. Experimental Results

The testing program produced a comprehensive dataset that characterizes the anisotropic swelling behavior of the expansive soil under varying stress conditions. Here, we present the key findings from the analysis of vertical swelling strain and lateral pressure responses measured across a range of controlled suction reductions.

Figure 5a illustrates the variations in the vertical swelling strain with matric suction reduction observed across all net normal stress conditions for the OVS and OHS test series. Several consistent trends were observed. Firstly, the swelling strains increased with decreasing suction as the soil moisture content rose for both test orientations. This behavior is consistent with the typical mechanisms of expansive soils gaining volume as water enters the diffused double layer of smectite clay plates.

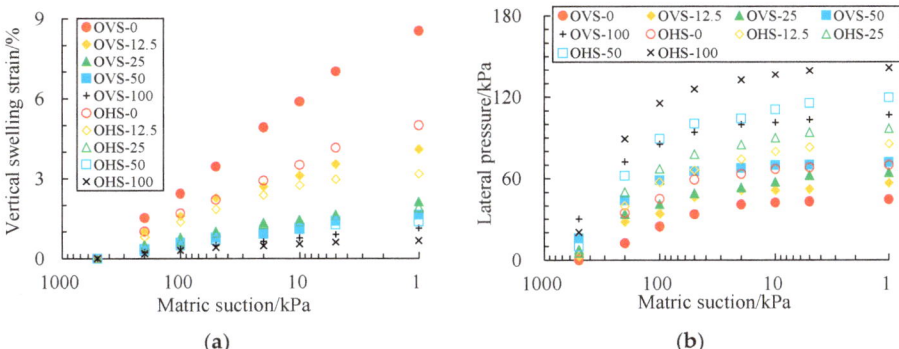

Figure 5. Variation in the (**a**) vertical swelling strain and (**b**) lateral pressure under different net normal stresses with matric suction.

Secondly, the strains in the vertical direction were significantly larger compared to the horizontal direction. At full saturation under zero net stress, the maximum vertical swell measured 8.54% in OVS, whereas only 4.99% horizontal swell occurred in the OHS tests. The vertical swelling strain in OVS was about 1.71 times that in OHS. This confirms the presence of intrinsic anisotropy, where clays expand more readily out of the plane of their layered structure due to the influence of depositional packing and consolidation stresses.

Thirdly, higher net normal stresses resulted in reduced vertical swell strains as confinement restricted volume changes. However, strains progressively increased with desaturation across all stress conditions, indicating a complex interaction between the applied stresses and changing suction states.

Figure 5b illustrates the variations in the measured lateral confining pressure with suction reduction. Once again, suction decreases induced growing pressures across all test series as soil expansive forces developed against the constant lateral confinement. Peak pressures often occurred within the initial high suction range above 50 kPa as the volume occupied by the adsorbed water layers increased the thicknesses of the diffused double layers.

Interestingly, lateral pressures exhibited the opposite behavior to vertical strains, with higher initial responses developing under elevated net stresses. For instance, maximum pressures of 44.7 kPa and 70.0 kPa were obtained at full saturation under zero net stress for OVS and OHS tests, yet these grew substantially larger under confinement. This confirms that confinement amplifies both vertical and lateral swelling capacities through stress–suction coupling effects. In addition, it should also be noted that the lateral pressures measured under zero net stress can be seen as pure swelling pressure, where the swelling pressure in the vertical direction (OHS-0) was 1.57 times that in the horizontal direction (OVS-0), also demonstrating an obvious swelling anisotropy as with swelling strain.

Notably, the OHS tests consistently produced higher lateral pressures than OVS runs across all suction–stress conditions, highlighting the greater development of expansive forces in the horizontal direction related to microstructural anisotropy.

In summary, the test results clearly demonstrated that the expansive soil exhibits anisotropic volumetric swelling strongly influenced by the stress state, moisture condition, and orientation of the layered mineral structure. These behaviors have significant implications for properly assessing and accommodating earth and swelling pressures in geostructure designs situated within expansive ground.

4. Developed Constitutive Model

4.1. Constitutive Model Expression

In a previous study, it was noted from the experimental results that the relationship between stress and strain could be considered an elastic process when the surcharge ranges from zero to the vertical swelling pressure measured under constant volume conditions [10]. The measured vertical swelling strain and lateral pressure under certain surcharges with saturated conditions were found to be quite close during the loading and unloading process [32]. Additionally, the earth pressure of unsaturated expansive soil would mobilize due to matric suction changes after rainfall. This single swelling process differs from the drying and wetting cyclical process, which can be regarded and assumed to be an elastic behavior. Therefore, to analyze the earth pressure of unsaturated expansive soil acting on a vertical retaining wall and investigate the mobilization of earth pressure distribution from the initial state to the saturation state, the interaction between the unsaturated expansive soil and the vertical retaining wall was simplified and regarded as a two-dimensional elastic problem.

Modifications were made to Fredlund's isotropic elastic model to characterize the anisotropic swelling behavior of expansive soil. The elastic modulus with respect to matric suction (H) was modified to consider two elastic moduli with respect to matric suction (H_v and H_h) in the vertical and horizontal directions, respectively. For simplicity, the elastic modulus with respect to net normal stress E was still considered isotropic. Therefore, the three-dimensional nonlinear elastic model can be further simplified as follows:

$$\begin{cases} d\varepsilon_h = \frac{d(\sigma_h - u_a)}{E} - \frac{\mu}{E} d(\sigma_h + \sigma_v - 2u_a) + \frac{ds}{H_h} \\ d\varepsilon_v = \frac{d(\sigma_v - u_a)}{E} - \frac{\mu}{E} d(\sigma_h + \sigma_h - 2u_a) + \frac{ds}{H_v} \end{cases}, \quad (1)$$

where ε_v and ε_h are the vertical and horizontal strain, respectively, in %; $(\sigma_v - u_a)$ and $(\sigma_h - u_a)$ are the vertical and horizontal net normal stress, respectively, in kPa; μ is the Poisson ratio; s is the matric suction, $s = u_a - u_w$, kPa; E is the elastic modulus with respect to net normal stress, in kPa; and H_v and H_h are the vertical and horizontal elastic moduli with respect to matric suction, respectively, in kPa.

4.2. Constitutive Parameters

In comparison with the original model, this modified constitutive model includes three elastic moduli, E, H_v, and H_h, all of which can be determined through modified unsaturated consolidation tests. In the modified unsaturated consolidation test, the specimen is subjected to constant net normal stress and gradually reduced matric suction, while always being subjected to lateral confinement, as shown in Figure 6.

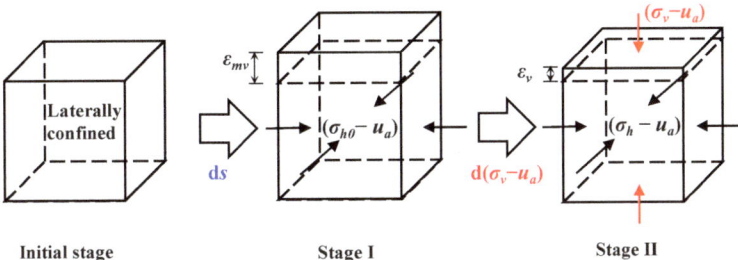

Figure 6. Stress state change of soil elements.

Assuming that the direction of the swelling is positive, Stage I demonstrates the stress state changes that occur in the soil elements of the specimen swelled under zero net normal stress from its initial matric suction to a specific matric suction level with lateral confinement. The lateral confining pressure without certain net normal stress is generated in the horizontal direction, and the maximum vertical swelling strain occurs in the vertical direction. The constitutive relationship at Stage I can be derived from Equation (1) and described by Equation (2):

$$\begin{cases} 0 = \frac{\mu-1}{E}d(\sigma_{h0} - u_a) + \frac{ds}{H_h} \\ d\varepsilon_{mv} = \frac{2\mu}{E}d(\sigma_{h0} - u_a) + \frac{ds}{H_v} \end{cases}, \quad (2)$$

$$d(\sigma_{h0} - u_a) = \frac{E}{(1-\mu)H_h}ds, \quad (3)$$

$$d\varepsilon_{mv} = \frac{2\mu}{1-\mu} \cdot \frac{ds}{H_h} + \frac{ds}{H_v}, \quad (4)$$

where σ_{h0} is the lateral confining pressure without certain net normal stress, and ε_{mv} is the maximum vertical swelling strain.

Equations (3) and (4) are derived by solving the previously derived equations to estimate the lateral confining pressure without certain net normal stress and the maximum vertical swelling strain at Stage I. The lateral confining pressure actually corresponds to the lateral swelling pressure associated with free swelling without certain net normal stress. In Stage II, the stress state changes occur in the soil elements of the specimen swelled under certain net normal stress from its initial matric suction to a specific matric suction level with lateral confinement. The lateral confining pressure under certain net normal stress is generated in the horizontal direction, and the vertical swelling strain under certain net normal stress occurs in the vertical direction. The constitutive relationship at Stage II can also be derived from Equation (1) and described by Equation (5):

$$\begin{cases} 0 = \frac{\mu-1}{E}d(\sigma_h - u_a) + \frac{\mu}{E}d(\sigma_v - u_a) + \frac{ds}{H_h} \\ d\varepsilon_v = -\frac{d(\sigma_v - u_a)}{E} + \frac{2\mu}{E}d(\sigma_h - u_a) + \frac{ds}{H_v} \end{cases}, \quad (5)$$

$$d(\sigma_h - u_a) = \frac{\mu}{1-\mu}d(\sigma_v - u_a) + \frac{E}{(1-\mu)H_h}ds, \quad (6)$$

$$d\varepsilon_v = -\frac{(1-\mu-2\mu^2)d(\sigma_v-u_a)}{(1-\mu)E} + \frac{2\mu}{1-\mu}\cdot\frac{ds}{H_h} + \frac{ds}{H_v}, \tag{7}$$

Comparing Equation (3) with Equation (6) and Equation (4) with Equation (7), it can be observed that these two pairs of equations have similar forms, with the difference being the presence of vertical net normal stress. In terms of elasticity, it can be understood that a vertical net normal stress ($\sigma_v - u_a$) is further loaded on the top of the specimen at Stage I. Under its influence, the vertical swelling strain decreases from the maximum value to the vertical swelling strain under surcharge, and the horizontal confining pressure generated in Stage I would further experience an increment and increase to ($\sigma_h - u_a$). During this period, the increment of matric suction is zero, namely $ds = 0$. The constitutive relationships from Stage I to Stage II can be described using Equation (8).

$$\begin{cases} 0 = \frac{\mu-1}{E}d(\sigma_h - \sigma_{h0}) + \frac{\mu}{E}d(\sigma_v - u_a) \\ d(\varepsilon_v - \varepsilon_{mv}) = -\frac{d(\sigma_v - u_a)}{E} + \frac{2\mu}{E}d(\sigma_h - \sigma_{h0}) \end{cases}, \tag{8}$$

$$E = \frac{(1-\mu-2\mu^2)d(\sigma_v - u_a)}{(1-\mu)d(\varepsilon_{mv} - \varepsilon_v)}, \tag{9}$$

where ($\varepsilon_v - \varepsilon_{mv}$) represents the reduction in vertical strain resulting from net normal stress.

Equation (9) is derived from Equation (8) to estimate the elastic modulus (E) with respect to the net normal stress. Once the net normal stress is loaded onto the specimen, it remains constant. Thus, the increment in net normal stress is zero, namely $d(\sigma_v - u_a) = 0$. The first term on the right-hand side of Equation (7) equals zero, rendering this equation identical to Equation (4). This indicates that the vertical swelling strain of the unsaturated expansive soil is due to a moisture increment consisting of two parts. In addition to the vertical strain resulting from the change in matric suction itself, the lateral swelling strain would also occur if it were not laterally confined. The lateral confinement results in the representation of this part in the vertical direction. However, as mentioned in Section 2.2, the maximum radial strain of the oedometer ring is 0.032%. Therefore, the latter part could be extremely small compared to the previous part and can be ignored. Hence, the vertical swelling strain in OVS ($\varepsilon_{v,OVS}$) and the vertical swelling strain in OHS ($\varepsilon_{v,OHS}$) can be described as shown in Equation (10):

$$\begin{cases} d\varepsilon_{v,OVS} = \frac{ds}{H_v} \\ d\varepsilon_{v,OHS} = \frac{ds}{H_h} \end{cases}, \tag{10}$$

$$H_v = \frac{ds}{d\varepsilon_{v,OVS}}, \tag{11}$$

$$H_h = \frac{ds}{d\varepsilon_{v,OHS}}, \tag{12}$$

Equations (11) and (12) are derived from Equation (10) to estimate the vertical and horizontal elastic moduli (H_v and H_h) with respect to matric suction, respectively. For the determined unsaturated expansive soil, the change in vertical swelling strain is caused by the coupling effect of the net normal stress and matric suction. These three elastic parameters are all influenced by the changes in net normal stress and matric suction, demonstrating the nonlinear elastic behavior during wetting. However, Equation (9) would be invalid if the soil is inundated without vertical net normal stress, whereas the elastic modulus should be a property of the material itself. Although it may change under the influence of external factors (stress state and boundary conditions, etc.), it should always have an initial value. Equation (9) would need to be further modified based on the test results to estimate the E without the net normal stress.

Furthermore, Poisson's ratio is also essential for the constitutive model. Unsaturated expansive soil undergoes significant volume changes after saturation, leading to substantial changes in dry density. Soils with smaller dry densities are more likely to deform, and those with larger Poisson ratios are more susceptible to this deformation. However, recent standards do not provide methods for measuring the Poisson's ratio of unsaturated soils, nor do they specify the size of specimens and the testing conditions of stress and strain that are required for determining Poisson's ratio. In engineering practice, Poisson's ratio is often assumed to be a constant value. The suggested range of values for Poisson's ratio ranges from 0.2 (dry sand) to 0.5 (saturated clay tested under undrained conditions) [10,33].

5. Determination of the Elastic Parameters

5.1. Elastic Modulus with Respect to Net Normal Stress

The elastic modulus with respect to the net normal stress (E) characterizes the compressibility of the soil skeleton. It is required as a parameter within the proposed constitutive model relating stress–strain responses under changing net normal stresses or suction conditions.

As mentioned above, both the denominator and the numerator on the right-hand side of Equation (9) would become zero when no net normal stress is loaded, rendering it unable to estimate the elastic modulus E in this state. The elimination method can be carried out if there is a certain relationship between the denominator and the numerator. Figure 7 illustrates the variation curves of the denominator ($\varepsilon_v - \varepsilon_{mv}$) with respect to the numerator ($\sigma_v - u_a$).

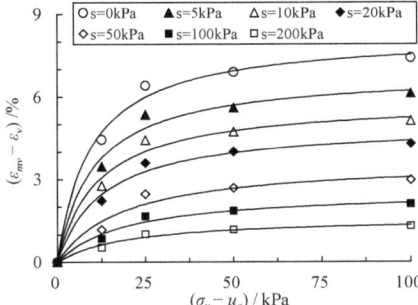

Figure 7. Variation curves of ($\varepsilon_{mv} - \varepsilon_v$) to ($\sigma_v - u_a$).

Figure 7 indicates that under the condition of constant matric suction, the increase in ($\varepsilon_{mv} - \varepsilon_v$) gradually increased with the increase in ($\sigma_v - u_a$), and the increment gradually decreased, tending to stabilize. The stress–strain relationship can be fitted in the form of a hyperbolic function, as shown in Equation (13). Table 3 shows that parameters a and b exhibited a strong correlation >0.95, validating the approach.

$$\varepsilon_{mvi} - \varepsilon_{vi} = \frac{a(\sigma_{vi} - u_a)}{1 + b(\sigma_{vi} - u_a)}, \tag{13}$$

where a and b are the fitting parameters.

Table 3. Fitting results of Equation (13).

Matric Suction (kPa)	a	b	R^2
200	0.0008	0.0524	0.9914
100	0.0014	0.0532	0.9908
50	0.0020	0.0545	0.9501
20	0.0039	0.0779	0.9829
10	0.0052	0.0882	0.9792
5	0.0067	0.0981	0.9814
0	0.0088	0.1070	0.9906

Substituting Equation (13) into Equation (9):

$$E = \frac{(1 - \mu - 2\mu^2)}{(1 - \mu)a/[1 + b(\sigma_{vi} - u_a)]}, \quad (14)$$

Comparing Equation (14) with Equation (9), Equation (14) is still valid in terms of estimating the elastic modulus E even in the absence of a vertical net normal stress. A series of elastic moduli E under different net normal stresses and matric suctions was estimated using Equation (14).

Figure 8 shows the variations in the calculated E values with changing net normal stress and suction states. Several trends were observed. E, with respect to net normal stress, decreased as matric suction decreased, showing a rapid reduction when the matric suction exceeded 20 kPa under a net normal stress of 50–100 kPa, while it gradually slowed down as the soil became increasingly saturated. With the decrease in net normal stress, the rapid reduction in E disappeared. Furthermore, under low net normal stress, matric suction had less impact on E than net normal stress. With an increase in net normal stress, the elastic modulus E under the same matric suction also increased, indicating that the influence of matric suction on E became much stronger. At the same matric suction level, a higher net normal stress led to a greater E. These results also highlight the fact that unsaturated expansive soil under low matric suction is more prone to deformation under external loads, and higher external loads enhance its resistance to deformation.

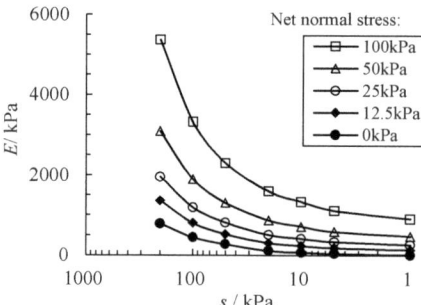

Figure 8. Variations in the elastic modulus E with different net normal stresses and suction states.

5.2. Elastic Modulus with Respect to Matric Suction

The elastic modulus with respect to matric suction reflects compressibility induced solely by suction changes independent of net stress effects. Both vertical (H_v) and horizontal (H_h) moduli were estimated to capture swelling anisotropy.

Equations (11) and (12) were applied to OVS and OHS test data to back-calculate H_v and H_h, respectively, from the slopes of the swelling strain–suction curves. Figure 9 presents the variations in the calculated H_v and H_h with suction reduction over different net normal stress levels.

Matric suction significantly influences the moduli of H_v and H_h. As matric suction decreases, both moduli monotonically decrease, with varying degrees of reduction for H_v and H_h. The moduli of H_v and H_h are relatively large when the matric suction is high, as the change in matric suction during this period does not significantly lead to changes in soil volume. Additionally, net normal stress also affects these moduli. Under the same matric suction, specimens subjected to higher net normal stresses have a larger elastic modulus than matric suction. This indicates that greater net normal stress leads to smaller swelling strain and larger swelling pressure. Consequently, the lateral swelling pressure, like the vertical swelling pressure, increases with net normal stress. The disparity between H_v and H_h can be considered a representation of swelling anisotropy on a macro scale.

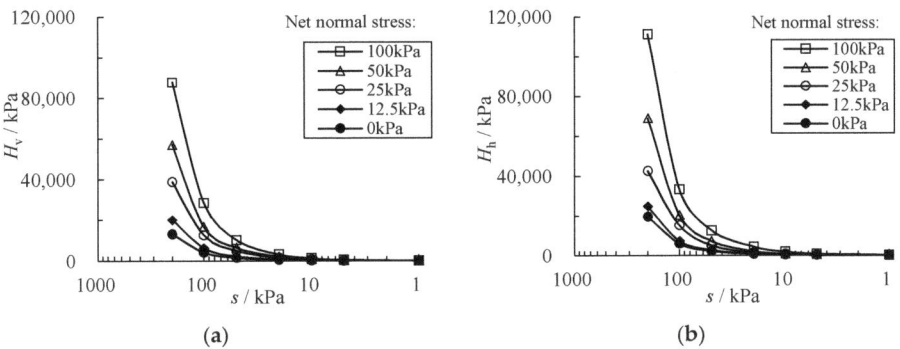

Figure 9. Variation curves of (**a**) H_v and (**b**) H_h with different matric suctions.

Notably, the moduli H_h exceeded H_v across all conditions, reflective of preferential horizontal restraint against intrinsically weaker lateral swelling. This separation quantifies the microstructural anisotropy manifestation in macroscopic stress–strain terms.

5.3. Prediction Method for Unsaturated Elastic Modulus

All of the elastic moduli calculated above are tangent moduli, regardless of whether they are E or H, while the calculation of lateral swelling pressure or lateral pressure is based on an incremental method, according to Equations (3) and (6). Therefore, in order to predict the unsaturated elastic modulus under certain net normal stress and matric suction states, the normalization of E by saturated E magnitude (E_{sat}) was subsequently performed, collapsing the data onto consistent power functions of normalized suction (Figure 10). The correlation coefficients exceeded 0.98, allowing predictive Equation (15) to estimate E_{unsat} from known saturated conditions. The values of the fitting parameters and their correlation coefficients are shown in Table 4. This simple expression captures modulus evolution, which is important for constitutive modeling.

$$E_{unsat} = E_{sat}\left[1 + \alpha \left(\frac{s}{s_0}\right)^\beta\right], \qquad (15)$$

where α and β are fitting parameters, and s_0 is the initial matric suction of the soil.

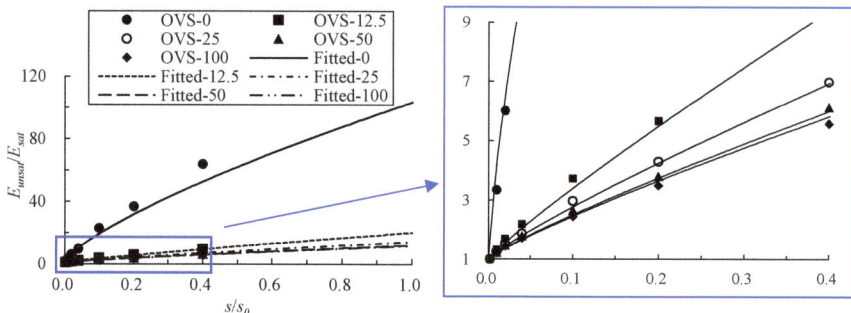

Figure 10. Normalization fitting curves of E_{unsat}/E_{sat} to s/s_0.

The unsaturated modulus with respect to matric suction can be predicted in the same way. To normalize the data, Figure 11 plots H_{vunsat}/H_{vsat} and H_{hunsat}/H_{hsat} versus s/s_0, collapsing onto single best-fit power curves, as per Equation (16). The values of the fitting parameters and their correlation coefficients are shown in Table 5. Very strong correlations (more than 0.99) affirmed the predictability of this expression in terms of estimating the unsaturated elastic modulus H_{unsat} from the saturated conditions.

$$H_{unsat} = H_{sat}\left[1 + \lambda\left(\frac{s}{s_0}\right)^{\eta}\right], \qquad (16)$$

where λ and η are the fitting parameters.

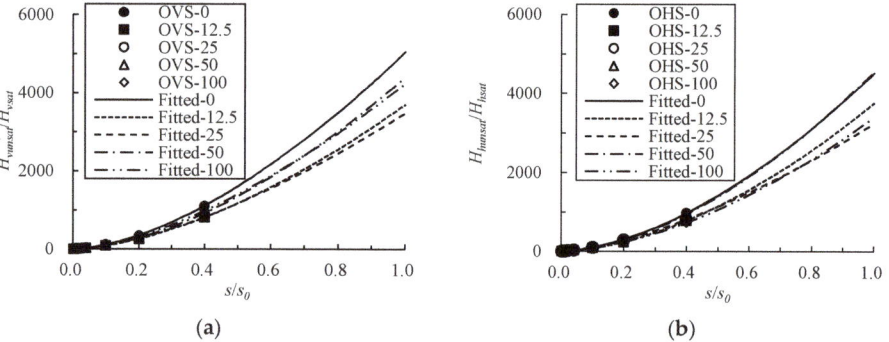

Figure 11. Normalization curves of (**a**) H_{vunsat}/H_{vsat} to s/s_0 and (**b**) H_{hunsat}/H_{hsat} to s/s_0.

Table 4. Fitting results between E_{unsat}/E_{sat} and s/s_0.

Net Normal Stress (kPa)	α	β	R^2
0	102.502	0.747	0.9851
12.5	19.224	0.904	0.9983
25	13.227	0.873	0.9986
50	11.047	0.866	0.9982
100	10.640	0.864	0.9960

Table 5. Fitting results between H_{unsat}/H_{sat} and s/s_0.

Net Normal Stress (kPa)	H_v			H_h		
	λ	η	R^2	λ	η	R^2
0	5050.221	1.648	0.9997	4518.053	1.673	0.9990
12.5	3694.508	1.646	0.9995	3750.679	1.710	0.9991
25	3479.687	1.567	0.9993	3232.893	1.502	0.9999
50	4396.977	1.694	0.9990	4553.960	1.712	0.9994
100	4229.299	1.585	0.9997	3393.036	1.676	0.9989

Moreover, it was observed that the datasets in Figure 11a,b were quite close to each other after normalization; hence, united fitting based on all of the datasets was further performed, and the fitting results show that the correlation coefficient is 0.9777, where the fitting parameter of λ is 4012.631 and η is 1.639, respectively. For convenient use in practical engineering applications, the united fitting method is recommended in the prediction of the unsaturated elastic modulus H_{unsat}.

The implementation of the proposed methods provides a practical means for determining the anisotropic expansive soil compressibility represented by H_{unsat}, which is a critical parameter within the constitutive framework for improved unsaturated expansive soil analyses.

6. Validation of Lateral Pressure Estimation

To evaluate the proposed techniques, lateral pressure estimations using the constitutive model were compared against experimental OVS and OHS test measurements. To further validate the anisotropy consideration, additional predictions were carried out treating H_v and H_h as equal (isotropic assumption) rather than directionally dependent, namely Fredlund's nonlinear elastic model. Table 6 summarizes the parameter values obtained for input from the analyses presented in Sections 4 and 5.

Table 6. Summary of the calculating parameters used in the estimation.

Net Normal Stress (kPa)	E_{sat} (kPa)	H_{vsat} (kPa)	H_{hsat} (kPa)	H_{isosat} (kPa)	α	β	λ_v	η_v	λ_h	η_h
0	12	12	20	34	102.502	0.747	5050.221	1.648	4518.053	1.673
12.5	134	24	31	55	19.224	0.904	3694.508	1.646	3750.679	1.710
25	261	47	52	97	13.227	0.873	3479.687	1.567	3232.893	1.502
50	470	61	72	124	11.047	0.866	4396.977	1.694	4553.960	1.712
100	901	88	152	175	10.640	0.864	4229.299	1.585	3393.036	1.676

Note: H_{isosat}: the isotropic elastic modulus with respect to matric suction, $H_{isosat} = (1 + \mu)/(1 - \mu) \cdot ds/d\varepsilon_v$; λ_v and η_v: the fitting parameters for estimating H_{vunsat}; λ_h and η_h: the fitting parameters for estimating H_{hunsat}.

Elastically isotropic behavior was assumed within the stress range under consideration. Namely, the elastic moduli E in the vertical and horizontal directions were considered to be the same. All of the test series for the OVS and OHS tests provided lateral pressure datasets covering net normal stresses ranging from 0 to 100 kPa under staged suction reductions. Predictions were generated using Equations (3) and (6) with the appropriate elastic moduli at given stress states calculated using Equations (15) and (16).

Figure 12a overlays the estimated and measured lateral pressure variations across the decreasing matric suction path for each test. Remarkably close correlations were observed regarding the fact that the datasets are distributed near both sides of the 1:1 perfect prediction line, demonstrating the suitability of the proposed constitutive relationships and prediction methods. However, as shown in Figure 12b, it presents significantly poorer alignment that would increasingly underestimate the lateral pressure of expansive soil by 5.8–61.0%, which can be a disaster for engineers designing geo-infrastructure in expansive soil distributed areas. In addition, the deviations between the measured and predicted lateral pressures were found to be relatively large at higher stress states, whether using the proposed method or the isotropic model. This may be due to the fact that the expansive soil has already entered the plasticity state under such large stress and even yielded, where the elastic constitutive model can no longer characterize its stress–strain behavior. Therefore, this proposed model and method are suggested for use in designing light structures with lateral confinements at shallow depths.

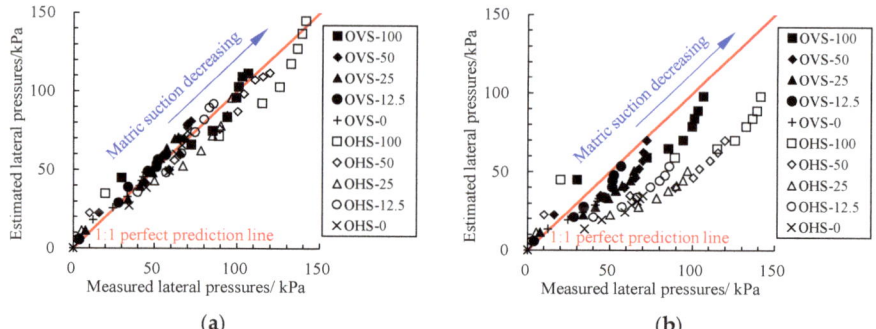

Figure 12. Comparison of the measured lateral pressure and the estimated lateral pressure by (**a**) the proposed method and (**b**) method without considering the anisotropic swelling behavior.

Five statistical indices were used to better evaluate the performance of the proposed method, including the correlation coefficient (R^2), refined Willmott index (RWI), mean arctangent absolute percentage error (MAAPE), root mean square error (RMSE), and mean absolute error (MAE). The model has larger R^2 and RWI, and smaller MAAPE, RMSE, and MAE performed best [34]. The calculation results of those statistical indices are summarized in Table 7.

Table 7. Summary of the calculating statistical indices for all test series.

Indices Test ID	R^2		RWI		MAAPE (%)		RMSE		MAE	
	ANI	ISO	ANI	ISO	ANI	ISO	ANI	ISO	ANI	ISO
OVS-0	0.9899	0.9898	0.9239	0.7610	/	/	2.6975	8.6487	1.99	7.45
OVS-12.5	0.9966	0.9712	0.9118	0.7788	9.9	20.4	2.7427	7.7028	2.35	6.86
OVS-25	0.9858	0.9761	0.8513	0.6464	12.2	30.8	4.4998	14.1332	3.96	13.52
OVS-50	0.9410	0.8940	0.7553	0.6935	13.4	21.9	7.0124	12.9584	6.46	11.63
OVS-100	0.9362	0.9038	0.7978	0.6529	11.8	21.6	8.3822	17.4199	7.32	16.81
OHS-0	0.9816	0.9882	0.8873	0.5856	/	/	5.3509	30.2147	4.27	27.86
OHS-12.5	0.9828	0.9751	0.8898	0.6022	16.7	47.5	5.2837	29.7645	4.63	27.77
OHS-25	0.9746	0.9549	0.8055	0.5631	22.7	54.3	11.1098	41.2384	10.06	38.76
OHS-50	0.9850	0.9193	0.8520	0.5633	18.6	50.7	9.3792	46.3975	8.65	44.06
OHS-100	0.9464	0.8835	0.7976	0.5681	17.9	43.2	15.3981	46.4962	13.52	45.22

Note: ANI: estimation using the proposed method (anisotropic consideration); ISO: estimation using Fredlund's nonlinear elastic model (isotropic consideration).

As depicted in Table 7, it can be observed that the proposed method that considers the swelling anisotropy performed reasonably well in terms of determining the lateral pressure of expansive soil, and it has a superior predictive ability with higher R^2 and RWI values and lower MAAPE, RMSE, and MAE values compared to the isotropic model.

In conclusion, validation with high-quality test measurements affirmed the ability of the anisotropic constitutive model and estimation techniques to predict lateral pressures. Significant improvement over isotropic assumptions justifies the consideration of intrinsic anisotropy for more realistic expansive soil modeling and design. The results demonstrate the effectiveness of the proposed framework in capturing true stress–strain–suction behavior. With further refinement, the approach holds promise as a practical tool for facilitating the wider usage of expansive soils in geotechnical applications through proper earth pressure assessments.

7. Conclusions

This study conducted a comprehensive experimental investigation into the anisotropic swelling behavior of expansive soils and developed predictive methodologies to estimate earth pressures considering this inherent anisotropy. Based on the results and findings, the following conclusions were drawn:

(1) Modified oedometer testing quantified clear anisotropy in expansive soil, with a maximum vertical swelling strain 1.71 times that of the horizontal direction. The swelling pressures were also directionally dependent, and the vertical swelling pressure was 1.57 times that of the horizontal one.

(2) A nonlinear elastic constitutive model was proposed incorporating vertical and horizontal elastic moduli with respect to matric suction to characterize swelling anisotropy. Three key elastic moduli were determined from the test data.

(3) The elastic moduli decreased nonlinearly with saturation and increased under higher confinement, exhibiting strong dependence on stress state and suction. The differences between the horizontal and vertical moduli quantify the macroscale manifestation of microstructural anisotropy.

(4) Simple predictive equations were developed to estimate unsaturated elastic moduli from saturated conditions via normalization. Validation affirmed the use of a constitutive model and predictive techniques as useful engineering tools for earth pressure assessments that consider expansive anisotropy.

In conclusion, these findings provide an improved understanding of more realistic characterization and utilization of expansive soils in geotechnical applications by properly accounting for their inherent anisotropic behavior. However, deviations between the measured and predicted lateral pressures were found to be relatively large at higher stress states; this proposed model and method are suggested to be used in designing light structures with lateral confinement at shallow depths. In addition, studies based on in situ soils and soils from other locations are necessary to further validate the methodology presented in this paper, and studies on swelling in an angular direction with respect to the direction of compaction should also be carried out.

Author Contributions: Conceptualization, Z.L. and R.Z.; methodology, Z.L. and R.Z.; validation, Z.L., T.L. and C.H.; formal analysis, Z.L. and T.L.; data curation, Y.Z. and C.H.; investigation, Z.L. and Y.Z.; writing—original draft preparation, Z.L. and Y.Z.; writing—review and editing, Z.L., T.L. and R.Z.; supervision, R.Z.; funding acquisition, Z.L., R.Z. and T.L. All authors have read and agreed to the published version of the manuscript.

Funding: This research was funded by the National Natural Science Foundations of China, grant numbers 52308436 and 51978085; the Research and Development Program of China National Railway Group Co., Ltd., grant number K2023G033; the Open Fund of National Key Laboratory of Green and Long-Life Road Engineering in Extreme Environment (Changsha University of Science & Technology), grant number kfj230106.

Institutional Review Board Statement: Not applicable.

Informed Consent Statement: Not applicable.

Data Availability Statement: The raw data supporting the conclusions of this article will be made available by the authors on request.

Conflicts of Interest: Author Zhengnan Liu was employed by the company Hunan Communications Research Institute Co., Ltd. The remaining authors declare that the research was conducted in the absence of any commercial or financial relationships that could be construed as a potential conflict of interest.

References

1. Puppala, A.J. Performance evaluation of infrastructure on problematic expansive soils: Characterization challenges, innovative stabilization designs, and monitoring methods. *J. Geotech. Geoenviron. Eng.* **2021**, *2021*, 147. [CrossRef]
2. Yao, H.; She, J.; Lu, Z.; Luo, X.; Xian, S.; Fang, R.; Chen, Z. Inhibition effect of swelling characteristics of expansive soil using cohesive non-swelling soil layer under unidirectional seepage. *J. Rock Mech. Geotech. Eng.* **2020**, *12*, 188–196. [CrossRef]
3. Miao, L.; Wang, F.; Ye, W.; Jiang, M.; Li, J.; Shi, S. Combined method limiting shrinkage–swelling behaviours of expansive soils in Huai'an, China. *Environ. Geotech.* **2021**, *8*, 334–344. [CrossRef]
4. Zheng, J.; Zhang, R.; Yang, H. Highway subgrade construction in expansive soil areas. *J. Mater. Civ. Eng.* **2009**, *21*, 154–162. [CrossRef]
5. Zada, U.; Jamal, A.; Iqbal, M.; Eldin, S.M.; Almoshaogeh, M.; Bekkouche, S.R.; Almuaythir, S. Recent advances in expansive soil stabilization using admixtures: Current challenges and opportunities. *Case Stud. Constr. Mater.* **2023**, *18*, e01985. [CrossRef]
6. Zhang, J.; Ding, L.; Li, F.; Peng, J. Recycled aggregates from construction and demolition wastes as alternative filling materials for highway subgrades in China. *J. Clean. Prod.* **2020**, *255*, 120223. [CrossRef]
7. Sarker, D.; Apu, O.S.; Kumar, N. Sustainable lignin to enhance engineering properties of unsaturated expansive subgrade soils. *J. Mater. Civ. Eng.* **2023**, *35*, 04023259. [CrossRef]
8. Zhang, R.; Liu, Z.; Zheng, J.; Lei, G. Utilisation of expansive soils as highway embankment materials in humid environments. *Int. J. Pavement Eng.* **2022**, *23*, 2176–2190. [CrossRef]
9. Cui, X.; Li, X.; Du, Y.; Bao, Z.; Zhang, X.; Hao, J.; Hu, Y. Macro-micro numerical analysis of granular materials considering principal stress rotation based on DEM simulation of dynamic hollow cylinder test. *Constr. Build. Mater.* **2024**, *412*, 134818. [CrossRef]
10. Liu, Y.; Vanapalli, S.K. Influence of lateral swelling pressure on the geotechnical infrastructure in expansive soils. *J. Geotech. Geoenviron. Eng.* **2017**, *143*, 04017006. [CrossRef]
11. Oh, W.T.; Vanapalli, S.K. Modeling the stress versus settlement behavior of shallow foundations in unsaturated cohesive soils extending the modified total stress approach. *Soils Found.* **2018**, *58*, 382–397. [CrossRef]
12. Nelson, J.D.; Chao, K.C.; Overton, D.D.; Nelson, E.J. *Foundation Engineering for Expansive Soils*; John Wiley & Sons: Hoboken, NJ, USA, 2015.
13. Qi, S.; Vanapalli, S.K. Influence of swelling behavior on the stability of an infinite unsaturated expansive soil slope. *Comput. Geotech.* **2016**, *76*, 154–169. [CrossRef]
14. Tu, H.; Vanapalli, S.K. Prediction of the variation of swelling pressure and 1-D heave of expansive soils with respect to suction using the soil water retention curve as a tool. *Can. Geotech. J.* **2016**, *53*, 1213–1234. [CrossRef]
15. Fredlund, D.G.; Morgenstern, N.R. Constitutive relations for volume change in unsaturated soils. *Can. Geotech. J.* **1976**, *13*, 261–276. [CrossRef]
16. Adem, H.H.; Vanapalli, S.K. Prediction of the modulus of elasticity of compacted unsaturated expansive soils. *Int. J. Geotech. Eng.* **2015**, *9*, 163–175. [CrossRef]
17. Han, Z.; Vanapalli, S.K. State-of-the-Art: Prediction of resilient modulus of unsaturated subgrade soils. *Int. J. Geomech.* **2016**, *16*, 04015104. [CrossRef]
18. Avsar, E.; Ulusay, R.; Sonmez, H. Assessments of Swelling Anisotropy of Ankara clay. *Eng. Geol.* **2009**, *105*, 24–31. [CrossRef]
19. Jia, L.-Y.; Chen, Y.-G.; Ye, W.-M.; Cui, Y.-J. Effects of a Simulated Gap on Anisotropic Swelling Pressure of Compacted GMZ Bentonite. *Eng. Geol.* **2019**, *248*, 155–163. [CrossRef]
20. Saba, S.; Cui, Y.-J.; Barnichon, J.-D.; Tang, A.M. Infiltration column for studying the lateral swell behavior of expansive clay. *Geotech. Test. J.* **2016**, *39*, 407–414. [CrossRef]
21. Zhu, Y.; Ye, W.; Wang, Q.; Lu, Y.; Chen, Y. Anisotropic Volume Change Behaviour of Uniaxial Compacted GMZ Bentonite under Free Swelling Condition. *Eng. Geol.* **2020**, *278*, 105821. [CrossRef]
22. Sahin, H.; Slowey, N.C.; Lytton, R.L. Volume measurement of expansive soils and its application during the design of a retaining wall in Texas. *J. Mater. Civ. Eng.* **2018**, *30*, 04018114. [CrossRef]
23. Zou, W.-L.; Han, Z.; Vanapalli, S.K.; Zhang, J.-F.; Zhao, G.-T. Predicting volumetric behavior of compacted clays during compression. *Appl. Clay Sci.* **2018**, *156*, 116–125. [CrossRef]
24. Li, J.; Zhang, J.; Zhang, A.; Peng, J. Evaluation on deformation behavior of granular base material during repeated load triaxial testing by discrete-element method. *Int. J. Geomech.* **2022**, *22*, 04022210. [CrossRef]
25. Zhang, R.; Liu, Z.; Zheng, J.; Zhang, J. Experimental evaluation of lateral swelling pressure of expansive soil fill behind a retaining wall. *J. Mater. Civ. Eng.* **2020**, *32*, 04019360. [CrossRef]
26. Rawat, A.; Baille, W.; Tripathy, S. Swelling behavior of compacted bentonite-sand mixture during water infiltration. *Eng. Geol.* **2019**, *257*, 105–141. [CrossRef]
27. Abbas, M.F.; Elkady, T.Y.; Al-Shamrani, M.A. Evaluation of strain and stress states of a compacted highly expansive soil using a thin-walled oedometer. *Eng. Geol.* **2015**, *193*, 132–145. [CrossRef]
28. Liu, Z.; Zhang, R.; Liu, Z.; Zhang, Y. Experimental study on swelling behavior and its anisotropic evaluation of unsaturated expansive soil. *Adv. Mater. Sci. Eng.* **2021**, *2021*, 6937240. [CrossRef]
29. *ASTM D1557-12e1*; Standard Test Methods for Laboratory Compaction Characteristics of Soil Using Modified Effort (56,000 ft-lbf/Ft3 (2700 kN-m/m3)). American Society for Testing Materials: West Conshohocken, PA, USA, 2012.

30. CCCC (China Communications Construction Co., Ltd.); First Highway Consultants Co., Ltd. *JTG C20-2011 Code for Highway Engineering Geological Investigation*; China Communication Press: Beijing, China, 2011.
31. *ASTM D2435/D2435M-11*; Standard Test Method for One-Dimensional Consolidation Properties of Soils Using Incremental Loading. American Society for Testing Materials: West Conshohocken, PA, USA, 2011.
32. Zhang, R.; Zhang, B.; Zheng, J.; Liu, Z. Modified lateral confined swelling tests on expansive soils. *Chin. J. Geotech. Eng.* **2018**, *40*, 2223–2230. (In Chinese)
33. Kumar, S.; Cao, D.T.; Vahedifard, F. Poisson's ratio characteristic curve of unsaturated soils. *J. Geotech. Geoenviron. Eng.* **2021**, *147*, 04020149. [CrossRef]
34. Raja, M.N.A.; Shukla, S.K. Predicting the settlement of geosynthetic-reinforced soil foundations using evolutionary artificial intelligence technique. *Geotext. Geomembr.* **2021**, *49*, 1280–1293. [CrossRef]

Disclaimer/Publisher's Note: The statements, opinions and data contained in all publications are solely those of the individual author(s) and contributor(s) and not of MDPI and/or the editor(s). MDPI and/or the editor(s) disclaim responsibility for any injury to people or property resulting from any ideas, methods, instructions or products referred to in the content.

Article

Investigation of the Effect of Relative Density on the Dynamic Modulus and Damping Ratio for Coarse Grained Soil

Ziying Huang [1], Sen Cai [2,3,4], Rongfen Hu [2,3,4], Jianfeng Wang [2,3,4], Mingjie Jiang [2,3,4],* and Jian Gong [2,3,4]

1. Faculty of Architecture, Civil and Transportation Engineering, Beijing University of Technology, Beijing 100124, China; huangziying@emails.bjut.edu.cn
2. College of Civil Engineering and Architecture, Guangxi University, Nanning 530004, China; 17788504842@163.com (S.C.); 19176598247@163.com (R.H.); 18751957312@163.com (J.W.); jiangong@gxu.edu.cn (J.G.)
3. Key Laboratory of Disaster Prevention and Structural Safety of Ministry of Education, Guangxi University, Nanning 530004, China
4. d. Key Laboratory of Disaster Prevention and Mitigation and Engineering Safety of Guangxi, Guangxi University, Nanning 530004, China
* Correspondence: 20180121@gxu.edu.cn

Abstract: As the critical dynamic parameters for soil, an extensive examination of the dynamic elastic modulus E_d and damping ratio λ in coarse-grained soil is of significant theoretical and practical importance. Currently, there is a scarcity of experimental equipment and methods for measuring the dynamic elastic modulus and damping ratio of coarse-grained soils. Moreover, studies examining the influence of relative density on these parameters in coarse-grained soils are largely absent. To investigate the behavior of the dynamic elastic modulus and damping ratio in coarse-grained soil under varying relative densities, a number of dynamic triaxial tests were conducted on a specific coarse-grained soil using the DYNTTS type dynamic triaxial test apparatus. The findings reveal that, under various gradations, the E_d of coarse-grained soils exhibits a decreasing trend with increasing dynamic strain, a trend that intensifies with higher relative densities. Additionally, as relative density increases, the degradation rate of the dynamic shear modulus ratio G_d/G_{dmax} to dynamic shear strain γ_d curve escalates. The maximum dynamic shear modulus G_{dmax} rises with increasing relative density D_r, displaying a linear relationship between G_{dmax} and D_r. Furthermore, both the increasing rate of λ to γ_d curve and the maximum damping ratio λ_{max} progressively diminish with the escalation of relative density D_r. Notably, the maximum damping ratio has a power function relationship with the relative density.

Keywords: dynamic elastic modulus; damping ratio; coarse-grained soil; relative density; maximum dynamic shear modulus

Citation: Huang, Z.; Cai, S.; Hu, R.; Wang, J.; Jiang, M.; Gong, J. Investigation of the Effect of Relative Density on the Dynamic Modulus and Damping Ratio for Coarse Grained Soil. *Appl. Sci.* **2024**, *14*, 6847. https://doi.org/10.3390/app14156847

Academic Editor: Tiago Miranda

Received: 18 June 2024
Revised: 21 July 2024
Accepted: 24 July 2024
Published: 5 August 2024

Copyright: © 2024 by the authors. Licensee MDPI, Basel, Switzerland. This article is an open access article distributed under the terms and conditions of the Creative Commons Attribution (CC BY) license (https://creativecommons.org/licenses/by/4.0/).

1. Introduction

Rockfill dams, a type of embankment dam constructed using rockfill materials, are increasingly preferred in Southwest China due to their strong adaptability to geological environments, the feasibility of using local materials, lower construction costs, and superior seismic performance [1,2]. The complex geological conditions and frequent seismic activities in this region make seismic performance a critical factor for the safety of these dams. A failure in seismic resistance could lead to catastrophic societal consequences. Thus, optimizing the seismic design of rockfill dams and enhancing their seismic performance are of paramount importance. In this context, the dynamic elastic modulus and damping ratio, as key parameters for soil dynamics, are the focal points in this analysis.

Coarse-grained soil, often employed as a filling material in rockfill dam projects, is chosen for its excellent engineering characteristics like high permeability, strength, and minimal compression deformation. Accurately determining its dynamic elastic modulus and damping ratio is crucial for the seismic design of rockfill dams. Consequently, in-depth research into these parameters holds significant theoretical and engineering value [3].

There has been substantial research by international scholars on the dynamic elastic modulus, the dynamic shear modulus, and damping ratio of coarse-grained soils. Studies from Sawangsuriya [4], Kokusho [5], Saxena [6], Li Yangbo [7], and others have indicated that the dynamic elastic modulus and damping ratio all trend to increase when pressure and frequency increase. The maximum dynamic elastic modulus of coarse-grained soil was empirically formulated by Wang [8], considering the confining pressure and frequency, based on extensive data from large-scale dynamic triaxial tests. Fang [9] conducted tests on limestone aggregate using a static and dynamic simple shear testing device, developing an estimation formula for the maximum dynamic shear modulus that considers the effects of confining pressure, consolidation ratio, gradation, and porosity characteristics. Du [10] investigated the influence of factors like the consolidation ratio on the dynamic modulus and damping ratio of materials used in dam construction, including dam shell, heart wall, and dam foundation fault materials, through dynamic triaxial tests. Research by Matsui [11] and Yasuhara [12], and subsequent work by Zhou [13], indicated that higher confining pressure and vibration frequencies increase soil stiffness and stabilize soil dynamics, leading to the development of a dynamic strain backbone curve model that considers vibration cycles and confining pressure.

Overall, the investigations into the dynamic modulus and damping ratio of coarse-grained soil have primarily focused on factors like confining pressure, consolidation ratio, vibration, and porosity characteristics. However, studies specifically addressing the impact of relative density on these parameters in coarse-grained soil are less frequent. Limited research, such as that by Fu [14] and Wang [15], has provided only qualitative insights, leaving the quantitative relationship between relative density and the dynamic modulus and damping ratio of coarse-grained soil largely unexplored. This gap highlights the current inadequacy in understanding the influence of relative density on these parameters, emphasizing the need for more quantitative research. Zhu [16,17] underscored the significance of relative density as a mechanical parameter reflecting the physical state of soil, heavily influencing the mechanical characteristics of coarse-grained soil. Therefore, quantitative experimental research into how relative density affects the dynamic modulus and damping ratio of coarse-grained soil is imperative.

Therefore, this study utilizes a GDS large-scale dynamic-static triaxial apparatus for dynamic triaxial testing on compacted samples of a specific coarse-grained soil. Leveraging the results from these tests, this research quantitatively examines the impact of relative density on the dynamic modulus and damping ratio of coarse-grained soil. Additionally, it formulates a computational model that precisely elucidates the correlation between the maximum dynamic shear modulus, the maximum damping ratio, and relative density, thereby contributing to an enhanced comprehension of the seismic behavior exhibited by rockfill dams.

2. Testing Apparatus and Program

2.1. Instruments and Equipment

In this study, the DYNTTS type coarse-grained soil dynamic triaxial testing system was employed. This system comprises a data acquisition device, a volume controller, a back pressure, a confining pressure controller, a mainframe that governs axial stress and displacement, and a data display unit, as depicted in Figure 1. The instrument's principal specifications include a maximum confining pressure of 1 MPa, an axial load capacity of 60 kN, a load vibration frequency ranging from 0 to 2 Hz, an axial displacement scope of 0 to 88 mm, and an axial force measurement precision of 0.0001 kN. This system is capable of conducting dynamic performance evaluations on samples measuring 300 mm in diameter and 600 mm in height. The experimental procedure encompasses five phases: sample preparation, saturation, consolidation, loading, and unloading, with further details provided in reference [18].

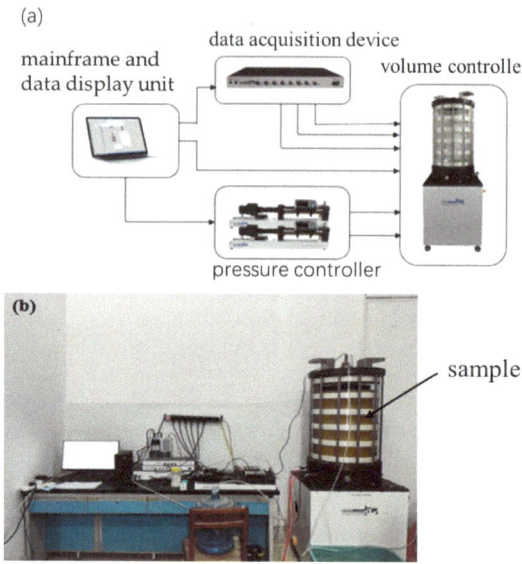

Figure 1. DYNTTS coarse-grained soil dynamic triaxial test system (**a**,**b**).

2.2. Specimen Preparation Standard

The soil material utilized by the experiments was sourced from the Pingnan Sanqiao construction site, consisting of sand, pebbles, and gravel. These particles are predominantly rounded and exhibit a grayish-white hue. Figure 2 displays the appearance of the various particle sizes in this material. Samples, labeled S1 to S3, were characterized by gradations, as depicted in Figure 3.

Figure 2. Sieved soil material for each grain group.

The sample preparation was based on the relative density standard, with the relative densities of each group of samples set at 0.9, 0.7, 0.5, and 0.3, respectively. To ensure the required density for each group during sample preparation, relative density tests were conducted according to the experimental gradation. The relative density tests were carried out using a surface vibratory compactor for coarse-grained soils, as shown in Figure 4. The relevant test parameters for this device are as follows: the inner diameter of the sample cylinder is 28 cm, the volume is 14,200 cm^3, the vibration frequency is 47.5 Hz, the excitation force ranges from 10 to 80 kN, and the static pressure exerted by the tamper plate is above 18 kPa.

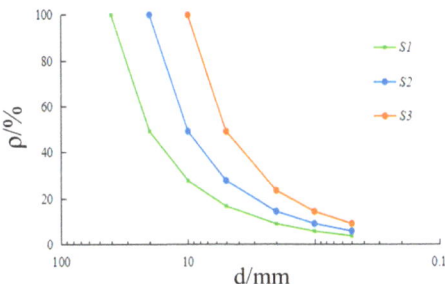

Figure 3. Gradation curves of experimental coarse-grained soils.

Figure 4. Surface vibratory compactor for coarse-grained soils.

By controlling the mass of the soil sample, the desired density for each group of samples can be achieved. The maximum dry density (ρ_{max}) of each experimental gradation was determined using the surface vibratory compaction method, and the minimum dry density (ρ_{min}) was determined using the loose filling method. The measured ρ_{max} and ρ_{min} for each gradation were then substituted into the relative density formula to calculate the dry density required to achieve the corresponding relative density, and, subsequently, the required mass of soil for each group of samples was derived.

The corresponding dry density values for these relative densities are detailed in Table 1.

Table 1. Dry density physical parameters.

Specimen Number	Maximum Particle Diameter/mm	Minimum Dry Density/(g·cm^{-3})	Maximum Dry Density/(g·cm^{-3})	Dry Density/(g·cm^{-3})			
				$D_r = 0.9$	$D_r = 0.7$	$D_r = 0.5$	$D_r = 0.3$
S1	40	1.884	2.244	2.202	2.122	2.048	1.979
S2	20	1.844	2.174	2.136	2.063	1.995	1.932
S3	10	1.798	2.1	2.065	1.999	1.937	1.879

2.3. Test Method

The corresponding dry density values for these relative densities are detailed in Table 1. The experiment was conducted based on the "Standard for Soil Test Method" (GB/T50123-2019) [18], using sample sizes of diameter 300 mm and height 600 mm. The process was divided into five steps: sample preparation, saturation, consolidation, loading, and sample removal. The specific details are as follows:

1. Sample Preparation:

The sample was directly placed on the instrument base. A layer of petroleum jelly was applied around the instrument base and the inside of the membrane holder to prevent water and air leakage during the experiment. After fixing the rubber membrane to the base and installing the membrane holder, a vacuum pump was used to draw air out, causing the rubber membrane to adhere to the holder. The test used air-dried material, forming the sample by controlling the compaction. The weighed test material was evenly divided into six portions, each portion was placed into the membrane holder in four layers, compacted, and roughened to achieve the predetermined dry density. After filling the sample, a vacuum was applied to maintain a negative pressure of 20 kPa, and then the membrane holder was removed.

2. Saturation:

After sample preparation, to ensure the sealed state during the experiment, the rubber ring around the instrument base was cleaned. After cleaning, the pressure chamber was installed and filled with water. Maintain a constant water temperature to control the environmental temperature during the testing process. The sample was saturated using the water head saturation method: after the pressure chamber was filled with water, water injection was stopped, and CO_2 was introduced from the bottom of the sample to replace the air in the pores. Then, air-free water was injected from the bottom, and once water emerged from the top, the water head saturation method was used to gradually saturate the sample from bottom to top. The saturation was considered complete when the pore pressure coefficient B value reached above 0.95.

3. Consolidation:

The sample was consolidated by controlling the stress. While maintaining constant confining pressure, the sample was subjected to drained consolidation with a consolidation ratio K_c of 2.0. Initially, isotropic consolidation was performed, and once the sample stabilized, the axial pressure was gradually increased to avoid severe deformation due to the sudden application of excessive axial pressure. Throughout the consolidation process, the sample's drainage was continuously monitored, and consolidation was considered complete when the drainage volume did not exceed 15 mL within 30 min.

4. Loading:

Stress-controlled loading was used in the experiment. A confining pressure of 200 kPa was selected. After consolidation, while maintaining the confining pressure constant, axial dynamic stress was applied in stages from small to large. Each level of dynamic stress was $\sigma_d = \pm 0.3\sigma_3, 0.4\sigma_3, 0.5\sigma_3, \ldots$, and the next level of loading could only proceed after completing the previous level. Each level of dynamic stress was cycled for six cycles, and the data from the third cycle was selected for analysis. Additionally, the vibration waveform used in the experiment was a sine wave with a vibration frequency of 0.33 Hz.

5. Sample Removal:

After completing all loading tasks, the confining pressure and axial pressure were gradually unloaded, data acquisition and control programs were turned off, the drainage valve was opened to empty the pressure chamber, and the pressure chamber was removed. Finally, the sample was dismantled and the site was cleaned.

3. Interpretation of Experimental Results

3.1. Relation of Dynamic Elastic Modulus and Dynamic Strain

For this analysis, data from average value to three cycles of each dynamic loading level were employed. The relationship curves depicting the dynamic strain (ε_d) against dynamic elastic modulus (E_d) for samples S1 to S3 are illustrated in Figure 5. The graph indicates that under a constant dynamic load, the decrease in relative density results in an increase in the dynamic strain experienced by specimens and a reduction in the rate at which the dynamic elastic modulus decreases. Specifically, it can be seen that ε_d of the sample with the same relative density (D_r) of 0.3 is larger. Under the same dynamic strain conditions, the sample with $D_r = 0.9$ showed the most significant decrease in the dynamic modulus. This variation is attributed to the transition from tight to loose contact among coarse- and fine-grained particles as Dr decreases, thereby diminishing the structural capacity to resist deformation. Consequently, under identical dynamic loads, a higher dynamic strain is observed. While the contact remains relatively firm at $D_r = 0.7$, resulting in a minor deviation from the curve with $D_r = 0.9$, the contact becomes considerably looser at $D_r = 0.5$ and 0.3, significantly reducing structural resistance, hence the notable disparity from the curve with $D_r = 0.9$.

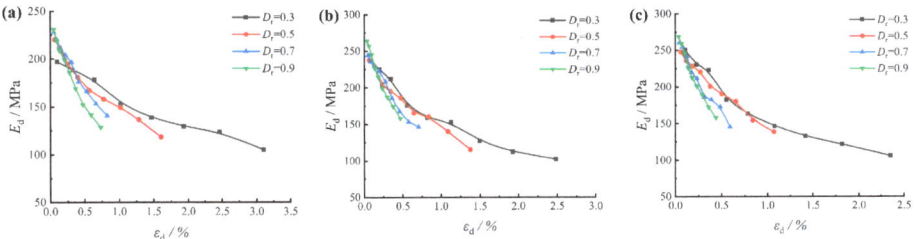

Figure 5. E_d-ε_d relationship curves: (**a**) D2-1, (**b**) D2-2, (**c**) D2-4.

A further comparative analysis of Figure 5a–c indicates, under identical density conditions, an increase in maximum particle size correlates with increasing dynamic elastic modulus and decreasing dynamic strain. This trend can be attributed to the denser packing of coarse- and fine-grained particles and enhanced inter-particle contact in samples with larger maximum particle sizes, leading to increased resistance to deformation.

3.2. Relation of the Dynamic Shear Modulus Ratio and Dynamic Shear Strain

Contemporary research on dynamic properties for coarse-grained soils predominantly employs the Hardin-Drnevich model [18]. This model describes the correlation between the dynamic shear strain (γ_d) and the dynamic shear modulus ratio (G_d/G_{dmax}) in coarse-grained soils, as per the following relationship:

$$\frac{G_d}{G_{dmax}} = \frac{1}{1 + \gamma_d/\gamma_r} \qquad (1)$$

where γ_r represents the reference shear strain.

Figure 6a–c depict the results of G_d/G_{dmax} and γ_d tests for samples S1 to S3 under varying relative densities, alongside their fitting curves based on Equation (1). These Figures demonstrate a strong correlation and a satisfactory fit between the experimental data and the fitting curves. Upon analyzing Figure 6, it is noted that the attenuation rate of G_d/G_{dmax} varies with different relative densities (D_r). In general, the higher the relative density D_r, the greater the rate of decay of G_d/G_{dmax} with increasing dynamic shear strain (γ_d), and the more pronounced the overall decay trend.

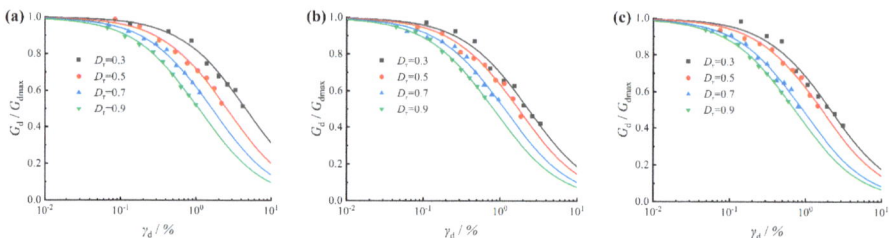

Figure 6. G_d/G_{dmax}-γ_d fitted relationship curves: (**a**) S1, (**b**) S2, (**c**) S3.

3.3. Relation of Dynamic Shear Strain and the Damping Ratio

Based on the existing studies on rockfill materials [19], the relationship of λ of soil and γ_d can be described as follows:

$$\lambda = \gamma_d/(c + d\gamma_d) \tag{2}$$

$$1/\lambda = c/\gamma_d + d \tag{3}$$

where c and d represent experimental parameters, with the inverse of the linear intercept d defining the maximum damping ratio λ_{max}.

Figure 7a–c delineate the relationship of λ of soil and γ_d samples S1 to S3 under varying relative densities. The curves reveal considerable disparities in the λ-γ_d relationships across different relative densities. For shear strains below 10^{-2}, λ progressively increases with rising γ_d. The rate of increase is more pronounced in samples exhibiting lower relative densities. Notably, the sample with a relative density (D_r) of 0.3 exhibits the most rapid augmentation in damping ratio, significantly outpacing those with D_r = 0.5, 0.7, and 0.9. These observations underscore the profound impact of compaction on the soil's energy dissipation capacity. Looser soils demonstrate easier energy dissipation, leading to higher damping ratios.

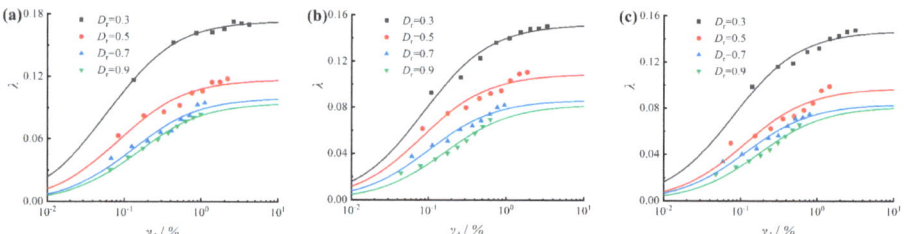

Figure 7. λ-γ_d fitted relationship curves: (**a**) S1, (**b**) S2, (**c**) S3.

4. Influence of Relative Density on the Maximum Dynamic Shear Modulus

By arranging 12 sets of dynamic triaxial test results of graded samples S1–S3 under different relative compactness D_r of 0.3, 0.5, 0.7, and 0.9, the relationship between the relative compactness D_r and the maximum dynamic shear modulus G_{dmax} was obtained, as depicted in Figure 8. Figure 8 illustrates that, for a constant maximum particle size, G_{dmax} incrementally increases with an increase in D_r. Further analysis and fitting of these 12 datasets using fitting software (origin) revealed a linear relationship between D_r and G_{dmax}, represented by this Equation:

$$G_{dmax} = eD_r + f \tag{4}$$

where e and f are parameters, with e being the slope and f representing the maximum dynamic shear modulus at D_r = 0.

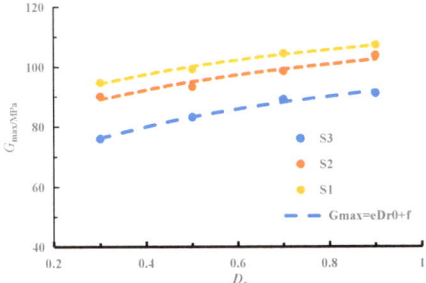

Figure 8. G_{dmax}–D_r fitted relationship curves.

Fitting these 12 datasets with Equation (4) and summarizing the results in Table 2 shows a high congruence between the fitted curves and experimental points, with coefficients of determination exceeding 0.96. The maximum discrepancy between the fitted and experimental values of G_{dmax} was less than 2%. Consequently, this study posits that the relationship between D_r and G_{dmax} can be effectively described by Equation (4). Consistent with these findings, Yang [20] reported, in his research using a resonant column apparatus on sand, that the relative density of sand has a linear positive correlation with its maximum dynamic shear modulus.

Table 2. Fitting results of Equation (4).

Specimen Number	Maximum Dynamic Shear Modulus		
	e	f	R^2
S1	25.653	69.060	0.961
S2	22.076	82.776	0.986
S3	21.066	88.061	0.975

5. Influence of Relative Density on the Maximum Damping Ratio

The maximum damping ratio (λ_{max}) of granular materials at various relative densities (D_r) is presented in Figure 9. Figure 9 shows that λ_{max} inversely correlates with D_r, decreasing as D_r increases, a trend that is opposite to that observed for the maximum dynamic shear modulus.

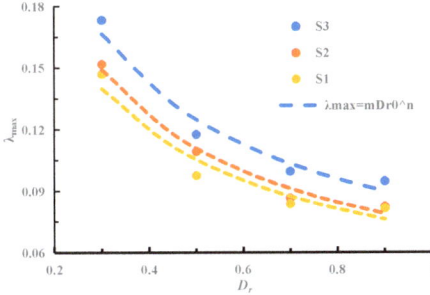

Figure 9. λ_{max} vs. D_r fitted relationship curves.

Figure 9 also reveals that the attenuation rate of λ_{max} progressively diminishes with increasing D_r. This is likely due to tighter particle contacts at higher D_r, resulting in smaller relative displacements under external forces, thereby leading to a reduced damping ratio.

Analysis and fitting of these 12 datasets using fitting software suggest that D_r and $\lambda_{\max}$ exhibit a power law relationship, expressed by this Equation:

$$\lambda_{\max} = mD_r^n \tag{5}$$

where m and n are parameters.

Fitting these 12 datasets with Equation (5) and summarizing the results in Table 3, Table 3 demonstrates a high congruence between the fitting curves and the experimental data, with coefficients of determination exceeding 0.93. The maximum discrepancy between the fitted and experimental values of $\lambda_{\max}$ was under 5%. Hence, this study posits that the relationship between relative density D_r and $\lambda_{\max}$ can be effectively described by Equation (5).

Table 3. Fitting results of Equation (5).

Specimen Number	Maximum Damping Ratio		
	m	n	R^2
S1	0.0072	−0.554	0.9533
S2	0.074	−0.58	0.978
S3	0.085	−0.563	0.957

6. Conclusions

This paper, through dynamic triaxial testing of 12 groups of coarse-grained soil samples at varying relative densities, investigates the impact of relative density on the dynamic elastic modulus and the damping ratio (λ) of coarse-grained soils. The conclusions are as follows:

1. The dynamic elastic modulus of coarse-grained soil progressively diminishes with increasing dynamic strain. The attenuation rate of dynamic elastic modulus escalates with increasing relative density; the rate of decay of the coarse-grained soil's normalized dynamic shear modulus with increasing dynamic shear strain also rises with an increase in relative density, with the attenuation trend becoming more distinct at higher relative density values. Additionally, the rate of increase in the damping ratio–dynamic shear strain relationship curve gradually decreases as relative density increases.
2. The maximum dynamic shear modulus of coarse-grained soil increases with an increase in relative density. An empirical formula has been established to describe the relationship between the maximum dynamic shear modulus and relative density of coarse-grained soil.
3. The maximum damping ratio of coarse-grained soil decreases progressively with increasing relative density. An empirical formula has been developed to delineate the relationship between the maximum damping ratio and relative density of coarse-grained soil.

The conclusions drawn in this article are helpful for the construction of coarse-grained soil engineering such as dams and retaining walls, and the formulas obtained can provide reference for further research on the dynamic performance of coarse-grained soil.

Author Contributions: Conceptualization, Z.H. and M.J.; methodology, R.H.; software, S.C.; formal analysis, J.W. and J.G.; resources, M.J.; data curation, Z.H.; writing—original draft preparation, M.J.; writing—review and editing, M.J.; project administration, M.J. and J.G.; funding acquisition, M.J. and J.G. All authors have read and agreed to the published version of the manuscript.

Funding: The authors gratefully acknowledge the financial support from a project from Guangxi Natural Science Foundation (No. 2021GXNSFBA196091), a project from Guangxi Science and Technology (No. AA23023016), a project from Inner Mongolia Transportation Department Construction Technology (No. NJ-2021-10).

Data Availability Statement: The data presented in this study are available on request from the corresponding author. The data are not publicly available due to privacy restrictions.

Conflicts of Interest: The authors declare no conflicts of interest.

References

1. Guo, Q. *Engineering Properties and Application of Coarse-Grained Soil*; Yellow River Conservancy Press: Zhengzhou, China, 1998.
2. Xu, Z. Key Technologies and Geotechnical Problems in Contemporary High Rockfill Dam Construction. *J. Geotech. Eng.* **2011**, *33*, 34–40.
3. Menq, F.Y.; Stokoe, K. *Linear Dynamic Properties of Sandy and Gravelly Soils from Large-Scale Resonant Tests*; A. A. Balkema: Lisse, The Netherlands, 2003.
4. Sawangsuriya, A.; Bosscher, P.J.; Edil, T.B. Alternative Testing Techniques for Modulus of Pavement Bases and Subgrades. In Proceedings of the Great Lakes Geotechnical & Geoenvironmental Conference, Milwaukee, WI, USA, 13 May 2005.
5. Kokusho, T. Cyclic Triaxial Test of Dynamic Soil Properties for Wide Strain Range. *Soils Found.* **1980**, *20*, 45–60. [CrossRef] [PubMed]
6. Saxena, S.K.; Reddy, K.R. Dynamic Moduli and Damping Ratios for Monterey No. 0 Sand by Resonant Column Tests. *Soils Found.* **1989**, *29*, 37–51.
7. Li, Y.; Zhang, J.; Zhu, Z.; Wang, X.; Shi, X. Research on Dynamic Characteristics of Coarse-Grained Soil for Railway Subgrade under Graded Loading. *J. Railw. Sci. Eng.* **2019**, *16*, 620–628.
8. Wang, J. Experimental Study on Dynamic Elastic Modulus and Damping Ratio of Coarse-Grained Soil. Master's Thesis, Central South University, Changsha, China, 2013.
9. Fang, E. Research on Dynamic Properties of Dam Building Materials. Thesis, Dalian University of Technology, Dalian, China, 2015.
10. Du, C.; Xie, H.; Xiao, M.; He, C.R.; He, J.D. Experimental Study on Dynamic Properties of Dam Building Materials in Seismic Areas. *J. Sichuan Univ. Eng. Sci. Ed.* **2016**, *48*, 39–44.
11. Matsui, T.; Bahr, M.A.; Abe, N. Estimation of Shear Characteristics Degradation and Stress-Strain Relationship of Saturated Clays after Cyclic Loading. *Soils Found.* **1992**, *32*, 161–172. [CrossRef]
12. Yasuhara, K. Post-cyclic Degradation of Saturated Plasticity Silts. *Cycl. Behav. Soils Liq. Phenom.* **2004**, 275–286.
13. Zhou, W.; Leng, W.; Liu, W.; Nie, R.S.; Yang, Q.; Zhao, C.Y. Study on Dynamic Characteristics and Backbone Curve Model of Saturated Coarse-Grained Soil under Low Confining Pressure Cyclic Loading. *Rock Soil Mech.* **2016**, *37*, 415–423.
14. Fu, H.; Han, H.; Ling, H. Experimental Study on the Influence of Density on Dynamic Properties of Coarse Particulate Materials. *J. China Inst. Water Resour. Hydropower Res.* **2014**, *12*, 437–441.
15. Wang, B. Study on Static and Dynamic Properties of Saturated Round Gravel Soil in Nanning Metro Area. Ph.D. Thesis, Guangxi University, Nanning, China, 2018.
16. Zhu, J.; Shi, J.; Luo, X.; Xu, J. Experimental Study on Stress-Strain-Strength Behavior of Sand with Different Densities. *Chin. J. Geotech. Eng.* **2016**, *38*, 336–341.
17. Zhu, J.; Guo, W.L.; Xu, J.C.; Chu, F.Y. DEM Analysis on Impact of Gradation and Compactness on Coarse-Grained Soil in Tri-Axial Test. *J. Chongqing Jiaotong Univ.* **2017**, *36*, 70–74.
18. Liu, X.; Zhang, J.; Liu, M. Exploration of Test Methods in GB/T 50123—2019 "Standards for Soil Test Methods". *Tianjin Constr. Sci. Technol.* **2020**, *30*, 1–4.
19. Hardin, B.O.; Drnevich, V.P. Shear Modulus and Damping in Soils: Design Equations and Curves. *Geotech. Spec. Publ.* **1972**, *98*, 667–692. [CrossRef]
20. Yang, P. Study on the Effect of Particle Grading and Compaction on the Dynamic Deformation Characteristics of Sand. Master's Thesis, Jiangsu University, Zhenjiang, China, 2021.

Disclaimer/Publisher's Note: The statements, opinions and data contained in all publications are solely those of the individual author(s) and contributor(s) and not of MDPI and/or the editor(s). MDPI and/or the editor(s) disclaim responsibility for any injury to people or property resulting from any ideas, methods, instructions or products referred to in the content.

Article

An Investigation of Particle Motion and Energy Dissipation Mechanisms in Soil–Rock Mixtures with Varying Mixing Degrees under Vibratory Compaction

Wei Wang [1], Wei Hu [2,3] and Shunkai Liu [2,3,*]

[1] School of Road and Bridge Engineering, Hunan Communication Engineering Polytechnic, Changsha 410132, China; wangwei@hnust.edu.cn
[2] School of Civil Engineering, Hunan University of Science and Technology, Xiangtan 411201, China; yilukuangben1982@163.com
[3] Hunan Province Key Laboratory of Geotechnical Engineering Stability Control and Health Monitoring, Hunan University of Science and Technology, Xiangtan 411201, China
* Correspondence: lsk1019@hnust.edu.cn

Abstract: Soil–rock mixture (S–RM) is a heterogeneous granular material commonly used in engineering applications, but achieving uniform particle mixing is challenging. This study investigated the effect of mixing homogeneity on the compaction of S–RM using the discrete element method (DEM). Specimens with varying degrees of mixing were modeled under realistic vibration loading. The results showed that a higher degree of mixing resulted in a smaller void ratio after compaction. The analysis of particle motion and energy dissipation revealed that not all particle motion during vibration compaction was aligned with the direction of the particle system. However, rotation was more prevalent and contributed to densification. Dashpot energy dissipation did not solely promote changes in the void ratio, while slip energy dissipation did lead to changes in the void ratio, but not entirely towards compaction. Rolling slip energy dissipation primarily occurred during the stage of void ratio changes and significantly promoted compaction. The change in strain energy aligned with the trend of the void ratio but did not directly contribute to its promotion.

Keywords: vibratory compaction; soil–rock mixture; degree of mixing; particle motion; energy dissipation

Citation: Wang, W.; Hu, W.; Liu, S. An Investigation of Particle Motion and Energy Dissipation Mechanisms in Soil–Rock Mixtures with Varying Mixing Degrees under Vibratory Compaction. *Appl. Sci.* **2023**, *13*, 11359. https://doi.org/10.3390/app132011359

Academic Editor: Tiago Miranda

Received: 27 September 2023
Revised: 11 October 2023
Accepted: 14 October 2023
Published: 16 October 2023

Copyright: © 2023 by the authors. Licensee MDPI, Basel, Switzerland. This article is an open access article distributed under the terms and conditions of the Creative Commons Attribution (CC BY) license (https://creativecommons.org/licenses/by/4.0/).

1. Introduction

Soil–rock mixture (S–RM) is a heterogeneous geotechnical material composed of coarse particles such as rock, gravel, and sand, and fine particles such as sand, clay, and silt. It is typically formed by seismic, collapse, landslide, and other actions during the Quaternary Period, and distributed in loose accumulations on steep slopes or beside ditches [1–4]. For instance, the 2008 Wenchuan earthquake in China triggered numerous landslides and debris flows in the subsequent years due to secondary factors like aftershocks and heavy rainfall. This led to widespread S–RM slopes in the mountainous regions of southwestern China [5,6]. S–RM formed by similar causes is also common in other areas [7,8].

S–RM offers numerous advantages, including its high strength, compactness, permeability, erosion resistance, and ability to utilize local materials [9]. Consequently, it is extensively utilized as a filler in subgrade engineering projects [10]. However, S–RM is a granular material that presents challenges in achieving a uniform mixing of particles with varying sizes, shapes, and material properties. Non-uniform mixing is a common occurrence in both natural and construction processes. For instance, during road construction, the coarse aggregates in S–RM tend to settle downwards due to their higher potential energy, resulting in layers with varying degrees of mixing [11,12].

The mixing degree is a measure of the heterogeneity of particle mixtures [13]. Current definitions primarily originate from the chemical, agricultural, construction, and medical fields, where they guide industrial production and quality evaluation. However, mixing degree indices are infrequently utilized in geotechnical engineering [14]. Previous research has demonstrated the significant influence of mixing degree on the local and global properties of granular materials [15]. However, limited studies have investigated its effect on the vibratory compaction of S–RM as a subgrade filler and the resulting negative effects on long-term road performance.

Subgrade compaction involves the consolidation of soils through mechanical methods such as static pressure, dynamic compaction, or vibration compaction [16]. These methods apply external energy to the soil, causing particle movements and rearrangements. Energy is transformed and dissipated during this process, specifically in terms of particle potential energy. The compaction process is fundamentally driven by particle movements and the resulting energy conversions under loading conditions. Thus, conducting statistical analyses on particle motions and energy consumption during compaction can offer a more comprehensive understanding of the compaction mechanism of S–RM (specific road material) under vibration loads, in comparison to macro-scale observations.

This paper employed numerical simulations using the discrete element method (DEM) to investigate the vibratory compaction process of S–RM with different degrees of mixing homogeneity. This study analyzed the relationships between changes in void ratio and particle movements, as well as energy dissipation during compaction. Furthermore, the effects of various vibration parameters on energy dissipation paths were examined. The findings will contribute to a deeper understanding of the vibration compaction mechanism for S–RM as a subgrade filler. This knowledge can serve as a more rational basis for selecting fillers, ensuring the quality and bearing capacity of compacted subgrades, and conducting stability assessments.

2. Discrete Element Modeling and Energy Consumption Calculation

2.1. Discrete Element Modeling of Soil–Rock Mixtures

The Particle Flow Code 3D (PFC3D) software was employed for the numerical simulations conducted in this study. The S–RM specimens used had a fixed coarse particle content of 50%. The mixing degree index (I) values, ranging from 0.0 to 1.0, were determined using the formulation proposed by Liu et al. [17]. The brief calculation principle is as follows:

The curves in Figure 1 represent the variation of coarse and fine aggregate content Vf with the normalized depth H/HB (HB is the height of the mixture) for different particle mixes, where the Arbitrary Line (black) is the arbitrary mix curve, and the Separation Line (blue) and the Uniform mixing Line (red) are the complete segregation curve and the uniform distribution curve, respectively. When the Arbitrary Line and the Uniform mixing Line do not coincide exactly, the total area As (shaded in Figure 1) enclosed by the two curves represents the degree of coarse aggregate segregation in the graded aggregates. The area bounded by the Separation Line, the Uniform mixing Line, and Lines AB and CD is the area of complete segregation (as shown in areas Ai and Aii). The mixing degree index (I) in this paper was calculated using Equation (1):

$$I = 1 - \frac{A_s}{A_i + A_{ii}} \tag{1}$$

Figure 2 illustrates the I value versus the depth of the curves for the six groups of specimens. In the figure, H represents the height from the bottom of the specimen, while HW denotes the total height. The specimens had dimensions of 800 mm × 800 mm × 600 mm and were enclosed by five rigid walls.

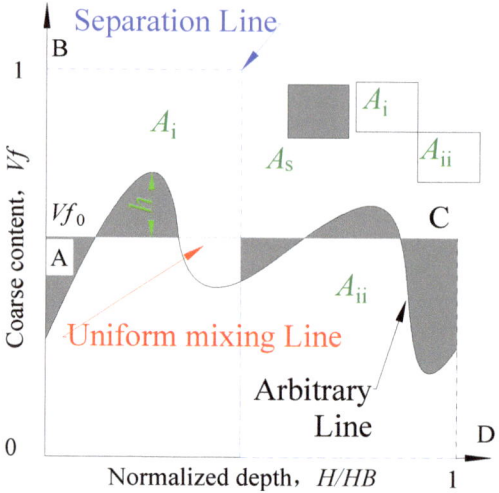

Figure 1. Schematic representation of the principles of calculating the indicators.

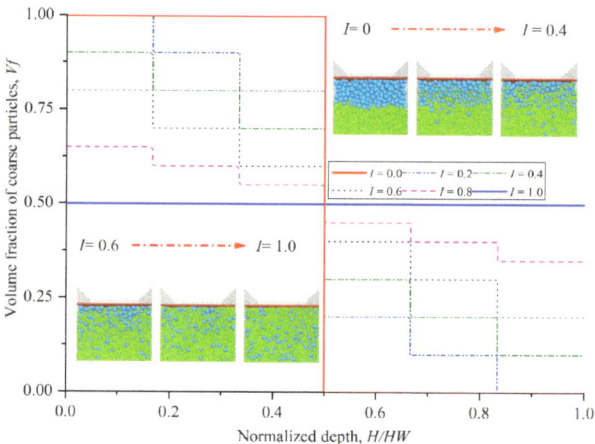

Figure 2. Variation curve of coarse particles with normalized depth under different I value.

The sample preparation process is as follows:

(1) Divide the specimen height into 10 equal layers. Generate specific numbers of coarse and fine particles in each layer based on the initial void ratio target of 0.7 and relative coarse/fine particle proportions in Figure 2.

(2) Reset the interparticle contact forces and velocities every 5 cycles until 20,000 cycles to eliminate excessive contacts.

(3) Allow the particles to settle under gravity to produce the initial specimen. The final I values match the targets.

The top of the specimen was equipped with an 800 mm × 800 mm × 2 mm loading plate, which contains a cluster composed of 6241 sub-spheres with a radius of 1 mm. The resulting model is depicted in Figure 2. To simulate the vibrations induced by field vibratory rollers, an excitation force was applied to the plate. This force followed a cosine wave pattern, and matched the magnitude and frequency of the field vibration compaction, as described by Equation (2):

$$F = -F_0(\cos(2\pi f \Delta t) + 1) \tag{2}$$

where F presents the excitation force; F_0 = 500 kN; f is the loading frequency; and Δt is the loading time. Given the focus of this study on particle motions and energy dissipation, important parameters included dashpot coefficients, sliding friction, and rolling friction. The contact stiffness and other relevant parameters were directly derived from triaxial model verifications and incorporated into the analysis [18].

Linear contact models were employed for particle interactions. Research indicates that both linear and nonlinear Hertz models can effectively represent the behaviors of granular materials [19]. The normal stiffness of a particle, k_n, is expressed in Equation (3):

$$k_n = \pi E_c r/(r_1 + r_2) \tag{3}$$

where E_c is the particle effective modulus; r_1 and r_2 are the contacting particle radii; and r is the smaller radius. In this study, the effective contact modulus of soil particles E_{cb} is 1.24×10^8 Pa, and the effective contact modulus of loaded plate particles E_{cl} is 3.31×10^9 Pa. Tangential stiffness k_s used a normal-to-tangential stiffness ratio $k^* = k_n/k_s$ between 1.0 and 1.5 for realistic materials [20,21]. Here $k^* = 4.0/3.0$ was applied. Density was set as 2650 kg/m^3, similar to actual granular geo-materials.

Dashpot was utilized to dissipate energy within the particle assembly during preparation and loading processes. Common forms of dashpot include local dashpot, which directly decreases particle velocities, and viscous dashpot, which introduces contact dashpot forces. The local dashpot coefficient, D_p, regulates the unbalanced forces, as demonstrated in Equation (4):

$$F_i^d = D_p\left(\left|F_i^d\right|\right)\text{sign}(v_i) \tag{4}$$

where D_p is the local dashpot coefficient; sign is the sign function; and v_i (i = 1–6) is the linear and angular velocities. Viscous dashpot introduces normal and tangential contact dashpot forces, as shown in Equation (5):

$$F_j^d = \left(2\beta_j \sqrt{\overline{m} k_j}\right)\dot{\delta}_j \tag{5}$$

where j = n, and s represents the normal and tangential directions of particle contact, respectively; $\beta_n = \beta_s = 0.7$; and $\overline{m}$ is the equivalent value of contacting particle mass (m_1 and m_2), $\overline{m} = m_1 m_2/(m_1+m_2)$. The contact between particles follows Coulomb's law of friction, that is $f_s \leq \mu_b f_n$, where f_n and f_s are normal and tangential contact forces. The static friction coefficient μ_b = 0.6. Particle shapes were incorporated via a rolling resistance model giving rotational moments, as shown in Equation (6):

$$M \leq \mu_r \overline{R} f_n \tag{6}$$

where μ_r = 0.25 is the rolling friction and $\overline{R}$ is the effective particle radius. Key mesoparameters are listed in Table 1. Coarse to fine particle diameter ratio d_c/d_f was 5.0. Previous studies have indicated that mechanical behavior remains relatively unchanged when the ratio exceeds 4.44, which corresponds to the situation where fine particles fill the voids between coarse particles [17,22]. Therefore, variations in particle size scales did not significantly influence the objectives of the current research.

Table 1. Mesoscopic parameters used in numerical simulations.

Parameter	Value
Particle density (kg/m^3)	2650
Local dashpot D_p	0.01
Normal viscous dashpot β_n	0.70
Tangential viscous dashpot β_s	0.70
Sliding friction μ_b	0.60
Rolling friction μ_r	0.25
Effective contact modulus E_{cb} (Pa)	1.24×10^8
Effective contact modulus of loaded plate E_{cl} (Pa)	3.31×10^9
Normal-to-tangential stiffness ratio k^*	4.0/3.0
Coarse particle diameter	40–60
Fine particle diameter	5–15

2.2. Energy Consumption Calculation

Energy consumption values are aggregated based on PFC principles. The reliability of these values is confirmed through experiments conducted on vibrating powder beds, with simulations aligning with the experimental results [23,24]. The formulations used are as follows:

(1) Sliding strain energy E_{st}:

Sliding strain energy (E_{st}) is the energy resulting from the elastic forces between contact points and stored within the system as potential energy. The formula for computing the sliding strain energy (E_{sst}) is:

$$E_{sst} = \sum_{i=1}^{k} \frac{1}{2} \left(\frac{f_{n,i}^2}{k_n} + \frac{\|f_{s,i}\|^2}{k_s} \right) \Big|_t \quad (7)$$

where $f_{n,i}$ and $f_{s,i}$ are the normal and tangential contact forces of the i-th contact; and t is the real time.

(2) Slip energy E_μ:

$$E_\mu = \sum_{i=1}^{k} \frac{1}{2} \left[(f_{s,i})_0 + f_{s,i} \right] \Delta \delta_{s,i}^\mu \Big|_t \quad (8)$$

where $f_{s,i}$ is the tangential force of the i-th contact at the time t; and $\Delta \delta_s^u$ is the relative tangential displacement increment $\Delta \delta_s$ in the sliding direction.

(3) Dashpot energy E_β:

Dashpot energy (E_β) denotes the overall energy dissipated by the damper, and its formula for calculation is as follows:

$$E_\beta = F^d \cdot \left(\dot{\delta} \Delta t \right) \quad (9)$$

$$\dot{\delta} = \dot{x}_c^i - \dot{x}_c^j \quad (10)$$

$$\dot{x}_c^i = \dot{x}^i + \omega^i \times (x_c - x^i) \quad (11)$$

where $\dot{\delta}$ is the relative velocity of particles; $\dot{x}_c^i$ and $\dot{x}_c^j$ are the velocities of the two particles at the contact point c, respectively; $\dot{x}^i$ and ω^i are the velocity and angular velocity of the i-th particle, respectively; x_c and x^i are the positions of contact point c and the center of gravity of the particle i, respectively.

(4) Rolling strain energy E_{rst}:

Rolling strain energy (E_{rst}) signifies the energy generated from particle contact and accumulated within the rolling spring. The formula for calculating this energy is as follows:

$$E_{\text{rst}} = \frac{1}{2}\frac{\|M_r\|^2}{k_r} \tag{12}$$

(5) Rolling slip energy $E_{\mu r}$:

Rolling slip energy ($E_{\mu r}$) pertains to the energy dissipation resulting from the occurrence of rolling slip between particles. The formula for calculating this energy is as follows:

$$E_{\mu r} = \frac{1}{2}[(M_r)_0 + M_r] \cdot \Delta\theta^{\mu r} \tag{13}$$

where $\Delta\theta^{\mu r}$ is the increment component bending $\Delta\theta$ in the sliding direction.

(6) Normal elastic work W_n:

$$W_n = \sum_{t=1}^{t}\sum_{m=1}^{k}\left[f_{\text{fn,ij}|t+\Delta t}\left(p_{n,i|t+\Delta t} - p_{n,i|t}\right) + f_{\text{fn,ji}|t+\Delta t}\left(p_{n,j|t+\Delta t} - p_{n,j|t}\right)\right] \tag{14}$$

where $f_{\text{fn,ij}|t+\Delta t}$ represents the normal elastic force generated on the surface of particle i due to the contact between particle i and particle j at $t + \Delta t$; $p_{n,i|t}$ represents the position of the i particle at time t; and other symbols are similar.

(7) Tangential elastic work W_t:

The amount of tangential elastic work due to friction is:

$$W_s = \sum_{t=1}^{t}\sum_{m=1}^{k}\left(f_{\text{fs,ij}|t+\Delta t}\delta_{si} + f_{\text{fs,ji}|t+\Delta t}\delta_{sj}\right) \tag{15}$$

where $f_{\text{fs,ij}}$ represents the tangential friction force generated on the surface of particle i; δ_{si} represents the overall movement of the contact point on the surface of particle i due to sliding and rotation within time Δt. Since W_s includes sliding friction work, the magnitude from tangential springs is:

$$W_t = W_s - E_\mu \tag{16}$$

3. Compaction Effect Analysis

3.1. Void Ratio Variation

During the vibratory compaction simulations, the settlement of the load plate and the void ratio were continuously monitored. Data were recorded at intervals of 1/8 cycle. The plate displacement increments between cycles were compared, and loading was terminated when the ratio fell below 0.1% for ten consecutive cycles, indicating volume stability.

Figure 3 illustrates the settlement of the load plate over time for different samples with varying degrees of particle mixing. The results demonstrated that the sedimentation of the particle system can be divided into two main stages: a rapid change phase and a stable phase. In the initial period ($t < 25T$), the sedimentation of the granular system experienced a significant increase, accompanied by a sharp decrease in the void ratio. Subsequently ($t > 25T$), the sedimentation and the void ratio of the particle system tended to stabilize, reaching a state of relative constancy.

Figure 4 presents the variations in void ratios and final values of the samples with different mixing degrees. The findings demonstrated that the uniformity of particle mixing had a substantial influence on densification under identical vibration loads. Specifically, the settlement decreased as the mixing degree increased for the same number of load cycles. Similarly, both the change in void ratio (Δe) and the final value (e_f) decreased monotonically as the homogeneity of mixing improved.

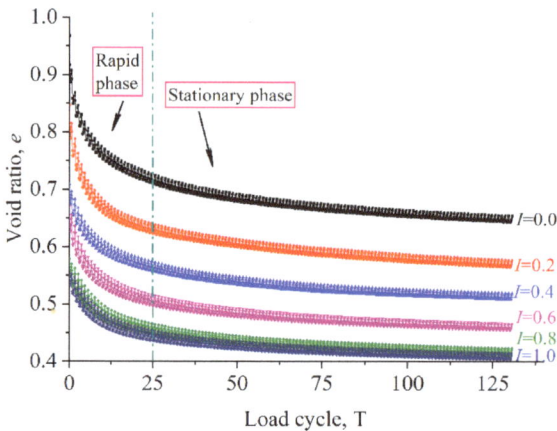

Figure 3. Changes in void ratio of particle system with load period.

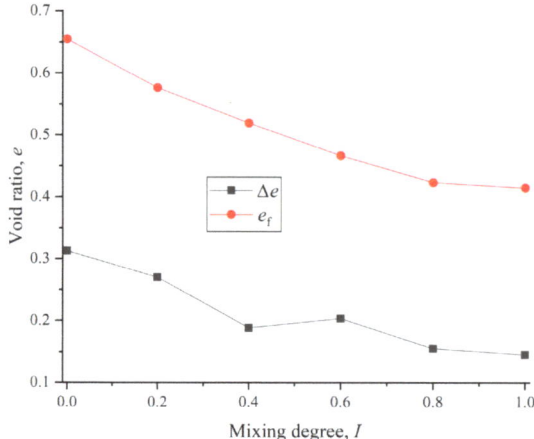

Figure 4. Variations in void ratio, final void ratio, and minimum void ratio.

3.2. Particle Motion Statistics and Analysis

Compaction primarily involves the rearrangement of particles as they approach each other and smaller particles enter the voids of larger particles through motion [25,26]. The primary particle movements associated with deformation are sliding and rotation [27,28]. Here, the particle displacement and rotation angle represent sliding and rotation amounts, respectively.

Figure 5 illustrates the average particle displacement and rotation angle as a function of load cycles for different mixing degrees. In terms of the duration of loading, both metrics gradually increased over time and closely aligned with the settlement trend shown in Figure 3. During the rapid densification phase ($t < 25T$), significant increases occurred, indicating substantial particle movements. As stabilization began ($t > 25T$), the values plateaued, reflecting the stabilization of particle movements.

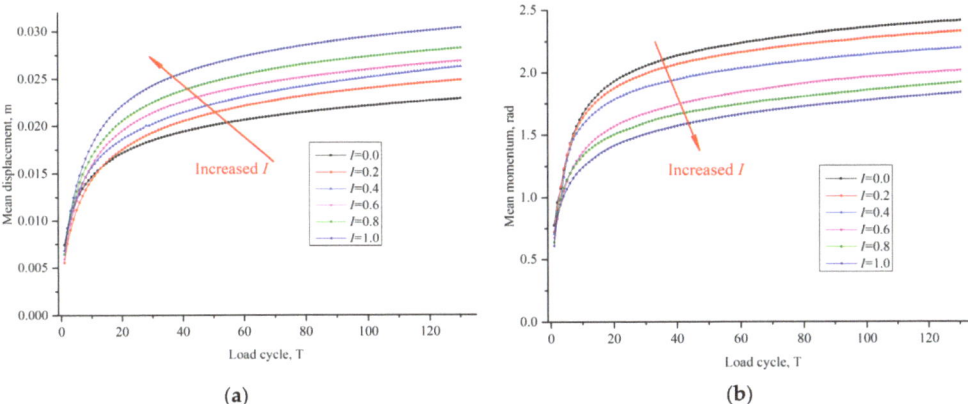

Figure 5. The average displacement and rotation angle of samples with different mixing degrees vary with load period: (**a**) displacement; and (**b**) rotation angle.

In terms of the effects of mixing degree, displacements and rotations did not exhibit clear trends during the early stages of loading ($t < 10T$), but divergence became apparent at the later stages ($t > 10T$). However, while the final void ratios systematically decreased with higher mixing degrees, displacements monotonically increased while rotations decreased. This suggested that particle movements during compaction did not necessarily promote densification. It is likely that more particles undergo reciprocal or even upward displacements, while rotations are biased towards compaction to achieve greater homogeneity.

3.3. Compactability Characterization

The previous sections have provided qualitative insights into the relationship between particle movement and compaction when considering mixing degrees. However, the strength of the correlation could not be adequately described. To address this, particle self-diffusion coefficients were introduced to quantify the association between displacements, system compactness, and mixing homogeneity.

On a microscopic level, particle rearrangements, approaching, and void-filling are a result of random motions induced by external excitation. Loading leads to random velocity fluctuations, similar to molecular thermal diffusion or eddy diffusion in turbulence. These fluctuations in velocity result in a non-uniform distribution of force chains and the continuous formation and breakage of contacts, prompting rearrangements and void filling. This particle diffusion process under vibration signifies a key mechanism of compaction.

Similar to the thermal velocities of gas molecules, the average squared magnitude of particle velocities is referred to as "granular temperature". Campbell et al. [29] computed the self-diffusion coefficient D by analyzing the growth rate of displacement variance over time, using the following formula:

$$D = \frac{\left\langle [s(t) - s(0)]^2 \right\rangle}{2t} \qquad (17)$$

where t is elapsed time; and $s(t)$ and $s(0)$ are particle displacements at times t and 0, respectively. In this study, $t = 130T$ was used.

Figure 6 illustrates the values of D for different mixing degrees. A consistent decrease was observed with improved homogeneity, closely aligning with the void ratio trends shown in Figure 4. This indicated that the particle diffusion ability, which represented the range of single particle motion, decreased, and compactability was reduced at higher mixing degrees.

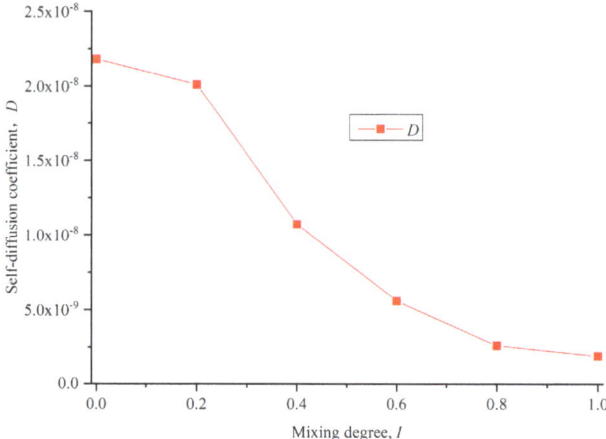

Figure 6. Self-diffusion coefficient varies with mixing degree.

4. Particle Energy Dissipation Mechanism

4.1. Verification of Energy Dissipation in Particle Systems

According to the law of conservation of energy, the energy input into the particle system (E_{input}) during vibratory compaction should equal the total energy dissipated (E_{total}) within the system. This principle has been verified in cyclic shear testing simulations by Christina et al. [30]. E_{total} comprises dashpot energy, slip energy, rolling slip energy, and strain energy (sliding and rolling). With the periodic cosine excitation on the load plate, E_{input} is calculated from the force–displacement curve:

$$E_{input} = \sum_{i=1}^{T} S_{Ti} = \sum_{i=1}^{T} \int_{\varepsilon_O}^{\varepsilon_A} F d\varepsilon \tag{18}$$

where T is the number of load cycles; F is the force magnitude; ε_0 is the displacement at the start of the cycle; and ε_A is the maximum displacement in the cycle.

Studies by Asmar et al. [31] on input and dissipated energy relationships showed the calculated E_{total} was always less than the actual E_{input}. This is because some energy (E_{art}) is neglected by artificial definitions, mainly normal and tangential elastic work, W_n and W_t, in Equations (15) and (16).

By introducing a correction and defining the total dissipated energy as $E'_{total} = E_{total} + E_{art}$, the comparison is presented in Figure 7. It was observed that E'_{total} closely matched E_{input}, confirming the dissipation calculations by PFC criteria appropriately represent the compaction mechanism energy pathways. This monitoring approach enhanced insights into meso-scale particle interactions and enabled a better understanding of macro-scale responses. However, it is crucial to verify that the calculated meso-scale energy dissipations correspond to the physical and mechanical behaviors observed at the macro-scale, as this is critical for mechanism analysis.

Figure 8 presents the cumulative input energy over load cycles for different mixing degrees. The increments of input energy decreased over time but experienced a significant rise before t < 25T, during periods of rapid void ratio changes. Afterward, the increments slowly increased. This can be attributed to the easier structural adjustments and greater efficiency of dissipation in the initial looser states. As densification proceeded, the presence of more compact and uniform particle contacts reduced sliding contacts and tangential creep, resulting in a severe limitation of energy dissipation and input [32,33]. The consistency observed with the void ratio–time patterns in Figure 3 supports the notion that energy input leads to void ratio reductions.

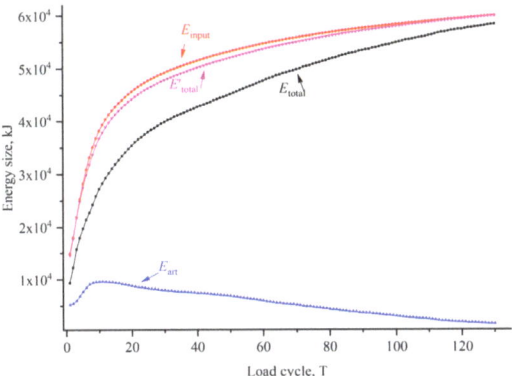

Figure 7. Comparison of the input energy with the corrected total dissipated energy.

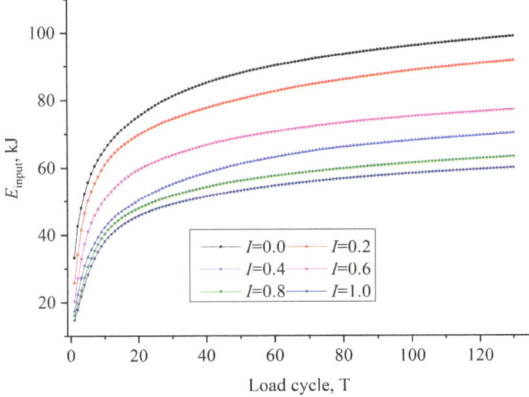

Figure 8. Variations in input energy with load period.

Figure 9 further displays the aligned energy input and void ratio trends over mixing degrees. Their monotonic decline with improving homogeneity visually confirms void ratio changes had direct correspondence to particle system energy input and thus total dissipation. Therefore, analyzing the compaction mechanism via energy dissipation pathways is reasonable.

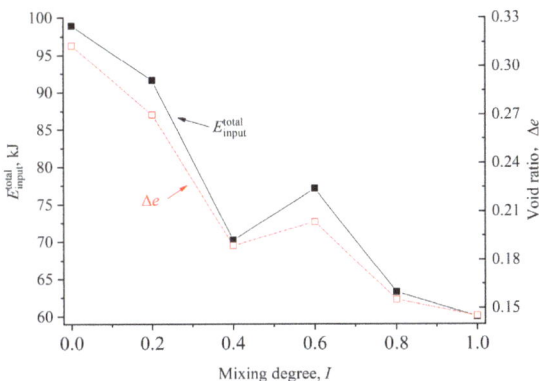

Figure 9. Input energy and void ratio changes with mixing degree.

4.2. Analysis of Energy Dissipation Path and Its Proportion

Different modes of energy dissipation play distinct roles in the changes in void ratio during vibratory compaction. Moreover, their relative contributions to the total dissipated energy will evolve as void ratio variations occur. Figure 10 illustrates the ratio of each dissipation component to the total energy over load cycles. As specific dissipation values exhibit considerable randomness within individual cycles, average trendlines over 10-cycle intervals were presented to showcase clearer tendencies over time.

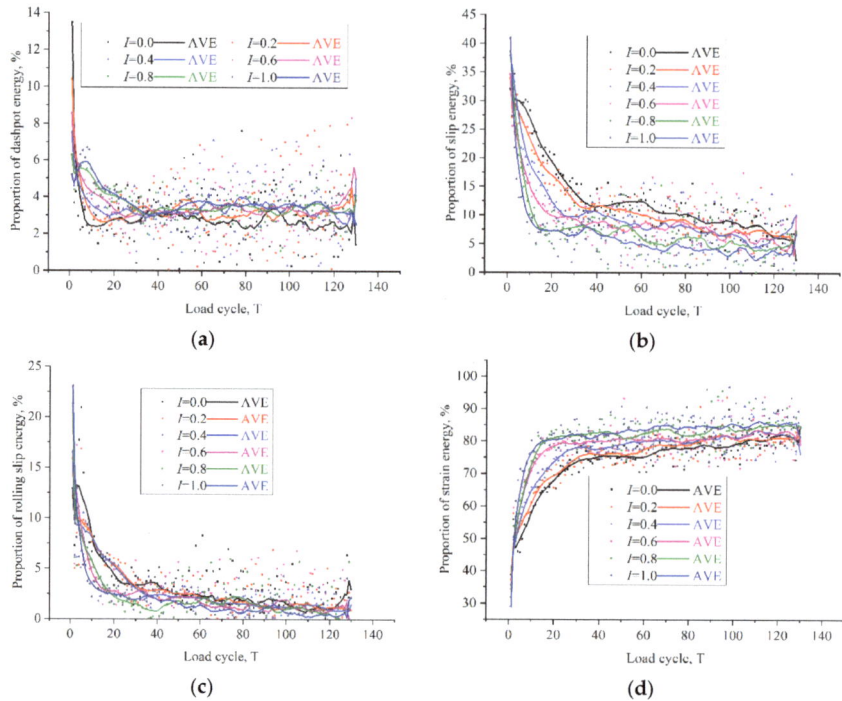

Figure 10. The proportion of energy consumption to total energy dissipation during a single load period: (**a**) dashpot energy; (**b**) slip energy; (**c**) rolling slip energy; and (**d**) strain energy.

Figure 10a shows dashpot energy accounting for 6–14% initially, before rapidly decreasing in the rapid void ratio change zone and slightly rising to 3–4% during stabilization. This implied dashpot did not wholly facilitate void ratio reductions since its proportion increased again once void ratio became approximately constant.

The slip energy proportion in Figure 10b ranged from 30 to 45% initially but quickly declined with void ratio changes and later stabilized between 5 and 12%. This agrees with past findings relating particle sliding and rotations to energy dissipation during compaction [34]. A certain magnitude continued even after stabilization, indicating sliding does not completely promote densification.

Figure 10c demonstrates rolling slip energy following a similar decreasing trend from initial 12–22% portions to near 0% at stability. In contrast with sliding dissipation, rolling slip energy primarily existed during void ratio variations and played an absolute role in enabling compaction.

As shown in Figure 10d, strain energy accounted for 30–40% initially before rapidly increasing with load cycles during void ratio reductions and maintaining a high 70–80% proportion at stability. Its evolution closely matched void ratio changes but did not directly facilitate compaction.

In summary, dashpot energy does not directly cause void ratio changes, sliding provides mixed densification effects, rolling predominantly enables compaction during void ratio variations, and strain energy passively reflects void ratio trends.

5. Parametric Studies on Energy Dissipation

The preceding sections have highlighted the varying influences of energy dissipation pathways during vibratory compaction. It is important to note that external load changes play a critical role in the evolution rates and final values of void ratio. Consequently, further investigation of energy dissipation under varied loading conditions can offer additional insights into the compaction mechanism. This section analyses homogeneous specimens consisting of 50% coarse particles, which were subject to different excitation forces and frequencies.

5.1. Excitation Force Effects

Excitation forces of 10 kN, 50 kN, 100 kN, and 500 kN were applied at a constant 35 Hz frequency. Figure 11 presents void ratio–time histories under the different forces. All samples progressively compacted but the compaction degree increased with higher forces, yielding lower final void ratios.

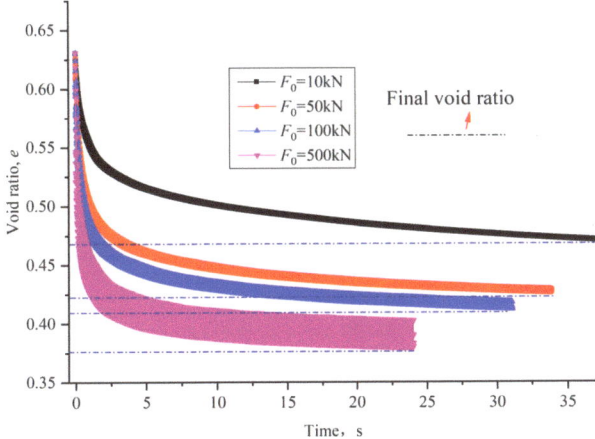

Figure 11. Changes in void ratio with time under different excitation forces.

Figure 12 illustrates the evolutions of energy dissipation components over time. It was observed that all values increased with increasing excitation, with cumulative dashpot, sliding, and rolling slip energy exhibiting a monotonous growth over time. Strain energy, on the other hand, experienced a rapid initial increase before descending to steady-state levels as the void ratio stabilized. When comparing the rate of increments, it can be noted that dashpot, sliding, and rolling slip energy exhibited greater growth in the zone of rapid void ratio change, which gradually slowed down and declined as the system approached stability. However, dashpot and sliding energies maintained small constant increases after reaching certain levels, while the convergence of rolling slip energy flattened completely.

With regard to the degree of compaction, the effectiveness and efficiency improved significantly with higher forces, up to a certain limit. While the void ratio differences gradually decreased from 50 kN to 100 kN and from 100 kN to 500 kN due to diminishing marginal returns, the energy consumption of the specimen continued to increase approximately linearly with the increase in excitation.

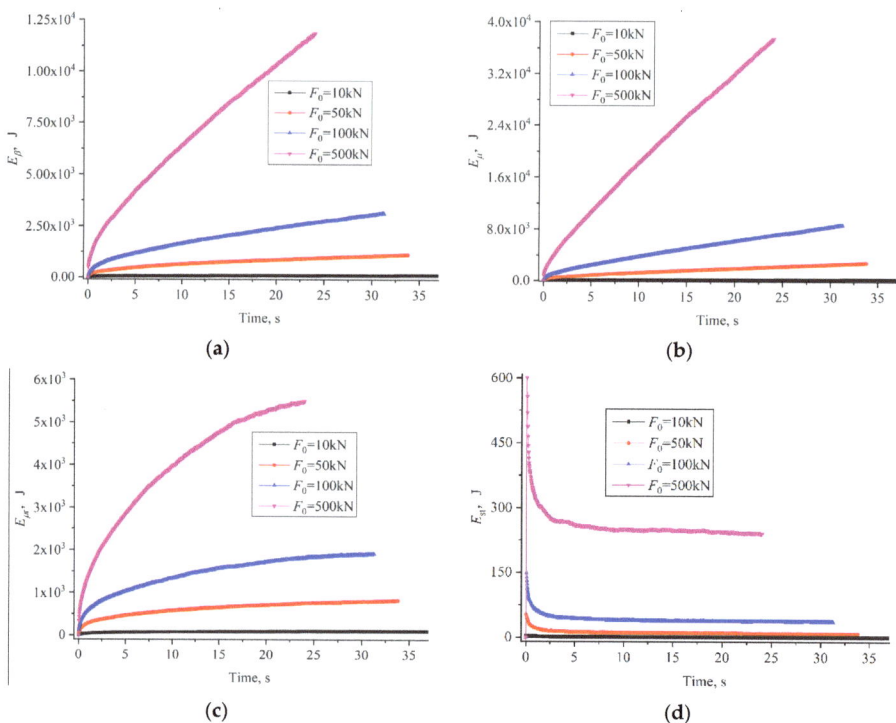

Figure 12. Energy dissipation pathway under different excitation forces: (**a**) dashpot energy; (**b**) sliding energy; (**c**) rolling slip energy; and (**d**) strain energy.

5.2. Excitation Frequency Effects

For a constant 50 kN excitation, frequencies of 25 Hz, 30 Hz, 35 Hz, and 40 Hz were analyzed. Figure 13 presents void ratio versus time plots for these different frequencies. It was observed that all samples underwent monotonic densification, with void ratios decreasing slightly faster at higher frequencies. However, the discrepancies in void ratio reduction were minor within identical loading durations. Therefore, the excitation frequency did not significantly affect the effectiveness or efficiency of S–RM compaction.

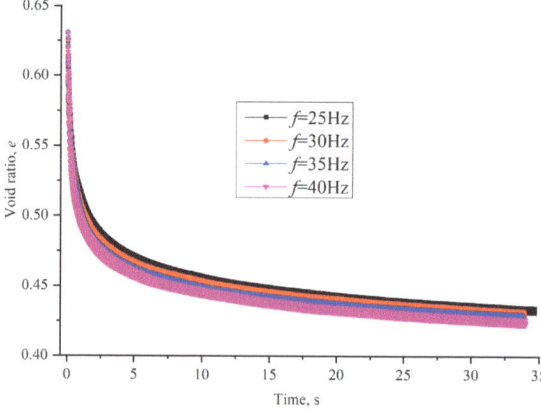

Figure 13. Changes in void ratio with time under different excitation frequencies.

Figure 14 displays the evolutions of the different dissipation components. In contrast to strain energy, which remained unaffected by frequency, dashpot, sliding, and rolling slip energy progressively increased with higher frequencies under the same loading period. This can be attributed to the fact that increased frequencies result in more loading cycles, leading to greater energy consumption. However, since strain energy depends on overall deformations during the given timeframe, the differences in its evolution across frequencies are negligible.

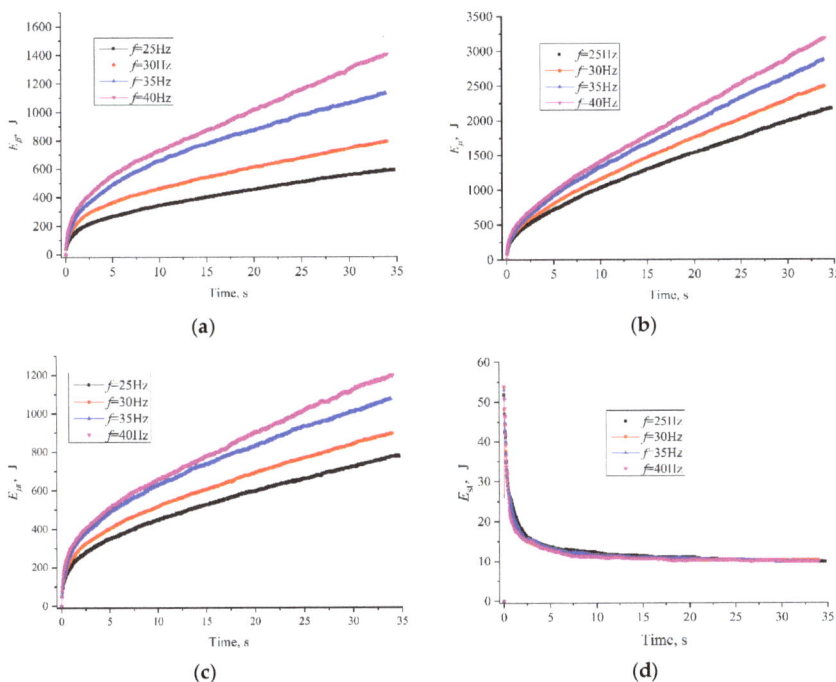

Figure 14. Energy dissipation pathway under different excitation frequencies: (**a**) dashpot energy; (**b**) sliding energy; (**c**) rolling slip energy; and (**d**) strain energy.

In summary, increasing excitation forces can significantly improve the degree of compaction up to a certain limit. However, it also leads to a substantial increase in energy consumption. On the other hand, adjusting the frequency within a typical range has a mild effect on compactness, without appreciable effects on energy dissipation. These trends provide valuable guidance for achieving target densification levels while optimizing energy inputs.

6. Conclusions

This research conducted DEM simulations of the vibratory compaction process in S–RM with varying degrees of mixing homogeneity. The study analyzed the relationships between void ratio changes, particle movements, and energy dissipations during compaction. Additionally, the influences of different excitation forces and frequencies on energy dissipation trends were examined. The key conclusions are summarized as follows:

(1) The mixing uniformity of S–RM significantly affects the compaction characteristics of the filler material. More homogeneous specimens exhibit smaller void ratios after compaction.

(2) Particle motions during vibratory compaction do not necessarily promote densification, although rotations are found to be more closely associated with the compaction process than displacements.

(3) The cumulative external load input energy corresponds to the total energy dissipated by the specimen, indicating that the compaction mechanism can be effectively studied through energy dissipation pathways. The consistent correlations observed between input energy, dissipated energy, and void ratio changes over time and mixing degree support this premise.

(4) Dashpot energy does not directly cause variations in void ratio, sliding provides ambiguous effects on densification, rolling predominantly facilitates compaction during changes in void ratio, and strain energy passively reflects void ratio trends.

In summary, this work provides insights into the underlying energy dissipation mechanisms that govern the densification of S–RM under vibratory loads. These findings contribute to more effective filler selection, improved vibratory compaction procedures, and enhanced predictions of subgrade quality and performance. Further efforts may involve experimental validations through instrumented laboratory vibratory compaction tests on S–RM specimens.

Author Contributions: Conceptualization, S.L.; methodology, S.L.; software, W.W.; validation, W.W. and W.H.; data curation, S.L.; writing—original draft preparation, W.W.; writing—review and editing, S.L.; supervision, W.H.; project administration, W.H.; funding acquisition, W.H. All authors have read and agreed to the published version of the manuscript.

Funding: This research was funded by the National Natural Science Foundation of China, grant number 52178332; and the Scientific Research Project of the Hunan Provincial Education Department, grant number 22C250.

Institutional Review Board Statement: Not applicable.

Informed Consent Statement: Not applicable.

Data Availability Statement: Data are contained within this article.

Conflicts of Interest: The authors declare no conflict of interest.

References

1. Xu, W.J.; Hu, L.M.; Gao, W. Random generation of the meso-structure of a soil-rock mixture and its application in the study of the mechanical behavior in a landslide dam. *Int. J. Rock Mech. Min. Sci.* **2016**, *86*, 166–178. [CrossRef]
2. Fan, X.; Scaringi, G.; Korup, O.; West, A.J.; Westen, C.J.; Tanyas, H.; Hovius, N.; Hales, T.C.; Jibson, R.W.; Allstadt, K.E.; et al. Earthquake-Induced Chains of Geologic Hazards: Patterns, Mechanisms, and Impacts. *Rev. Geophys.* **2019**, *57*, 421–503. [CrossRef]
3. Wang, F.; Fan, X.; Yunus, A.P.; Siva Subramanian, S.; Alonso-Rodriguez, A.; Dai, L.; Xu, Q.; Huang, R. Coseismic landslides triggered by the 2018 Hokkaido, Japan (Mw 6.6), earthquake: Spatial distribution, controlling factors, and possible failure mechanism. *Landslides* **2019**, *16*, 1551–1566. [CrossRef]
4. Qi, Q.; Nie, Y.; Wang, X.; Liu, S. Exploring the effects of size ratio and fine content on vibration compaction behaviors of gap-graded granular mixtures via calibrated DEM models. *Powder Technol.* **2023**, *415*, 118156. [CrossRef]
5. Fan, X.; Juang, C.H.; Wasowski, J.; Huang, R.; Xu, Q.; Scaringi, G.; van Westen, C.J.; Havenith, H.-B. What we have learned from the 2008 Wenchuan Earthquake and its aftermath: A decade of research and challenges. *Eng. Geol.* **2018**, *241*, 25–32. [CrossRef]
6. Xu, Q.; Zhang, S.; Li, W.L.; van Asch, T.W.J. The 13 August 2010 catastrophic debris flows after the 2008 Wenchuan earthquake, China. *Nat. Hazards Earth Syst. Sci.* **2012**, *12*, 201–216. [CrossRef]
7. Wen-Jie, X.; Qiang, X.; Rui-Lin, H. Study on the shear strength of soil–rock mixture by large scale direct shear test. *Int. J. Rock Mech. Min. Sci.* **2011**, *48*, 1235–1247. [CrossRef]
8. Dong, H.; Peng, B.; Gao, Q.-F.; Hu, Y.; Jiang, X. Study of hidden factors affecting the mechanical behavior of soil–rock mixtures based on abstraction idea. *Acta Geotech.* **2021**, *16*, 595–611. [CrossRef]
9. Li, J.; Zhang, J.; Yang, X.; Zhang, A.; Yu, M. Monte Carlo simulations of deformation behaviour of unbound granular materials based on a real aggregate library. *Int. J. Pavement Eng.* **2023**, *24*, 2165650. [CrossRef]
10. Yao, Y.; Li, J.; Ni, J.; Liang, C.; Zhang, A. Effects of gravel content and shape on shear behaviour of soil-rock mixture: Experiment and DEM modelling. *Comput. Geotech.* **2022**, *141*, 104476. [CrossRef]
11. Huilin, L.; Yurong, H.; Gidaspow, D.; Lidan, Y.; Yukun, Q. Size segregation of binary mixture of solids in bubbling fluidized beds. *Powder Technol.* **2003**, *134*, 86–97. [CrossRef]

12. Combarros, M.; Feise, H.J.; Zetzener, H.; Kwade, A. Segregation of particulate solids: Experiments and DEM simulations. *Particuology* **2014**, *12*, 25–32. [CrossRef]
13. Chang, J.; Li, J.; Hu, H.; Qian, J.; Yu, M. Numerical Investigation of Aggregate Segregation of Superpave Gyratory Compaction and Its Influence on Mechanical Properties of Asphalt Mixtures. *J. Mater. Civ. Eng.* **2023**, *35*, 04022453. [CrossRef]
14. Dai, B.-B.; Yang, J.; Liu, F.-T.; Gu, X.-Q.; Lin, K.-R. A new index to characterize the segregation of binary mixture. *Powder Technol.* **2020**, *363*, 611–620. [CrossRef]
15. Azema, E.; Preechawuttipong, I.; Radjai, F. Binary mixtures of disks and elongated particles: Texture and mechanical properties. *Phys. Rev. E* **2016**, *94*, 042901. [CrossRef] [PubMed]
16. Zhang, Z.-T.; Wang, Y.-H.; Gao, W.-H.; Hu, W.; Liu, S.-K. Permanent Deformation and Its Unified Model of Coal Gangue Subgrade Filler under Traffic Cyclic Loading. *Appl. Sci.* **2023**, *13*, 4128. [CrossRef]
17. Liu, S.; Hu, W.; Gong, J.; Nie, Z. An improved index of mixing degree and its effect on the strength of binary geotechnical mixtures. *Granul. Matter* **2021**, *24*, 6. [CrossRef]
18. Liu, S.; Nie, Y.; Hu, W.; Ashiru, M.; Li, Z.; Zuo, J. The Influence of Mixing Degree between Coarse and Fine Particles on the Strength of Offshore and Coast Foundations. *Sustainability* **2022**, *14*, 9177. [CrossRef]
19. Zhao, S.; Evans, T.; Zhou, X. Effects of curvature-related DEM contact model on the macro-and micro-mechanical behaviours of granular soils. *Géotechnique* **2018**, *68*, 1085–1098. [CrossRef]
20. Goldenberg, C.; Goldhirsch, I. Friction enhances elasticity in granular solids. *Nature* **2005**, *435*, 188–191. [CrossRef]
21. Zhu, Y.; Gong, J.; Nie, Z. Shear behaviours of cohesionless mixed soils using the DEM: The influence of coarse particle shape. *Particuology* **2021**, *55*, 151–165. [CrossRef]
22. Zhou, W.; Xu, K.; Ma, G.; Yang, L.; Chang, X. Effects of particle size ratio on the macro- and microscopic behaviors of binary mixtures at the maximum packing efficiency state. *Granul. Matter* **2016**, *18*, 81. [CrossRef]
23. Matchett, A.J.; Yanagida, T.; Okudaira, Y.; Kobayashi, S. Vibrating powder beds: A comparison of experimental and Distinct Element Method simulated data. *Powder Technol.* **2000**, *107*, 13–30. [CrossRef]
24. Yanagida, T.; Matchett, A.J.; Coulthard, J.M. Energy dissipation of binary powder mixtures subject to vibration. *Adv. Powder Technol.* **2001**, *12*, 227–254. [CrossRef]
25. Huang, M.; Yao, Z. Explicit model for cumulative strain of saturated clay subjected to cyclic loading. *Chin. J. Geotech. Eng.* **2011**, *33*, 325–331.
26. Mo, H.; Shan, Y.; Li, H.; Liu, S.; Chen, J. Energy-based method for analyzing accumulative plastic strain growth of tailing silt. *Chin. J. Geotech. Eng.* **2017**, *39*, 1959–1966.
27. Zhao, C.; Li, C.; Hu, L. Rolling and sliding between non-spherical particles. *Phys. A* **2018**, *492*, 181–191. [CrossRef]
28. Wang, Y.; Alonso-Marroquin, F.; Guo, W.W. Rolling and sliding in 3-D discrete element models. *Particuology* **2015**, *23*, 49–55. [CrossRef]
29. Campbell, C.S. Self-diffusion in granular shear flows. *J. Fluid Mech.* **1997**, *348*, 85–101. [CrossRef]
30. Denissen, C. A Micromechanical Study of Energy Dissipation Mechanisms in Granular Soils Subjected to Cyclic Loading. Master's Thesis, Southern Methodist University, Dallas, TX, USA, 2009.
31. Asmar, B.N.; Langston, P.A.; Matchett, A.J.; Walters, J.K. Energy monitoring in distinct element models of particle. *Adv. Powder Technol.* **2003**, *14*, 43–69. [CrossRef]
32. Pilbeam, C.C.; Vaišnys, J.R. Acoustic velocities and energy losses in granular aggregates. *J. Geophys. Res.* **1973**, *78*, 810–824. [CrossRef]
33. Yu, T.; Zhang, G.-H.; Sun, Q.-C.; Zhao, X.-D.; Ma, W.-B. Dynamic effective mass and power dissipation of the granular material under vertical vibration. *Acta Phys. Sin.* **2015**, *64*, 044501.
34. Liu, S.; Li, H.; Shan, Y.; Li, K.; Ba, L. Energy method for analyzing dynamic pore water pressure model for tailing soil. *Chin. J. Geotech. Eng.* **2016**, *38*, 2051–2058.

Disclaimer/Publisher's Note: The statements, opinions and data contained in all publications are solely those of the individual author(s) and contributor(s) and not of MDPI and/or the editor(s). MDPI and/or the editor(s) disclaim responsibility for any injury to people or property resulting from any ideas, methods, instructions or products referred to in the content.

Article

Permanent Deformation and Its Unified Model of Coal Gangue Subgrade Filler under Traffic Cyclic Loading

Zong-Tang Zhang [1,2], Yan-Hao Wang [1], Wen-Hua Gao [3,*], Wei Hu [1] and Shun-Kai Liu [1]

1. Hunan Provincial Key Laboratory of Geotechnical Engineering for Stability Control and Health Monitoring, Hunan University of Science and Technology, Xiangtan 411201, China; zzt@hnust.edu.cn (Z.-T.Z.)
2. College of Civil Engineering, Tongji University, Shanghai 200092, China
3. Hunan Software Vocational and Technical University, Xiangtan 411201, China
* Correspondence: gwh@hnust.edu.cn

Abstract: Using coal gangue as subgrade filler can not only solve the environmental problems of coal mine waste accumulation but also decrease the subgrade cost, which has important theoretical and practical significance. A series of cyclic triaxial tests was carried out using the large-scale dynamic and static triaxial apparatus (LSDSTA) to investigate the permanent deformation (ε) of coal gangue subgrade filler (CGSF) under cyclic loading. Experimental grading was designed by using the fractal model grading equation (FMGE), and then well-grading limits of CGSF were captured. The relationship curve between ε and the numbers of cyclic loading (N) can be divided into three stages, i.e., the rapid growth phase, the deceleration growth phase, and the approaching stability phase. N = 1000 can be used as the criterion for reaching the stable stage of CGSF. The effect of confining pressure (σ'_3) on ε is related to the level of σ'_3. The effect of σ'_3 on ε is significant when σ'_3 is smaller, whereas the influence of σ'_3 on ε is smaller when σ'_3 is larger. Furthermore, the influence of grading (D_f) on ε of coal gangue samples is significant. With the increase of D_f, ε first increases and then decreases, reflecting that there is an obvious optimal grading for coal gangue samples under cyclic loading. Moreover, the effect of compaction degree (D_c) on ε of CGSF depends on the level of D_c. ε is hardly affected when D_c is smaller, whereas increasing D_c has a significant effect on restraining ε when D_c is bigger. In addition, according to the analysis of the permanent deformation curve for CGSF, the unified calculation model of permanent deformation for CGSF under cyclic loading is established. Compared with the existing permanent deformation models, the proposed model in this paper can better describe the permanent deformation of CGSF under cyclic loading. Finally, the model parameters are analyzed, and the model is verified.

Keywords: dynamic behaviors; cyclic loading; permanent deformation; coal gangue subgrade filler; large-scale triaxial test

Citation: Zhang, Z.-T.; Wang, Y.-H.; Gao, W.-H.; Hu, W.; Liu, S.-K. Permanent Deformation and Its Unified Model of Coal Gangue Subgrade Filler under Traffic Cyclic Loading. *Appl. Sci.* **2023**, *13*, 4128. https://doi.org/10.3390/app13074128

Academic Editor: Alberto Campagnolo

Received: 20 February 2023
Revised: 14 March 2023
Accepted: 22 March 2023
Published: 24 March 2023

Copyright: © 2023 by the authors. Licensee MDPI, Basel, Switzerland. This article is an open access article distributed under the terms and conditions of the Creative Commons Attribution (CC BY) license (https://creativecommons.org/licenses/by/4.0/).

1. Introduction

Coal gangue is a waste material associated with the process of coal mine construction, coal exploitation, accounting for 15–20% of coal production. Now, more than 6 billion tons of coal gangue are accumulated on the surface of mining areas in China, and its emission has leaped to the top of China's industrial solid waste [1–3]. However, compared with the amount of released coal gangue, the utilization rate of coal gangue in China is low, resulting in a large amount of surplus coal gangue piled up on the useful land for a long time. The long-term accumulation of coal gangue has caused great harm to the surrounding environment [4,5]: ① A large number of useful land resources (such as cultivated land, forest land, and mining sites) are occupied. ② Dust particles easily float in the air, and coal gangue self-ignition produces many harmful gases, resulting in serious air pollution. ③ The piled-high coal gangue easily causes landslides, debris flow and other geological disasters. ④ Accumulated coal gangue seriously affects the surrounding landscape environment. Therefore, the effective utilization of coal gangue has great theoretical and practical significance.

The effective utilization of coal gangue waste has always been a hot topic that concerns many scholars. The physical and chemical characteristics of coal gangue are similar to natural gravel, so coal gangue can be broken down into a coarse aggregate of concrete, which can decrease the exploitation of natural gravel but can also save costs and avoid a series of hazards caused by it [6–8]. Hence, the study on coal gangue concrete has been focused on by many scholars in recent years [9,10], and the results indicate that the mechanical behaviors of coal gangue concrete, made by replacing a certain amount of gravel with coal gangue, are close to that of ordinary concrete of the same grade. Zhao et al. [11] investigated the effect of partial replacement of fly ash with natural loess on gangue-cemented paste backfill (GCPB) performance. Gangue-cemented paste backfill specimens with varying loess doses were produced, and then the rheological properties, macroscopic strength, and microstructural evolution of GCPB were examined. Zhao et al. [12] studied the activation and hydration mechanisms of composite activated coal gangue geopolymer, and the results show that coal gangue can be employed as a primary cementitious material after being modified by the proposed activation method. Su et al. [13] studied the influence of thermally activated coal gangue powder on the structure of the interfacial transition zone in concrete.

However, compared with traditional concrete, the investigation of the coal gangue concrete still shows many deficiencies. The consumption of coal gangue used as subgrade filler is tremendous, which can effectively solve the problem of coal gangue accumulation. Chen et al. [14] studied the effect of the compactive effort and initial particle gradings on the particle size distribution of mineral waste slag based on screening tests and analyzed the effects of different factors such as the compactive effort, moisture content, coarse grain content (CGC, mass proportion of particles with sizes greater than 5 mm), and forming methods on the engineering properties of mineral waste slag to determine the reasonable roadbed construction parameters. In addition, the research on coarse aggregate subgrade filler has a great reference value for coal gangue subgrade filler [15–17].

As mentioned above, coal gangue is widely used as subgrade filler. The coal gangue subgrade is affected by the traffic dynamic loading in the actual environment. However, there is little research reporting the dynamic behaviors of coal gangue, especially considering coarse particles, used as subgrade filler under traffic cyclic loading. Hence, a series of cyclic triaxial tests was carried out using the LSDSTA to research the permanent deformation of CGSF (the maximum particle size is 60 mm) under cyclic loading. The purposes of this study are to (1) study the permanent deformation of coal gangue used as subgrade filler so as to realize resource utilization, (2) explore the effect of σ'_3, D_f, and D_c on the permanent deformation to further understand the mechanical properties of CGSF, and (3) establish the unified model of permanent deformation in order to apply this to different types of permanent deformation.

2. Laboratory Testing Program

2.1. Tested Materials and Apparatus

The original tested material of the specimens was crushed coal gangue, which was collected from a coal mine in Xiangtan city. The waste coal gangue in this mine is shown in Figure 1. Nearly 15 tons of coal gangue were transported to the laboratory for indoor tests and research. The original particle size of coal gangue not only contains fine particles less than 0.075 mm, but also includes stones of tens of centimeters. It should be noted that the maximum particle size allowed by the test equipment in this test does not exceed 60 mm. Considering that the specimens in this test were prepared manually, CGSF with particle sizes greater than 60 mm were removed. The color of coal gangue particles is black and black-gray, and the coal gangue has not experienced spontaneous combustion. Coal gangue particles are angular, sharp, and hard with a rough surface and an irregular shape. The CGSF was dried to constant weight in an oven at 105–110 °C (more than 24 h), and then the standard sieve tests with aperture sizes of 60, 40, 20, 10, 5, 2, 0.5, and 0.075 mm were carried out. Coal gangue particles of each group after sieving tests were displayed in Figure 2. According to the JTG 3430-2020 Chinese standard for soil test method [18], the natural moisture content of CGSF is 2.20–2.98%, the liquid limit, the plastic limit, and the plasticity index of fine particles are 31.46%, 20.57%, and 10.89%, respectively. The coal gangue of this coal mine mainly includes sandstone, limestone, shale, and mudstone.

Figure 1. The waste coal gangue of a coal mine.

Figure 2. Coal gangue particles after sieving tests.

An LSDSTA manufactured by Chengdu Donghua Zhuoyue Technology Co., Ltd. (Chengdu, China), was used in this test, which is shown in Figure 3. The specimen sizes allowed by the LSDSTA are D = 300 mm and H = 600 mm. The ratio between the triaxial specimen diameter and the maximum particle size should not be smaller than 5 [19–21]; therefore, the maximum particle size allowed by LSDSTA in this test is no greater than 60 mm, and then the effect of specimen size can be neglected. The LSDSTA mainly includes the following parts: (1) a data acquisition system through a computer, (2) a testing machine control system, (3) a triaxial pressure cover, (4) an axial loading system, (5) a volumetric strain measurement system, and (6) a sample preparation mold, which are shown in Figure 3. The LSDSTA can automatically collect test parameters, such as axial load and displacement, confining pressure, pore pressure, and volumetric strain, as well as realize the static shear test and cyclic dynamic loading test. In addition, the large-scale triaxial tests and the same specimen size were widely used in the previous studies, e.g., Cai et al. [20] and Leng et al. [21], which guarantees the reliability of this apparatus.

Figure 3. The large-scale dynamic and static triaxial instrument.

2.2. Specimen Preparation and Testing Program

The only way to characterize the grading of granular materials is to use the grading curve. The grading curve contains a large amount of data; however, it lacks quantitative indicators. Hence, it is difficult to make the comparison of the particle size distribution with different gradings of granular materials. In order to completely express the grading of particles and quantitatively analyze the relationship between grading and relevant mechanical indexes, the grading of granular materials is quantified by establishing the grading equations with mathematical formulas, which has great significance for engineering practice and academic research. In this test, the method of artificial sample preparation according to FMGE was used, and the FMGE is defined as [22–24]

$$P_i = \left(\frac{d_i}{d_{max}}\right)^{3-D_f} \times 100\% \quad (1)$$

where D_f represents the fractal dimension, d_i presents the particle size (mm), P_i denotes the cumulative mass percentage with particle size less than d_i (%), and d_{max} indicates the maximum particle size (mm).

The control parameters of well grading for CGSF are the coefficient of uniformity (C_U) and the coefficient of curvature (C_C), and the calculation formulas are as follows [25,26]:

$$C_u = \frac{d_{60}}{d_{10}} \quad (2)$$

$$C_c = \frac{(d_{30})^2}{d_{10} d_{60}} \quad (3)$$

where d_{60}, d_{30}, and d_{10} refer to the particle size corresponding to the passing percentage of 60%, 30%, and 10% in the grading curve, respectively (mm).

CGSF with well grading satisfies $C_u \geq 5$ and $1 \leq C_c \leq 3$. Furthermore, combining Equations (1)–(3), the range of well grading can be captured based on the FMGE:

$$1.89 = 3 - \frac{\lg 6}{\lg 5} \leq D_f \leq 3 - \frac{\lg(\frac{3}{2})}{\lg 3} = 2.63 \quad (4)$$

According to Equation (4), 4 groups of tests with different fractal dimensions, i.e., D_f = 1.89, 2.13, 2.37, and 2.61, were designed to carry out the experimental research, and the test design grading curve is shown in Figure 4. A cylindrical specimen with D = 300 mm and H = 600 mm was utilized in this test; D and H are the diameter and height of the specimen, respectively. According to the Chinese Standard of Soils for Highway Engineering [18], the maximum dry density of the specimen can be obtained. Compaction degree, which was widely used for the triaxial test and situ construction [27,28], is calculated as follows:

$$D_c = \frac{\rho}{\rho_{max}} \times 100 \tag{5}$$

where ρ_{max} denotes the maximum dry density (g/cm^3), ρ is the dry density of the specimen (g/cm^3), and D_c represents the compaction degree (%).

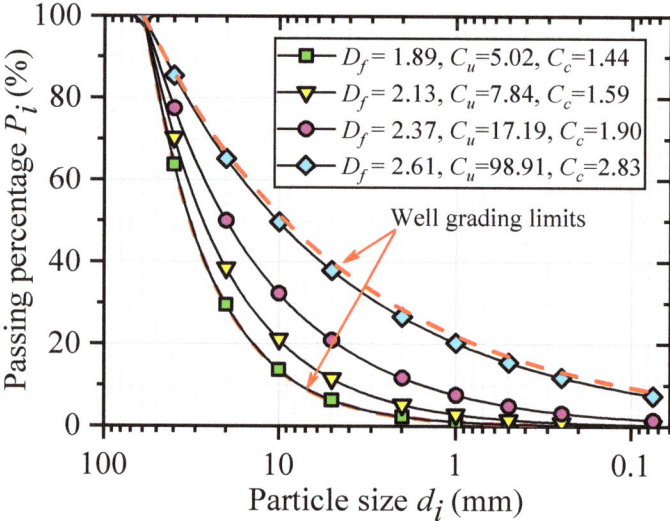

Figure 4. Particle size distribution of the tested materials.

In this test, the compaction degree was used to control the preparation of specimens and $D_c = 90\%$, 93%, and 96% were adopted. In addition, the compaction degree meets the requirements of the road base and subbase materials [18].

Figure 5 shows the process of the large triaxial tests. First, the above drying CGSF (as displayed in Figure 2) should be well mixed according to the designed grading curve (as shown in Figure 4). The specimen prepared in this test was too large and heavy at the laboratory. Therefore, the specimen was compacted with a compaction hammer in a mold in five layers (as shown in Figure 5a). Before placing CGSF on the next layer, the surface of the previously compacted layer was scraped to a depth of about 20 mm to guarantee well-interlocking vertically adjacent layers, just as in other studies [20,29,30]. The target compaction degree of the CGSF specimen was reached by controlling the thickness of each individual layer and the mass of added CGSF. After compaction, a rubber membrane was used to enclose the specimen, and the top and bottom of the specimen were tied with rubber ropes. Figure 5b displays the prepared sample.

Then, the specimen was put in the triaxial pressure cover. All of the specimens were saturated by back pressure before loading, as described by Kong et al. [31], Cai et al. [20], Chen et al. [32], and Wu et al. [33]. The specimens were considered completely saturated when the pore pressure coefficient B was larger than 0.95. After that, the required effective confining pressure was applied to the specimen to complete the isotropic consolidation.

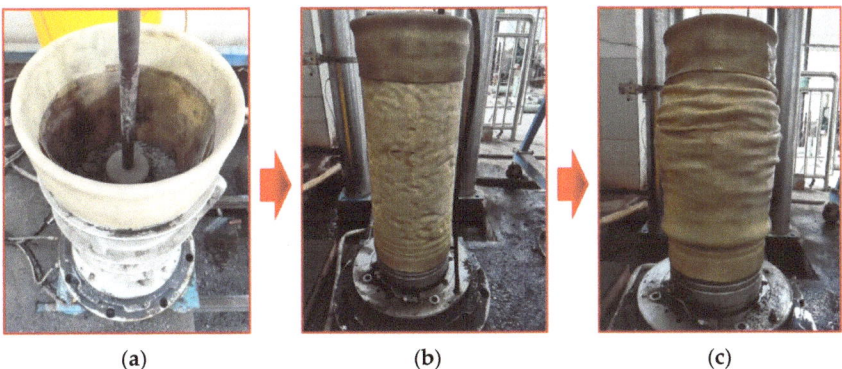

Figure 5. The process of the large triaxial tests: (**a**) compacting in the mold; (**b**) the prepared sample; (**c**) failed sample after the test.

The research shows that traffic loading is different from the sine wave, but very similar to the half-sine wave [34]. Therefore, the half-sine wave was used to simulate the traffic cyclic dynamic loading. The dynamic loading frequency was chosen as 1 Hz in these tests, which was also used in [21,34]. This paper mainly focuses on the permanent deformation of CGSF, and the confining pressures (i.e., effective consolidation stress), σ_3', of 50, 100, and 150 kPa were selected in this test. The cyclic dynamic loading in railway subgrade is generally distributed between 35 kPa and 185 kPa [35,36]. Therefore, the axial dynamic stress amplitude was taken as 180 kPa in the separate loading test of each sample, and each specimen was loaded with 30,000 numbers of half-sine wave separately in this test. In addition, Wang et al. [37] studied the permanent deformation of reinforced gravelly soil filler under cyclic loading with dynamic stress amplitudes of 90 kPa and 135 kPa.

The test scheme design is shown in Table 1. The large-scale triaxial test can investigate the mechanical properties with large-size particles, which is closer to the engineering practice. Hence, the large-scale triaxial test has been widely used in recent years. Three groups of parallel tests were carried out at the same time under each test condition, and one group was randomly selected for key analysis. The loading process in this test is shown in Figure 6.

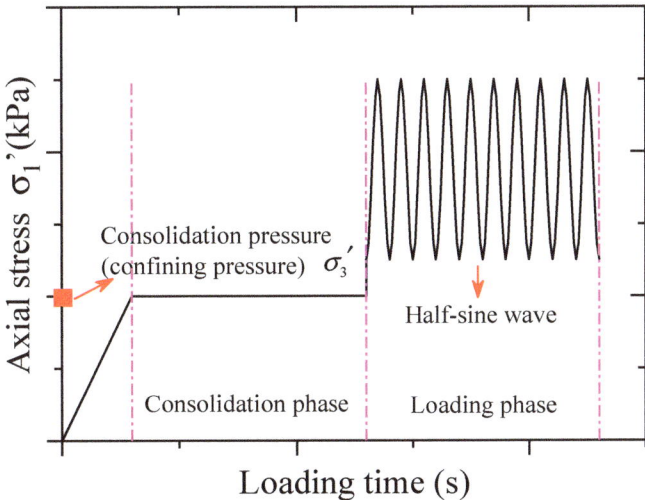

Figure 6. Loading process under cyclic loading.

Table 1. Test scheme design.

Specimen Number	D_f	σ_3' (kPa)	D_c (%)
DT01	2.37	50	93
DT02	2.37	100	93
DT03	2.37	150	93
DT04	2.37	50	90
DT05	2.37	50	96
DT06	2.61	50	93
DT07	2.13	50	93
DT08	1.89	50	93

3. Permanent Deformation Analysis

The monitoring data show that the permanent deformation of the subgrade under the traffic cyclic loading is very considerable and even has an obvious impact on the normal operation of the project [36]. Therefore, accurate analysis and prediction of the permanent deformation for the subgrade have important theoretical and practical significance for the normal use and safe operation of the completed project and for the guidance of future project construction.

According to the theory of elastoplastic mechanics [35], the axial strain of a coal gangue sample under cyclic loading includes elastic strain ε^e and plastic strain ε^p, namely:

$$\varepsilon_1 = \varepsilon^e + \varepsilon^p \tag{6}$$

where ε_1 represents the axial strain of the specimen; ε^e denotes the elastic strain; and ε^p indicates plastic strain.

The elastic strain will recover during the loading and unloading process, while the plastic strain cannot recover and will gradually accumulate, resulting in the failure of the sample. Therefore, the cumulative plastic strain causes permanent deformation, and the permanent deformation (ε) studied in this paper is the cumulative plastic strain under cyclic loading. The calculation diagram is shown in Figure 7.

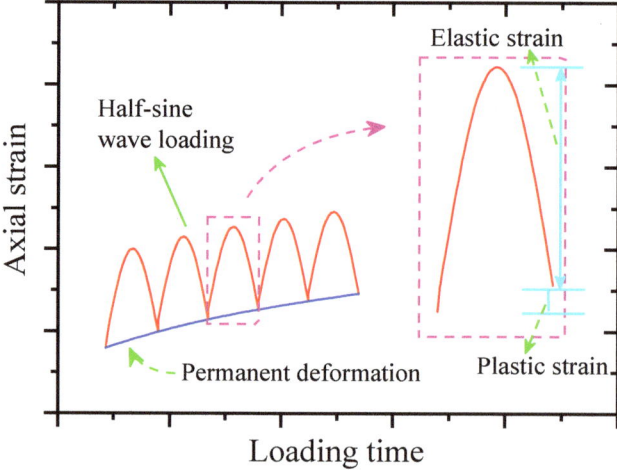

Figure 7. Schematic diagram of the permanent deformation calculation.

3.1. Effect of Confining Pressure on the Permanent Deformation

According to the above test scheme, the relationship between the permanent deformation (ε) and the numbers of cyclic loading (N) with different confining pressures is shown in Figure 8. The following can be seen from Figure 8: (1) The relationship curve between ε and N can be divided into three stages. The first stage is the rapid growth phase, and the curve has approximately linear growth. The second stage is the deceleration growth phase; the curve growth rate slows down obviously, and the curve gradient decreases gradually. The third stage is the approaching stability phase, and the permanent deformation closes to stable. (2) As observed in Figure 8, ε decreases by 2.79% when the confining pressure increases from 50 kPa to 100 kPa, whereas ε decreases by only 0.30% when the confining pressure increases from 100 kPa to 200 kPa. Hence, the effect of confining pressure on ε is related to the level of confining pressure. When the confining pressure is smaller, its effect on ε is significant, whereas when the confining pressure is larger, its influence on ε is smaller. This also reflects that the effect of traffic cyclic loading on subgrade decreases with the increase of subgrade depth.

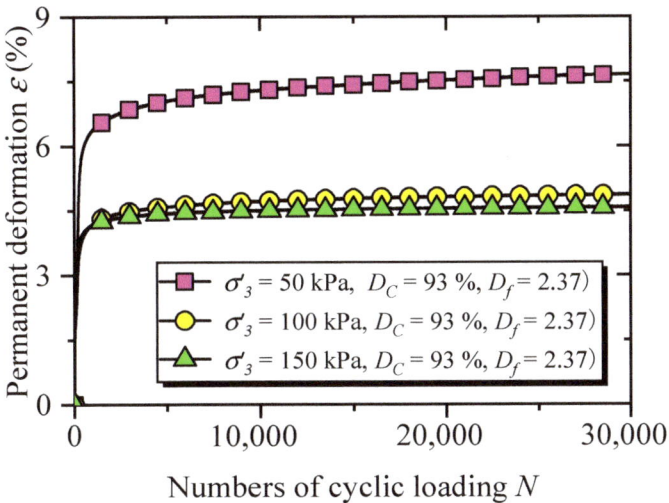

Figure 8. The relationship between ε and N with different confining pressure values.

3.2. Effect of Grading on the Permanent Deformation

The relationship between ε and N with different gradings is displayed in Figure 9. As demonstrated in Figure 9: (1) ε increases approximate linear when N is less than 400. The growth rate of ε begins to slow down and gradually decreases when $400 \leq N \leq 1000$. ε tends to be stable when N is more than 1000. The abovementioned laws apply to the final stability relationship curve between ε and N. Therefore, $N = 1000$ can be used as a criterion for reaching the stable stage of CGSF, which can guide the later test loading and coal gangue subgrade engineering. (2) Under the condition of maximum fine particle content (D_f = 2.61), the coal gangue sample will fail (ε reaches 15%) rapidly when N is very small (N = 535). Moreover, in these four groups of tests, ε of the coal gangue sample is the smallest when D_f = 2.13. Hence, the influence of grading, i.e., particle size distribution, on ε of coal gangue samples is significant. With the increase of the fractal dimension (D_f), ε first decreases and then increases, reflecting that there is an obvious optimal grading for coal gangue samples under cyclic loading. Wu et al. [26,38] studied the compaction characteristics of coarse aggregates for embankment dams using the surface vibration compaction test and lateral compression test, which showed that there is an optimal grading of coarse aggregate. In addition, through the large-scale vibration compaction test and static shear test, the authors of [39] also investigated the influence of grading on the compaction and strength of CGSF, and then the optimal grading, i.e., $2.04 \leq D_f \leq 2.55$, was captured using FMGE. The reason for this phenomenon is related to the contact relationship and interlocking relationship between coarse and fine particles. These conclusions are all consistent with this study.

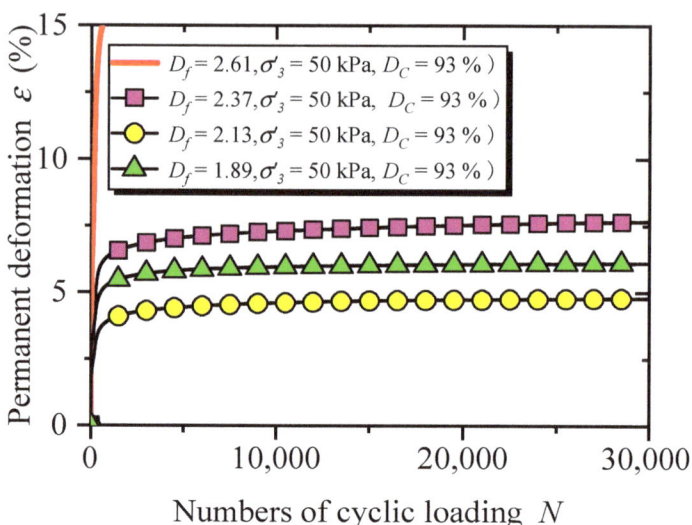

Figure 9. Relationship between ε and N with different grading parameters.

3.3. Effect of Compaction Degree on the Permanent Deformation

The evolution of ε versus N with different compaction degree values is displayed in Figure 10. As demonstrated in Figure 10: (1) The relationship between ε and N with different compaction degree values is consistent with the variation laws under different confining pressures and grading parameters. (2) When the compaction degree increases from 90% to 93%, the development of ε is hardly affected. However, when the compaction degree increases from 93% to 96%, increasing compaction degree has a significant effect on restraining ε. Therefore, the effect of compaction degree on ε of CGSF depends on the level of compaction degree. ε is hardly affected when the compaction degree is smaller, whereas increasing the compaction degree has a significant effect on restraining ε when the compaction degree is bigger.

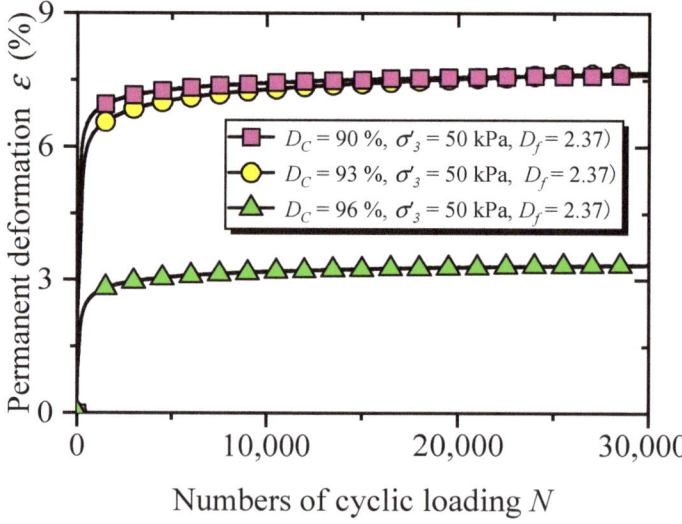

Figure 10. Evolution of ε versus N with different compaction degree values.

4. Unified Model of Permanent Deformation

4.1. Comparative Analysis of Existing Models

The establishment of a permanent deformation model has always been the focus of many scholars. The most widely used model was proposed by Monismith et al. [40], which was defined as:

$$\varepsilon = \alpha_1 N^{\beta_1} \tag{7}$$

where ε indicates the permanent deformation, N represents the numbers of cyclic loading, and α_1 and β_1 are the fitting parameters of this model.

The permanent deformation model proposed by Li et al. [35] was defined as:

$$\varepsilon = \alpha_2 \left(1 - e^{-\beta_2 N}\right) \tag{8}$$

where α_2 and β_2 are the fitting parameters.

Liu et al. [41] proposed the following permanent deformation model:

$$\varepsilon = \alpha_3 + \beta_3 \ln N \tag{9}$$

where α_3 and β_3 are the fitting parameters.

Wang et al. [37] proposed the permanent deformation model as follows:

$$\varepsilon = \frac{N}{\alpha_4 + \beta_4 N + \gamma_4 N^{0.5}} \tag{10}$$

where α_4, β_4, and γ_4 are the fitting parameters.

According to the relationship between ε and N presented in Figures 8–10, the permanent deformation of CGSF under cyclic loading is analyzed using a data-fitting method based on the above models in Equations (7)–(10). Analysis shows that fitting parameters of CGSF in Equation (10) cannot be obtained. Hence, Equation (10) is not investigated in this paper. The fitting parameters are displayed in Table 2.

Table 2. Model parameters.

Specimen Number	DT01	DT02	DT03	DT04	DT05	DT06	DT07	DT08
α_1	3.9085	2.8126	3.2501	4.9523	1.6604	12.1707	2.5312	3.7737
β_1	0.0667	0.0550	0.0345	0.0432	0.0693	0.0323	0.0635	0.0482
R^2	0.8159	0.7709	0.7050	0.7170	0.8585	0.3876	0.8570	0.7742
α_2	7.3600	4.7367	4.4983	7.4476	3.2039	16.5600	4.6217	5.9533
β_2	0.0033	0.0041	0.0102	0.0062	0.0031	0.0051	0.0033	0.0047
R^2	0.6947	0.7091	0.5936	0.7042	0.6320	0.8911	0.6038	0.6182
α_3	2.8128	2.2945	3.0339	4.4157	1.1584	11.2994	1.9108	3.2612
β_3	0.4808	0.2584	0.1558	0.3216	0.2163	0.5537	0.2866	0.2850
R^2	0.8560	0.8095	0.7321	0.7494	0.8980	0.4149	0.8937	0.8091

According to the correlation coefficient (R^2) of fitting parameters in Table 2, the existing permanent deformation model cannot accurately enough describe the permanent deformation of CGSF under cyclic loading, and R^2 values are all less than 0.9. The permanent deformation curve can be divided into three types [42]: (1) Stable/attenuation type, where ε first increases with the increase of N and then tends to stay at a stable value when N achieves a larger value. (2) Failure type, where ε will increase sharply until the specimen fails when N reaches a bigger value. (3) Criticality type, where ε distributes between (1) and (2). The existing permanent deformation model can describe the variation of one certain type of the mentioned curves well; however, there is a lack of a unified model of permanent deformation used for different types of permanent deformation curves. Therefore, it is necessary to put forward a unified model which can be generally applicable to different types of permanent deformation based on the mentioned CGSF tests.

4.2. Establishment of Unified Model for Permanent Deformation

Based on the above analysis of the permanent deformation curve for CGSF and the comparative analysis of existing models, the relationship between ε and N is analyzed using regression using MATLAB, and then the unified calculation model of permanent deformation for CGSF under cyclic loading is established:

$$\varepsilon = \frac{pN}{q+N} \quad (11)$$

where p and q are the model parameters.

The model parameters in Equation (11) are solved using the least square method, that is:

$$\sum_{i=1}^{n}\left[\varepsilon - \frac{pN}{q+N}\right]^2 = \min\left\{\sum_{i=1}^{n}\left[\varepsilon - \frac{pN}{q+N}\right]^2\right\} \quad (12)$$

The model parameters obtained by Equations (11) and (12) are shown in Table 3. Figure 11 presents the comparative analysis of R^2 for the above permanent deformation models, i.e., Equations (7)–(9), and Figure 12 shows the comparison between the proposed model and the test curve. It can be seen from Table 3, Figures 11 and 12, compared with the existing permanent deformation models, that the proposed model in this paper can better describe the permanent deformation of CGSF under cyclic loading. The R^2 of the proposed model is bigger than 0.9, which is larger than the other models. The correctness of the model is preliminarily verified.

Table 3. Parameters of the proposed model.

Specimen Number	DT01	DT02	DT03	DT04	DT05	DT06	DT07	DT08
p	7.5179	4.8175	4.5371	7.5381	3.2774	16.7341	4.7171	6.0390
q	178.5503	135.5844	55.5003	87.8797	193.5777	84.8601	172.0490	111.6893
R^2	0.9165	0.9391	0.9031	0.9279	0.9104	0.9675	0.9034	0.9152

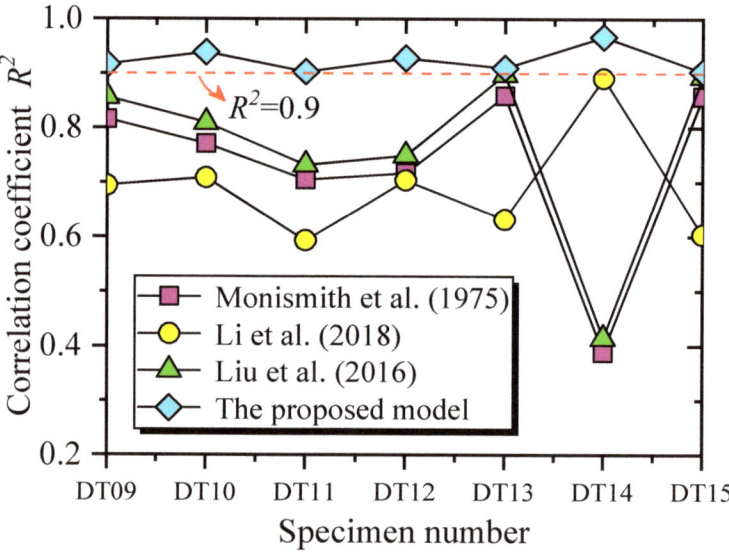

Figure 11. Correlation coefficient comparison of permanent deformation models [35,40,41].

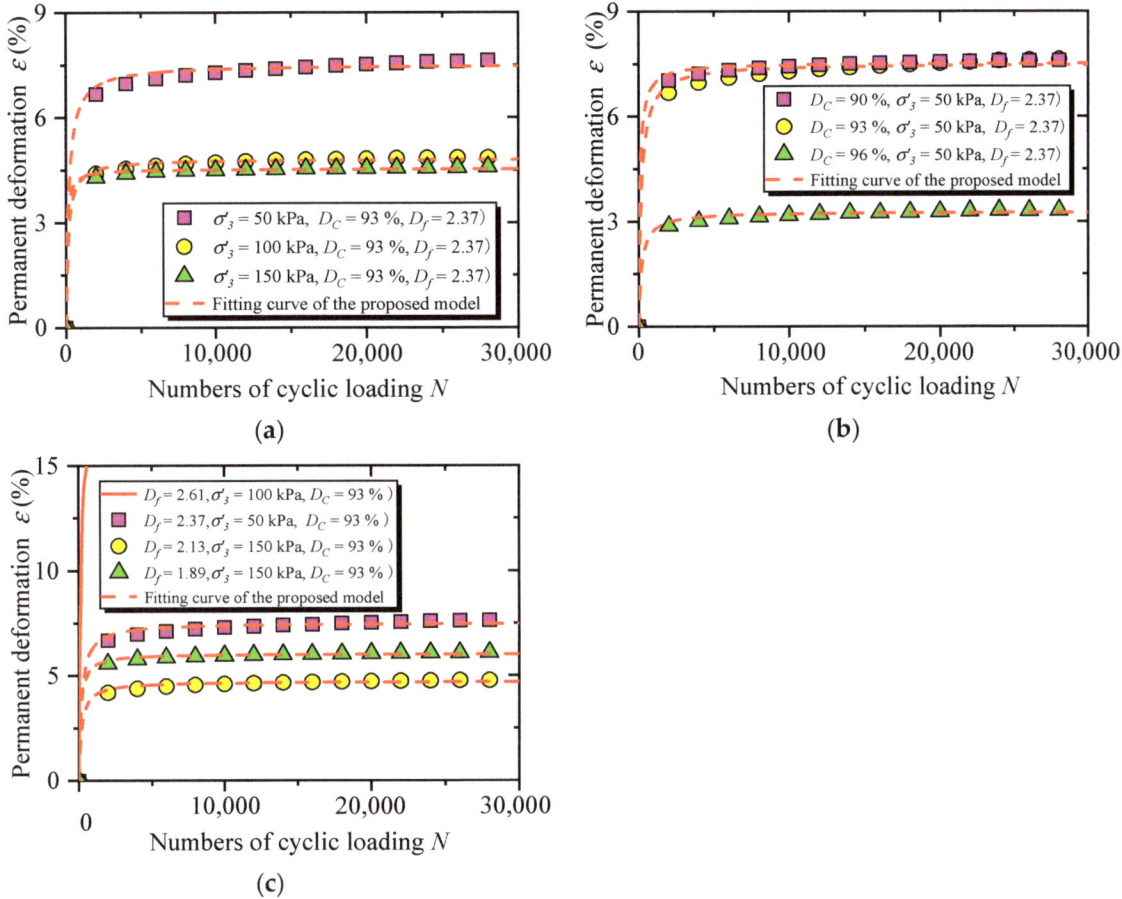

Figure 12. Comparison between the proposed model and the test curve: (**a**) under different confining pressure conditions, (**b**) under diverse compaction degree conditions, and (**c**) under various grading conditions.

4.3. Model Parameter Analysis

Based on the test data of the DT02 specimen, i.e., $\sigma'_3 = 100$ kPa, $D_f = 2.37$, and $D_c = 93\%$, the physical meaning of the proposed model (Equation (11)) parameters is analyzed by changing the model parameter values, as shown in Figure 13 (the model parameters of fitting curve in Figure 13 are $p = 4.8175$, $q = 135.5844$).

It can be seen from Figure 13 that, when q is constant, the N required before the permanent deformation curve tends to be stable is basically unchanged with the increase of p, whereas the stable value of the permanent deformation curve increases accordingly. Therefore, p reflects the permanent deformation in the stable stage. The greater p occurs with the bigger permanent deformation. Similarly, when p is constant, with the increasing q, the permanent deformation at the stable stage remains unchanged, whereas the N required before the curve tends to be stable increases. Hence, q indicates the N required before the permanent deformation curve tends to be stable, and the greater N required before the permanent deformation curve reaches the stable stage occurs with a larger q.

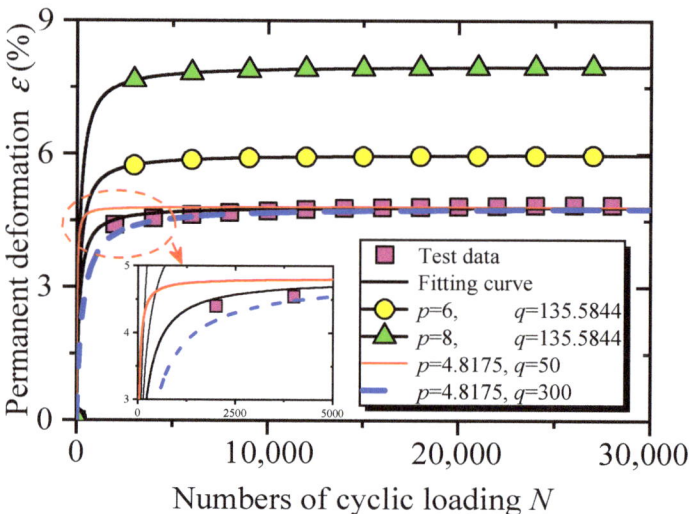

Figure 13. Model parameters analysis.

The above analysis studies the physical meaning of the model parameters by changing the parameter values. Then, the correctness of the above model parameter analysis will be further verified from a mathematical point of view.

For the unified model of permanent deformation, i.e., Equation (11), when N tends to be 0:

$$\lim_{N \to 0} \varepsilon = \lim_{N \to 0} \frac{pN}{q+N} = 0 \tag{13}$$

Before test loading, the permanent deformation of the sample is 0, and the model is consistent with the actual situation. When the coal gangue sample experiences a large number of cyclic loadings:

$$\lim_{N \to \infty} \varepsilon = \lim_{N \to \infty} \frac{pN}{q+N} = \lim_{N \to \infty} \frac{p}{\frac{q}{N}+1} = p \tag{14}$$

According to Equation (14), when N is large enough, the denominator approaches 1, and the maximum value of permanent deformation is equal to p. Therefore, p reflects the permanent deformation in the stable stage. For Equation (14), the smaller N required before the permanent deformation curve reaches the stable stage occurs with the lesser q. It can be seen that the analysis of model parameters from the perspective of mathematics and test curve is consistent.

4.4. Model Validation

The test data of Figure 8a in Li et al. [35], Figure 3 in Wang et al. [37], and Figure 3a in Mei et al. [43] were selected to verify the correctness of the unified model of permanent deformation in this paper. Figure 14a–c display the fitting effect of the test data in the above research and the permanent deformation model established in this paper. It can be seen from Figure 14 that the permanent deformation model established in this paper can describe the permanent deformation test results in the existing research well, thus verifying the correctness of this model. In addition, three types of the permanent deformation curve in Figure 14 can be described well by the unified model of permanent deformation in this study, which shows the universal applicability of the model in this paper.

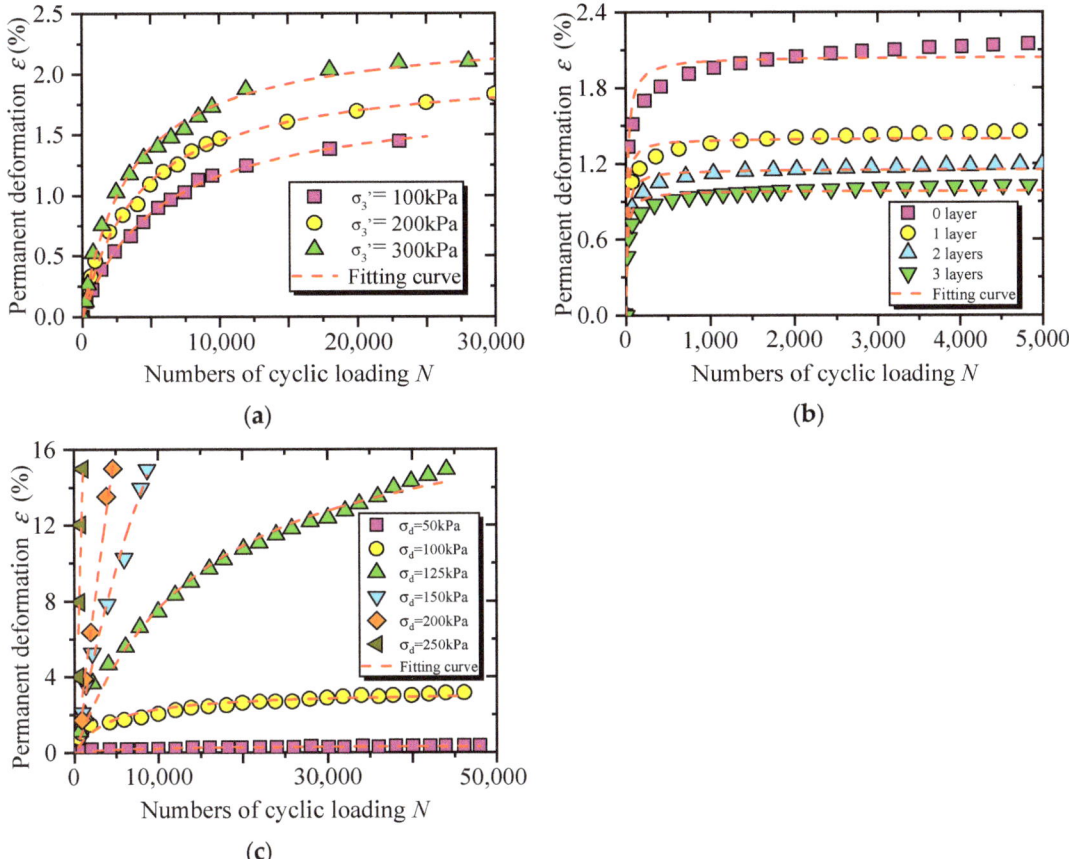

Figure 14. Model validation. Test data were extracted from: (**a**) Li et al. [35], (**b**) Wang et al. [37], and (**c**) Mei et al. [43].

5. Conclusions

The following conclusions can be drawn from the investigation described above.

(1) Experimental grading was designed by using FMGE, and the well-grading limits of CGSF were captured based on the FMGE, i.e., the grading is uniform when $1.89 \leq D_f \leq 2.63$.

(2) The relationship curve between ε and N can be divided into three stages, i.e., the rapid growth phase, the deceleration growth phase, and the approaching stability phase. $N = 1000$ can be used as a criterion for reaching the stable stage of CGSF, which can guide the later test loading and coal gangue subgrade engineering.

(3) The effect of confining pressure on ε is related to the level of confining pressure. The effect of confining pressure on ε is significant when the confining pressure is smaller, whereas the influence of confining pressure on ε is smaller when the confining pressure is larger.

(4) The influence of grading on ε of coal gangue samples is significant. With the increase of D_f, ε first increases and then decreases, reflecting that there is an obvious optimal grading for coal gangue samples under cyclic loading.

(5) The effect of compaction degree on ε of CGSF depends on the level of compaction degree. ε is hardly affected when the compaction degree is smaller, whereas increasing compaction degree has a significant effect on restraining ε when the compaction degree is bigger.

(6) According to the analysis of the permanent deformation curve for CGSF, the unified calculation model of permanent deformation for CGSF under cyclic loading was established. Compared with the existing permanent deformation models, the proposed model in this paper can better describe the permanent deformation of CGSF under cyclic loading. Then, the model parameters were analyzed and the model was verified.

Author Contributions: Investigation, Z.-T.Z., Y.-H.W., W.-H.G., W.H. and S.-K.L. All authors have read and agreed to the published version of the manuscript.

Funding: This research was funded by the National Natural Science Foundation of China, Grant No. 52208341; the Natural Science Foundation of Hunan Province, Grant No. 2020JJ4019; and the Scientific Research Project of the Hunan Provincial Education Department, Grant No. 21C0360.

Data Availability Statement: Not applicable.

Conflicts of Interest: The authors declare no conflict of interest.

References

1. Zhang, Y.; Ling, T.-C. Reactivity activation of waste coal gangue and its impact on the properties of cement-based materials—A review. *Constr. Build. Mater.* **2020**, *234*, 117424. [CrossRef]
2. Zhao, Y.; Qiu, J.; Ma, Z.; Sun, X. Eco-friendly treatment of coal gangue for its utilization as supplementary cementitious materials. *J. Clean. Prod.* **2021**, *285*, 124834. [CrossRef]
3. Li, J.; Huang, Y.; Ouyang, S.; Guo, Y.; Gao, H.; Wu, L.; Shi, Y.; Zhu, L. Transparent characterization and quantitative analysis of broken gangue's 3D fabric under the bearing compression. *Int. J. Min. Sci. Technol.* **2022**, *32*, 335–345. [CrossRef]
4. Ma, D.; Duan, H.; Liu, J.; Li, X.; Zhou, Z. The role of gangue on the mitigation of mining-induced hazards and environmental pollution: An experimental investigation. *Sci. Total Environ.* **2019**, *664*, 436–448. [CrossRef] [PubMed]
5. Chen, X.; Zheng, L.; Dong, X.; Jiang, C.; Wei, X. Sources and mixing of sulfate contamination in the water environment of a typical coal mining city, China: Evidence from stable isotope characteristics. *Environ. Geochem. Health* **2020**, *42*, 2865–2879. [CrossRef]
6. Xiao, G.; Yang, G.; Jixi, C.; Ruyi, Z. Deterioration mechanism of coal gangue concrete under the coupling action of bending load and freeze–thaw. *Constr. Build. Mater.* **2022**, *338*, 127265. [CrossRef]
7. Wu, Q.-h.; Weng, L.; Zhao, Y.-l.; Feng, F. Influence of infilling stiffness on mechanical and fracturing responses of hollow cylindrical sandstone under uniaxial compression tests. *J. Cent. South Univ.* **2021**, *28*, 2485–2498. [CrossRef]
8. Wu, Q.; Weng, L.; Zhao, Y.; Zhao, F.; Peng, W.; Zhang, S. Deformation and cracking characteristics of ring-shaped granite with inclusion under diametrical compression. *Arab. J. Geosci.* **2020**, *13*, 681. [CrossRef]
9. Li, Y.; Liu, S.; Guan, X. Multitechnique investigation of concrete with coal gangue. *Constr. Build. Mater.* **2021**, *301*, 124114. [CrossRef]
10. Qiu, J.; Zhu, M.; Zhou, Y.; Guan, X. Effect and mechanism of coal gangue concrete modification by fly ash. *Constr. Build. Mater.* **2021**, *294*, 123563. [CrossRef]
11. Zhao, B.; Zhai, D.; Xin, J.; Guo, Y.; Wang, J.; Wei, Q.; Wang, H.; Tang, R. Rheological properties, mechanical characteristics, and microstructures of gangue-cemented paste backfill: Linking to loess doses. *Arab. J. Geosci.* **2022**, *15*, 244. [CrossRef]
12. Zhao, Y.; Yang, C.; Li, K.; Qu, F.; Yan, C.; Wu, Z. Toward understanding the activation and hydration mechanisms of composite activated coal gangue geopolymer. *Constr. Build. Mater.* **2022**, *318*, 125999. [CrossRef]
13. Su, Z.; Li, X.; Zhang, Q. Influence of thermally activated coal gangue powder on the structure of the interfacial transition zone in concrete. *J. Clean. Prod.* **2022**, *363*, 132408. [CrossRef]
14. Chen, M.; Wen, P.; Wang, C.; Chai, Z.; Gao, Z. Evaluation of particle size distribution and mechanical properties of mineral waste slag as filling material. *Constr. Build. Mater.* **2020**, *253*, 119183. [CrossRef]
15. Li, J.; Zhang, J.; Yang, X.; Zhang, A.; Yu, M. Monte Carlo simulations of deformation behaviour of unbound granular materials based on a real aggregate library. *Int. J. Pavement Eng.* **2023**, *24*, 2165650. [CrossRef]
16. Li, J.; Zhang, J.; Zhang, A.; Peng, J. Evaluation on Deformation Behavior of Granular Base Material during Repeated Load Triaxial Testing by Discrete-Element Method. *Int. J. Geomech.* **2022**, *22*, 04022210. [CrossRef]
17. Yao, Y.; Li, J.; Ni, J.; Liang, C.; Zhang, A. Effects of gravel content and shape on shear behaviour of soil-rock mixture: Experiment and DEM modelling. *Comput. Geotech.* **2022**, *141*, 104476. [CrossRef]
18. JTG 3430-2020; Test Methods of Soils for Highway Engineering. China Communications Press: Beijing, China, 2020. (In Chinese)
19. Chen, W.B.; Yin, J.H.; Feng, W.Q.; Borana, L.; Chen, R.P. Accumulated Permanent Axial Strain of a Subgrade Fill under Cyclic High-Speed Railway Loading. *Int. J. Geomech.* **2018**, *18*, 04018018. [CrossRef]
20. Cai, Y.Q.; Chen, J.Y.; Cao, Z.G.; Gu, C.; Wang, J. Influence of Grain Gradation on Permanent Strain of Unbound Granular Materials under Low Confining Pressure and High-Cycle Loading. *Int. J. Geomech.* **2018**, *18*, 04017156. [CrossRef]
21. Leng, W.; Xiao, Y.; Nie, R.-s.; Zhou, W.; Liu, W. Investigating Strength and Deformation Characteristics of Heavy-Haul Railway Embankment Materials Using Large-Scale Undrained Cyclic Triaxial Tests. *Int. J. Geomech.* **2017**, *17*, 04017074. [CrossRef]

22. Zhang, Z.-T.; Gao, W.-H. Effect of different test methods on the disintegration behaviour of soft rock and the evolution model of disintegration breakage under cyclic wetting and drying. *Eng. Geol.* **2020**, *279*, 105888. [CrossRef]
23. Zhang, Z.-T.; Gao, W.-H.; Wang, X.; Zhang, J.-Q.; Tang, X.-Y. Degradation-induced evolution of particle roundness and its effect on the shear behaviour of railway ballast. *Transp. Geotech.* **2020**, *24*, 100388. [CrossRef]
24. Zhang, Z.-T.; Gao, W.-H.; Zeng, C.-F.; Tang, X.-Y.; Wu, J. Evolution of the disintegration breakage of red-bed soft rock using a logistic regression model. *Transp. Geotech.* **2020**, *24*, 100382. [CrossRef]
25. Zhu, J.G.; Guo, W.L.; Wen, Y.F.; Yin, J.H.; Zhou, C. New Gradation Equation and Applicability for Particle-Size Distributions of Various Soils. *Int. J. Geomech.* **2018**, *18*, 04017155. [CrossRef]
26. Wu, E.L.; Zhu, J.G.; Chen, G.; Wang, L. Experimental study of effect of gradation on compaction properties of rockfill materials. *Bull. Eng. Geol. Environ.* **2020**, *79*, 2863–2869. [CrossRef]
27. García-de-la-Oliva, J.L.; Moreno-Robles, J. Granular sub-ballast compaction control methods in high-speed railway lines. Spanish experience. *Transp. Geotech.* **2019**, *19*, 135–145. [CrossRef]
28. Trinh, V.N.; Tang, A.M.; Cui, Y.-J.; Dupla, J.-C.; Canou, J.; Calon, N.; Lambert, L.; Robinet, A.; Schoen, O. Mechanical characterisation of the fouled ballast in ancient railway track substructure by large-scale triaxial tests. *Soils Found.* **2012**, *52*, 511–523. [CrossRef]
29. Lenart, S.; Koseki, J.; Miyashita, Y.; Sato, T. Large-scale triaxial tests of dense gravel material at low confining pressures. *Soils Found.* **2014**, *54*, 45–55. [CrossRef]
30. Wichtmann, T.; Rondón, H.A.; Niemunis, A.; Triantafyllidis, T.; Lizcano, A. Prediction of Permanent Deformations in Pavements Using a High-Cycle Accumulation Model. *J. Geotech. Geoenviron. Eng.* **2010**, *136*, 728–740. [CrossRef]
31. Kong, X.; Liu, J.; Zou, D.; Liu, H. Stress-Dilatancy Relationship of Zipingpu Gravel under Cyclic Loading in Triaxial Stress States. *Int. J. Geomech.* **2016**, *16*, 04016001. [CrossRef]
32. Chen, G.; Wu, Q.; Zhao, K.; Shen, Z.; Yang, J. A Binary Packing Material–Based Procedure for Evaluating Soil Liquefaction Triggering during Earthquakes. *J. Geotech. Geoenviron. Eng.* **2020**, *146*, 04020040. [CrossRef]
33. Wu, Q.; Ma, W.j.; Liu, Q.; Zhao, K.; Chen, G. Dynamic shear modulus and damping ratio of rubber-sand mixtures with a wide range of rubber content. *Mater. Today Commun.* **2021**, *27*, 102341. [CrossRef]
34. Huang, B.; Ding, H.; Chen, Y. Simulation of high-speed train load by dynamic triaxial tests. *Chin. J. Geotech. Eng.* **2011**, *33*, 195–202. (In Chinese)
35. Li, Y.; Zhang, J.; Zhu, Z.; Wang, X.; Yu, Z. Accumulated deformation of gravel filler of subgrade under cyclic loading. *Adv. Eng. Sci.* **2018**, *50*, 130–137. (In Chinese)
36. Wang, C.; Chen, Y. Study on effect of traffic loading induced static deviator stress on undrained cyclic properties of saturated soft clay. *Chin. J. Geotech. Eng.* **2007**, *29*, 1742–1747. (In Chinese)
37. Wang, J.; Chang, Z.; Tang, Y.; Tang, Y. Dynamic triaxial test analysis of reinforced gravel soil under cyclic loading. *Rock Soil Mech.* **2020**, *41*, 2851–2860. (In Chinese)
38. Wu, E.; Zhu, J.; Guo, W.; Zhang, Z. Effect of Gradation on the Compactability of Coarse-Grained Soils. *KSCE J. Civ. Eng.* **2020**, *24*, 356–364. [CrossRef]
39. Zhang, Z.; Gao, W.; Liu, C.; Liu, Z.; Feng, X. Experimental study on the effect of gradation on the compaction and strength characteristics of coal gangue subgrade filler. *J. Eng. Geol.* **2022**. (In Chinese) [CrossRef]
40. Monismith, C.L.; Ogawa, N.; Freeme, C.R. Permanent deformation characteristics of subgrade soils due to repeated load. *Transp. Res. Rec.* **1975**, *537*, 1–17.
41. Liu, B.; Pham, D.P.; Su, Q.; Gui, B. Deformation characteristics of subgrade graded gravel with different water contents. *Rock Soil Mech.* **2016**, *37*, 1365–1372. (In Chinese)
42. Mu, R.; Huang, Z.; Pu, S.; Yao, Z.; Cheng, X. Accumulated deformation characteristics of undisturbed red clay under cyclic loading and dynamic constitutive relationship. *Rock Soil Mech* **2020**, *S2*, 1–10. (In Chinese)
43. Mei, H.; Leng, W.; Nie, R.; Li, Y. Study on dynamic behavior and permanent deformation characteristics of coarse-grained soil. *J. Huazhong Univ. of Sci. Technol. (Nat. Sci. Ed.)* **2019**, *47*, 113–119. (In Chinese)

Disclaimer/Publisher's Note: The statements, opinions and data contained in all publications are solely those of the individual author(s) and contributor(s) and not of MDPI and/or the editor(s). MDPI and/or the editor(s) disclaim responsibility for any injury to people or property resulting from any ideas, methods, instructions or products referred to in the content.

Article

Effects of Lime Content on Road Performance of Low Liquid Limit Clay

Jinli Zhang [1], Hai Li [2,*], Junhui Peng [2,*] and Zhe Zhang [2]

[1] Anhui Transportation Holding Group Co., Ltd., Hefei 230088, China; 18756062813@163.com
[2] National Engineering Research Center of Highway Maintenance Technology, Changsha University of Science and Technology, Changsha 410114, China
* Correspondence: lihai@stu.csust.edu.cn (H.L.); pjh@csust.edu.cn (J.P.)

Abstract: Low liquid limit clay has a low plastic index, displays poor strength, and is sensitive to water, and its mechanical qualities decline as the water content changes, making it difficult to employ directly in the construction process. Adding lime is a fantastic way to improve it. The influence of lime concentration on the road performance of low liquid limit clay is investigated in this research using a limit water content test, compaction test, and California bearing ratio test. The results show that the original plain soil does not meet the requirements of highway subgrade filling, and the basic properties of subgrade soil are improved to varying degrees after adding lime, resolving the problem regarding the original well-cultivated soil's inability to meet the requirements of construction. The plastic limit of the improved soil increased by roughly 3% as the lime content increased, but the maximum dry density decreased dramatically by 9.03%, 5.71%, and 5.98%, respectively. With an increase of 57.3% in lime content and compaction times, the California bearing ratio increases dramatically. The ideal moisture content rises as the lime content rises. The optimal dosage is 6%, according to a rigorous study of several performance metrics.

Keywords: low liquid limit clay; lime improvement; CBR; compaction; liquid plastic limit

Citation: Zhang, J.; Li, H.; Peng, J.; Zhang, Z. Effects of Lime Content on Road Performance of Low Liquid Limit Clay. *Appl. Sci.* **2023**, *13*, 8377. https://doi.org/10.3390/app13148377

Academic Editor: Syed Minhaj Saleem Kazmi

Received: 21 April 2023
Revised: 18 July 2023
Accepted: 18 July 2023
Published: 20 July 2023

Copyright: © 2023 by the authors. Licensee MDPI, Basel, Switzerland. This article is an open access article distributed under the terms and conditions of the Creative Commons Attribution (CC BY) license (https://creativecommons.org/licenses/by/4.0/).

1. Introduction

The Yellow and Yangtze River basins in China include a considerable number of low liquid limit clays. The use of low liquid limit clay as roadbed filler in the construction of expressways in this area is unavoidable. However, because of the low liquid limit, poor plasticity index, low strength, and water sensitivity, the mechanical properties of low liquid limit clay deteriorate with water changes [1,2], making it difficult to compact in roadbed construction. Because of its water sensitivity, water migration is common as the environment changes, affecting road performance [3]. The elastic modulus is significantly influenced by the stress state and water content of compacted clay. This directly affects road service [4]. In addition, it is simple to create roadbed collapse and pavement cracking if it is employed during the active period of a highway, which will directly impact the safety of traffic operation. To meet the performance requirements for the road, it is crucial to improve the low liquid limit clay.

Presently, bad soil is typically improved using physical (soil compaction, etc.) and chemical approaches. The three primary additions utilized in chemical stability are lime, cement, and fly ash [5–9]. Due to its low cost, positive effects, and practical construction, lime has drawn the interest of several researchers and produced many research-related findings. In Yan'an City, Gao et al.'s [10] research looked at the impact of dry density and lime content on the hydraulic conductivity and microstructure of loess. Due to the negative logarithmic correlation between hydraulic conductivity and dry density, adding lime will make loess less hydraulically conductive at the same dry density. However, lime addition causes a decrease in dry density at a specific level of compaction because of increased flocculation and aggregation. Al-Mukhtar et al.'s study of the main geotechnical properties of untreated and lime-treated compacted FoCa clay samples used X-ray diffraction, thermogravimetric analysis, scanning electron microscopy (SEM), and transmission electron microscopy (TEM) [11]. The findings demonstrate that lime-treated clay has additional layers of accumulation, altered clay particles, and a higher calcium content at the particle border. By conducting studies on lime-stabilized loess with various moisture levels and temperatures, Bao Weixing [12] looked at the features of lime stability and internal mineral changes at high temperatures. The pozzolanic reaction, crystallization reaction, and lime ripening reaction all contribute to the strength improvement of lime-stabilized loess. The response rate of these processes can be accelerated by high temperatures. Eades and Grim [13] claim that the lime stabilization process consists mostly of two steps. It may take several hours or days to finish the first stage of alteration. According to the soil's mineralogical makeup, cation exchange, flocculation, carbonization, and various short-term pozzolanic reactions take place at this stage. The pozzolanic process can also increase strength and durability, which is the second stage. In order to assess the effects of compaction delay and ambient temperature on the physical, mechanical, and hydraulic properties of lime-treated expansive clay, Hatim Ali [14] conducted a number of tests. Al-Mukhtar et al.'s [15] research examined the effects of a 10% lime treatment on several clay minerals. The consumption of lime on the curing time was assessed using an atomic absorption device, revealing the mechanism underlying the mineral reaction and the short- and long-term curing of lime soil subgrade. Malkathi [16] conducted studies to lower the clay and silt content in CSEB manufacturing and discovered the stability of lime and lime-cement combinations as stabilizers. According to the test results, lime-stabilized blocks can be utilized for single-layer construction, and lime combined with cement stabilizer results in blocks with greater compressive strength than lime alone. Noorzad [17] conducted triaxial tests, including the Atterberg limit, standard invigilation compaction, unconfined compressive strength, and unconsolidated undrained strength, to assess the impacts of the stabilizer type, variable curing duration, and different lime-sludge ratio. The results of the tests indicate that sludge and lime can improve the maximum strength. The fundamental interactions between lime and clay during the stabilization process have also been extensively researched and elucidated. They contend that the four reactions listed below—cation exchange, flocculation and agglomeration, lime carbonization, and finally, volcanic ash reaction—are responsible for the improved performance of lime-stabilized soil [18–26]. The strength of lime soil is produced through a pozzolanic reaction, which is the most important process. There are only a few studies on low liquid limit clay, and the majority of them are about new roadbeds, while a small number of them are about road reconstruction and expansion. The aforementioned studies primarily concentrate on the mechanism of the lime improvement of poor soil, and the research objects are primarily expansive soil and saline soil, etc.

The effectiveness of lime as a stabilizer has also been thoroughly researched by academics. Raheem et al. [27] stabilized lime with 5–25% lime content utilizing laterite as the test object. Compressed stabilized earth blocks (CSEB) were stabilized with lime by Ramirez et al. [28], and the ideal lime concentration was 28%. Lime was employed as a stabilizer by Guettala et al. [29] to alter the proportion of clay to sand, and they found that 8% was the best dosage. Lime is another stabilizer used by Ngowi [30], and the ideal dosage is 15%. Lime is used by Akpokodje [31] as a stabilizer to provide the best lime content in various material proportions. According to a review of earlier studies by Bogas et al. [32], the optimal lime level is between 6% and 12%. The findings of the pertinent research that the aforementioned academics conducted on lime as a stabilizer are displayed in Table 1. The ideal lime content range is often between 6% and 15%, however there is no precise and optimum value of lime content for diverse uses and types of improved soil.

Table 1. The best dosage of lime under different coating [28–32].

	Application	Optimum Content
Literature [28]	CSEB	28%
Literature [29]	Sand and clay	8%
Literature [30]	CSEB	15%
Literature [31]	Clay and silt	6–12%
Literature [32]		6–12%

In conclusion, lime has a wide variety of applications and has a good application effect in improving expansive soil, red clay, and other soils. Relevant studies have also produced fruitful outcomes, but there are still some limitations. For example, the studies mentioned above mostly concentrate on the research mechanism, while there is a dearth of study on low liquid limit clay, new roadbeds, and rehabilitation and expansion. In order to identify the representative low liquid limit clay, this paper analyzes its natural moisture content, particle gradation composition, boundary moisture content, compaction test results, and California bearing ratio (CBR value) as specific research indicators. It then modifies this clay by adding digestion lime to study its basic performance indicators. The optimum lime content of subgrade filling provides a reference and guidance for construction. It provides a feasible disposal idea for road construction.

2. Testing Program

2.1. Basic Properties of Low Liquid Limit Clay

The soil samples used in this paper are from the Hefei-Dagudian section of the Shanghai-Shanxi Expressway reconstruction and expansion project; the soil samples of three different project soil fields are chosen for research. The three soil samples returned from different project soil fields are marked as soil sample A, soil sample B, and soil sample C, respectively. Figure 1 depicts the soil sampling site and some soil samples that have been classified.

(**a**) Soil field to take soil   (**b**) Soil samples

Figure 1. Soil field and Soil samples.

(1) Natural moisture content

After the return of the undisturbed soil samples from the soil field, the natural moisture content was tested by the drying method. The test is conducted strictly in line with Highway Soil Test Specification JTG3430-2020. Five samples are taken for each soil sample in order to confirm the validity of the test results, and the average value is used to represent the natural water content of the undisturbed soil. Table 2 displays the test results.

Table 2. Natural moisture content of soil sample.

Sample	Sample Moisture Content (%)					
	1	2	3	4	5	Average
A	24.8	23.3	25.2	28.1	29.1	26.1
B	25.7	25.4	25.5	22.7	24.2	24.7
C	20.6	21.9	20.2	20.3	24.0	21.4

(2) Particle grading

In order to analyze the gradation composition of soil samples with a particle size range of 0.075~60 mm, a particle screening test was carried out by Highway Geotechnical Test Procedure JTG3430-2020. The test steps are as follows: Firstly, the samples were weighed according to the regulations, and the samples were passed through a 2 mm sieve in batches. Samples larger than 2 mm were passed through coarse sieves at all levels larger than 2 mm from a large to small order. The soil left on the sieve is weighed separately. If the amount of soil under the 2 mm sieve is too much, it can be reduced to 100~800 g by quartering. Samples less than 2 mm were passed through a fine sieve at all levels from a large to small order. Shaking can be carried out by a shaker. The shaking time is generally 10~15 min. Starting from the sieve with the largest pore size, each sieve is taken down in sequence, and shaken with the hand on the white paper until the number of sieves per minute is no more than 1% of the residual mass of the sieve. The leaking soil particles should be put into the next sieve, and the soil samples left on each sieve should be brushed with a soft brush and weighed separately. The difference between the total mass of the soil under the sieve and the total mass of the sample before the sieve should not be greater than 1% of the total mass of the sample before the sieve. Finally, three soil sample gradations are obtained through experiments, as shown in Figure 2. Figure 2 shows that the mass percentage of soil sample A (less than 0.075 mm) is 93.2%, the mass percentage of soil sample B (less than 0.075 mm) is 61.8%, and the mass percentage of soil sample C (less than 0.075 mm) is 93.5%.

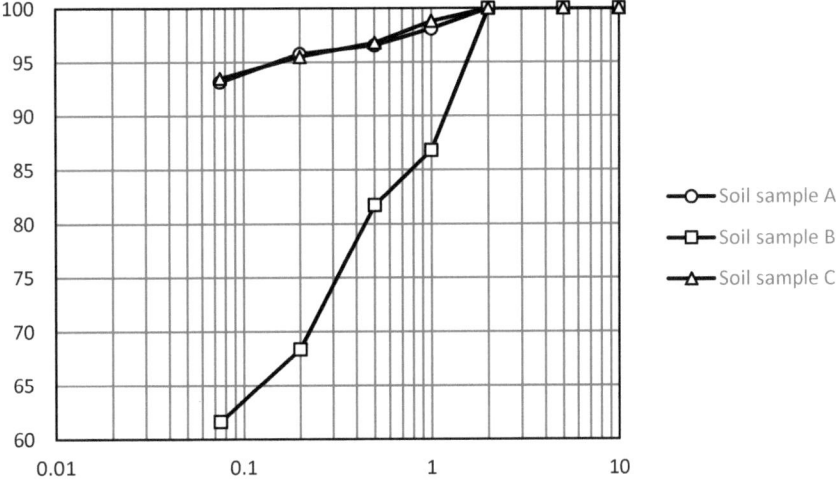

Figure 2. Soil sample gradation.

2.2. Preparation of Digestion Lime

The digestion lime that was collected from the lime digestion site is the lime digestion lime that was used in this article. Since the digestion lime retrieved from the site contains some water, it cannot be used to directly prepare the test soil for this paper's purposes. Before being utilized for the test, it needs to be processed. The following are the precise therapy steps: The site's recovered digestion lime samples were dried for 24 h in an oven at

105 °C. A 0.5 mm sieve was used for screening, and a lime that was less than 0.5 mm thick was used for this test. Figure 3 depicts the particular test procedures.

Figure 3. Lime preparation for test.

2.3. Test Scheme

The following three experiments were conducted in this experiment to examine the changing rule of the boundary moisture content of subgrade filling with varying lime contents: California bearing ratio test (CBR), compaction test, and boundary moisture content test. The design documentation was consulted for the engineering filler's required lime content in the test lime soil configuration. The lime content in the areas where the degree of compaction is 93% and 94% is 4%, and the lime content in the 96% area is 6%. Therefore, the test involved in this paper is sets up six lime contents of 0%, 1%, 2%, 4%, 6%, 8%, and the corresponding lime content is mixed with the test soil to prepare the lime soil used in the test. After the preparation of the test soil samples, the road performance tests, such as the limit water content, compaction test, and CBR value test, were carried out according to the test procedures. The specific test plan is shown in Table 3. Each group of experiments was repeated three times, and the average value was removed for subsequent analysis.

Table 3. Test schedule.

	Lime Content of Soil Sample A	Lime Content of Soil Sample B	Lime Content of Soil Sample C
Water ratio limit test	0%, 1%, 2%, 4%, 6%, 8%	0%, 1%, 2%, 4%, 6%, 8%	0%, 1%, 2%, 4%, 6%, 8%
compaction test	0%, 1%, 2%, 4%, 6%, 8%	0%, 1%, 2%, 4%, 6%, 8%	0%, 1%, 2%, 4%, 6%, 8%
CBR	0%, 1%, 2%, 4%, 6%, 8%	0%, 1%, 2%, 4%, 6%, 8%	0%, 1%, 2%, 4%, 6%, 8%

2.4. Test Method

The liquid-plastic limit of soil is determined by a combined liquid-plastic limit tester, which reflects the interaction between soil particles and water, and can indirectly reflect the engineering properties of soil. These are the test steps: In order to ensure that the water content of the soil samples was controlled within the liquid limit (point a), and slightly larger than the plastic limit (point c) and the intermediate state (point b), of the two, 200 g of treated soil samples were taken and separately put into three soil containers. A soil cutter was used to mix the soil, which was then sealed for over 18 h. After scraping the surface and setting it on the lifting seat, the lifting knob was steadily turned clockwise while the adjusted soil sample was inserted into the test cup. The indicator light turned on instantly, stopped rotating, and pressed the "measurement" button to wait for the test to finish the reading when the soil sample made contact with the cone tip. The previous steps were repeated until the test was over. A portion of the sample must be taken after the test has finished in order to determine the water content. The weight of the cone is 100 g.

A compaction test is a technique that involves hammering soil samples to determine the soil's propensity for compaction. This technique involves hammering soil samples with varying water contents using various compaction techniques to produce the maximum dry bulk density and ideal water content, which serves as the foundation for the design and construction of filling engineering. Samples were made with varying amounts of lime content, including 0%, 1%, 2%, 4%, 6%, and 8%. Dry heavy compaction was used in the compaction test, with 3 compaction layers and 98 compaction times for each layer. After compaction was completed, the sample in the cylinder was pushed out with the demolding instrument to determine the wet density of the sample, and then the representative soil sample was taken from the center of the sample to measure its water content, which was calculated as 0.1%.

3. Test Results and Analysis

3.1. Limit Moisture Content

The measured result was mapped, and the horizontal coordinate was lime content and the vertical coordinate was moisture. The test results are shown in Figure 4.

Figure 4 shows that while the plastic limit of the three soil samples increases to some degree with an increase in lime content, the liquid limit of the three soil samples does not become more obvious. For soil sample A (plain soil), the respective liquid limit, plastic limit, and plastic index values were 48.9%, 21.2%, and 27.7%. For soil sample B (plain soil), the liquid limit, plastic limit, and plastic index were 48.6%, 25.2%, and 23.3%, respectively. The plain soil type C has a liquid limit, plastic limit, and plastic index of 39.2%, 21.4%, and 17.8%, respectively.

Soil sample A's liquid limit, plastic limit, and plastic index were 48.6%, 24.2%, and 24.5% when the lime level exceeded 6%. Soil sample B had a plastic index of 19.6%, a plastic limit of 47.7%, and a plastic limit of 28.1%. Soil sample C had a liquid limit, plastic limit, and plastic index of 38.6%, 24.5%, and 14.1%, respectively. The three different types of soil samples all had their plastic limits raised by 3%, 2.9%, and 3.1%, respectively. Soil sample A's plastic limit had a propensity towards stability. The deplasticity index reduces with an increase in the plastic limit to some extent when the liquid limit does not increase evidently. This is because certain ion exchanges, carbonation, crystallization, and pozzolanic actions exist in lime-improved soil, which leads to the plastic limit of each soil sample increasing with the increase in lime content, while the plastic index decreases correspondingly.

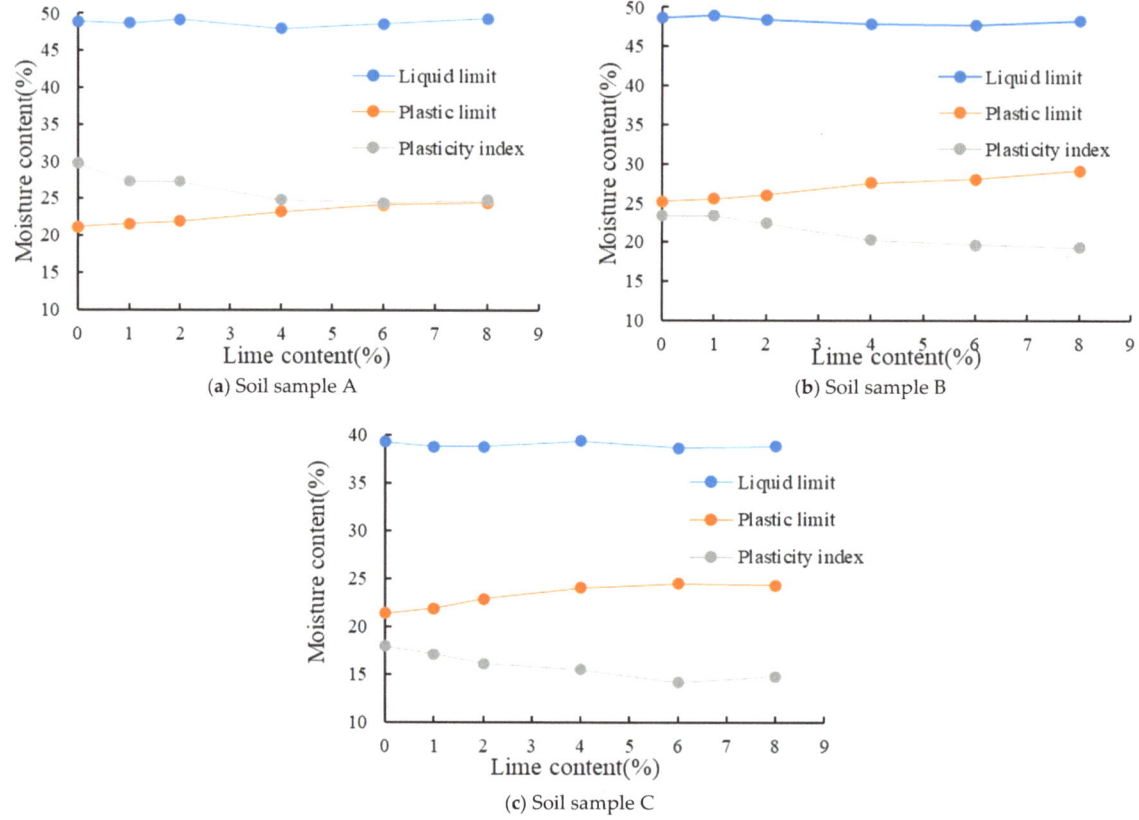

Figure 4. Boundary moisture content test results.

Combined with the undisturbed soil particle grading obtained above, it can be seen from Highway Geotechnical Test Procedure JTG3430-2020 that the mass percentage of the fine grain groups of all soil samples is greater than 50%, the liquid limit of all soil samples is less than 50%, and the plasticity index is greater than 7%, indicating that these three soil samples are all low liquid limit clays (CL).

3.2. Compaction Test

The relationship curve between dry density and water content is drawn. The horizontal coordinate represents water content and the vertical coordinate represents dry density. The test results are shown in Figures 5–7.

It can be seen from the figure that the maximum dry density of lime-stabilized soil reaches its peak as the ash content of soil samples A and B increases from 0% to 8%, and reaches its peak when the ash content of soil sample B reaches 6%. Soil sample A decreased from 1.77 g/cm^3 to 1.61 g/cm^3 by 9.03%; soil sample B decreased from 1.75 g/cm^3 to 1.65 g/cm^3 by 5.71%; soil sample C decreased from 1.84 g/cm^3 to 1.73 g/cm^3 by 5.98%; and when lime content exceeded 6%, the maximum dry density decreased less. At the same time, with the increase in the ash mixing rate from 0% to 6%, the optimal water content has basically reached the maximum. Sample A increased from 14.7% to 16.7% (13.6%), sample B increased from 14.5% to 17.2% (18.6%), and sample C increased from 15.1% to 17.4% (15.2%). However, when the ash content increased from 6% to 8%, the improvement effect of increased lime dosage on low liquid limit clay was no longer obvious. The decrease in dry density is small, and the optimal water content is basically unchanged. On the one hand, the water consumption of the improved soil is due to the exchange of Ca^{2+} in the lime with other cations on the soil surface. On the other hand, as lime dissolves and hydrates in the soil, the soil is pressed in real time, requiring more water to reduce the friction between particles for optimal compaction. Therefore, with different lime dosage, water consumption is also different, so the change in optimal water content is also different. Therefore, it can be concluded that 6% ash content is a reasonable dosage of improved low liquid limit clay in this area.

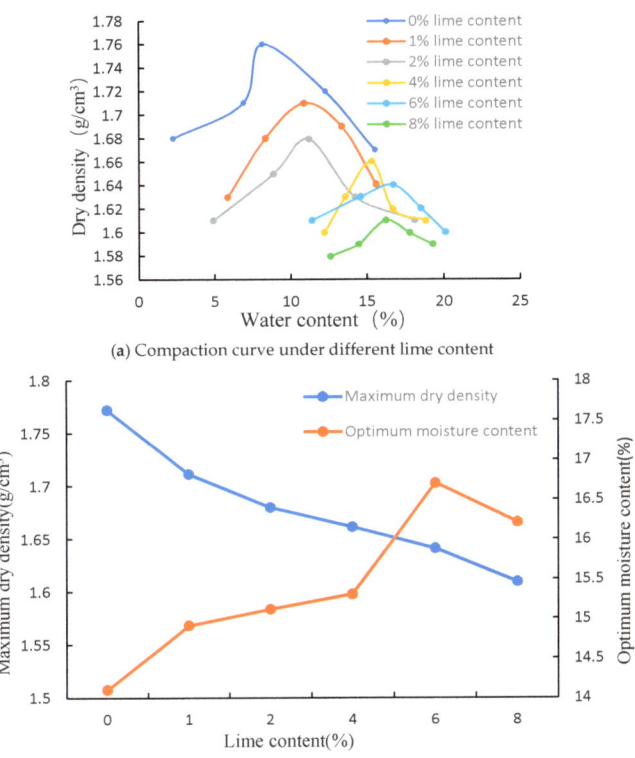

Figure 5. Compaction test results of soil sample A.

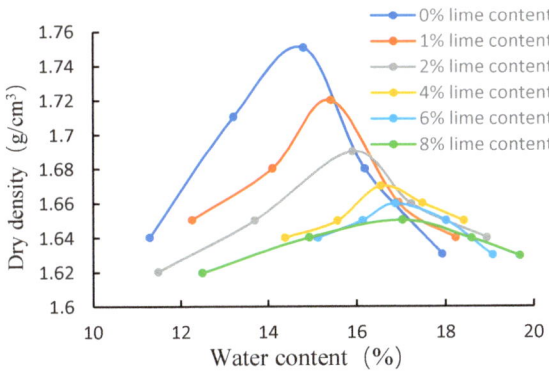

(**a**) Compaction curve under different lime content

Figure 6. *Cont.*

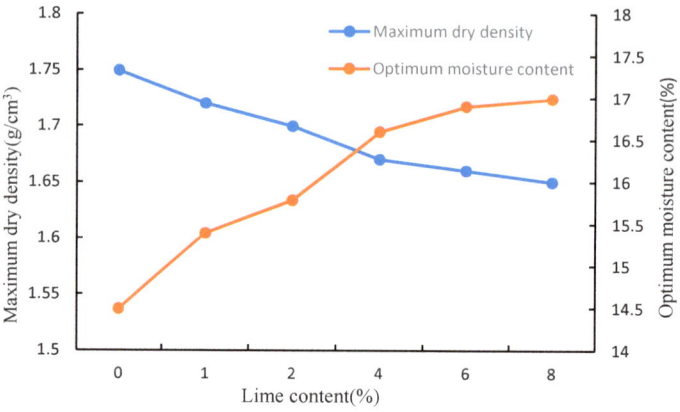

(**b**) Variation of compaction results under different lime content

Figure 6. Compaction test results of soil sample B.

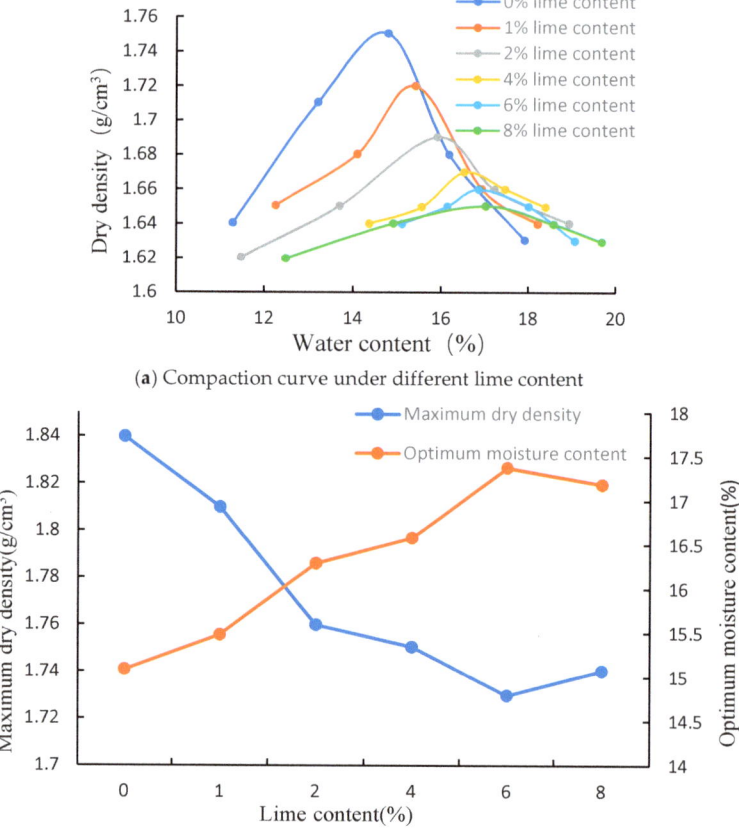

(**a**) Compaction curve under different lime content

(**b**) Variation of compaction results under different lime content

Figure 7. Compaction test results of soil sample C.

3.3. CBR

The carrying capacity of soil foundation materials and the soil foundation's resistance to deformation are measured using the CBR value. It is an important signal while constructing a roadbed. The bearing capacity of a material is defined as its ability to endure deformation under a local load, and standard gravel is used as the benchmark. This capacity is denoted by their relative ratio CBR value. Prior to the experiment, the specimen that has been prepared in accordance with the test guidelines must be immersed in water. In order to calculate the change in the humidity density of the specimen, the specimen is weighed after being removed from the solution and allowed to drain for 15 min. Following the results of the last compaction test, the sample for this test was prepared using 30, 50, and 98 compaction times. During sample preparation, the lime content was still 0%, 1%, 2%, 4%, 6%, and 8%, and the ideal moisture content was chosen. The results of the CBR test are displayed in Figures 8–10.

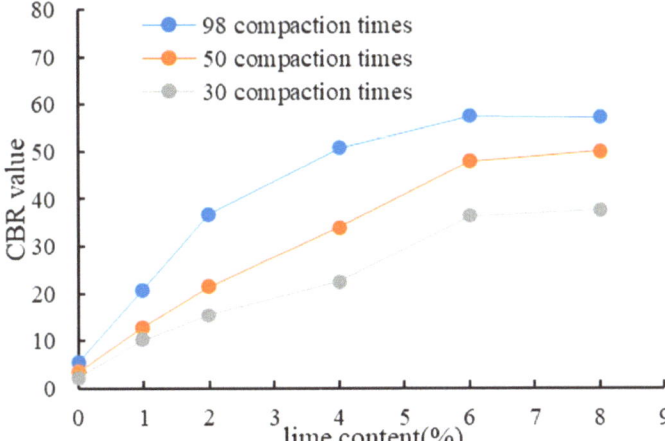

Figure 8. CBR test results of soil sample A.

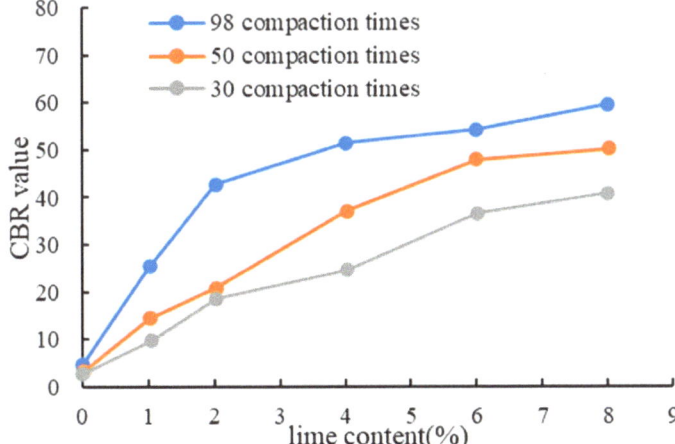

Figure 9. CBR test results of soil sample B.

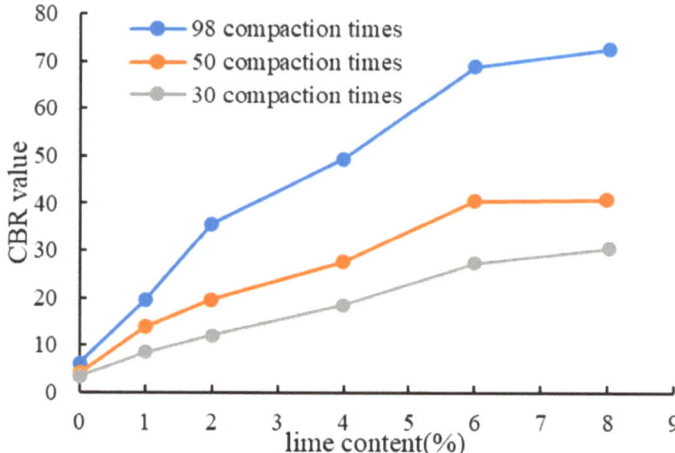

Figure 10. CBR test results of soil sample C.

It can be seen from the figure that with the increase in compaction times, the CBR values of stabilized soil with different ash content increase. In the case of the same compaction times, the CBR value increased by a large margin before 6%. When the ash content increased again, the increase was not obvious, and the curve tended to be stable. Taking the test with 98 times of compaction as an example, when the ash content increases from 0 to 6%, the CBR value increases from 5.4% to 57.3%. When the ash content increases again, the CBR value does not increase significantly or even decrease to 56.9. It shows that the increase in ash content can significantly improve the water stability of low liquid limit clay. It can be concluded that the ash content of 6% is a reasonable dose for improving low liquid limit clay in this area.

Longer compaction times improve the CBR value of stabilized soil with varied lime levels, mostly for the following two reasons: When lime first absorbs water from the soil, a lot of heat is emitted as the volume expands, which evaporates the water and improves the soil's quality. Second, some lime reacts with carbon dioxide in the atmosphere to form calcium carbonate, a weakly-bonding material that increases the soil's CBR value and strength to some level.

4. Discussions

In view of the problem mentioned above that the original engineering soil does not meet the filling requirements, this paper improved the original soil by mixing ash. At the same time, the improvement effect is judged by comparing the basic properties of undisturbed soil and lime-doped soil before and after mixing.

The addition of lime has little effect on the liquid plastic limit, and the plastic limit of the three soil samples is about 3%. This shows that the addition of lime does not change the plastic limit property of soil liquid considerably, but the addition of lime has a great effect on dry density and water content. As can be seen from Figures 5–7, the curve of water content and dry density presents the following rules with the increase in lime content: First, with the increase in lime content, the maximum dry density corresponding to the curve gradually decreases, while the optimal water content gradually increases. Moreover, the effect of lime improvement on the CBR value is also obvious. With the increase in compaction times, the CBR value of the soil sample will be increased to a certain extent. With the increase in lime content, the CBR value gradually increases, and basically stabilizes when the lime content reaches 6%. Following the addition of lime, the basic physical characteristics of the original soil, such as the liquid-plastic limit, CBR, and optimal water content, can be enhanced due to the aforementioned interaction between lime and bad soil, allowing the bad soil that did not initially meet the filling requirements to do so.

Ion exchange, carbonation, and crystallization will occur throughout the process of enhancing low liquid limit clay with lime mixing, resulting in an increase in the plastic limit of each soil sample with an increase in lime concentration and a corresponding decrease in the plastic index. On the one hand, the interchange of Ca^{2+} in the lime with other cations on the surface of the soil particle is what causes the water loss of the improved soil. On the other hand, more water is required to produce the best compaction effect because the dissolution and hydration of lime in the soil causes soil to be compressed in real time [18].

Compared with other treatment methods, such as replacement, lime improvement has the following advantages: first, lime improvement is convenient in construction, as it does not need to be transported back and forth to shorten the construction period and save costs; second, the price of lime is low, and the improvement of 1 m3 bad soil only needs about 60 rmb; finally, the technology of lime improved soil is mature, mixing is simple, and there is no complicated process.

5. Conclusions

In this research, the CBR test, compaction test, and limit water content test are used to assess and compare the differences between lime-improved soil and an untouched soil sample. The results of this inquiry were as follows:

1. After lime digestion improves the initial low liquid limit clay, the liquid limit essentially stays the same, the plastic limit increases as the lime content rises, and the plastic index gradually declines. After lime is introduced to the soil, ions from the lime and the soil exchange, causing the clay particles to form a granular structure. The rise in the plastic limit often remains steady once the lime content reaches 6%. It is also shown that a low liquid limit clay mixture with lime has a reasonable ash concentration of about 6%. When the lime content is 6%, the maximum dry densities are 1.61 g/cm^3, 1.65 g/cm^3, and 1.73 g/cm^3, respectively. The optimal water content was 16.7%, 17.2%, and 17.4%, respectively.
2. The CBR value of the soil samples under various compaction durations considerably rose with an increase in ash content, showing that ash mixing had improved the water stability of low liquid limit clay containing sand. The acceptable ash content is 6% at the same time. When the lime content is 6% and the compaction times are 98, the CBR values are 57.4%, 54.2%, and 68.9%, respectively.
3. The ideal water content and CBR value of the clay with low liquid limit are clearly impacted by the amount of dissolved lime added. The ideal water content falls as the incorporation amount increases, while the CBR value rises.
4. Plain soil does not meet the filling requirements of subgrade in areas 93, 94, and 96 of expressways. The performance of the improved soil has been improved to varying degrees after the ash mixing improvement, and it can meet the filling requirements of subgrade in areas 93, 94, and 96. According to the test, the most reasonable ash mixing amount of the improved soil is determined to be 6%.

Author Contributions: Conceptualization, J.Z.; Investigation, Z.Z.; Writing—original draft, H.L.; Project administration, J.P. All authors have read and agreed to the published version of the manuscript.

Funding: This research was funded by the Science and technology project of Anhui Transportation Holding Group Co., Ltd. (JKKJ-2020-16).

Data Availability Statement: Some or all data, models, or code that support the findings of this study are available from the corresponding author upon reasonable request.

Conflicts of Interest: The authors declare no conflict of interest.

References

1. Zhang, J.; Chen, Y.; Wu, H. Measurement of water content of red clays using X-ray CT. *Intl. J. E Sci. Eng.* **2015**, *8*, 31–35.
2. Zhang, J.; Jiang, Q.; Zhang, Y.; Dai, L.; Zheng, J. Nondestructive measurement of water content and moisture migration of unsaturated red clays in South China. *Adv. Mater. Sci. Eng.* **2015**, *2015*, 542538. [CrossRef]

3. Zhang, J.; Li, F.; Zeng, L.; Peng, J.; Li, J. Numerical simulation of the moisture migration of unsaturated clay embankments in southern China considering stress state. *Bull. Eng. Geol. Environ.* **2020**, *80*, 11–24. [CrossRef]
4. Zhang, J.; Peng, J.; Zheng, J.; Yao, Y. Predicting moisture-dependent resilient modulus for compacted clays in south China. In Proceedings of the Transportation Research Board 97th Annual Meeting, Washington, DC, USA, 7–11 January 2018.
5. Shimobe, S.; Karakan, E.; Sezer, A. Improved dataset for establishing novel relationships between compaction characteristics and physical properties of soils. *Bull. Eng. Geol. Environ.* **2021**, *80*, 8633–8663. [CrossRef]
6. Karakan, E.; Demir, S. Effect of fines content and plasticity on undrained shear strength of quartz-clay mixtures. *Arab. J. Geosci.* **2018**, *11*, 743. [CrossRef]
7. Di Sante, M.; Evelina, F.; Francesco, M.; Virginia, B. Influence of delayed compaction on the compressibility and hydraulic conductivity of soil-lime mixtures. *Eng. Geol.* **2015**, *185*, 131–138. [CrossRef]
8. Li, J.; Zhang, J.; Yang, X. Monte Carlo simulations of deformation behaviour of unbound granular materials based on a real aggregate library. *Int. J. Pavement Eng.* **2023**, *24*, 2165650. [CrossRef]
9. Peng, J.; Hu, H.; Zhang, J. Rapid testing and prediction of soil-water characteristic curve of subgrade soils considering stress state and degree of compaction. *J. Rock Mech. Geotech. Eng.* **2023**. [CrossRef]
10. Gao, Y.; Qian, H.; Li, X.; Chen, J.; Jia, H. Effects of lime treatment on the hydraulic conductivity and microstructure of loess. *Environ. Earth Sci.* **2018**, *77*, 529. [CrossRef]
11. Al-Mukhtar, M.; Khattab, S.; Jean-Francois, A. Microstructure and geotechnical properties of lime-treated expansive clayey soil. *Eng. Geol.* **2012**, *139–140*, 17–27. [CrossRef]
12. Bao, W.; Wang, H.; Lai, H.; Chen, R. Experimental study on strength characteristics and internal mineral changes of Lime-stabilized loess under High-Temperature. *Constr. Build. Mater.* **2022**, *351*, 128945. [CrossRef]
13. Eades, J.L.; Grim, R.E. *Reaction of Hydrated Lime with Pure Clay Minerals in Soil Stabilization*; Highway Research Board Bulletin: Washington, DC, USA, 1960.
14. Ali, H.; Mohamed, M. The effects of compaction delay and environmental temperature on the mechanical and hydraulic properties of lime-stabilized extremely high plastic clays. *Appl. Clay Sci.* **2017**, *150*, 333–341. [CrossRef]
15. Al-Mukhtar, M.; Abdelmadjid, L.; Alcover, J.-F. Lime consumption of different clayey soils. *Appl. Clay Sci.* **2014**, *95*, 133–145. [CrossRef]
16. Malkanthi, S.N.; Balthazaar, N.; Perera, A.A.D.A.J. Lime stabilization for compressed stabilized earth blocks with reduced clay and silt. *Case Stud. Constr. Mater.* **2019**, *12*, e00326. [CrossRef]
17. Noorzad, R.; Motevalian, S. Improvement of Clayey soil with lime and industrial sludge. *Geotech. Geol. Eng.* **2018**, *36*, 2957–2966. [CrossRef]
18. Cao, P.; Wang, F.; Yan, L. Experimental study on CBR value of Lime-improved clay. *Chin. J. Rock Mech. Eng.* **2011**, *33*, 305–308.
19. Ingles, O.; Metcalf, J. *Soil Stabilization: Principles and Practice*; Butterworths: Sidney, Australia, 1972.
20. Little, D.N. *Fundamentals of the Stabilization of Soil with Lime*; National Lime Association: Arlington, VA, USA, 1996; Volume 332, pp. 1–20.
21. Boardman, D.; Glendinning, S.; Rogers, C.D.F. Development of stabilisation and solidification in lime–clay mixes. *Geotechnique* **2001**, *51*, 533–543. [CrossRef]
22. Rao, S.M.; Shivananda, P. Role of curing temperature in progress of lime-soil reactions. *Geotech. Geol. Eng.* **2005**, *23*, 79–85. [CrossRef]
23. Amer, A.; Mattheus, F. *Expansive Soils: Recent Advances in Characterization and Treatment*; Taylor & Francis Group/Balkema: London, UK, 2006.
24. Muzahim, A.; Abdelmadjid, L.; Alcover, J.-F. Behaviour and mineralogy changes in lime-treated expansive soil at 20 °C. *Appl. Clay Sci.* **2010**, *50*, 191–198.
25. Olivier, C.; Jean-Claude, A.; Tangi-Le, B.; Dimitri, D. Microstructure and hydraulic conductivity of a compacted lime-treated soil. *Eng. Geol.* **2011**, *123*, 187–193.
26. Wang, Y.; Cao, D. Experimental study on CBR value of modified expansive soil. *Chin. J. Rock Mech. Eng.* **2004**, *S1*, 4396–4399.
27. Raheem, A.A.; Bello, O.A.; Makinde, O.A. A comparative study of cement and lime stabilized lateritic interlocking blocks. *Pac. J. Sci. Technol.* **2010**, *11*, 27–34.
28. Rafael, A.; Pedro, M.; Jacobo, M.; Delia, C.-A.; Yadira, G.-P. The use of sugarcane bagasse ash and lime to improve the durability and mechanical properties of compacted soil blocks. *Constr. Build. Mater.* **2012**, *34*, 296–305.
29. Guettala, A.; Houari, H.; Mezghiche, B.; Chebili, R. Durability of lime stabilized earth blocks. *Courrier du Savoir* **2002**, *2*, 61–66.
30. Ngowi, A.B. Improving the traditional earth construction: A case study of Botswana. *Constr. Build. Mater.* **1997**, *11*, 1–7. [CrossRef]
31. Akpokodje, E.G. The stabilization of some arid zone soils with cement and lime. *Q. J. Eng. Geol. Hydrogeol.* **1985**, *18*, 173–180. [CrossRef]
32. Bogas, J.A.; Silva, M.; Gomes, M.D.G. Unstabilized and stabilized compressed earth. blocks with partial Incorporation of recycled aggregates. *Int. J. Archit. Herit.* **2018**, *13*, 569–584. [CrossRef]

Disclaimer/Publisher's Note: The statements, opinions and data contained in all publications are solely those of the individual author(s) and contributor(s) and not of MDPI and/or the editor(s). MDPI and/or the editor(s) disclaim responsibility for any injury to people or property resulting from any ideas, methods, instructions or products referred to in the content.

Article

Safety and Effect of Fly Ash Content on Mechanical Properties and Microstructure of Green Low-Carbon Concrete

Zhijie Chen [1], Maohui Li [2,*] and Lei Guan [1,*]

[1] China Academy of Safety Science and Technology, Beijing 100012, China
[2] School of Materials Science & Engineering, North Minzu University, Yinchuan 750021, China
* Correspondence: lmnlmb@126.com (M.L.); gsandaye@163.com (L.G.)

Abstract: Based on the promotion and application of green and low-carbon technology, this study aims to develop a high-safety performance cement concrete incorporating a large dosage of fly ash (FA). The safety and effect of FA content on the mechanical properties of FA composited cement were studied through compressive strength, flexural strength, and microscopic tests. The results show that when the FA replaced 20% cement, the properties of concrete were the best in this study. The flexural strengths and compressive strengths of the standard cured concrete for 28 days with 20% FA content are 0.82 MPa and 4.32 MPa larger than that of the pure cement concrete. The XRD and SEM analysis suggested that the mechanical properties of the composite cement FA system are improved significantly since the replacement of cement by FA promotes secondary hydration of calcium hydroxide in the concrete, leading to a more compact and safe interface between cement and FA.

Keywords: low-carbon concrete; fly ash; mechanical property; microstructure; high-safety performance

Citation: Chen, Z.; Li, M.; Guan, L. Safety and Effect of Fly Ash Content on Mechanical Properties and Microstructure of Green Low-Carbon Concrete. *Appl. Sci.* **2024**, *14*, 2796. https://doi.org/10.3390/app14072796

Academic Editor: Laurent Daudeville

Received: 2 March 2023
Revised: 12 April 2023
Accepted: 12 April 2023
Published: 27 March 2024

Copyright: © 2024 by the authors. Licensee MDPI, Basel, Switzerland. This article is an open access article distributed under the terms and conditions of the Creative Commons Attribution (CC BY) license (https://creativecommons.org/licenses/by/4.0/).

1. Introduction

Concrete is still an engineering material with the largest usage and the widest application range in construction projects since it has good plasticity, economy, high-strength, and durability [1]. Cement is an important component of concrete, and a lot of CO_2 is emitted into the atmosphere during its production [2]. Cement production accounts for about 10% of the world's current annual CO_2 emissions, which is about 32.3 billion tones [3]. Ordinary Portland cement (OPC) requires a lot of energy to produce, and the manufacturing process releases toxic CO_2 into the environment. Large amounts of CO_2 emission leads to the greenhouse effect and aggravates global warming. A large portion of the waste produced in the manufacturing process is dumped and disposed of in landfills, damaging the soil and causing environmental pollution [4]. Since the sustainable development model of the social economy has been proposed, the protection of the environment and ecology is required in the production, use, maintenance, and reuse of concrete [5]. Meanwhile, climate anomalies caused by greenhouse gas emissions have become the focus of global attention, and the concrete industry is responsible for excessive emission of CO_2 and other greenhouse gases [6]. The low carbon life aims to achieve the lower energy consumption and lower CO_2 emission, which has received people's response and recognition [7]. The concept of green high-performance concrete can be summarized as saving resources and energy, not damaging the environment, helpong the environment, aiding sustainable development, and ensuring the healthy and happy survival of human offspring [8]. This philosophy has raised attention of the performance improvement and energy conservation of concrete [9,10]. Therefore, it is an inevitable choice for the future development of engineering materials to make the cement concrete industry moving towardslow-carbon and sustainable development.

As an important link in sustainable development, the preparation methods of green and low-carbon concrete have been developed and promoted successively. The mechanical properties of concrete are affected by many factors, such as temperature and loading ratio [11,12]. Previous studies demonstrated that the reasonable composition ratio of mineral admixtures and recycled aggregates can greatly improve the performance of composite admixtures [13–15]. On the one hand, the compaction method and microstructure of concrete are also important factors affecting its performance [16]. Şengün, et al. [17] investigated the effect of four compaction techniques on the performance of concrete after 28 days through uniaxial compression and splitting tests. Results showed that the mechanical properties and mixing parameters of concrete are closely related to compacted density. On the other hand, an appropriate amount of mineral admixtures can achieve an effective supply of cement materials and improve the technical performance at a low cost [18,19]. Matar and Barhoun [20] found that the waterproofing admixture presents a strong inhibiting effect on the micro-cracking of the concrete surface by producing calcium silicate hydrates. Ji, et al. [21] performed laboratory tests to evaluate the hydration properties of concrete by adding magnesium slag, and the results suggest that a magnesium slag content of 30% can improve the working performance of concrete in frost resistance and crack resistance. Therefore, a series of mineral admixtures provide a convenient solution to enhance the mechanical properties of concrete considering the low-carbon and sustainability requirements.

A large amount of fly ash (FA) is produced in the coal industry every year as a by-product with a low utilized value [22]. At present, given that the utilization rate of FA is about 50% in the world, a lot of FA waste is piled up in landfills, occupying much arable land and space [23]. Zhang, et al. [24] calculated the CO_2 emissions and cost of the concrete with FA addition and suggested that the effect of FA content on CO_2 emissions is more obvious for higher-strength concrete. Uliasz-Bocheńczyk and Mokrzycki [25] reported the relative contribution of FA to reduce CO_2 emissions is higher than 15% in the production process. Based on the above consideration, many studies declared that FA can be applied suitably as a substitute for cement to meet the needs of hydration products in concrete preparation, which is also an effective measure to produce low-carbon concrete [26]. Therefore, the exploration of FA admixture has become a research topic of green low-carbon concrete [27]. In addition, the usage of FA in concrete not only improves concrete performance but also provides an economical and effective way to consume FA [28]. The existing study found that the main chemical components of FA, as a pozzolanic material, are SiO_2, Al_2O_3, CaO, Fe_2O_3, and a small number of unburned carbon particles [29]. Its major phases are vitreous aluminum silica and a small amount of quartz, mullite, and other minerals. A large number of vitreous substances are the main source of the gelling activity of FA and have potential hydration reactivity [30]. The activation methods of FA mainly include calcium treatment, single alkali excitation (lime, sodium silicate), sulfate excitation ($CaSO_4$, Na_2SO_4), physical fine grinding or physical fine grinding combined with chemical activators, etc. Hwang and Huynh [31] obtained fine ash with a particle size of less than 45 μm by a wind separation method, which can improve the strength and working performance of concrete. Fan, et al. [32] demonstrated that the slurry fluidity and backfill strength of the cement material mixed with FA can meet the mining requirements of filling cement. Karakurt and Bayazıt [33] suggested that the strength of FA concrete may be obviously improved by activating the activity of FA with chemical admixtures. Poletanovic, et al. [34] found that the method of the combination of composite activation, mechanical activation, and chemical activator could enhance the activity of FA more significantly. Concrete consumption creates a large carbon footprint in the environment. Fly ash (FA), rice husk ash (RHA), and silica fume (SF) can replace cement in proper proportions to reduce CO_2 emissions. FA affects the set-up time and sulfate resistance of concrete and can improve the workability of concrete mixtures. Conversely, the high surface area of SF particles reduces workability. A high LOI ratio indicates that RHA may evaporate when the concrete is exposed to high temperatures. FA and RHA, as substitutes for cement, have no adverse effect on the compressive strength of concrete, whereas the incorporation of SF into concrete can improve the overall compressive strength, tensile strength, and elastic modulus of concrete. SF not only improves the bond between the cement paste and the aggregate but also has a key advantage as an alternative to cement due to its ability to reduce the permeability of concrete [35]. It has been established that the mechanical strength of concrete will be affected when the replacement level of RHA and SF synergies is above 30%, and that concrete with a continued increase in RHA content will have lower mechanical strength than ordinary concrete. When the RHA content is increased to a certain extent, higher flexural strength can be obtained, and the durability of the concrete can be improved [36]. The combination of FA and nS is adopted to replace ordinary Portland cement (OPC), which significantly improves the mechanical properties of environmentally friendly concrete and the form of the cement matrix. At the same time, homogenization of the cement matrix promotes structural alignment of the composite materials mixed with FA and nS and reduces the carbon footprint of cement-based materials [37]. In addition, the research on the properties of FA concrete mainly focuses on the physical and chemical properties of the material, whereas the research and test data on the mechanical properties of concrete are relatively few. Therefore, the mechanical properties of FA concrete are investigated in depth in this study.

This study aimed to explore the high safety performance of green and low-carbon concrete. The improvement effect of FA on the performance of the composite Portland-cement–FA system was investigated. Under the condition that the amount of binder and water, the ratio of water to the binder, and the total amount of material used in the specimen are equal, the concrete was prepared by adding the FA content instead of cement. Through the mechanical properties test, XRD, and SEM analysis, the influence law of FA content on the road performance of concrete was comprehensively discussed. The research results provide support for the future study of FA content in concrete from both theoretical and data aspects and obtains the optimal FA content.

2. Materials and Methods
2.1. Materials

This study used Portland cement, which comes from a cement plant in Ningxia.

Cement is a type of binder that can bond at room temperature. It can set and harden to adhere to sand, brick, stone, and other building materials. The chemical composition of cement contains the most Fe_2O_3 content and quite a lot of SiO_2.

Fe_2O_3 in cement is responsible for the cement's acting as a flux in the high-temperature manufacturing process. It combines with Ca and Al_2O_3 to form C2F, which is the main component of cement hardness. SiO_2 is responsible for reacting with lime to form $2CaO·SiO_2$ and $3CaO·SiO_2$, and the correct proportion of SiO_2 plays an important role in improving cement strength.

Table 1 presents the test results of physical and mechanical properties, which meet the requirements of construction performance.

Table 1. Physical and mechanical properties of tested cement.

	Setting Time (min)		Compressive Strength (MPa)		Flexural Strength (MPa)		Specific Surface Area (m²/kg)	Water Content of Normal Consistency (%)
	Initial	Final	3 d	28 d	3 d	28 d		
Result	107	161	23.5	45.2	5.4	8.6	347	27.4
Limit	≥45	≤600	≥22	≥42.5	≥4.0	≥6.5	—	≤30

Table 2 displays the chemical compositions of Portland Cement.

Table 2. Chemical compositions of cement.

Chemical Composition	SiO_2	Al_2O_3	CaO	Fe_2O_3	MgO	SO_3
Cement	22.4%	3.17%	5.2%	58.85%	2.53%	2.40%

The coarse sand produced in Xiamen was used as the fine aggregate. With a fineness modulus of 3.4, the coarse sand is in zone II. The water content is 3%. The apparent density is 2590 kg/m³, and the mud content is 1.8%.

Crude FA comes from Tianjin. The specific surface area is 252 m²/kg, and the fineness (0.044 mm square hole sieve residue) is 20.2%. The water demand ratio is 98%. Table 3 lists the main chemical composition of FA.

Table 3. Chemical composition of FA.

Chemical Composition	SiO_2	Al_2O_3	CaO	Fe_2O_3	SO_3	Cl^-	Alkali Content
FA	48.73%	22.48%	3.87%	9.84%	0.93%	0.02%	2.11%

Clean drinking water or fresh water is used in the design of the concrete mix in this study. The water quality must be tested as the following requirements to ensure it is available for concrete preparation.

(1) Sulfate content (measured by SO_4^{2-}) should be less than 0.0027 mg/mm³;
(2) Salt content should not exceed 0.005 mg/mm³;
(3) PH should not be less than 4.6;
(4) Do not contain oil, mud, and other harmful impurities.

2.2. FA Addition

The objective is to study the impact of FA content on the working performance of concrete, based on the same water–cement ratio, water–binder ratio, water consumption, the amount of cementing material, and the total amount of material used in specimens, according to the equal substitution method adopted in concrete mix design, the FA content was, respectively, compared with the total content of 0, 5%, 10%, 15%, 20%, 25%, 30%, 35%, 40%, 45%, and 50% in this test.

2.3. Testing Design

The slump and density of the specimen were measured before assembling. Then, a standard test mold, according to the Method of Test method of mortar strength (ISO method), was used to make concrete test specimens, and the mold was removed after 24 h. After the test pieces were made, they were placed in a standard curing box (relative humidity 98%, temperature 20 °C) for curing. After the standard curing for 3 days, 7 days, and 28 days, respectively, concrete test specimens with a size of 40 mm × 40 mm × 160 mm were applied to obtain the compressive strength and flexural strength. According to the Chinese Standard for test method of mechanical properties on ordinary concrete (GB/T 50081-2002), the concrete specimens were prepared and standard cured as shown in Figure 1. Table 4 lists the mix ratio design scheme of concrete specimens. Concrete was prepared by substituting cement schemes with different FA content according to the test schemes shown in Table 4. Three identical test specimens were poured in each group, and 11 control groups of concrete test specimens were tested after standard curing at 3, 7, and 28 days.

Figure 1. Concrete specimens in the preparation process: (**a**) test piece to be cured, (**b**) cured sample.

Table 4. Experimental scheme of cement replaced by FA.

Serial Number	Water Cement Ratio	Water Binder Ratio	Water/g	Standard Sand/g	Material of Cementation/g	FA/%	Cement/%
B1	0.55	0.33	247.5	1350	450	0	100
B2	0.55	0.33	247.5	1350	450	5	95
B3	0.55	0.33	247.5	1350	450	10	90
B4	0.55	0.33	247.5	1350	450	15	85
B5	0.55	0.33	247.5	1350	450	20	80
B6	0.55	0.33	247.5	1350	450	25	75
B7	0.55	0.33	247.5	1350	450	30	70
B8	0.55	0.33	247.5	1350	450	35	65
B9	0.55	0.33	247.5	1350	450	40	60
B10	0.55	0.33	247.5	1350	450	45	55
B11	0.55	0.33	247.5	1350	450	50	50

2.4. Mechanical Property Evaluation Parameters

The mechanical behavior of concrete is obviously dependent on FA content, cement type, cement grade, aggregate type, concrete placement, age, the porosity of cement stone, and field conditions [38]. Experimental evaluation is an important tool to understand the changes in mechanical properties of concrete with material design. The laboratory tests of the same concrete mix design under different FA content were performed in this study. According to the measured data, the mechanical property evaluation parameters can be reasonably determined. Through the above comprehensive analysis, the flexural strength can be calculated as shown in Equation (1). The flexural strength of concrete test specimens is key evaluation index of concrete in mechanical properties.

$$f_f = \frac{FL}{bh^2} \cdot 1.5 \tag{1}$$

where f_f is the flexural strength of concrete cube specimen (MPa); F is the failure load under flexure (N); L is the distance between two fulcrums (mm); b is the section width of the specimen (mm); h is the section height of the specimen (mm).

In the flexural strength test, the specimen was installed according to Figure 2. The b and h of the sample are 40 mm, and the loading head is a rigid cylinder with a diameter of 25 mm and hinged support. The average of the three specimens in each group is taken as the test result. After being removed from the curing place, the specimen should be tested in time and the surface of the specimen should be wiped clean. The application of loads should be uniform and continuous. The loading rate was 0.05–0.08 mm/s.

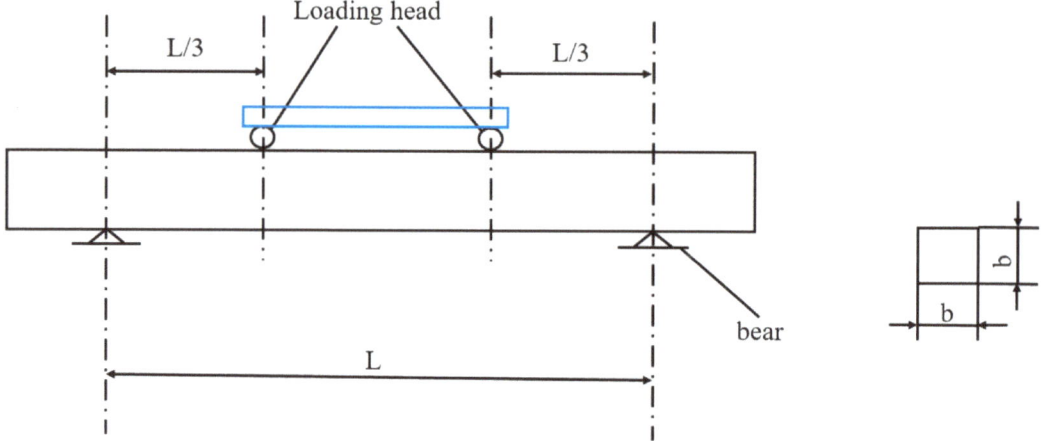

Figure 2. Test scheme of flexural strength.

After standard curing to the specified age, tested specimens were taken out for determination. The strength of the compression test is obtained by Equation (2).

$$f_{cc} = \frac{F}{A} \quad (2)$$

where: f_{cc} is the compressive strength (MPa); F is the failure load (N); A is the bearing area of the specimen (mm^2).

The compressive strength of each test group was treated as required by the Chinese standard for the evaluation of concrete compressive strength (GB/T 50107-2010). After removal from the curing site, the specimen shall be tested in time, and the surface of the specimen and the upper and lower bearing plates shall be wiped clean. In the test process, the load should be continuous and uniform, and the loading rate was 0.5–0.8 MPa/s. When the loading value was recorded after the failure, the testing data was obtained from three specimens.

The X-ray diffraction (XRD) test was measured by a SHIMADZU (Kyoto, Japan) X-ray diffractometer, as shown in Figure 3. Mainly for the test of concrete ground into powder, the test range is −3–150°, the full spectrum of <±0.02° deviation, and the concrete can withstand up to 120 kg. The scanning speed of the equipment is 0.01~120°/min. In this test, the scanning speed of 80°/min can be used to determine the phase composition of permeable concrete samples.

Scanning electron microscopy (SEM) was used in this study. The scanning electron microscope was produced by SHIMADZU, and the instrument model was ZEISS Merlin Compact (Jena, Germany). The reaction products of FA, mineral powder, and silica fume at different ages in pervious concrete were tested from a microscopic point of view. The microscopic mechanism of the influence of admixture on the performance of pervious concrete was analyzed. The magnification of the SEM image was 10,000 times, and the scale was 10 μm.

Figure 3. FRINGE CLASS diffraction instrument.

3. Results and Discussions

3.1. Influence of FA Content on Mechanical Properties of Concrete

After the standard curing for 3, 7, and 28 days, the concrete specimens were tested for flexural strength and compressive strength based on different FA content (0–50%). The results are shown in Figure 4. In addition, the standard error lines were added in Figure 4, to describe the differences in the results of the three parallel tests.

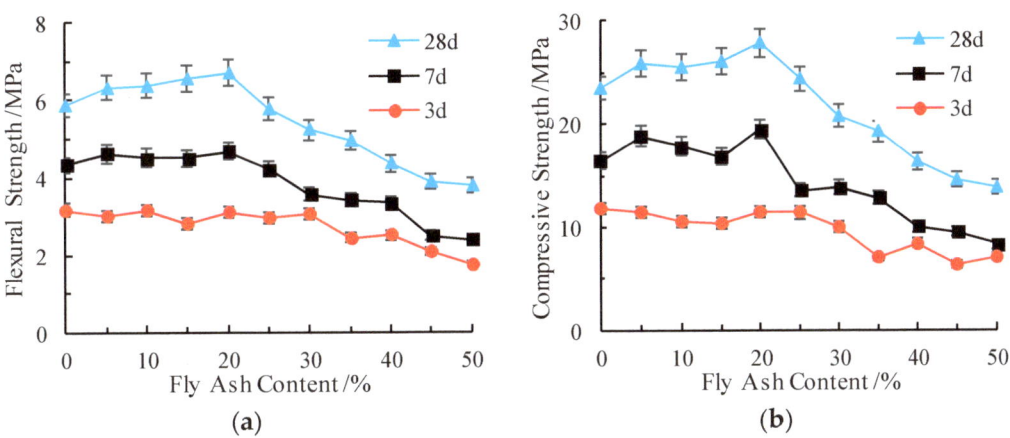

Figure 4. Effect curve of FA content on mechanical properties of concrete: (**a**) flexural strength; (**b**) compressive strength.

Results show that under the condition of keeping the concrete mix unchanged, and the standard curing for 3 days flexural strength of concrete slowly decreased with the increase of FA content. In particular, the flexural strength of the curve decreases rapidly after the inflection point of 20% content. When the FA content is 20%, the flexural strength is 3.09 MPa. When the FA content is 50%, the flexural strength is 1.76 MPa, which is also the minimum flexural strength of concrete after 3 days of standard curing. The flexural strength of concrete after 7 days of standard curing increases slowly with the increase of the FA content and then decreases rapidly. When the FA content is 20%, the flexural strength is 4.68 MPa, which is also the maximum flexural strength of concrete after 7 days of standard curing. As can be seen from Figure 4b, after the incorporation of FA, the variation law of concrete's compressive strength is consistent with that of its SF on the whole. Basically, it showed a trend of a slow increase at first and then a gradual decrease. When the FA content is 20%, compressive strength at 3 days of standard curing age is 11.48 MPa, at 7 days of standard curing age is 19.46 Mpa, and at 28 days of standard curing age is 27.81 MPa. When the FA content is 50%, compressive strength at 3 days of standard curing age is 7.08 MPa, compressive strength at 7 days of standard curing age is 8.31 Mpa, and compressive strength at 28 days of standard curing age is 13.87 MPa.

Compared with the concrete specimens without FA, the flexural strength of concrete after 3 days of standard curing and the compressive strength of concrete after FA incorporation show little change. Compared with the untreated concrete, after 28 days of standard curing, the flexural strength and the compressive strength of concrete with 20% FA increased by 0.82 MPa and 4.32 MPa, respectively. With the increase of the standard curing age, the volcanic ash effect of FA is further released, which can not only keep the flexural strength of concrete but also improve the overall mechanical properties of concrete due to the active characteristics of FA. Therefore, from the perspective of industrial solid waste utilization and reducing carbon emissions in cement production, the experimental results show that the optimal content of FA is 20%.

FA as an admixture of concrete has been extensively studied, and most of the studies are consistent with the law of change in the compressive and flexural strength of concrete after the addition of FA. As the age increases, it basically shows a trend of fast growth at the beginning and slow growth at the end. At the same time, the experimental results show that the relative percentage values of the compressive strength of cement concrete, Portland concrete, and high-performance concrete with FA content of 15% and 20% are significantly larger than those of the other mixtures. The optimal FA content in this study is 20%, which is in line with most experimental results on the mechanical properties of concrete materials with FA content [39,40].

3.2. Phase Analysis of FA after Incorporation

After the standard curing for 3 days and 7 days, the concrete XRD test was conducted based on the FA content of 0% and 20%, respectively, to observe their micromorphology and qualitatively study their hydration products. Then the macroscopic difference is explained from the microscopic mechanism, and the impact of FA on the road performance of concrete is further explored. The XRD test was used to analyze and determine the content of amorphous calcium silicate hydrate (C-S-H) gel, and the test results are shown in Figure 5.

XRD is mainly used to analyze the crystal changes in the slurry before and after the hydration reaction of pervious concrete, so as to qualitatively analyze the hydration reaction effect of admixture added to pervious concrete. Figure 5 shows the XRD pattern of concrete after 3 days of the standard curing. It can be seen from Figure 5a that the main phases of concrete without FA are SiO_2, $CaCO_3$, $Ca(OH)_2$, and Ca_2SiO_4, whereas the main phases of concrete mixed with 20% FA are SiO_2, $CaCO_3$, $Ca(OH)_2$, and C-S-H, which can be seen from Figure 6b. The formation of C-S-H gel indicates that the incorporation of FA promotes the hydration of cement clinker in concrete. With the increase of C-S-H gel content, the porosity of the cementing material decreases, the material becomes dense, the connected porosity of the permeable concrete decreases, and the reaction speed in the system is improved. The content of $Ca(OH)_2$ and SiO_2 in the system was gradually reduced. The results also present the correspondence in the XRD spectrum phase peak.

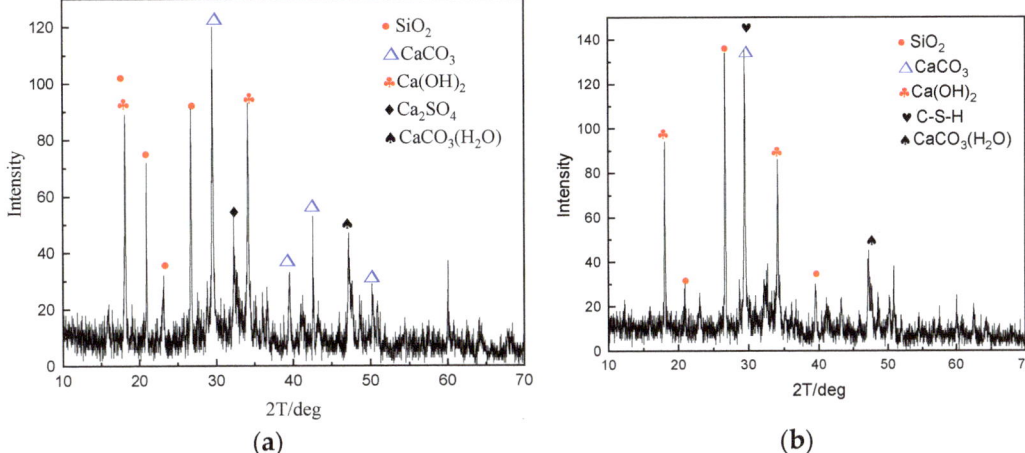

Figure 5. XRD patterns of the hydration products of concrete after 3 days of the standard curing: (**a**) concrete without FA; (**b**) concrete mixed with 20% FA.

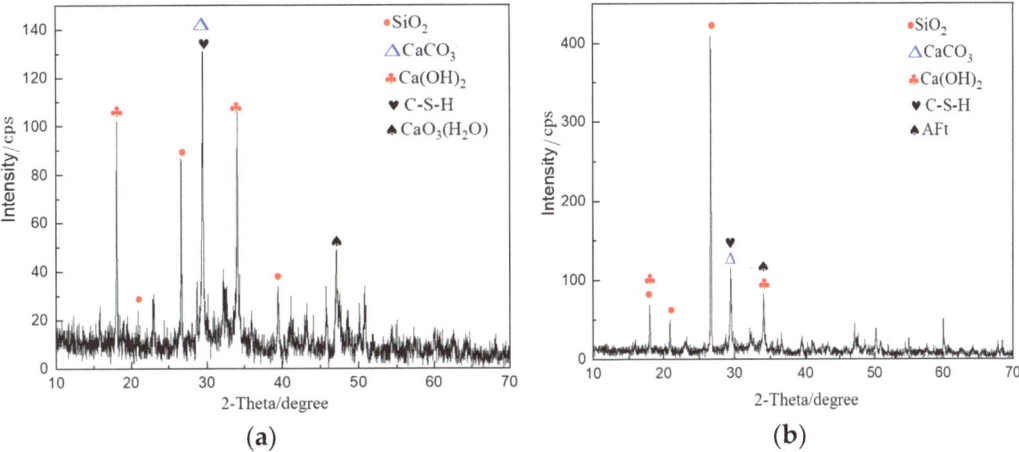

Figure 6. XRD patterns of the hydration products of concrete after 7 days of the standard curing: (**a**) concrete without FA; (**b**) concrete mixed with 20% FA.

Figure 6 shows the XRD pattern of concrete after 7 days of the standard curing, from which it can be seen that the main phases of concrete without FA are SiO_2, $CaCO_3$, $Ca(OH)_2$, and C-S-H. The main phases of concrete mixed with 20% FA are SiO_2, $CaCO_3$, $Ca(OH)_2$, C-S-H, and columnar ettringite (AFt). Compared with the XRD pattern of FA content in 3 days of curing standard, after 7 days of curing standard, the FA added in concrete can replace cement significantly, and exerts an active pozzolanic effect. AFt was further formed by a secondary reaction of calcium hydroxide due to the active pozzolanic effect.

3.3. Microstructure Analysis of FA after Incorporation

The hydration of Portland cement produces many chemical compounds, including the C-S-H, the calcium aluminate hydrate gel (C-A-H), the lamellar calcium hydroxide (CH) crystals, the Aft, and the irregular petal-shaped calcium sulfide aluminate hydrate (AFm) [41]. Figure 7 shows the SEM images of the standard curing for 3 days and 7 days of concrete without FA.

 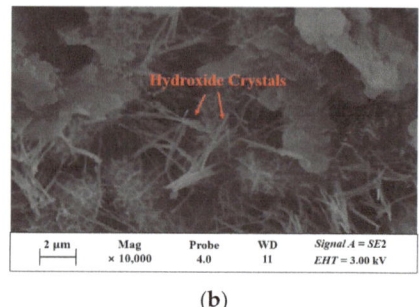

(a)   (b)

Figure 7. SEM images of concrete without FA after the standard curing for (**a**) 3 days and (**b**) 7 days.

The early hydration rate of pure cement concrete specimens is faster. In Figure 7a, there are a large number of hexagonal plate calcium hydroxide crystals, large cracks can be seen in the structure of the specimen, and the structure is loose. In Figure 7b, hydration has occurred in most of the composite Portland cement clinker minerals in the structure at the standard curing for 7 days, forming a large number of calcium hydroxide crystals, which is significantly more than at the standard curing for 3 days, and the internal structure of the concrete is denser.

Figure 8 shows the SEM images of concrete at the standard curing for 3 days and 7 days when 20% FA is added. A large number of fibrous, network, sheet, and flocculent C-S-H gels appeared in the specimen structure, and a large number of rod-like ettringite was generated in Figure 8a. At this time, the calcium hydroxide was not obvious, and most of them were interwoven C-S-H gel and AFt. In Figure 8b, the active substance in the FA is rehydrated with calcium hydroxide, and the interface between cement colloid and FA tends to be dense. The FA in the concrete structure presents a state of approximately spherical particles, and the pores of the structure are accompanied by FA particles without hydration reaction (active reactants appear on the surface) and cube crystals. There are more rod-like ettringite in the interior. With the increase in curing time, the hydration reaction of concrete structure specimens is continuously strengthened, and the activity of FA is gradually stimulated. In Figure 8, it can be clearly seen that the specimens of concrete structures at the standard curing for 7 days contain a large number of needle-rod substances, which are denser than those at the standard curing for 3 days.

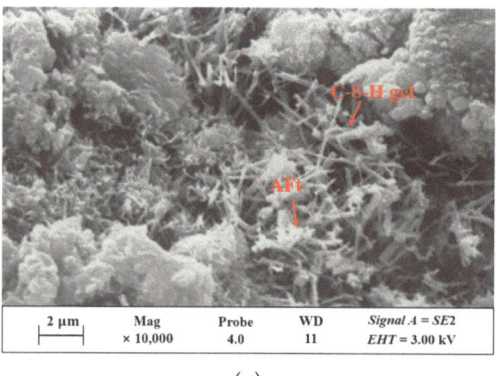 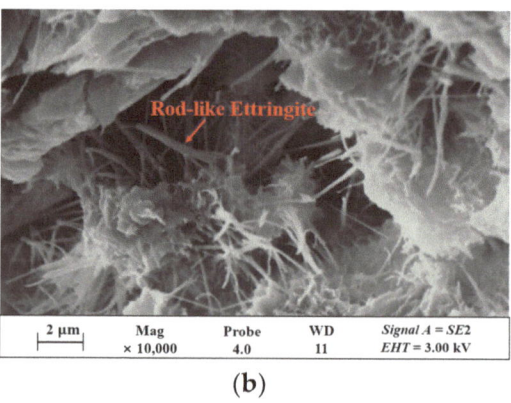

(a)   (b)

Figure 8. SEM images of FA mixed with 20% concrete after the standard curing for (**a**) 3 days and (**b**) 7 days.

In conclusion, with the increase of FA content, the volcanic ash effect is continuously intensified, spherical particles of concrete microstructure surround a large number of hydration products, and the specimen structure becomes loose. However, with the extension of the standard curing age, the types of hydration products increase, and there are unhydrated FA particles, a large number of needle-like ettringite, and a small amount of calcium hydroxide.

From the analysis of the microstructure test results, it can be seen that the internal structure density of the standard curing 7 day concrete in this study is better than that of ordinary concrete of the same age after adding 20% FA. With most FA as the concrete admixture of the micro test study, it is concluded that the holes and cracks in the internal structure of concrete are effectively filled, forming a density skeleton system, its standard curing of 7 and 28 days concrete structure is consistently denser.

In order to reduce the footprint of cement production, the cement was partially replaced by FA. Calculations based on carbon emissions in the carbon footprint suggest that the higher the FA content, the higher the low-carbon response of the concrete. Further research and optimization of FA characteristics ensure that the mechanical properties of the cement mix will correspondingly further reduce the carbon footprint.

4. Conclusions

This study aims to improve the safety performance of a green low-carbon concrete by FA content based on mechanical property tests and microscopic results of FA content. The main findings were listed as follows.

(1) The optimal FA content in green low-carbon concrete is 20%. After 28 days of standard curing, the flexural strength and compressive strength of the concrete with 20% FA increased by 0.82 MPa and 4.32 MPa, respectively;
(2) XRD analysis shows that the formation time of C-S-H and AFt phase in FA-doped concrete is earlier. In addition, the incorporation of FA promotes hydration reactions that rehydrate $Ca(OH)_2$ in the system;
(3) SEM analysis revealed that the microstructure of the concrete mixed with 20% FA is mainly composed of fibrous C-S-H gels and rod-like ettringite, and the cement colloids and FA between the interfaces tend to be dense, ensuring the safety properties of the concrete;
(4) This study only provides a qualitative description of the carbon footprint, and computational models should be used to quantify carbon reduction capabilities in the future.

Author Contributions: Conceptualization, Z.C. and M.L.; methodology, Z.C. and M.L.; formal analysis, Z.C. and M.L.; investigation, Z.C.; validation, M.L.; data curation, Z.C. and M.L. writing—original draft, Z.C. and M.L.; writing—review and editing, Z.C. and L.G.; visualization, Z.C. and L.G.; supervision, L.G.; resources, L.G.; project administration, L.G.; funding acquisition, M.L. and L.G. All authors have read and agreed to the published version of the manuscript.

Funding: The study is supported by the Key Research and Development Program in Ningxia Hui Autonomous Region, grant number 2022BDE02002, and the Key Research and Development Program in Xinjiang Uygur Autonomous Region, grant number 2022B01050.

Data Availability Statement: The data used to support the findings of this study are included within the article.

Conflicts of Interest: The authors declare no conflict of interest.

References

1. Ren, K.; Liu, C.; Wu, Z.; An, H.; Qu, J.; Zhang, H.; Lv, S. Laboratory investigation on performance of waste-oil cutback asphalt as prime coat on cement stabilized macadam base. *Constr. Build. Mater.* **2023**, *365*, 129965. [CrossRef]
2. Benhelal, E.; Zahedi, G.; Shamsaei, E.; Bahadori, A. Global strategies and potentials to curb CO_2 emissions in cement industry. *J. Clean. Prod.* **2013**, *51*, 142–161. [CrossRef]
3. Gao, T.; Shen, L.; Shen, M.; Liu, L.; Chen, F.; Gao, L. Evolution and projection of CO_2 emissions for China's cement industry from 1980 to 2020. *Renew. Sustain. Energy Rev.* **2017**, *74*, 522–537. [CrossRef]

4. Thumrongvut, J.; Seangatith, S.; Phetchuay, C.; Suksiripattanapong, C. Comparative Experimental Study of Sustainable Reinforced Portland Cement Concrete and Geopolymer Concrete Beams Using Rice Husk Ash. *Sustainability* **2022**, *14*, 9856. [CrossRef]
5. Wei, J.; Cen, K. Empirical assessing cement CO_2 emissions based on China's economic and social development during 2001–2030. *Sci. Total Environ.* **2019**, *653*, 200–211. [CrossRef] [PubMed]
6. Ke, J.; Zheng, N.; Fridley, D.; Price, L.; Zhou, N. Potential energy savings and CO_2 emissions reduction of China's cement industry. *Energy Policy* **2012**, *45*, 739–751. [CrossRef]
7. Bridge, G.; Bouzarovski, S.; Bradshaw, M.; Eyre, N. Geographies of energy transition: Space, place and the low-carbon economy. *Energy Policy* **2013**, *53*, 331–340. [CrossRef]
8. Sun, W.; Zhang, Y.; Liu, S.; Zhang, Y. The influence of mineral admixtures on resistance to corrosion of steel bars in green high-performance concrete. *Cem. Concr. Res.* **2004**, *34*, 1781–1785. [CrossRef]
9. Green, B.H.; Moser, R.D.; Scott, D.A.; Long, W.R. Ultra-high performance concrete history and usage by the Corps of Engineers. *Adv. Civ. Eng. Mater.* **2014**, *4*, 132–143. [CrossRef]
10. Qian, D.; Yu, R.; Shui, Z.; Sun, Y.; Jiang, C.; Zhou, F.; Ding, M.; Tong, X.; He, Y. A novel development of green ultra-high performance concrete (UHPC) based on appropriate application of recycled cementitious material. *J. Clean. Prod.* **2020**, *261*, 121231. [CrossRef]
11. Wei, H.; Zhang, H.; Li, J.; Zheng, J.; Ren, J. Effect of loading rate on failure characteristics of asphalt mixtures using acoustic emission technique. *Constr. Build. Mater.* **2023**, *364*, 129835. [CrossRef]
12. Ozbakkaloglu, T.; Gholampour, A.; Xie, T. Mechanical and durability properties of recycled aggregate concrete: Effect of recycled aggregate properties and content. *J. Mater. Civ. Eng.* **2018**, *30*, 04017275. [CrossRef]
13. Sharma, R.; Jang, J.G.; Bansal, P.P. A comprehensive review on effects of mineral admixtures and fibers on engineering properties of ultra-high-performance concrete. *J. Build. Eng.* **2022**, *45*, 103314. [CrossRef]
14. Sun, J.; Zhang, P. Effects of different composite mineral admixtures on the early hydration and long-term properties of cement-based materials: A comparative study. *Constr. Build. Mater.* **2021**, *294*, 123547. [CrossRef]
15. Wang, L.; Yao, Y.; Li, J.; Tao, Y.; Liu, K. Review of Visualization Technique and Its Application of Road Aggregates Based on Morphological Features. *Appl. Sci.* **2022**, *12*, 10571. [CrossRef]
16. Chang, J.; Li, J.; Hu, H.; Qian, J.; Yu, M. Numerical Investigation of Aggregate Segregation of Superpave Gyratory Compaction and Its Influence on Mechanical Properties of Asphalt Mixtures. *J. Mater. Civ. Eng.* **2023**, *35*, 04022453. [CrossRef]
17. Şengün, E.; Alam, B.; Shabani, R.; Yaman, I. The effects of compaction methods and mix parameters on the properties of roller compacted concrete mixtures. *Constr. Build. Mater.* **2019**, *228*, 116807. [CrossRef]
18. Langaroudi, M.A.M.; Mohammadi, Y. Effect of nano-clay on workability, mechanical, and durability properties of self-consolidating concrete containing mineral admixtures. *Constr. Build. Mater.* **2018**, *191*, 619–634. [CrossRef]
19. Yu, R.; Spiesz, P.; Brouwers, H. Development of an eco-friendly Ultra-High Performance Concrete (UHPC) with efficient cement and mineral admixtures uses. *Cem. Concr. Compos.* **2015**, *55*, 383–394. [CrossRef]
20. Matar, P.; Barhoun, J. Effects of waterproofing admixture on the compressive strength and permeability of recycled aggregate concrete. *J. Build. Eng.* **2020**, *32*, 101521. [CrossRef]
21. Ji, G.; Peng, X.; Wang, S.; Hu, C.; Ran, P.; Sun, K.; Zeng, L. Influence of magnesium slag as a mineral admixture on the performance of concrete. *Constr. Build. Mater.* **2021**, *295*, 123619. [CrossRef]
22. Herath, C.; Gunasekara, C.; Law, D.W.; Setunge, S. Performance of high volume fly ash concrete incorporating additives: A systematic literature review. *Constr. Build. Mater.* **2020**, *258*, 120606. [CrossRef]
23. Sharma, V.; Akhai, S. Trends in utilization of coal fly ash in India: A review. *J. Eng. Des. Anal.* **2019**, *2*, 12–16.
24. Zhang, Y.; Liu, M.; Xie, H.; Wang, Y. Assessment of CO_2 emissions and cost in fly ash concrete. In *Environment, Energy and Applied Technology, Proceedings of the 2014 International Conference on Frontier of Energy and Environment Engineering (ICFEEE 2014), Taipei City, Taiwan, 6–7 December 2014*; Taylor & Francis Group: Oxfordshire, UK, 2014; pp. 327–331.
25. Uliasz-Bocheńczyk, A.; Mokrzycki, E. The potential of FBC fly ashes to reduce CO_2 emissions. *Sci. Rep.* **2020**, *10*, 9469. [CrossRef]
26. Cho, Y.K.; Jung, S.H.; Choi, Y.C. Effects of chemical composition of fly ash on compressive strength of fly ash cement mortar. *Constr. Build. Mater.* **2019**, *204*, 255–264. [CrossRef]
27. Sandanayake, M.; Gunasekara, C.; Law, D.; Zhang, G.; Setunge, S.; Wanijuru, D. Sustainable criterion selection framework for green building materials—An optimisation based study of fly-ash Geopolymer concrete. *Sustain. Mater. Technol.* **2020**, *25*, e00178. [CrossRef]
28. Elchalakani, M.; Basarir, H.; Karrech, A. Green concrete with high-volume fly ash and slag with recycled aggregate and recycled water to build future sustainable cities. *J. Mater. Civ. Eng.* **2017**, *29*, 04016219. [CrossRef]
29. Xie, J.; Wang, J.; Rao, R.; Wang, C.; Fang, C. Effects of combined usage of GGBS and fly ash on workability and mechanical properties of alkali activated geopolymer concrete with recycled aggregate. *Compos. Part B Eng.* **2019**, *164*, 179–190. [CrossRef]
30. Matsumoto, S.; Ogata, S.; Shimada, H.; Sasaoka, T.; Kusuma, G.J.; Gautama, R.S. Application of coal ash to postmine land for prevention of soil erosion in coal mine in Indonesia: Utilization of fly ash and bottom ash. *Adv. Mater. Sci. Eng.* **2016**, *2016*, 8386598. [CrossRef]
31. Hwang, C.-L.; Huynh, T.-P. Evaluation of the performance and microstructure of ecofriendly construction bricks made with fly ash and residual rice husk ash. *Adv. Mater. Sci. Eng.* **2015**, *2015*, 891412. [CrossRef]

32. Fan, C.; Wang, B.; Zhang, T. Review on cement stabilization/solidification of municipal solid waste incineration fly ash. *Adv. Mater. Sci. Eng.* **2018**, *2018*, 5120649. [CrossRef]
33. Karakurt, C.; Bayazıt, Y. Freeze-thaw resistance of normal and high strength concretes produced with fly ash and silica fume. *Adv. Mater. Sci. Eng.* **2015**, *2015*, 830984. [CrossRef]
34. Poletanovic, B.; Dragas, J.; Ignjatovic, I.; Komljenovic, M.; Merta, I. Physical and mechanical properties of hemp fibre reinforced alkali-activated fly ash and fly ash/slag mortars. *Constr. Build. Mater.* **2020**, *259*, 119677. [CrossRef]
35. Al-Mansour, A.; Chow, C.L.; Feo, L.; Penna, R.; Lau, D. Green concrete: By-products utilization and advanced approaches. *Sustainability* **2019**, *11*, 5145. [CrossRef]
36. Tayeh, B.A.; Alyousef, R.; Alabduljabbar, H.; Alaskar, A. Recycling of rice husk waste for a sustainable concrete: A critical review. *J. Clean. Prod.* **2021**, *312*, 127734. [CrossRef]
37. Golewski, G.L. Combined Effect of Coal Fly Ash (CFA) and Nanosilica (nS) on the Strength Parameters and Microstructural Properties of Eco-Friendly Concrete. *Energies* **2023**, *16*, 452. [CrossRef]
38. Li, J.; Zhang, J.; Yang, X.; Zhang, A.; Yu, M. Monte Carlo simulations of deformation behaviour of unbound granular materials based on a real aggregate library. *Int. J. Pavement Eng.* **2023**, *24*, 2165650. [CrossRef]
39. Tosti, L.; van Zomeren, A.; Pels, J.R.; Comans, R.N. Technical and environmental performance of lower carbon footprint cement mortars containing biomass fly ash as a secondary cementitious material. *Resour. Conserv. Recycl.* **2018**, *134*, 25–33. [CrossRef]
40. Gao, X.; Yu, Q.L.; Lazaro, A.; Brouwers, H.J.H. Investigation on a green olivine nano-silica source based activator in alkali activated slag-fly ash blends: Reaction kinetics, gel structure and carbon footprint. *Cem. Concr. Res.* **2017**, *100*, 129–139. [CrossRef]
41. Uchechukwu, E.A. Effect of addition of sawdust ash to clay bricks. *Civ. Eng. Environ. Syst.* **2006**, *23*, 263–270. [CrossRef]

Disclaimer/Publisher's Note: The statements, opinions and data contained in all publications are solely those of the individual author(s) and contributor(s) and not of MDPI and/or the editor(s). MDPI and/or the editor(s) disclaim responsibility for any injury to people or property resulting from any ideas, methods, instructions or products referred to in the content.

Article

Discussing the Negative Pressure Distribution Mode in Vacuum-Preloaded Soft Foundation Drainage Structures: A Numerical Study

Ming Lei [1,2], Jin Chang [1,2,*], Jianqing Jiang [1,2] and Rui Zhang [1,2]

[1] College of Civil Engineering, Changsha University, Changsha 410022, China; lm2656717@163.com (M.L.); lh201314@163.com (J.J.); z20190809@ccsu.edu.cn (R.Z.)
[2] Hunan Engineering Research Center for Intelligent Construction of Fabricated Retaining Structures, Changsha 410022, China
* Correspondence: changjin1906@126.com

Abstract: The aim of this paper is to clarify the negative pressure distribution in drainage structures of soft foundations reinforced by vacuum preloading. The focus of this study was an actual engineering project, the Beijing–Shanghai high-speed railway; four different soil consolidation models were established using FLAC^{3D} to consider various loading conditions. The consolidation process of the soft foundation was calculated and analyzed in detail. The results show that (1) the settlement developed rapidly within the first 30 days, slowed during the period between 20 and 30 days, and finally stabilized. (2) The settlement curves obtained from the four different models were highly consistent with the site monitoring curve for the first 5 days, after which point significant differences appeared. (3) During the first 20 days, the pore water pressure decreased noticeably within the depth range of 0–18 m. Between days 20 and 30, the rate of pore water pressure decrease slowed down, and after the 30th day, the pore water pressure remained constant at all depths. (4) Vacuum preloading affected the soil to a depth of approximately 16 m. A concave or linear distribution of negative pressure in the drainage structure was found to be a reasonable assumption, providing a reference for the numerical analysis of vacuum preloading.

Keywords: negative pressure distribution; settlement; pore water pressure; numerical simulation; vacuum preloading

Citation: Lei, M.; Chang, J.; Jiang, J.; Zhang, R. Discussing the Negative Pressure Distribution Mode in Vacuum-Preloaded Soft Foundation Drainage Structures: A Numerical Study. Appl. Sci. **2023**, 13, 6297. https://doi.org/10.3390/app13106297

Academic Editor: Chiara Bedon

Received: 27 April 2023
Revised: 17 May 2023
Accepted: 19 May 2023
Published: 21 May 2023

Copyright: © 2023 by the authors. Licensee MDPI, Basel, Switzerland. This article is an open access article distributed under the terms and conditions of the Creative Commons Attribution (CC BY) license (https://creativecommons.org/licenses/by/4.0/).

1. Introduction

Thick, soft soil layers are widely distributed in coastal areas of China. These soil layers are characterized by a high void ratio, high water content, low permeability coefficient, and low strength. To build structures on such soft soil, it is necessary to reinforce the foundation.

The vacuum preloading method is a mature and low-cost technique used to strengthen soft foundations in the field of drain consolidation. This method was first proposed by W. Kjellman in 1952 [1], and since then, civil engineering scholars at home and abroad have conducted practical applications, tests, and theoretical research on this method. In terms of theoretical analysis, various researchers, such as Barron [2], Horne [3], Hansbo [4], Yoshikuni and Nakanodo [5], Onoue [6], Dong [7], Lin et al. [8], Liu et al. [9], etc., have developed sand drain consolidation theory with reference to the consolidation calculation method of surcharge preloading, changing the load boundary conditions to derive accurate analytical solutions of consolidation suitable for vacuum preloading. However, these methods are not convenient for practical application and promotion due to their simplification of assumptions, obscure and complex derivation processes, large numbers of parameters, and extensive requirements. In terms of numerical calculations, many researchers, such as Cheung et al. [10], Hird et al. [11], Indraratna and Redana [12], Zeng et al. [13], Chai et al. [14],

Sha et al. [15], Bergado et al. [16], Nguyen et al. [17], and Wang et al. [18], have conducted extensive research, including two-dimensional simulation, three-dimensional simulation, and sand drain simplification, considering smearing and other factors. However, few studies have been conducted on the negative pressure distribution mode of the vertical drain body under vacuum preloading. The plane strain model is usually used to represent the actual three-dimensional situation in the concrete implementation process. Although many engineering examples have been used to obtain relatively ideal results, the seepage and mechanical effects of soft foundations under vacuum preloading are three-dimensional, so a three-dimensional model should be applied in research. In the process of theoretical exploration and practical application, the mechanical and fluid disturbances of soft foundations strengthened by vacuum preloading are significant. Therefore, it is essential to analyze the settlement and pore pressure of soft foundations under this construction method using the fluid–solid coupling method, as suggested by Zhao et al. [19] and Liu et al. [20].

FLAC3D finite-difference method software based on the LaGrangian continuum method is a suitable option for conducting such analysis. This software has a strong analytical ability, making it suitable for complex engineering problems involving the mechanical seepage coupling of geotechnical materials. Compared to other finite element software, FLAC3D has the following advantages. (1) FLAC3D adopts the "mixed discrete method", which is more accurate and reasonable than the "discrete integration method" commonly used in the finite element method. (2) There are no numerical barriers to simulating physically unstable processes with FLAC3D. (3) FLAC3D uses an explicit difference method to solve differential equations. It can conveniently calculate stress increments and unbalanced forces and track the evolution process of the system. (4) FLAC3D can simulate a large number of units with less memory, making it particularly suitable for operation on microcomputers.

In the present study, fluid–solid coupling analysis of soft soil under the combined action of vacuum and surcharge was simulated Using FLAC3D.

We utilized the FLAC3D finite-difference method software to model and calculate the soil consolidation process under vacuum preloading for specific projects while varying the negative pressure distributions of the drainage body and keeping other conditions constant. The calculated results were compared with measured values to assess the impact of different negative pressure distributions on soil consolidation. This study is significant, given its aim of improving the accuracy of soft foundation settlement and pore pressure calculation.

2. Engineering Background

The soft foundation reinforcement test section for the Beijing–Shanghai high-speed railway was located in Kunshan, China. Specifically, the section from k0 + 276.51 to k0 + 515 was strengthened using the vacuum preloading + plastic drain board drainage consolidation method, with a reinforcement depth of 14.5~18.5 m. The plastic drain boards were arranged in a quincunx shape with a spacing of 1.2 m, and a 0.8 m thick sand cushion layer with a geogrid was placed on top of the plastic drain board. The vacuum pressure under the membrane was maintained at a minimum of 80 kPa. The consolidated foundation soil layer primarily consisted of muddy silty clay with high compressibility and low strength. Figure 1 displays the calculation section.

The settlement of the foundation surface was measured using settlement plates and an N4 leveling instrument. Specifically, one settlement plate was buried at the midline of the road bed, with another at the midline of the left lane and a third at the shoulder of the right lane. The layered settlement of the foundation was tested using settlement tubes, magnetic rings, and an R40 settlement monitoring instrument. The settlement tube was buried near the centerline of the right lane close to the centerline of the road bed. The pore water pressure was measured using MSY pore water pressure gauges and a frequency instrument. Ten water pressure gauges were buried at intervals of 2 m, beginning 2 m below the surface near the center of the section. These test components are shown in Figure 2. Vacuum preloading lasted for 56 days, from 26 April to 20 June, after which time the embankment was formally filled.

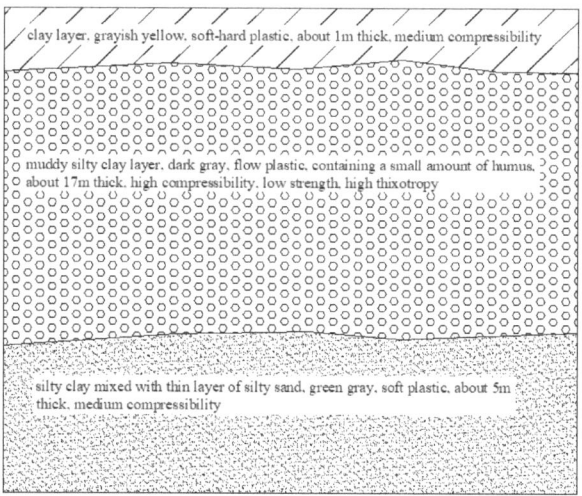

Figure 1. Soil layer distribution of the calculation section.

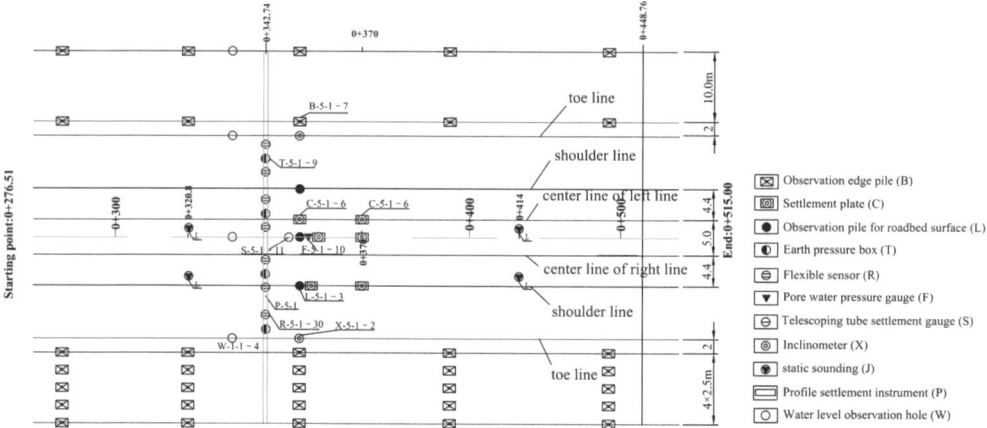

Figure 2. The layout plan of the test components.

3. Numerical Analysis Calculation Mode

FLAC (Fast Lagrangian Analysis of Continua) software, which uses the LaGrangian continuum method, was utilized for finite-difference numerical calculations. Initially, FLAC was developed for geotechnical and mining engineering applications. The strong analytical capabilities of the FLAC software for complex engineering problems make it adaptable to civil engineering, transportation, water conservancy, and other fields. FLAC^{3D} can be used to simulate the consolidation process of geotechnical materials, making it suitable for the study of the consolidation behavior of soil under vacuum preloading.

3.1. Constitutive Model and Seepage Model

Among numerous constitutive models of rock and soil, the Mohr Coulomb plastic constitutive model is the most universal. The Mohr Coulomb plastic constitutive model is suitable for materials that yield under shear stress, such as loose or cemented granular soil [21–25]. Geotechnical engineering problems often involve the action of pore water pressure, such as groundwater in the foundation, the seepage of earth dams, and the dewatering of foundation pits. When analyzing problems involving pore water pressure, FLAC^{3D} has two calculation modes that can be applied depending on whether fluid calculation is set up, namely, the seepage mode and non-seepage mode. Therefore, the use of the Mohr Coulomb plastic constitutive model to simulate the stress–strain relationship of soil and the anisotropic seepage model to simulate the anisotropic seepage characteristics of soil has practical significance. The calculation parameters are presented in Tables 1 and 2.

Table 1. Calculation parameters of the constitutive model.

Series	Clay	Smear Layer of Clay	Muddy Silty Clay	Smear Layer of Muddy Silty Clay	Silty Clay	Sand Drain
Compressive modulus, E_s/MPa	4.61	4.61	4.35	4.35	8.77	11.66
Poisson's ratio	0.47	0.47	0.55	0.55	0.49	0.3
Cohesion, c/kPa	14	14	3.7	3.7	4	0
Internal friction angle, φ/°	15.5	15.5	18.9	18.9	26.7	36
Bulk density, γ/kN·m^{-3}	19.2	19.2	17.8	17.8	18.8	19
Water content, ω/%	31.9	31.9	44.4	44.4	35	/

Table 2. Calculation parameters of the seepage model.

Series	Clay	Smear Layer of Clay	Muddy Silty Clay	Smear Layer of Muddy Silty Clay	Silty Clay	Sand Drain
Horizontal permeability coefficient, $k_{h100-200}$ /cm/s	0.40×10^{-7}	0.35×10^{-7}	1.44×10^{-7}	1.30×10^{-7}	0.41×10^{-7}	3×10^{-2}
Vertical permeability coefficient, $k_{v100-200}$ /cm/s	0.52×10^{-7}	0.53×10^{-7}	0.68×10^{-7}	0.69×10^{-7}	0.57×10^{-7}	3×10^{-2}

Density of water: 1000 kg/m^3; Biot modulus: 4×10^9 Pa.

3.2. Gridding

Based on the soil layer distribution map of the calculation section, a single sand drain consolidation model grid was established. To convert the plastic drain board into a sand drain with a radius of 0.05 m, the formula $r_w = \alpha(a+b)/4$ (where a is the width of the drain board, b is the thickness of the drain board, and α is the conversion factor) was used. The smear layer radius was taken as 3 times 0.15 m, and the affected area radius was taken as 7 times 0.35 m. The thickness of the clay layer is 1 m. The thickness of the muddy silty clay layer is 17 m. The bottom of the sand drain is flush with the bottom of the muddy silty clay layer, and the depth of the sand drain is 18 m. The thickness of the silty clay layer is 5 m.

This paper defines each soil layer as a group, the sand drain as a group, and the smear layer near the sand drain in different soil layers as a group. A total of six groups are defined: clay, muddy silty clay, silty clay, smear layer of clay, smear layer of muddy silty clay, and sand drain.

As the single sand drain foundation was axisymmetric, only one-quarter was taken for calculation. A cylindrical peripheral gradient radial grid was applied in the clay layer and muddy silty clay layer. A cylindrical peripheral gradient radial grid, cylindrical shell grid, and cylindrical grid were applied in the silty clay layer. A cylindrical grid was applied in the sand drain. A cylindrical shell grid was applied in the smear layers. The calculation model was 1.4 m wide and 23 m deep, divided into 2576 units and 3346 nodes, as depicted in Figure 3.

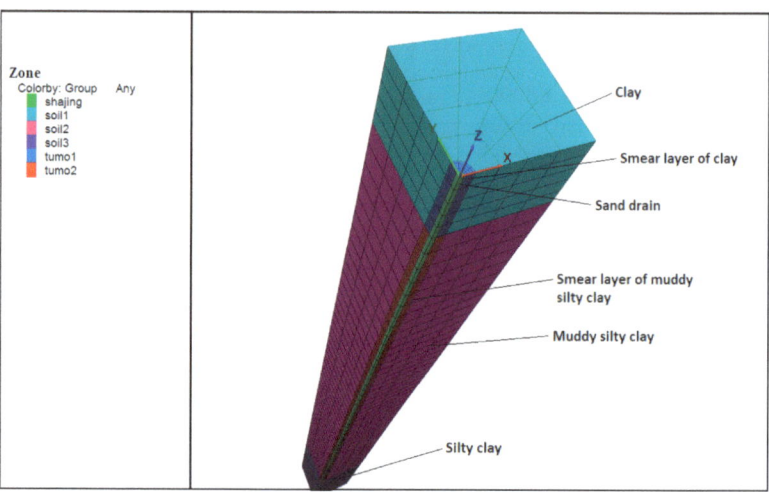

Figure 3. Computational model.

3.3. Boundary and Initial Conditions

The model had a free boundary on the top surface and a fixed boundary on the bottom surface, with no displacement in any direction. The four sides of the model had no horizontal displacement but allowed for vertical displacement due to the constraints of the surrounding soil. All sides of the hexahedron model were considered permeable boundaries.

The groundwater level was assumed to be flush with the ground, and the static pore water pressure at the ground node was set to 0, which increased linearly along the depth with a gradient of 10 kPa. The initial stress state was set as the gravity field. The density of each group was assigned, and the gravity acceleration was set to calculate the initial stress distribution for each group. After the calculation reached equilibrium, the deformation and the rate of the entire model node were assigned a value of 0.

A coordinate system was established for pore water pressure and sand drain height, with the center of the sand drain bottom as the origin, as shown in Figure 4.

In the fluid–solid coupling numerical analysis, the pore water pressure at the top node of the sand drain was assumed to be -80 kPa, as the vacuum degree under the membrane in the field exceeded 80 kPa within 8 h. The influence range of vacuum action was set at the bottom of the sand drain, where there was hydrostatic pressure but no negative excess pore pressure caused by vacuum, i.e., 0 kPa. Therefore, four models of pore water pressure distribution were assumed along the axial direction of the sand drain, as shown in Figure 3:

(1) "Concave" parabolic distribution: According to the standard parabolic equation ($x^2 = -2py(p > 0)$) and coordinate points (18, -80), $p = 2.025$, so $y = -x^2/4.05$. Because the distribution was concave relative to the vertical axis of the sand well, it is referred to as a "concave" parabola.
(2) "Convex" parabolic distribution: $y = (x - 18)^2/4.05 - 80$ was calculated according to the translation transformation of the parabolic equation obtained in (1). Because the distribution was convex relative to the vertical axis of the sand drain, it is referred to as a "convex" parabola.
(3) Linear distribution: The linear equation across the origin was $y = -40x/9$.
(4) Uniform distribution: The equation was $y = -80$.

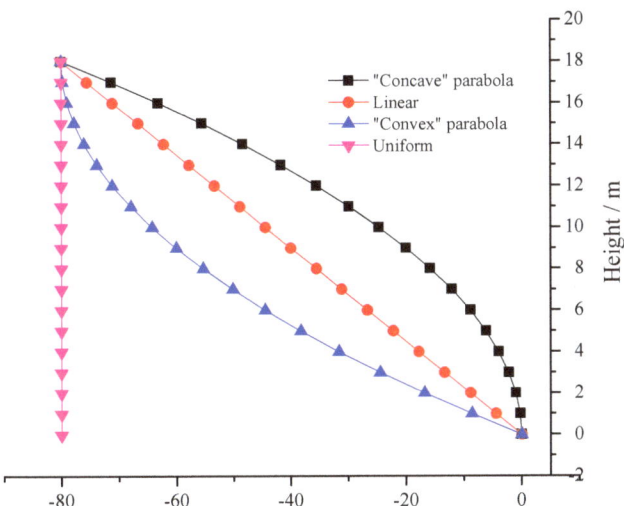

Figure 4. Distribution pattern of pore water pressure along the sand well.

The subcycle command flow was compiled to realize the application of a vacuum load under the above four working conditions. The unbalanced force ratio was set to 10^{-4}. The master–slave program method was adopted to solve the problem. The number of mechanical substeps was subordinate to the number of seepage substeps, and the seepage time was set as 4.8384×10^6 s.

4. Analysis of Calculation Results

4.1. Settlement Analysis

Figures 5–8 display the settlement–time calculation curves for the four negative pore water pressure distribution modes along the sand drain, namely, the "concave" parabola, "convex" parabola, linear distribution, and uniform distribution. The legend represents the depth from the surface. The results demonstrate that the settlement of the soft foundation increased rapidly during the first 30 days and then gradually slowed down, finally reaching a stable state. The surface soil was subject to the most settlements, which decreased with increasing depth. Settlement changes were faster and more significant closer to the surface and slower and less noticeable further away from the surface. On the 56th day, the surface settlement reached 82.40 cm under the "concave" parabolic distribution of pore water pressure, 93.95 cm under the "convex" parabolic distribution of pore water pressure, 81.69 cm under the linear distribution of pore water pressure, and 109.33 cm under the uniform distribution of pore water pressure. The settlement–time curve at a depth of 22 m was almost horizontal. On the 56th day, the settlement deformation at a depth of 22 m reached 2.74 cm, 2.83 cm, 2.75 cm, and 3.27 cm for each of the four conditions, respectively, indicating that the vacuum effect was minimal at a depth of 22 m.

After vacuuming, within 8 h, the vacuum under the membrane reached over 80 kPa. Negative pore water pressure was transmitted vertically from the sand cushion layer under the membrane to the sand drains, causing a change in pore pressure in the sand drains. Then, the negative pore pressure in the sand drains was transmitted to the surrounding soil. Finally, the soil underwent consolidation under the negative pore pressure. The vertical distribution pattern of the pore pressure in the sand drains determined the horizontal transmission strength of the pore pressure in the surrounding soil. From the assumptions of the four types of sand drain pore pressure distribution modes, it could be known that under the "concave" parabolic distribution mode, the average pore pressure was the smallest, while under the uniformly distributed model, the average pore pressure was the largest. So, it could be inferred that the consolidation settlement of soil was in descending order:

uniform distribution mode, "convex" parabolic distribution mode, linear distribution mode, and "concave" parabolic distribution mode.

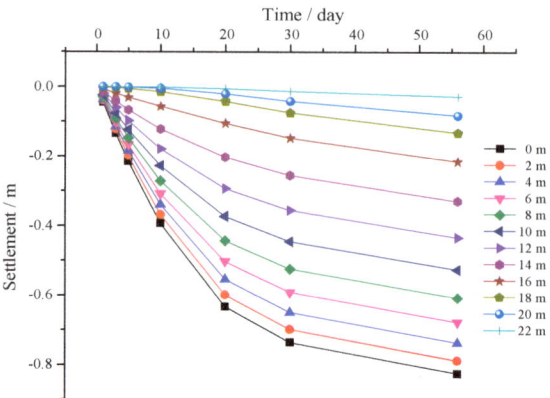

Figure 5. Settlement–time curve under "concave" parabolic distribution.

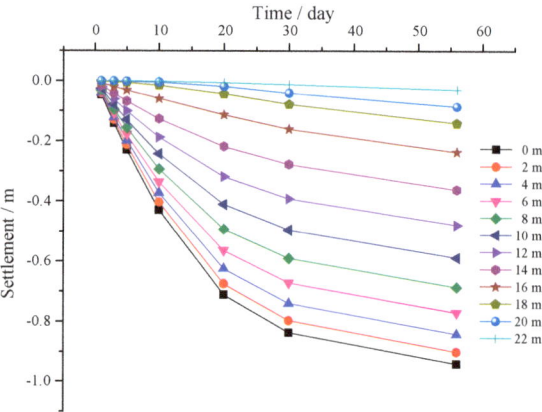

Figure 6. Settlement–time curve under "convex" parabolic distribution.

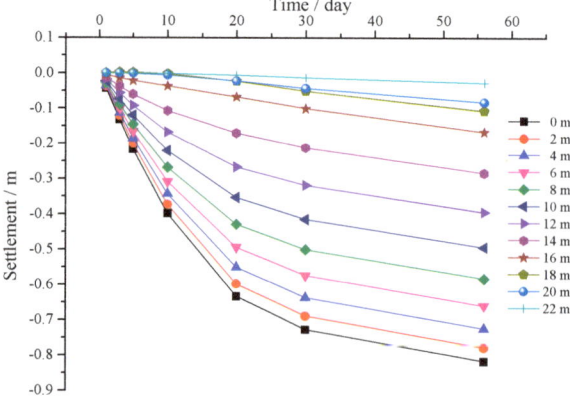

Figure 7. Settlement–time curve under linear distribution.

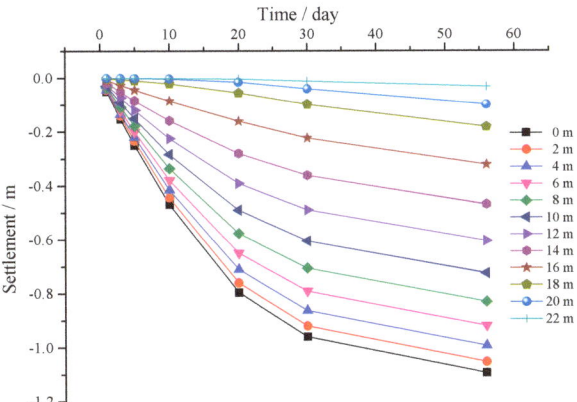

Figure 8. Settlement–time curve under uniform distribution.

Figures 9 and 10 depict the settlement–time calculation curves and measured value curves at depths of 0 m and 4 m under the four different pore water pressure distribution modes. The qualitative development trend of the four calculation curves was consistent with the measured values. During the first 5 days, the four calculated curves were highly consistent with the curves of the measured values. However, a large gap between the four calculated curves and the measured values was observed between days 5 and 30. The maximum difference between the calculated settlement value and the measured settlement value under the concave parabolic and linear distributions occurred around the 10th day, reaching 8.95 cm. The maximum difference between the calculated settlement value and the measured settlement value under the "convex" parabolic distribution occurred around the 30th day, reaching 12.53 cm. The maximum difference between the calculated settlement value and the measured settlement value under uniform distribution also occurred around the 30th day, reaching 24.87 cm. After 30 days, the calculated settlement curve and the measured settlement curve under the "concave" parabolic and linear distributions had a high degree of coincidence, with differences of 0.724–2.4 cm and 0.01–1.65 cm, respectively. However, the difference between the calculated settlement value and the measured settlement value under the "convex" parabolic and uniform distributions was consistent with the difference around the 30th day.

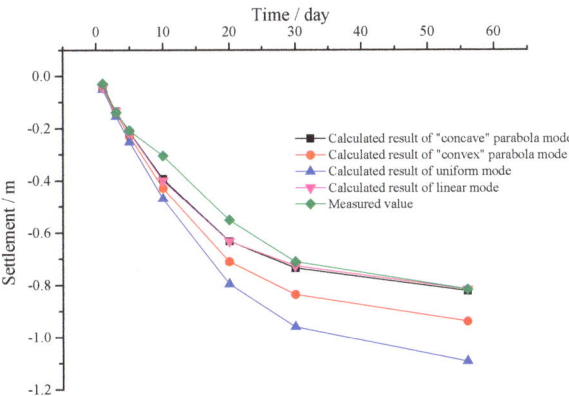

Figure 9. Settlement–time curve of four distributions at a 0 m depth.

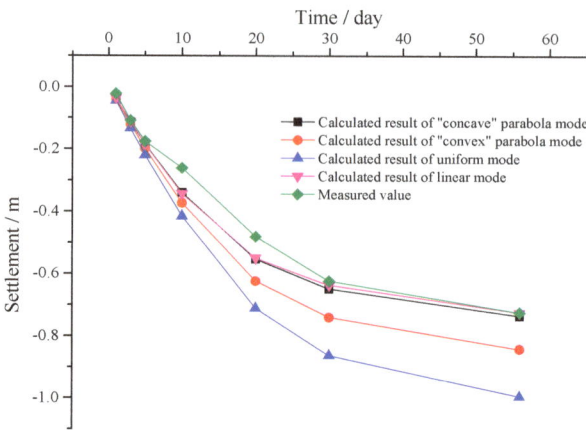

Figure 10. Settlement–time curve under four distributions, measured at a 4 m depth.

Many simplifications and assumptions were applied in the calculation model, such as assuming that the three soil layers were horizontal and homogeneous with the sand drain and smear layer and that the soil parameters remained constant. However, in reality, the soil layer was not horizontal or homogeneous due to its complex geological origin, and the soil parameters changed gradually during stress deformation, which resulted in the calculated curve being smooth, whereas the measured curve was more variable. During the first 5 days, the vacuum effect had little impact on the soil mass, and the settlement at each depth was minimal, resulting in highly consistent values between the four calculated curves and the curve of measured values. Between days 5 and 30, the vacuum negative pore water pressure was gradually transferred from the sand drain to a wider range of soil layers, resulting in rapid settlement of the soil mass at each depth. However, due to the complex structure of the soil mass and the anisotropy of negative pore water pressure transmission, the distribution of pore water pressure at each point in the soil mass was extremely unbalanced, resulting in a large deviation between the calculated value curve and the measured value curve. After 30 days, the calculated settlement values under the "concave" parabola and linear distributions gradually became consistent with the measured settlement values, whereas the difference between the calculated and measured settlement values under the "convex" parabola and uniform distributions remained at the same level as between days 5 and 30. After 30 days, the unbalanced pore water pressure in the soil gradually reached equilibrium and stabilized at a constant value. The pore water pressure at the same depth within the influence range of vacuum action was basically the same, indicating that the isotropic pressure values at each point at the same depth were consistent. The pore water pressure at different depths tended to have different constant values, and the isotropic pressure values at various points at different depths also differed.

From the settlement calculation curve, using the two setting modes: "concave" parabolic and linear pore water pressure modes, the calculation results were significantly better than those yielded using "convex" parabolic and uniform distribution modes. The linear setting mode was slightly better than the "concave" parabolic setting mode.

In the numerical calculation of the vacuum preloading reinforcement of soft foundation, the pore pressure in the sand cushion and sand drains under the membrane can rapidly decrease to a constant value in a short period of time, so the sand cushion and sand drains can be regarded as negative pressure boundaries. We can assign and adjust the node pore pressure of the sand cushion and sand drain area to achieve the loading effect of vacuum load. Based on the calculation results of the four negative pressure distribution modes of sand drains in the article, the calculation results using smaller pore pressure distribution modes (linear distribution mode and "concave" parabolic distribution mode) are in line with the actual situation on site. Since the consolidation settlement curve in the linear mode is very close to the measured curve (especially the final consolidation settlement), we selected the surface settlement time curve in this mode for asymptotic fitting and obtained the calculation formula and coefficients, as shown in Figure 11.

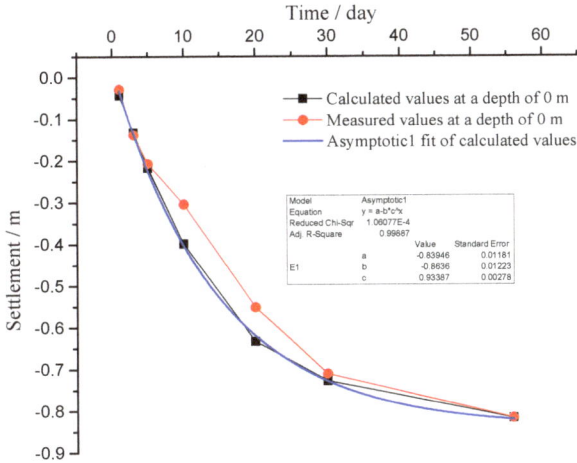

Figure 11. Asymptote fitting curve of calculated values.

4.2. Pore Water Pressure Analysis

Figures 12 and 13 show the change curve of pore water pressure at each depth of the soil mass over time under the concave parabola and convex parabola distribution modes.

During the calculation, we assumed that the initial value of pore water pressure at each point in the soil was hydrostatic pressure, i.e., a positive value, as the groundwater level was flush with the top surface of the model. After applying negative pore water pressure due to vacuum preloading to the top surface of the model and sand drains, the pore water pressure at each point in the soil decreased to varying degrees. Between 0 and 20 days, the pore water pressure decreased most obviously within a depth of 18 m. Between 20 and 30 days, the rate of pore water pressure decrease was significantly reduced and gradually became stable. After 30 days, the pore water pressure at each depth was basically unchanged and maintained at a constant value.

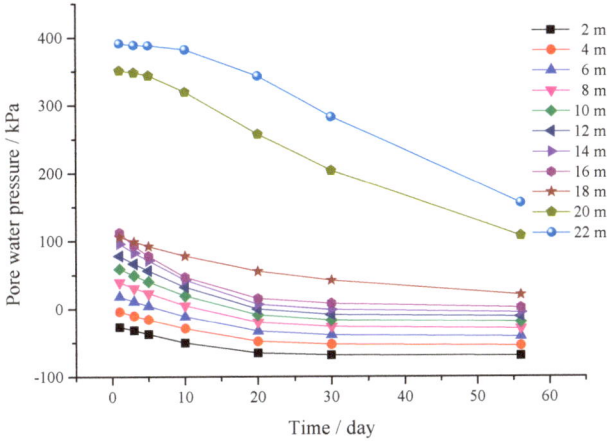

Figure 12. Pore water pressure–time curve under a "concave" parabolic distribution.

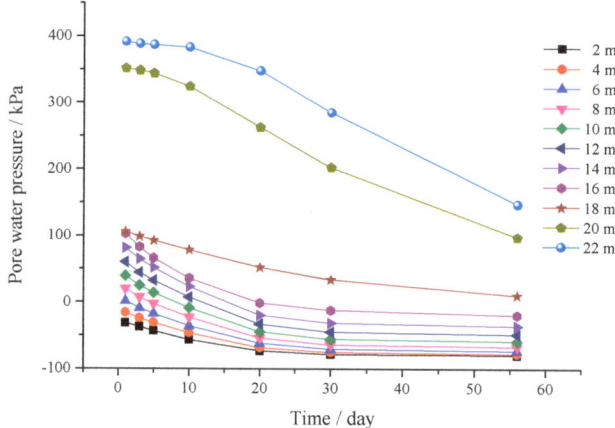

Figure 13. Pore water pressure–time curve under a "convex" parabolic distribution.

The pore water pressure at a depth of 2 m under the concave parabolic distribution was −69.17 kPa, that under the convex parabolic distribution was −79.59 kPa, that under the uniform distribution was −80.28 kPa, and that under the linear distribution was −72.20 kPa. The pore water pressure at a 16 m depth under the concave parabolic distribution was 1.79 kPa, and that under the linear distribution was 5.84 kPa. The pore water pressure at an 18 m depth under the convex parabolic distribution was 10.52 kPa, and that under the uniform distribution was −5.38 kPa, indicating that the vacuum preloading influence depth was approximately 16 m under the "concave" parabola and linear distributions and approximately 18 m under the "convex" parabola and uniform distributions. Combining the comparison and analysis results between the settlement calculation and the measured values proved that the influence depth of vacuum preloading was approximately 16 m.

Vacuum preloading causes a decrease in pore pressure in the soil. The greater the absolute value of negative pore pressure is, the better the consolidation effect of the soil is. However, the impact range of vacuum preloading on soil is limited. The maximum negative pore pressure is one atmospheric pressure that is impossible to achieve. The distribution pattern of pore pressure in sand drains for numerical calculation should be consistent with the actual situation. From the above settlement analysis, it can be seen that the linear distribution mode and the "concave" parabolic distribution mode are more in line with the actual situation. Due to the different mean values of the four sand drain pore pressure distribution modes, we can also infer that the decreasing values of pore pressure in soil are in descending order: uniform distribution mode, "convex" parabolic distribution mode, linear distribution mode, and "concave" parabolic distribution mode.

Figure 14 shows the pore water pressure–time change curve in soil under the four distribution modes at a 2 m depth.

Figures 15 and 16 show the pore water pressure–time curves of the four models and measured values at 4 m and 6 m depths.

The measured pore water pressure curve had a large dispersion, which may have been caused by various factors, such as equipment error, construction activity, and human errors during monitoring. However, this curve can qualitatively explain some of the phenomena. The pore water pressure–time curve obtained by the logarithmic fitting of the measured values was found to be closest to the calculated value of the linear distribution model.

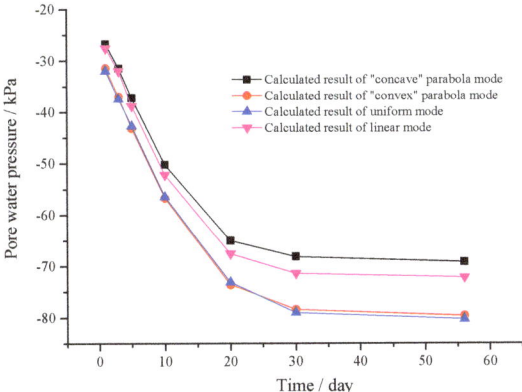

Figure 14. Pore water pressure–time curve under four distribution modes at a 2 m depth.

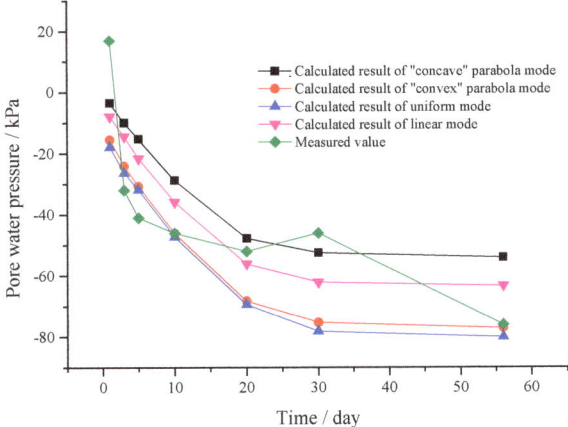

Figure 15. Pore water pressure–time curves of the four different distribution models and the measured results at a 4 m depth.

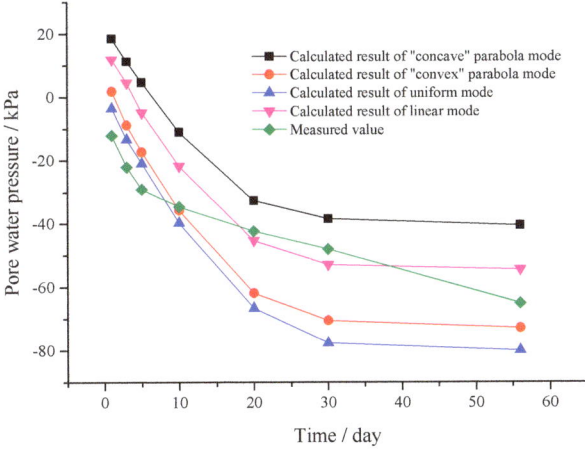

Figure 16. Pore water pressure–time curves of four distribution models and measured values at a 6 m depth.

5. Conclusions

The Beijing–Shanghai high-speed railway test section project used a fluid–solid coupling calculation model in FLAC^{3D} software to establish four modes of negative pore water pressure distribution along the sand drain: concave parabola, convex parabola, linear, and uniform distribution. The soil consolidation process was simulated and calculated, and the results were compared with the measured values of the project. The following conclusions were drawn.

The settlement of the soft foundation developed rapidly in the first 30 days, slowed down after 30 days, and eventually tended to stabilize. The settlement was most significant near the surface and gradually decreased with depth. The settlement–time curve at a depth of 22 m was nearly horizontal, indicating a weak vacuum effect at that depth.

Within the first 5 days of vacuum preloading, the settlement calculation curves for all four distribution modes were highly consistent with the measured settlement curves. Between days 5 and 30, there was a significant gap between the calculated and measured values. After 30 days, the settlement curves for the concave parabolic and linear distribution modes coincided closely with the measured settlement curves, with differences ranging from 0.724 to 2.4 cm and from 0.01 to 1.65 cm, respectively. However, the differences between the calculated and measured settlement values for the convex parabolic and uniform distribution modes were consistent with the differences observed around day 30.

The calculation results for the concave parabolic and linear pore water pressure modes were better than those for the convex parabolic and uniform distribution modes. The linear setting mode was slightly better than the concave parabolic setting mode.

During the first 20 days, the pore water pressure dropped most significantly within the depth range of 0–18 m. Between days 20 and 30, the rate of the pore water pressure decrease was significantly reduced and eventually became stable. After 30 days, the pore water pressure at each depth was essentially constant.

The influence depth of vacuum preloading for the concave parabolic and linear distribution modes was approximately 16 m, whereas the influence depth for the convex parabolic and uniform distribution modes was approximately 18 m. A comparison of the calculated settlement and the measured settlement showed that the influence depth of vacuum preloading was approximately 16 m.

This article did not consider the impact of group sand drains. Therefore, we will consider this impact in future research.

Author Contributions: M.L.: Conceptualization and writing—original draft. J.C.: Data curation and formal analysis. R.Z.: Software. J.J.: Validation. All authors have read and agreed to the published version of the manuscript.

Funding: This work was supported by the National Natural Science Foundation of China (42107166), Hunan Provincial Natural Science Foundation (No. 2021JJ40632, 2021JJ30758, and 2022JJ40521), Key project of Teaching Reform Research in Hunan Province (HNJG-2021-0209), Changsha Municipal Natural Science Foundation (No. kq2202065 and kq2202063), and Hunan Provincial Department of Education Project (No. 22B08253).

Institutional Review Board Statement: Not applicable.

Informed Consent Statement: Not applicable.

Data Availability Statement: All data, models, and code generated or used during the study are available from the corresponding author by request.

Conflicts of Interest: The authors declare no conflict of interest.

References

1. Kjellman, W. Consolidation of clay soil by means of atmospheric pressure. In Proceedings of the Conference on Soil, Zurich, Switzerland, 16–27 August 1953.
2. Barronr, A. Consolidation of fine-grained soils by drain wells. *Trans. Am. Soc. Civ. Eng.* **1948**, *113*, 718–754. [CrossRef]

3. Horne, M.R. The consolidation of a stratified soil with vertical and horizontal drainage. *Int. J. Mech. Sci.* **1964**, *6*, 187–197. [CrossRef]
4. Hansbo, S. Consolidation of fine-grained soils by prefabricated drains. In Proceedings of the 10th International Conference on Soil Mechanics and Foundation Engineering, Stockholm, Sweden, 15–19 June 1981; Volume 3, pp. 677–682.
5. Yoshikuni, H.; Nakanodo, H. Consolidation of soils by vertical drain wells with finite permeability. *Soils Found.* **1974**, *14*, 35–46. [CrossRef]
6. Onoue, A. Consolidation by vertical drains taking well resistance and smear into consolidation. *Soils Found.* **1988**, *28*, 165–174. [CrossRef] [PubMed]
7. Dong, Z. *Analytical Theory of Consolidation of Sand Drain Foundation under Surcharge and Vacuum Preloading*; Chinese Science and Technology Library: Beijing, China, 1997.
8. Lin, W.-A.; Jiang, W.-H.; Zhan, L.-T. General analytical solution for consolidation of sand-drained foundation considering the vacuum loading process and the time-dependent surcharge loading. *Rock Soil Mech.* **2021**, *42*, 1829–1838.
9. Liu, S.; Sun, H.; Geng, X.; Cai, Y.; Shi, L.; Deng, Y.; Cheng, K. Consolidation considering increasing soil column radius for dredged slurries improved by vacuum preloading method. *Geotext. Geomembr.* **2022**, *50*, 535–544. [CrossRef]
10. Cheung, Y.K.; Lee, P.K.; Xie, K.H. Some remarks on two and three dimensional consolidation analysis of sand-drained ground. *Comput. Geotech.* **1991**, *12*, 73–87. [CrossRef]
11. Hird, C.C.; Russel, D.; Cinicioglu, F. Modeling the effect of vertical drains in two-dimensional finite element analysis of embankments on soft ground. *Can. Geotech. J.* **1995**, *32*, 795–807. [CrossRef]
12. Indraratna, B.; Redana, I.W. Numerical modeling of vertical drains with smear and well resistance installed in soft clay. *Can. Geotech. J.* **2000**, *37*, 132–145. [CrossRef]
13. Zeng, G.; Wang, T.; Gu, R. Some Aspects of Sand-drained Ground. *J. Zhejiang Univ. Tecnol.* **1981**, *1*, 1–7.
14. Chai, J.C.; Shen, S.L.; Miura, N. Simple method of modeling PVD-Improved subsoil. *J. Geotech. Geoenviron. Eng.* **2001**, *127*, 965–972. [CrossRef]
15. Sha, L.; Liu, H.; Wang, G. Finite element analysis on large deformations of dredger fill improved by combined vacuum and surcharge preloading. *J. Zhejiang Univ. Technol.* **2021**, *49*, 140–146.
16. Bergado, D.T.; Jamsawang, P.; Jongpradist, P.; Likitlersuang, S.; Pantaeng, C.; Kovittayanun, N.; Baez, F. Case study and numerical simulation of PVD improved soft Bangkok clay with surcharge and vacuum preloading using a modified air-water separation system. *Geotext. Geomembr.* **2022**, *50*, 137–153. [CrossRef]
17. Nguyen, T.N.; Bergado, D.T.; Kikumoto, M.; Dang, P.H.; Chaiyaput, S.; Nguyen, P.-C. A simple solution for prefabricated vertical drain with surcharge preloading combined with vacuum consolidation. *Geotext. Geomembr.* **2021**, *49*, 304–322. [CrossRef]
18. Wang, D.; Wei, D.; Lin, G.; Zheng, J.; Tang, Z.; Fan, L.; Yuan, B. Finite Element Analysis of Vertical and Horizontal Drainage Structures under Vacuum Combined Surcharge Preloading. *Hindawi Ltd.* **2021**, *2021*, 1–11. [CrossRef]
19. Zhao, Y.; Tang, J.; Chen, Y.; Zhang, L.; Wang, W.; Wan, W.; Liao, J. Hydromechanical coupling tests for mechanical and permeability characteristics of fractured limestone in complete stress–strain process. *Environ. Earth Sci.* **2017**, *76*, 24. [CrossRef]
20. Liu, J.; Zhao, Y.; Tan, T.; Zhang, L.; Zhu, S.; Xu, F. Evolution and modeling of mine water inflow and hazard characteristics in southern coalfields of China: A case of Meitanba mine. *Int. J. Min. Sci. Technol.* **2022**, *32*, 513–524. [CrossRef]
21. Chen, Y.; Xu, D. *FLAC/FLAC3D Fundamentals and Engineering Examples*, 2nd ed.; China Water Power Press: Beijing, China, 2013; pp. 229–230.
22. Chang, J.; Li, J.; Hu, H.; Qian, J.; Yu, M. Numerical Investigation of Aggregate Segregation of Superpave Gyratory Compaction and Its Influence on Mechanical Properties of Asphalt Mixtures. *J. Mater. Civ. Eng.* **2023**, *35*, 04022453. [CrossRef]
23. Nariman, N.A.; Hamdia, K.; Ramadan, A.M.; Sadaghian, H. Optimum Design of Flexural Strength and Stiffness for Reinforced Concrete Beams Using Machine Learning. *Appl. Sci.* **2021**, *11*, 8762. [CrossRef]
24. Chang, J.; Xu, Y.F.; Xiao, J.; Wang, L.; Jiang, J.Q.; Guo, J.X. Influence of acid rain climate environment on deterioration of shear strength parameters of Natural residual expansive soil. *Transp. Geotech.* **2023**, 101017. [CrossRef]
25. Klyuev, R.; Bosikov, I.I.; Egorova, E.V.; Gavrina, O.A. Assessment of mining-geological and mining technical conditions of the Severny pit with the use of mathematical models. *Sustain. Dev. Mt. Territ.* **2020**, *3*, 418–427. [CrossRef]

Disclaimer/Publisher's Note: The statements, opinions and data contained in all publications are solely those of the individual author(s) and contributor(s) and not of MDPI and/or the editor(s). MDPI and/or the editor(s) disclaim responsibility for any injury to people or property resulting from any ideas, methods, instructions or products referred to in the content.

Article

Shaking Table Testing and Numerical Study on Aseismic Measures of Twin-Tube Tunnel Crossing Fault Zone with Extra-Large Section

Fengbing Zhao [1,*], Bo Liang [1], Ningyu Zhao [1,2] and Bolin Jiang [3]

1. School of Civil Engineering, Chongqing Jiaotong University, No. 66, Xuefu Road, Nan'an District, Chongqing 400074, China; liang_laoshi@126.com (B.L.); zny2008@163.com (N.Z.)
2. State Key Laboratory of Mountain Bridge and Tunnel Engineering, No. 66, Xuefu Road, Nan'an District, Chongqing 400074, China
3. Chongqing Vocational Institute of Engineering, Chongqing 402260, China; bolinjiang@cqvie.edu.cn
* Correspondence: zhao.fengbing@163.com

Abstract: As transportation networks continue to expand into mountainous regions with high seismic activity, ensuring the seismic safety of tunnels crossing active faults has become increasingly crucial. This study aimed to enhance our understanding of the impact of fault zones on the seismic behavior of tunnels and to provide optimized seismic design recommendations through a comprehensive experimental and numerical investigation. The focus of this research is the Xiangyangshan Highway Tunnel in China, which intersects a significant longitudinal fault. Large-scale shake table tests were performed on 1:100 scale physical models of the tunnel to analyze the seismic responses under various ground motion excitations. Detailed three-dimensional finite difference models were developed in FLAC3D and calibrated based on the shake table results. The tests indicated that strains, earth pressures, and accelerations experience localized amplification within 10–20 m of the fault interface compared to undisturbed ground sections. Common seismic mitigation measures, such as rock grouting, seismic joints, and shock absorption layers, were observed to effectively reduce the amplified seismic demands. Grouting, in particular, led to an average reduction of up to 56.3% in circumferential strain and 38.5% in earth pressure. It was concluded that 6 m thick grouted zones and 20 cm thick rubber interlayers between tunnel lining shells provide optimal structural reinforcement against the effects of fault zones. This study provides valuable insights for improving the seismic resilience of underground transportation corridors in seismically active regions.

Keywords: extra-large section tunnel; shaking table test; surrounding rock grouting; shock absorption layer; seismic joint; fault

1. Introduction

With rapid urbanization and economic development, the construction of transportation infrastructure has significantly accelerated throughout China in recent decades. The expansion of highways, high-speed railways, and underground metro networks has increasingly focused on effectively traversing complex terrain, particularly in mountainous regions [1–3]. Consequently, tunnels have become crucial for facilitating continuous travel through areas with challenging geological conditions. However, tunnels that cross active faults or are situated in high seismic zones are especially susceptible to earthquake damage, which can jeopardize structural integrity and public safety [4]. As a result, the optimized seismic design of tunnels is of utmost importance from both engineering and societal standpoints.

Numerous seismic zones with frequent seismic activity are located in Southwest and Northwest China. The construction of large-section tunnels in areas affected by active faults and high-intensity seismic zones presents an unavoidable challenge. In accordance with

the Specification for Seismic Design of Highway Tunnels (JTG 2232-2019) [5], the Standard for Seismic Design of Underground Structures (GB/T 51336-2018) [6], the Code for Seismic Design of Railway Engineering (GB 50111-2006) [7], and other standards, measures such as surrounding rock reinforcement, seismic joints, lining reinforcement, and extension of open spaces can be implemented for tunnel linings in high-intensity areas. While engineers and scholars have studied and compiled some effective vibration control measures for these tunnels with complex adverse site conditions, further research is still needed to investigate the vibration control mechanisms and key parameters of these measures [1].

In high-intensity seismic areas, shallow tunnel structures are more susceptible to severe deformation or even damage. Moreover, in mountainous regions, the complex geological conditions exacerbate the degree of structural damage [8]. Currently, scholars have developed mature theories on earthquake damage types, dynamic response characteristics, and laws governing ordinary mountain tunnels [5,6]. Previous studies have also demonstrated that shallow tunnels located within or near fault zones experience more severe deformations and damages compared to those in homogeneous ground. However, there is relatively limited research on the seismic dynamic response laws of shallow buried sections of extra-large highway tunnels.

The common anti-vibration measures outlined in the aforementioned Chinese standards include surrounding rock reinforcement methods, such as grouting reinforcement and anchor reinforcement, as well as lining reinforcement methods like concrete strength improvement, lining thickening, and steel mesh lining. In 2016, Xu et al. [9] conducted shaking table tests on these measures, analyzing their anti-vibration effects and studying the action mechanism and impact of seismic measures for mountain tunnels. While such measures have demonstrated effectiveness through small-scale shaking table tests, their vibration control mechanisms and key parameters require further elucidation, especially for tunnels with deep burial in complex fault settings.

Numerical dynamic analysis and shaking table tests are commonly employed to investigate anti-vibration measures for tunnels. The numerical dynamic time-history analysis method of the full model can comprehensively describe the dynamic interaction of surrounding rock and the tunnel, fully accounting for the geometric irregularity and medium inhomogeneity of the site [10]. This method is the most practical approach for predicting the effects of various anti-vibration measures prior to their implementation in tunnels and underground structures. Shaking table test methods are divided into centrifuge shaking table tests and ordinary shaking table tests, each with the characteristic of strictly controlling the research parameters of the test object and being unaffected by external environmental and natural conditions [11]. General shaking table test equipment is typically large and can conduct large-scale model tests, with relatively minimal model size effects on the test. In contrast, the model size in centrifuge tests is generally small, and the test results are easily influenced by boundary effects [12]. Given the characteristics of these research methods, the numerical dynamic analysis method is generally utilized to analyze the dynamic response characteristics of the tunnel structure, and subsequently, the shaking table test is employed to validate the dynamic response characteristics, yielding significant effects.

Common numerical analysis methods include the finite element method, finite difference method, discrete element method, and others. The finite element method is commonly implemented using software such as ANSYS 10.0 and ABAQUS 6.11, while the finite difference method typically utilizes software like FLAC3D 9.0. Xie [13], in 2013, employed the finite element analysis method to compare and evaluate the seismic behavior of a tunnel with different cross-sectional shapes, focusing on a portal segment in a shallow-built tunnel located in a seismic region with strong motion. Similarly, Salemi et al. [14], in 2018, investigated the behavior of the concrete lining of circular shallow tunnels in sedimentary urban areas under seismic loads using an integration of numerical and metaheuristic techniques. Furthermore, Momenzadeh et al. [15], in 2019, explored the function of the tunnel lining under static and seismic conditions by combining the response surface method, the Hasofer-

Lind reliability concept, and the finite element method, with a focus on the reliability of the lining system of a small underground tunnel in the soil. An et al. [16], in 2021, established an ABAQUS finite element model to clarify the influence of fiber-reinforced concrete lining structure on the seismic performance of an urban shallow-buried rectangular tunnel. Additionally, Jian et al. [17], in 2022, applied the finite element method to examine the influence of the thickness of a shock absorption layer on the seismic effect of an urban shallow-buried double-arch rectangular tunnel. Moreover, Liu et al. [18], in 2022, employed full dynamic time history analysis to investigate the interaction in the transversal direction of an arched tunnel buried in a stratified soil in Hohhot, China. A numerical parametric analysis was conducted to elucidate critical response characteristics.

Shaking table tests for tunnels are used to validate numerical calculation results or theoretical analysis findings, and to independently analyze the dynamic response characteristics of tunnel structures. The comparative analysis of several anti-vibration measures by Xu et al. [9] falls into the latter category. Shaking table model tests were conducted to investigate the seismic behaviors of a double box utility tunnel with joint connections and the surrounding soil [19]. Liang et al. [20] investigated the seismic behavior of a shield tunnel with an ultra-large diameter of 15 m passing through a soft-hard stratum using a series of 1/30 scaled shaking table model tests and numerical simulations. Additionally, in 2022, Zhang et al. [21] studied the seismic performance of a shield tunnel under near-field ground motion, conducting a series of large-scale shaking table tests.

This study aimed to enhance the understanding of seismic performance for an extra-large cross-section highway tunnel crossing faults through a comprehensive experimental and numerical investigation. A representative case tunnel in Southwest China was selected as the research object. Shaking table tests were initially conducted on physical models to reveal strain, earth pressure, and acceleration distributions with and without control measures, including surrounding rock grouting, seismic joints, and shock absorption layers. Based on the test results, finite difference analyses were then performed to optimize key parameters of the grouting thickness and the shock absorption layer thickness. The findings provide practical seismic design recommendations applicable to similar tunnels constructed in complex fault environments.

2. Case Study Tunnel

The case study tunnel selected for this research is the Xiangyangshan Tunnel located along the Qujing-Kunming Expressway in Yunnan Province, Southwest China. The Xiangyangshan tunnel is situated in the middle of the eastern Yunnan platform fold belt. The geological structure is highly intricate, particularly with a well-developed fault structure. The clearance width of a single tunnel on the standard section is 15.53 m, and the maximum excavation area is 167.6 m^2. It is a three-lane extra-large section highway tunnel. The tunnel is designed as a left and right tunnel with a typical shallow buried section and a double tunnel spacing of 23.07 m. The cross-sectional dimensions of the lining structure and the tunnel's portal site under construction are illustrated in Figure 1. The surrounding rock mass of the tunnel is categorized as grades V_2 to III_1, as assessed in accordance with the Chinese industry standard "Code for Design of Road Tunnel (JTG D70-2004)" [22]. The tunnel exhibits numerous fault fracture zones, developed joints, and fissures, leading to a rock mass that is relatively fragmented and unstable.

Based on the geological survey report, three low-resistance fractures have been identified in the surrounding rock of the tunnel, suspected to be structural fracture zones. The shallow rock in the tunnel area exhibits significant weathering, resulting in poor rock integrity. The deep joint fissures range from underdeveloped to moderately developed, with the surface primarily featuring two sets of joint fissures, which are detrimental to the stability of the surrounding rock of the tunnel.

Figure 1. Tunnels cross section parameters and its portal site under construction: (**a**) cross section parameters; (**b**) the portal site under construction.

The basic seismic intensity of the tunnel site area is rated at VIII on China's intensity scale. However, to account for the critical function of the expressway, a design fortification intensity of IX degree (strong earthquake level) was adopted for seismic design and control measures. The peak ground acceleration value for tunnel analysis was conservatively set at 0.4 g. Three types of input earthquake waves were incorporated into the subsequent physical model tests, namely the El-Centro, Taft, and artificial synthetic waves. The former two consist of seismic wave records from renowned historical earthquakes, whereas the latter are artificial seismic waves generated using probability function techniques. These waves represent different seismic characteristics that the tunnel may encounter. The peak value of original records was also adjusted and used in these physical model tests when input.

3. Shake Table Model Tests

To experimentally investigate the seismic responses of the Xiangyangshan Tunnel and evaluate potential vibration control measures, physical model tests were conducted on a large-scale shake table. This section describes the testing methodology and presents the results obtained, which provide valuable data for calibrating numerical models and optimizing anti-seismic designs.

3.1. Model Design and Fabrication

Given the intricate and time-consuming nature of the model testing process, as well as the extended duration required for each experiment, only two tunnel models were constructed. Considering the research scope and testing conditions, the geometric similarity ratio of the test model is set at 1/100. The geotechnical model is designed to have dimensions of 91 cm in total height, 200 cm in total length, and 137 cm in total width, with a mass density of 1. The elastic modulus similarity ratio is 1/100, and other physical quantities are scaled accordingly based on the principles of similarity. The physical parameters and similarity relationships between the model and prototype are outlined in Table 1. Table 2 provides detailed information on the setup conditions of the two test models. Figures 2 and 3 show the size and preparation of the shake table model.

Table 1. Physical parameters and similarity relationships between experimental models and prototypes.

Physical Parameters	Similarity Relationships	Physical Parameters	Similarity Relationships
Stress σ	1/137.5	Time T	1/11.72604
Strain ε	1/1.375	Frequency f	1/0.08528
Elastic modulus E	1/100	Velocity v	1/11.72604
Poisson's ratio μ	1	Accelerate a	1/0.727263
Density ρ	1/1.375	gravitational acceleration g	1
Length L	1/100	Cohesive force c	1/137.5
Displacement u	1/137.5	Damping C	1/1612.33
Force F	1/1375000	Stiffness K	1/10000

Table 2. Model setup details.

Model	Setting Conditions	Proposed Research Content	Model Overall Size
Model 1	The fault has a dip of 90 degrees and a width of 20 m, and the tunnel is a two-hole tunnel with a small clearance distance. The left tunnel does not have any anti-vibration measures and is supported by general V surrounding rock conditions. In contrast, grouting is used to reinforce the surrounding rock in the right tunnel. The grouting is carried out at intervals of the entire ring with a thickness of 4 m. Different reinforcement lengths are set before and after the longitudinal upper fault, with lengths of 25 m and 35 m, respectively.	(1) Seismic response characteristics of an extra-large section tunnel. (2) Strengthening effect of grouting reinforcement on surrounding rock in fault-related areas.	137 cm × 200 cm × 91 cm based on similarity ratio calculation.
Model 2	The fault has a dip of 90 degrees and a width of 20 m, and the tunnel is a two-hole tunnel with a small clearance distance. Both the left and right tunnels are supported by Class V surrounding rock. The left tunnel is equipped with seismic joints, while the right tunnel is provided with shock absorption layers. Different reinforcement ranges are set before and after the longitudinal upper fault, with lengths of 25 m and 35 m, respectively.	(1) Establishing the strengthening effect of seismic joints. (2) Establishing the strengthening effect of the shock absorption layer.	

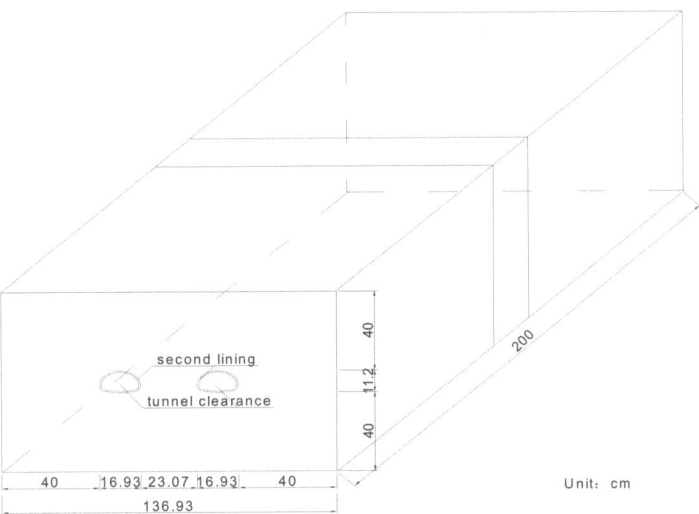

Figure 2. Size of the shaking table model.

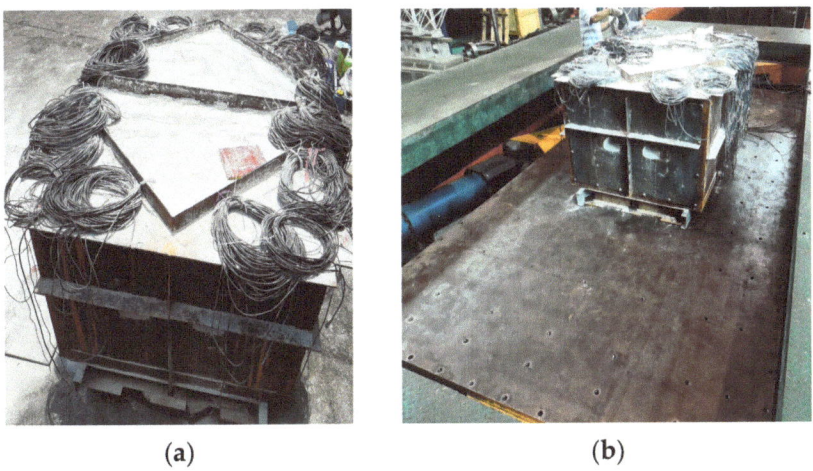

Figure 3. Descriptions of (**a**) model completion and (**b**) mounting on shaking table.

3.2. Instrumentation and Measurement

Strain sensors were positioned at designed monitoring sections A–A, B–B, C–C, D–D, E–E, F–F, G–G, H–H, I–I, J–J, and K–K (refer to Figure 4). A total of six strain gauge measuring points were placed on the outer surface of a single tunnel lining (see Figure 5). Each measuring point was equipped with two longitudinal and circumferential test channels, denoted by the symbol "Y" for strain measurement. Dynamic earth pressure testers and accelerometers were installed in sections C–C, D–D, E–E, F–F, G–G, H–H, and I–I. A dynamic earth pressure gauge (marked by the symbol "○" and sequentially labeled with number after the letter P in Figure 6) was positioned near the middle of each tunnel vault and left wall, respectively. An accelerometer was arranged at the top of the model box tunnel for each X/Y direction, and another accelerometer was placed at the bottom plate of the model box for each X/Y/Z direction. Additionally, two accelerometers were positioned at the middle of the right wall and the vault, one for each X/Y/Z direction.

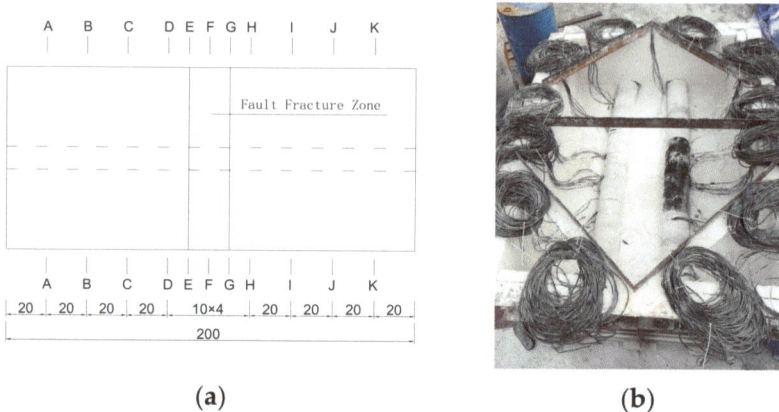

Figure 4. Diagram of (**a**) longitudinal numbering of monitoring sections and (**b**) sensor arrangement.

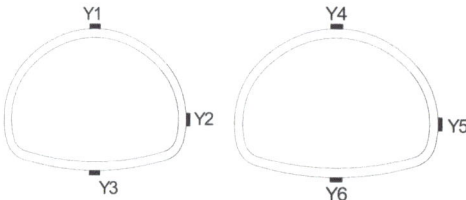

Figure 5. Arrangement of strain gauges within a single tunnel section.

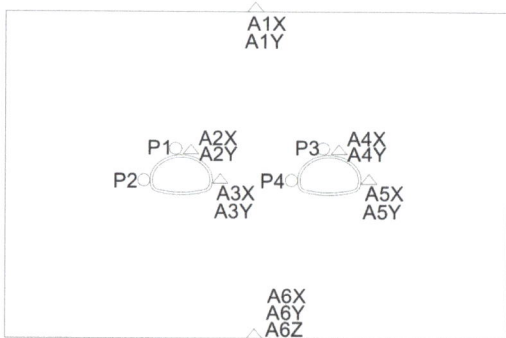

Figure 6. Layout of accelerometers and earth pressure gauges in the model cross-section.

3.3. Loading Protocols

The experimental scenarios involved exposing models to a range of input ground motions derived from scaled prototype earthquake data. The testing parameters for both models remained uniform, as outlined in Table 3. Four distinct seismic input levels were employed, specifically 0.25 A, 0.50 A, 0.75 A, and 1 A, with "A" denoting the peak value of the design seismic wave. Consistent peak amplitudes were maintained for identical El Centro, Taft, and artificial waves at each intensity level to facilitate the comparative analysis of structural reactions across various ground motion attributes.

Table 3. Model test conditions.

No.	Loading Model	Input Seismic Wave	Seismic Input Mode	Model Loading Intensity
1	Model 1 and Model 2	White noise	Bottom synchronous input X, Y, Z direction vibration	Load seismic wave peak 0.10 A
2	Model 1 and Model 2	El-Centro wave	Bottom input X direction vibration	Load seismic wave peak 0.25 A
3	Model 1 and Model 2	Taft wave	Bottom input X direction vibration	Load seismic wave peak 0.25 A
4	Model 1 and Model 2	Artificial wave	Bottom input X direction vibration	Load seismic wave peak 0.25 A
5	Model 1 and Model 2	White noise	Bottom synchronous input X, Y, Z direction vibration	Load seismic wave peak 0.10 A
6	Model 1 and Model 2	El-Centro wave	Bottom input X direction vibration	Load seismic wave peak 0.5 A
7	Model 1 and Model 2	Taft wave	Bottom input X direction vibration	Load seismic wave peak 0.5 A
8	Model 1 and Model 2	Artificial wave	Bottom input X vibration	Load seismic wave peak 0.5 A
9	Model 1 and Model 2	White noise	Bottom synchronous input X, Y, Z direction vibration	Load seismic wave peak 0.10 A
10	Model 1 and Model 2	El-Centro wave	Bottom input X direction vibration	Load seismic wave peak 0.75 A
11	Model 1 and Model 2	Taft wave	Bottom input X direction vibration	Load seismic wave peak 0.75 A
12	Model 1 and Model 2	Artificial wave	Bottom input X direction vibration	Load seismic wave peak 0.75 A
13	Model 1 and Model 2	White noise	Bottom synchronous input X, Y, Z direction vibration	Load seismic wave peak 0.10 A
14	Model 1 and Model 2	El-Centro wave	Bottom input X direction vibration	Load seismic wave peak 1 A
15	Model 1 and Model 2	Taft wave	Bottom input X direction vibration	Load seismic wave peak 1 A
16	Model 1 and Model 2	Artificial wave	Bottom input X direction vibration	Load seismic wave peak 1 A

Before excitation, a low-amplitude white noise signal was utilized to consolidate the soil model, and white noise scanning was introduced each time the peak acceleration value was adjusted to observe the dynamic behavior of the system model. White noise with a maximum amplitude of 0.1 g was applied in scenarios 1, 11, 21, and 31 to eliminate initial residual deformations and other variables. The original design seismic wave acceleration peak value was 0.4 g, equivalent to 4.0 m/s^2, with a vibration duration of 40.00 s. Following adjustments based on the similarity principle, the acceleration peak value was revised to 5.5 m/s^2, and the vibration duration was set at 3.4112 s. Consequently, the maximum peak value "A" of the seismic wave was established at 5.5 m/s^2.

3.4. Results and Analysis

3.4.1. Strain Analysis

The assessment of circumferential and longitudinal strain along the tunnel's axial direction under different seismic wave excitations and anti-vibration strategies was carried out using the findings from the model tests, illustrated in Figures 7–9. The testing segment of the tunnel model is positioned within the vertical range of 90–110 cm.

In general, the circumferential and longitudinal strains within and around the fault section (90–110 cm) displayed slightly higher values compared to other undisturbed ground segments when they were subjected to the three input ground motions. This indicated that the boundary effects of the fault zone reached a certain distance into the surrounding intact rock.

After incorporating anti-vibration measures, the strain distributions exhibited a more evenly spread pattern along the tunnel axis in contrast to the initial condition without any interventions. Additionally, the peak strain values decreased with the implementation of these controls. Although certain local strain readings displayed slight increments, these variations were presumed to have stemmed from minor testing inaccuracies.

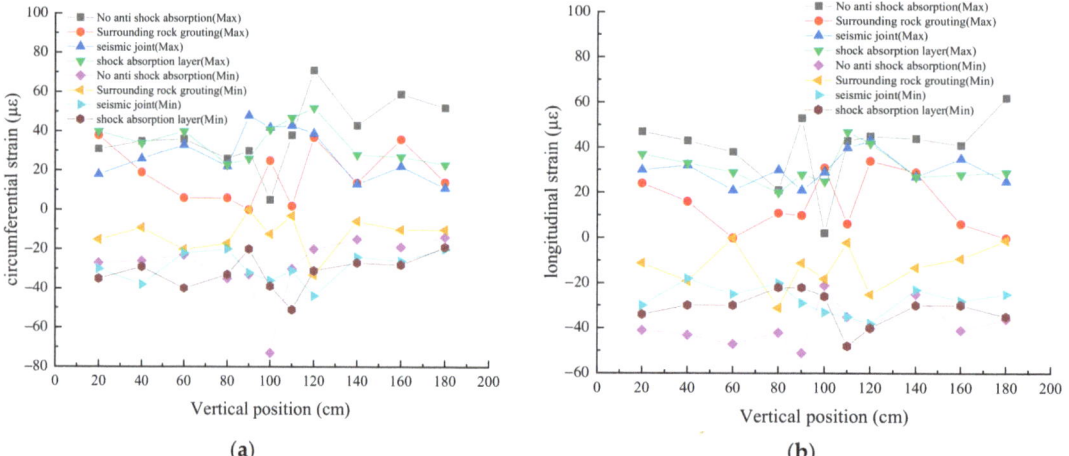

Figure 7. Peak distribution of (**a**) circumferential and (**b**) longitudinal strain increments along the longitudinal direction of the tunnel under the El-Centro wave.

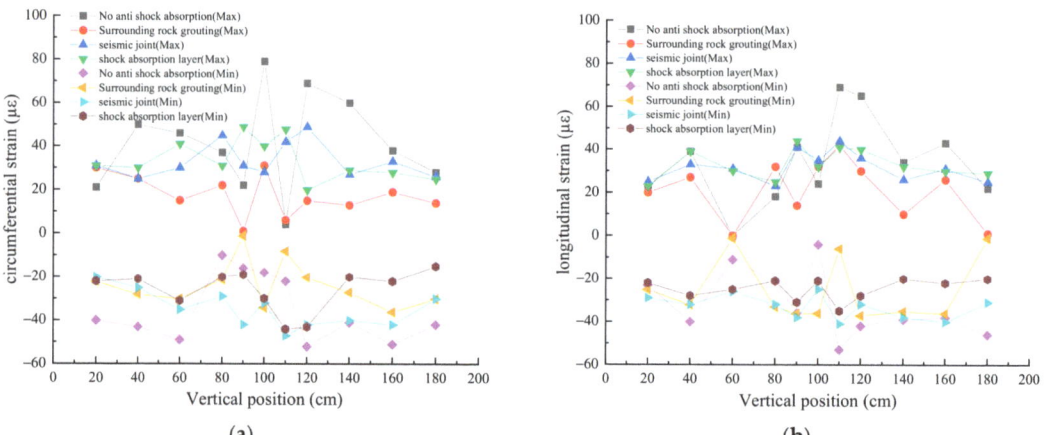

Figure 8. Peak distribution of (**a**) circumferential and (**b**) longitudinal strain increments along the longitudinal direction of the tunnel under the Taft wave.

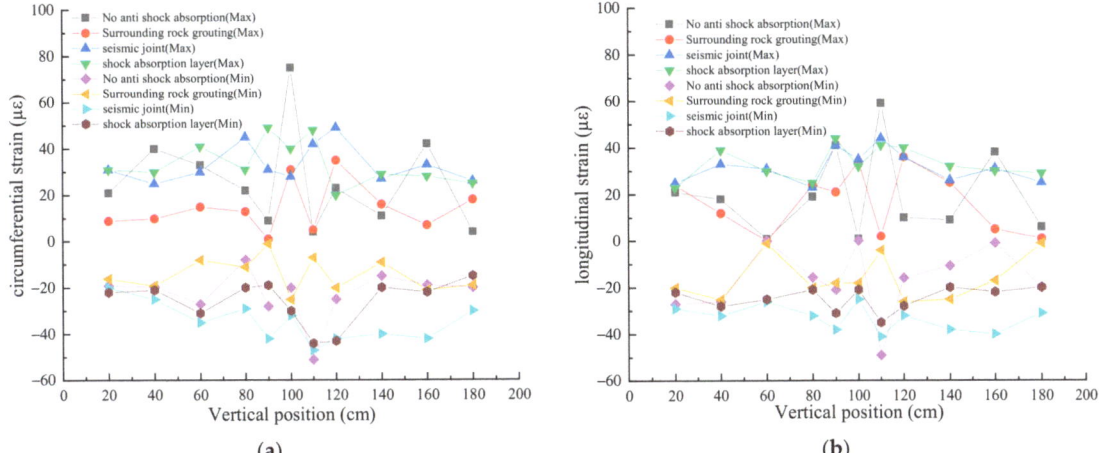

Figure 9. Peak distribution of (**a**) circumferential and (**b**) longitudinal strain increments along the longitudinal direction of the tunnel under the artificial wave.

In particular, when subjected to El-Centro wave excitation (refer to Figure 7), the introduction of anti-seismic measures effectively mitigated strain responses. In the absence of these measures, the maximum and minimum circumferential strain values were recorded at 71 με and −73 με, respectively. Subsequent to the implementation of interventions such as surrounding rock grouting, seismic joints, and shock absorption layers, reductions in strain levels were evident. Specifically, the maximum circumferential strain decreased to 38 με, 48 με, and 52 με, corresponding to the reduction ratios of −46.5%, −32.4%, and −26.8%, respectively. Similarly, the minimum circumferential strain values decreased to −33 με, −38 με, and −51 με, with reduction ratios of −54.8%, −47.9%, and −30.1%. As for longitudinal strain, the initial maximum value in the absence of measures was recorded at 62 με. Post-grouting, seismic joints installation, and shock absorption layer application, this figure decreased to 34 με, 43 με, and 47 με, respectively. The reduction ratios for longitudinal strain were calculated at −45%, −30.64%, and −24.2%.

Under Taft wave excitation, as illustrated in Figure 8, the implementation of surrounding rock grouting, seismic joints, and shock absorption layers effectively reduced strains. The reduction ratios of maximum circumferential strain were −60.8%, −38%, and −38%, respectively, for each measure. Meanwhile, the reduction ratios of minimum circumferential strain were −33.3%, −7.8%, and −13.7%, respectively. In terms of longitudinal strain, the reduction ratios of maximum strain were −53.6%, −36.2%, and −36.2% following the application of the three controls. The reduction ratios of minimum longitudinal strain were −30.2%, −22.6%, and −34%, respectively.

Similar trends were observed under artificial wave excitation, as depicted in Figure 9. In this case, the reduction ratios of maximum circumferential strain were −53.3%, −34.7%, and −34.7% with each control. The reduction ratios of minimum circumferential strain were −51.9%, −9%, and −14.8%, respectively. For longitudinal strain, the reduction ratios of maximum strain ranged from −39% to −25.4%, while the reduction ratios of minimum strain ranged from −47% to −16.3%.

Furthermore, the analysis indicated a shift in the locations of peak strain at the fault interface section after the installation of seismic joints and shock absorption layers, demonstrating the effectiveness of these measures against fault zone amplification effects.

3.4.2. Earth Pressure Analysis

Figure 10 illustrates the peak distribution of lining earth pressure increments along the tunnel longitudinal direction under different anti-vibration measures implemented in the model tests. Generally, the earth pressure increments near the fault section were slightly higher than in other intact sections under all three input ground motions. The distribution became more uniform after the application of anti-seismic controls.

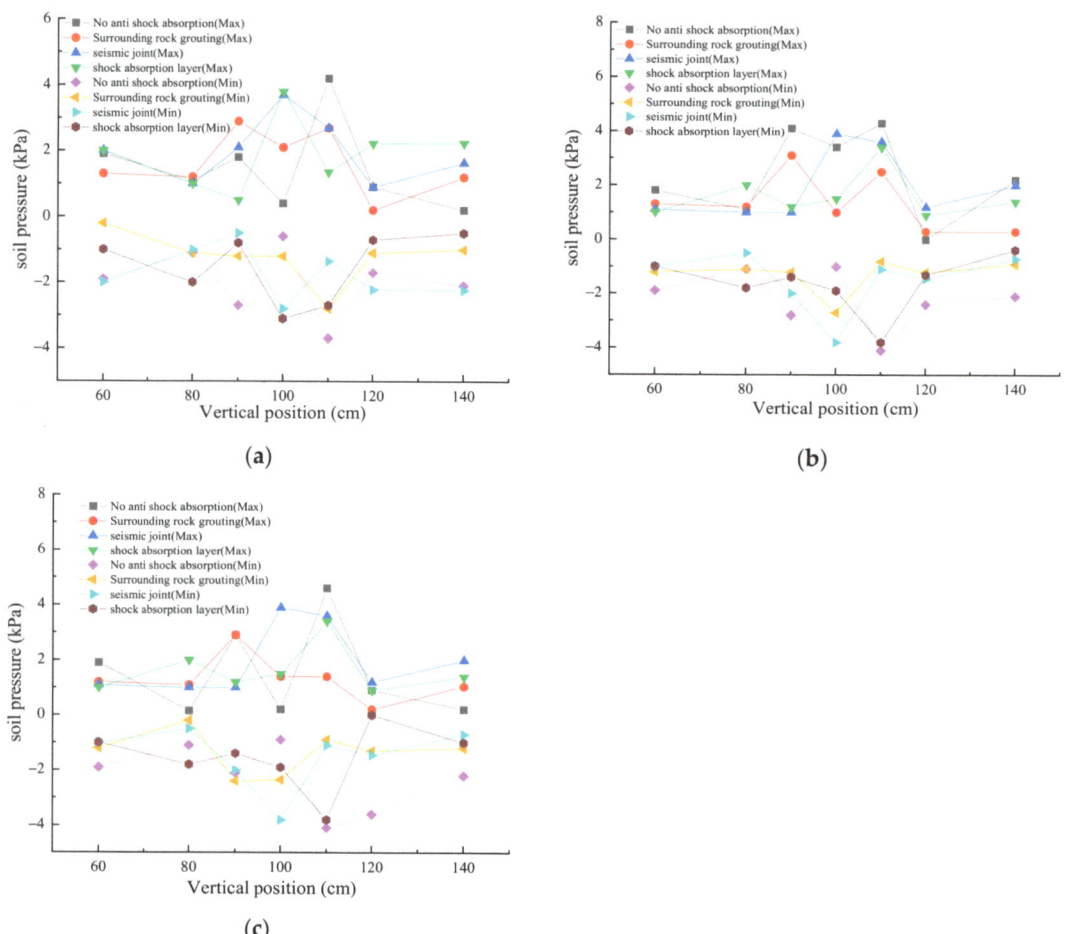

Figure 10. Increment peak distribution of lining earth pressure along the longitudinal direction of the tunnel: (**a**) El-Centro wave; (**b**) Taft wave; (**c**) artificial wave.

In Figure 10a, it was evident that under El-Centro wave excitation, the maximum and minimum increments of lining earth pressure were 4.2 kPa and −3.7 kPa, respectively, without seismic measures. After grouting, installing seismic joints, and incorporating a shock absorption layer, the maximum increment of lining earth pressure decreased to 2.9 kPa, 3.7 kPa, and 3.8 kPa, respectively, with reduction ratios of −40%, −12%, and −9.5%. Simultaneously, the minimum increment of lining earth pressure was −2.8 kPa, −2.8 kPa, and −3.1 kPa, respectively, with reduction ratios of −24.3%, −24.3%, and −16.2%.

In Figure 10b, under Taft wave excitation, following the grouting of surrounding rock, installation of anti-seismic joints, and implementation of shock absorption layers, the reduction ratio for the maximum increment of lining earth pressure was −28%, −9.3%, and −20.9%, respectively. Similarly, the reduction ratio for the minimum increment of lining earth pressure was −34%, −7.3%, and −7.3%, respectively. In Figure 10c, under artificial wave excitation, after the completion of grouting, installation of anti-seismic measures, and integration of shock absorption layers, the reduction ratio for the maximum increment of lining earth pressure was −37%, −15.2%, and −26.1%, respectively. Additionally, the reduction ratio for the minimum increment of lining earth pressure was −41.4%, −7.3%, and −7.3%, respectively.

Furthermore, the analysis of the peak position of earth pressure indicated that the peak position of earth pressure on the fault interface section changed after the installation of seismic joints and shock absorption layers.

3.4.3. Acceleration Analysis

Figures 11–13 illustrate the distribution of peak acceleration values in the X and Y axis along the tunnel section under different anti-vibration measures implemented in the model tests. The results revealed dynamic shifts in the peak positions of X-axis and Y-axis acceleration within the tunnel section when subjected to three different types of wave excitations, in contrast to scenarios lacking anti-vibration interventions. With the implementation of anti-vibration measures, the distribution of acceleration increments in the tunnel section exhibited a more uniform pattern, thus successfully managing the acceleration peaks in both the X and Y axes.

In Figure 11, it was observed that under El-Centro wave excitation, the maximum and minimum values of acceleration in the X axis were 7.2 m/s^2 and −7.1 m/s^2, respectively, without seismic measures. After grouting, installing anti-seismic joints, and incorporating a shock absorption layer, the maximum value of acceleration in the X axis decreased to 5.2 m/s^2, 5.2 m/s^2, and 6.3 m/s^2, respectively, with reduction ratios of −27.8%, −27.8%, and −12.5%, while the minimum value of acceleration in the X axis was −5.2 m/s^2, −5.2 m/s^2, and −6.5 m/s^2, respectively, with reduction ratios of −26.8%, −26.8%, and −8.5%. Without seismic measures, the maximum and minimum values of acceleration in the Y axis were 5.3 m/s^2 and −5.2 m/s^2, respectively. After grouting, setting seismic joints, and incorporating a shock absorption layer, the maximum acceleration in the Y axis decreased to 2.3 m/s^2, 4.8 m/s^2, and 4.8 m/s^2, respectively, with reduction ratios of −56.6%, −9.4%, and −9.4%, while the minimum acceleration in the Y axis was −2.8 m/s^2, −4.9 m/s^2, and −4.8 m/s^2, respectively, with reduction ratios of −46.2%, −7.55%, and −7.7%, respectively.

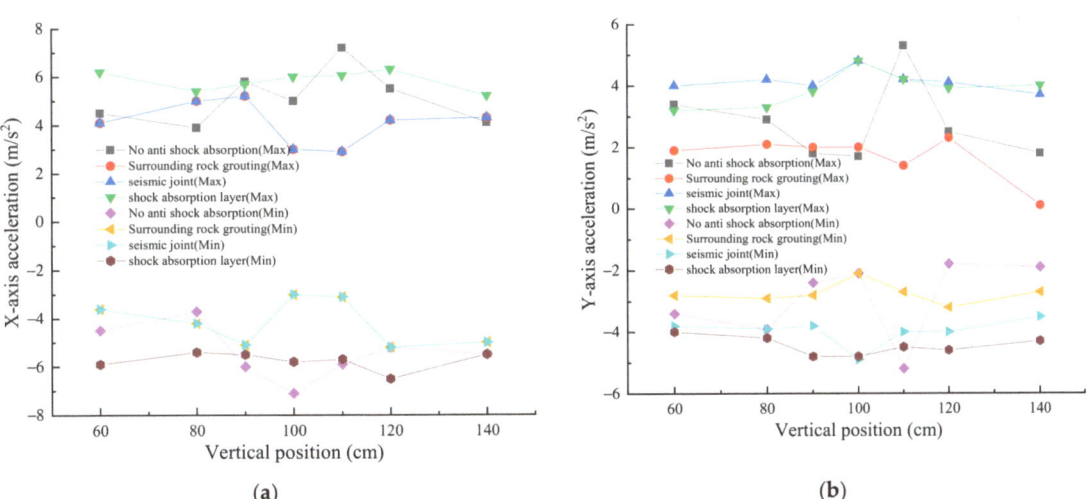

Figure 11. Distribution of (**a**) X-axis and (**b**) Y-axis acceleration peak value along tunnel longitudinal direction under El-Centro wave.

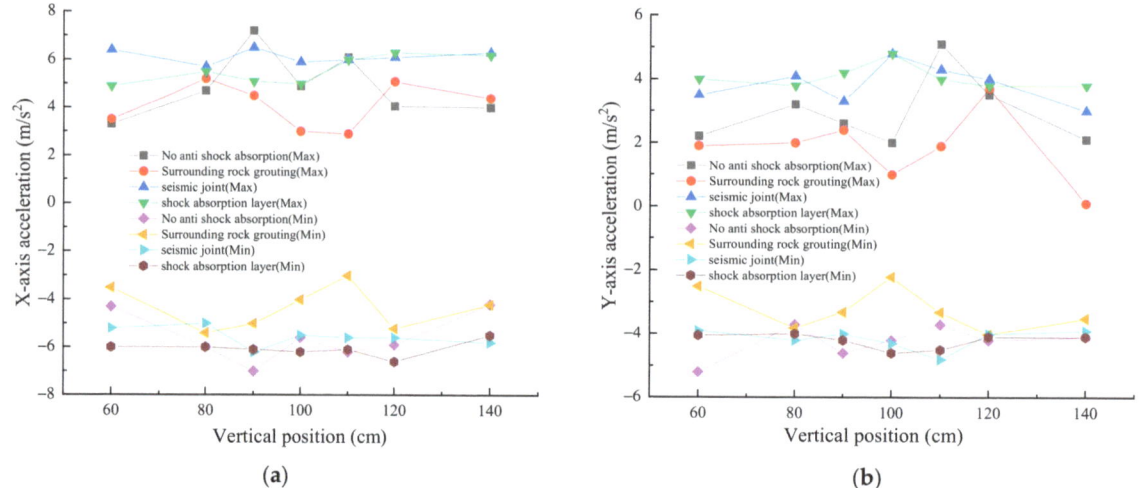

Figure 12. Distribution of (**a**) X-axis and (**b**) Y-axis acceleration peak value along tunnel longitudinal direction under Taft wave.

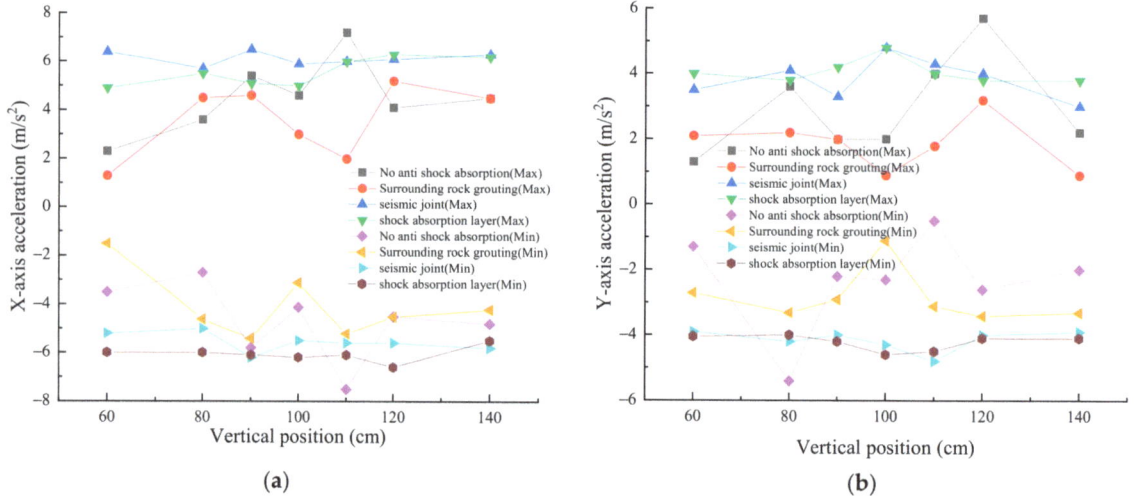

Figure 13. Distribution of (**a**) X-axis and (**b**) Y-axis acceleration peak value along tunnel longitudinal direction under artificial wave.

From Figure 12, it was evident that under Taft wave excitation, after grouting of surrounding rock, setting of seismic joints, and incorporating a shock absorption layer, the reduction ratio of the maximum acceleration in the X axis was −27.8%, −9.7%, −12.5%, respectively, while the reduction ratio of the minimum acceleration in the X axis was −22.9%, −11.4%, −5.7%, respectively. The reduction ratio of the maximum acceleration in the Y axis was −27.5%, −5.9%, −5.9%, respectively, and the reduction ratio of the minimum acceleration in the Y axis was −27%, −7.7%, −11.5%, respectively.

Likewise, from Figure 13, under artificial wave excitation, after grouting of surrounding rock, setting of seismic joints, and incorporating a shock absorption layer, the reduction ratio of the maximum acceleration in the X axis was −27.8%, −9.7%, −12.5%, respectively, while the reduction ratio of the minimum acceleration in the X axis was −28%, −17.3%, −12%, respectively. The reduction ratio of the maximum acceleration in the Y axis was

−43.8%, −15.8%, −15.8%, respectively, and the reduction ratio of the minimum acceleration in the Y axis was −37%, −11.1%, −14.8%, respectively.

Furthermore, the analysis of the peak position of acceleration indicated that the peak position of acceleration at the fault interface section changed after the installation of seismic joints and shock absorption layers.

3.4.4. Discussion

Based on the aforementioned test results, it was apparent that strain, earth pressure, and acceleration were slightly larger along the fault section and its vicinity under the excitation of three waveforms. In most cases, the index amplification effect was most pronounced at the interface of the fault zone surrounding rock. This demonstrated that the presence of a fault zone had a significant amplification effect on the acceleration, principal stress, and lining stress of the tunnel lining structure. The amplification effect extended a certain distance from the boundary surface of the surrounding rock of the fault zone to the complete surrounding rock section, with the maximum extension being 10 m. It was advisable to extend the minimum length of seismic fortification at both ends of the fault section by 10 to 20 m beyond the specifications outlined for tunnels with the recommended section in the Chinese industry standard (JTG D70-2004). Furthermore, after the installation of seismic joints and shock absorption layers, there were alterations in the positions of the maximum seismic response peaks at the fault interface sections.

To comprehensively analyze the shock absorption effect of surrounding rock grouting, seismic joints, and shock absorption layer, the maximum reduction ratio of strain, earth pressure, and acceleration peak values for each seismic measure was summarized in Table 4. In general, the trends in anti-vibration effects across various waveform excitations remained largely consistent, affirming the reliability of the model test outcomes.

Table 4. Analysis of anti-vibration effect.

Anti-Shock Measures	Waveform	Maximum Reduction Ratio (%)				
		Circumferential Strain	Longitudinal Strain	Earth Pressure	X-Axis Acceleration	Y-Axis Acceleration
Surrounding rock grouting	El-Centro wave	−54.8%	−45%	−40%	−27.8%	−56.6%
	Taft wave	−60.8%	−53.6%	−34%	−27.8%	−27.5%
	Artificial wave	−53.3%	−47%	−41.4%	−28%	−43.8%
	Average	−56.3%	−48.5%	−38.5%	−27.9%	−42.6%
Seismic joints	El-Centro wave	−47.9%	−30.64%	−24.3%	−27.8%	−9.4%
	Taft wave	−38%	−36.2%	−9.3%	−11.4%	−7.7%
	Artificial wave	−34.7%	−30.5%	−15.2%	−17.3%	−15.8%
	Average	−40.2%	−32.4%	−16.3%	−18.8%	−11.0%
Shock absorbing layer	El-Centro wave	−30.1%	−24.2%	−16.2%	−12.5%	−9.4%
	Taft wave	−38%	−36.2	−20.9%	−12.5%	−11.5%
	Artificial wave	−34.7%	−28.6	−26.1%	−12.5%	−15.8%
	Average	−34.3%	−29.7%	−21.1%	−12.5%	−12.2%

A comprehensive analysis revealed that the reinforcement of surrounding rock through grouting, the installation of seismic joints, and the addition of a shock absorption layer had noticeable seismic effects. Following the grouting reinforcement, the reduction ratios of hoop strain, longitudinal strain, earth pressure, peak acceleration value in the X direction, and peak acceleration value in the Y direction were −56.3%, −48.5%, −38.5%, −27.9%, and −42.6%, respectively. Subsequently, after the installation of seismic joints, the reduction ratios of hoop strain, longitudinal strain, earth pressure, X acceleration peak, and Y acceleration peak were −40.2%, −32.4%, −16.3%, −18.8%, and −11.0%, respectively. Finally, with the addition of the shock absorption layer, the reduction ratios of hoop strain, longitudinal strain, earth pressure, X acceleration peak, and Y acceleration peak were −34.3%, −29.7%,

−21.1%, −12.5%, and −12.2%, respectively. These results indicated that the seismic effects of seismic joints and shock absorption layers were similar, with the grouting reinforcement of surrounding rock exhibiting more significant effects than the former two.

4. Numerical Simulation

Following the validation achieved with the shake table experiments, extensive numerical analyses were conducted using the FLAC3D finite difference program. The objectives were to complement the physical model tests through more comprehensive parametric investigations and ultimately optimize key seismic control parameters for the design of Xiangyangshan Tunnel traversing the longitudinal fault zone.

4.1. Theoretical Basis

In numerical computations for models, the damping form typically adopts linear Rayleigh damping. In this case, the damping matrix [C] is represented as a linear combination of the mass matrix [M] and the stiffness matrix [K], as depicted in Equation (1) [23].

$$[C] = \alpha[M] + \beta[K], \quad (1)$$

where α and β can be determined by assuming that the damping ratio for a specific second-order frequency is known.

The damping constant can be expressed using two frequencies of different magnitudes as follows:

$$\left. \begin{array}{l} \alpha = \frac{2(\xi_j \omega_i - \xi_i \omega_j)}{(\omega_i + \omega_j)(\omega_i - \omega_j)} \omega_i \omega_j \\ \beta = \frac{2(\xi_i \omega_i - \xi_j \omega_j)}{(\omega_i + \omega_j)(\omega_i - \omega_j)} \end{array} \right\}, \quad (2)$$

where ξ_i and ξ_j are the damping ratios of the *i*-th and *j*-th order circular frequencies (ω_i and ω_j), respectively.

In general, engineering structures are usually assumed to have a damping ratio that remains relatively constant over a wide frequency range, with a typical value of 0.05 often used. The physical and mechanical parameters of the boundary elements in practical applications are determined by the materials of the adjacent surrounding rock medium, and specific calculation formulas can be found in the reference [24].

The input method for seismic waves acting on the computational model adopts the form of inputting stress waves at the viscoelastic artificial boundary, which is known as the equivalent boundary force method [25]. This method requires that the equivalent load applied to the artificial boundary makes the stress and displacement on the boundary identical to the original wave field. At this juncture, the equivalent boundary stress $F_B(t)$ can be expressed as follows:

$$F_B(t) = \sigma_B(t) + C\dot{u}_B(t) + Ku_B(t), \quad (3)$$

where $\sigma_B(t)$ represents the stress at the artificial boundary of the infinite domain model; $\dot{u}(t)$ and $u(t)$ represent the vibration velocity and displacement at the artificial boundary. C and K, respectively, denote the damping coefficient and spring elasticity coefficient set at the artificial boundary.

When accounting for the fluctuation effects of the normal and tangential waves at the artificial boundary, researchers have analyzed the incident wave field of seismic waves in spherical coordinates and derived expressions for the vertical incident P-wave and S-wave at the artificial boundary, respectively [26].

Considering the incident non-attenuated S-wave in the far field, the corresponding expression is:

$$F_{BT}(t) = 2\rho C_S \dot{u}_B(t) + \frac{2G}{R} u_B(t), \qquad (4)$$

where R represents the distance from the artificial boundary to the ground or structure; G represents the shear modulus of the adjacent medium in the artificial boundary region; λ and ρ represent the Lamé constants and density of the corresponding medium.

4.2. Computational Model

Based on the experimental model size and parameter design, a three-dimensional numerical model was constructed, as illustrated in Figure 14. Solid elements were used to simulate both the surrounding rock and the secondary lining, while the initial support was represented by shell structure elements [27]. The surrounding rock was modeled using the Mohr–Coulomb yield criterion and an elastic-plastic incremental constitutive relationship, whereas the secondary lining and initial support were characterized by a linear elastic constitutive model. Excavation simulation was carried out utilizing the "model null" function in FLAC3D, with a maximum grid size of 5 m. The model boundary conditions were defined using the free field mesh technology within FLAC3D software to establish free field boundaries, with a viscous boundary applied at the base. The free field boundary comprised four side-layered free field meshes surrounding the model and four corner-point layered free field meshes [28], connected to the main grid via dampers to mimic an infinite field model. The seismic input wave at the base corresponded to the renowned El-centro wave mentioned earlier.

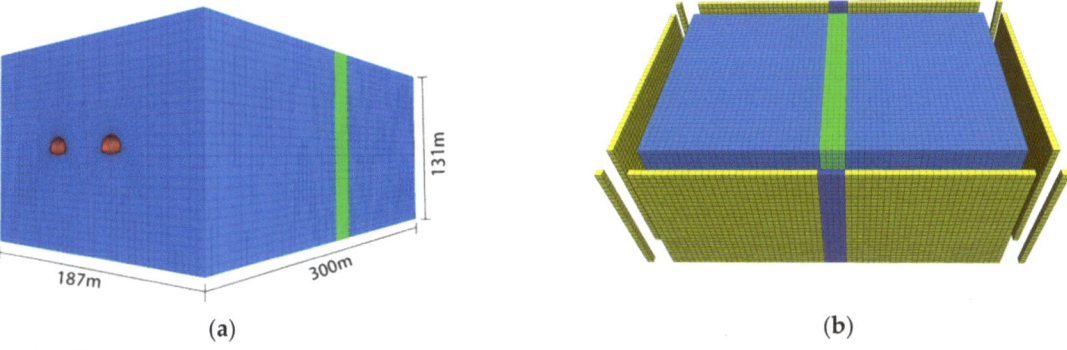

Colour explanation:
Red: tunnel lining; Blue: surrounding rock; Green: fault rock; yellow and deep blue: boundary

Figure 14. Diagram of numerical model: (**a**) model grid; (**b**) boundary conditions.

4.3. Validation of Numerical Model

Before conducting parametric studies, it was essential to validate the model against shake table test results to ensure the accuracy of the solution and the applicability of the findings to the prototype tunnel design. Accelerations recorded at identical points along tunnel sections under bottom-input El-Centro excitations showed partly agreement between simulation and physical experimentation (Figure 15). This confirmed the numerical model's capability to basically capture soil–structure interaction and seismic response using equivalent FLAC3D techniques.

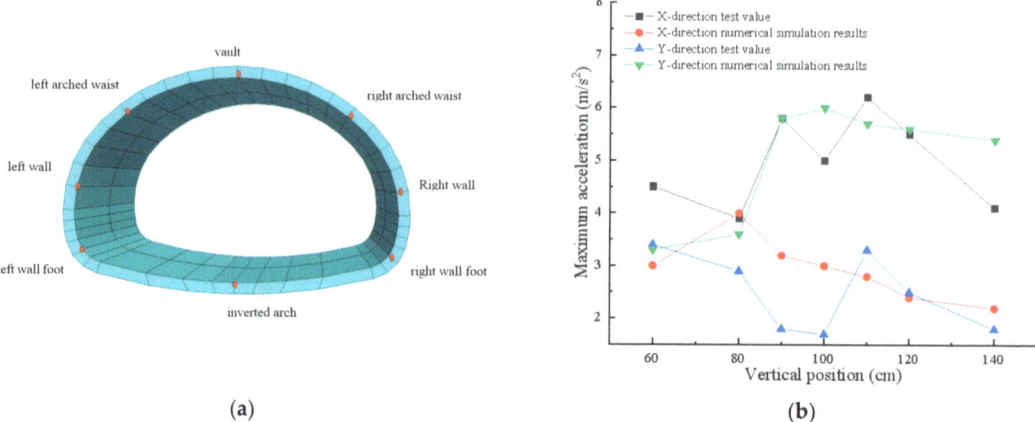

(a)　　　　　　　　　　　　　　　(b)

Figure 15. Validation of numerical simulation: (**a**) lining cross section and monitoring points; (**b**) comparison of numerical simulation results with model test results.

4.4. Parametric Study of Controls

With validated simulation capabilities, two key anti-vibration measures, namely surrounding rock grouting and shock-absorbing layer insertion, were systematically optimized through numerical experimentation. The evaluation focused on their effectiveness in reducing peak accelerations and stresses in the vicinity of the fault.

4.4.1. Grouting Layer Thickness

In conjunction with current relevant research findings, this section focused on selecting grouting reinforcement surrounding the tunnel rock with grouting layer thicknesses of 2 m, 4 m, and 6 m as seismic fortification measures for the tunnel, and investigated the anti-vibration mechanism of grouting reinforcement surrounding the rock. For the calculation results of peak values of horizontal acceleration (positive and negative) and principal stress at key positions of the tunnel under different grouting thickness conditions, refer to Figures 16 and 17.

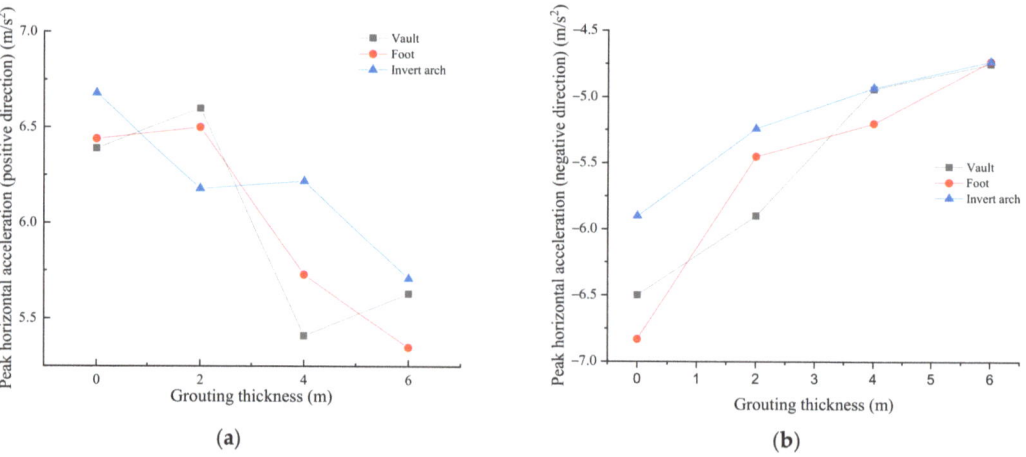

(a)　　　　　　　　　　　　　　　(b)

Figure 16. Effect of grouting thickness on horizontal acceleration in (**a**) positive and (**b**) negative directions.

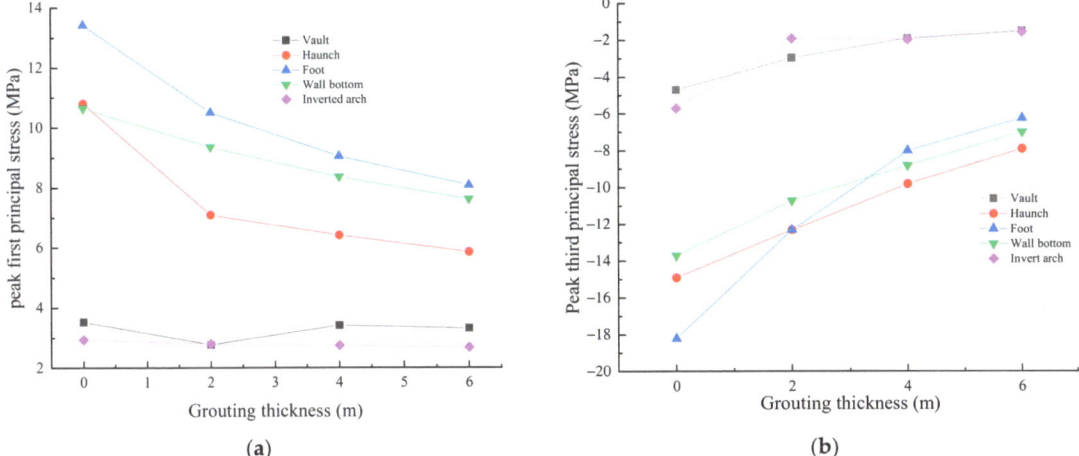

Figure 17. Effect of grouting thickness on (**a**) first and (**b**) third principal stresses.

The results in Figure 16 indicated that radial grouting had a similar effect on reducing acceleration at the vault, arch toe, and inverted arch. The maximum acceleration in the fault fracture zone notably decreased with an increase in grouting layer thickness. When the grouting layer thickness was 6 m, the maximum acceleration response peak value of the tunnel lining was only 5.35 m/s^2, approximately 17% lower than that without a grouting layer. This was attributed to the significantly enhanced strength of the surrounding rock in the fracture zone after grouting reinforcement, gradually strengthening the constraint of the surrounding rock on the lining structure and reducing the lithological difference between the fracture zone and the intact surrounding rock on both sides.

Furthermore, the acceleration distribution along the longitudinal direction of the tunnel was analyzed. In general, the acceleration response at the fracture zone was larger than that at positions far away from the fracture zone. When the grouting layer thickness was 6 m, the acceleration response peak at the fracture zone position approached that at the intact section of surrounding rock, and the acceleration longitudinal distribution curve became gentler. It could be inferred that when the grouting layer thickness increased to a certain extent, the influence of the fracture zone on the lining essentially disappeared due to the reinforcement of the fractured rock mass around the tunnel over a large range, and the acceleration response curve along the longitudinal direction of the tunnel tended to become horizontal.

In Figure 17, it was evident that the first principal stress and the third principal stress in the tunnel lining structure decreased significantly with the continuous increase in the thickness of the grouting layer at the location of the fault zone and its vicinity. When the thickness of the grouting layer was 2 m, 4 m, and 6 m, respectively, the maximum reduction in the first principal stress was 34%, 41%, and 46%, with the largest reduction occurring at the crown and the base of the wall. The reduction in stress at the crown and invert was not significant. The highest reduction rate of the third principal stress was close to 73%, with the largest reduction occurring at the crown and invert.

Through comparative analysis, it was concluded that the decrease in stress response due to the grouting layer was more significant than the acceleration. This was attributed to the enhanced self-stabilizing ability of the surrounding rock after grouting reinforcement, which increased the constraint force on the tunnel and reduced the external load transmitted from the surrounding rock to the lining under seismic action.

In summary, when the thickness of the grouting layer is 6 m, the principal stress in the tunnel meets the code requirements, the acceleration response of the tunnel along the full length fluctuates within a small range, and the amplification effect of the acceleration on the lining at the fault zone is already minimal. Further increasing the thickness of the grouting layer no longer has a significant effect. It is suggested that the thickness of the grouting layer should be around 6 m.

4.4.2. Shock Absorbing Layer Thickness

In this section, the shock-absorbing layer was positioned using the "surrounding rock-initial support-shock absorbing layer-secondary lining" method. Four thicknesses were considered: 10 cm, 15 cm, 20 cm, and 30 cm, and compared with the condition without a shock absorbing layer. The peak horizontal accelerations (positive and negative) and peak principal stresses at critical locations in the tunnel for different shock absorbing layer thickness conditions are depicted in Figures 18 and 19.

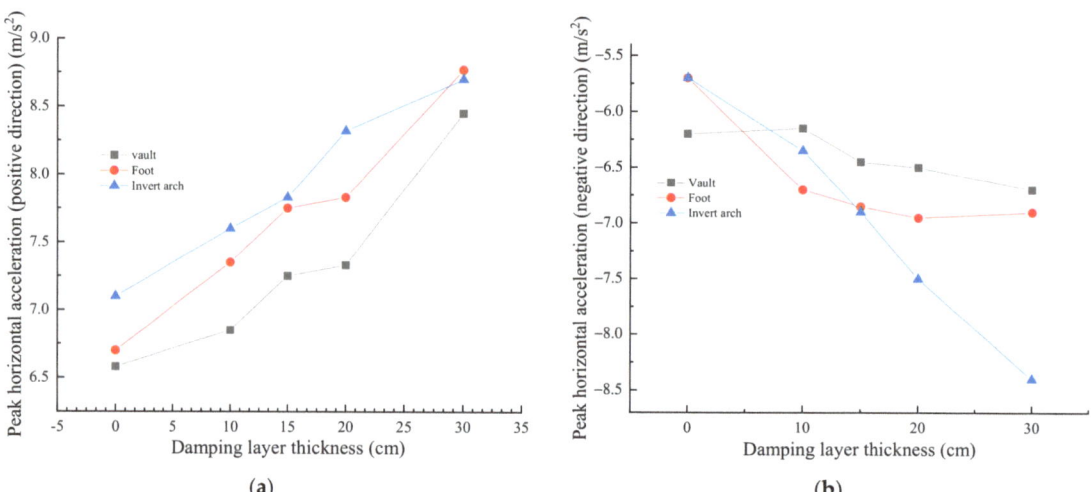

Figure 18. Effect of shock absorbing layer thickness on horizontal acceleration in (**a**) positive and (**b**) negative directions.

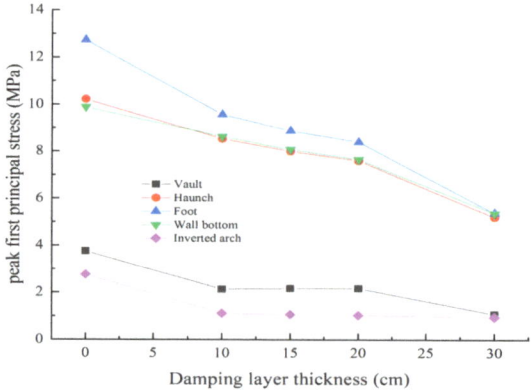

Figure 19. Effect of shock absorbing layer thickness on the first principal stress.

The findings from Figure 18 indicated that the amplification factor of the horizontal acceleration at various points of the lining at the fault zone of the extra-large section tunnel aligned with the trend of the change in the thickness of the seismic isolation layer relative to the original seismic wave acceleration. It increased with the thickness of the seismic isolation layer, and the horizontal acceleration at the crown position was slightly larger than that at the springing and the crown. In the absence of a seismic isolation layer, the maximum acceleration response peak value along the full length of the lining at the fault zone was 6.56 m/s^2, approximately 1.89 times larger than the original seismic wave acceleration. With a 10 cm thickness of the seismic isolation layer, the acceleration at the crown increased by 1.97 times, and with a 15 cm thickness, the acceleration at the crown was amplified by 2.09 times. At 20 cm thickness, the amplification factor of the crown acceleration was 2.11 times. The amplification factor of the acceleration exhibited a slowing trend as the thickness of the seismic isolation layer changed from 15 cm to 20 cm. When the thickness of the seismic isolation layer was 30 cm, the amplification factor of the acceleration was 2.52 times, showing an increasing trend again. Upon comparing the acceleration distribution patterns of the fault section and the intact surrounding rock section, it was found that at this point, the difference in horizontal acceleration between the two was the largest.

Combined with related research findings, the initial analysis suggests that the trend of increasing acceleration response with the thickness of the shock absorbing layer can be attributed to the lower and softer elastic modulus of the shock absorbing layer. This leads to reduced restraint on the lining structure, resulting in an amplified acceleration response of the tunnel under seismic action. This observation underscores the need for particular attention in practical engineering anti-seismic efforts.

Figure 19 illustrated that the inclusion of a shock absorbing layer led to a significant reduction in the first principal stress value of the lining structure at the location of the fault fractured zone in the tunnel. Compared to the absence of a shock absorbing layer, the maximum reduction in the first principal stress was nearly 62% after the installation of the shock absorbing layer, with the most pronounced effect observed at the crown and invert positions. The reduction rate slightly increased with the thickness of the shock absorbing layer and gradually stabilized. When the thickness of the shock absorbing layer was below 20 cm, for every 5 cm increase in thickness, the reduction rate consistently remained around 5%. However, once the thickness of the shock absorbing layer exceeded 20 cm, the additional shock absorbing effect became limited. It was recommended that the thickness of the shock absorbing layer should be 20 cm, and potentially increased conservatively if necessary.

4.4.3. Overall Analysis

The comparative analysis of horizontal acceleration and maximum reduction amplitude of principal stress of the tunnel under different grouting thickness of surrounding rock and shock absorbing layer thickness conditions is presented in Table 5.

Table 5. Analysis of numerical results.

Parameters		Grouting Thickness of Surrounding Rock			Shock Absorbing Layer Thickness			
		2 m	4 m	6 m	10 cm	15 cm	20 cm	30 cm
Horizontal acceleration	Maximum reduction ratio/%	−20%	−24%	−31%	17%	21%	23%	46%
	Appearance position	Arch foot	Arch foot	Arch foot	Arch foot	Inverted arch	Arch foot	Inverted arch
Principal stress	Maximum reduction ratio/%	−68%	−65%	−73%	−60%	−61%	−62%	−65%
	Appearance position	Inverted arch	Inverted arch	Inverted arch	Inverted arch	Inverted arch	Inverted arch	Inverted arch

The comparative analysis showed that grouting in the surrounding rock significantly reduced the principal stress and acceleration of the tunnel structure, while the installation of a shock absorbing layer notably reduced the stress of the tunnel, albeit with an increase in acceleration. The existence of a damping layer may lead to a decrease in the impedance of the medium in the outer extension region of the tunnel lining, consequently amplifying the acceleration response. Nonetheless, the stress response of the lining is mitigated due to the diminished deformation modulus in this zone. Both grouting in the surrounding rock and the installation of a shock absorbing layer had a stronger control effect on principal stress than on acceleration, with the maximum reduction amplitudes being 73% and 65%, respectively. The maximum amplitude of principal stress was located at the inverted arch, whereas the maximum amplitude of acceleration was situated at the arch foot and inverted arch. These findings warranted increase attention in practical applications.

Through comparing and analyzing the distribution of peak principal stress and acceleration in tunnel structures under varying operational parameters, it is observed that as the thickness of the damping layer increases, there is a decrease in the peak value of the first principal stress. Meanwhile, the reduction amplitude of the third principal stress peak initially decreases and then increases with thickness. Opting for a 20 cm thick shock absorber layer provides superior shock absorption benefits. A thicker grouting layer results in a greater reduction in peak principal stress. Notably, the seismic resistance effect is more pronounced for grouting thicknesses ranging from 4–6 m, with a recommended thickness of 6 m for optimal application.

5. Conclusions

Similar to the conclusions drawn from field investigations and research literature on many historical earthquakes, it was also concludes that most serious seismic damage happens to fault fracture zone [29], and the following conclusions were given based on the above analysis.

(1) Under the excitation of three waveforms, strain, earth pressure, and acceleration all showed a tendency to be slightly higher along the longitudinal direction of the tunnel at the fault section and its surroundings. The most significant amplification effect was observed at the interface between the fault zone and the surrounding rock. This amplification effect extends from the boundary of the surrounding rock to the entire surrounding rock, with a maximum extension distance of 10 m. It is recommended that the minimum length of seismic fortification at both ends of the fault section in tunnels with large spans should be extended by 10 to 20 m beyond that specified for tunnels with the standard section in the Chinese industry standard (JTG D70-2004).

(2) In general, the variation in the anti-vibration effect under different waveform excitations remained largely consistent, affirming the accuracy of the model test results. Following the implementation of seismic joints and shock-absorbing layers, there were changes in the positions of the maximum seismic response peaks at fault interface sections. Grouting reinforcement of the surrounding rock, installation of seismic joints, and incorporation of shock-absorbing layers all demonstrated noticeable seismic effects. The seismic impact of seismic joints and shock-absorbing layers was comparable, whereas the reinforcement effect of grouting on the surrounding rock surpassed that of the other two measures.

(3) As the thickness of the grouting layer increased, there was a significant decrease in both the acceleration and the peak value of principal stress in the tunnel structure. The influence of the grouting layer on stress response was more pronounced than on acceleration, with the maximum reduction in principal stress reaching up to 73%. When the grouting layer thickness reached 6 m, the tunnel principal stress complied with the code requirements. At this thickness, the acceleration response peak value at the fracture zone position approached that of the intact section of the surrounding rock, the longitudinal distribution curve of acceleration became gentler, the amplification effect of lining acceleration at the fracture zone position diminished significantly, and the impact of further increasing the grouting layer thickness became negligible. It was recommended that the grouting layer thickness be maintained at approximately 6 m.

(4) The horizontal acceleration of the lining at the fault of an extra-large section tunnel increased with the thickness of the shock-absorbing layer. When the shock-absorbing layer thickness was 30 cm, the acceleration amplification reached 2.52 times, representing the largest difference. The installation of a shock-absorbing layer could significantly reduce the first principal stress value of the lining structure at the fault fracture zone, with the maximum reduction rate nearing 62%. Initially, the reduction rate slightly increased with the thickness of the shock-absorbing layer and gradually stabilized. Once the shock-absorbing layer thickness exceeded 20 cm, the effectiveness of further increasing the thickness became limited. It was recommended to maintain the shock-absorbing layer thickness at 20 cm.

Author Contributions: Conceptualization, F.Z. and B.L.; methodology, B.L. and N.Z.; software, F.Z. and B.L.; validation, F.Z., B.L. and N.Z.; formal analysis, B.L. and B.J.; investigation, F.Z. and B.L.; resources, F.Z. and B.L.; data curation, F.Z. and B.J.; writing—original draft preparation, F.Z. and N.Z.; writing—review and editing, F.Z., B.L. and B.J.; visualization, B.L.; supervision, B.L.; project administration, B.L. All authors have read and agreed to the published version of the manuscript.

Funding: This research was funded by the Science and Technology Research Project of Chongqing Education Commission, grant number (with grant number KJQN202205802, KJQN202303436, KJQN202305802, and KJQN202304301), Construction Science and Technology Plan Project of Chongqing (with number Chengke Zi 2023 No. 1-10) and General Program of Natural Science Foundation of Chongqing (with number CSTB2022NSCQ-MSX0661).

Institutional Review Board Statement: Not applicable.

Informed Consent Statement: Not applicable.

Data Availability Statement: Data will be made available on request.

Conflicts of Interest: The authors declare no conflicts of interest.

References

1. Editorial Department of China Journal of Highway and Transport. Review on China's Traffic Tunnel Engineering Research: 2022. *China J. Highw. Transp.* **2022**, *35*, 1–40. (In Chinese)
2. Gong, J.; Tang, G.; Wang, W.; Fan, L. As of the End of 2021, Statistics on the Situation of Railway Tunnels in China and an Overview of the Design and Construction of the Gaoligongshan Tunnel. *Tunn. Constr.* **2022**, *42*, 508–517. (In Chinese)
3. Hong, K.; Feng, H. Development Trends and Views of Highway Tunnels in China over the Past Decade. *China J. Highw. Transp.* **2020**, *33*, 62–76. (In Chinese)
4. Khan, M.S.; Khan, Z.A.; Sadique, M.R.; Alam, M.M. Seismic Behaviour of Double Arched Tunnel: A Review. *IOP Conf. Ser. Earth Environ. Sci.* **2021**, *796*, 012043. [CrossRef]
5. JTG 2232-2019; Ministry of Transport of the People's Republic of China. Specification for Seismic Design of Highway Tunnels. China Communication Press: Beijing, China, 2022. (In Chinese)
6. GB/T 51336-2018; Ministry of Housing and Urban Rural Development of the People's Republic of China, State Administration for Market Regulation. Standard for Seismic Design of Underground Structures. China Architecture & Building Press: Beijing, China, 2019. (In Chinese)
7. GB 50111-2006; The Ministry of Railways of the People's Republic of China. Code for Seismic Design of Railway Engineering. China Planning Press: Beijing, China, 2009. (In Chinese)
8. Asakura, T.; Shiba, Y.; Matsuoka, S.; Oya, T.; Yashiro, K. Damage to mountain tunnels by earthquake and its mechanism. *Doboku Gakkai Ronbunshu.* **2000**, *659*, 27–38. [CrossRef] [PubMed]
9. Xu, H.; Li, T.; Xia, L.; Zhao, J.X.; Wang, D. Shaking table tests on seismic measures of a model mountain tunnel. *Tunn. Undergr. Space Technol. Inc. Trenchless Technol. Res.* **2016**, *60*, 197–209. [CrossRef]
10. Tsinidis, G.; de Silva, F.; Anastasopoulos, I.; Bilotta, E.; Bobet, A.; Hashash, Y.M.; He, C.; Kampas, G.; Knappett, J.; Madabhushi, G.; et al. Seismic behaviour of tunnels: From experiments to analysis. *Tunn. Undergr. Space Technol. Inc. Trenchless Technol. Res.* **2020**, *99*, 103334. [CrossRef]
11. Prasad, S.K.; Towhata, I.; Chandradhara, G.P.; Nanjundaswamy, P. Shaking table tests in earthquake geotechnical engineering. *Curr. Sci. Geotech. Earthq. Hazards* **2004**, *87*, 1398–1404.
12. Liu, J.; Liu, X.; Wang, Z.; Zhao, D. Dynamic Centrifuge Model Test of a Soil-structure Interaction System. *China Civ. Eng. J.* **2010**, *43*, 114–121. (In Chinese) [CrossRef]
13. Xie, H.T. Numerical Analysis on Influence of Cross Section Shape on Earthquake Resistant Capability of Shallow-Buried Tunnel. *Appl. Mech. Mater.* **2013**, *405*, 1292–1296. [CrossRef]

14. Salemi, A.; Mikaeil, R.; Haghshenas, S.S. Integration of Finite Difference Method and Genetic Algorithm to Seismic analysis of Circular Shallow Tunnels (Case Study: Tabriz Urban Railway Tunnels). *KSCE J. Civ. Eng.* **2018**, *22*, 1978–1990. [CrossRef]
15. Momenzadeh, M.; Koopialipoor, M.; Tootoonchi, H.; Khalili, F.; Khorami, S.; Khorami, S. Investigation of Seismic Reliability Index in Shallow Underground Tunnels by Combining Three Methods of Surface Response, Hasofer–Lind and Finite Element Method. *Geotech. Geol. Eng.* **2019**, *37*, 3903–3914. [CrossRef]
16. An, D.; Chen, Z.; Cui, G. Research on Seismic Performance of Fiber Concrete Lining Structure of Urban Shallow-Buried Rectangular Tunnel in Strong Earthquake Area. *KSCE J. Civ. Eng.* **2021**, *25*, 2748–2757. [CrossRef]
17. Wang, J.; Hu, Y.; Fu, B.; Shan, H.; Wei, H.; Cui, G. Study on Antiseismic Effect of Different Thicknesses of Shock Absorption Layer on Urban Shallow Buried Double Arch Rectangular Tunnel. *Shock. Vib.* **2022**, *2022*, 4863756. [CrossRef]
18. Liu, S.; Liu, S.; Lu, S.; Ma, F.; Pei, G. Seismic Behaviour of Shallow Tunnelling Method Tunnels Accounting for Primary Lining Effects. *Buildings* **2022**, *13*, 20. [CrossRef]
19. Zhang, W.; Han, L.; Feng, L.; Ding, X.; Wang, L.; Chen, Z.; Liu, H.; Aljarmouzi, A.; Sun, W. Study on seismic behaviors of a double box utility tunnel with joint connections using shaking table model tests. *Soil Dyn. Earthq. Eng.* **2020**, *136*, 106118. [CrossRef]
20. Liang, J.; Xu, A.; Ba, Z.; Chen, R.; Zhang, W.; Liu, M. Shaking table test and numerical simulation on ultra-large diameter shield tunnel passing through soft-hard stratum. *Soil Dyn. Earthq. Eng.* **2021**, *147*, 106790. [CrossRef]
21. Zhang, S.; Yang, Y.; Yuan, Y.; Li, C.; Qiu, J. Experimental investigation of seismic performance of shield tunnel under near-field ground motion. *Structures* **2022**, *43*, 1407–1421. [CrossRef]
22. JTG D70-2004. Ministry of Transport of the People's Republic of China. Code for Design of Road Tunnel. China Communication Press: Beijing, China, 2004. (In Chinese)
23. ALMahdi, F.; Fahjan, Y.; Doğangün, A. Critical remarks on Rayleigh damping model considering the explicit scheme for the dynamic response analysis of high rise buildings. *Adv. Struct. Eng.* **2021**, *24*, 1955–1971. [CrossRef]
24. Gu, Y.; Liu, J.-B.; Du, Y.-X. 3D consistent viscous-spring artificial boundary and viscous-spring boundary element. *Eng. Mech.* **2007**, *24*, 31–37. (In Chinese)
25. Liu, J.; Lu, Y. A direct method for analysis of dynamic soil-structure interaction. *China Civ. Eng. J.* **1998**, *31*, 55–64. (In Chinese)
26. Zhang, B.; Li, S.; Yang, X.; Wang, X. Research on seismic wave input with three-dimensional viscoelastic artificial boundary. *Rock Soil Mech.* **2009**, *30*, 774–778. (In Chinese)
27. Zhou, Q.; Zhou, J.; Ma, H.; Li, X.; Zhang, L. An improved algorithm for the optimization of the primary tensioning force of the steel pipe arch rib section. *J. Transp. Eng.* **2020**, *20*, 93–99. (In Chinese)
28. Zhou, Q.; Zhou, J.; Feng, P.; Xin, L.; Jing, S.; Zheng, G. Full-Scale Experimental Study on Temperature Field of Large-Diameter CFST Arch Bridges under Strong Radiation and Large Daily Ambient Temperature Difference. *J. Civ. Struct. Health Monit.* **2022**, *12*, 1247–1263. [CrossRef]
29. Lai, J.; He, S.; Qiu, J.; Chen, J.; Wang, L.; Wang, K.; Wang, J. Characteristics of seismic disasters and aseismic measures of tunnels in Wenchuan earthquake. *Environ. Earth Sci.* **2017**, *76*, 1–19. [CrossRef]

Disclaimer/Publisher's Note: The statements, opinions and data contained in all publications are solely those of the individual author(s) and contributor(s) and not of MDPI and/or the editor(s). MDPI and/or the editor(s) disclaim responsibility for any injury to people or property resulting from any ideas, methods, instructions or products referred to in the content.

Article

Fibre-Microbial Curing Tests and Slope Stability Analysis

Weijian Jiang, Wen Yi * and Lei Zhou

School of Civil Engineering, Central South University of Forestry & Technology, Changsha 410004, China; jwj980305jwj@163.com (W.J.); 18774537803@163.com (L.Z.)
* Correspondence: yiwengangbiao@163.com

Abstract: In response to the deformation resistance deficiency and poor toughness characteristics of soil after microbial curing, a combination of fibre reinforcement technology and microbial curing technology was used to conduct microbial curing tests using basalt fibres and denitrifying bacteria. In this paper, the effects of fibre on the strength and toughness of soil consolidation were analysed by unconfined compressive strength test and direct shear test, and the stability of reinforced slope was analysed by numerical simulation. The results show the following. (1) Basalt fibre can effectively improve the characteristics of brittle damage of microbially consolidated soil while increasing the compressive and shear strength. (2) Fibre dosing and fibre length have important effects on the mechanical properties of microbially consolidated soil. (3) The appropriate amount of basalt fibre can promote the generation of calcium carbonate. (4) The plastic strain area of the slope decreases after microbial reinforcement and the maximum equivalent plastic stress decreases by 65 kPa.

Keywords: basalt fibres; microbial-induced calcite precipitation; slope stability

1. Introduction

Microbially induced calcium carbonate deposition (MICP) is an emerging geotechnical improvement technology that uses calcium carbonate cemented soil particles produced by microbial metabolic activities to enhance the physical and mechanical characteristics of geotechnical bodies [1,2]. This has great potential for application in many fields including soil mechanical modification, embankment erosion resistance, and prevention of heavy metal ion pollution [3–7]. The use of microorganisms to reinforce the slope surface improves the stability of the slope while improving the soil, facilitating plant growth, and being ecologically friendly.

MICP technology has received wide attention from researchers at home and abroad because of its simplicity of operation, high efficiency of reinforcement, and lack of pollution to the environment [8], and much research has been conducted on the engineering properties of MICP-modified soils [9–18]. Chu et al. [19] used MICP technology to improve sandy soils to form a weakly permeable crust layer, which served the purpose of enhancing impermeability in engineering. Liu Lu et al. [20] used a microbial curing method to treat dikes, and the experimental results showed that the treated dikes improved the erosion resistance. Li Chi [21] used microbially induced calcium carbonate precipitation (MICP) technology combined with adsorbent materials to cure/stabilise the remediation of Zn-Pb composite heavy metal contaminated soil, revealing the remediation mechanism of MICP technology to treat Zn-Pb heavy metal contaminated soil. Liu Xiaojun [22] used MICP technology for soil site fracture remediation and curing. These studies showed that MICP, as an emerging soil consolidation technology, has potential practical engineering value and can be applied to various fields. However, the strength and toughness of materials are usually opposed to each other, and some studies have shown that microbially cured soils exhibit significant brittle characteristics [23], which to some extent inhibits the application of MICP technology in practical engineering. Therefore, it is necessary to investigate how to improve the toughness of microbially cured specimens.

Citation: Jiang, W.; Yi, W.; Zhou, L. Fibre-Microbial Curing Tests and Slope Stability Analysis. *Appl. Sci.* **2023**, *13*, 7051. https://doi.org/10.3390/app13127051

Academic Editor: Syed Minhaj Saleem Kazmi

Received: 27 April 2023
Revised: 4 June 2023
Accepted: 9 June 2023
Published: 12 June 2023

Copyright: © 2023 by the authors. Licensee MDPI, Basel, Switzerland. This article is an open access article distributed under the terms and conditions of the Creative Commons Attribution (CC BY) license (https://creativecommons.org/licenses/by/4.0/).

Studies have demonstrated that by adding discrete short filament fibres as reinforcement to the soil, the soil becomes substantially less brittle when it fractures, increasing its strength [24]. Through indoor research, Yetimoglu et al. [25] observed that fibre reinforcement has no discernible impact on peak shear strength, but that it can ameliorate sandy soil shear brittle damage by increasing the residual shear strength of the soil sample by increasing the amount of fibre admixture. According to Shao et al. [26], adding fibres to sandy soil had an impact on its shear strength, lowering strength loss after the peak strength and improving the nature of brittle damage. Wei Li et al. [27] used wheat-straw-fibre-reinforced seaside saline soil and found that fibre reinforcement increased the cohesion c of saline soil substantially, and its resistance to deformation was greatly enhanced.

For this reason, this paper uses a combination of fibre reinforcement technology and microbial curing technology for soil curing tests. Based on the unconfined compressive strength test and direct shear test, the effects of basalt fibre on the mechanical properties of microbial soil consolidation are analysed, and a three-dimensional slope model is established by ABAQUS finite element software to analyse the stability of the slope after microbial consolidation.

2. Materials and Methods

2.1. Test Soil

The soil used for the test is taken from Longlang Expressway, Xinhua County, Loudi City, Hunan Province. This soil is clayey, and its physical parameters are listed in Table 1.

Table 1. Physical parameters of clay.

Optimum Moisture Content/%	Maximum Dry Density/g·cm^{-3}	Liquid Limit/%	Plasticity Index
16.8	1.68	35	18.6

2.2. Test Fibres

The fibres used for the test were basalt short-cut fibres. Compared with ordinary synthetic fibre, basalt fibre has obvious advantages in tensile strength, elastic modulus, impermeability, and freeze–thaw resistance, overcoming the shortcomings of synthetic fibres that are easily pulled off when cracks expand. Referring to Abd Al-kaream et al.'s [28] formulation study of polypropylene fibres for soft soil improvement, the fibres were added to the soil at 0, 0.1, 0.2, 0.3, 0.4, 0.5, and 0.6 by mass. The fibre is produced by Zhejiang Haining Anjie Composite Material. A photograph is shown in Figure 1, and the physical and mechanical properties are listed in Table 2.

Figure 1. Basalt short-cut fibre.

Table 2. Physical and mechanical properties of fibre.

Physical and Mechanical Indicators	Monofilament Diameter/μm	Specific Gravity/g·cm^{-3}	Modulus of Elasticity/GPa	Tensile Strength/MPa
Parameters	7~15	2.63~2.65	91~110	3000~4800

2.3. Bacterial Solution for Test

The microorganisms used were paracoccus, a type of denitrifying bacteria, purchased at the Shanghai Conservation Biotechnology Center (SHBCC). Denitrifying Bacillus is a heterotrophic, parthenogenic anaerobic bacterium that can survive in the medium of nitrate. It acts as a nitrogen source, reducing nitrate to nitrite and further reducing nitrite to ammonia and free nitrogen under insufficient soil oxygen. The medium consists of 5 g peptone, 3 g beef paste, 5 g sodium chloride, 15 g agar, and 1000 mL distilled water, and the specific method of activating the culture includes the following steps:

(1) The strain is added to sterile water, gently shaken to dissolve, and inoculated on slant medium. After inoculation is complete, it is placed in an incubator for incubation, with the incubator temperature set at 30 °C and time set at 24 h, and finally placed in a refrigerator at 4 °C for backup.

(2) The ingredients were weighed into triangular flasks according to the medium recipe, the agar was heated and melted, and the pH of the medium was adjusted to 7.0 using a solution of sodium hydroxide at a concentration of 1 mol/L. The triangular flask is added with a plunger and wrapped and placed in an autoclave for sterilisation, the sterilisation temperature is set at 120 °C, and the sterilisation time is set at 30 min.

(3) After autoclaving, the triangular flasks were placed on a sterile operating table to cool. The cultured colonies were inoculated into the agar-free culture medium by aseptic operation and incubated for 36–48 h in an intelligent shaker set at an ambient temperature of 30 °C and a shaker speed of 150 r/min.

2.4. Test Cementing Solution

The cementing solution was a mixture of calcium chloride ($CaCl_2$), sodium nitrite ($NaNO_2$), and potassium nitrate (KNO_2). Among them, sodium nitrite and potassium nitrate provide nitrogen sources in the denitrification process of denitrifying bacteria, while calcium chloride provides calcium sources; calcium chloride is also the fixing solution of the bacterial solution, and calcium ions and bacterial cell walls have adsorption effects, which facilitate bacteria attachment to the surface of negatively nucleated soil particles and play the role of fixing bacteria. The sedimentation and cementation principle of denitrifying bacteria is the combination of carbonate ions and calcium ions to produce the cementation $CaCO_2$ precipitate. $CaCO_2$ adheres to the surface of soil particles and connects the loose particles by wrapping and filling the gaps between particles. The specific reaction equations are (1)–(3) [29].

$$5CH_3COO^- + 8NO_3^- + 13H^+ \rightarrow 10CO_2 + 4N_2 + 14H_2O \quad (1)$$

$$CO_2 + H_2O \leftrightarrow HCO_3^- + H^+ \quad (2)$$

$$Ca^{2+} + HCO_3^- + OH^- \rightarrow CaCO_3(s) + H_2O \quad (3)$$

2.5. Specimen Preparation Steps

(1) The lower bedding block of the test mould was placed into the lower part of the test mould but exposed by approximately 2 cm.

(2) According to the sample preparation standards, four equal portions of soil and basalt short-cut fibre were weighed, and the two were mixed and stirred, layered into the mould, and lightly compacted with a tamping rod to a predetermined height (20 mm per layer). After the sample was completed, the upper mat with the test mould was placed into the test mould, and the upper mat was exposed to approximately 2 cm.

(3) A peristaltic pump was used to inject 50 mL of bacterial solution at a rate of 5 mL/min, and after standing for 4 h, the same volume of cementing solution was injected at a rate of 10 mL/min and allowed to stand for 6–8 h to ensure that the microorganisms reacted fully within the specimen.

(4) A peristaltic pump was used to inject 50 mL of cementing solution into the specimen at a rate of 10 mL/min at an interval of 12 h. The injection was stopped after reaching a predetermined number of treatments, and water was continuously and slowly injected from the top of the specimen to clean the inside of the specimen to terminate the microbial curing process.

2.6. Test Method

2.6.1. Compressive Strength Test without Lateral Limit

A strain-controlled unconfined compression tester is used, and the processed specimen is tested according to the Highway Geotechnical Test Procedure JTG3430-2020, see [30] (pp. 213–217). The loading rate of unconfined compressive strength is kept at 1.0 mm/min until the specimen breaks the ring to end the test. The compression test schematic is shown in Figure 2.

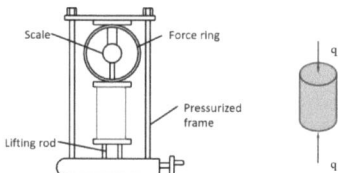

Figure 2. Schematic diagram of compressive test.

2.6.2. Calcium Carbonate Content Determination Test

The acid washing method was used to measure the calcium carbonate content inside each specimen separately. The modified specimens were dried in an oven at 100 °C until constant weight, and the mass of the specimen and calcium carbonate was recorded as m1. A sufficient amount of dilute hydrochloric acid was added and soaked for a period of time, and when no bubbles were generated in the solution, the calcium carbonate in the specimen was considered to have reacted completely. After rinsing the sample with distilled water several times and then putting it into the oven to dry, the mass of the treated sample was m2. The difference between m1 and m2 is the mass of calcium carbonate produced.

2.6.3. Direct Shear Test

After the specimen is compacted, each layer is weighed and filled with 30 g of soil in the ring knife, and the test is carried out with quadruple direct shear in accordance with the Highway Geotechnical Test Procedure JTG3430-2020, see [30] (p. 185). The shear rate set to 0.8 mm/min and recorded every 10 s. After the shear is finished, the shear force and vertical pressure are removed, and the test block is taken out to end the test. The shear test schematic is shown in Figure 3.

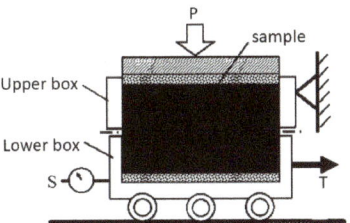

Figure 3. Schematic diagram of shear test.

3. Results and Discussion

3.1. Stress–Strain Curve

The stress–strain curves of denitrifying bacterial consolidated soil under different reinforcement conditions were basically the same. The specimens with 0.4 fibre dosing and a 12 mm fibre length were analysed as an example, as shown in Figure 4, where σ is the stress and ε is the strain.

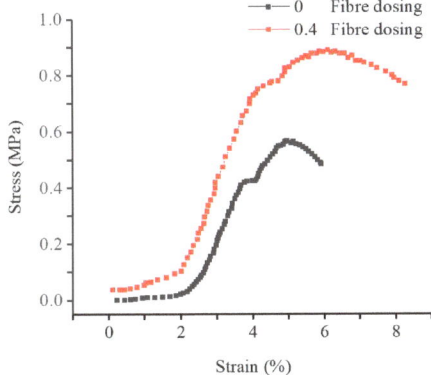

Figure 4. Stress–strain curve.

It is obvious from the figure that the stress peak of the 0.4 fibre-doped specimen is higher and the stress peak appears later compared with the non-fibre-doped specimen. This is because on the one hand, the presence of fibre promotes the generation of calcium carbonate, the integrity and strength of the specimens are improved, and the stress limit that the specimens can withstand is increased. On the other hand, when cracks appear inside the specimens, the tensile force generated by the fibre inhibits the further development of the cracks, and the stress of the specimens rises slowly and reaches its peak. At the same time, it can be seen that the stress of the specimens with 0.4 fibre dosing decreases more slowly. It is obvious that the addition of fibre can effectively enhance the strength and toughness of the specimens after curing with denitrifying bacteria and improve the brittle damage characteristics of the soil.

3.2. Effect of Fibre Admixture on Strength of Specimens

Figure 5 shows the variation in the unconfined compressive strength of the specimens with different fibre lengths with respect to the fibre admixture. From Figure 5, it can be seen that after the treatment of denitrifying bacteria, the originally loose soil can be effectively solidified and present a higher strength. When basalt fibres were added to the soil, the unconfined compressive strength of the specimens was further improved. For example, the unconfined compressive strengths of the corresponding specimens were 526 kPa, 612 kPa, 674 kPa, and 886 kPa when the fibre dosing amount was 0, 0.1, 0.2, and 0.3 at a 12 mm fibre length, respectively. Overall, the unconfined compressive strength of the specimens tended to increase and then decrease with increasing fibre dosing, reaching peak strengths of 886 kPa and 918 kPa at 0.3 and 0.4 fibre dosing, respectively. This is because the interaction between the fibres and soil particles in the soil sample can limit the relative sliding of the fibres, which provides the fibres with an ability to bear the external load and transfer the load and reduce the stress concentration in the soil sample. The addition of an appropriate amount of fibre in microbial soil consolidation can improve the strength of soil, and the optimal fibre admixture is between 0.3 and 0.4.

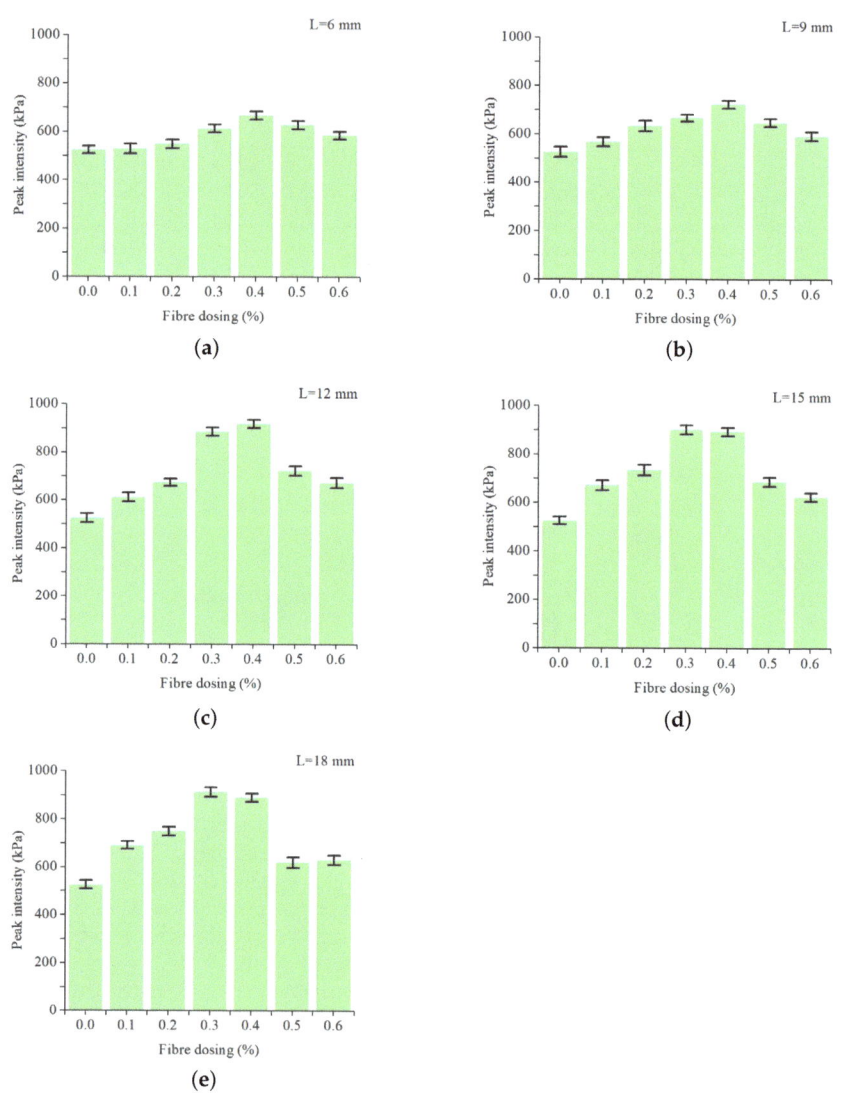

Figure 5. Effect of fibre dosing on peak strength. (**a**) Effect of fibre dosing on peak strength at 6 mm fibre length. (**b**) Effect of fibre dosing on peak strength at 9 mm fibre length. (**c**) Effect of fibre dosing on peak strength at 12 mm fibre length. (**d**) Effect of fibre dosing on peak strength at 15 mm fibre length. (**e**) Effect of fibre dosing on peak strength at 18 mm fibre length.

3.3. Effect of Fibre Length on Strength of Specimens

Figure 6 reflects the variation in the lateral limitless compressive strength of the specimens with fibre length for different fibre dosing amounts. It can be seen from the figure that when the fibre dose is too low (0.1, 0.2, 0.3, 0.4), the unconfined compressive strength of the specimen increases with increasing fibre length. When the fibre dose is too high (0.5, 0.6), the unconfined compressive strength of the specimen increases with increasing fibre length and then decreases. When the fibre length is 12 mm, the basalt fibre has the most obvious effect on denitrifying bacteria.

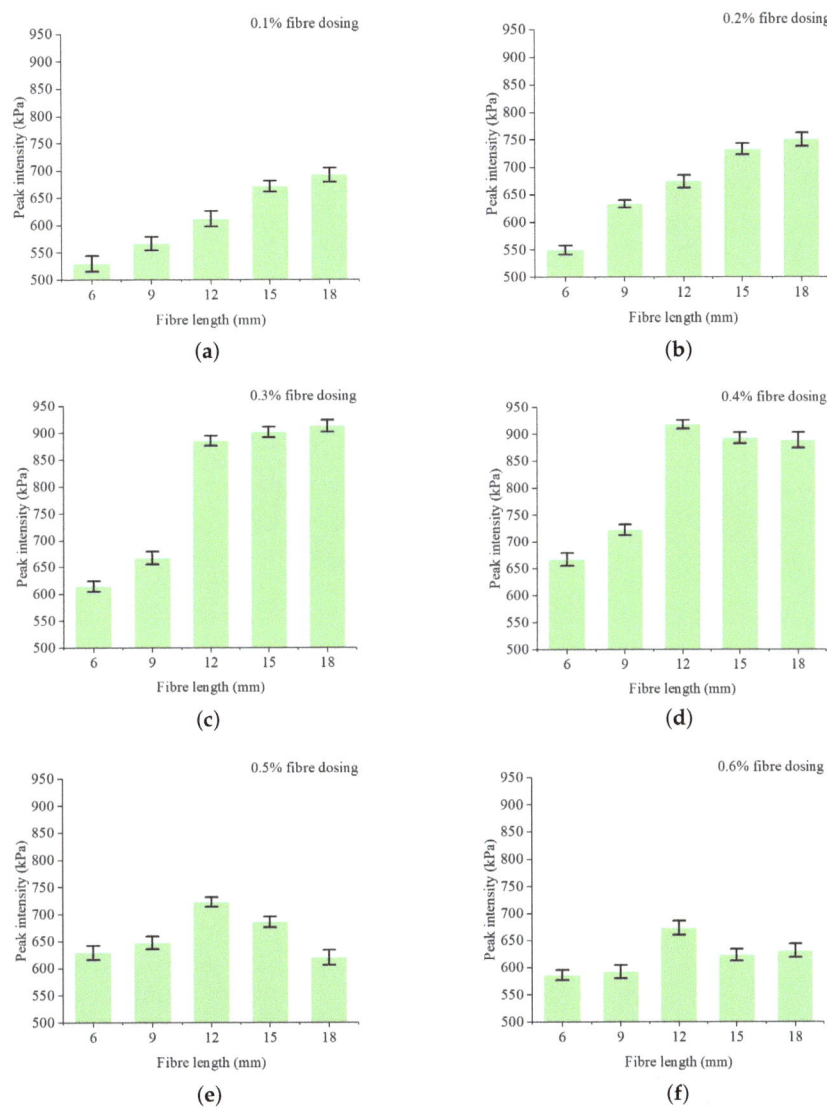

Figure 6. Effect of fibre length on peak strength. (**a**) Effect of fibre length on peak strength with 0.1 fibre content. (**b**) Effect of fibre length on peak strength with 0.2 fibre content. (**c**) Effect of fibre length on peak strength with 0.3 fibre content. (**d**) Effect of fibre length on peak strength with 0.4 fibre content. (**e**) Effect of fibre length on peak strength with 0.5 fibre content. (**f**) Effect of fibre length on peak strength with 0.6 fibre content.

3.4. Calcium Carbonate Content

Figure 7 shows the calcium carbonate content in the specimens with different fibre doping and gives the unconfined compressive strength of each specimen. It can be seen from the figure that the lowest calcium carbonate content of 1.91 was found in the specimens without fibre dosing, while the highest calcium carbonate content of 6.56 and 6.34 was found in the specimens with fibre dosing of 0.3 and 0.4. The overall trend of calcium carbonate content increased and then decreased with increasing fibre dosing, but the decrease in calcium carbonate content after reaching the peak was not obvious. This occurred mainly because calcium carbonate was attached to the soil particles after generation, and the addition of fibre increased the 'colonisation area' available for microorganisms. However, the volume of pores inside the soil body is certain, and with the increase in fibre incorporation, the pores inside the soil body are gradually occupied by fibres, which compresses the growth environment of microorganisms and leads to the restriction of microorganism growth and has a negative effect on the amount of calcium carbonate production. Therefore, it can be inferred that the addition of fibres in the soil is beneficial to the production of calcium carbonate, and the highest content of calcium carbonate is achieved at 0.3 and 0.4 fibre admixture, but the addition of excessive fibres is detrimental to the production of calcium carbonate.

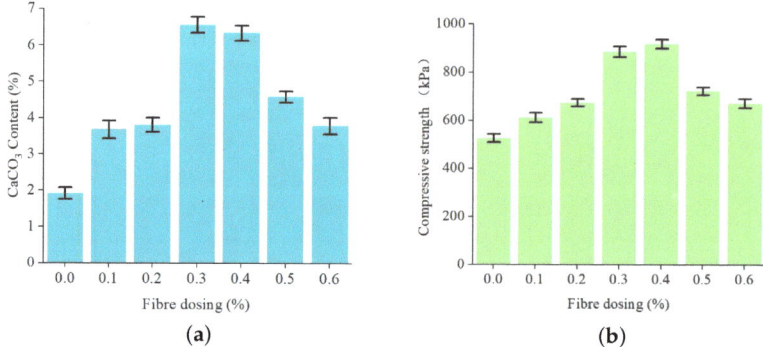

Figure 7. (a) Effect of fibre dosing on $CaCO_3$ content at 12 mm. (b) Effect of fibre dosing on unconfined compressive strength at 12 mm.

3.5. Shear Strength

Figure 8 shows the relationship between vertical pressure and shear strength for different fibre dosing. From the figure, it can be seen that the maximum shear strength of the plain soil is 96 kPa and the maximum shear strength of the soil is 114 kPa when the fibre admixture is 0. This indicates that the microbial curing technology can improve the shear strength of the clay soil with a maximum increase of 118.9. With an increase in fibre content, the shear strength increases and then decreases, and the maximum shear strength of 163 kPa is reached at 0.3 fibre admixture.

Figures 9 and 10 show the relationship between fibre dosing and cohesion and internal friction angle. With an increase in fibre dosing, the cohesion and internal friction angle increase and then decrease, and they all reach their maxima when the fibre dosing is 0.3. This is because excessive fibre content will inhibit the formation of calcium carbonate and thus reduce the shear strength of soil. Therefore, the cohesiveness and internal friction angle of the soil mass will decrease. On the whole, the cohesion and internal friction angle of reinforced soil are generally higher than those of unreinforced soil.

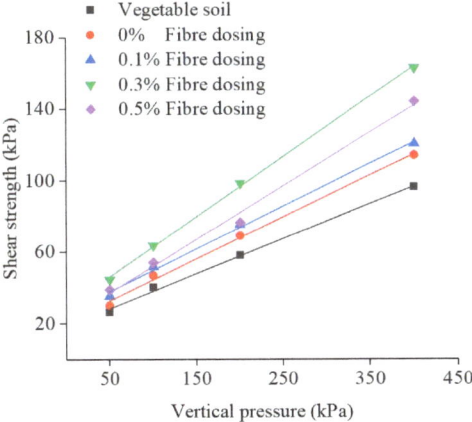

Figure 8. Relationship between shear strength and vertical pressure.

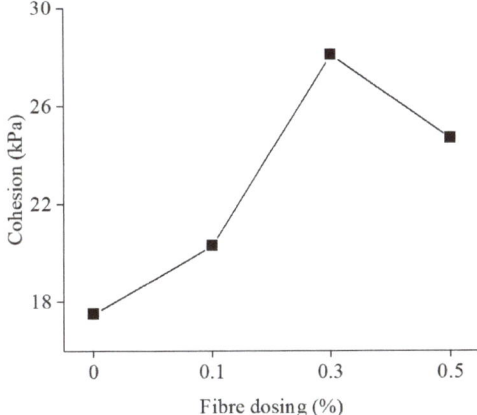

Figure 9. Fibre dosing and cohesion relationship.

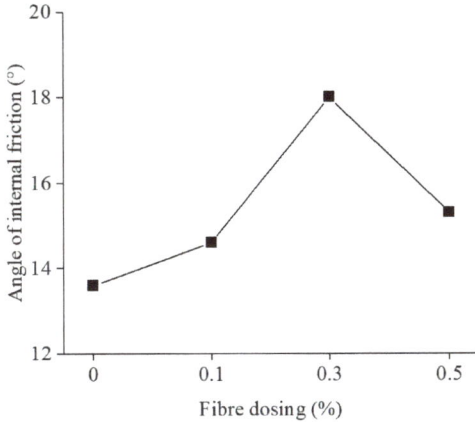

Figure 10. Relationship between fibre dosing and internal friction angle.

4. Numerical Simulation

4.1. Finite Element Basic Principle of Strength Reduction Method

The strength reduction method is a widely used analysis method in slope stability analysis. It is calculated by substituting the cohesion and internal friction angle into the finite element model, with the reduction factor of the slope just reaching the damage state as the safety factor, the essence of which is that the cohesion and internal friction angle of the material gradually decrease. This results in the stress of a unit not being matched with the strength or beyond the yield surface, and the unbearable stress is gradually transferred to the surrounding soil units. When a continuous sliding surface appears, the soil is destabilised.

4.2. Model Construction

Using the Longlang Expressway in Loudi city, Hunan Province, as the base project, ABAQUS software was used to establish a three-dimensional slope model with a length of 25 m, width of 7 m, height of 13 m, and slope of 1:1.5. Microbial reinforcement treatment was carried out along the vertical slope direction, and the reinforcement thickness was 1 m. The model assumed that the soil was an ideal elastic–plastic body, and the Mohr–Coulomb model was used. According to the experimental results, the soil before microbial reinforcement is taken as density $\rho = 1.78$ g/cm^{-3}, elastic modulus $E = 10$ MPa, Poisson's ratio $\mu = 0.35$, cohesion $c = 13$ kPa, and internal friction angle $\varphi = 11.7°$, and after microbial reinforcement is taken as density $\rho = 1.96$ g/cm^{-3}, elastic modulus $E = 10$ MPa, Poisson's ratio $\mu = 0.35$, cohesion $c = 25.95$ kPa, and internal friction angle $\varphi = 15.6°$. The cohesion and internal friction angle vary with the field variables, and the range of field variables varies between 0.5 and 3. The boundary conditions are set in ABAQUS load to constrain the displacements in the x, y, and z directions at the bottom of the model, constrain the displacements in the y directions before and after the model, constrain the displacements in the x directions to the left and right of the model, and apply the gravity force in the z-axis direction to the model as a whole. The mesh division of the slope model adopts eight-node linear hexahedral cells (C3D8), and the calculation area is divided into a total of 2415 cells.

4.3. Stability Analysis

4.3.1. Plastic Zone Analysis

The plastic strain clouds before and after the finite element simulation analysis of microbial reinforcement are shown in Figure 11.

From the above figure, it can be seen that when t = 0.2, the plastic zone appears above the foot of the slope, and when t = 0.25, the plastic zone above the foot of the slope expands and extends to the inner part of the slope and gradually connects with the plastic zone inside the slope. When t = 0.34, the plastic zone basically penetrates, and the slope is destabilised. Comparing the plastic strain clouds before and after microbial reinforcement, it can be seen that at t = 0.2, the strain in the plastic zone at the foot of the slope after microbial reinforcement is lower and the strain inside the slope body is higher, but the value is smaller than the strain inside the slope body before microbial reinforcement. This may occur because after the slope surface is reinforced by microorganisms, the microorganisms have not completely penetrated into the interior of the soil body and have less influence on the interior of the slope body. The subsequent development of the plastic zone is roughly similar before and after microbial reinforcement. The analysis of the strain cloud diagram at the time of complete penetration shows that the maximum plastic strain before microbial reinforcement appears at the foot of the slope, and the corresponding stress reaches 239.3 kPa, while the maximum plastic strain after microbial reinforcement also appears at the foot of the slope, but its distribution range is greatly reduced, and the maximum stress value is lowered to 174.5 kPa.

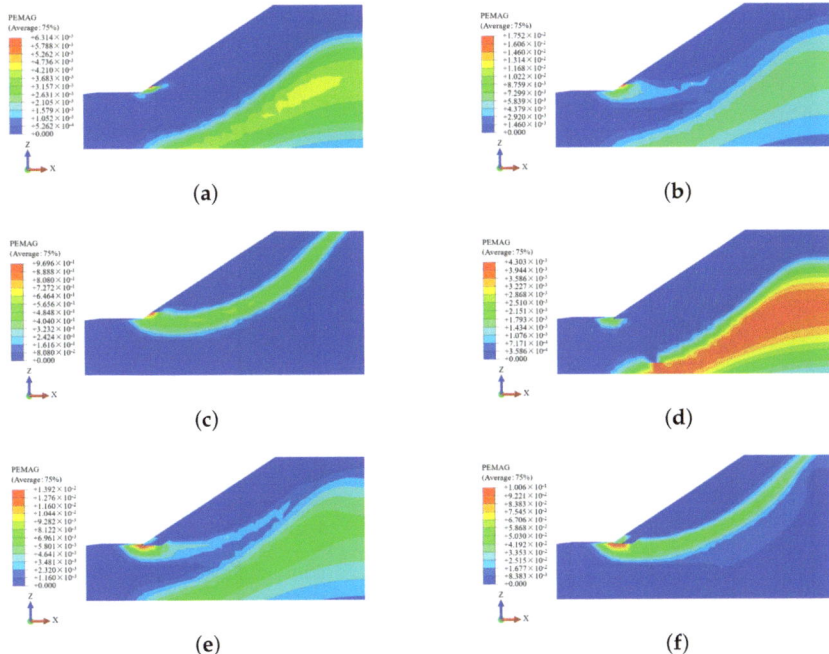

Figure 11. (**a**) Equivalent plastic strain cloud before microbial reinforcement at t = 0.2. (**b**) Equivalent plastic strain cloud before microbial reinforcement at t = 0.25. (**c**) Equivalent plastic strain cloud before microbial reinforcement at t = 0.34. (**d**) Equivalent plastic strain cloud after microbial reinforcement at t = 0.2. (**e**) Equivalent plastic strain cloud after microbial reinforcement at t = 0.25. (**f**) Equivalent plastic strain cloud after microbial reinforcement at t = 0.34.

4.3.2. Displacement Cloud Analysis

Figure 12 shows the total displacement, X-directional displacement, total displacement vector, and X-directional displacement vector of the slope after microbial reinforcement derived by the intensity reduction method. Analysis of Figure 12a shows that the maximum displacement of the slope is 1.36 cm, the area of the maximum displacement is located at the foot of the slope, and the displacement gradually decreases in a circular shape with this position as the centre downward. Figure 12b shows the X-direction displacement. From the X-direction displacement, we can see the location of the potential sliding surface of the slope and the range of the potential landslide area. The total displacement vector map in Figure 12c clearly shows the location and regional range of the sliding surface of the slope, which forms a circular arc-shaped sliding surface from the top of the slope to the foot of the slope. Figure 12d shows the X-direction displacement vector diagram. The X-direction specified by the calculation model points to the inside of the slope body in the positive direction. From the diagram, it can be seen that the maximum displacement in the X-direction is 1.34 cm, the displacement produced is the displacement of the landslide sliding outward, the sliding surface can be clearly seen, and the displacement of the soil below the sliding surface is basically zero.

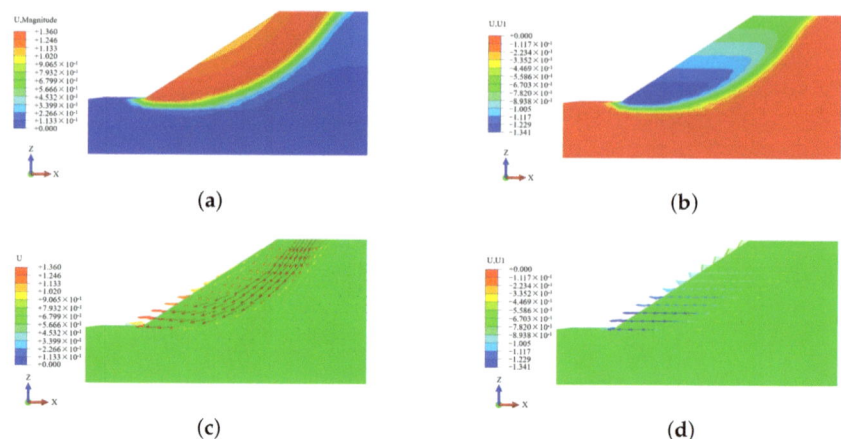

Figure 12. (**a**) Total displacement cloud after microbial reinforcement. (**b**) X-direction displacement cloud after microbial reinforcement. (**c**) Total displacement vector diagram after microbial reinforcement. (**d**) X-direction displacement vector diagram after microbial reinforcement.

4.3.3. Calculation of Safety Coefficient

Nodal 1622 at the top of the slope is selected as the characteristic point, and the graphs related to the safety coefficient and displacement in the process of discounting are obtained. From Figures 13 and 14, two obvious inflection points can be seen. The appearance of the inflection points indicates that the slope is unstable or close to damage when the plastic stress of the slope increases and the displacement increases suddenly. If the inflection point of displacement is used as the stability index of the slope, then it can be concluded that the safety coefficient of the slope without microbial reinforcement Fs = 1.16, and the safety coefficient of the slope after microbial reinforcement Fs = 1.41, the safety coefficient after reinforcement is increased by 21.5 percent, and the reinforcement effect is obvious. If the nonconvergence of numerical analysis calculation is used as an index to evaluate the stability of slope, then it can be concluded that the safety factor of slope without microbial reinforcement Fs = 1.18, the safety factor of slope after microbial reinforcement Fs = 1.46, and the safety factor after reinforcement is increased by 23.7 percent.

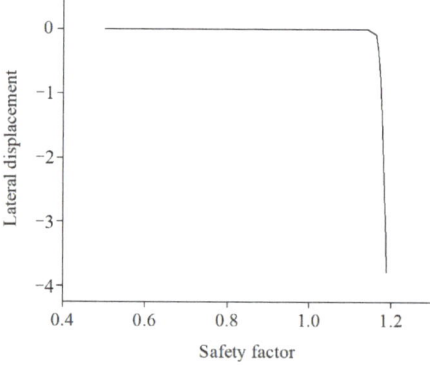

Figure 13. Relationship between safety factor and lateral displacement before microbial reinforcement.

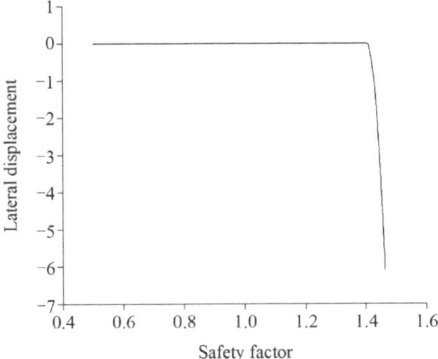

Figure 14. Relationship between safety factor and lateral displacement after microbial reinforcement.

5. Conclusions

In this paper, the mechanical properties of basalt fibre-reinforced microbially consolidated soil were studied by conducting unconfined compressive strength tests and direct shear tests and analysing the stability of the slope after microbial reinforcement in terms of plastic zone characteristics, displacement clouds, and safety factors through finite element numerical simulations. The following conclusions were obtained:

(1) The combination of fibre reinforcement technology and MICP technology can significantly improve the compressive and shear strength of the soil and improve the characteristics of brittle soil after microbial curing.

(2) The incorporation of basalt fibres has an important influence on the mechanical properties of denitrifying bacterial consolidated soil. When the fibre admixture is low, the unconfined compressive strength of the soil increases with increasing fibre length, and when the fibre admixture is high, the strength tends to increase and then decrease with increasing fibre length. The optimal fibre admixture is between 0.3 and 0.4, and the best fibre length is 12 mm.

(3) The effect of increasing basalt fibre incorporation on the calcium carbonate content of the soil after microbial curing tends to increase and then decrease. This is because after the fibre is added to the soil, the area where calcium carbonate can be colonised increases, and when the fibre is increasingly added, the internal void of the soil is gradually occupied by the fibre, and the growth of microorganisms is restricted. This has a negative impact on the generation of calcium carbonate.

(4) The development of the plastic zone of the slope before and after microbial reinforcement is generally similar, but the scope of the plastic zone after reinforcement is reduced as a whole, especially in the reinforced area of the slope, and the maximum equivalent plastic stress is decreased by 65 kPa.

(5) The safety coefficient of the slope before microbial reinforcement was 1.16, and the safety coefficient after reinforcement was 1.41. The stability of the slope was obviously strengthened.

Author Contributions: Conceptualization, W.J. and W.Y.; methodology, W.J.; software, W.J.; validation, W.J., W.Y. and L.Z.; formal analysis, W.J.; investigation, W.J.; resources, W.Y.; data curation, L.Z.; writing—original draft preparation, W.J.; writing—review and editing, W.J.; visualization, W.J.; supervision, W.J.; project administration, W.J.; funding acquisition, W.Y. All authors have read and agreed to the published version of the manuscript.

Funding: This research was funded by Hunan Provincial Transportation Science and Technology Project. The project names are "Research on Key technologies of Road slope Ecological landscape restoration in ecologically fragile Areas" and "Research on microbial improvement of ecological protection technology for strongly weathered coal gangue slopes", grant numbers are 201803 and 202212 respectively.

Institutional Review Board Statement: Not applicable.

Informed Consent Statement: Not applicable.

Data Availability Statement: All data, models, and code generated or used during the study appear in the submitted article.

Conflicts of Interest: The authors declare that they have no conflict of interest.

References

1. Whiffin, V.S. Microbial $CaCO_3$ Precipitation for the Production of Biocement. Ph.D. Thesis, Murdoch University, Perth, Australia, 2004.
2. DeJong, J.T.; Fritzges, M.B.; Nüsslein, K. Microbially induced cementation to control sand response to undrained shear. *J. Geotech. Geoenviron. Eng.* **2006**, *132*, 1381–1392. [CrossRef]
3. Yang, Z.; Cheng, X.; Li, M. Engineering properties of MICP-bonded sandstones used for historical masonry building restoration. In Proceedings of the Geo-Frontiers 2011: Advances in Geotechnical Engineering, Dallas, TX, USA, 13–16 March 2011. [CrossRef]
4. Li, M.; Cheng, X.H.; Guo, H.X. Heavy metal removal by biomineralization of urease producing bacteria isolated from soil. *Int. Biodeterior. Biodegrad.* **2013**, *76*, 81–85. [CrossRef]
5. Shanahan, C.; Montoya, B.M. Erosion reduction of coastal sands using microbial induced calcite precipitation. In Proceedings of the Geo-Chicago, Chicago, IL, USA, 14–18 August 2016. [CrossRef]
6. Shanahan, C.; Montoya, B.M. Strengthening coastal sand dunes using microbial-induced calcite precipitation. In Proceedings of the Geo-Congress 2014: Geo-Characterization and Modeling for Sustainability, Atlanta, GA, USA, 23–26 February 2014. [CrossRef]
7. Zhao, Q.; Li, L.; Li, C.; Li, M.; Amini, F.; Zhang, H. Factors affecting improvement in engineering properties of geomaterials by microbial-induced calcite precipitation. *Geotechnics* **2019**, *40*, 2525–2546.
8. Qian, C.X.; Wang, A.H.; Wang, X. Advances of soil improvement with bio-grouting. *Geotech. Mech.* **2015**, *36*, 1537–1548. [CrossRef]
9. He, J.; Chu, J.; Gao, Y.; Liu, H. Research advances in biogeotechnologies. *Chin. J. Geotech. Eng.* **2016**, *38*, 643–653. [CrossRef]
10. Li, M.; Li, L.I.N.; Zhang, Z.D.; Li, C. Review, outlook and application technology design on soil improvement by microbial induced calcium carbonate precipitation. *China Civ. Eng. J.* **2016**, *2016*, 80–87.
11. Martinez, B.C.; DeJong, J.T.; Ginn, T.R.; Montoya, B.M.; Barkouki, T.H.; Hunt, C.; Tanyu, B.; Major, D. Experimental optimization of microbial-induced carbonate precipitation for soil improvement. *J. Geotech. Geoenviron. Eng.* **2013**, *139*, 587–598. [CrossRef]
12. Al Qabany, A.; Soga, K.; Santamarina, C. Factors affecting efficiency of microbially induced calcite precipitation. *J. Geotech. Geoenviron. Eng.* **2012**, *138*, 992–1001. [CrossRef]
13. Montoya, B.M.; DeJong, J.T.; Boulanger, R.W.; Wilson, D.W.; Gerhard, R.; Ganchenko, A.; Chou, J.C. Liquefaction mitigation using microbial induced calcite precipitation. In Proceedings of the GeoCongress 2012, Oakland, CA, USA, 25–29 March 2012. [CrossRef]
14. He, J.; Chu, J.; Ivanov, V. Mitigation of liquefaction of saturated sand using biogas. *Géotechnique* **2013**, *63*, 267–275. [CrossRef]
15. Bao, R.; Li, J.; Li, L.; Cutright, T.J.; Chen, L.; Zhu, J.; Tao, J. Effect of microbial induced calcite precipitation on surface erosion of granular soils: Proof of concept. In Proceedings of the TRB Annual Meeting, Washington, DC, USA, 7–11 January 2017. [CrossRef]
16. Zhang, X.; Chen, Y.; Liu, H.; Zhang, Z.; Ding, X. Performance evaluation of a micp-treated calcareous sandy foundation using shake table tests. *Soil Dyn. Earthq. Eng.* **2020**, *129*, 105959. [CrossRef]
17. Xiao, P.; Liu, H.; Xiao, Y.; Stuedlein, A.W.; Evans, T.M. Liquefaction resistance of bio-cemented calcareous sand. *Soil Dyn. Earthq. Eng.* **2018**, *107*, 9–19. [CrossRef]
18. Xiao, P.; Liu, H.; Stuedlein, A.W.; Evans, T.M.; Xiao, Y. Effect of relative density and bio-cementation on the cyclic response of calcareous sand. *Can. Geotech. J.* **2019**, *56*, 1849–1862. [CrossRef]
19. Chu, J.; Ivanov, V.; Stabnikov, V.; Li, B. Microbial method for construction of aquaculture pond in sand. *Géotechnique* **2013**, *63*, 871–875. [CrossRef]
20. Liu, L.; Shen, Y.; Liu, H.L.; Chu, J. Application of bio-cement in erosion control of levees. *Rock Soil Mech.* **2016**, *37*, 3410–3416. [CrossRef]
21. Li, C.; Tian, L.; Dong, C.; Zhang, Y.; Wang, Y. Experimental study on zinc-lead composite contaminated soil solidified/stabilized by MICP technology combined with porous silicon adsorption materials. *Geotechnics* **2022**, *43*, 307–316. [CrossRef]
22. Liu, X.; Gao, X.; Pan, C.V. Experimental study on shear strength of cracks in MICP solidified soil sites. *J. Civ. Eng.* **2022**, *55*, 88–94.
23. Cui, M.J.; Zheng, J.J.; Zhang, R.J.; Lai, H.J.; Zhang, J. Influence of cementation level on the strength behaviour of bio-cemented sand. *Acta Geotech.* **2017**, *12*, 971–986. [CrossRef]
24. Tang, C.; Shi, B.; Gao, W. Study on the effect of polypropylene fiber and cement on the strength of cohesive soil and the mechanism. *J. Eng. Geol.* **2007**, *15*, 108–113.

25. Yetimoglu, T.; Salbas, O. A study on shear strength of sands reinforced with randomly distributed discrete fibers. *Geotext. Geomembranes* **2003**, *21*, 103–110. [CrossRef]
26. Shao, W.; Cetin, B.; Li, Y.; Li, J.; Li, L. Experimental investigation of mechanical properties of sands reinforced with discrete randomly distributed fiber. *J. Geotech. Geoenviron. Eng.* **2014**, *32*, 901–910. [CrossRef]
27. Wei, L.; Chai, S.X.; Cai, H.Z.; Li, M. Triaxial shear strength and deviatoric stress-strain of saline soils reinforced with wheat straws. *J. Civ. Eng.* **2012**, *45*, 109–114.
28. Abd Al-kaream, K.W.; Fattah, M.Y.; Hameedi, M.K. Compressibility and Strength Development of Soft Soil by Polypropylene Fiber. *Int. J. Geomate* **2022**, *22*, 91–97. [CrossRef]
29. Liu, H.; Xiao, P.; Xiao, Y.; Chu, J. State-of-the-artreview of biogeotechnology and its engineering applications. *J. Civ. Environ. Eng.* **2019**, *41*, 1–14. [CrossRef]
30. Transport and Communications Department. *Test Methods of Soils for Highway Engineering*; People's Transport Publications Society: Beijing, China, 2020.

Disclaimer/Publisher's Note: The statements, opinions and data contained in all publications are solely those of the individual author(s) and contributor(s) and not of MDPI and/or the editor(s). MDPI and/or the editor(s) disclaim responsibility for any injury to people or property resulting from any ideas, methods, instructions or products referred to in the content.

Article

Experiments on the State Boundary Surface of Aeolian Sand for Road Building in the Tengger Desert

Zhigang Ma [1,2] and Xuefeng Li [1,2,*]

1. School of Physics and Electronic-Electrical Engineering, Ningxia University, Yinchuan 750021, China
2. Solid Mechanics Institute, Ningxia University, Yinchuan 750021, China
* Correspondence: lixuefeng1928@163.com

Abstract: As a special road-building material widely distributed in desert areas, critical state soil mechanics is used to study the mechanical properties of sand and make up for the lack of research on its engineering characteristics. A series of drained and undrained triaxial compression tests with a loading rate of 0.12 mm/min medium-density aeolian sands taken from Tengger Desert in the northwest of China was carried out to obtain the three-dimensional state boundary surface. The test results reveal that the strength gained from drained and undrained tests increased, respectively, linearly and non-linearly with the increase of the effective confining pressure. Affected by the variation of pore pressure and shear rate, the undrained strength was higher than the drained strength at low effective confining pressures, and the two types of strengths tend to be consistent when the effective confining pressure becomes greater than 800 kPa. The volumetric changes of the aeolian specimens transition from dilatation to contraction when the effective confining pressures increase. The investigation of the strength, deformation and failure characteristics gives rise to the shape parameters of its state boundary surface, which provides not only a basis for the constitutive modelling of the aeolian sand, but also a reference for roadbed construction and other foundation engineering in desert areas.

Keywords: aeolian sand; triaxial test; state boundary surface; strength characteristics; deformation

1. Introduction

The state boundary surface is the unique physical state relationship formed by effective stress paths of soil in a three-dimensional space composed of generalized normal stress, shear stress and specific volume, and it provides an outer limit to the combinations of effective stress and specific volume which the soil can reach [1]. In road building, it can predict the limit state of aeolian sand subgrade failure. The state boundary surface is the basis of critical state soil mechanics and is crucial in studies of the soil mechanical properties, which have been widely used to study the mechanical behaviors of remodeled clay. Aeolian sand is a special material for roadbed filling, which is widely distributed in desert areas, while there are only a few basic experiments for engineering applications. Moreover, the basic experimental results related to critical states are rather scarce. In recent years, much infrastructure, such as highways, railways, transmission lines and other projects, has been built in desert areas. In addition, the numerical simulation of the dynamic response of multi-layer pavement under a moving load is gradually enriched [2,3]. However, the lack of research on the mechanical properties of aeolian sand has seriously restricted the geotechnical application in desert areas. Therefore, experimental characteristics of the state boundary surface of aeolian sand is urgently required for a better understanding the mechanical behaviour of this material.

Currently, most of the existing research on aeolian sands focuses on their engineering aspects, such as particle-size distribution, compaction characteristics, bearing capacity, shear resistance and proportioned concrete [4–6]. The particle-size distribution of aeolian sand in several regions was analysed by different researchers, for instance, Li et al. [7] for the Tengger Desert, Liu et al. [8] for the Mu Us Desert, Ning et al. [9], Guo et al. [10] for the Badain Jaran Desert, Zhang et al. [11] for the Qinghai Lake East Sandy Land, etc. These studies provide rich references for the construction of a foundation treatment in desert areas. Other researchers, e.g., Yuan et al. [12], Li et al. [13], Yin et al. [14], studied the compaction characteristics of aeolian sand. Du et al. [15], Yu et al. [16], Yi et al. [17] and Zheng et al. [18] studied the shear strength characteristics in different desert regions. Yin et al. [19] and Li et al. [20] studied the bearing capacity characteristics of aeolian sand foundations. Although the existing research has accumulated valuable engineering experience for foundation construction in desert areas, a systematic and in-depth triaxial test study is needed to better obtain the unique characteristics of its physical state.

So far aeolian sand has been rarely studied in triaxial tests. Some authors have studied the dynamic properties of aeolian sand with dynamic triaxial tests, e.g., Deng [21], Song [22], Liu [23], Song et al. [24], Liu et al. [25], Luo et al. [26] and Bao et al. [27]. Other authors focus on the static strength of sand. For instance, Li et al. [28] studied the strength characteristics of cement-improved aeolian sand; Badanagki [29] obtained the shear strength and stiffness of aeolian sand in the Sahara Desert, Libya, by a series of drained and undrained triaxial tests; Song [24] obtained the strength characteristics of the aeolian sand in the Mu Us Desert, China, at different stress paths, densities and moisture contents; Qureshi et al. [30] obtained the strength and softening resistance of aeolian sand treated by biopolymer in Al-Sharqia desert; Souza et al. [31] determined the critical state parameters of aeolian sand in Natal, Brazil by triaxial tests with different initial densities; Wei et al. [32] obtained the mechanical properties of aeolian sand and fly ash at different proportions. In particular, Li Xuefeng et al. [33–35] studied the characteristics of deformation, strength and failure of aeolian sand in the Tengger Desert, China at different spatial stress states, different densities and multiple confining pressures. All in all, the unique mechanical properties of aeolian sand have attracted increasing popularity, but some other aspects, such as the critical state, phase transformation and dilatancy of aeolian sand at different stress states and stress paths, need to be studied further. In particular, the determination of its state boundary surface is rarely reported.

In this paper, a series of triaxial drained and undrained tests on the medium-density specimens were conducted to obtain the unique relationship of the state boundary surface of the aeolian sand taken from the Tengger Desert in China. The mechanical responses are measured at different confining pressures. The critical state lines, phase transformation lines and dilatancy characteristics are determined. According to the unique relationship between the stress state and the volume state, the state boundary surface in the p-q-e space is established. The test results improve our understanding of the mechanical response and helps to establish a reasonable constitutive relationship for aeolian sand.

2. Test Method
2.1. Test Apparatus

The triaxial apparatus used in the test was produced by Ningxi Soil Apparatus in Nanjing, China, which can be controlled by stress or strain (Figure 1). The triaxial apparatus is mainly composed of a host, a pressure controller, and a multi-channel communication digital acquisition apparatus. The apparatus is controlled by a single chip computer, and each part can work independently. Multi-channel communication can collect and process data in real time. The apparatus can perform various stress path tests and drained or undrained triaxial tests, in which the drained triaxial test can obtain the real strength of the material, and the undrained triaxial test corresponding to the rapid construction can obtain the pore pressure development. The size of the cylindrical specimen is $\Phi 39.1$ mm $\times$ 80 mm, the axial load range is 0~30 kN, and its measurement accuracy is $\pm 1\%$. The range of the confining pressure controller is 0~1.99 MPa, the range of the back pressure controller is 0~0.99 MPa, and the control accuracy is $\pm 0.5\%$FS (Full Scale).

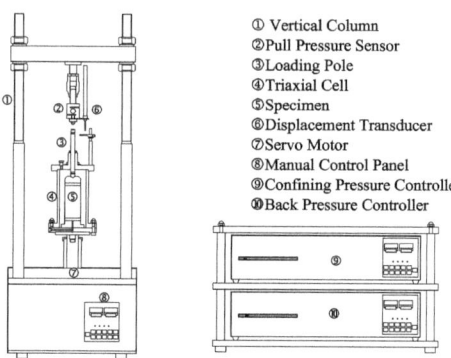

Figure 1. SLB-1 triaxial apparatus, Nanjing, China.

2.2. Test Material

The sand specimen is aeolian sand sampled from the Tengger Desert, China. The Tengger Desert is a typical enrichment area of aeolian sand. Aeolian sand in this area is a special granular material with heterogeneity, cohesionless, uniform particle size, strong permeability and remarkable anisotropy characteristics. The compaction curve has bimodal characteristics, which is also a type of collapsible soil [36]. Therefore, the sand tested in this paper is widely representative. Figure 2 shows the microscopic image of the used sand.

The mass of the aeolian sand with a particle size larger than 0.075 mm exceeds 85% of the total mass. The moisture content of natural aeolian sand is 0.14%; the maximum dry density is 1.68 g/cm^3; the minimum dry density is 1.40 g/cm^3; the specific gravity of sand is 2.67; the maximum void ratio is 0.907, and the minimum void ratio is 0.589. The coefficient of nonuniformity C_u is 1.31, the coefficient of curvature C_c is 2.66, and the fine particle content is less than 5%. According to the "Engineering Classification Standard of Soil" (GB/T 50145-2007), the sand is classified as poorly graded sand. Table 1 shows the particle-size distribution of aeolian sand measured by the sieving method (the data in Table 1 are the average results of three sieving tests). In the table, the sieve mass with a particle size of 0.1~0.25 mm is 750.8 g, accounting for 75.08% of the total mass of the sample, which is the highest particle size of aeolian sand.

Table 1. Particle size gradation of aeolian sand in the Tengger Desert.

Mass of sample taken for fine sieve analysis = 1000 g				
Sand mass on 2 mm sieve = 0 g			The percentage of sand less than 0.075 mm in the total sand mass = 1.23%	
Sand mass under 2 mm sieve = 1000 g			The percentage of sand less than 2 mm in the total sand mass = 100%	
Particle Size/mm	Cumulative Sand Mass on the Sieve/g	Mass of Sand with Particle Size Smaller than the Aperture/g	The Mass Percentage of Sand with a Particle Size Smaller than the Aperture/%	The Mass Percentage of Total Sand Whose Particle Size Is Smaller than the Aperture /%
0	0	0	0	0
0.075	12.3	12.3	1.23	1.23
0.1	131.3	143.6	13.13	14.36
0.25	750.8	894.4	75.08	89.44
0.5	104.4	998.8	10.44	99.88
1	1.2	1000	0.12	100

2.3. Test Process and Scheme

The specimen preparation process was completed by using a split mould, a rubber membrane and a vacuum pump. The vacuum was used to make the rubber membrane close to the inner wall of the split mould. The multiple sieving pluviation method is used for the specimen preparation. The process of specimen preparation and specimen installation is shown in Figure 3. The relative density D_r is controlled to be 0.5, the dry density ρ_d = 1.53 g/cm^3, and the initial void ratio e_0 = 0.745 (medium density). After the specimen was prepared, it was necessary to vacuum the specimen through an exhaust hole on the top cap of the specimen to ensure the stability of the specimen size. To this end, a negative pressure of 20 kPa inside the specimen was maintained to fix the shape of the specimen. Afterwards, two steps of hydraulic saturation and back pressure saturation were performed to saturate the specimens. After the saturation reaches higher than 95%, the specimen consolidation and triaxial drained and undrained shear test were carried out with reference to ASTM (D7181-11).

Figure 2. Microscopic image of test material (0.5 mm/grid).

Figure 3. Specimen preparation and specimen installation.

To obtain the state boundary surface of the aeolian sand in the three-dimensional space, it is necessary to obtain the effective stress paths and strength and deformation at different confining pressures. For this purpose, the drained and undrained triaxial tests at the confining pressure σ_3 of 50, 100, 200, 400 and 800 kPa were designed. The key control parameters of the test scheme were detailed in Table 2.

Table 2. Triaxial test control parameters.

Material Type	Saturability	Effective Confining Pressure σ_3 (kPa)	Drained Conditions	Strain Loading Rate (mm/min)
Aeolian sand	More than 95%	50 100 200 400 800	I. Drained II. Undrained	0.12

3. Test Results

3.1. Stress-Strain Relationships

Figure 4a,b shows the variation of the generalized shear stress and volumetric strain with axial strain under the drained conditions. Due to the complex and diverse in natural particle shapes of the aeolian sand (Figure 1), the particle internal friction is strong, resulting in obvious nonlinear characteristics in the stress-strain curves. At a low effective confining pressure ($\sigma_3 \leq 100$ kPa), the specimens exhibit strain hardening behaviour, and at a high effective confining pressure, they show strain-softening behaviours. The higher the effective confining pressure, the more obvious the softening characteristic, the greater the elastic modulus, the higher the peak strength, and the longer the elastic-plastic stage. At low effective confining pressure, the aeolian sand first undergoes contraction deformation and then dilates until failure is achieved. Meanwhile, the characteristics of contraction and dilatation are affected significantly by the effective confining pressure. With the increase of the effective confining pressure, the volumetric changes develop from dilatation to contraction. While the effective confining pressure reaches 800 kPa, only the contraction deformation occurs (compared to the initial volume of the specimen).

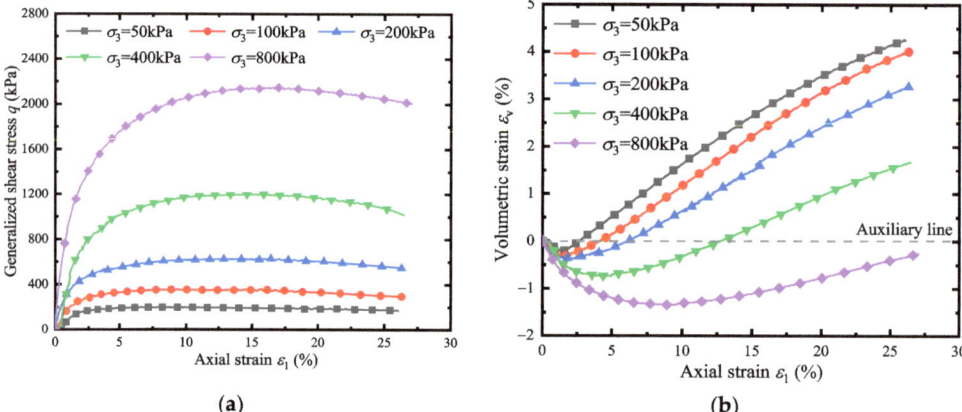

Figure 4. Relationships between stress and volumetric strain with axial strain at drained condition. (**a**) Stress-strain relationships. (**b**) Volumetric strain-strain relationships.

Figure 5a,b show the variation of generalized shear stress and pore pressure with axial strain under undrained conditions. Figure 5a shows that the stress-strain relationships are softened only at relatively low effective confining pressures (e.g., 50, 100 and 200 kPa), and hardened at high effective confining pressures (>200 kPa). A greater effective confining pressure gives rise to a greater elastic modulus and a higher peak strength. Compared with the stress-strain relationships under the drained condition, the peak stress point of the undrained test is higher and the elastic-plastic stage is longer under the same load conditions. The results suggest that the undrained shear rate needs to be reduced to fully dissipate the excess pore pressure. Figure 5b shows the variation of pore pressure, implying that the dilatancy increases gradually with the increase of effective confining pressure. At low effective confining pressure, the negative pore pressure generally increases, while at high effective confining pressure, the pore pressure increases generally. It also shows that only dilation occurs at low effective confining pressure, while only contraction occurs at high effective confining pressure. This is consistent with the results obtained from drained tests. However, pore pressure has a greater influence on the stress-strain relationships under undrained conditions, and aeolian sand is more prone to dilatancy failure.

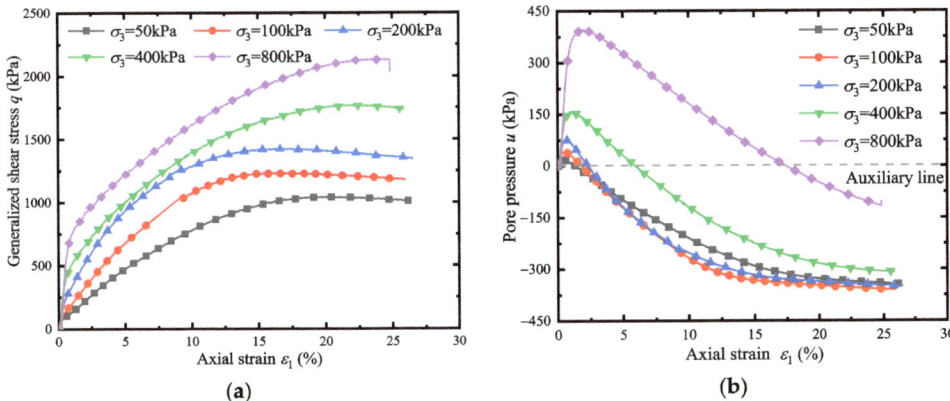

Figure 5. Relationships between stress and pore pressure with axial strain under undrained conditions. (**a**) Stress-strain relationships. (**b**) Pore pressure-strain relationships.

Figure 6 shows the variation of pore pressure coefficient A with axial strain. Skempton [37] reported that the specimen contracts for $A > 0$, and it dilates at $A < 0$. Therefore, in Figure 6, the pore pressure and strain relationships above auxiliary line $A = 0$ are contraction, and below auxiliary line $A = 0$ is dilation. The test results of the pore pressure coefficient A also show that the deformation and failure mode of the aeolian sand is dilatation under undrained conditions, and the contraction part only occurs within 2% of the axial strain.

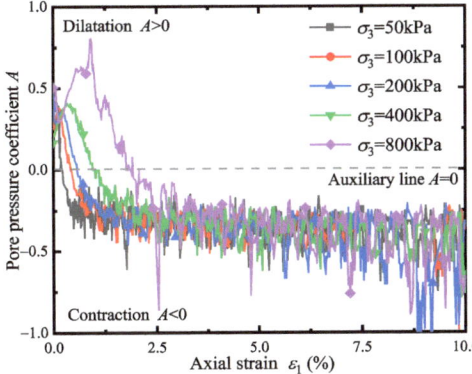

Figure 6. Relationships between pore pressure coefficient and axial strain.

Figure 7a,b shows the relationships between axial strain and radial strain under drained and undrained conditions. The relationships between the axial strain and radial strain change linearly under drained condition. As the effective confining pressure increases, the slope of the linear relationship increases negatively, indicating that the aeolian sand has an initial anisotropy, and the initial anisotropy decreases with the increase of the effective confining pressure continuously. Figure 7b shows that the relationships between the axial strain and radial strain change linearly under undrained conditions, which always satisfies the equation $\varepsilon_1 = -2\varepsilon_3$. The anisotropy characteristic is not obvious, which may be related to the loading rate of the test.

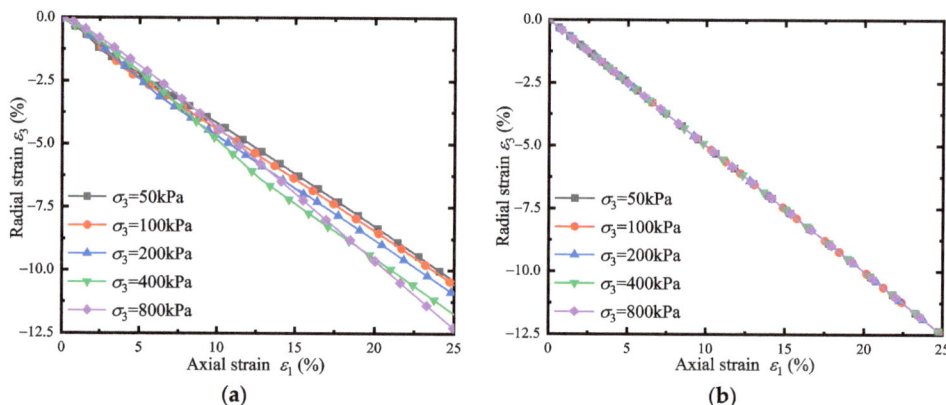

Figure 7. Relationships between axial strain and radial strain. (**a**) Drained. (**b**) Undrained.

Figures 8a,b and 9a,b show the relationships between generalized stress ratio η and generalized shear strain ε_s of aeolian sand and the relationships between ε_s/η and ε_s under drained and undrained conditions, respectively. Comparing Figures 8a and 9a, it can be concluded that the peak stress ratio decreases gradually with the increase of effective confining pressure in both the drained and undrained tests, but the peak stress ratio of the drained condition is slightly higher than that of the undrained condition. The shape of the η-ε_s relationship for drained and undrained conditions are significantly different. Under undrained conditions, the stress ratio has an obvious peak value, and the peak stress ratio decreases slightly with the increase of ε_s. In Figures 8b and 9b, the ε_s/η-ε_s relationships are linear under drained and undrained conditions. The slope of the straight line increases with the increase of the effective confining pressure under the drained condition, but the change of the slope is small under an undrained condition.

Wood et al. [38] used the peak generalized stress ratio to represent the characteristics of the softening curve and proposed a hyperbolic model characterized by the stress ratio and the shear strain, which reads:

$$\frac{\eta}{\eta_{max}} = \frac{\varepsilon_s}{B + \varepsilon_s} \qquad (1)$$

where B is the test constant and η_{max} is the peak value of the generalized stress ratio. The transformation form is as follows.

$$\frac{\varepsilon_s}{\eta} = \frac{B}{\eta_{max}} + \frac{\varepsilon_s}{\eta_{max}} \qquad (2)$$

Our test results are consistent with the hyperbolic model proposed by Wood et al. [38]. The slope of the ε_s/η-ε_s curve increases gradually with the increase of effective confining pressure under drained conditions, indicating that softening increases gradually. The slope of the ε_s/η-ε_s curve under undrained conditions is significantly higher than that under drained conditions, indicating that the softening phenomenon is more obvious.

Figure 10 shows the variation of peak shear stress and peak friction angle with effective confining pressure under drained and undrained conditions. The black curve in the figure increases linearly, indicating that the generalized peak shear stress increases linearly with the increase of effective confining pressure under both drained and undrained conditions. However, the undrained strength is greater than the drained strength at low effective confining pressure, and the drained and undrained strength becomes the same as the effective confining pressure increases. All the purple curves show a nonlinear decreasing trend, indicating that the peak friction angle decreases nonlinearly with the increase of effective confining pressure. At low effective confining pressure, the peak friction angles of the two test conditions are quite different, but at high effective confining pressure they are close to the same.

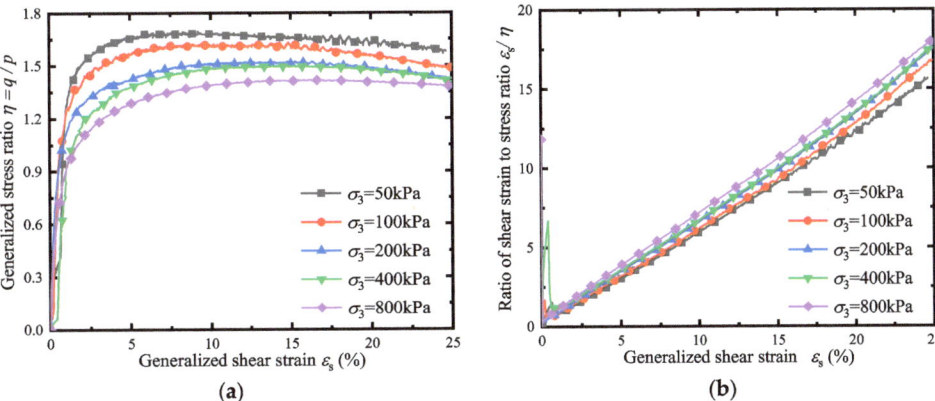

Figure 8. η-ε_s relationships and ε_s/η-ε_s relationships under drained condition. (**a**) η-ε_s relationships under drained condition. (**b**) ε_s/η-ε_s relationships under drained condition.

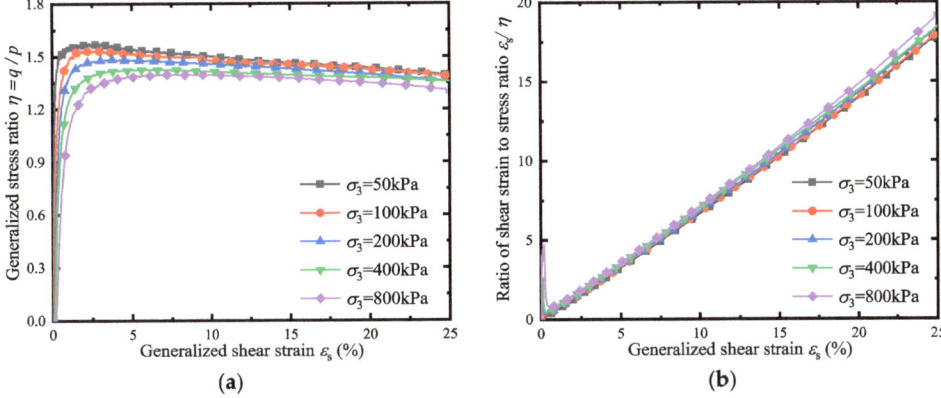

Figure 9. η-ε_s relationships and ε_s/η-ε_s relationships under undrained condition. (**a**) η-ε_s relationships under undrained condition. (**b**) ε_s/η-ε_s relationships under undrained condition.

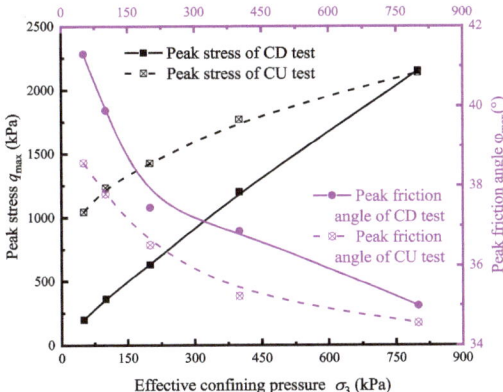

Figure 10. The relationships between q_{max}~σ_3 and φ_{max}~σ_3 under drained and undrained conditions.

3.2. State Boundary Surface

Figure 11 plots the critical state line and phase transformation line in the p-q space under drained and undrained conditions and gives the slopes of the two-state lines. The green points in Figure 11a are the phase transformation points, which are the inflection points where the void ratio changes from decrease to increase, and it is also the transformation point of volumetric change from contraction to dilation. The phase transformation point is determined according to the corresponding stress state point, as the void ratio increment is 0. Figure 11 shows that the critical state line and phase transformation line determined by the undrained triaxial test are slightly lower than those determined by the drained triaxial test, due to the change of pore pressure and shear rate, and the variation range is less than 5%. The test results show that the aeolian sand has a unified critical state line and phase transformation line.

The critical state line and phase transformation line of aeolian sand in the p-q space can be expressed linearly by the following equations:

$$q = M_{\text{CSL1}} p \quad (3)$$

$$q = M_{\text{PTL1}} p \quad (4)$$

where M_{CSL1} and M_{PTL1} are the slopes of the critical state line and the phase transformation line in p-q space, respectively.

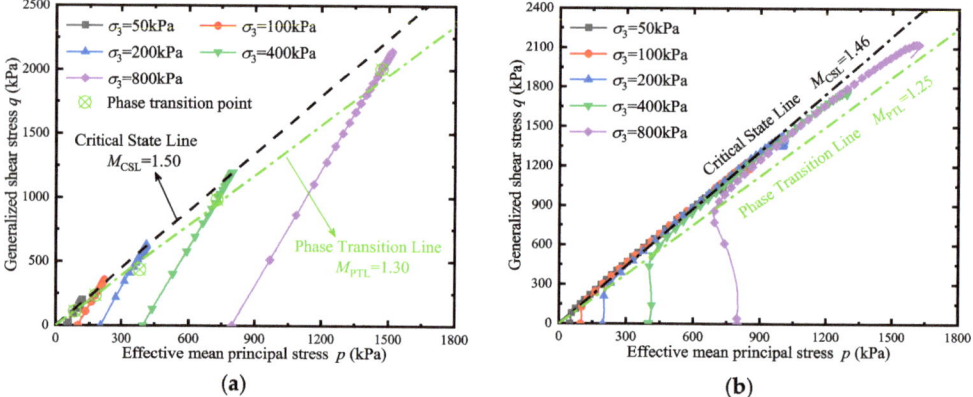

Figure 11. Effective stress path for drained and undrained test. (**a**) Effective stress path for drained test. (**b**) Effective stress path for undrained test.

The information in Figure 12 shows the critical state line, phase transformation line and normal consolidation line under drained conditions, which can be represented by linear relations. At the same effective confining pressure, with the increase of $\ln p$, the void ratio decreases first and then increases rapidly to the critical state (compared to the consolidated void ratio). At different effective confining pressures, with the increase of effective confining pressure and $\ln p$, the decreased degree of void ratio increases gradually compared with the consolidated void ratio. While the effective confining pressure is greater than 800 kPa, the void ratio is always smaller than the consolidation void ratio, and the aeolian sand undergoes only contractive deformation under this condition. The studies of Verdugo and Ishihara [39], Riemer and Seed [40] show that the critical state characteristics of cohesionless soil are significantly different from those of clay, and the critical state line is no longer unique in the $\ln p$-e space, due to the anisotropy of the soil. In this study, the specimen adopts the same specimen preparation method and is sheared under triaxial conditions, so the critical state lines, phase transformation lines and normal consolidation lines of aeolian sand in e-$\ln p$ space can be expressed by linear equations as expressed by Equations (5)–(7), respectively.

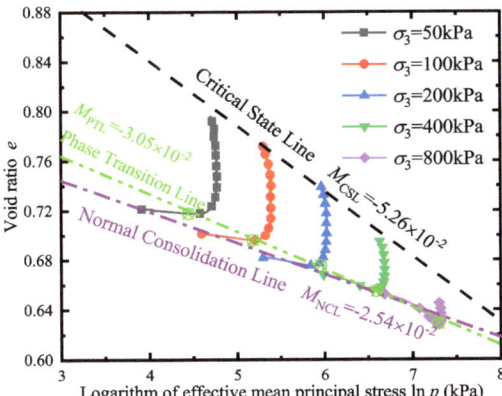

Figure 12. e-$\ln p$ relationships under drained conditions.

$$e_{\text{CSL}} = M_{\text{CSL2}} \ln p + e_C \quad (5)$$

$$e_{\text{PTL}} = M_{\text{PTL2}} \ln p + e_P \quad (6)$$

$$e_{\text{NCL}} = M_{\text{NCL}} \ln p + e_N \quad (7)$$

where e_{CSL2}, e_{PTL2} and e_{NCL} are the void ratios corresponding to the critical state line, the phase transformation line and the normal consolidation line at any p, respectively. M_{CSL2}, M_{PTL2} and M_{NCL} are the slopes of the critical state line, phase transformation line and normal consolidation line in $\ln p$-e space, respectively. e_C, e_P and e_N are the void ratios corresponding to the critical state line, phase transformation line and normal consolidation line at $p = 1$ kPa, respectively.

Figure 13 shows the e-q relationships of aeolian sand under drained conditions. The shape characteristics of the critical state line and the phase transformation line in the e-q space are exponential. Moreover, as q increases, the void ratio decreases compared with the consolidated void ratio, and the specimen contracts. At low and medium effective confining pressure, the void ratio increases rapidly to a critical state after reaching the phase transformation point. At high effective confining pressures, the void ratio increases and q decreases, and the specimen show strain softening behaviours. At low effective confining pressures, and the dilatation characteristics are significant. The higher the effective confining pressure, the greater the peak shear stress. The critical state lines and phase transformation lines in e-q space are nonlinear. The critical state line and phase transformation line can be used to predict the development trend of voids under different test conditions. According to Equations (3) and (5), the critical state line in e-q space can be expressed as follows:

$$q = M_{\text{CSL1}} p = M_{\text{CSL1}} \exp \frac{e_{\text{CSL}} - e_C}{M_{\text{CSL2}}} \quad (8)$$

Based on Equations (4) and (6), the phase transformation line in e-q space can be expressed as follows:

$$q = M_{\text{PTL1}} p = M_{\text{PTL1}} \exp \frac{e_{\text{PTL}} - e_P}{M_{\text{PTL2}}} \quad (9)$$

Figure 14 shows the critical state characteristic curve of aeolian sand in e-p-q space. The three-dimensional surface composed of e, p and q is the state boundary surface or Roscoe surface. The curve connected by the transformation points where the void ratio first decreases and then increases at different stress states is defined as the phase transformation state line, which reflects the state transformation from contraction to dilation. While the granular material is sheared to failure, the curve composed of the effective stress path, void ratio and average effective stress is defined as the critical state line. The three-dimensional critical state line can be expressed in Equations (5) and (7), and reads:

$$\begin{cases} e_{CSL} = M_{CSL2} \ln p + e_C \\ q = M_{CSL1} \exp \frac{e_{CSL} - e_C}{M_{CSL2}} \end{cases} \quad (10)$$

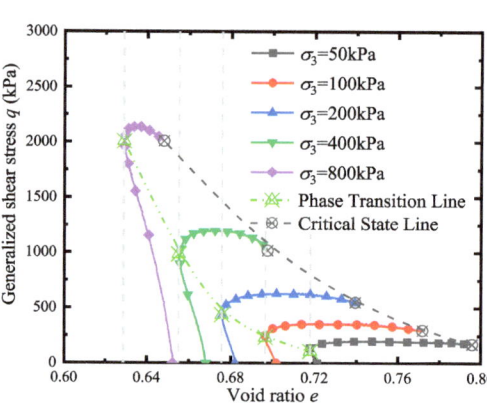

Figure 13. e-q relationships under drained conditions.

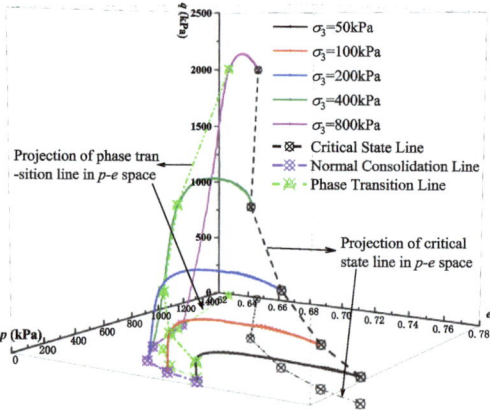

Figure 14. State boundary surface in three-dimensional space.

The three-dimensional phase transformation line can be expressed in Equations (6) and (8), and reads:

$$\begin{cases} e_{PTL} = M_{PTL2} \ln p + e_P \\ q = M_{PTL1} \exp \frac{e_{PTL} - e_P}{M_{PTL2}} \end{cases} \quad (11)$$

The test results take into account the dilatancy characteristics for the establishment of the state boundary surface, so the state boundary surface is quite different from that of remodelled clay proposed by Roscoe [1]. The state boundary surface describes the unique relationship among the stress state, strength and void ratio of aeolian sand. The spatial critical state line and phase transformation line shown in Figure 14 and their descriptive Equations (9) and (10) can better describe and predict the quantitative relationship between stress state characteristics and volume state characteristics in the three-dimensional space.

4. Conclusions

In this paper, the state boundary surface and deformation and failure characteristics of aeolian sand in the Tengger Desert, China are studied through a series of drained and undrained triaxial tests. The following conclusions can be drawn from this study:

(1) The generalized peak shear stress of aeolian sand increases linearly with the increase of effective confining pressure under drained and undrained conditions; the undrained strength is greater than the drained strength at low effective confining pressure, and the strength is close to the same with the increase of effective confining pressure. The peak friction angle decreases nonlinearly with the increase of effective confining pressure. The peak friction angle of the two test conditions is quite different at low effective confining pressure and is close to the same at high effective confining pressure.

(2) At low and medium effective confining pressures, the dilatancy is obvious. With the increase of effective confining pressures, the dilatancy develops to contraction. At high effective confining pressures, it only contracts. The development of pore pressure under undrained conditions also reflects a similar law.

(3) The medium-density specimen of aeolian sand obtained by the multiple sieving pluviation method has strong initial anisotropy. With the increase of effective confining pressure, the effect of initial anisotropy gradually weakens. While the effective confining pressure is 800 kPa, the initial anisotropy has almost no effect on the deformation characteristics. The initial anisotropy characteristics of the undrained test are not obvious, and the relationships between axial strain and radial strain always satisfy the relationship $\varepsilon_1 = -2\varepsilon_3$.

(4) The three-dimensional state boundary surface of aeolian sand considering dilatancy is quite different from that of remoulded clay. The study of the state boundary surface and the determination of critical state line and phase transformation line equations in three-dimensional space describe the unique state relationship formed by the generalized normal stress, shear stress and void ratio accurately, which can predict the quantitative relationship between stress state and volumetric state reasonably. The state boundary parameters can provide the basis for the establishment of the constitutive model of aeolian sand and provide basic test support for the geotechnical design, construction and maintenance of foundations, roadbeds and another foundation engineering in desert areas.

Author Contributions: Conceptualization, Z.M. and X.L.; methodology, X.L.; validation, Z.M., X.L.; formal analysis, X.L.; investigation, Z.M.; resources, X.L.; data curation, Z.M.; writing—original draft preparation, Z.M.; writing—review and editing, Z.M. and X.L.; visualization, Z.M.; supervision, X.L.; funding acquisition, X.L. All authors have read and agreed to the published version of the manuscript.

Funding: This work was financially supported by the Projects for Leading Talents of Science and Technology Innovation of Ningxia (No. KJT2019001), the National Natural Science Foundation of China (No. 12162028), and the innovation team for multi-scale mechanics and its engineering applications of Ningxia Hui Autonomous Region (2021), and these supports are gratefully acknowledged.

Institutional Review Board Statement: Not applicable.

Informed Consent Statement: Informed consent was obtained from all subjects involved in the study.

Data Availability Statement: The data used to support the findings of this study are available from the corresponding author upon request.

Conflicts of Interest: The authors declare no conflict of interest.

References

1. Schofield, A.N.; Wroth, P. *Critical State Soil Mechanics*; McGraw-Hill: London, UK, 1968; Volume 310.
2. Li, J.; Zhang, J.; Yang, X.; Zhang, A.; Yu, M. Carlo simulations of deformation behaviour of unbound granular materials based on a real aggregate library. *Int. J. Pavement. Eng.* **2023**. [CrossRef]
3. Fan, H.; Zhang, J.; Zheng, J. Dynamic response of a multi-layered pavement structure with subgrade modulus varying with depth subjected to a moving load. *Soil. Dyn. Earthq. Eng.* **2022**, *160*, 107358. [CrossRef]
4. Wang, X.Y.; Liu, M.H.; Liu, X.; Jia, S.Y.; Xu, Z. Study on mechanical properties and carbon emissions of desert sand and machine—Made sand concrete. *China Civ. Eng. J.* **2022**, *55*, 23–30. [CrossRef]
5. Wang, H.; Huang, X.; Xie, B. Strength and deformation properties of structural lightweight concrete under true tri-axial compression. *Case Stud. Constr. Mater.* **2019**, *11*, e00269. [CrossRef]
6. Wang, Y.H.; Chu, Q.; Han, Q. Filling effect of kubuqi aeolian sand on different classifications of river sand. *J. Build. Mater.* **2021**, *24*, 191–198.
7. Dong, Z.B.; Cui, X.J. Grain-size characteristics of transverse dune during different developmental stages in the southeastern edge of the Tengger Desert. *J. Desert Res.* **2015**, *35*, 129–135. [CrossRef]
8. Liu, Z.Y.; Jin, H.L.; Liu, B.; Xue, W.P. Desert evolution during the mid holocene reflected by grain-size variation of aeolian sand and paleosoil sequence records from Mu Us sandy land. *J. Desert Res.* **2019**, *39*, 88–96.
9. Ning, K.; Li, Z.L.; Wang, N.A.; Sun, J.W.; Shao, W.W. Spatial characteristics of grain size and its environmental implication in the Badain Jaran Desert. *J. Desert Res.* **2013**, *33*, 642–648.
10. Guo, F.; Sun, D.H.; Wang, F.; Li, Z.J.; Li, B.F. Grain-size distribution pattern of the depositional sequence in central Badain Jaran Desert andits genetic interpretation. *Mar. Geol. Quat. Geol.* **2014**, *34*, 165–173.
11. Zhang, D.S.; Tian, L.H.; Lu, R.J.; Tang, Q.L.; Shi, H. Grain-size features of aeolian deposits in the eastern shore of Qinghai lake. *Arid. Land Geogr.* **2013**, *36*, 203–211.
12. Yuan, Y.Q.; Wang, X.C. Experimental research on compaction characteristics of aeolian sand. *Chin. J. Geotech. Eng.* **2007**, *29*, 360–365. [CrossRef]
13. Li, Z.Y.; Cao, Y.W.; Liang, N.X.; Mei, Y.J. Compaction mechanism of aeolian sand. *China J. Highw. Transp.* **2006**, *19*, 6–11.
14. Yin, Y.Z.; Wang, Y.L. Study of Key Parameters in the Process of Aeolian Sand Compactibility. *Appl. Mech. Mater.* **2014**, 278–282. [CrossRef]
15. Du, X.L.; Yang, J.B.; Zhang, X.F. Research on relationships between shear strength index and in-situ indexes of desert sand. *Rock Soil Mech.* **2005**, *26*, 837–840. [CrossRef]
16. Yu, Y.F.; Zhang, X.F.; Jiao, Q.X.; Zhao, Y.M. Research on engineering properties of desert sands in Taklimakan Desert. *J. Desert Res.* **2007**, *27*, 362–366.
17. Yi, F.; Hong, C.; Xue, Y.Z.; Kaidi, Z. Shear strength of aeolian sand sediments. *Trans. ASABE* **2018**, *61*, 583–590. [CrossRef]
18. Zheng, M.L.; Wang, Q.Q.; Chen, W.; Gao, Y.; Zhang, S.; Zhu, L.L. Materials characteristics and shear strength of aeolian sand in different areas. *China Sci.* **2021**, *16*, 415–421.
19. Yin, Y.Z.; Wang, Y.L. Determine the Shear Strength of Aeolian Sand and Bearing Capacity. *Appl. Mech. Mater.* **2014**, *580*, 165–168. [CrossRef]
20. Li, Y.; Zhang, D.; Wu, C. Sensitivity study of the bearing capacity and pile-soil stress ratio for aeolian sand foundation treated with CFG piles. *Rev. TÉCnica De La Fac. De Ing. Univ. Del Zulia* **2017**, *39*, 124–135.
21. Deng, Y.H.; Li, X.A.; Wang, Z.J.; Song, Y.X.; Pen, J.B. Study on dynamic strength of the aeolian sand inmaowusu desert area. *Eng. Mech.* **2012**, *29*, 281–286.
22. Song, Y.X. Test Study on the Mechanical Property of the Aeolian Sand and the Bearing Capacity of the Aeolian Sand Ground of Mu Us Desert. Ph.D. Thesis, Chang'an University, Xi'an, China, 2011.
23. Liu, D.; Yang, X.; Wang, J.; Mao, Z.J. Study on Static Strength of Aeolian Sand before and after Cyclic Loading. *Appl. Mech. Mater.* **2014**, *580*, 191–194. [CrossRef]
24. Song, Y.; Zhang, X.D.; Zhang, X. Experimental study on the characteristics of weakened subgrade of aeolian soil along the Beijing-Shenyang super rail. *J. Saf. Environ.* **2014**, *14*, 69–73.
25. Liu, D.P.; Yang, X.H.; Wang, Y.W. Study on the plastic strain characteristics of aeolian sand under cyclic loading. *J. Wuhan Univ. Technol.* **2014**, *36*, 103–108.
26. Luo, J.W.; Li, X.A.; Zhao, N.; Zhou, J.; Zhao, X.K. Experimental study on dynamic characteristics of sandy loess of aeolian sand to loess transitional origin. *J. Eng. Geol.* **2016**, *24*, 915–923.
27. Bao, J.Q.; Xing, Y.M.; Liu, L. Dynamic characteristics of reinforced aeolian sands with geogrid. *Ind. Constr.* **2019**, *49*, 77–81+107.
28. Li, J.; Wang, F.; Yi, F.; Wu, F.; Liu, J.; Lin, Z. Effect of freeze-thaw cycles on triaxial strength property damage to cement improved aeolian sand (CIAS). *Materials* **2019**, *12*, 2801. [CrossRef] [PubMed]
29. Badanagki, M. Shear Strength and Stiffness of a Sahara Sand from Libya. Ph.D. Thesis, Colorado State University, Fort Collins, CO, USA, 2011.
30. Qureshi, M.U.; Chang, I.; Al-Sadarani, K. Strength and durability characteristics of biopolymer-treated desert sand. *Geomech. Eng.* **2017**, *12*, 785–801. [CrossRef]
31. Souza Júnior, P.L.; Santos Júnior, O.F.; Fontoura, T.B.; Freitas Neto, O.D. Drained and undrained behavior of an aeolian sand from Natal, Brazil. *Soils Rocks São Paulo* **2020**, *43*, 263–270. [CrossRef]

32. Wei, X.; Gao, C.; Ai, K.; Zhao, J.; Xu, L. Mechanical Interpretation of Effects of Aeolian FineSands on Coal Fly Ash in Northern Shaanxi Province, China. *Adv. Civ. Eng.* **2020**. [CrossRef]
33. Li, X.; Xu, W.; Chang, L.; Yang, W. Shear Behaviour of Aeolian Sand with Different Density and Confining Pressure. *Appl. Sci.* **2022**, *12*, 3020. [CrossRef]
34. Li, X.; Ma, Z.; Lu, W.; Wang, Y. True-Triaxial Drained Test of Tengger Desert Sand. *Adv. Civ. Eng.* **2020**, *2020*, 8851165. [CrossRef]
35. Li, X.F.; Lu, W.N.; Ma, Z.G.; Tuo, N. The Undrained Characteristics of Tengger Desert Sand from True Triaxial Testing. *Adv. Civ. Eng.* **2021**, *2021*, 6320397. [CrossRef]
36. Li, J.S.; Zhang, Y.Z. Undrained monotonic and dynamic triaxial properties of the aeolian sand. In *IOP Conference Series: Earth and Environmental Science*; IOP Publishing: Bristol, UK, 2019; Volume 242, p. 062010.
37. Skempton, A. Effective stress in soils, concrete and rocks. *Sel. Pap. Soil Mech.* **1984**, *1032*, 4–16.
38. Wood, D.M.; Belkheir, K. Strain softening and state parameter for sand modelling. *GÉOtechnique* **1994**, *44*, 335–339. [CrossRef]
39. Verdugo, R.; Ishihara, K. The steady state of sandy soils. *Soils Found.* **1996**, *36*, 81–91. [CrossRef] [PubMed]
40. Riemer, M.F.; Seed, R.B. Factors affecting apparent position of steady-state line. *J. Geotech. Geoenvironmental Eng.* **1997**, *123*, 281–288. [CrossRef]

Disclaimer/Publisher's Note: The statements, opinions and data contained in all publications are solely those of the individual author(s) and contributor(s) and not of MDPI and/or the editor(s). MDPI and/or the editor(s) disclaim responsibility for any injury to people or property resulting from any ideas, methods, instructions or products referred to in the content.

Article

Performance Assessment of Existing Asphalt Pavement in China's Highway Reconstruction and Expansion Project Based on Coupling Weighting Method and Cloud Model Theory

Ying Xu [1], Xixin Shi [1,*] and Yongsheng Yao [2]

[1] China Merchants Chongqing Highway Engineering Testing Center Co., Ltd., Chongqing 400067, China; xuying12568@163.com
[2] College of Traffic & Transportation, Chongqing Jiaotong University, Chongqing 400074, China; yaoyongsheng23@cqjtu.edu.cn
* Correspondence: shixixin2024@163.com

Abstract: In China, a substantial portion of highway asphalt pavements are no longer capable of accommodating increasing traffic volumes and necessitate renovation and expansion. Prior to commencing such activities, it is crucial to evaluate the performance of the existing asphalt pavements. This study developed a novel normal cloud framework integrating a comprehensive weighted indicator system for existing asphalt pavement. Five key performance indicators including riding quality index (RQI), rutting area ratio (R_r), cracking area ratio (C_r), patching area ratio (P_r), and pavement structural strength index (PSSI) were selected to holistically represent the pavement condition in highway renovation and expansion projects. Subsequently, a method was proposed to determine the weights of these indicators by integrating the analytic hierarchy process (AHP) and entropy. A normal cloud model was constructed to address data characteristics and representation of indicator fuzziness/randomness through digital cloud modeling. The model was applied to 12 sections of the Jingjintang Expressway (Tianjin section). The results revealed only one section where the normal cloud model differed from the pavement maintenance quality assessment (PQI) model. The 3D ground-penetrating radar detection results of this different section indicated that the normal cloud model more closely aligned with the road structure condition. Compared to absolute pass/fail criteria of the traditional PQI model, the cloud model offered enhanced sensitivity to define graded condition assessments essential for reconstruction planning and decision analysis. Therefore, the normal cloud model is more suitable for assessing the performance of existing asphalt pavements in highway reconstruction and extension projects compared to the PQI model.

Keywords: road engineering; pavement performance; evaluation; weights; normal cloud model

1. Introduction

With rapid economic development and the increase in traffic volumes in China, many early-built highways now require renovation and expansion due to deteriorating pavement conditions [1,2]. Highway reconstruction aims to improve transportation efficiency, stimulate economic growth, and enhance quality of life for residents. However, current standards for assessing asphalt pavement performance in China, i.e., the Highway Performance Assessment Standards (JTG 5210-2018), are insufficient to guide reconstruction works [3]. Therefore, developing a performance assessment indicator system and evaluation models for existing asphalt pavements is imperative in highway renovation and expansion projects.

Numerous studies have explored indicator systems and models for assessing existing asphalt pavement in highway renovation and expansion projects in China. Xiong et al. [4] employed non-destructive testing (NDT) systems to establish a decision-making framework for pavement maintenance in renovation and expansion projects. Li et al. [5] utilized artificial field surveys, ground-penetrating radar (GPR), and a falling-weight deflectometer

(FWD) to inspect existing asphalt pavements in highway reconstruction and expansion projects, subsequently developing a corresponding decision-making framework. While these are pioneering detection methods, the main challenge lies in comprehensive analysis and utilization of inspection results. The rapid progress of computer technology has offered a plethora of valuable tools for conducting comprehensive pavement performance evaluations. Notably, fuzzy mathematics [6], grey theory [7], neural networks [8], entropy theory [9,10], and support vector machines [11], among others, were initially applied for the comprehensive evaluation of pavement performance. However, there are still several key issues that require further discussion concerning the proper application of these tools in road surface evaluation [12–15].

Li Deyi, an academician from the Chinese Academy of Engineering, proposed the cloud model theory based on fuzzy mathematics and statistical mathematics to realize the mapping and conversion between uncertain linguistic values and accurate values, better describing the randomness, fuzziness, and relevance of variables [16]. Since their inception, cloud models have achieved success across diverse fields through natural language processing, data mining, decision analysis, and intelligent control [17–19]. Fu [17] and Yang et al. [20] reviewed the generality and flexibility of cloud models in dealing with complex problems and multi-indicator system problems. Cloud models have been preliminarily applied in pavement performance assessment. Xiao and Fan [21] analyzed the fuzziness, randomness, and discreteness in the process of pavement condition evaluation, established a pavement condition evaluation model based on the comprehensive weight and cloud model, and verified the model's correctness through engineering applications. Wei et al. [22] established an entropy weight-cloud model for evaluating pavement performance and compared the calculated results of the model with those of the matter element model, confirming the feasibility of the model. He et al. [23] combined the gray level co-occurrence matrix (GLCM) algorithm and the cloud model theory to construct a damage identification and evaluation model for pavements. However, applications of cloud models in evaluating pavement performance remain limited. Moreover, existing studies neglect reconstruction project particulars by not discussing indicator systems tailored for such work.

This study established an evaluation model based on a comprehensive weighting method and the normal cloud model theory for assessing the performance of existing asphalt pavement in highway renovation and expansion projects, taking into account the fuzziness and randomness inherent in the assessment. The application of the normal cloud model in the performance evaluation of existing asphalt pavement for highway renovation and expansion projects necessitated addressing the following two issues:

(1) A rational performance assessment indicator system.
(2) Determination of the weights for the evaluation indicators.

Based on a synthesis of existing research results, and expert experience, this study selected five key indicators to construct a performance assessment indicator system for existing asphalt pavement in highway reconstruction and expansion projects. These five indicators were the riding quality index (RQI), rutting area ratio (R_r), cracking area ratio (C_r), patching area ratio (P_r), and the pavement structural strength index (PSSI). The weights of the evaluation indicators were determined through the analytic hierarchy process (AHP) and entropy. Furthermore, the existing asphalt pavement performance assessment model was established based on the AHP–entropy and normal cloud model. Finally, the feasibility of the method was verified using the detection data from the renovation and expansion project of the Jingjintang Expressway (Tianjin section).

Specifically, this study made the following contributions: It selected indicators suitable for evaluating the performance of existing asphalt pavement in highway renovation and expansion projects and obtained the weights of the indicators through subjective and objective weighting methods. A normal cloud model for evaluating the existing asphalt pavement in highway renovation and expansion projects was established, and the correctness of the model was verified through engineering applications. The applicability of the model for existing asphalt pavement in highway renovation and expansion projects was demonstrated with high confidence when compared with the PQI evaluation results.

2. Comparative Analysis of Old Pavement Evaluation Models

The oldest worldwide model for assessing asphalt pavement performance is the present serviceability index (PSI) established by the American Association of State Highway Officials (AASHO) in the 1960s [24]. The introduction of the PSI marked a significant milestone in the road management sector. The AASHO established threshold indicators for road surface condition, with a PSI of 2.5 for primary roads and 2.0 for secondary roads. If the PSI fell below the specified threshold, remedial technical measures should be considered for maintenance. Subsequently, many countries adopted PSI variations tailored to their contexts, including the ride comfort index (RCI) in Canada, the maintenance condition index (MCI) in Japan, and the pavement quality index (PQI) model in China [25].

While pioneering, these early models primarily relied on limited regression analysis and contemporary expert knowledge, which presents issues when evaluating aged pavements in reconstruction projects. Firstly, evaluation data itself demonstrates randomness, complexity, and fuzziness characteristics difficult to fully capture through single-factor regression. This can induce discrepancies between modeled and actual relationships between factors and outputs. Secondly, the models were mainly developed for maintenance and repair rather than reconstruction, requiring investigation into their suitability given reconstruction's unique demands.

Notably, the widely used PQI model in China incorporates indices like overall cracking, rutting, depression, and others [24]. However, related research shows cracks and ruts, respectively, account for over 60% and 30% of pavement distress on Chinese highways [23]. The PQI model does not sufficiently prioritize these predominant failure modes. Furthermore, the PQI calculation equally weights all indices, which may not optimally guide decisions if a particular problem drastically worsens. Fixed weights cannot flexibly reflect actual priorities and importance levels for reconstruction projects.

In summary, while pioneering works, conventional models exhibit several shortcomings limiting applicability to aged pavement performance appraisal for major reconstruction projects. A new approach considering data characteristics and project requirements is warranted to scientifically guide engineering decision-making. The proposed normal cloud framework addresses the abovementioned issues by enabling holistic representation of indicators, weights, and condition fuzziness.

3. Construction of Performance Assessment Indicator System for Existing Asphalt Pavement in Highway Renovation and Expansion Project

The current assessment of asphalt pavement performance in China primarily relies on the PQI evaluation model, with the calculation formula of this model shown in Equation (1).

$$\text{PQI} = w_{\text{PCI}}\text{PCI} + w_{\text{RQI}}\text{RQI} + w_{\text{RDI}}\text{RDI} + w_{\text{PBI}}\text{PBI} + w_{\text{PWI}}\text{PWI} + w_{\text{SRI}}\text{SRI} + w_{\text{PSSI}}\text{PSSI} \quad (1)$$

where PQI, PCI, RQI, RDI, PBI, PWI, SRI, and PSSI, respectively, represent the pavement maintenance quality index, pavement surface condition index, riding quality index, pavement rut depth, pavement bumpiness index, pavement wear index, pavement surface skid resistance index, and pavement structural strength index; w_{PCI}, w_{RQI}, w_{RDI}, w_{SRI}, w_{PBI}, w_{PWI}, and w_{PSSI}, respectively, represent the weights of PCI, RQI, RDI, PQI, SRI, PBI, PWI, and PSSI in the PQI model; and w_{PSSI} takes a value of 0.

According to Equation (1), the PQI model incorporates elements such as surface condition, riding quality, skid resistance, rutting, etc. However, further discussion is needed on the following aspects to evaluate the performance of existing asphalt pavement in highway renovation and expansion projects:

(1) PSSI is not factored into the PQI calculation, rendering the model unable to reflect the pavement's structural condition.

(2) Indicators such as PBI, PWI, and SRI, which are associated with pavement safety, are seldom considered in the pavement design of highway renovation and expansion projects, leading to redundant indicators.
(3) The weights assigned to these indicators are fixed, resulting in a lower PQI evaluation when a particular indicator deteriorates, which may not effectively guide decision-making in the design of the asphalt pavement for highway renovation and expansion projects.

The primary objective of assessing asphalt pavement performance in highway renovation and expansion projects is to gauge the condition of existing asphalt pavement. Thus, when establishing a performance assessment indicator system for existing asphalt pavement in highway renovation and expansion projects, it is crucial to highlight common issues and accurately reflect the pavement's load-bearing capacity. Based on the aforementioned considerations, it is evident that there is a need to develop a new performance assessment indicator system for existing asphalt pavement in highway renovation and expansion projects. Drawing from existing literature [26–28], five asphalt pavement performance evaluation indicators were selected, including RQI, R_r, C_r, P_r, and PSSI, to construct a comprehensive performance assessment indicator system for existing asphalt pavement in highway renovation and expansion projects. These five indicators provide a holistic view of pavement performance across various dimensions, as illustrated in Figure 1.

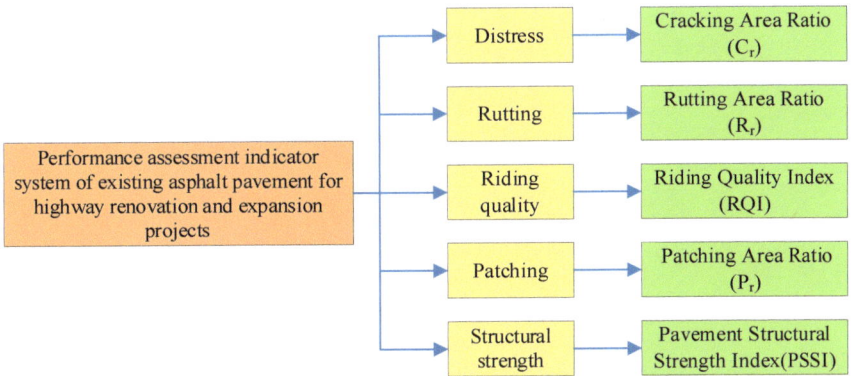

Figure 1. Performance assessment indicator system of existing asphalt pavement in renovation and expansion projects.

The calculation methods for RQI and PSSI are based on the Chinese standard (JTG 5210-2018) [3]. The calculation methods for R_r, C_r, and P_r are presented in Equations (2)–(4), respectively.

$$R_r = \frac{A_R}{A} \times 100\% \qquad (2)$$

$$C_r = \frac{A_C}{A} \times 100\% \qquad (3)$$

$$P_r = \frac{A_P}{A} \times 100\% \qquad (4)$$

where A_R represents the pavement surface area with a rutting depth greater than 7 mm, calculated by multiplying the rutting length (m) by 0.4 m; A_C denotes the crack area, encompassing alligator cracking, block cracking, transverse cracks, and longitudinal cracks, and the area is determined according to the standard JTG 5210-2018 [3]; A_P signifies the patching area; and A represents the survey area.

4. Evaluation Model Based on AH–Entropy and Normal Cloud Model
4.1. Cloud Model-Related Theories

Academician Li Deyi [29] introduced the theory of the cloud model in 1995. The cloud model serves as a framework for converting qualitative concepts into quantitative data, with the cloud digital features and cloud generator playing pivotal roles in its theoretical application. The cloud generator facilitates the bidirectional transformation between qualitative concepts and quantitative data.

4.1.1. Definition of Normal Cloud Model

Definition 1. *Consider U as the universe of discourse, and let C be a qualitative concept in U. If $x \in U$ is a random instantiation of concept C, where x follows a distribution $x \sim N(Ex, En'^2)$, $En' \sim N(En, He^2)$, then the degree of certainty that x belongs to concept C is satisfied by:*

$$\mu(x) = \exp\left\{-\frac{(x-Ex)^2}{2Ex'^2}\right\} \tag{5}$$

The distribution of x within the universe U is referred to as a normal cloud or a second-order normal cloud.

From Definition 1, it is evident that the normal cloud model can capture not only the fuzziness of concepts through membership functions $u(x)$ but also the randomness associated with these membership functions $u(x)$. This highlights a key distinction between the normal cloud model and type-2 fuzzy sets: the normal cloud model is capable of characterizing both the fuzziness of uncertain concepts and their inherent randomness.

4.1.2. Digital Features of Normal Cloud Model

According to the definition in Section 4.1.1, the normal cloud model encompasses three numerical features: Ex, En, and He. Among these, Ex represents the expectation, En denotes the entropy, and He signifies the entropy of entropy, known as hyper entropy. A degenerate cloud drops into a normal distribution when $Ex = 0$. If $Ex = 0$ and $En = 0$, then $x = Ex$ and $\mu(x) = 1$. A larger He indicates a heavier tail in the distribution of the random variable x. Ex serves as the central value of the cloud droplet distribution in the domain space, representing the qualitative concepts most accurately. En measures the uncertainty of qualitative concepts, determined by the randomness and fuzziness of the concept. It not only reflects the probability degree of cloud droplets but also mirrors the fuzziness of qualitative concepts. Hyper entropy He is an uncertainty measure of entropy En, determined by the randomness and fuzziness of entropy, primarily reflecting the aggregation of uncertainty in qualitative concepts [30]. The cloud image comprises a specific number of cloud droplets, as shown in Figure 2. In this study, the number of cloud droplets is set at 3000, determined through a comparison of cloud images composed of varying numbers of cloud droplets.

4.1.3. Positive Cloud Generator

The generator is a specific algorithm employed to convert qualitative concepts and quantitative data in cloud models, with two types: positive cloud generator and backward cloud generator. The positive cloud generator facilitates the transformation from qualitative concepts to quantitative values. The cloud is generated from the cloud parameters (Ex, En, and He), as shown in Figure 3.

Utilizing the cloud drops generated by the positive generator of the cloud model, a normal cloud model for pavement condition evaluation can be established through the following main steps:

Step 1: Obtain the digital feature entropy Ex and hyper entropy He of the cloud model based on the measured data of pavement condition evaluation indicators.

Step 2: Generate a normal random number En' using statistical methods based on the obtained digital features of the cloud model, $En' \sim N(Ex, He^2)$.

Step 3: Calculate the uncertainty value $\mu(x) = \exp\left\{-\frac{(x-Ex)^2}{2En'^2}\right\}$ based on the generated normal random number En' to generate a cloud drop (x,u).

Step 4: Repeat the aforementioned three steps until n cloud drops are generated, and the normal cloud model is depicted by the cloud drops.

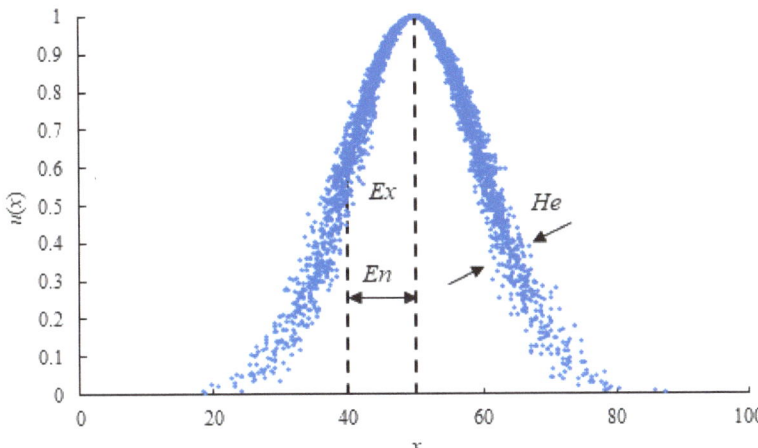

Figure 2. The cloud image (in the figure, $Ex = 50$, $En = 10$, $He = 1$).

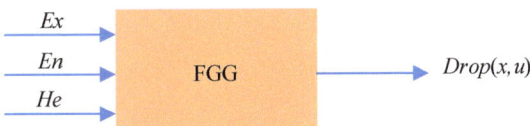

Figure 3. Positive cloud generator.

4.2. Determination of Combination Weights

Prior to employing cloud models to assess pavement performance conditions, it is crucial to determine appropriate indicator weights. Weighting methods encompass subjective, objective, and comprehensive approaches. Subjective methods include the AHP [31], the Delphi method [32], and the scoring method [33], among others. Objective methods comprise the entropy method [34], CRITIC method [35], and principal component analysis (PCA) [36], among others. Subjective methods can reasonably establish weights, ensuring alignment with actual importance; however, they may lack objectivity. Objective methods offer clarity in the calculation process and objective weighting but may fail to capture evaluators' varying degrees of importance placed on different indicators, potentially leading to disparities between attribute weights and actual importance. Upon reviewing existing research findings, the AHP method was selected for subjective weighting, entropy weighting for objective weighting, and a combination of both methods to derive comprehensive weights.

4.2.1. Deriving Subjective Weights with AHP

The calculation procedure of AHP [37] is outlined as follows:

Step 1: Invite experts to conduct pairwise comparisons of the performance evaluation indicators of the current asphalt pavement in highway renovation and expansion projects, assigning scores based on their relative importance. The specific scores and corresponding scale meanings are detailed in Table 1.

Table 1. Fundamental scale of absolute numbers.

Intensity of Importance	Definition	Explanation
1	Equal Importance	Two indicators contribute equally to the objective
3	Moderate importance	Experience and judgement slightly favor one indicator over another
5	Strong importance	Experience and judgement strongly favor one indicator over another
7	Very strong or demonstrated importance	An indicator is favored very strongly over another; its dominance is demonstrated in practice
9	Extreme importance	The evidence favoring one indicator over another is of the highest possible order of affirmation
2, 4, 6, 8	The median value of the above judgment	—
Reciprocals of above	If indicator *i* has one of the above non-zero numbers assigned to it when compared with indicator *j*, then *j* has the reciprocal value when compared with *i*	—

Step 2: Construct a judgment matrix based on expert scoring. Assuming there are n evaluation indicators, the judgment matrix $A = (a_{ij})_{n \times n}$ is as follows:

$$A = \begin{bmatrix} a_{11} & a_{12} & \cdots & a_{n1} \\ a_{11} & a_{22} & \cdots & a_{n2} \\ \cdots & \cdots & \cdots & \cdots \\ a_{n1} & a_{n2} & \cdots & a_{nn} \end{bmatrix} \tag{6}$$

where the element a_{ij} of the judgment matrix is determined from Table 1 based on expert opinions.

Step 3: Compute the maximum eigenvalue $\lambda_{\max}$ of matrix A according to Equation (7) and derive the weight matrix W accordingly:

$$\lambda_{\max} = \sum_{i=1}^{n} \frac{(AW)}{nW_i} = \frac{1}{n}\sum_{i=1}^{n} \frac{(AW)_i}{W_i} \tag{7}$$

where:

$$AW = \begin{bmatrix} (AW)_1 \\ (AW)_2 \\ \cdots \\ (AW)_n \end{bmatrix} = \begin{bmatrix} a_{11} & a_{12} & \cdots & a_{1n} \\ a_{21} & a_{22} & \cdots & a_{2n} \\ \cdots & \cdots & \cdots & \cdots \\ a_{n1} & a_{n2} & \cdots & a_{nm} \end{bmatrix} \times \begin{bmatrix} \omega_1 \\ \omega_2 \\ \cdots \\ \omega_4 \end{bmatrix} \tag{8}$$

Step 4: Consistency verification. This study employed a composite indicator CI for assessing consistency.

4.2.2. Deriving Objective Weights with Entropy

In information theory, the definition of information entropy is as follows:

$$H(x) = -\sum_{i} p(x_i) \ln p(x_i) \tag{9}$$

where, x represents a random variable, and $p(x)$ represents the output probability function, $p(x_i) \in [0, 1]$, $\sum p(x_i) = 1$.

According to Equation (9), a higher variability of the variable corresponds to a greater entropy, signifying that is carries a larger amount of information. Information entropy primarily indicates the extent of variation in indicators. A high entropy for a specific evaluation indicator suggests that the indicator provides more information in the comprehensive evaluation, resulting in a higher corresponding weight. Conversely, a lower weight is assigned. In cases where the evaluation values of an indicator are identical, it conveys no information and is assigned a weight of 0 in the comprehensive evaluation. The weight calculation process for the entropy method is detailed as follows [34,38]:

Step 1: Construct the original matrix. Assuming the number of evaluation indicators is n and the number of evaluation objects is m, an original matrix $B = (b_{ij})_{m \times n}$ can be constructed as follows:

$$B = \begin{bmatrix} b_{11} & b_{12} & \cdots & b_{1n} \\ b_{21} & b_{22} & \cdots & b_{2n} \\ \cdots & \cdots & \cdots & \cdots \\ b_{m1} & b_{m2} & \cdots & b_{mn} \end{bmatrix} \tag{10}$$

where b_{ij} represents the jth indicator detection result of the ith evaluation object.

Step 2: The indices B_{ij} are normalized. The positive indicator is calculated as follows:

$$b'_{ij} = \frac{b_{ij} - \min\{b_{ij}, \ldots, b_{nj}\}}{\max\{b_{1j}, \ldots, b_{nj}\} - \min\{b_{ij}, \ldots, b_{nj}\}} \tag{11}$$

The negative indicator is calculated as follows:

$$b'_{ij} = \frac{\min\{b_{ij}, \ldots, b_{nj}\} - b_{ij}}{\max\{b_{1j}, \ldots, b_{nj}\} - \min\{b_{ij}, \ldots, b_{nj}\}} \tag{12}$$

Step 3: Determining the proportion of evaluation indicators in the scheme is achieved as follows:

$$p_{ij} = \frac{b'_{ij}}{\sum_{i=1}^{m} b'_{ij}}, i = 1, 2, \ldots, m; j = 1, 2, \ldots, n \tag{13}$$

Step 4: Calculate entropy. The computation of entropy for the evaluation indicators is as follows:

$$H_j = -k \sum_{i=1}^{m} p_{ij} \ln p_{ij}, j = 1, 2, \ldots, n, k = \frac{1}{\ln m} \tag{14}$$

where H_j is the entropy of the jth indicator. If $p_{ij} = 0$, then $p_{ij} \ln p_{ij} = 0$, while ensuring $H_j \in [0, 1]$.

Step 5: Calculate entropy weights. The calculation of the entropy weights for the evaluation indicators is as follows:

$$\omega_j = \frac{1 - H_j}{n - \sum_{i=1}^{n} H_j}, j = 1, 2, \ldots, n \tag{15}$$

where w_j is the entropy weight of the jth indicator, $w_j \in [0, 1]$, $\sum_{j=1}^{n} \omega_j = 1$.

4.2.3. Determination of Comprehensive Weights

The formula for calculating the comprehensive weight is as follows [39]:

$$\omega_i = \frac{\omega 1_i \omega 2_i}{\sum_{i=1}^{n} \omega 1_i \omega 2_i} \quad (16)$$

where w_i is the combination weight, and $w1$ and $w2$ are the weights calculated by the AHP and entropy method, respectively.

4.3. Performance Ratings of Evaluation Indicators for Existing Asphalt Pavement in Highway Renovation and Expansion Projects

The PQI model and its sub-indicators categorize the performance of asphalt pavement into five classifications: excellent, good, average, poor, and failed. This study adopted the PQI level classification approach and also categorized the five evaluation indicators of existing asphalt pavement in highway renovation and expansion projects—namely, RQI, R_r, C_r, P_r, and PSSI—into the same five categories: excellent, good, average, poor, and failed. While the performance ratings for RQI and PSSI can be determined using the Chinese standard JTG 5210-2018 [3], there are currently no relevant references for R_r, C_r, and P_r. This study established the performance ratings of R_r, C_r, and P_r. The specific performance ratings of evaluation indicators are shown in Table 2.

Table 2. Performance ratings of evaluation indicators for the existing asphalt pavement in highway renovation and expansion project.

Performance Rating	RQI	R_r	C_r	P_r	PSSI
Excellent	≥90, <100	≥0, <1	≥0, ≤0.5	≥0, ≤5	≥90, <100
Good	≥80, <90	≥1, <5	>0.5, ≤3.5	>5, ≤10	≥80, <90
Average	≥70, <80	≥5, <10	>3.5, ≤10	>10, ≤20	≥70, <80
Poor	≥60, <70	≥10, <25	>10, ≤25	>20, ≤50	≥60, <70
Failed	≥0, <60	≥25, <50	>25, ≤50	>50, ≤80	≥0, <60

4.4. Calculation of Digital Features for Normal Cloud Model

The digital features of the normal cloud model for evaluating the performance condition of existing asphalt pavement in highway renovation and expansion projects can be calculated according to Equations (17)–(19):

$$Ex = (c_{ij}^1 + c_{ij}^2)/2 \quad (17)$$

$$En = (c_{ij}^1 - c_{ij}^2)/2.335 \quad (18)$$

$$He = k \quad (19)$$

where Ex is the expectation; En is the entropy; and He is the entropy of entropy; c_{ij}^1 and c_{ij}^2 are the upper and lower limits of the corresponding performance ratings for each evaluation indicator; and k is a constant that can be adjusted according to the degree of ambiguity of the actual problem. The value of k in this study uniformly takes 0.1.

The normal cloud model for evaluating the performance condition of existing asphalt pavement in highway renovation and expansion projects is constructed using the positive generator. The calculation procedure for the positive generator is detailed in Section 4.1.3. This study adopted a value of n = 3000.

4.5. Calculation of Membership Degree for Normal Cloud Model

Based on the normal cloud model in Section 4.4, the membership degree $\mu(x)$ of each evaluation indicator at different performance levels can be calculated. Utilizing Equation

(20), the comprehensive membership degree of the performance evaluation of existing asphalt pavement in highway renovation and expansion projects is determined.

$$F = \sum_{i=1}^{n} u(x_{ij})\omega_i, i = 1, 2, \ldots, n \quad (20)$$

where F is the comprehensive membership degree of the performance ratings, $u(x_{ij})$ is the membership degree of the ith indicator at the jth evaluation level, and w_i is the comprehensive weight of the ith indicator.

The performance level S for the existing asphalt pavement in highway renovation and expansion projects is determined based on the principle of maximum membership degree.

$$S = \max(F_1, F_2, \ldots, F_n) \quad (21)$$

4.6. Flow of Evaluation System for Combination Weighting and Normal Cloud Model

The construction process of the evaluation model for existing asphalt pavement in highway renovation and expansion projects, based on AHP–entropy and the normal cloud model, is as follows:

(1) Determination of the comprehensive weight of evaluation indicators.
(2) Determination of performance ratings for the indicators.
(3) Calculation of the comprehensive certainty degree of the normal cloud.
(4) Determination of the performance rating for existing asphalt pavement.

The flow of the evaluation system for combination weighting and the normal cloud model is shown in Figure 4.

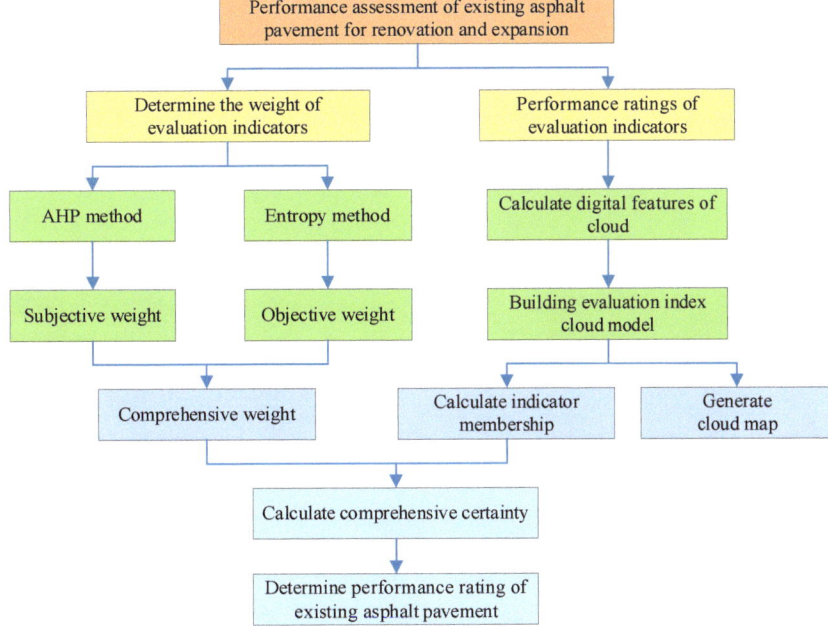

Figure 4. Flow chart of evaluation system for combination weighting and normal cloud model.

5. Case Study

5.1. Engineering Background

The application project for this model is the renovation and expansion project of the Jingjintang Expressway (Tianjin section). The Jingjintang Expressway, approved as the first expressway by the State Council for construction and the first cross-provincial expressway in China, was fully completed and opened to traffic in September 1993, and has been in operation for nearly 30 years. The Tianjin Municipal Transportation Commission approved the application report for the renovation and expansion project of the Jingjintang Expressway (Tianjin section) on 29 December 2022, signifying the official commencement of the project's implementation phase. However, before the implementation of the renovation and expansion project, it is essential to analyze and evaluate the current performance of the existing highway pavement, and then systematically formulate the utilization strategy for the existing pavement structure. Against this backdrop, this study selected sections K67 to K70 to conduct pavement performance inspections and verified this model based on the inspection data. The results for RQI, R_r, C_r, P_r, and PSSI are shown in Table 3. The measurement and calculation methods of RQI and PSSI are in accordance with Chinese standard (JTG 5210-2018) [3], while the calculation methods for R_r, C_r, and P_r are based on Equations (2)–(4).

Table 3. Inspection data of sections K67 to K70.

Number	Stake	Direction	Lane	RQI	R_r	C_r	P_r	PSSI
1	K67–K68	Forward	Light traffic	93.71	0.832	0.311	0.234	99.95
2	K68–K69	Forward	Light traffic	93.06	0.876	0.286	0.167	99.94
3	K69–K70	Forward	Light traffic	93.74	0.756	0.437	0.209	99.99
4	K67–K68	Forward	Heavy traffic	94.01	0.955	0.799	0.289	99.98
5	K68–K69	Forward	Heavy traffic	94.12	0.917	0.741	0.197	99.92
6	K69–K70	Forward	Heavy traffic	94.29	0.866	0.568	0.213	99.98
7	K67–K68	Reverse	Light traffic	94.80	0.452	0.149	0.251	99.73
8	K68–K69	Reverse	Light traffic	94.92	0.291	0.046	0.255	99.82
9	K69–K70	Reverse	Light traffic	95.23	0.856	0.144	0.324	99.81
10	K67–K68	Reverse	Heavy traffic	92.81	0.398	0.091	0.195	99.66
11	K68–K69	Reverse	Heavy traffic	94.50	0.321	0.052	0.312	99.88
12	K69–K70	Reverse	Heavy traffic	93.82	1.672	0.471	0.364	99.89

5.2. Evaluation Results of PQI Model

The PQI model, currently the primary pavement performance evaluation approach in China, was applied to the inspection data from section K67 to K70. Table 4 presents the PQI evaluation results. The PQI rating of the forward heavy traffic lane in sections K67 to K68 and K68 to K69 was good, while the rest of the sections were rated as excellent. Overall, the PQI rating of section K67 to K70 is excellent. Among the various sub-indicators, the PBI and PCI indicators are slightly lower, whereas the RQI, PBI, SRI, and PSSI indicators are better.

Table 4. Evaluation results of the PQI evaluation model.

Number	Stake	Direction	Lane	Sub-Indicators						PQI	Performance Rating
				PCI	RQI	RDI	PBI	SRI	PSSI		
1	K67–K68	Forward	Light traffic	87.67	93.71	94.28	100.00	94.74	99.95	92.41	Excellent
2	K68–K69	Forward	Light traffic	88.08	93.06	92.97	100.00	93.88	99.94	92.08	Excellent
3	K69–K70	Forward	Light traffic	85.81	93.74	93.87	100.00	92.46	99.99	91.48	Excellent
4	K67–K68	Forward	Heavy traffic	81.82	94.01	89.67	100.00	96.35	99.98	89.93	Good
5	K68–K69	Forward	Heavy traffic	81.73	94.12	89.71	100.00	96.65	99.92	89.95	Good

Table 4. Cont.

Number	Stake	Direction	Lane	Sub-Indicators						PQI	Performance Rating
				PCI	RQI	RDI	PBI	SRI	PSSI		
6	K69–K70	Forward	Heavy traffic	82.49	94.29	91.16	100.00	96.27	99.98	90.46	Excellent
7	K67–K68	Reverse	Light traffic	90.90	94.80	97.41	100.00	96.18	99.73	94.48	Excellent
8	K68–K69	Reverse	Light traffic	92.58	94.92	97.65	100.00	95.65	99.82	95.09	Excellent
9	K69–K70	Reverse	Light traffic	93.96	95.23	98.00	100.00	94.76	99.88	95.63	Excellent
10	K67–K68	Reverse	Heavy traffic	90.18	92.81	95.09	75.00	95.93	99.66	90.76	Excellent
11	K68–K69	Reverse	Heavy traffic	91.16	94.50	94.09	100.00	97.57	99.81	94.13	Excellent
12	K69–K70	Reverse	Heavy traffic	85.50	93.82	95.91	100.00	95.11	99.89	91.97	Excellent

The measurement and calculation methods of PCI, RDI, PBI, and SRI are in accordance with Chinese standard (JTG 5210-2018) [3]. Among sub-indicators, PCI and PBI values were slightly lower, while RQI, PWI, SRI, and PSSI performed better. PCI reflects surface distresses like cracking and rutting that predominantly impact Chinese highways [23]. The relatively lower PCI scores, thus, provide useful insight regarding pavement distress conditions. However, the PQI model assigns all sub-indicators equal weighting regardless of predominant distresses or reconstruction priorities.

5.3. Evaluation Results of Normal Cloud Model

Based on the calculation steps outlined in Section 4 and the data presented in Table 3, the calculation results of the combination weighting-normal cloud model can be derived, as illustrated in Table 5. Membership degrees at each performance level ("Excellent", "Good", etc.) were calculated using Equation (20) to determine comprehensive membership values.

Table 5. Evaluation results of normal cloud model.

Number	Membership Degree of Inspection Values in Performance Ratings					Normal Cloud Model	PQI Model
	Excellent	Good	Average	Poor	Failed		
1	0.798	0.374	0.042	0.028	0.002	Excellent	Excellent
2	0.815	0.373	0.041	0.028	0.077	Excellent	Excellent
3	0.646	0.399	0.047	0.029	0.002	Excellent	Excellent
4	0.275	0.519	0.062	0.032	0.004	Good	Good
5	0.307	0.500	0.059	0.031	0.002	Good	Good
6	0.449	0.445	0.052	0.030	0.002	Excellent	Excellent
7	0.970	0.254	0.009	0.020	0.001	Excellent	Excellent
8	0.640	0.265	0.033	0.024	0.002	Excellent	Excellent
9	0.734	0.334	0.037	0.027	0.002	Excellent	Excellent
10	0.726	0.283	0.034	0.025	0.002	Excellent	Excellent
11	0.660	0.269	0.033	0.025	0.002	Excellent	Excellent
12	0.093	0.668	0.080	0.037	0.003	Good	Excellent

Table 5 shows the membership degrees and resultant model/PQI ratings. Several notable aspects emerged:

(a) Sections rated "Good" by PQI (forward lanes K67–K68 and K68–K69) exhibited higher membership in the "Good" class using the cloud model (0.519, 0.500).

(b) Section K69–K70 reverse lane demonstrated higher membership in "Good" (0.668) versus "Excellent" (0.093).

(c) Other sections generally aligned between the two approaches, with membership heavily favoring the identical rating.

These results demonstrate the cloud model's ability to more sensitively represent indicator fuzziness and randomness, generating intermediate membership degrees where conventional methods deliver absolute ratings. This continuous evaluation scale is valuable for reconstruction project planning requiring graded condition assessments.

5.4. Results of 3D Radar Detection

To validate the results obtained from the normal cloud model, 3D ground-penetrating radar (GPR) detection was conducted on the reverse heavy traffic lanes of sections K68–K69 and K69–K70. GPR is a well-established nondestructive technique that has seen increasing usage for pavement subsurface investigation to supplement visual condition surveys.

A Malå ProEx 600 MHz shielded antenna system was employed for data collection. This frequency facilitated the necessary 1–1.2 m penetration depth required to evaluate key structural layers like the asphalt–base interface and aggregate base essential for reconstruction decision-making. Continuous profiling was performed at 14 channels spaced 10.5 cm along wheel-paths and between using an integrated positioning console. This configuration ensured collection of high-resolution 3D condition imagery suitable for detailed structural analysis. The 3D radar detection and processing software utilized in this study were provided by Chengdu Guimu Robot Co., Ltd. Chengdu Guimu Robot Co., Ltd. is a supplier of pavement non-destructive testing equipment located in Chengdu, China.

The 3D radar detection results were assessed based on the impact area, with the calculation method for the impact area being the sum of the areas affected by looseness, sub-grade settlement, and cracking. The calculation method for the cracking impact area involved multiplying the cracking length by a width of 0.4 m. All areas represented horizontally projected areas. The data presented in Table 6 were automatically computed using the software provided by Chengdu Guimu Robot Co., Ltd.

Table 6. 3D radar detection results (reverse heavy traffic lane).

Stake	Layer	Looseness (m^2)	Cracking (m^2)	Settlement (m^2)	Total Area (m^2)
K68–K69	Base layer	1224.6	0.0	/	
	Subbase layer	32.2	46.4	/	1326.0
	Subgrade	0.0	/	22.9	
K69–K70	Base layer	1667.7	0.0	/	
	Subbase layer	10.7	0.0	/	1678.0
	Subgrade	1.5	/	0.0	

Results showed that the reverse heavy traffic lane of section K69–K69 exhibited various types of structural issues, including looseness, cracking, and settlement, whereas there was only one type of issue in the reverse heavy traffic lane of section K69–K70. However, in terms of impact area, the total area affected by internal structural issues in the reverse heavy traffic lane of section K69–K70 was 1678 m^2, while it was 1326 m^2 in the reverse heavy traffic lane of section K68–K69. The total area affected by internal issues in the reverse heavy traffic lane of section K69–K70 was 126.5% of that in the reverse heavy traffic lane of section K68–K69. Therefore, based on the results of the 3D radar detection, the performance rating of the reverse heavy traffic lane in section K68–K69 was better than that of the reverse heavy traffic lane in section K69–K70.

In summary, these subsurface conditions validated the normal cloud model evaluation of the reverse lane in section K69–K70 as "good" versus the PQI assessment of "excellent". GPR objectively verifies increased subsurface impact warranting a lower rating than assigned previously. This reinforces the normal cloud approach's sensitivity in differentiating conditions where conventional methods may overlook subtle deterioration.

6. Conclusions

The AHP and entropy methods are utilized to determine subjective and objective weights, respectively, and a combination of these two methods is employed to derive comprehensive weights for evaluating indicators of existing asphalt pavement in highway reconstruction and expansion projects. Building upon the derived indicator weights, a performance assessment model for existing asphalt pavement in highway renovation and expansion projects is established, integrating combination weighting and the normal cloud model. This model is applied and validated in the renovation and expansion project of the Jingjintang Expressway (Tianjin section) highway reconstruction and expansion project. The research findings can be summarized as follows:

(a) The normal cloud framework addressed limitations of conventional methods by addressing input data characteristics and reconstructing the fuzziness and randomness inherent to pavement evaluation.

(b) Application to a reconstruction project case study yielded evaluation results demonstrating good consistency with objective 3D GPR detection. The cloud model exhibited an enhanced ability to discern marginal variations in condition and generate continuous membership outputs versus absolute ratings. This improves its utility for reconstruction and extension planning demand of graded condition assessments.

In conclusion, the proposed model establishes an innovative and practical means of appraising existing pavement informed by engineering fundamentals. It provides reconstruction and extension project managements with an effective decision support tool capturing input ambiguities. The cloud theoretic methodology also displays potential for continued refinement and wider pavement management applications

Author Contributions: Conceptualization, Y.X. and X.S.; methodology, Y.X.; software, X.S.; validation, Y.Y.; formal analysis, Y.Y.; investigation, Y.X. and X.S.; resources, Y.X.; data curation, Y.X.; writing—original draft preparation, Y.X. and X.S.; writing—review and editing, X.S. and Y.Y.; visualization, X.S.; supervision, Y.Y.; project administration, Y.X.; funding acquisition, Y.X. All authors have read and agreed to the published version of the manuscript.

Funding: This research was funded by Chongqing Transportation Bureau Science and Technology Project, grant number 2021-04.

Institutional Review Board Statement: Not applicable.

Informed Consent Statement: Not applicable.

Data Availability Statement: The raw data supporting the conclusions of this article will be made available by the authors on request.

Conflicts of Interest: The authors declare that this study received funding from Chongqing Transportation Bureau Science and Technology. The funder had the following involvement with the study: Acquisition and analysis of pavement detection data.

References

1. Cheng, Y.L. Construction Technology Urumqi outer ring expressway road reconstruction project expansion. *Appl. Mech. Mater.* **2014**, *587*, 965–970. [CrossRef]
2. Pan, X.; Xu, M.; Jia, J.; Xia, Y.; Chen, Q. Evaluation model of highway reconstruction and expansion scheme based on multiple attribute decision making. *Adv. Civ. Eng.* **2022**, *2022*, 3764557. [CrossRef]
3. JTG 5210-2018; Highway Performance Assessment Standards. T.M.o.C.o.t.P.R.o.: Beijing, China, 2018.
4. Xiong, C.; Yu, J.; Zhang, X. Use of NDT systems to investigate pavement reconstruction needs and improve maintenance treatment decision-making. *Int. J. Pavement Eng.* **2023**, *24*, 2011872. [CrossRef]
5. Li, J.; Liao, C.; Xiong, C.; Chen, C.; Wang, Z.; Wu, C.; Li, S.; Li, W.; Xu, X. Research on distresses detection, evaluation and maintenance decision-making for highway pavement in reconstruction and expansion project. *Case Stud. Constr. Mater.* **2023**, *19*, e02451. [CrossRef]
6. Soncim, S.P.; De Oliveira, I.C.S.; Santos, F.B. Development of fuzzy models for asphalt pavement performance. *Acta Scientiarum. Technol.* **2019**, *41*, e35626. [CrossRef]

7. Zhang, D.-b.; Li, X.; Zhang, Y.; Zhang, H. Prediction method of asphalt pavement performance and corrosion based on grey system theory. *Int. J. Corros.* **2019**, *2019*, 2534794. [CrossRef]
8. Vyas, V.; Singh, A.P.; Srivastava, A. Prediction of asphalt pavement condition using FWD deflection basin parameters and artificial neural networks. *Road Mater. Pavement Des.* **2021**, *22*, 2748–2766. [CrossRef]
9. Li, J.; Wei, H.; Yao, Y.; Hu, X.; Wang, L. Contribution modeling on condition evaluation of asphalt pavement using uncertainty measurement and entropy theory. *Adv. Mater. Sci. Eng.* **2021**, *2021*, 9995926. [CrossRef]
10. Wei, H.; Liu, Y.; Li, J.; Liu, L.; Liu, H. Reliability Investigation of Pavement Performance Evaluation Based on Blind-Number Theory: A Confidence Model. *Appl. Sci.* **2023**, *13*, 8794. [CrossRef]
11. Sun, Q.; Wang, G.; Sui, Y.; Zakaria, I. Pavement Performance Evaluation of Asphalt Expressway Based on Machine Learning Support Vector Machine. *Wirel. Commun. Mob. Comput.* **2022**, *2022*, 6011916. [CrossRef]
12. Shen, J.; Du, S.; Luo, Y.; Luo, J.; Yang, Q.; Chen, Z.F. Method and application research on fuzzy comprehensive evaluation based on cloud model. *Fuzzy Syst. Math.* **2012**, *26*, 115.
13. Guo, X.; Liu, S.; Wu, L.; Gao, Y.; Yang, Y. A multi-variable grey model with a self-memory component and its application on engineering prediction. *Eng. Appl. Artif. Intell.* **2015**, *42*, 82–93. [CrossRef]
14. Rosa, J.P.; Guerra, D.J.; Horta, N.C.; Martins, R.M.; Lourenço, N.C. Overview of Artificial Neural Networks. In *Using Artificial Neural Networks for Analog Integrated Circuit Design Automation*; Springer: Cham, Switzerland, 2020; pp. 21–44.
15. Van der Auweraer, S.; Boute, R.N.; Syntetos, A.A. Forecasting spare part demand with installed base information: A review. *Int. J. Forecast.* **2019**, *35*, 181–196. [CrossRef]
16. Li, D.; Cheung, D.; Shi, X.; Ng, V. Uncertainty reasoning based on cloud models in controllers. *Comput. Math. Appl.* **1998**, *35*, 99–123. [CrossRef]
17. Fu, B.; Li, D.-G.; Wang, M.-K. Review and prospect on research of cloud model. *Appl. Res. Comput.* **2011**, *28*, 420–426.
18. Liu, W.; Zhu, J.; Chiclana, F. Large-scale group consensus hybrid strategies with three-dimensional clustering optimisation based on normal cloud models. *Inf. Fusion* **2023**, *94*, 66–91. [CrossRef]
19. Mattioli, V.; Basili, P.; Bonafoni, S.; Ciotti, P.; Westwater, E.J. Analysis and improvements of cloud models for propagation studies. *Radio Sci.* **2009**, *44*, 1–13. [CrossRef]
20. Yang, J.; Wang, G.; Liu, Q.; Guo, Y.; Liu, Y.; Gan, W.; Liu, Y. Retrospect and prospect of research of normal cloud model. *Chin. J. Comput.* **2018**, *3*, 724–744.
21. Xiao, M.; Fan, L. Study on Comprehensive Evaluation of Pavement Condition Based on Comprehensive Integration Weighting Method and Cloud Model. In *Green and Intelligent Technologies for Sustainable and Smart Asphalt Pavements*; CRC Press: Boca Raton, FL, USA, 2021; pp. 437–444.
22. Wei, Z.; Li, J.; Zhang, N. Performance Evaluation Model of Urban Road Asphalt Pavement Based on Attribute Hierarchical Model and Entropy Weight Method. In Proceedings of the CICTP 2022, Changsha, China, 8–11 July 2022; pp. 2221–2231.
23. He, J.; Shao, L.; Li, Y.; Wang, K.; Liu, W. Pavement damage identification and evaluation in UAV-captured images using gray level co-occurrence matrix and cloud model. *J. King Saud Univ. Comput. Inf. Sci.* **2023**, *35*, 101762. [CrossRef]
24. Qin, R.; Li, T.; Liu, H. Study of the Evaluation Model about Old Asphalt Pavement Service Performance of Freeway. In Proceedings of the 2009 International Conference on New Trends in Information and Service Science, Beijing, China, 30 June–2 July 2009; pp. 187–190.
25. Yang, S.; Guo, M.; Liu, X.; Wang, P.; Li, Q.; Liu, H. Highway performance evaluation index in semiarid climate region based on fuzzy mathematics. *Adv. Mater. Sci. Eng.* **2019**, *2019*, 6708102. [CrossRef]
26. Onayev, A.; Swei, O. IRI deterioration model for asphalt concrete pavements: Capturing performance improvements over time. *Constr. Build. Mater.* **2021**, *271*, 121768. [CrossRef]
27. Marcelino, P.; Lurdes Antunes, M.d.; Fortunato, E. Comprehensive performance indicators for road pavement condition assessment. *Struct. Infrastruct. Eng.* **2018**, *14*, 1433–1445. [CrossRef]
28. Li, J.; Qin, Y.; Zhang, X.; Shan, B.; Liu, C. Emission Characteristics, Environmental Impacts, and Health Risks of Volatile Organic Compounds from Asphalt Materials: A State-ofthe-Art Review. *Energy Fuels* **2024**, *38*, 4787–4802. [CrossRef]
29. Li, D.; Du, Y. *Artificial Intelligence with Uncertainty*; CRC Press: Boca Raton, FL, USA, 2017.
30. Gong, Y.; Dai, L.; Hu, N. A triangular cloud model and cloud generator algorithm. *Open Cybern. Syst. J.* **2016**, *10*, 192–201. [CrossRef]
31. Vaidya, O.S.; Kumar, S. Analytic hierarchy process: An overview of applications. *Eur. J. Oper. Res.* **2006**, *169*, 1–29. [CrossRef]
32. Sprenkle, D.H.; Piercy, F.P. *Research Methods in Family Therapy*; Guilford Press: New York, NY, USA, 2005.
33. Ramadhan, R.H.; Al-Abdul Wahhab, H.I.; Duffuaa, S.O. The use of an analytical hierarchy process in pavement maintenance priority ranking. *J. Qual. Maint. Eng.* **1999**, *5*, 25–39. [CrossRef]
34. Golan, A.; Maasoumi, E. Information theoretic and entropy methods: An overview. *Econom. Rev.* **2008**, *27*, 317–328. [CrossRef]
35. Diakoulaki, D.; Mavrotas, G.; Papayannakis, L. Determining objective weights in multiple criteria problems: The critic method. *Comput. Oper. Res.* **1995**, *22*, 763–770. [CrossRef]
36. Paul, L.C.; Suman, A.A.; Sultan, N. Methodological analysis of principal component analysis (PCA) method. *Int. J. Comput. Eng. Manag.* **2013**, *16*, 32–38.
37. Saaty, T.L. Decision making with the analytic hierarchy process. *Int. J. Comput. Eng. Manag.* **2008**, *1*, 83–98. [CrossRef]

38. Li, Y.; Wang, Y.; Wu, Q.; Gu, X. The Quality Assessment of Pavement Performance Using the Entropy Weight-Variable Fuzzy Sets Model. *Math. Probl. Eng.* **2022**, *2022*, 5016050. [CrossRef]
39. Al-Aomar, R. A combined ahp-entropy method for deriving subjective and objective criteria weights. *Int. J. Ind. Eng.* **2010**, *17*, 12–24.

Disclaimer/Publisher's Note: The statements, opinions and data contained in all publications are solely those of the individual author(s) and contributor(s) and not of MDPI and/or the editor(s). MDPI and/or the editor(s) disclaim responsibility for any injury to people or property resulting from any ideas, methods, instructions or products referred to in the content.

Article

Reliability Investigation of Pavement Performance Evaluation Based on Blind-Number Theory: A Confidence Model

Hui Wei [1,2,3], Yunyao Liu [2], Jue Li [4,*], Lihao Liu [4] and Honglin Liu [2]

1. Engineering Research Center of Catastrophic Prophylaxis and Treatment of Road & Traffic Safety of Ministry of Education, Changsha University of Science & Technology, Changsha 410114, China; wh@csust.edu.cn
2. School of Traffic & Transportation Engineering, Changsha University of Science & Technology, Changsha 410114, China; 21101030060@stu.csust.edu.cn (Y.L.); hlliu@huuc.edu.cn (H.L.)
3. Xiangjiang Laboratory, Changsha 410205, China
4. College of Traffic & Transportation, Chongqing Jiaotong University, Chongqing 400074, China; aprleo@mails.cqjtu.edu.cn
* Correspondence: lijue1207@cqjtu.edu.cn

Abstract: The evaluation of in-service pavements' performance is a complex system that encompasses a variety of uncertain factors. These uncertainties include random, fuzzy, gray, and unascertained information, and their interrelationships are intricate, making comprehensive quantification unachievable. Nonetheless, current highway management organizations rely on a comprehensive indicator, namely, the Pavement Quality Index (PQI), to assess the level of pavement performance. This paper introduces a novel approach that employs blind number theory to evaluate the reliability of pavement performance test data. The proposed method aims to enhance the representativeness of PQI and is demonstrated using detection data from highway asphalt pavements in Hunan Province. The method takes into account the probability distribution characteristics of evaluation metrics and incorporates the blind number representation format of PQI. A confidence model for pavement performance evaluation is established to assess the reliability of pavement detection results. The method also integrates expert empowerment and entropy weight to consider both the subjectivity of evaluation and the objectivity of measured data. The method presented in this study has demonstrated superior performance compared to traditional evaluation index systems. This is attributed to the effective utilization of blind information to accurately characterize the discreteness of pavement performance indexes. Consequently, pavement performance can be quantitatively graded based on anticipated issues and data.

Keywords: pavement performance evaluation; reliability study; confidence model; entropy weight method; blind-number theory

1. Introduction

In the field of pavement engineering, one crucial aspect that affects the grade of pavement performance is the occurrence of distresses or diseases in asphalt pavements over time [1]. These distresses can manifest in various forms, such as cracks, potholes, rutting, and surface deterioration [2]. The pavement management system (PMS) encompasses a comprehensive range of interconnected activities, including road planning, design, construction, maintenance, evaluation, and research [3]. Its primary objective is to optimize the utilization of various resources such as capital, labor, machinery, materials, and energy [4]. Within the PMS framework, the maintenance management system plays a crucial role. It aims to maximize available resources to maintain optimal pavement performance throughout the entire life cycle [5]. Evaluating the service performance of pavements at different stages of their life cycle is essential to proactively address necessary repairs before they reach critical failure conditions [6]. By implementing maintenance management systems, it becomes possible to reduce maintenance and repair costs while ensuring the safety of transportation networks [7]. The assessment of pavement performance is a key component of maintenance management and directly impacts the quality of highway service [8]. Therefore, accurately evaluating the grade of pavement performance is of paramount importance.

To enhance the objectivity and persuasiveness of the evaluation process, numerous quantitative analysis studies have been conducted to assess pavement performance. Majidifard et al. [9] employed novel machine learning techniques to predict rut depth, thereby enhancing the accuracy of rut curves. Fan and Dai [10] devised a comprehensive pavement performance evaluation method that considers five performance indexes. Olowosulu et al. [11] utilized a fuzzy evaluation method, presenting a novel framework for accurate assessment and analysis of flexible pavement performance. Li et al. [12] proposed an enhanced entropy weight analytic hierarchy process for evaluating pavement maintenance. In recent years, evaluation models have expanded to machine learning models, including the BP neural network [13], NARX neural network [14], and TOPSIS theory [15]. These models employ single or comprehensive evaluation indexes to gain insights into the actual pavement condition, thereby providing a scientific foundation for maintenance decision-making schemes and designs [16,17]. However, current research on pavement performance evaluation primarily focuses on single evaluation indexes, with limited consideration given to the weight of individual evaluation indexes, comprehensive evaluation methods, and reliability analysis of comprehensive evaluation indexes.

With the rapid expansion of highway transportation demand in China, there has been significant construction of highway infrastructure, leading to increased research on pavement performance evaluation methods [18]. The Pavement Quality Index (PQI) is a comprehensive indicator that encompasses sub-indexes such as the Pavement Condition Index (PCI), Riding Quality Index (RQI), Rutting Depth Index (RDI), and Skidding Resistance Index (SRI) [19]. These sub-indexes are weighted to derive the comprehensive evaluation index, which provides an overall assessment of pavement condition [20]. In engineering applications, the evaluation of pavement performance often relies on the average value and discrete grade of the performance indexes [21]. The average value approach calculates the mean of the observed data along the entire road section, while the discrete grade approach involves statistical analysis to determine the proportions of excellent, good, fair, poor, and very poor road conditions based on unit pavement performance evaluation results [22]. However, the evaluation method based on the average value tends to compress the information contained in the data, potentially leading to the neglect of important details. Predictions based solely on the average value may result in symmetric dispersion around the average index value, which can misrepresent the actual pavement condition [23]. Moreover, the process of converting continuous unit-kilometer metrics to discrete pavement levels can mask detailed information about pavement performance, further contributing to evaluation inaccuracies [24]. To address these limitations, it is important to consider more advanced evaluation methods that capture the variability and nuances of pavement performance [25]. This may involve incorporating additional factors, such as the weight of individual evaluation indexes, the use conditions of each measuring point, and the reliability analysis of the comprehensive evaluation index [26]. Utilizing more sophisticated techniques can improve the objectivity and accuracy of pavement performance evaluation, providing a solid foundation for maintenance decision-making and design.

In this study, the probability function of each evaluation index parameter is established to gain insights into the probability distribution characteristics of pavement performance evaluation metrics. Fitting tests are conducted to analyze various influencing factors. By utilizing probability distribution methods, it becomes possible to analyze potential indicators per kilometer without losing information due to averaging and discretization of evaluation results [27]. This approach ensures the maximum retention and utilization of all indicator data at the unit kilometer level. However, it is important to note that due to the different distribution forms of variables, a unified equation form cannot be adopted when dealing with each index. Each evaluation index may follow a distinct probability distribution, and therefore, specific distribution functions need to be employed for accurate analysis. Furthermore, pavement performance evaluation often involves uncertain information, including randomness, fuzziness, gray areas, and unascertained factors [28]. Incorporating statistical techniques to handle uncertainty becomes crucial in accurately assessing pavement performance and making informed decisions. By considering the probability distribution characteristics and addressing uncertainties, this study aims to enhance the understanding of pavement performance evaluation and provide a more comprehensive and reliable assessment of the condition of highway pavements.

Therefore, this study presents the concept of blind-number theory and its application in evaluating the performance of pavement surfaces. A reliability framework for the pavement evaluation indicator using blind numbers is proposed. This framework integrates obscured data into the evaluation system, ensuring that it remains unaffected by probability distribution functions. By clearly defining the evaluation grade and its corresponding confidence, the rigor of the evaluation process is enhanced.

2. Testing Methods for Pavement Performances

2.1. Evaluation Indexes and Data Collection Methods

Accurate assessment of pavement performance is crucial in maintenance management, as it plays a pivotal role in determining the condition of pavements. Various factors such as climate, region, traffic load, and pavement materials contribute to the deterioration of pavements, leading to issues like ruts, cracks, pits, and oil flooding. The Highway Performance Assessment Standard (JTG H20) requires the use of the PQI for evaluating pavement performance in China. The PQI is calculated based on the PCI, RQI, RDI, and SRI, as defined in Equation (1).

$$PQI = w_{PCI}PCI + w_{RQI}RQI + w_{RDI}RDI + w_{SRI}SRI \tag{1}$$

where w_{PQI}, w_{RQI}, w_{RDI}, and w_{SRI} are the calculated weights of PCI, RQI, RDI, and SRI, respectively.

The data for the test object were collected using a laser-based 3D road intelligent detection vehicle [29]. This vehicle enabled comprehensive coverage of all the pavement performance indexes mentioned in the study. The collection of pavement condition data was carried out on expressways located in plain, hilly, and mountainous terrains of a province in China. These specific sections were carefully chosen to represent a diverse range of engineering geological conditions, variations in traffic load, complexities in pavement structure, and performance characteristics of pavement materials. The outcomes of the investigation provide valuable insights into how different conditions influence the probability distribution of pavement performance evaluation indicators.

2.2. Probability Distribution Analyses of Evaluation Indexes

In this study, several probability distributions, including Normal, Log-Logistic, Log-Logistic (3P), Logistic, and Lognormal, were used to analyze the probability distribution characteristics of the evaluation indexes. By employing different probability functions [30], probability distribution characteristics of the pavement performance evaluation indexes were determined.

To validate the appropriateness of the selected probability distributions for the evaluation indexes, fitting tests were conducted using the probability functions. These tests aimed to assess how well the probability distributions fit the observed data for the pavement performance evaluation indicators. Table 1 lists three typical fitting methods of probability results, providing insights into the suitability of the probability distributions for the evaluation indexes.

Table 1. Fitting test method of pavement performance evaluation index.

Type	Test Method
Kolmogorov–Smirnov Test	$D = \max\limits_{1 \leq i \leq n} (F(x_i) - \frac{i-1}{n}, \frac{i}{n} - F(x_i))$
Anderson–Darling Goodness Test	$A^2 = -n - \frac{1}{n}\sum\limits_{i=1}^{n}(2i-1) \cdot [\ln F(X_i) + \ln(1 - F(X_{n-i+1}))]$
Chi-Squared Goodness Test	$\chi^2 = \sum\limits_{i=1}^{k}\frac{(O_i - E_i)^2}{E_i}, E_i = F(x_2) - F(x_1)$

In the context of statistical hypothesis testing, H_0 represents the assumption that the observed data conform to the specified distribution, while H_1 suggests that the data deviate from the specified distribution.

Let $x_1, \ldots, x_n$ denote a series of random samples extracted from the theoretical probability density function $F(x)$, with n representing the number of sample sequences. Based on the predetermined significance level (typically 0.05) in the hypothesis test, the critical value is determined by referencing the appropriate table. If the test statistic D exceeds the critical value, the null hypothesis H_0 is rejected; otherwise, it is accepted.

$F_n(x)$ represents the empirical cumulative probability density function. By comparing the test statistic A^2 with the critical value size of each distribution cluster, it is determined at the given significance level α (e.g., 0.01, 0.05, etc.) whether to accept or reject the null hypothesis H_0.

O_i is the observed frequency of the sample falling in the i-th interval, whereas E_i signifies the expected frequency of the sample falling within the same interval. $F(x)$ denotes the probability density function of the calculated sample, and x_1 and x_2 specify the range of interval i.

2.3. Analysis Framework Pavement Performance Reliability

2.3.1. Principle of Blind-Number Theory

According to the degree of completeness, information can be categorized into two types: deterministic information and uncertain information. Deterministic information refers to information that is known to be complete and certain. On the other hand, uncertain information refers to information that is known to be incomplete and uncertain. Specifically, many factors affect pavement performance, such as pavement structure, traffic volume, pavement and base materials, engineering geological conditions, and environmental factors. All of these influencing factors have uncertainty, and their performance on pavement performance varies.

When dealing with incomplete and uncertain information, mathematical methods are commonly used to process blind information comprehensively. Blind information refers to information that lacks complete knowledge or certainty. To handle blind information, a mathematical tool called a blind number is utilized. A blind number is essentially a gray function that operates on a set of rational gray numbers, with its value varying between 0 and 1.

The study supposes that $H(I)$ represents the set of interval-type gray numbers formed by the gray interval a_i, where each a_i belongs to $H(I)$. If $\alpha_i \in [0, 1]$ for $i = 1, 2, \ldots, n$, the gray function in $H(I)$ can be defined as $f(x)$, as shown in Equation (2). If $i \neq j$, $a_i \neq a_j$, and $\sum^n \alpha_i = \alpha \leq 1$, the $f(x)$ should be called a blind number, which can be expressed by Equation (3) [30].

$$f(x) = \begin{cases} \alpha_i, & x = a_i \ (i = 1, 2, \cdots, n) \\ 0, & other \end{cases} \quad (2)$$

$$\{[a_1, a_n], f(x)\} \quad (3)$$

where n is the order of $f(x)$; α_i is the confidence of the value a_i of $f(x)$; α is the total confidence of $f(x)$. The greater n, the greater the accuracy of the blind number $f(x)$.

The probability distributions described by Equations (3) and (4) represent the likelihoods associated with various intervals of the blind numbers $A^\wedge$ and $B^\wedge$. The symbols "$\oplus$" "$\ominus$" "$\otimes$" "$\oslash$" denote the four arithmetic operations applied to the blind numbers. $A^\wedge$ and $B^\wedge$ can be any element within the matrix of possible values, expressed as $A \otimes B$, where $i = 1, 2 \ldots k$ and $j = 1, 2 \ldots m$. To illustrate the blind number operation using addition, this study considers $x_1, x_2, \ldots, x_k$ and $y_1, y_2, \ldots, y_n$ as lists of real numbers in descending order, referred to as the sequence of possible values for $A^\wedge$ and $B^\wedge$. The vertical side of a matrix is denoted by $x_1, x_2, \ldots, x_k$, while the horizontal edge is represented by $y_1, y_2, \ldots, y_m$. The bounded matrix is perpendicular horizontal and vertical axes, and the possible values of $A^\wedge$ and $B^\wedge$ are associated with the edges and matrices, as depicted in Table 2.

$$A^\wedge = f(x) = \begin{cases} \alpha_i, x = x_i (i = 1, 2, \ldots k) \\ 0 \end{cases} \quad (4)$$

$$B^\wedge = g(x) = \begin{cases} \beta_j, x = y_j (i = 1, 2, \ldots m) \\ 0 \end{cases} \quad (5)$$

Table 2. The possible values of $A^\wedge$ and $B^\wedge$ with edge sum matrix.

x_1	$x_1 + y_1$	$x_1 + y_2$	...	$x_1 + y_j$	...	$x_1 + y_m$
x_2	$x_2 + y_1$	$x_2 + y_2$	...	$x_2 + y_j$	...	$x_2 + y_m$
⋮	⋮	⋮	⋮	⋮	⋮	⋮
x_i	$x_i + y_1$	$x_i + y_2$	...	$x_i + y_j$	...	$x_i + y_m$
⋮	⋮	⋮	⋮	⋮	⋮	⋮
x_k	$x_k + y_1$	$x_k + y_2$	...	$x_k + y_j$	...	$x_k + y_m$
	y_1	y_2	...	y_j	...	y_m

Based on the above assumptions, the confidence of the event $A/B \geq r$, is shown in Equation (6).

$$P\{A/B \geq r\} = \sum_{x_i - y_j \geq r} f(x_i) g(y_j) \quad (6)$$

where B can be the classification threshold of a certain evaluation standard, usually a real value; r is a known real number determined according to the requirements of the actual problem.

Construct the confidence matrix with edge product for $A^\wedge$ and $B^\wedge$, where $f(x_1), f(x_2), \ldots, f(x_k)$ and $g(y_1), g(y_2), \ldots, g(y_k)$ represent the vertical and horizontal sides of the matrix with an edge, referred to as the confidence sequence of $A^\wedge$ and $B^\wedge$. The horizontal and vertical axes of the matrix with an edge are perpendicular lines. The resulting confidence matrix obtained by performing an edge product on $A^\wedge$ and $B^\wedge$ is presented in Table 3.

Table 3. The confidence band-edge product matrix of $A^\wedge$ and $B^\wedge$.

$f(x_1)$	$f(x_1)g(y_1)$	$f(x_1)g(y_2)$	...	$f(x_1)g(y_i)$	...	$f(x_1)g(y_m)$
$f(x_2)$	$f(x_2)g(y_1)$	$f(x_2)g(y_2)$	...	$f(x_2)g(y_i)$	...	$f(x_2)g(y_m)$
⋮	⋮	⋮	⋮	⋮	⋮	⋮
$f(x_i)$	$f(x_i)g(y_1)$	$f(x_i)g(y_2)$	...	$f(x_i)g(y_i)$	...	$f(x_i)g(y_m)$
⋮	⋮	⋮	⋮	⋮	⋮	⋮
$f(x_k)$	$f(x_k)g(y_1)$	$f(x_k)g(y_2)$	...	$f(x_k)g(y_i)$	...	$f(x_k)g(y_m)$
	$g(y_1)$	$g(y_2)$	...	$g(y_i)$	...	$g(y_m)$

2.3.2. Confidence Modeling of Pavement Quality Index

Due to the inherent uncertainty in pavement detection information, all indicators of pavement performance evaluation conform to specific probability distributions. Based on the aforementioned blind number theory, if the PCI, RQI, RDI, and SRI are all considered blind numbers, they can be expressed as follows:

$$P\hat{CI} = \{[PCI_1, PCI_n], f_1(PCI)\} \tag{7}$$

$$R\hat{QI} = \{[RQI_1, RQI_m], f_2(RQI)\} \tag{8}$$

$$R\hat{DI} = \{[RDI_1, RDI_i], f_3(PCI)\} \tag{9}$$

$$S\hat{RI} = \{[SRI_1, SRI_j], f_4(SRI)\} \tag{10}$$

Therefore, this study uses the blind number representation of the pavement quality index, as shown in Equation (10).

$$P\hat{QI} = w_{PCI} \otimes P\hat{CI} \oplus w_{RQI} \otimes R\hat{QI} \oplus w_{RDI} \otimes R\hat{DI} \oplus w_{SRI} \otimes S\hat{RI} \tag{11}$$

In reliability calculations, the reliability of the representative value is defined as the ratio of the occurrence frequency of a single indicator to the total frequency. The credibility of the representative value can be determined using the traditional probability density function method. In cases where the amount of data is limited, the frequency of data occurrence can also be analyzed. The thresholds for different performance levels in pavement performance evaluation are established: 90 for excellent, 80 for good, 70 for medium, and 60 for bad. According to the blind number theory, the reliability of pavement serviceability for excellent and good grades can be indicated in Equations (12) and (13).

$$R_{P\hat{QI}}(90) = \frac{1}{90} \otimes P\hat{QI} \tag{12}$$

$$R_{P\hat{QI}}(80) = \frac{1}{80} \otimes P\hat{QI} \tag{13}$$

3. Analysis of Examples

3.1. Statistical Result Analysis

To fulfill the requirements of probability function analysis and fitting tests for pavement performance evaluation metrics, an operational program was developed for analysis and calculation. The statistical results are shown in Table 4. The probability density and fitting analysis results of PCI, RQI, RDI, SRI, and other indicators are presented in Figure 1. The analysis of the results indicated that when comparing PCI, RQI, RDI, and SRI using the Kolmogorov–Smirnov and Anderson–Darling test methods, the Log-Logistic (3P) distribution provided the most suitable fitting results. When using the Chi-Squared method for comparison, the Log-Logistic (3P) distribution yielded the best fitting results for RQI and RDI. The PCI achieved the best result through Logistic fitting method, followed by Log-Logistic (3P) fitting. However, the SRI obtained the best result through Log-Logistic fitting. By comprehensively comparing the calculation results from all three methods, it can be concluded that the probability density distributions of PCI, RQI, RDI, and SRI can be effectively characterized by the Log-Logistic (3P) distribution.

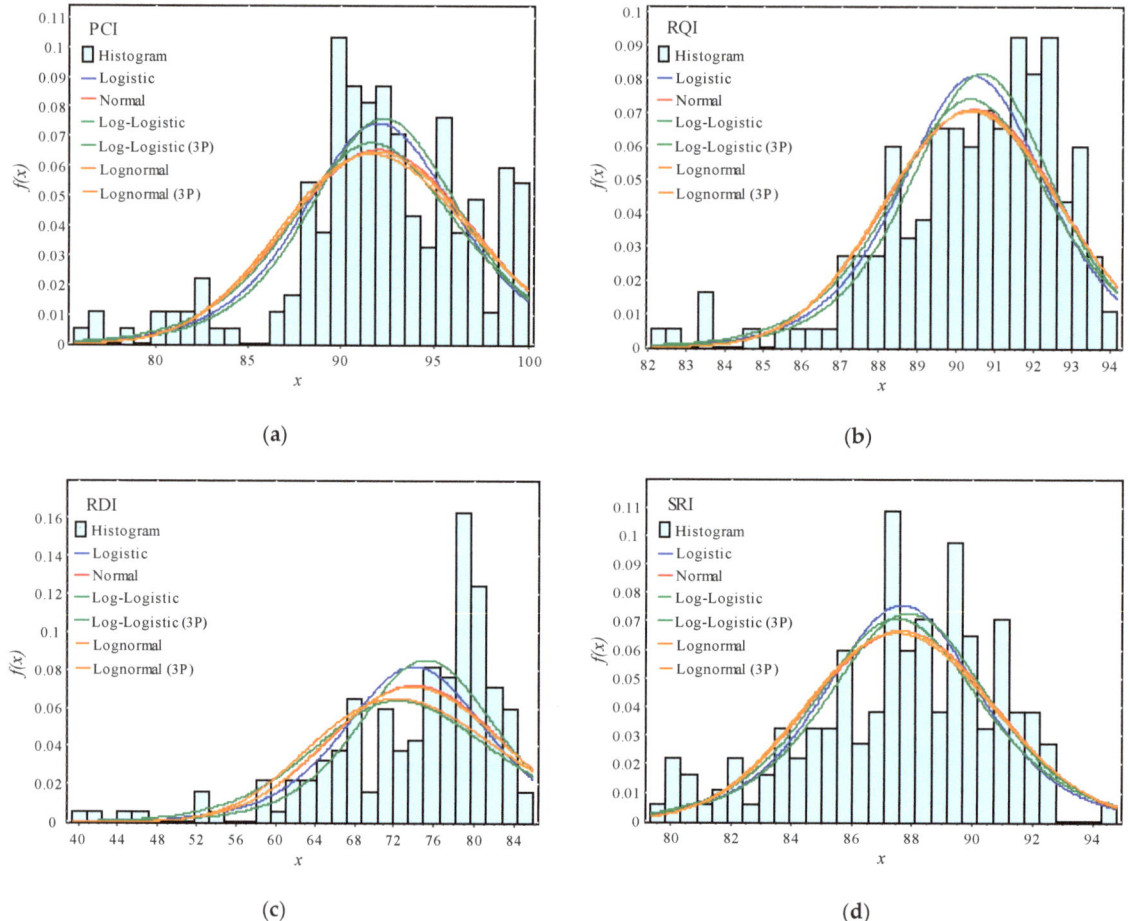

Figure 1. Comparison of probability density of pavement performance indexes and fitting analysis results: (**a**) PCI; (**b**) RQI; (**c**) RDI; (**d**) SRI.

The cumulative probability density functions of PCI, RQI, RDI, and SRI, as well as the comparison between measured values and fitting values, are presented in Figures 2 and 3. In the case of the PCI, the Log-Logistic (3P) fitting is not effective in the range of [80, 85], meaning that the fitted function does not accurately represent the distribution of the index within this range. However, the fitting becomes stable and reliable in the range of [85, 100], indicating that the fitted function accurately represents the distribution of the PCI within this range. For the RQI, the Log-Logistic (3P) fitting is not effective in the ranges of [82, 87] and [93, 94], suggesting that the fitted function does not accurately represent the distribution of the index within these ranges. However, the fitting becomes stable and reliable in the range of [87, 93], indicating that the fitted function accurately represents the distribution of the RQI within this range. The overall trend of the RDI obtained through Log-Logistic (3P) fitting to the cumulative probability density function is evident. This suggests that the fitted function accurately represents the distribution of the RDI across its entire range. Similarly, the cumulative probability density function of the SRI obtained through Log-Logistic (3P) fitting shows an ideal effect within the range of [84, 92] and is stable and reliable. This indicates that the fitted function accurately represents the distribution of the SRI within this range.

The measured and fitted values of pavement performance indicators are compared using Log-Logistic (3P) fitting. In the range of the PCI [0, 0.6], the fitting results fluctuate significantly, and the fitting effect is poor. In the range of [0.6, 0.9], the fitting results fluctuate slightly and are distributed on both sides of the line, indicating relative reliability and stability. For the RQI, in the range of [0, 0.2] and [0.5, 1], the fitting results fluctuate greatly, and the fitting effect is poor. However, in the range of [0.2, 0.5], the fitting results fluctuate slightly and are distributed on both sides of the straight line, indicating stability and reliability. The fitting values obtained for the RDI fluctuate around the actual values, with local fluctuations being significant. In the range of the SRI [0.4, 0.9], the fitting values exhibit a high correlation with the measured values, indicating a better effect.

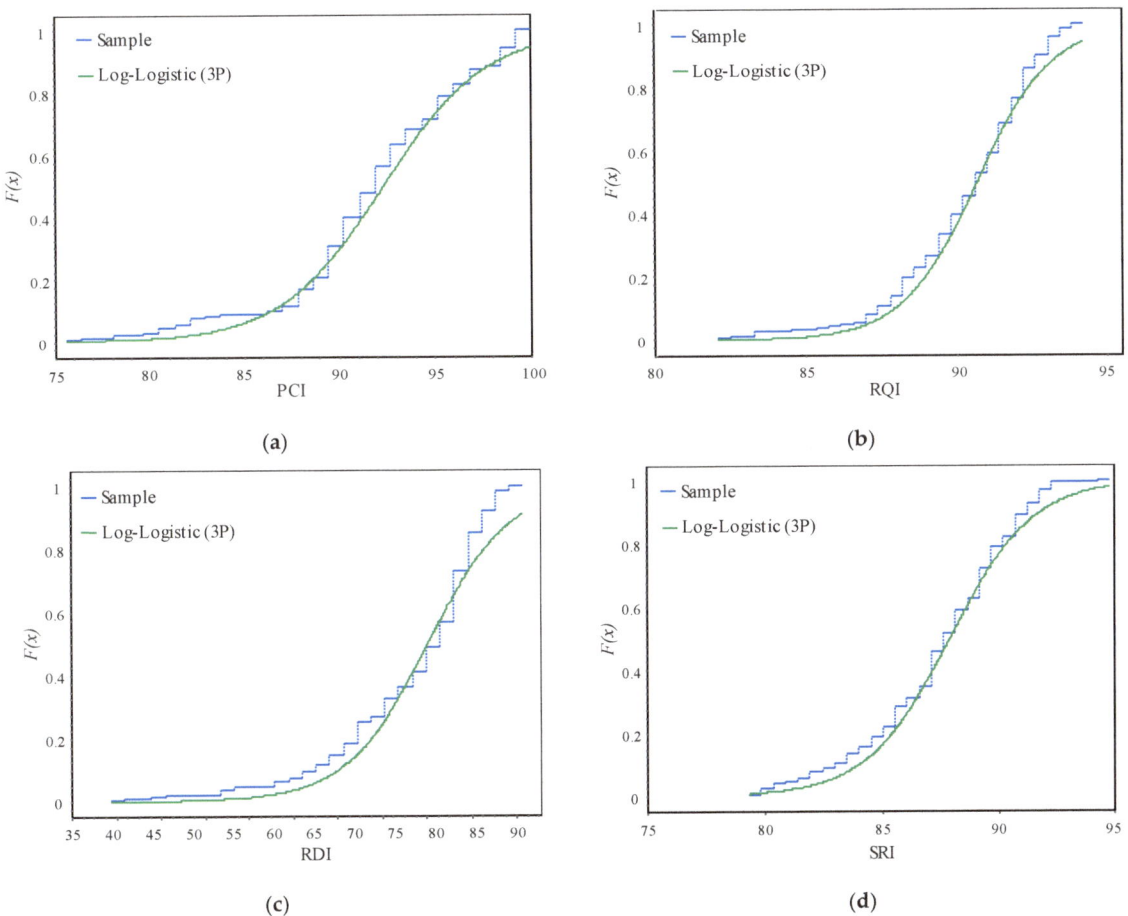

Figure 2. Cumulative probability density function of pavement performance evaluation indexes: (**a**) PCI; (**b**) RQI; (**c**) RDI; (**d**) SRI.

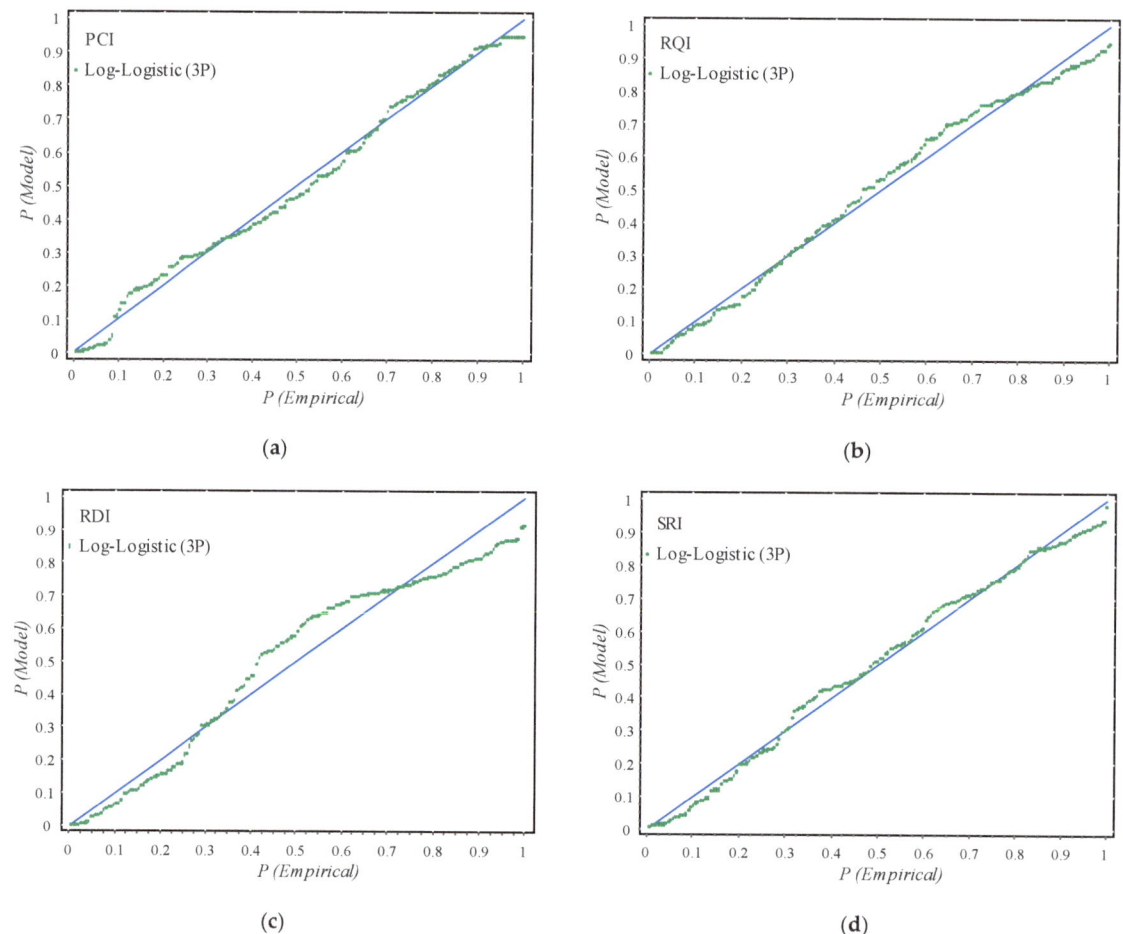

Figure 3. Comparison of measured values and fitting values of pavement performance indexes: (**a**) PCI; (**b**) RQI; (**c**) RDI; (**d**) SRI.

Indeed, studying the probability distribution characteristics of asphalt pavement performance evaluation indexes is an important research endeavor. The analysis conducted above indicates that the PCI, RQI, RDI, and SRIes do not follow a normal distribution entirely, and the probability distribution of pavement performance evaluation indexes varies. The gradual decay of pavement performance over time is influenced by various factors such as climate, geology, traffic load, material properties, and structural geometry parameters. Consequently, the probability distribution of pavement performance evaluation indexes will also change throughout different stages of the pavement's life cycle. The current deterministic evaluation method, which employs fixed weights, is insufficient to meet the practical requirements of the project. To ensure accurate and reliable pavement performance evaluation, it is crucial to consider the probabilistic nature of these indexes and incorporate appropriate statistical models or methods for analysis.

Table 4. Comparison of fitting function statistical test results of pavement performance indexes.

Serial Number	Distribution Function	Kolmogorov–Smirnov		Anderson–Darling		Chi-Squared	
		Statistic	Sort	Statistic	Sort	Statistic	Sort
PCI	Log-Logistic	0.10416	5	2.5466	5	18.017	6
	Log-Logistic (3P)	0.05657	1	1.3167	1	8.0729	2
	Logistic	0.07701	2	1.6292	2	6.5873	1
	Lognormal	0.10857	6	3.0129	6	17.641	5
	Lognormal (3P)	0.10026	4	2.5372	4	13.059	4
	Normal	0.09952	3	2.3536	3	13.057	3
RQI	Log-Logistic	0.08961	5	2.83	6	14.394	3
	Log-Logistic (3P)	0.06286	1	1.6038	1	10.768	1
	Logistic	0.09492	6	2.3974	2	11.416	2
	Lognormal	0.08381	4	2.8015	5	19.881	6
	Lognormal (3P)	0.07966	3	2.6147	4	18.457	5
	Normal	0.07928	2	2.4687	3	15.721	4
RDI	Log-Logistic	0.169	6	9.2652	6	79.025	6
	Log-Logistic (3P)	0.10865	1	4.6751	1	41.345	1
	Logistic	0.16246	4	6.3528	2	60.395	2
	Lognormal	0.16794	5	8.9946	5	77.588	5
	Lognormal (3P)	0.15262	2	6.606	4	63.712	4
	Normal	0.15298	3	6.4046	3	62.267	3
SRI	Log-Logistic	0.09108	6	2.1105	6	5.8546	1
	Log-Logistic (3P)	0.0554	1	1.2219	1	8.7292	5
	Logistic	0.07973	2	1.8442	4	10.447	6
	Lognormal	0.08903	5	2.031	5	7.0076	4
	Lognormal (3P)	0.08081	3	1.7982	3	6.5312	3
	Normal	0.08172	4	1.6595	2	6.3648	2

3.2. Confidence Analysis Based on Blind-Number Theory

Taking into account the uncertainty associated with randomness, fuzziness, grayness, and uncertainty in the evaluation of pavement performance, the blind number theory is employed to establish blind number expressions for pavement performance evaluation indexes. Additionally, a confidence model is developed to analyze the confidence of pavement performance. The integration of blind information into the evaluation system ensures that it remains unaffected by probability distribution functions. This approach not only provides a clear assessment grade for pavement performance but also assigns corresponding credibility to the assessment grade, thereby enhancing the scientific nature of the evaluation. The sample data and weight coefficients used in this study are based on the research conducted by Li, Wei, Yao, Hu, and Wang [12]. By utilizing Equations (14)–(16), blind numbers and reliabilities for the pavement performance indexes are computed, as shown in Table 5.

$$P\hat{QI} = w_{PCI} \otimes P\hat{CI} \oplus w_{RQI} \otimes R\hat{QI} \oplus w_{RDI} \otimes R\hat{DI} \oplus w_{SRI} \otimes S\hat{RI} \quad (14)$$

$$R_{PQI}(90) = \frac{1}{90} \otimes P\hat{QI} \quad (15)$$

$$R_{PQI}(80) = \frac{1}{80} \otimes P\hat{QI} \quad (16)$$

Table 5. Confidence results for intervals of pavement performance.

No.	PQI (Grade)	PQI^ (Grade)	$K_{PQI^\wedge}$ (90)	$K_{PQI^\wedge}$ (80)
1	83.64	73.31757	0.81464	0.91647
2	83.79	76.23695	0.847077	0.952962
3	84.89	76.85353	0.853928	0.960669
4	85.98	78.84341	0.876038	0.985543
5	84.90	80.23577	0.891509	1.002947
6	87.01	81.69958	0.907773	1.021245
7	84.92	82.01217	0.911246	1.025152
8	85.45	82.64352	0.918261	1.033044
9	84.96	82.85526	0.920614	1.035691
10	87.14	82.93161	0.921462	1.036645
11	84.72	83.26604	0.925178	1.040826
12	87.61	83.40383	0.926709	1.042548
13	87.67	83.48033	0.927559	1.043504
14	86.60	84.10160	0.934462	1.051270
15	86.36	84.60134	0.940015	1.057517
16	87.76	84.83564	0.942618	1.060446
17	87.91	84.84281	0.942698	1.060535
18	87.86	85.12389	0.945821	1.064049
19	88.06	85.74850	0.952761	1.071856
20	89.21	86.82397	0.964711	1.085300
21	89.70	87.03685	0.967076	1.087961
22	89.23	87.35512	0.970612	1.091939
23	89.22	87.47873	0.971986	1.093484
24	88.56	87.48089	0.972010	1.093511
25	89.42	87.75188	0.975021	1.096899
26	88.19	88.27680	0.980853	1.103460
27	89.83	88.34652	0.981628	1.104331
28	89.83	88.36494	0.981833	1.104562
29	90.35	88.42565	0.982507	1.105321
30	90.16	88.50354	0.983373	1.106294
31	89.74	88.56722	0.984080	1.107090
32	90.57	88.84937	0.987215	1.110617
33	89.18	88.98633	0.988737	1.112329
34	90.39	89.02159	0.989129	1.112770
35	90.99	89.17456	0.990828	1.114682
36	91.41	89.56480	0.995164	1.11956
37	90.84	89.72866	0.996985	1.121608
38	91.94	90.05702	1.000634	1.125713
39	92.94	90.97604	1.010845	1.137200
40	92.00	91.01112	1.011235	1.137639

The results of these calculations are presented in Table 4. It is evident that the calculated PQI^ results do not align with those obtained using the current standard. The PQI^ interval determined by the current standard is [83.64, 92.94], whereas the PQI interval computed is [73.32, 91.01]. Three of the judgment values for the optimal pavement performance evaluation grade exceed 1, indicating that the confidence of judgment values greater than 1 in the sample group is 0.075. There are 36 judgment values for the good pavement performance evaluation grade that surpass 1, signifying a confidence of 0.9 or 90% for judgment values greater than 1 in the sample group. Moreover, confidence is considered as 1 for values exceeding 0.9. According to the current standard, the evaluation outcome indicates that 30 samples are classified as good, while 10 samples are deemed excellent. For instance, considering sample 14, the current standard assigns a PQI evaluation result of 83.64, corresponding to a good evaluation grade. However, when employing the information entropy weight determination calculation for PQI^, the result is 73.32, indicating a medium evaluation grade. These evaluation results differ significantly.

Analyzing the pavement performance sample data reveals that the evaluation grade for the RDI is poor, while the PCI, RQI, and SRI receive excellent and good evaluation grades, respectively. The current standard assigns weights of 0.35 and 0.4 to the PCI and RQI, respectively, while the weight assigned to the pavement rutting depth index is relatively small [31]. Consequently, the overall pavement evaluation result becomes overly optimistic. In contrast, Li, Wei, Yao, Hu, and Wang [12] adopt the information entropy weight determination method, which considers the difference in evaluation indexes and reflects the contribution rate of these indexes to the system. This approach leads to an improved weight for the road rutting depth index. By comparing the scores provided by different experts, it is observed that the weight determination using information entropy weight aligns more closely with the actual road condition level.

Through the proposed confidence model for pavement performance analysis, not only is the evaluation level of pavement performance clearly defined, but the corresponding confidence for each evaluation level is also provided. Moreover, it significantly expands the application scope of pavement performance confidence analysis.

4. Conclusions and Outlook

This study has examined the probability distribution characteristics of the evaluation index for asphalt pavement performance and introduced the concept of blind-number theory to investigate the confidence model for analyzing the confidence of asphalt pavement performance. The key findings are as follows:

(1) The Pavement Condition Index (PCI), Riding Quality Index (RQI), Rutting Depth Index (RDI), and Skidding Resistance Index (SRI) of pavement facilities do not exhibit complete adherence to the normal distribution. Furthermore, the probability distribution of the pavement performance evaluation index differs.

(2) A blind-number expression for the pavement performance evaluation index is developed in this study. Additionally, a confidence model for analyzing the confidence of pavement performance is constructed using the method of determining the weight information entropy weight of the pavement performance evaluation index. The model effectively integrates blind information into the pavement performance evaluation system, making it independent of the probability distribution function.

(3) Compared to the traditional method, the proposed confidence model for pavement performance confidence analysis has several advantages. Firstly, it provides a clear evaluation level for pavement performance, allowing for a more precise assessment. Secondly, it also assigns corresponding credibility to the evaluation level, which enhances the scientific and rational nature of the evaluation process. This improvement ensures that the evaluation takes into account the confidence of the data and the assessment results.

Overall, the confidence model significantly enhances the scientific rigor and advanced nature of pavement performance evaluation, thereby expanding the application scope of pavement performance confidence analysis and enabling more accurate and reliable assessments across a wide range of scenarios. In future research, it is highly recommended to expand the sample size to enhance the richness and representativeness of the data. By incorporating a larger number of samples, the confidence model can comprehensively reflect the performance of pavements under diverse road sections and conditions, thereby enhancing its accuracy and reliability. While this study covers several critical pavement performance evaluation indexes, future investigations should consider incorporating additional relevant indexes, such as traffic flow and climate conditions, which also exert significant influence on pavement performance. The careful consideration of these additional factors can further enhance the applicability and prediction capability of the confidence model.

Moreover, future work should focus on expanding and refining the credibility model of pavement performance based on blind number theory, thereby increasing its applicability to road projects in different regions and under varying conditions. This will provide road maintenance activities with more scientific and reliable decision support. By continuously advancing the credibility model, road engineers can make well-informed decisions regarding maintenance strategies, ensuring the long-term functionality and safety of transportation networks in diverse geographical locations and environmental conditions.

Author Contributions: Conceptualization, H.W. and J.L.; methodology, H.W.; software, Y.L.; validation, Y.L., L.L. and H.L.; formal analysis, L.L.; investigation, H.W. and Y.L.; resources, H.W.; data curation, Y.L. and H.L.; writing—original draft preparation, H.W., J.L. and L.L; writing—review and editing, Y.L. and J.L.; visualization, H.L.; supervision, H.W.; project administration, H.W.; funding acquisition, J.L. All authors have read and agreed to the published version of the manuscript.

Funding: This research was funded by the National Natural Science Foundation of China (grant number 52278436, 52208426), the Science and Technology Innovation Program of Hunan Province (grant number 2022RC1024), the National Key R & D Program of China (grant number 2021YFB2601200), the Foundation of Engineering Research Center of Catastrophic Prophylaxis and Treatment of Road & Traffic Safety of Ministry of Education (kfj220402), the Special Financial Aid to the Post-Doctorate Research Project of Chongqing (grant number 2021XM1012), and the Xiangjiang Laboratory Project (grant number 22XJ01009).

Institutional Review Board Statement: Not applicable.

Informed Consent Statement: Not applicable.

Data Availability Statement: Not applicable.

Conflicts of Interest: The authors declare no conflict of interest.

References

1. Upadrashta, D.; Yang, Y. Experimental investigation of performance reliability of macro fiber composite for piezoelectric energy harvesting applications. *Sens. Actuators A Phys.* **2016**, *244*, 223–232. [CrossRef]
2. Ren, S.; Liu, X.; Lin, P.; Jing, R.; Erkens, S. Toward the long-term aging influence and novel reaction kinetics models of bitumen. *Int. J. Pavement Eng.* **2022**, 1–16. [CrossRef]
3. Shon, H.; Cho, C.-S.; Byon, Y.-J.; Lee, J. Autonomous condition monitoring-based pavement management system. *Autom. Constr.* **2022**, *138*, 104222. [CrossRef]
4. Shon, H.; Lee, J. Integrating multi-scale inspection, maintenance, rehabilitation, and reconstruction decisions into system-level pavement management systems. *Transp. Res. Part C: Emerg. Technol.* **2021**, *131*, 103328. [CrossRef]
5. de Bortoli, A.; Baouch, Y.; Masdan, M. BIM can help decarbonize the construction sector: Primary life cycle evidence from pavement management systems. *J. Clean. Prod.* **2023**, *391*, 136056. [CrossRef]
6. Sultan, S.A.; Guo, Z. Evaluating life cycle costs of perpetual pavements in China using operational pavement management system. *Int. J. Transp. Sci. Technol.* **2016**, *5*, 103–109. [CrossRef]
7. Cano-Ortiz, S.; Pascual-Munoz, P.; Castro-Fresno, D. Machine learning algorithms for monitoring pavement performance. *Autom. Constr.* **2022**, *139*, 104309. [CrossRef]
8. García-Segura, T.; Montalbán-Domingo, L.; Llopis-Castelló, D.; Lepech, M.D.; Sanz, M.A.; Pellicer, E. Incorporating pavement deterioration uncertainty into pavement management optimization. *Int. J. Pavement Eng.* **2022**, *23*, 2062–2073. [CrossRef]
9. Majidifard, H.; Jahangiri, B.; Rath, P.; Contreras, L.U.; Buttlar, W.G.; Alavi, A.H. Developing a prediction model for rutting depth of asphalt mixtures using gene expression programming. *Constr. Build. Mater.* **2021**, *267*, 120543. [CrossRef]
10. Fan, W.; Dai, L. Pavement evaluation with AHP based on expert's assessment. In Proceedings of the 2015 23rd international conference on Geoinformatics, Wuhan, China, 19–21 June 2015; pp. 1–3.
11. Olowosulu, A.; Kaura, J.; Murana, A.; Adeke, P. Development of framework for performance prediction of flexible road pavement in Nigeria using Fuzzy logic theory. *Int. J. Pavement Eng.* **2022**, *23*, 3809–3818. [CrossRef]
12. Li, J.; Wei, H.; Yao, Y.; Hu, X.; Wang, L. Contribution modeling on condition evaluation of asphalt pavement using uncertainty measurement and entropy theory. *Adv. Mater. Sci. Eng.* **2021**, *2021*, 9995926. [CrossRef]
13. He, L.; Zhu, H.; Gao, Z. Performance evaluation of asphalt pavement based on BP neural network. *NeuroQuantology* **2018**, *16*, 537–545. [CrossRef]
14. Song, Z.; Sun, F.; Zhang, R.; Du, Y.; Li, C. Prediction of road network traffic state using the NARX neural network. *J. Adv. Transp.* **2021**, *2021*, 2564211. [CrossRef]
15. Bao, Q.; Ruan, D.; Shen, Y.; Hermans, E.; Janssens, D. Improved hierarchical fuzzy TOPSIS for road safety performance evaluation. *Knowl.-Based Syst.* **2012**, *32*, 84–90. [CrossRef]
16. Abed, A.; Thom, N.; Neves, L. Probabilistic prediction of asphalt pavement performance. *Road Mater. Pavement Des.* **2019**, *20*, S247–S264. [CrossRef]
17. Li, J.; Liu, T.; Wang, X.; Yu, J. Automated asphalt pavement damage rate detection based on optimized GA-CNN. *Autom. Constr.* **2022**, *136*, 104180. [CrossRef]

18. Marcelino, P.; de Lurdes Antunes, M.; Fortunato, E.; Gomes, M.C. Machine learning approach for pavement performance prediction. *Int. J. Pavement Eng.* **2021**, *22*, 341–354. [CrossRef]
19. Hanandeh, S. Introducing mathematical modeling to estimate pavement quality index of flexible pavements based on genetic algorithm and artificial neural networks. *Case Stud. Constr. Mater.* **2022**, *16*, e00991. [CrossRef]
20. Elhadidy, A.A.; El-Badawy, S.M.; Elbeltagi, E.E. A simplified pavement condition index regression model for pavement evaluation. *Int. J. Pavement Eng.* **2021**, *22*, 643–652. [CrossRef]
21. Damirchilo, F.; Hosseini, A.; Mellat Parast, M.; Fini, E.H. Machine Learning Approach to Predict International Roughness Index Using Long-Term Pavement Performance Data. *J. Transp. Eng. Part B Pavements* **2021**, *147*, 04021058. [CrossRef]
22. Kaya, O.; Ceylan, H.; Kim, S.; Waid, D.; Moore, B.P. Statistics and artificial intelligence-based pavement performance and remaining service life prediction models for flexible and composite pavement systems. *Transp. Res. Rec.* **2020**, *2674*, 448–460. [CrossRef]
23. Wojtkiewicz, S.F.; Khazanovich, L.; Gaurav, G.; Velasquez, R. Probabilistic numerical simulation of pavement performance using MEPDG. *Road Mater. Pavement Des.* **2010**, *11*, 291–306. [CrossRef]
24. Piryonesi, S.M.; El-Diraby, T.E. Examining the relationship between two road performance indicators: Pavement condition index and international roughness index. *Transp. Geotech.* **2021**, *26*, 100441. [CrossRef]
25. Bashar, M.Z.; Torres-Machi, C. Performance of machine learning algorithms in predicting the pavement international roughness index. *Transp. Res. Rec.* **2021**, *2675*, 226–237. [CrossRef]
26. Gong, M.; Zhang, H.; Liu, Z.; Fu, X. Study on PQI standard for comprehensive maintenance of asphalt pavement based on full-cycle. *Int. J. Pavement Eng.* **2022**, *23*, 4277–4290. [CrossRef]
27. Jia, X.; Woods, M.; Gong, H.; Zhu, D.; Hu, W.; Huang, B. Evaluation of network-level data collection variability and its influence on pavement evaluation utilizing random forest method. *Transp. Res. Rec.* **2021**, *2675*, 331–345. [CrossRef]
28. Han, C.; Ma, T.; Chen, S. Asphalt pavement maintenance plans intelligent decision model based on reinforcement learning algorithm. *Constr. Build. Mater.* **2021**, *299*, 124278. [CrossRef]
29. Pandey, A.K.; Iqbal, R.; Maniak, T.; Karyotis, C.; Akuma, S.; Palade, V. Convolution neural networks for pothole detection of critical road infrastructure. *Comput. Electr. Eng.* **2022**, *99*, 107725. [CrossRef]
30. Hu, A.; Bai, Q.; Chen, L.; Meng, S.; Li, Q.; Xu, Z. A review on empirical methods of pavement performance modeling. *Constr. Build. Mater.* **2022**, *342*, 127968. [CrossRef]
31. Yu, J.; Zhang, X.; Xiong, C. A methodology for evaluating micro-surfacing treatment on asphalt pavement based on grey system models and grey rational degree theory. *Constr. Build. Mater.* **2017**, *150*, 214–226. [CrossRef]

Disclaimer/Publisher's Note: The statements, opinions and data contained in all publications are solely those of the individual author(s) and contributor(s) and not of MDPI and/or the editor(s). MDPI and/or the editor(s) disclaim responsibility for any injury to people or property resulting from any ideas, methods, instructions or products referred to in the content.

Article

Field Data Analysis of Pavement Marking Retroreflectivity and Its Relationship with Paint and Glass Bead Characteristics

Laura N. Mazzoni [1,*], Kamilla Vasconcelos [1], Orlando Albarracín [2], Liedi Bernucci [1] and Guilherme Linhares [3]

[1] Department of Transportation Engineering, Polytechnic School of the University of São Paulo, São Paulo 05508-070, Brazil; kamilla.vasconcelos@usp.br (K.V.); liedi@usp.br (L.B.)
[2] Department of Production Engineering, Mackenzie Presbyterian University, São Paulo 01221-040, Brazil; orlando.albarracin@mackenzie.br
[3] Arteris S.A., São Paulo 04506-000, Brazil; guilherme.linhares@arteris.com.br
* Correspondence: laura.mazzoni@usp.br

Featured Application: White water-based paints with high-volume solids and well-graded glass beads, characterized by uniformity and curvature coefficients, improve pavement marking service life.

Abstract: Pavement marking retroreflectivity, a critical factor for safe driving, depends on the characteristics of both the paint and the embedded glass beads. However, traditional methods for predicting pavement marking service life often overlook these materials properties. This study investigates the influence of paint and glass bead characteristics on pavement marking retroreflectivity performance and addresses the characterization of glass bead size distribution by the coefficient of uniformity and curvature. Three field test sites on a Brazilian highway with various paint and glass bead combinations were evaluated. A statistical model, GAMLSS (Generalized Additive Model for Location, Scale, and Shape), was adjusted to evaluate the performance of the markings' retroreflectivity as a function of paint and glass bead characteristics. The model revealed that well-graded glass beads increased retroreflectivity by around 10%, while paints with a higher volume of solids improved service life around 65%. Therefore, the results show that acrylic water-based paints with higher volumes of solids and well-graded glass beads with better shape characteristics should be preferred to improve pavement markings' retroreflectivity and service life. The statistical model identified the key characteristics with the greatest impact on pavement marking retroreflectivity, offering valuable insights for real-world applications, which will assist pavement marking practitioners and road authorities in selecting appropriate materials to achieve enhanced durability.

Keywords: road markings; test sites; GAMLSS; particle shapes; gradation; volume solids

Citation: Mazzoni, L.N.; Vasconcelos, K.; Albarracín, O.; Bernucci, L.; Linhares, G. Field Data Analysis of Pavement Marking Retroreflectivity and Its Relationship with Paint and Glass Bead Characteristics. *Appl. Sci.* **2024**, *14*, 4205. https://doi.org/10.3390/app14104205

Academic Editors: Jue Li, Junhui Zhang, Junfeng Gao, Junhui Peng and Wensheng Wang

Received: 25 March 2024
Revised: 28 April 2024
Accepted: 29 April 2024
Published: 15 May 2024

Copyright: © 2024 by the authors. Licensee MDPI, Basel, Switzerland. This article is an open access article distributed under the terms and conditions of the Creative Commons Attribution (CC BY) license (https://creativecommons.org/licenses/by/4.0/).

1. Introduction

1.1. Road Safety and Pavement Markings' Retroreflectivity

During the last decades, traffic crashes have become a worldwide concern. The last UN General Assembly established the Second Decade of Action for Road Safety 2021–2030 with a target to reduce death and injuries caused by traffic by a minimum of 50% by the year 2030 [1]. The report recommends ensuring safe road use by guaranteeing that road infrastructure considers the needs of all road users and is designed to facilitate safe behaviors, including the use of clear and intuitive pavement markings [1].

Pavement markings are one of the most important features for roads due to their contribution to road safety improvement. Due to their relatively low cost and broad availability, pavement markings are a low-cost solution to reduce traffic crashes, especially in developing countries [2]. However, adequate pavement markings must present visibility during the day by the contrast of the marking material with the pavement surface, and their nighttime visibility depends on the retroreflectivity provided by the glass beads in the pavement markings.

Retroreflectivity is an engineering measure of the efficiency of the pavement markings' ability to reflect the light from vehicle's headlights back to the light source. Pavement markings' retroreflectivity is measured by the coefficient of retroreflected luminance (R_L, mcd/m^2/lx) given by the ratio of the luminance (brightness to the driver from the markings surface, mcd/m^2) and the illuminance, in lux (lx), of the vehicles' headlight on the marking [3,4]. Retroreflectivity (R_L) is most required in low-light and nighttime conditions to improve the readability and perception of the information provided by pavement markings.

The improvement and maintenance of pavement markings' retroreflectivity correlate to a reduction in traffic crash rates [3,5]. Higher values of retroreflectivity reduce the detection distance of pavement markings, especially for elderly drivers [6], which improves their reaction time. In addition, studies have shown that pavement marking retroreflectivity values higher than 200 mcd/lx/m^2 are related to a lower number of traffic crashes. Moreover, the maintenance of pavement markings' quality presents a positive effect on road safety [7].

1.2. Performance of Pavement Markings' Retroreflectivity

Pavement markings present retroreflectivity due to the glass beads applied on their surface. The characteristics of the glass beads have a great influence on the retroreflectivity levels. Smadi et al. [8] assessed the size distribution (gradation), color, shape, and air inclusion of glass beads and evaluated the influence of these properties on the initial retroreflectivity of laboratory and field samples. The authors evaluated 30 glass bead samples and could not define a definitive relationship. However, the general trends observed showed that samples with higher percentages of round and larger particles, clearer beads, and low air inclusion tended to increase the initial retroreflectivity value.

Pavement markings' retroreflectivity decreases over time. Frequent snow removal activities, traffic, and dirt accumulation scratch the glass beads' surface, which accelerates the degradation rate of retroreflectivity due to the loss of a polished surface [9]. Moreover, retroreflectivity degradation also occurs due to the loss of glass beads and dirt accumulation on the pavement markings' surface, which reduces the reflectorized area [10]. The glass beads' loss depends on the marking material used; the selection of the type of binder must consider costs and performance [11]. In addition, materials' characteristics are evaluated by laboratory tests to guarantee their quality prior to application.

Retroreflectivity values and their rates of decrease depend on the traffic volume and composition, as well as climatic conditions such as rain, solar radiation, and temperature. Due to the difficulty of reproducing traffic and weather characteristics in the laboratory, pavement markings' performance are usually evaluated by field tests [12–20]. Experimental test sites are expensive and require long periods to produce results, but they are necessary for the proper evaluation of materials' performance.

1.3. Degradation Models

The data collected from the experimental test sites provide information regarding the decrease in retroreflectivity over time, and the results can be used to predict the retroreflectivity value expected at a given time by statistical modeling. Statistical models provide details regarding the service life of pavement markings based on the variables and characteristics included to fit the data.

Prediction of the end of pavement markings' service life started during the 1990s. The initial approaches considered linear or logarithmic models to predict the retroreflectivity as a function of age and initial R_L [12,13]. The authors evaluated the retroreflectivity data from pavement markings with different marking materials, considering paints, tapes, thermoplastic, and others. Since then, statistical models and analyzed data have evolved to more complex models using machine learning methods [20]. Table 1 presents several studies from the literature that proposed statistical models with the data from experimental test sites, including the main exploratory variables and the materials considered.

Table 1. Summary of retroreflectivity prediction models in the literature.

Author/Year	Exploratory Variables Included in the Model	Materials
Zhang and Wu, 2010 [15]	Age	Tape, water-based paint, thermoplastic, and experimental materials
Hummer et al., 2011 [16]	Age and R_L initial *	Water-based paint
Robertson et al., 2013 [17]	Age, R_L initial *, lane and shoulder width, difference and R_L percentage difference, and traffic volume and cumulative traffic volume	Water-based and high-build paint
Sitzabee et al., 2013 [18]	Age, R_L initial *, traffic volume, glass bead type, and line position	Polyurea
Babić et al., 2019 [19]	Age, R_L initial *, line position, and winter maintenance	Solvent-based paint, thermoplastic, and cold plastic

* R_L initial = initial retroreflectivity value.

Most of the studies presented in Table 1 predicted retroreflectivity as a function of age and the initial retroreflectivity value. Traffic volume was also frequently included in the models as a significant variable to the degradation rate of retroreflectivity. Furthermore, with the exception of Sitzabee et al. [18], all the researchers evaluated at least two different marking materials. However, Sitzabee et al. [18] evaluated the impact of glass bead variation by comparing the performance of standard and highly reflective beads and comparing their impact on the service life of pavement markings.

Despite all the studies including more than one material type as a source of variation, none of them included an explanatory variable to describe the influence of distinct materials on the degradation rate or on the retroreflectivity value predicted. The authors adjusted different degradation models to evaluate the retroreflectivity and the degradation rate of pavement markings using different materials. In addition, the authors grouped the data based on the material type and did not present any differentiation regarding variations in the same material type, for example, by manufacturer.

1.4. Objective

It is important to quantify the impact of different paints and glass beads. The choice of different materials will change their properties and characteristics. However, existing studies in the literature fail to discuss the influence of material properties or characteristics on retroreflectivity value or pavement markings' service life. Identifying and quantifying material properties' impact on retroreflectivity degradation is crucial during material selection prior to application.

The objective of this paper is to identify the contribution of basic characteristics of paints and glass beads, evaluated through laboratory tests, on the retroreflectivity performance of pavement markings. This analysis is based on data collected at three experimental test sites at a Brazilian highway and fitted to a statistical model. The results will assist pavement marking practitioners and road authorities in selecting appropriate materials to achieve enhanced durability.

2. Materials and Methods

2.1. Materials

In this research, seven white acrylic resin water-based paints were evaluated: A, B, C, D, E, F, and G. All the paints were commercial paints, from distinct manufacturers. Paints A, B, C, D, E, and G are traditional traffic paints, whereas paint F is expected to exhibit superior performance, as indicated by the manufacturer.

The glass beads used in this study were from five distinct manufacturers: α, β, ω, δ, and ε. Two glass bead gradations (IIA and IIC), following the guidelines of Brazilian standard ABNT NBR 16184 [21], were selected from manufacturers α, β, ω, and ε. The glass beads selected from manufacturer δ were two gradations (Type 2 and Type 3) according to AASHTO M247 [22]. Figure 1 presents the grain size distribution ranges of the gradations used.

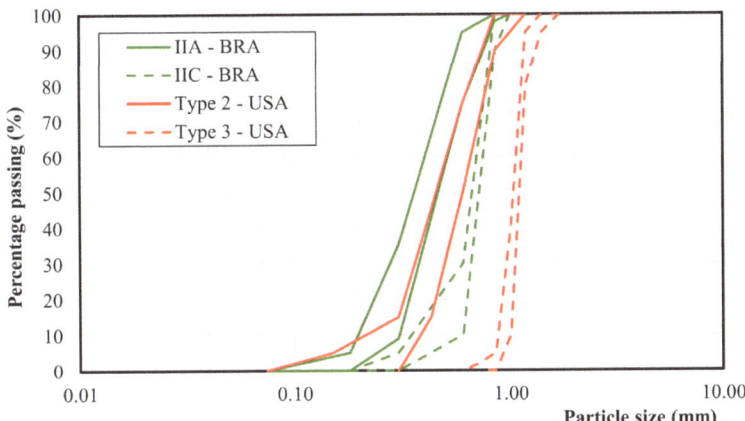

Figure 1. Grain size distribution ranges of glass beads IIA and IIC from NBR 16184 (BRA) [21] and Type 2 and Type 3 from AASHTO M247 (USA) [22].

2.2. Methods

All the paints were characterized regarding their consistency [23], specific gravity [24], and volume solids [25]. These methods were selected based on the common practices of Brazilian agencies for quality acceptance of traffic paints due to the simplicity of the tests. The glass beads' size distribution and shape characteristics were evaluated according to the procedure described in AASHTO R98 [26].

2.3. Experimental Design

The retroreflectivity data used in this study were collected from three experimental test sites where the pavement markings were subjected to the real weather and traffic conditions. Test site 1, test site 2, and test site 3 were monitored from 2016–2017, 2018–2020, and 2020–2022, respectively. All the test sites were constructed at the same road section with the same characteristics and were subjected to similar climatic conditions. Figure 2 shows the toll plaza where the test sites were located.

Figure 2. Experimental test site view [27].

Experiments on highways require special attention because they involve several safety aspects. The experiment used the lines transversal to traffic as recommended by NTPEP [28]. This experimental setup presents the following advantages: all stripes can be placed close together in a short length of highway, which allows for the quick measurement of retroreflectivity; all materials are subjected to the same conditions of traffic and weather; and all the stripes are hit by vehicles, which accelerates the experiment. Although transversal stripes do not represent the real condition of markings, since they are applied longitudinally [5], transversal stripes provide similar results to overall pavement markings' degradation [29,30]. Figure 3a shows one example of the test site on the day of application and Figure 3b shows the stripes after being subjected to traffic for 11 months.

(a) (b)

Figure 3. Experimental test site 2: (**a**) day of construction; (**b**) 11 months after construction (zoomed in on the right lane).

Due to the high traffic volume of the highway, traffic interruptions for frequent retroreflectivity measurements would cause speed reductions and safety issues. Therefore, the test sites were constructed in a toll plaza rather than a free rolling section because drivers are aware and warned of a speed reduction, which avoids misunderstandings and safety issues. All the test sites were placed after the toll cabin and were subjected to the effect of vehicles' acceleration. The test sites were located on highway BR-381 (an important road in the southeastern region of Brazil with very heavy traffic of 2.27×10^7 ESALs for a 10-year project). The traffic volume at this road section is approximately 17,000 vehicles/day, of which 35% are heavy vehicles.

The retroreflectivity values were collected several times during the monitoring period and the intervals between the measurements were random due to limitations on traffic interruption or wet surfaces caused by rain. In case of rain, the data collection was rescheduled to at least 24 h after the rain ended. The measurements were collected only during the day on a dry surface with a portable retroreflectometer with 30 m geometry, as prescribed by ASTM E1710 [4]. The equipment measurement error was ±5.0%, according to the manufacturer. The retroreflectivity was measured at the positions of the right and left wheel paths and the value considered herein is the average value between both readings for each stripe. These positions were selected due to their accelerated degradation since the retroreflectivity at the wheel path tends to present values around 50% lower than the center and edges [31].

Each experimental test site used different paints, glass beads, and glass bead application rates (ARs), which generated several material combinations, as shown in Figure 4. All the paints were applied with a wet thickness of 500 μm, and no anti-skid was used.

Test site 1 was constructed in July 2016 and the retroreflectivity data were collected for 11 months until June 2017. During this period, the retroreflectivity was measured 30 times, which generated over 6500 data points. The materials evaluated were two commercial paints, A and B, and two application rates of glass beads from three different manufacturers (α, β, and ω). This study used the gradations IIA and IIC from ABNT NBR 16184 [21] (Figure 1). The selected glass bead application rates (GB-ARs) were 70% IIA + 30% IIC (7030Br) and 100% IIA (100Br), regarding the total mass of glass beads applied at a rate of 400 g/m². For the application at the test site, the two paints were combined with the beads available, which resulted in 12 different material combinations, as shown in Figure 4.

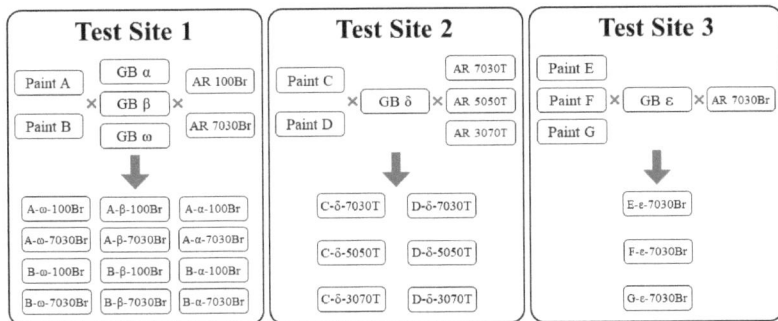

Figure 4. Experimental matrix for test sites 1, 2, and 3.

Test site 2 was constructed in September 2018 and the retroreflectivity data were monitored over 24 months until October 2020. The retroreflectivity was measured 39 times, generating over 7000 data points. The materials evaluated were two commercial paints, C and D, and three different application rates of two glass bead gradations from the same manufacturer (δ). The paints were provided by a resin manufacturer. The glass beads conformed to the AASHTO M247 [22] requirements. This study used the Type 2 and Type 3 gradations (Figure 1). The selected glass bead application rates (GB-ARs) were: 70% Type 2 + 30% Type 3 (7030T), 50% Type 2 + 50% Type 3 (5050T), and 30% Type 2 + 70% Type 3 (3070T), regarding the total mass of glass beads applied at a rate of 600 g/m². For the application at the test site, the two paints were combined with the three application rates, resulting in 6 different combinations, as shown in Figure 4.

Test site 3 was constructed in December 2020 and the retroreflectivity data were monitored over 18 months until August 2022. The retroreflectivity was measured 15 times, generating over 5500 data points. The materials evaluated were three commercial paints, E, F, and G, and one application rate of glass beads from one manufacturer (ε) applied at the same application rate. The glass beads followed the recommendation of Brazilian standards ABNT NBR 16184 [21] and this study used the gradations IIA and IIC in Figure 1. The selected glass bead application rate (GB-AR) was 70% IIA + 30% IIC (7030Br), regarding the total mass of glass beads applied at a rate of 400 g/m². For the application at the test site, the three paints were combined with the glass beads available, which resulted in 3 different material combinations, as shown in Figure 4.

3. Material Characterization Results

3.1. Paint Characterization

The paints were characterized regarding their consistency [23], specific gravity [24], and volume solids [25] prior to the application, and Table 2 presents the results.

Table 2. Basic characterization of paints.

Parameter	Limits *	Paint						
		Test Site 1		Test Site 2		Test Site 3		
		A	B	C	D	E	F	G
Consistency (KU)	$80 \leq KU \leq 95$	97	89	96	101	92	89	90
Specific gravity (g/cm³)	≥ 1.59	1.74	1.70	1.75	1.71	1.70	1.70	1.70
Volume solids (%)	≥ 62.0	63.8	64.2	62.0	60.5	66.0	65.0	65.0

* Limits according to ABNT NBR 13699 [32].

The consistency results in Table 2 show that paints B, E, F, and G were in accordance with the limits required, while paints A, C, and D were out of the range. Although they are considered inadequate for use based on the specification ABNT NBR 13699 [32], the materials were used for research purposes and applied at the test sites to identify the impact of such characteristics on the paint performance. Regarding the specific gravity, all the paints were in accordance with the required value, which indicates that the paints presented adequate balance and formulation. Considering the volume solids, the parameter evaluates the percentage of the paint's volume without the volatile fraction, therefore representing the dried paint's thickness as a percentage of the wet thickness.

3.2. Glass Bead Characterization

The glass beads' size distribution and shape characteristics were evaluated according to the procedure of AASHTO R98 [26]. Figures 5–7 present the grain size distributions, thickness-to-length distributions, and sphericity distributions, respectively, for each glass bead composition and application rate.

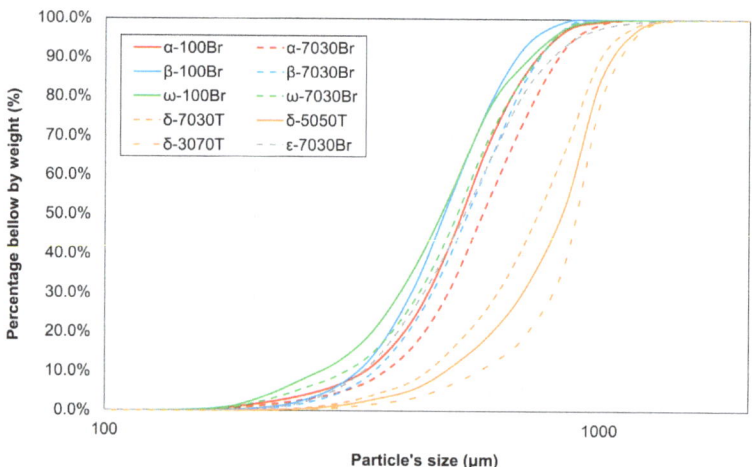

Figure 5. Grain size distributions of glass beads.

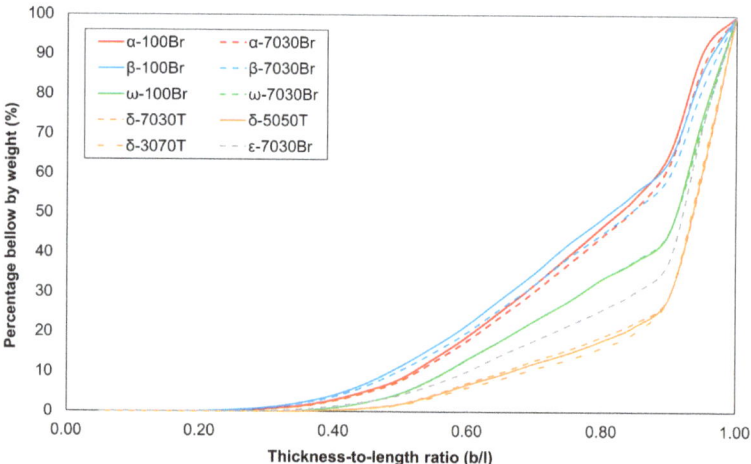

Figure 6. Thickness-to-length ratio (b/l) distributions of glass beads.

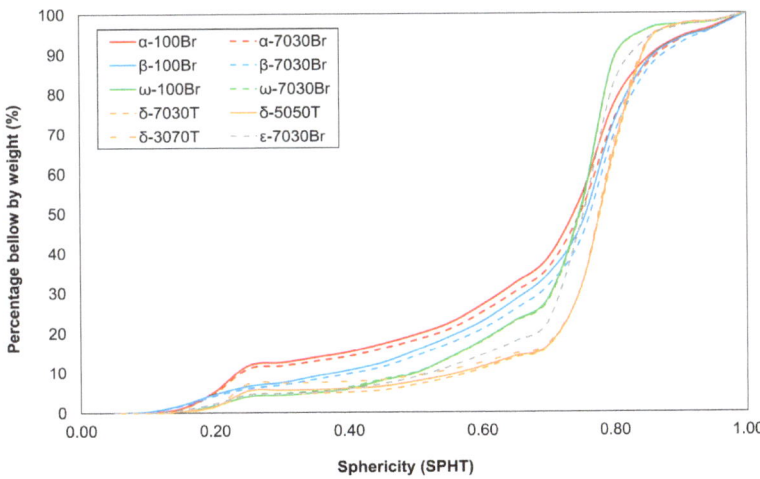

Figure 7. Sphericity (SPHT) distributions of glass beads.

The size distributions of the glass beads (Figure 5) present a large variation due to their gradations or manufacturers. The glass bead compositions δ-7030T, δ-5050T, and δ-3070T present larger particles than the other compositions. Regarding the other compositions, β-100Br and ω-100Br present the smallest particles, but all the compositions present similar size distributions.

The distributions of the thickness-to-length ratio (b/l) in Figure 6 show that compositions δ-7030T, δ-5050T, and δ-3070T present the same distribution of thickness-to-length ratio, with around 78% of round particles (b/l higher than 0.85), as required by AASHTO R98 [26]. The compositions ε-7030Br and ω-100Br present 70% and 65% of particles with b/l higher than 0.85, while the other compositions present less than 50% of round particles.

Regarding the sphericity distribution in Figure 7, all glass beads present poor shape properties considering the threshold of sphericity required by AASHTO R98 [26] to classify the particles as round (SPHT > 0.93), since all the compositions present less than 10% of round particles. Therefore, the lack of sphericity that all these glass beads present may lead to low retroreflectivity values when they are applied on the pavement markings [8,33].

Since the results of the glass bead characterization are distribution curves, the analysis of results is mainly qualitative. However, to compare the glass beads' composition and use their characteristics as variables in the statistical model, some parameters were obtained from the distributions of the grain size, thickness-to-length ratio, and sphericity to discretize the results.

The size distribution of glass beads was evaluated considering whether the composition is well graded, or not, by the coefficients of uniformity (C_U) and curvature (C_C) commonly employed in soil mechanics for analyzing granular materials [34,35]. The coefficient of uniformity is defined by Equation (1):

$$C_U = \frac{D_{10}}{D_{60}}, \qquad (1)$$

where D_{10} and D_{60} correspond to the diameter (particle size) at which 10% and 60% of particles are smaller, respectively. The coefficient of uniformity (C_U) evaluates the uniformity of a granular material. The material is considered uniform if C_U is lower than 2, i.e., the particles' size distribution is concentrated at one size range. The coefficient of curvature (C_C) is described by Equation (2):

$$C_C = \frac{D_{10}{}^2}{D_{10} \times D_{60}}, \qquad (2)$$

where D_{30} corresponds to the diameter (particle size) at which 30% of particles are smaller. The coefficient of curvature (C_C) identifies whether the particles' size distribution of the granular materials is continuous or not, i.e., presents a proportional percentage of several particle sizes. The material presents a continuous distribution if C_C is between 1 and 3. Continuous distribution characterizes well-graded sands and aggregates because it presents particles with several diameters that cause interlock and package between grains since the smaller particles will fill the voids between the larger particles [36]. This behavior is interesting for glass beads because a well-graded glass bead composition will present several embedment depths, which will improve the pavement markings' service life [33].

To characterize the thickness-to-length ratio curve, the parameters considered were bl_{20}, bl_{50}, and bl_{80}, which correspond to the thickness-to-length ratio at which 20%, 50%, and 80% of the particles, respectively, are lower than that value. Analogously, the characterization of the sphericity distribution curve considers the parameters $SPHT_{20}$, $SPHT_{50}$, and $SPHT_{80}$. Table 3 presents the results of the parameters used to characterize the glass beads' compositions.

Table 3. Characterization parameters for the glass beads' compositions.

Glass Bead	Parameters										
	D_{10} *	D_{30} *	D_{60} *	C_U	C_C	bl_{20}	bl_{50}	bl_{80}	$SPHT_{20}$	$SPHT_{50}$	$SPHT_{80}$
α-7030Br	0.368	0.489	0.625	1.698	1.040	0.62	0.84	0.93	0.53	0.75	0.82
α-100Br	0.335	0.450	0.557	1.663	1.085	0.61	0.82	0.92	0.51	0.74	0.81
β-7030Br	0.348	0.457	0.577	1.658	1.040	0.60	0.84	0.94	0.59	0.76	0.83
β-100Br	0.323	0.415	0.520	1.610	1.025	0.57	0.81	0.93	0.56	0.75	0.82
ω-7030Br	0.305	0.430	0.553	1.813	1.096	0.67	0.91	0.98	0.62	0.74	0.78
ω-100Br	0.270	0.494	0.518	1.919	1.745	0.67	0.91	0.98	0.62	0.74	0.78
δ-7030T	0.447	0.620	0.810	1.812	1.062	0.81	0.93	0.97	0.71	0.77	0.82
δ-5050T	0.485	0.698	0.886	1.827	1.134	0.83	0.93	0.97	0.71	0.77	0.82
δ-3070T	0.568	0.805	0.928	1.634	1.229	0.85	0.93	0.97	0.71	0.77	0.82
ε-7030Br	0.348	0.457	0.577	1.658	1.040	0.60	0.84	0.94	0.59	0.76	0.83

* Diameter in mm.

The glass beads are fine granular materials with their particles' size distribution inside a small size range. Therefore, glass beads present uniform size distribution with C_U values varying from 1.6 to 2.0. The glass beads also present well-graded (continuous) gradation, confirmed by the C_C, which is desirable for proper retroreflectivity performance over time.

4. Test Site Results: Statistical Analysis

The data collected at experimental test sites 1, 2, and 3 yielded over 19,000 retroreflectivity values, encompassing the characteristics of paints, glass beads, and the test site itself. Relying solely on graphical analysis for evaluating pavement markings' performance would introduce bias into the qualitative analysis results. To ensure a robust results analysis and to quantify the impact of each variable on retroreflectivity values and pavement markings' performance, statistical analysis was conducted.

In this section, the Generalized Additive Models for Location, Scale, and Shape (GAMLSSs) are implemented due to their flexibility in addressing a wide range of distributions and incorporating random effects to account for data correlation [37,38]. The GAMLSSs can be understood as an extension of the Generalized Linear Models (GLMs). The model was adjusted and its parameters were estimated using the *gamlss* library of the software R version 4.2.2 [39].

In the descriptive analysis, it was observed that the distribution of retroreflectivity is positively skewed. Therefore, a Weibull distribution was considered in this study to be suitable for modeling the positive random variable (retroreflectivity) representing values until the end of service. It is worth noting that the normal distribution did not fit the data well, as expected based on the data distribution. Let y'_{ijk} be a vector representing the retroreflectivity observed for i paint characteristics during a j time period of days after painting at the k test site. Conditional on the random effects u, assume that the elements of y are independent and follow a Weibull distribution.

Thus, the Weibull regression model considered is described by Equation (3):

$$Y_{ij}|u \sim \text{Weibull}(.)$$

$$\ln(\mu_{ijk}) = (\theta_0 + u_k) + \sum_{j=1}^{8} \theta_{1,j} X_{t,j} + \theta_2 X_{v.sol} + \theta_3 X_{bl50} + \theta_4 X_{CU} + \theta_5 X_{CC} + \theta_6 X_{spht_{20}}$$
$$+ \sum_{j=1}^{8} \theta_{7,j} X_{t,j \times v.sol} + \theta_8 X_{CU \times CC},$$

(3)

where μ_{ijk} is the mean of the response variable related to the explanatory variables through the logarithm link function. The explanatory variables considered in this study are paints' volume solids ($X_{v.sol}$), glass beads' coefficient of uniformity (X_{CU}), coefficient of curvature (X_{CC}), and shape characteristics ($X_{spht_{20}}$ and $X_{bl_{50}}$), and the dichotomous time variables $X_{t,1} = (0, 20]$, $X_{t,2} = (20, 40]$, $X_{t,3} = (40, 60]$, $X_{t,4} = (60, 80]$, $X_{t,5} = (80, 100]$, $X_{t,6} = (100, 200]$, $X_{t,7} = (200, 300]$, and $X_{t,8} = (300, 800]$, which represent the time periods (days elapsed since the test site construction) during which retroreflectivity was observed. Note that parentheses brackets indicate an open interval, not including a start point, while a closed interval includes the end point and is denoted with the square brackets, as a mathematical notation. Thus, if $X_{t,j} = 1$, the retroreflectivity was mensurated in the first 20 days of application of the pavement marking; the other time variables assume a value of zero in this case. Categorizing the time variable helps to evaluate changes in the degradation rate of pavement markings over time, which is not linear. It is important to highlight that the variable time accounts for the effect of traffic and weather on the pavement marking degradation.

The continuous variables $X_{v.sol}$, X_{CU}, X_{CC}, and $X_{bl_{50}}$ represent the values of these properties obtained from the characterization tests. On the other hand, the variable $X_{spht_{20}}$ is dichotomous and assumes a value of one when the $SPHT_{20}$ of the paint is higher than 0.59, or zero otherwise. Finally, the $\theta' = (\theta_0, \ldots, \theta_8)$ vector represents the fixed parameters to be estimated using maximum likelihood [37,38], and the random intercept u_k with $k = 1, 2, 3$ was considered to deal with the variability of the measurement at a distinct test site.

During the model selection process, other variables, such as paint consistency and density, were considered. However, these variables were insignificant to the model (*p*-value > 0.05). Therefore, only variables contributing to the model significance were included in Equation (3). In addition, interactions between explanatory variables were also considered. Interactions evaluate whether the association between the target variable and the independent variable varies based on the value of another independent variable. The interactions between all variables were considered in the model.

The final model presented in Equation (3) includes the variables and interactions selected using a stepwise algorithm based on the Akaike information criterion (AIC) [37,38]. The interpretability of the final model was also considered during the selection process. It is worth noting that a data cleansing process was conducted on the retroreflectivity dataset with the intention of removing any typos or outliers. Retroreflectivity values lower than 70 mcd/m²/lx were also excluded from the dataset to simulate an experiment, using as the interruption criteria the end of service life as considered by the MUTCD [40].

4.1. Model Adjustment

The data was adjusted to the model proposed in Equation (3), and the parameters were estimated using the *gamlss* library of the software R [39]. Table 4 presents the estimates of the parameters, their standard errors, and the *p*-values. All variables were found to be significant at a 5.0% significance level. Despite the variable $X_{v.sol}$ not being significant, it was kept in the model due to its significant interaction with time.

To validate the adequacy of the fitted model, a residual analysis was run, and Figure 8 presents the diagnostic plots of the normalized randomized quantile residuals [41]. The diagnostic plots in Figure 8 show that there is no violation of the model assumptions, and the residuals are normally distributed, confirming the adequacy of the fitted data to the model.

Table 4. The model's estimated parameters.

	Variable	Parameter	Estimate	Standard Error	p-Value
Main effects	Intercept	θ_0	−7.330	0.362	<0.001
	$X_{t,2}$: (20, 40]	$\theta_{1,2}$	−5.850	0.640	<0.001
	$X_{t,3}$: (40, 60]	$\theta_{1,3}$	−8.822	0.587	<0.001
	$X_{t,4}$: (60, 80]	$\theta_{1,4}$	−8.281	0.720	<0.001
	$X_{t,5}$: (80, 100]	$\theta_{1,5}$	−10.195	0.612	<0.001
	$X_{t,6}$: (100, 200]	$\theta_{1,6}$	−11.199	0.421	<0.001
	$X_{t,7}$: (200, 300]	$\theta_{1,7}$	−11.308	0.590	<0.001
	$X_{t,8}$: (300, 800]	$\theta_{1,8}$	−88.414	0.627	<0.001
	V.sol	θ_2	−0.003	0.005	0.404
	bl_{50}	θ_3	0.011	0.005	<0.001
	C_U	θ_4	6.652	0.113	<0.001
	C_C	θ_5	9.055	0.150	<0.001
	$SPHT_{20}$	θ_6	0.186	0.054	<0.001
Interactions	V.sol × $X_{t,2}$: (20, 40]	$\theta_{7,2}$	0.090	0.010	<0.001
	V.sol × $X_{t,3}$: (40, 60]	$\theta_{7,3}$	0.133	0.009	<0.001
	V.sol × $X_{t,4}$: (60, 80]	$\theta_{7,4}$	0.118	0.011	<0.001
	V.sol × $X_{t,5}$: (80, 100]	$\theta_{7,5}$	0.148	0.010	<0.001
	V.sol × $X_{t,6}$: (100, 200]	$\theta_{7,6}$	0.159	0.007	<0.001
	V.sol × $X_{t,7}$: (200, 300]	$\theta_{7,7}$	0.156	0.010	<0.001
	V.sol × $X_{t,8}$: (300, 800]	$\theta_{7,8}$	0.120	0.010	<0.001
	$C_U × C_C$	θ_8	−4.841	0.078	<0.001

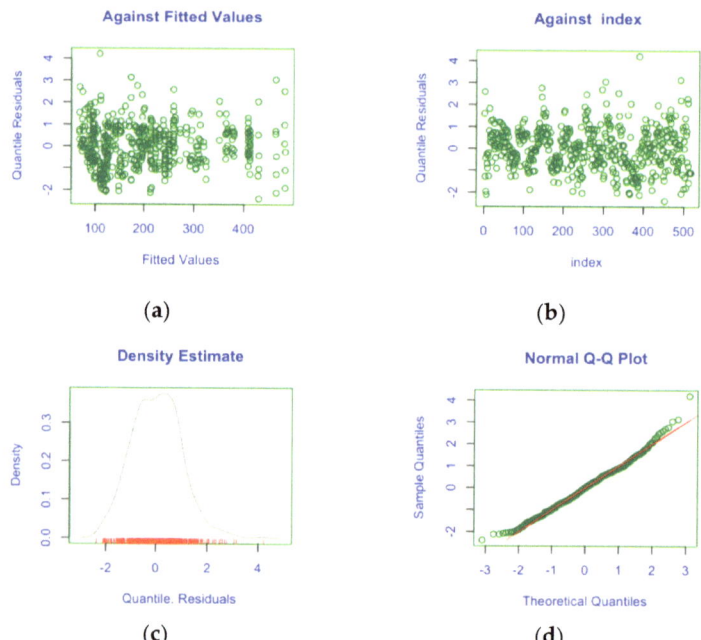

Figure 8. Model's diagnostic plots: (**a**) Residuals × Fitted Values; (**b**) Residuals × Index; (**c**) Residuals distribution; (**d**) Normal Q-Q plot.

4.2. Results Analysis

Given the model results, the coefficients obtained may be interpreted to analyze the variables' impact on the average retroreflectivity. It is worth mentioning that in the time variable, the category $X_{t,1} = (0, 20]$ is the reference category. Therefore, the effects of the other time variables are interpreted in comparison to $X_{t,1}$.

Regarding the covariates without interactions, it is noteworthy that the parameter estimates for the $X_{bl_{50}}$ and $X_{spht_{20}}$ variables are positive, indicating that an increase in their values is associated with an increase in the mean retroreflectivity. Enhancing the roundness of glass beads (X_{bl50}) by 0.1 results in an average increase of 11.59% in retroreflectivity because $\exp(\theta_3 \times X_{bl_{50}}) - 1 = \exp(0.011 \times 0.1 \times 100) - 1 = 0.1159$. Analogously, the impact of glass beads' sphericity on the pavement markings may be calculated as $\exp(\theta_6 \times X_{spht_{20}}) - 1 = \exp(0.186 \times 1) - 1 = 0.205$, i.e., pavement markings with glass beads with a sphericity higher than 0.59 present retroreflectivity, on average, 20.5% higher when compared to pavement markings with glass beads with sphericity lower than 0.59. These parameters characterize the glass beads' shape, and the results confirm the importance of shape to retroreflectivity [8].

To analyze the impact of C_U and C_C on retroreflectivity, it is necessary to consider the interaction between these variables. The size and gradation of glass beads also impact the retroreflectivity. However, an evaluation of glass beads' size and gradation beyond the granulometric curves or even the quantification of different beads' gradation on retroreflectivity was not found in the literature. Therefore, the evaluation of the coefficients related to C_U and C_C is important to understand the grain size distribution contribution to retroreflectivity. Since there is an interaction between C_U and C_C, their impact on retroreflectivity must be evaluated simultaneously.

A higher coefficient of uniformity indicates a large range of sizes for glass beads, while higher coefficient of curvature indicates the equivalent distribution of several particles' sizes. The increase in retroreflectivity related to higher C_U and C_C values shows the importance of selecting well graded glass beads. The improvement of retroreflectivity occurs due to the distribution of several glass bead sizes on the pavement markings' surface since the larger particles fall on the paint surface first, and then the smaller particles fill the voids between the larger beads, which expands the area of the markings covered with glass beads. Thus, there is a higher area available to reflect light and improve the night visibility of pavement markings [10].

Supposing a glass bead sample with $X_{CU} = 1.700$, an increase in X_{CC} by 0.1 will improve the retroreflectivity, on average, by 8.71%. The difference between the R_L before ($X_{CC_1} = 1.0$) and after the C_C increase ($X_{CC_2} = 1.1$) may be calculated as $\exp[(\theta_4 \times X_{CU} + \theta_5 \times X_{CC_2} - \theta_8 \times X_{CU} \times X_{CC_2}) - (\theta_4 \times X_{CU} + \theta_5 \times X_{CC_1} - \theta_8 \times X_{CU} \times X_{CC_1})] - 1 = \exp[(6.652 \times 1.700 + 9.055 \times 1.1 - 4.841 \times 1.700 \times 1.1) - (6.652 \times 1.700 + 9.055 \times 1.0 - 4.841 \times 1.700 \times 1.0)] - 1 = 8.71\%$.

Regarding the paint's characteristics, the effect of the variable $X_{v.sol}$ on the retroreflectivity is analyzed considering the different time periods in which the retroreflectivity was measured. An increase of one unit in the volume of solids leads to an average decrease in retroreflectivity of 0.23% when measured within 20 days after the application of the pavement marking. However, this decrease is not statistically significant (p-value = 0.404).

The volume solids of paints are associated with pavement markings' durability. The estimates of the parameters of the time intervals obtained at the model adjustment show that the decrease in retroreflectivity over time depends on the volume solids. Supposing a pavement marking using a paint with V.sol = 62.0, the retroreflectivity decreases, on average, by 24.38% ($\exp(\theta_4 \times X_{t,2} + \theta_{7,2} \times X_{t,2} \times X_{V.sol}) - 1 = \exp(-5.850 \times 1 + 0.090 \times 1 \times 62) - 1 = 0.2438$) at the time interval $X_{t,2} = (20, 40]$ when compared to the initial time interval. Analogously, the time interval $X_{t,3} = (40, 60]$ presents, on average, 43.50% lower retroreflectivity values. Regarding the other time intervals, the reduction in retroreflectivity is, on average, 62.36% for $X_{t,4} = (60, 80]$, 63.51% for $X_{t,5} = (80,100]$, 74.08% for $X_{t,6} = (100,200]$, 80.30% for $X_{t,7} = (200,300]$, and 74.64% for $X_{t,8} = (300,800]$. The volume solids is an important characteristic because it evaluates the percentage of paint's volume without the volatile fraction, thus representing the percentage of the dried paint's thickness compared to the wet thickness. Therefore, this parameter influenced the retroreflectivity over time instead of the initial retroreflectivity.

Retroreflectivity decreases progressively over time, but the model's estimated parameters show that the reduction over time is not linear. There is a severe decrease for the first 100 days (until $X_{t,5}$) and a relative continuous reduction for the other time intervals. However, the retroreflectivity reduction is more intense for the time interval $X_{t,7}$ than the time interval $X_{t,8}$, which shows that the estimated retroreflectivity is higher for interval $X_{t,8}$ than $X_{t,7}$. This occurs because the evaluation of time as an interval accounts for the seasonal variation of retroreflectivity, which may present higher values after rain due to surface cleaning, as reported by Salles et al. [42].

Considering a one-unit increase in the volume solids of paints, the retroreflectivity improves by 9.15% when it shifts from being measured within the time interval $X_{t,1} = (0, 20]$ to being measured within the interval $X_{t,2} = (20, 40]$. Analogously, the average retroreflectivity improvement is, on average, 14.0%, 12.3%, 15.7%, 17.0%, 16.6%, and 12.6% for time intervals $X_{t,3}$, $X_{t,4}$, $X_{t,5}$, $X_{t,6}$, $X_{t,7}$, and $X_{t,8}$, respectively.

The positive contribution of volume solids to the average retroreflectivity shows that the retroreflectivity decreases slower for paints with higher volume solids, i.e., higher volume solids paints reduce the degradation rate of pavement markings' retroreflectivity.

An increase in paints' volume solids contributes to the occurrence of the retroreflectivity peak and improves the expected service life of pavement markings. The V.sol is responsible for the thickness of the paints' film on the pavement surface after the drying of paint. Higher V.sol leads to higher dry paint thickness compared to lower V.sol paints if they are applied at the same wet thickness. Therefore, the glass beads present higher embedment depths that will require more wear to remove the particles from the markings' surface, which improves the service life of pavement markings.

Finally, random effects were incorporated into the model to deal with the variability between the test sites. The random effect in the intercept for the variable u_k refers to each test site, in which $u_1 = -0.1097$ for test site 1, $u_2 = -0.0082$ for test site 2, and $u_3 = 0.1179$ for test site 3. The intercepts indicates that the retroreflectivity values were, on average, higher for test site 3, followed by test site 2 and test site 1, respectively. The results show that, even with the higher concentration of glass beads at test site 2 (600 g/m^2), the retroreflectivity values were most impacted by material characteristics.

5. Discussion

This research evaluated three experimental test sites of pavement markings in a Brazilian road and proposed a statistical model to assess the quantitative impact of the characteristics of the water-based paints with acrylic resin and the characteristics of the glass beads used on the retroreflectivity value over time for the test sites. The analysis of the coefficients' estimates was important to quantify the impact of each materials' characteristic on the retroreflectivity and on the pavement markings' service life.

5.1. Glass Bead Characteristics

The glass beads' shape has a strong impact on the initial retroreflectivity of the pavement markings [8]. Regarding the coefficients of the properties of shape, both bl$_{50}$ and SPHT$_{20}$ present a positive impact on the retroreflectivity; however, the SPHT$_{20}$ has a stronger contribution to the retroreflectivity improvement than bl$_{50}$. In addition, the glass beads evaluated in this research present poor shape properties considering the threshold of sphericity to classify the particles as round (SPHT > 0.93), while a much larger percentage of particles for all glass beads may be classified as round considering the thickness-to-length ratio (b/l > 0.85). Therefore, considering the glass beads evaluated herein, they meet the requirements of shape, b/l > 0.85, more easily than the requirements for sphericity, SPHT > 0.93. Moreover, SPHT is harder to achieve and has a higher impact on the retroreflectivity. Thus, it is recommended that the glass beads evaluated herein should present better shape characteristics, mainly sphericity.

The previous study reporting the impact of glass bead gradation on pavement markings' retroreflectivity also discretized the size distribution, but evaluated it as a rank between the samples evaluated [8]. This research calculated and attributed two coefficients commonly used to classify granular materials in soil mechanics, the coefficients of uniformity (C_U) and curvature (C_C), to characterize the size distribution of each glass bead sample. The results of both coefficients are in a short range, which might indicate the need of proposing a specific classification range for glass beads. Ultimately, the estimates of the model's coefficients showed that the improvement of glass beads' gradation by C_C is more important than the uniformity (C_U). The coefficients could evaluate, discretize, and differentiate the glass beads' size distributions.

Based on the results, the expected coefficient of uniformity for glass beads must range around 1.5 to 1.9 to guarantee the absence of fine particles that reduce the retroreflectivity or larger particles that will cause a lack of embedment depth and premature failure of pavement markings. Regarding the coefficient of curvature, the results obtained range around 1.05 to 1.20; this may be an adequate range to guarantee a well-graded glass bead to improve R_L. It is important to highlight that these ranges are only premises based on the results obtained herein. However, it is recommended to calculate the C_U and C_C for other glass beads to observe how they impact the retroreflectivity and evaluate whether the coefficients can be used to create a new range or not.

5.2. Paint Characteristics

The paints were evaluated regarding their consistency, specific gravity, and volume solids. In order to fit the data to the statistical model proposed in this research, the only significant variable was the volume solids. An increase in this variable causes a non-significant reduction in the initial retroreflectivity; however, considering the interaction with time, an increase in volume solids reduces the degradation rate of retroreflectivity over time, i.e., improves the service life of pavement markings.

Despite the limitation of using only the volume solids as a paint characteristic, the model captured the expected tendency of retroreflectivity. It is important to highlight that other characteristics of paints impact pavement markings' retroreflectivity. The results obtained by the analysis of the model's coefficients show that using white water-based paints with acrylic resin and higher volume solids could improve pavement markings' performance, i.e., considering commercial paints with similar characteristics, in which it is not possible to adjust the formulation, the one with higher volume solids should be chosen because it may present a better performance over time.

6. Conclusions

This research analyzed the retroreflectivity data collected from pavement markings at Brazilian test sites under real traffic action subjected to tropical climate conditions. It adjusted a statistical model to evaluate the influence of paint and glass bead characteristics on pavement markings' service life.

The research demonstrated the importance of the proper characterization of paints and glass beads before field application. Paints' volume solids are an important characteristic for pavement markings' durability since higher values of volume solids in paints were found to enhance pavement markings' durability. Regarding the glass beads, the results emphasize the importance of their shape on the initial retroreflectivity. Moreover, the research addresses the characterization of glass beads' size distribution as a discrete value, facilitating comparison based on gradation.

The research findings offer guidance for pavement marking practitioners and road authorities in selecting materials. By understanding the impact of paint characteristics and glass bead properties on retroreflectivity, practitioners can make informed choices regarding suitable paint and glass beads. Moreover, improving pavement markings' service life reduces the maintenance frequency and, consequently, reduces road safety issues.

From the results obtained, it is possible to conclude that white water-based paints with higher volume solids are preferable for improving pavement markings' service life. In addition to the importance of glass beads' shape characteristics regarding sphericity

(SPHT) and thickness-to-length ratio (b/l), it is also recommended to characterize the glass beads' grain size distribution by the coefficients of uniformity and curvature.

It is important to emphasize that this research does not aim to reduce or replace the characterization tests of paints and glass beads. Rather, it evaluates which parameters most significantly affect the retroreflectivity to improve the acceptance limits of these materials. Furthermore, the results obtained herein are based on a restricted number of materials subjected to specific climate conditions and traffic. Therefore, the application of this research must be carefully conducted, considering only white acrylic water-based paints and glass beads with characteristics similar to those evaluated herein.

Author Contributions: Conceptualization, L.N.M. and L.B.; methodology, L.N.M., O.A., G.L. and K.V.; validation, L.N.M. and O.A.; formal analysis, L.N.M., K.V., O.A. and L.B.; resources, L.B., K.V. and G.L.; writing—original draft preparation, L.N.M. and O.A.; writing—review and editing, L.N.M., K.V., L.B., O.A. and G.L.; visualization, L.N.M., G.L. and O.A.; supervision, K.V. and L.B.; project administration, L.B.; funding acquisition, L.B., K.V. and G.L. All authors have read and agreed to the published version of the manuscript.

Funding: This study was funded in part by the Coordenação de Aperfeiçoamento de Pessoal de Nível Superior-Brasil (CAPES)-Finance Code 001 and by Recurso para Desenvolvimento Tecnológico (RDT) from concessionary Autopista Fernão Dias with the supervision of Agência Nacional de Transportes Terrestres (ANTT).

Institutional Review Board Statement: Not applicable.

Informed Consent Statement: Not applicable.

Data Availability Statement: Restrictions apply to the availability of these data. Data were obtained from Autopista Fernão Dias and are available from the authors with the permission of Autopista Fernão Dias.

Conflicts of Interest: Author Guilherme Linhares was employed by the company Arteris S.A. The remaining authors declare that the re-search was conducted in the absence of any commercial or financial relationships that could be construed as a potential conflict of interest.

References

1. WHO-World Health Organization. *Global Plan for the Decade of Action for Road Safety 2021–2030*; World Health Organization: Geneva, Switzerland, 2021.
2. Burghardt, T.E.; Mosböck, H.; Pashkevich, A.; Fiolić, M. Horizontal Road Markings for Human and Machine Vision. In *Proceedings of the Transportation Research Procedia*; Elsevier: Amsterdam, The Netherlands, 2020; Volume 48.
3. Smadi, O.; Souleyrette, R.R.; Ormand, D.J.; Hawkins, N. Pavement Marking Retroreflectivity Analysis of Safety Effectiveness. *Transp. Res. Rec.* **2008**, *2056*, 17–24. [CrossRef]
4. E1710-11; Standard Test Method for Measurement of Retroreflective Pavement Marking Materials with CEN-Prescribed Geometry Using a Portable. American Society for Testing and Materials: West Conshohocken, PA, USA, 2011.
5. Carlson, P.J.; Park, E.S.; Kang, D.H. Investigation of Longitudinal Pavement Marking Retroreflectivity and Safety. *Transp. Res. Rec.* **2013**, *2337*, 59–66. [CrossRef]
6. Guan, Y.; Hu, J.; Wang, R. Study on the Enrichment of Pavement Marking Width and Retroreflectivity on Elderly Drivers' Safety. *Transp. Res. Rec.* **2024**. [CrossRef]
7. Babić, D.; Fiolić, M.; Babić, D.; Gates, T. Road Markings and Their Impact on Driver Behaviour and Road Safety: A Systematic Review of Current Findings. *J. Adv. Transp.* **2020**, *2020*, 1–19. [CrossRef]
8. Smadi, O.; Hawkins, N.; Aldemir-Bektas, B.; Carlson, P.; Pike, A.; Davies, C. Recommended Laboratory Test for Predicting the Initial Retroreflectivity of Pavement Markings from Glass Bead Quality. *Transp. Res. Rec. J. Transp. Res. Board* **2014**, *2440*, 94–102. [CrossRef]
9. Wenzel, K.M.; Burghardt, T.E.; Pashkevich, A.; Buckermann, W.A. Glass Beads for Road Markings: Surface Damage and Retroreflection Decay Study. *Appl. Sci.* **2022**, *12*, 2258. [CrossRef]
10. Zhang, G.; Hummer, J.E.; Rasdorf, W. Impact of Bead Density on Paint Pavement Marking Retroreflectivity. *J. Transp. Eng.* **2010**, *136*, 773–781. [CrossRef]
11. Babić, D.; Burghardt, T.E.; Babić, D. Application and Characteristics of Waterborne Road Marking Paint. *Int. J. Traffic Transp. Eng.* **2015**, *5*, 150–169. [CrossRef]
12. Andrady, A.L. *Pavement Marking Materials: Assessing Environment Friendly Performance*; National Academy Press: Washington, DC, USA, 1997; ISBN 0309060648.

13. Lee, J.T.; Maleck, T.L.; Taylor, W.C. Pavement Marking Material Evaluation Study in Michigan. *ITE J. Institute Transp. Eng.* **1999**, *69*, 44.
14. Abboud, N.; Bowman, B.L. Cost- and Longevity-Based Scheduling of Paint and Thermoplastic Striping. *Transp. Res. Rec.* **2002**, *1974*, 55–62. [CrossRef]
15. Zhang, Y.; Wu, D. Methodologies to Predict Service Lives of Pavement Marking Materials. *J. Transp. Res. Forum* **2010**, *45*, 5–18. [CrossRef]
16. Hummer, J.E.; Rasdorf, W.; Zhang, G. Linear Mixed-Effects Models for Paint Pavement-Marking Retroreflectivity Data. *J. Transp. Eng.* **2011**, *137*, 705–716. [CrossRef]
17. Robertson, J.; Sarasua, W.; Johnson, J.; Davis, W. A Methodology for Estimating and Comparing the Lifecycles of High-Build and Conventional Waterborne Pavement Markings on Primary and Secondary Roads in South Carolina. *Public Work. Manag. Policy* **2013**, *18*, 360–378. [CrossRef]
18. Sitzabee, W.E.; White, E.D.; Dowling, A.W. Degradation Modeling of Polyurea Pavement Markings. *Public Work. Manag. Policy* **2013**, *18*, 185–199. [CrossRef]
19. Babić, D.; Ščukanec, A.; Babić, D.; Fiolić, M. Model for Predicting Road Markings Service Life. *Balt. J. Road Bridg. Eng.* **2019**, *14*, 341–359. [CrossRef]
20. Mousa, M.R.; Mousa, S.R.; Hassan, M.; Carlson, P.; Elnaml, I.A. Predicting the Retroreflectivity Degradation of Waterborne Paint Pavement Markings Using Advanced Machine Learning Techniques. *Transp. Res. Rec.* **2021**, *2675*, 483–494. [CrossRef]
21. NBR 16184:2021; Sinalização Horizontal Viária—Esferas e Microesferas de Vidro—Requisitos e Métodos de Ensaio. Associação Brasileira de Normas Técnicas:: Rio de Janeiro, RJ, Brazil, 2021.
22. AASHTO M247-13; Standard Specification for Glass Beads Used in Pavement Markings. American Association of State Highway and Transportation Officials: Washington, DC, USA, 2013.
23. D562-14; Standard Test Method for Consistency of Paints Measuring Krebs Unit (KU) Viscosity Using a Stormer-Type Viscometer. American Society for Testing and Materials: West Conshohocken, PA, USA, 2014.
24. D1475-13; Standard Test Method for Density of Liquid Coatings, Inks, and Related Products. American Society for Testing and Materials: West Conshohocken, PA, USA, 2013.
25. D2792-17; Standard Practice for Solvent and Fuel Resistance of Traffic Paint. American Society for Testing and Materials: West Conshohocken, PA, USA, 2017.
26. AASHTO R98-20; Standard Practice for Standard Practice for Determination of Size and Shape of Glass Beads Used in Traffic Markings by Means of Computerized Optical Method. American Association of State Highway and Transportation Officials: Washington, DC, USA, 2020.
27. Google Earth 10.49.0.0 Test Site View (22°54′31″ S 46°25′29″ W). Available online: https://www.google.com/earth/about/ (accessed on 12 March 2024).
28. NTPEP. *NTPEP Best Practices Manual*; American Association of State Highway and Transportation Officials: Washington, DC, USA, 2004.
29. Zhang, Y.L.; Pike, A.M.; Ge, H.C.; Carlson, P.J. Comparison of Designs of Field Test Decks for Pavement Marking Materials. *Transp. Res. Rec.* **2011**, *5*, 95–102. [CrossRef]
30. Pike, A.M.; Songchitruksa, P. Predicting Pavement Marking Service Life with Transverse Test Deck Data. *Transp. Res. Rec. J. Transp. Res. Board* **2015**, *2482*, 16–22. [CrossRef]
31. Mazzoni, L.N.; Ho, L.L.; Vasconcelos, K.L.; Bernucci, L.L.B. Probabilistic Service Life Model of Pavement Marking by Degradation Data. *Transp. Res. Rec.* **2022**, *2676*, 328–340. [CrossRef]
32. NBR 13699:2021; Sinalização Horizontal Viária-Tinta à Base de Resina Acrílica Emulsionada Em Água. Associação Brasileira de Normas Técnicas: Rio de Janeiro, RJ, Brazil, 2021.
33. Migletz, J.; Fish, J.K.; Graham, J.L. *Roadway Delineation Practices Handbook*; Federal Highway Administration: Washington, DC, USA, 1994.
34. Chai, X.; Sheng, Y.; Liu, J.; Xu, Y.; Liu, H. Experimental Study on the Mechanical Properties of Saturated Tailing Sand with Different Particle Sizes. *Appl. Sci.* **2022**, *12*, 12231. [CrossRef]
35. Daghistani, F.; Abuel-Naga, H. Evaluating the Influence of Sand Particle Morphology on Shear Strength: A Comparison of Experimental and Machine Learning Approaches. *Appl. Sci.* **2023**, *13*, 8160. [CrossRef]
36. Pinto, C. *De S. Curso Básico de Mecânica Dos Solos*, 3rd ed.; Oficina dos Textos: São Paulo, SP, Brazil, 2006.
37. Stasinopoulos, M.D.; Rigby, R.A.; Heller, G.Z.; Voudouris, V.; De Bastiani, F. *Flexible Regression and Smoothing: Using GAMLSS in R*; CRC Press: Chapman and Hall/CRC: New York, NY, USA, 2017; ISBN 1351980378.
38. Rigby, R.A.; Stasinopoulos, M.D.; Heller, G.Z.; De Bastiani, F. *Distributions for Modeling Location, Scale, and Shape: Using GAMLSS in R*; Chapman and Hall/CRC: New York, NY, USA, 2019; ISBN 0429298544.
39. Stasinopoulos, D.M.; Rigby, R.A. Generalized Additive Models for Location Scale and Shape (GAMLSS) in R. *J. Stat. Softw.* **2008**, *23*, 1–46. [CrossRef]
40. Federal Highway Administration. *Manual on Uniform Traffic Control Devices for Streets and Highways (MUTCD)*, 11th ed.; Federal Highway Administration: Washington, DC, USA, 2023.

41. Dunn, P.K.; Smyth, G.K. Randomized Quantile Residuals. *J. Comput. Graph. Stat.* **1996**, *5*, 236–244. [CrossRef]
42. Salles, L.S.; Pereira, D.D.S.; Texeira, D.L.K.; Specht, L.P. Road Markings Retroreflectivity Experimental Assessment Observarions on Rainfall, Dirt, Retreflectometer Geometry and Minumum Requirements. In Proceedings of the 95th Annual Meeting of Transportation Research Board, Washington, DC, USA, 10–14 January 2016.

Disclaimer/Publisher's Note: The statements, opinions and data contained in all publications are solely those of the individual author(s) and contributor(s) and not of MDPI and/or the editor(s). MDPI and/or the editor(s) disclaim responsibility for any injury to people or property resulting from any ideas, methods, instructions or products referred to in the content.

Article

A Case Study of Pavement Foundation Support and Drainage Evaluations of Damaged Urban Cement Concrete Roads

Weiwei Wang [1], Wen Xiang [1], Cheng Li [1,*], Songli Qiu [2], Yujin Wang [2], Xuhao Wang [1], Shanshan Bu [3] and Qinghua Bian [4,*]

[1] Key Laboratory for Special Area Highway Engineering of Ministry of Education, Chang'an University, Xi'an 710064, China; wwwang@chd.edu.cn (W.W.); 2021121169@chd.edu.cn (W.X.); wangxh@chd.edu.cn (X.W.)
[2] Ningbo Communications Engineering Construction Group Co., Ltd., Ningbo 315099, China; 2022221291@chd.edu.cn (S.Q.); 2021121179@chd.edu.cn (Y.W.)
[3] College of Transportation Engineering, Chang'an University, Xi'an 710064, China; bssglxy@chd.edu.cn
[4] Gansu Road & Bridge Construction Group Shanjian Technology Company, Lanzhou 730314, China
* Correspondence: cli@chd.edu.cn (C.L.); wangzhifeng@chd.edu.cn (Q.B.)

Abstract: Surface cracks and joint deteriorations are typical premature failures of urban cement concrete pavement. However, traffic loads on the urban pavement are much lower than those on highways. Limited research has been conducted to investigate the causes of accelerated damage in urban cement concrete roads. To investigate the foundation issues that may cause the accelerated damage of urban cement concrete pavements, in this study, field evaluations were conducted to assess pavement foundation support and drainage conditions. Field visual inspections, Ground Penetrating Radar (GPR) survey, Dynamic Cone Penetrometer (DCP) test, and the Core-Hole Permeameter (CHP) test were performed. In urban residential areas with inadequate subgrade bearing capacity, cement concrete pavements are prone to early damage. Foundations with a higher content of coarse particles exhibit a higher CBR value, which can extend the service life of the pavement. The compaction of foundation materials near sewer pipelines and manholes is insufficient, leading to non-uniform support conditions. Moreover, the permeability of the foundation material can influence the service life of pavement surface structures. Foundation materials with fewer fine particles enhance drainage performance, contributing to a longer service life for PCC pavements. In areas with inadequate drainage, water accumulation reduces the bearing capacity of the foundation, thereby accelerating pavement deterioration. The poor bearing capacity and drainage conditions of the foundation lead to cavities between the surface layer and foundation material thus yielding stress concentrations on the pavement surface, which cause the formation of pavement surface cracks.

Keywords: urban cement concrete pavement; pavement foundation; filed test; support condition; drainage

1. Introduction

The use of concrete for road pavements is typical of several nations and regions, particularly in North America and parts of Asia such as India [1,2]. With the variable climate in North America and the hot and humid conditions in parts of Asia, urban roads mainly are Portland Cement Concrete (PCC) pavements due to their good durability. The design service life for PCC pavement in various specifications is usually over 20 years. In concrete pavements, cracking is one of the major types of premature damage [3–5]. Previous studies have shown that road damage in urban areas arises from a variety of interconnected factors [6–8]. Primarily, these issues originate from foundation problems, such as bearing capacity and drainage performance [9,10].

Past research shows that traffic loads can cause accumulated damage in concrete [11–14] and different types of traffic loads, such as light and heavy vehicles, have different long-term effects on PCC pavements [15–17]. Nemati and Uhlmeyer [18] replaced the original asphalt pavement at intersections with PCC pavement to tackle the issue of rutting caused by high traffic volumes and traffic loads, thereby prolonging the service life of the pavement. However, traffic loads on the urban pavement are much lower than those on highways [19]. Therefore, the insufficient foundation support or subbase stiffness of urban pavements may lead to accelerated damage and affect the service life [20–22]. Khoury et al. [23] discovered that the stiffness of the foundation is a crucial factor influencing the initiation of cracks in PCC slabs. This finding was substantiated through field survey experiments, which involved comparing the performance of two sections of Portland Cement Concrete pavements. Beckemeyer et al. [24] found that Jointed Plain Concrete Pavement (JPCP) designs are more prone to top-down cracking when the base layer consists of untreated Open-Graded Subbase (OGS) materials due to insufficient foundation support. Therefore, it is important to investigate the causes of premature failure in PCC pavements from the perspective of base layer bearing capacity.

Additionally, damage to PCC pavements can be affected by structural design and base layer drainage [25–28]. Zhu et al. [29] evaluated the performance of unbonded concrete overlays of PCC pavements in Ohio and found that damage caused by water accumulation within the structure seriously affected its serviceability. To address the issue of water accumulation on urban roads in India during the monsoon season, Joshi and Dave [30] constructed a permeable concrete pavement to study its permeability. Due to the large pore structure of previous concrete pavements, their strength and freeze-thaw resistance is significantly lower compared to traditional concrete pavements. This limitation hinders their widespread use [31,32]. Moreover, highly permeable materials allow water to infiltrate the interior of the concrete, leading to the corrosion of reinforcing steel, and ultimately resulting in the cracking of the road surface [33–35]. It is essential to investigate the early damage caused by water accumulation in traditional concrete pavements.

Environmental factors play a crucial role in the performance of pavements. The temperature and humidity variations in seasonally frozen or wet-freeze regions during different seasons can significantly affect the performance and response of PCC pavements [36]. Temperature fluctuations may cause concrete to expand or contract, thereby causing cracks [37]. High humidity levels can slow down the drying process of concrete, affecting its hardening and strength development. Additionally, humidity influences the freeze-thaw cycles, accelerating corrosion in reinforced concrete [38,39]. Glinicki et al. [40] conducted a study on a section of highway in a wet-freeze climate region that experienced premature damage and discovered that the alkali-silica reaction was one of the reasons for the early deterioration of the concrete pavement. PCC pavements in seasonally frozen or wet-freeze regions are more susceptible to premature failure.

Limited research has been conducted specifically addressing accelerated damage caused by urban cement concrete roads. Getachew et al. [41] and Magdi [42] conducted field surveys to assess road damage caused by inadequate drainage. They reviewed the condition of road and ground drainage infrastructure and explored the reasons for poor drainage. They attributed drainage problems to the irrational design of drainage systems and a lack of proper maintenance. Few studies focus on the impact of sewer pipelines under the pavement on the cracking of urban cement concrete pavements.

This study examines the service conditions of PCC pavements in seasonal frost regions. In seasonal frost regions, premature failure of cement concrete pavements often occurs due to the lack of systematic quality control methods. Research specifically addressing the accelerated damage to urban cement concrete roads is limited, prompting local governments to investigate the causes of early failures. Consequently, experimental tests were conducted at sites exhibiting early failures to examine the influence of foundation materials, bearing capacity, and drainage performance. By comparing sites with varying extents of cracking and surface damage, this research aims to assess how enhanced bearing capacity and drainage capabilities affect pavement service life, to provide insights for the design and maintenance of urban cement concrete pavements. To achieve these objectives, field visual inspections, Ground Penetrating Radar (GPR) surveys, Dynamic Cone Penetrometer (DCP) tests, Core-Hole Permeameter (CHP) tests, laboratory particle size analysis, liquid limit (LL), and plastic limit (PL) tests were performed at six test sites.

2. Site Conditions

In this study, a total of six test sites selected for investigation were in one city located in a seasonal frost region, the area where the city is located experiences four distinct seasonal changes, with hot summers, averaging around 30 °C, and cold winters, with an average temperature of about −6 °C. These sections are typical of those observed to be suffering accelerated in the form of surface cracks, joint deterioration, and D-cracking. For the six test sites, two types of pavement surface design were followed: Continuous Reinforced Concrete Pavement (CRCP) and Jointed Plain Concrete Pavement (JPCP) typically as shown in Figure 1. The steel bars were embedded at the mid-depth of the slab at 1.5 m spacing in both transverse and longitudinal directions, with overlap at the longitudinal joints. The other locations were unreinforced but did contain dowels across the transverse joints.

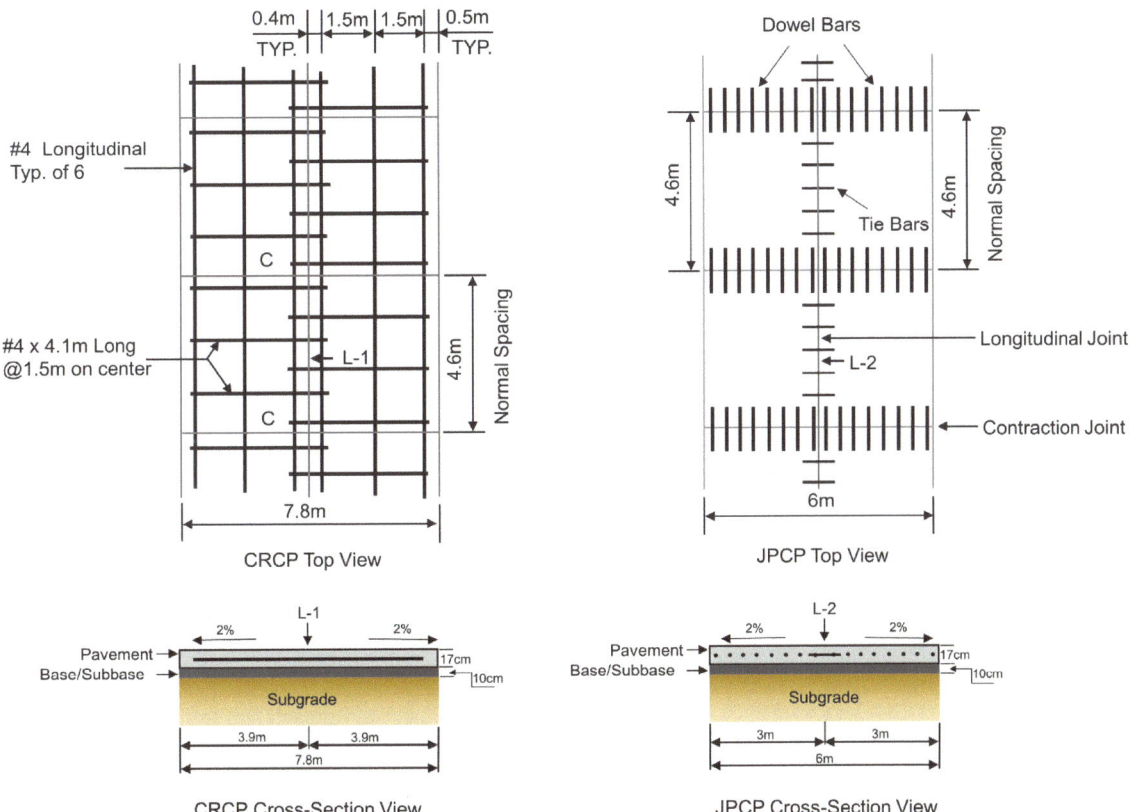

Figure 1. The design schematic of the two pavement types.

Figure 2 provides photos of the locations of the six test sites. The test site ID is named after the surface design type, service age, and site number. The diagram indicates that all test sites are within residential areas, subjected to traffic loads considerably lower than those on highways, with a load limit of 36 tons. Located on a secondary road, Site CRCP-23-B likely experiences even lighter vehicle traffic in comparison to the other sites, which are on the main roads of the residential area. Furthermore, Site CRCP-12 is positioned at the intersection of two roads and the Site CRCP-12 is close to a manhole and sewer pipelines.

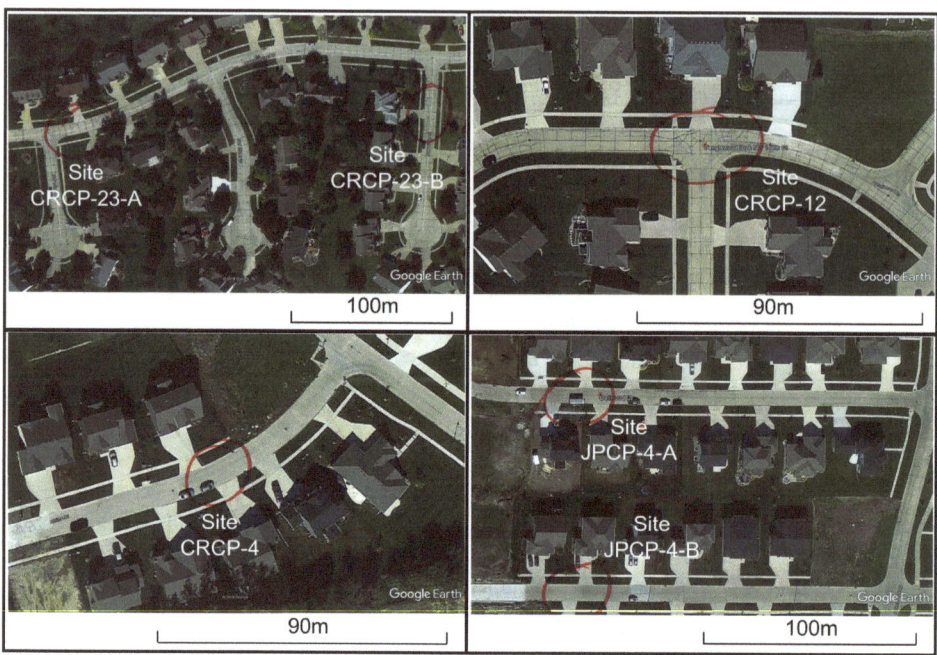

Figure 2. Aerial images of six selected testing sections (The parts marked with red circles are the specific test sites).

3. Test Methods

3.1. Method Introduction

In this study, field tests were performed to evaluate the performance of support and drainage conditions of pavement foundations. Laboratory soil index property tests were conducted on pavement foundation samples collected after drilling core holes. Table 1 summarizes the testing methods and corresponding test objectives.

Table 1. The field-testing methods and corresponding objectives.

Test Type	Test Name	Test Objective
Filed testing	Field visual inspections	• Determine the extent and location of cracks and joint deterioration
	Ground Penetrating Radar (GPR) Scan	• Determine the surface thickness and rebar location • Locate possible cavities beneath the slabs • Determine the coring locations
	Dynamic Cone Penetrometer (DCP) Test	• Evaluate the in-situ bearing capacity of pavement foundation materials in terms of CBR
	Core-Hole Permeameter (CHP) Test	• Evaluate in-situ hydraulic conductivity of pavement foundation materials
Laboratory testing	Particle size analysis and Atterberg limits test	• Determine the soil index properties and Unified Soil Classification System (USCS) classifications of the pavement foundation materials

Field visual inspections, GPR, CHP, and DCP tests aimed at assessing the performance of the pavement foundation of the test sites.

The GPR test is a nondestructive method commonly used to assess pavement thicknesses, determine locations of rebar, and identify defects such as voids within or beneath the pavement surface. In this study, a ground-coupled 1600 MHz antenna (model SIR-20, manufactured by GSSI) installed on a survey cart was used to collect three-dimensional (3D) information for the top 46 cm of the selected test sections, as shown in Figure 3.

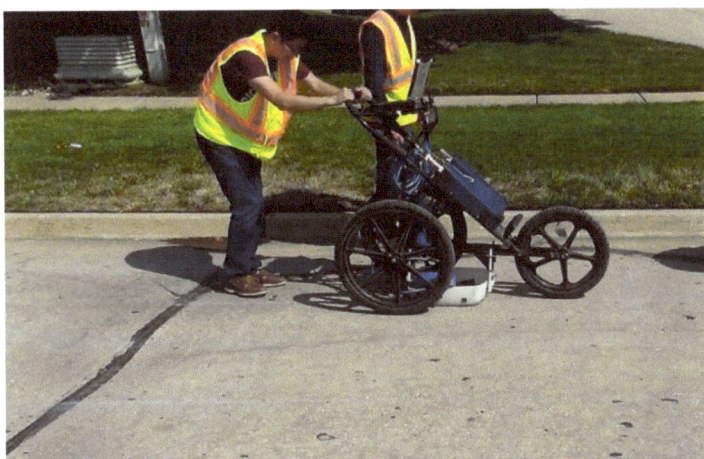

Figure 3. GPR survey conducted on a test site.

The DCP test was used to assess bearing capacity in terms of an empirically correlated CBR of pavement foundation materials. The test was performed in accordance with ASTM D6951 [43]. The test involves driving a conical point with a base diameter of 2 cm using an 8 kg hammer dropped at 57 cm. The penetration depth per blow was measured, which is referred to as the dynamic cone penetration index (DCPI). The DCPI was measured as follows for the various demonstration sections and used in the empirical correlations of Equations (1)–(3) to estimate the in situ CBR values.

For all soils except CL soils with CBR < 10 and CH soils,

$$DCP - CBR = \frac{292}{DCPI \times 25.4^{1.12}} \qquad (1)$$

For CL soils with CBR < 10,

$$DCP - CBR = \frac{1}{DCPI \times 0.432283} \qquad (2)$$

For CH soils,

$$DCP - CBR = \frac{1}{DCPI \times 0.072923} \qquad (3)$$

The CHP test was performed to evaluate the drainage performance of the foundation materials. The test uses the falling head method to measure the in-situ permeability of the foundation layers after drilling cores, the corresponding test device as shown in Figure 4.

In this testing methodology, a core hole with a diameter of 15 cm is bored through the pavement surface down to the underlying support layer. Subsequently, the testing apparatus is inserted into the borehole. To ensure an airtight seal within the interior of the core hole, an inflatable rubber tube is employed, inflated to an air pressure between 20 to 25 psi. The procedure includes the systematic recording of the water head loss rate from the apparatus, observed continuously over a period ranging from 20 to 60 min. The hydraulic conductivity (K_{CHP}) of the tested layer is calculated using Equation (4) following the approach described in ASTM D6391 [44].

$$K_{CHP} = R_t G_1 \frac{\ln(H_1/H_2)}{t_2 - t_1} \qquad (4)$$

$$R_t = \frac{2.2902 \times 0.9842^T}{T^{0.1702}} \quad (5)$$

$$G_1 = \left(\frac{\pi d^2}{11 D_1}\right)\left[1 + a\left(\frac{D_1}{4 b_1}\right)\right] \quad (6)$$

where H_1 and H_2 are effective heads (cm) at time t_1 and t_2 (s), respectively, R_t is the ratio of kinematic viscosity of permeant at the temperature of the test during time increment t_1 to t_2 to that of water at 20 °C, T is the temperature of the test permeant (20 °C), d is the inside diameter of the standpipe (3.6 cm for the top standpipe and 33 cm for the middle standpipe), D_1 is the inside diameter of the bottom casing (12.7 cm), b_1 is the thickness of the tested layer (cm), and a is 0 for the infinite depth of the tested layer (i.e., $b_1 > 20 D_1$).

Figure 4. The CHP device was installed in a concrete core hole.

After the field DCP and CHP tests, foundation materials were sampled from the core holes. The laboratory particle size analysis, liquid limit, and plastic limit tests were conducted on the samples to determine the soil index properties and Unified Soil Classification System (USCS) classifications of the pavement materials. The particle size analysis tests were conducted in accordance with ASTM D422 [45]. The particle size analysis consists of two parts: sieve analysis and hydrometer analysis. Sieve analysis was performed on particles retained on a 0.075 mm sieve, and hydrometer tests were used to determine the proportions of silt and clay particles smaller than the 0.075 mm sieve. The liquid limit, plastic limit, and plasticity index of the materials were determined in accordance with ASTM D4318 [46]. The wet preparation method was followed to prepare the samples. The liquid limit tests were performed according to the multi-point liquid limit method, and at least three points were measured for each material. The plastic limit tests were performed using the ASTM plastic limit rolling device. The particle size analysis, liquid limit, and plastic limit test results were used to classify the samples in accordance with ASTM D2487 [47] and ASTM D3282 [48].

3.2. Design of Experiments

Based on the visual inspections and GPR test results, locations of surface cracks, rebars, and cavities in base layers can be determined, as shown in Figure 5 thus determining the coring locations for further material laboratory tests. At least two 15 cm cores were extracted from each test slab, including a non-cracked full core. After drilling cores, DCP and CHP tests were performed in the core holes to evaluate the in-situ bearing capacity and drainage performance of the foundation materials, respectively.

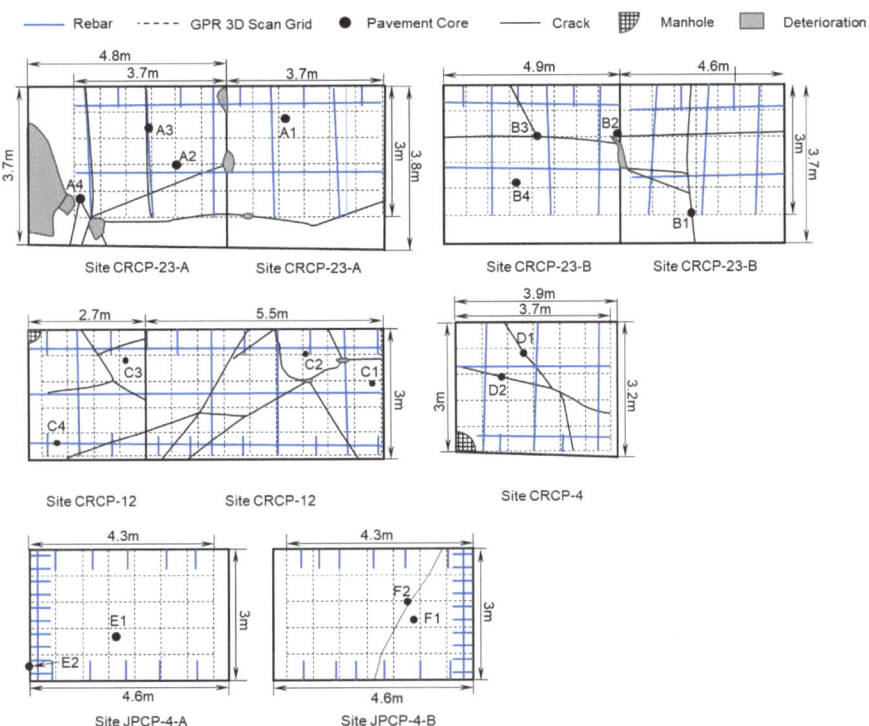

Figure 5. The schematics of the locations of rebar, testing grid, pavement cores, cracks, manholes, and deterioration of the selected slabs at all sites.

In this study, material samples were collected from all core holes at each test site and subjected to laboratory particle size analysis, liquid limit, and plastic limit tests. These tests were conducted once at each site. The DCP test was performed on all core holes at each site, with the average of all DCP-CBR values at each test site determining the representative DCP-CBR value of the test sites. The CHP tests were carried out on two to four core holes at each site. Selected core holes included those without cracks, with cracks, and at joint locations.

4. Results and Discussion
4.1. Field Visual Inspection Results

Figure 6 provides photos of the typical surface conditions of the six test sites. In general, all sites with JPCP pavement designs exhibited similar distress patterns, consisting of longitudinal and transverse cracking with varying degrees of joint deterioration. The sites with younger JPCP pavement appeared to exhibit less distress.

Figure 6. Typical pavement conditions of the six test sites.

Sites CRCP-23-A and B were constructed at the same time with the same design. The service life of the two sites was 23 years at testing time, and both yielded similar surface damage including significant longitudinal cracking. However, CRCP-23-A showed more joint deterioration and D-cracking.

The surface thickness and reinforcement design of the Sites CRCP-12 and CRCP-4 were the same as those of CRCP-23-A and B. However, even though the service life of the two sites was much shorter, similar surface damage can be observed. Both yielded some random surface cracking and joint damage.

Sites JPCP-4-A and JPCP-4-B were constructed using the JPCP design as shown in Figure 1. The service life of both sites is four years. Site JPCP-4-A exhibited good pavement conditions without any visible surface damage. Site JPCP-4-B had one slab yielding a transverse crack, with no evidence of joint deterioration.

4.2. Evaluation of Pavement Foundation Support Conditions

Subgrade material samples were collected from the core holes at each test site to determine the material index properties of the foundation materials on each site. Laboratory particle size analysis, Liquid Limit (LL) test, and Plastic Limit (PL) test were conducted on the samples collected from core holes to determine the particle size distribution and soil index properties according to the Unified Soil Classification System (USCS) and AASHTO classifications.

The soil classification test results are summarized in Table 2. The Sites CRCP-23-A, CRCP-4, JPCP-4-A, and JPCP-4-B were classified as Sandy Lean Clay (USCS group symbol: CL). The Sites CRCP-23-B and CRCP-12 were classified as Clayey Sand (USCS group symbol: SC). The plasticity values of the subgrade materials were approximately identical for all the sites. This uniformity in plasticity indicates a certain consistency in the behavior of the materials when subjected to moisture changes.

Table 2. Soil classification results of the foundation surface materials of the six test sites.

Index Properties	Site CRCP-23-A	Site CRCP-23-B	Site CRCP-12	Site CRCP-4	Site JPCP-4-A	Site JPCP-4-B
Liquid Limit, LL (%)	31	31	34	30	33	32
Plastic Limit, PL (%)	13	12	16	14	14	12
Plasticity Index (%)	18	19	18	16	19	20
AASHTO classification	A-6(7)	A-2-6(1)	A-6(5)	A-6(6)	A-6(9)	A-6(9)
USCS classification	CL	SC	CL	CL	CL	SC
USCS group name	Sandy lean clay	Clayey sand	Clayey sand	Sandy lean clay	Sandy lean clay	Sandy lean clay

The particle size distribution curves of the foundation materials of the six test sites are shown in Figure 7. The foundation materials at Sites CRCP-23-A, CRCP-4, JPCP-4-A, and JPCP-4-B were similar. The foundation material at Sites CRCP-23-B and CRCP-12 contained more sand and fewer fine materials. Relevant research [49–51] indicates that a higher content of coarse aggregates can enhance the stability and drainage performance of the subgrade. Following this, DCP and CHP tests will be conducted at all test sites to measure the bearing capacity and drainage performance of the foundation.

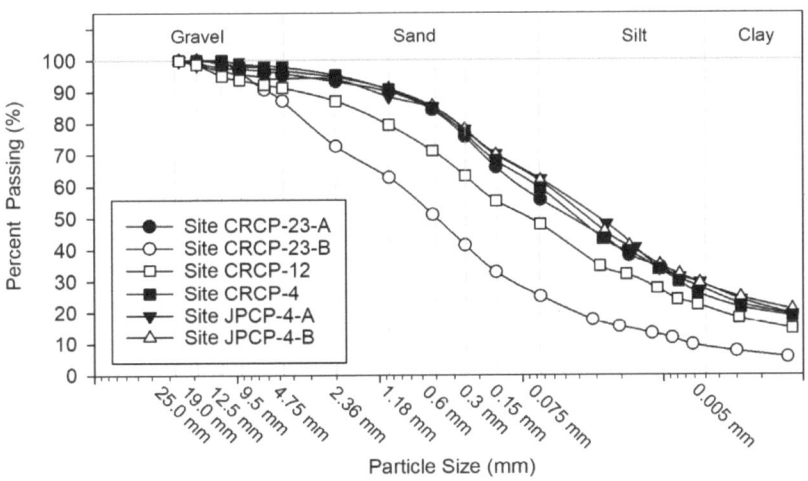

Figure 7. Sieve analysis results of the foundation surface materials of the six test sites.

The DCP tests were conducted to quantitatively analyze the bearing capacity of the pavement foundation. For each test site, two to four core holes were selected to conduct DCP tests after drilling surface cores. The testing blows, DCPI, and CBR versus depth profiles of the six sites are shown in Figure 8. Based on the test results, the pavement foundation-bearing capacity conditions of the six sites can be separated into two groups. The DCP-CBR values of sites CRCP-23-A, JPCP-4-A, and JPCP-4-B were relatively uniform, and no obvious boundary can be observed in their DCP-CBR profiles. However, for sites

CRCP-23-B, CRCP-12, and CRCP-4, the DCP-CBR values of the top 250 mm foundation material are very different from those of the bottom materials. The top layers of sites CRCP-12 and CRCP-4 are much softer than their bottom materials. This led to noticeably premature failures compared to sites JPCP-4-A and JPCP-4-B, despite their shorter service life, as illustrated in Figure 6.

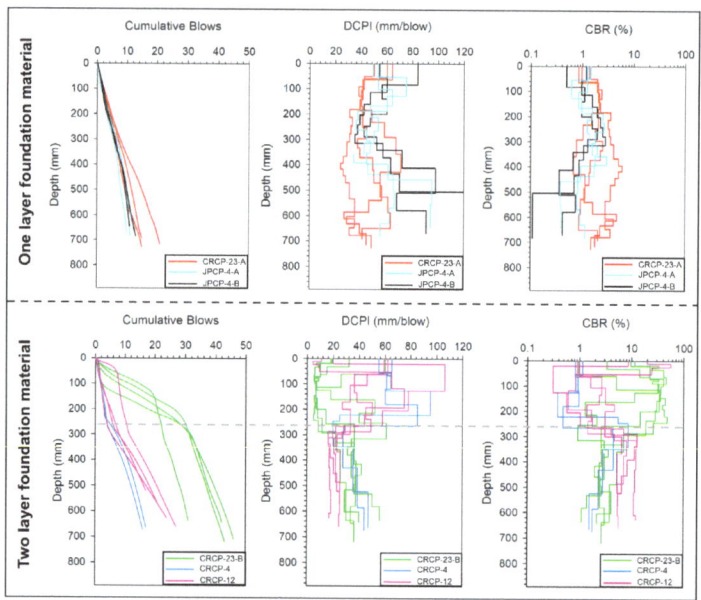

Figure 8. DCP test results versus depth profiles of the foundation materials of the test sites.

To evaluate the relative support conditions of the six test sites, the in-situ DCP-CBR values are compared to the Iowa Statewide Urban Design and Specifications (SUDAS) rating [52], which was developed to evaluate the support conditions for subbase and subgrade layers of rigid and flexible pavement systems based on the CBR values. Figure 9 compares the DCP-CBR of the two groups of test sites with the SUDAS rating.

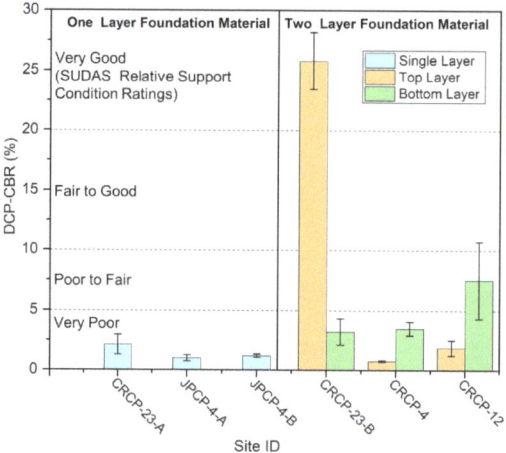

Figure 9. Comparison of DCP test results with the SUDAS pavement foundation relative support condition rating.

At all test sites, the top layer of site CRCP-23-B was rated as very good support conditions, which is much higher than that of the bottom material and other sites. The difference is caused by material gradation. The top layer material of CRCP-23-B contains a higher gravel content than those of other sites as shown in Figure 7. This indicates that a higher content of coarse particles can significantly enhance the bearing capacity of the foundation.

The average DCP-CBR values of sites CRCP-23-A, JPCP-4-A, and JPCP-4-B are below 5%, which are rated as very poor support conditions. Regarding sites CRCP-23-B, CRCP-4, and CRCP-12, the top subgrade layer of sites CRCP-4 and CRCP-12 showed lower average DCP-CBR values than the bottom materials, corresponding to very poor support. At site CRCP-23-B the average CBR of the top layer was approximately eight times higher than that of the bottom material. The average DCP-CBR of the top layer was 25.8%, indicating good support. Compared to CRCP-4, despite having the same service life, sites JPCP-4-A and JPCP-4-B exhibited lighter pavement damage but still had lower bearing capacities. This phenomenon is attributed to the pavement design approach of Jointed JPCP. The reinforcement placement method in CRCP may more readily lead to stress concentration areas, thereby resulting in cracks. Additionally, field observations noted well-sealed joints at Sites JPCP-4-A and JPCP-4-B. Similarly, compared to Site CRCP-23-A, despite having the same service life, site CRCP-23-A showed more joint deterioration and D-cracking, as shown in Figure 6. This suggests that higher bearing capacity can help delay deterioration, thereby extending the service life of the pavement. However, despite this higher bearing capacity of the top layer, Figure 2 demonstrates that severe random cracking still occurred at this site. It indicates that the bearing capacity of the foundation is influenced by both the bearing capacities of the top and bottom layers. Even if the top layer of the foundation has good support conditions, poor support of the bottom layer similarly affects the overall bearing capacity of the foundation, ultimately leading to premature failure of PCC pavement.

4.3. Evaluation of Pavement Foundation Drainage Performance

The drainage performance of the pavement foundation layer significantly affects the performance and durability of the pavement surface system. At the CRCP-12 site, Photos taken during the field investigation process are shown in Figure 10a. Field observations revealed severe random and corner cracking in the pavement and the water accumulated close to the curb. The water accumulation can cause insufficient bearing capacity of the foundation. Reduction in the bearing capacity of the subgrade materials may not only lead to a non-uniform support condition but also cause subgrade erosion. Additionally, the test section of the site CRCP-12 is close to a manhole and sewer pipelines (i.e., green paint marks the pipeline directions in Figure 10), where the subgrade material is likely less well-compacted, which makes it more susceptible to scoured and loose material. The GPR scan results show that a 5 cm thick layer was observed between the concrete and the bottom foundation layer as shown in Figure 10b. This was confirmed by the observation at the bottom of the core hole shown in Figure 10c. This further suggests that the pressure-injected layer was applied to address the erosion and loosening of less compacted materials.

To quantitatively assess the drainage performance of pavement foundation materials, the CHP tests were performed in core holes at each site. The CHP test results are summarized in Table 3. Tests performed on surface crack locations were marked as cracks, tests on regular surface locations were labeled as regular, and tests performed at joints were marked as joints.

The calculated hydraulic conductivity values (K_{CHP}) for the core holes without cracks are denoted as regular as shown in Table 3 and are representative of each testing site. The foundation layers provide better drainage at sites CRCP-23-B and CRCP-12, which have fewer fine particles than the other sites as shown in Figure 7. It seems to indicate that more coarse particles and fewer fines are beneficial for better permeability. Figure 6 shows that the CRCP-23-A had more joint deterioration and D-cracking. It indicated that the permeability of the foundation material with relatively fewer fine particles yields good drainage performance, which may lead to a longer service life of the PCC pavement surface structure.

Figure 10. (**a**) Faulted concrete slab, (**b**) GPR 2D scan result, and (**c**) injected material at Site CRCP-12.

Table 3. CHP test results of subgrade materials in each site.

Test Site	Core Number	Test Location	K_{CHP} (m/day)
Site CRCP-23-A	A1	Regular	0.52
	A2	Cracks	8.44
	A3	Cracks	0.31
	A4	Cracks	17.34
Site CRCP-23-B	B1	Cracks	6.95
	B4	Regular	4.05
Site CRCP-12	C4	Regular	3.44
Site CRCP-4	D1	Cracks	0.58
	D2	Cracks	2.59
Site JPCP-4-A	E1	Regular	0.24
	E2	Joint	0.09
Site JPCP-4-B	F1	Regular	0.21
	F2	Cracks	0.64

The foundation layers provide very poor drainage at the other sites, at site JPCP-4-A, the CHP test result for the core hole at a joint is very low. It indicates that the joints at this site were well-sealed, effectively preventing water infiltration. The K_{CHP} at site CRCP-4 is low but still higher than that of sites JPCP-4-A and JPCP-4-B, suggesting that the foundation of site CRCP-4 has greater permeability. Figure 6 indicates that despite having the same service life, site CRCP-4 exhibited more significant premature failure than the other two sites. This could potentially be related to water entering the foundation, leading to the washout of foundation materials and consequently resulting in insufficient bearing capacity of the subgrade. Additionally, the CHP test results indicate that most core holes with cracks show higher permeability compared to those without cracks. This suggests that the cracks allow water to more easily seep into the foundation, resulting in higher flow rates beneath the cracked slabs.

Figure 11 shows the observed cracking pattern and corresponding GPR scan results at site CRCP-23-A. Figure 11a shows a photo taken during the field investigation, also depicting water accumulation near the curb and severe random cracks and corner cracks on the pavement. The cracks allow water to seep into the foundation, which may accelerate the corrosion of the rebar. The GPR survey, as illustrated in Figure 11b,d, indicates the potential existence of a predictable pattern in the occurrence of crack locations. The GPR results seem to indicate the formation of random cracks within the concrete slab, especially in areas between the rebars. This pattern suggests that the cracking might initiate at or near one of the rebars. The occurrence of cracks between the rebars could be attributed to stress concentrations or material defects due to rebar corrosion in these areas.

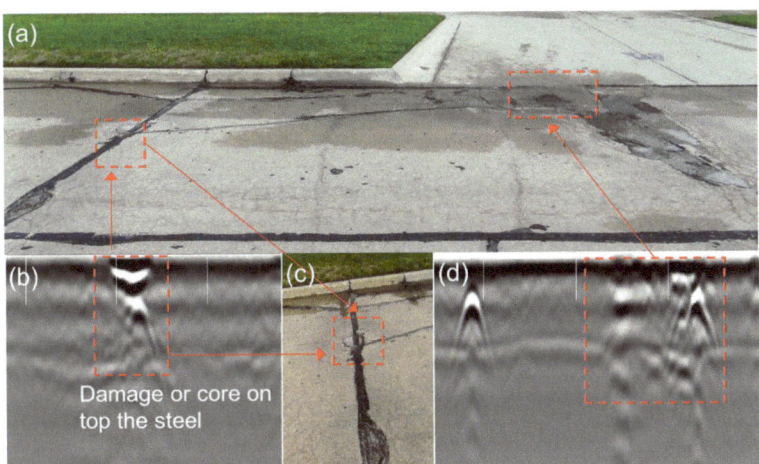

Figure 11. (**a**) Distresses observed at site CRCP-23-A, (**b**) GPR 2D scan result, (**c**) Magnified view of part of the distress, (**d**) GPR 2D scan result.

Further investigation was conducted by drilling a core A3, from a transverse crack to determine if the crack originated from the rebar, as depicted in Figure 12a. The GPR result and field observations results show that two small transverse cracks propagated along the transverse rebars, also shown in Figure 12a,b. However, observation of core A3 shown in Figure 12c illustrates that the interface may not be the cracking initiation point. Instead, it may behave as a stress concentration area where the initiated cracks may follow the rebars to propagate. The DCP results shown in Figure 9 and CHP results shown in Table 3 illustrate the poor bearing capacity and drainage performance at site CRCP-23-A, which indicate that when the subgrade layer is not strong enough, lacking the necessary strength, it fails to adequately support vehicular loads. This could result in the formation of stress concentration areas in the areas around the rebars, leading to the development and propagation of cracks in these specific regions.

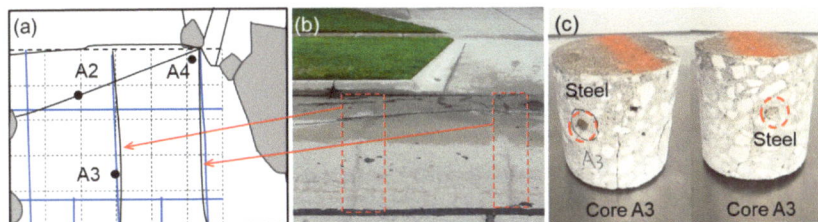

Figure 12. (**a**) Schematic of crack locations, reinforced bars, and cores, (A2, A3, and A4 are the labels for the core sampling locations) (**b**) transverse cracks that developed along the transverse rebars, and (**c**) images of Core A3 at Site CRCP-23-A.

Furthermore, at site CRCP-23-B, special attention was paid to the intersection of severe transverse and longitudinal cracks at core B3, as shown in Figure 13a,b. After drilling the core sample, an unexpectedly large gravel particle was found beneath core B3, as depicted in Figure 13c. It suggested a stress concentration area might have formed beneath the core B3 under the influence of vehicular loads. Additionally, the presence of the large gravel particle could have altered the direction of crack propagation, preventing it from following the path of the reinforcing bars.

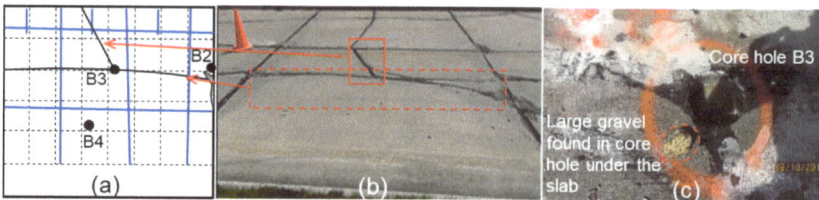

Figure 13. (**a**) Schematic of crack locations, reinforced bars, and cores, (B2, B3, and B4 are the labels for the core sampling locations) (**b**) location of the cracks, and (**c**) a large gravel particle in core hole B3 at site CRCP-23-B.5.

5. Conclusions

This study aims to explore potential foundational issues that may lead to the accelerated damage of urban cement concrete pavements in seasonal frost regions. To achieve the objectives, a total of six test sites designed by CRCP and JPCP methods were selected for field evaluations. Field visual inspections, GPR surveys, DCP tests, and CHP tests were performed to assess the support and drainage conditions of pavement foundation materials. The key findings of this field study are listed below:

(1) In urban residential areas where the subgrade bearing capacity is insufficient, cement concrete pavements often suffer premature failure. Foundations with a higher content of coarse particles exhibit a higher CBR value, which can extend the service life of the pavement. Urban roads contain sewer pipelines under the pavement, which lead to less compaction of foundation materials. The less compacted foundation will result in non-uniform bearing capacity and support conditions.

(2) The permeability of the foundation material with relatively fewer fine particles yields good drainage performance, which leads to a longer service life of the PCC pavement surface structure. For subgrades with poor drainage, water tends to accumulate near curbs or in low-lying areas, significantly reducing the bearing capacity of the foundation, and thereby accelerating pavement deterioration. The cracks allow water to more easily penetrate the foundation and potentially wash away foundation materials, resulting in non-uniform support conditions and accelerating the formation of cracks.

(3) For the pavement design type of CRCP, the poor bearing capacity and drainage conditions of the foundation lead to cavities between the surface layer and foundation material thus yielding stress concentrations on the pavement surface, which cause the formation of pavement surface cracks.

Author Contributions: Methodology, C.L. and X.W.; experiment, C.L. and W.X.; supervision, S.Q. and Q.B.; validation, Y.W. and S.B.; writing—original draft, W.W.; writing—review and editing, C.L. and W.W.; funding acquisition, C.L. and S.B. All authors have read and agreed to the published version of the manuscript.

Funding: This study was supported by the National Science Foundation of Shaanxi Province (2022JQ-743), the National Natural Science Foundation Project (52178185), the fellowship of China Postdoctoral Science Foundation, (Grant No. 2021MD703885), and the Fundamental Research Funds for the Central Universities, CHD (No. 300102212208).

Institutional Review Board Statement: Not applicable.

Informed Consent Statement: Not applicable.

Data Availability Statement: The data presented in this study are available on request from the corresponding author. Some data are related to research projects, and are not provided for the time being.

Acknowledgments: The authors would like to acknowledge the guidance and support provided by Peter C. Taylor and Jeramy C. Ashlock at Iowa State University. The assistance of the City of Clive, Iowa is also appreciated. The authors are also very grateful to the editor and anonymous reviewers for their valuable comments and suggestions on this paper.

Conflicts of Interest: Authors Songli Qiu and Yujin Wang were employed by the Ningbo Communications Engineering Construction Group Co, Ltd. Author Qinghua Bian was employed by the Gansu Road & Bridge Construction Group Shanjian Technology Company. The remaining authors declare that the research was conducted in the absence of any commercial or financial relationships that could be construed as a potential conflict of interest.

References

1. Naik, T.R. Sustainability of concrete construction. *Pract. Period. Struct. Des. Constr.* **2008**, *13*, 98–103. [CrossRef]
2. Kolawole, J.T.; Babafemi, A.J.; Paul, S.C.; du Plessis, A. Performance of concrete containing Nigerian electric arc furnace steel slag aggregate towards sustainable production. *Sustain. Mater. Technol.* **2020**, *25*, e00174. [CrossRef]
3. *IRC:58-2015*; Guidelines for the Design of Plain Jointed Rigid Pavements for Highways. Indian Roads Congress: New Delhi, India, 2011.
4. *NCHRP 1-37A*; Guide for Mechanistic-Empirical Design of New and Rehabilitated Pavement Structures. Transportation Research Board: Washington, DC, USA, 2004.
5. PCA. *Thickness Design for Concrete Highway and Street Pavements*; Portland Cement Association: Skokie, IL, USA, 1984.
6. Barr, B.; Hoseinian, S.B.; Beygi, M.A. Shrinkage of concrete stored in natural environments. *Cem. Concr. Compos.* **2003**, *25*, 19–29. [CrossRef]
7. Persson, B. Eight-year exploration of shrinkage in high-performance concrete. *Cem. Concr. Res.* **2002**, *32*, 1229–1237. [CrossRef]
8. West, R.P.; Holmes, N. Predicting moisture movement during the drying of concrete floors using finite elements. *Constr. Build. Mater.* **2005**, *19*, 674–681. [CrossRef]
9. Moody, E.D. Transverse Cracking Distress in Long-Term Pavement Performance Jointed Concrete Pavement Sections. *Transp. Res. Rec.* **1998**, *1629*, 6–12. [CrossRef]
10. Zhan Hong, D.L.-L. Research on Crack Mechanism of Portland Cement Concrete Pavements. *J. Chongqing Jiaotong Univ.* **2016**, *27*, 405–407.
11. Ioannides, A.M. *Fracture Mechanics Applications in Pavement Engineering: A Literature Review*; Contract No. DACA39-94-C-0121; US Army Engineer Waterways Experiment Station: Vicksburg, MS, USA, 1995.
12. Barenberg, E.J. Factors affecting fatigue failure of concrete. In Proceedings of the Workshop on Fracture Mechanics for Concrete Pavements: Theory to Practice, Copper Mountain, CO, USA, 10–12 August 2005.
13. Ioannides, A.M. Fracture Mechanics in Pavement Engineering: The Specimen-Size Effect. *Transp. Res. Rec.* **1997**, *1568*, 10–16. [CrossRef]
14. Darter, M.I. Concrete slab versus beam fatigue models. In Proceedings of the Second International Workshop on the Design and Evaluation of Concrete Pavements, Siguenza, Spain, 4–5 October 1990; pp. 139–164.
15. Lu, Y.N.; Xiao, T.L. Stress Analysis of Cement Concrete Pavement under Overweight Loads. In Proceedings of the 2nd International Conference on Structures and Building Materials (ICSBM), Hangzhou, China, 9–11 March 2012; p. 949.
16. Smit, M.S.; Kearsley, E.P.; Jacobsz, S.W. The effect of relative stiffness on soil-structure interaction under vehicle loads. In Proceedings of the 9th International Conference on Physical Modelling in Geotechnics (ICPMG), London, UK, 17–20 July 2018; pp. 185–190.
17. Su, Y.H.; Xin, S.Z.; Shi, J.N.; Zhang, Z.H. Stress Analysis of Cement Concrete Pavement with Special Heavy Mine Vehicle. In Proceedings of the International Conference on Future Energy, Environment, and Materials (FEEM), Hong Kong, China, 12–13 April 2012; pp. 722–729.
18. Nemati, K.M.; Uhlmeyer, J.S. Accelerated construction of urban intersections with Portland Cement Concrete Pavement (PCCP). *Case Stud. Constr. Mater.* **2021**, *14*, e00499. [CrossRef]
19. Titus-Glover, L.; Mallela, J.; Darter, M.I.; Voigt, G.; Waalkes, S. Enhanced Portland Cement Concrete Fatigue Model for StreetPave. *Transp. Res. Rec.* **2005**, *1919*, 29–37. [CrossRef]
20. Amalia, Y.; Fatimah, E.; Oktaviani, C.Z. Principal Component Analysis Application for Determining Factors Influencing Drainage Construction Process in Residential Areas. *J. Phys. Conf. Ser.* **2022**, *2394*, 012042. [CrossRef]
21. Titus-Glover, L.; Hein, D.; Rao, S.; Smith, K.L. Impact of Increasing Roadway Construction Standards on Life-Cycle Costs of Local Residential Streets. *Transp. Res. Rec.* **2006**, *1958*, 44–53. [CrossRef]
22. Weiss, W.J.; Shah, S.P. Restrained shrinkage cracking: The role of shrinkage reducing admixtures and specimen geometry. *Mater. Struct.* **2002**, *35*, 85–91. [CrossRef]

23. Khoury, I.; Sargand, S.; Hatton, D.C. Impact of base type on performance of rigid pavement: A case study. *Int. J. Pavement Eng.* **2022**, *23*, 888–899. [CrossRef]
24. Beckemeyer, C.; Khazanovich, L.; Thomas Yu, H. Determining Amount of Built-in Curling in Jointed Plain Concrete Pavement: Case Study of Pennsylvania 1-80. *Transp. Res. Rec.* **2002**, *1809*, 85–92. [CrossRef]
25. Kim, S.; Ceylan, H.; Gopalakrishnan, K.; Yang, B. How Are the Subsurface Drainage Outlets in Iowa Roadways with Recycled Concrete Aggregate Base Performing? In Proceedings of the Geotechnical and Structural Engineering Congress 2016, Phoenix, AZ, USA, 14–17 February 2016; pp. 1295–1302.
26. Oyediji, R.; Lu, D.; Tighe, S.L. Impact of flooding and inundation on concrete pavement performance. *Int. J. Pavement Eng.* **2021**, *22*, 1363–1375. [CrossRef]
27. Rodden, R.; Ferrebee, E.; Sullivan, S.; Covarrubias, J.; Nantasai, B. Comparison of Modern Concrete Pavement Performance Predictions, Thickness Requirements, and Sensitivity to Joint Spacing (Poster). In Proceedings of the TAC 2017: Investing in Transportation: Building Canada's Economy—2017 Conference and Exhibition of the Transportation Association of Canada, Toronto, ON, Canada, 24–27 September 2017.
28. Shafiee, M.; Maadani, O. Investigation of climate change impacts on early-age cracking of jointed plain concrete pavements in Canada. *Can. J. Civ. Eng.* **2022**, *49*, 1121–1127. [CrossRef]
29. Zhu, J.; Sargand, S.; Green, R.; Khoury, I. Performance assessment of unbonded concrete overlays of concrete pavements in Ohio: A forensic practice. *J. Perform. Constr. Facil.* **2020**, *34*, 04020050. [CrossRef]
30. Joshi, T.; Dave, U. Construction of pervious concrete pavement stretch, Ahmedabad, India—Case study. *Case Stud. Constr.* **2022**, *16*, e00622. [CrossRef]
31. Weiss, P.T.; Kayhanian, M.; Gulliver, J.S.; Khazanovich, L. Permeable pavement in northern North American urban areas: Research review and knowledge gaps. *Int. J. Pavement Eng.* **2019**, *20*, 143–162. [CrossRef]
32. Da Costa, F.B.P.; Haselbach, L.M.; da Silva Filho, L.C.P. Pervious concrete for desired porosity: Influence of w/c ratio and a rheology-modifying admixture. *Constr. Build. Mater.* **2021**, *268*, 121084. [CrossRef]
33. Denison, W.B. Performance of Pervious Portland Cement Concrete by Field and Laboratory Testing, Including Void Structure, Unit Weight, Compressive and Flexural Strength. In Proceedings of the Conference on Pervious Concrete, Tampa, FL, USA, 4 December 2011; pp. 17–26.
34. Kevern, J.T. Evolution of Portland cement pervious concrete construction. In Proceedings of the 5th International Structural Engineering and Construction Conference, Las Vegas, NV, USA, 22–25 September 2009; pp. 473–478.
35. Ibrahim, A.; Mahmoud, E.; Yamin, M.; Patibandla, V.C. Experimental study on Portland cement pervious concrete mechanical and hydrological properties. *Constr. Build. Mater.* **2014**, *50*, 524–529. [CrossRef]
36. Mccracken, J.K.; Asbahan, R.E.; Vandenbossche, J.M. *Response Characteristics of a Jointed Plain Concrete Pavement to Applied and Environmental Loads-Phase II Final Report*; Pennsylvania Department of Transportation: Harrisburg, PA, USA, 2008.
37. Deschenes, R.A., Jr.; Giannini, E.R.; Drimalas, T.; Fournier, B.; Hale, W.M. Effects of Moisture, Temperature, and Freezing and Thawing on Alkali-Silica Reaction. *ACI Mater. J.* **2018**, *115*, 575. [CrossRef]
38. Nazeer, M.; Kapoor, K.; Singh, S.P. Pervious concrete: A state-of-the-art review. *J. Mater. Eng. Struct.* **2020**, *7*, 417–437.
39. Nguyen-Van, D.; Nguyen-Tuan, T.; Pham-Thanh, T. Experimental study on pervious cement and pervious geopolymer concretes using sea sand and seawater. *Int. J. Geomate* **2022**, *23*, 63–71. [CrossRef]
40. Glinicki, M.A.; Jóźwiak-Niedźwiedzka, D.; Antolik, A.; Dziedzic, K.; Dąbrowski, M.; Bogusz, K. Diagnosis of ASR damage in highway pavement after 15 years of service in wet-freeze climate region. *Case Stud. Constr. Mater.* **2022**, *17*, e01226. [CrossRef]
41. Kebede, G. Assessment of the Effect of Urban Road Surface Drainage: A Case Study at Ginjo Guduru Kebele of Jimma Town. *Int. J. Sci. Technol. Soc.* **2015**, *3*, 194. [CrossRef]
42. Zumrawi, M. Investigating surface drainage problem of roads in Khartoum state. *Int. J. Civ. Eng. Technol.* **2016**, *7*, 91–103.
43. *ASTM D6951*; Standard Test Method for Use of the Dynamic Cone Penetrometer in Shallow Pavement Applications. Annual Book of ASTM Standards. ASTM: West Conshohocken, PA, USA, 2015.
44. *ASTM D6391*; Standard Test Method for Field Measurement of Hydraulic Conductivity Using Borehole Infiltration. Annual Book of ASTM Standards. ASTM: West Conshohocken, PA, USA, 2011.
45. *ASTM D422-03*; Standard Test Method for Particle-Size Analysis of Soils. Annual Book of ASTM Standards. ASTM: West Conshohocken, PA, USA, 2007.
46. *ASTM D4318*; Standard Test Methods for Liquid Limit, Plastic Limit, and Plasticity Index of Soils. Annual Book of ASTM Standards. ASTM: West Conshohocken, PA, USA, 2017.
47. *ASTM D2487-11*; Standard Practice for Classification of Soils for Engineering Purposes (Unified Soil Classification System (USCS)). Annual Book of ASTM Standards. ASTM: West Conshohocken, PA, USA, 2011.
48. *ASTM D3282*; Standard Practice for Classification of Soils and Soil-Aggregate Mixtures for Highway Construction Purposes. Annual Book of ASTM Standards. ASTM: West Conshohocken, PA, USA, 2015.
49. Mishra, S.; Sachdeva, S.N.; Manocha, R. Subgrade Soil Stabilization Using Stone Dust and Coarse Aggregate: A Cost Effective Approach. *Int. J. Geosynth. Ground Eng.* **2019**, *5*, 20. [CrossRef]

50. Wang, K.; Tang, L.; Tian, S.; Ling, X.; Cai, D.; Liu, M. Experimental investigation and prediction model of permeability in solidified coarse-grained soil under freeze-thaw cycles in water-rich environments. *Transp. Geotech.* **2023**, *41*, 101035. [CrossRef]
51. Zhuang, W.; Li, S.; Deng, Q.; Chen, M.; Yu, Q. Effects of coarse aggregates size on dynamic characteristics of ultra-high performance concrete: Towards enhanced impact resistance. *Constr. Build. Mater.* **2024**, *411*, 134524. [CrossRef]
52. SUDAS. *Design Manual, Chapter 6—Geotechnical. Statewide Urban Design and Specifications (SUDAS)*; Institute for Transportation, Iowa State University: Ames, IA, USA, 2015.

Disclaimer/Publisher's Note: The statements, opinions and data contained in all publications are solely those of the individual author(s) and contributor(s) and not of MDPI and/or the editor(s). MDPI and/or the editor(s) disclaim responsibility for any injury to people or property resulting from any ideas, methods, instructions or products referred to in the content.

Article

Long-Term Maintenance Planning Method of Rural Roads under Limited Budget: A Case Study of Road Network

Chao Han [1,2,3], Jiuda Huang [2,*], Xu Yang [1], Lili Chen [2] and Tao Chen [2]

[1] Highway Institute, Chang'an University, Xi'an 710061, China; hc1527@jsti.com (C.H.); yang.xu@chd.edu.cn (X.Y.)
[2] JSTI.GROUP Co., Ltd., Nanjing 211112, China; hjd984@jsti.com (L.C.); cll295@jsti.com or ct985@jsti.com (T.C.)
[3] NERC-ARM, National Engineering Research Center of Advanced Road Materials, Nanjing 210019, China
* Correspondence: hjd984@outlook.com; Tel.: +86-15951965112

Abstract: At present, the task of maintaining and managing rural roads in China is becoming increasingly severe. To solve the problems of insufficient scheme benefits, complex feasible solutions, and low optimization efficiency in long-term maintenance planning of rural road networks under a limited budget, it is urgent to develop maintenance decision-making models and optimization methods suitable for rural roads in China. This paper focuses on the critical aspects of performance evaluation, prediction, and decision-making. Firstly, this paper proposes evaluation indicators and maintenance countermeasures suitable for rural roads, combining them with the characteristics of rural road performance degradation. Based on different treatment measure levels, RPCI and RRQI performance prediction models are established. On this basis, an improved heuristic optimization method is proposed, which realizes rapid optimization of the most cost-effective solution. Finally, the model and method proposed in this paper are applied to the case analysis of 10 rural roads in Haimen City, generating 171 optimal maintenance sections, further verifying the feasibility and effectiveness of the model. The study provides a theoretical basis for the scientific management of rural road maintenance.

Keywords: rural roads; prediction models; improved heuristic methods; maintenance benefits; maintenance strategy

1. Introduction

Rural roads in foreign countries are typically referred to as county, township, and village or low-volume roads in China. Rural roads are a critical component of China's road network, essential for rural economic and social development. China began large-scale rural road construction in 2003, with a total length of 4.5314 million kilometers by the end of 2022, accounting for 84.6% of all roads. A developed rural highway transportation network has been established, centered around county towns, with townships as nodes and village groups as the network.

In recent years, rural road development in China has shifted from construction to maintenance due to the rapid growth of the scale of rural road construction. With limited maintenance funds, local road management departments face challenges in managing such a vast mileage of rural roads effectively while improving maintenance fund utilization efficiency and guaranteeing road service levels. The current maintenance and management system applies high-grade road maintenance decision-making without considering differences in pavement structure, traffic volume, and funding budgets, leading to issues like unreasonable pavement performance evaluations and inadequate scientific maintenance decision-making in actual management processes.

Therefore, it is necessary to establish a decision-making method for rural road surface maintenance through systematic research. Selectively locating maintenance sections and measures can effectively maintain a high level of service for rural roads.

Research on low-flow rural road maintenance decision-making has been conducted abroad. Pantha [1] et al. (2010) used Geographic Information System (GIS) to determine the priority map of pavement maintenance in the Himalayas and developed a budget, time, and resource-constrained decision model for rural road maintenance. Mergi [2] et al. (2012) evaluated pavement conditions using the Pavement Condition Index (PCI) and adopted a "worst PCI priority" strategy for Sudan's rural road networks. Mathew [3] et al. (2015) created a dual-objective deterministic optimization model for rural road network maintenance and proposed a constrained genetic algorithm as the optimization tool. Torres-Machi [4] et al. (2017) studied the impact of road environmental performance on road maintenance decision management, integrating technical, economic, and environmental aspects into maintenance plan design, and developed a tool for SUS optimization design.

Agarwa [5] et al. (2017) studied Indian rural roads and found that maintenance decisions primarily depend on functional, structural, and importance conditions, proposing a two-stage optimization process. Pasindu [6] et al. (2020) established a multi-objective decision-making framework based on pavement structure type selection to address funding, technology, and human resource issues in low-traffic rural road maintenance, providing tools for local highway planning and decision-making. Yogesh [7] et al. (2023) researched and developed a long-term rural road network planning method, applied ant colony optimization, and found it to be 14% more efficient than existing models through verification analysis.

Pavement maintenance decision-making has widely employed various methods, from simple ranking to complex mathematical planning. However, each method has limitations in solving real-world optimization problems. For instance, the ranking method is straightforward but lacks holistic conservation planning over the entire period. It struggles with sorting multiple objectives (Kabir [8] et al. 2014, Choi [9] 2015, Abu Dabous [10] et al. 2019). The mathematical planning model considers different sections, schemes, and time series within the road network but suffers from unstable solutions and slow processing for large-scale problems (Fecarotti [11] et al. 2021). Artificial intelligence methods like genetic algorithms, artificial neural networks, and fuzzy set theory have high processing power but are sensitive to environmental factors, require ample sample sizes, learn slowly, and may not yield long-term optimal solutions (Han [12] et al. 2021, Hanandeh [13] et al. 2022, Mohimenul [14] et al. 2023).

To address the issues of inadequate scheme accuracy, complex decision-making, and low optimization efficiency in rural road maintenance with limited budgets, this paper proposes a maintenance decision model suitable for rural roads. The model combines heuristic optimization algorithms and aims to maximize overall benefits throughout the life cycle by considering pavement performance. By establishing a reasonable decision model and optimization algorithm, the scheme can be quickly and accurately optimized. A case study of 10 rural roads in Haimen City, Jiangsu province, with a total road network length of 280 km is conducted to research the application of long-term maintenance planning from 2023 to 2036. The model determines a maintenance strategy with a reasonable budget and best benefits, verifying its feasibility and effectiveness. This scientifically and effectively guides rural road maintenance management in China.

2. Research Conditions and Methods

2.1. Key Indicators and Conditions

2.1.1. Pavement Performance Evaluation

Considering the characteristics of low road grade (mainly Grade III and IV roads), slow driving speed (not higher than 60 km/h), and small traffic load in rural roads in China, it is often not necessary to select all road performance indicators as evaluation parameters in the actual evaluation of their road conditions (Tang [15] et al. 2021, Shtayat [16] et al.

2020). Therefore, according to the actual road characteristics of the rural road network in the Jiangsu province, this paper ignores the requirements for pavement anti-skid performance and rutting. Two key indicators, namely, the Rural Road Pavement Surface Condition Index (RPCI) and the Rural Road Pavement Riding Quality Index (RRQI), are mainly used for calculation and evaluation, as shown in the following Formulas (1) and (2) and Table 1. In addition, in order to further understand the internal conditions of rural roads, this paper also supplements the evaluation of the internal health status of the pavement based on the RIPCI auxiliary index based on bottom-finding radar, as shown in Equation (3) (this index is not included in the comprehensive evaluation as an influencing factor to evaluate the road condition attenuation).

$$RPCI = 100 - a_0 CR^{a_1} - \sum W_i N_i \quad (1)$$

$$RRQI = \frac{100}{1 + a_2 e^{a_3 IRI}} \quad (2)$$

$$RIPCI = 100 - 15 * IDI^{0.412} \quad (3)$$

where CR is Pavement Cracking Ratio; IRI is International Roughness Index; IDI is the Inner Pavement Distress Ratio; a_0, a_1, a_2, and a_3 are related calculation parameters; N_i is the number of different types of damage within the surveyed road section; W_i is a unit deduction for different types of damage.

Table 1. Key evaluation indicators and grading standards for pavement performance.

Evaluating Indicator		Evaluation Grade			
		Excellent	Good	Average	Inferior and Poor
Pavement damage	RPCI	≥90	≥80	≥70, <80	<70
	CR (%)	≤0.4	≤2.6, <0.4	>2.6, ≤7.8	>7.8
Pavement driving quality	RRQI	≥90	≥80, <90	≥70, <80	<70
	IR (m/km)	≤3.0	>3.0, ≤4.7	>4.7, ≤5.8	>5.8

2.1.2. Maintenance Measures and Effects

This paper recommends the selection of typical maintenance technologies suitable for rural roads, given their large maintenance scale, complex road shape, low maintenance funds, and low level of mechanization. The recommended measures include five strength grades: P1 (slurry sealing layer), P2 (thin layer cover), P3 (crushed stone regeneration: using a multi hammer crusher to break the old road surface into smaller particle sizes, compacting it with a roller, and then adding a new road structure), P4 (milling and repaving one layer), and P5 (milling and repaving two layers). By calculating the costs of each different maintenance technology and evaluating previous engineering application effects, this paper provides the cost and improvement in pavement damage (RPCI) and driving quality (RRQI) after implementation, as shown in Table 2.

Table 2. Maintenance technology cost and effect after implementation.

Measures	Cost (China RMB) ¥/m²	Life/ Year	Implementation Effect (Improvement Value)	
			RPCI	RRQI
P1: slurry sealing layer	29	2–4	MIN (100, RPCI + 10)	MIN (100, RRQI + 10)
P2: thin layer cover	90	4–6	MIN (100, RPCI + 10)	MIN (100, RRQI + 10)
P3: crushed stone regeneration	72	4–6	MIN (100, RPCI + 20)	MIN (100, RRQI + 20)
P4: milling and repaving 1 layer	134	6—8	100	100
P5: milling and repaving 2 layers	298	7–9	100	100

2.1.3. Treatment Conditions

When conducting multi-year maintenance planning for rural roads, multiple treatment strategies can be applied for one pavement performance state. This paper uses a decision tree model to analyze and determine the maintenance strategies for county and township roads, selecting RPCI and RRQI as key decision indicators and different strength level measures as treatment plans. By setting reasonable treatment thresholds, decision tree models for the maintenance of asphalt and cement pavements in different combination states are established, as shown in Figures 1 and 2.

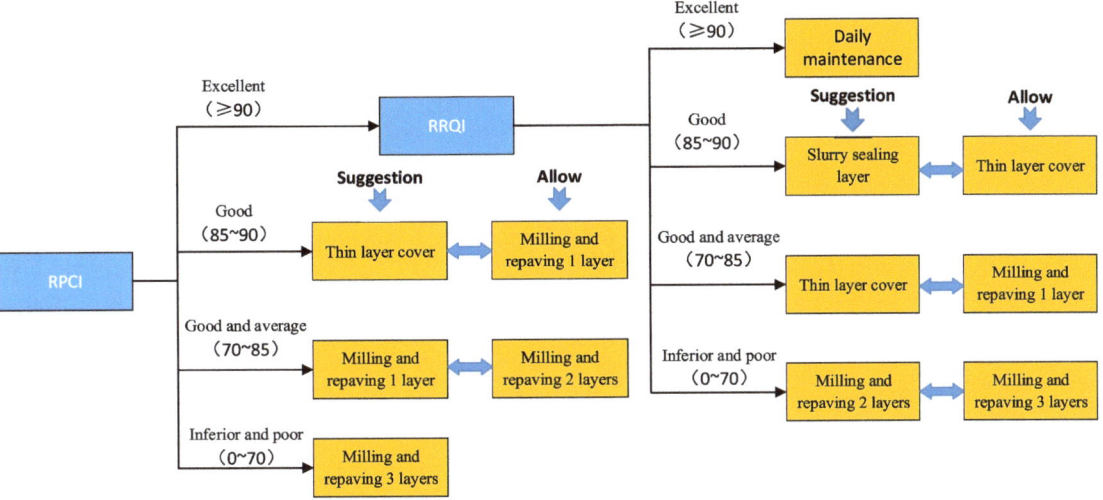

Figure 1. Decision tree for rural road asphalt pavement maintenance.

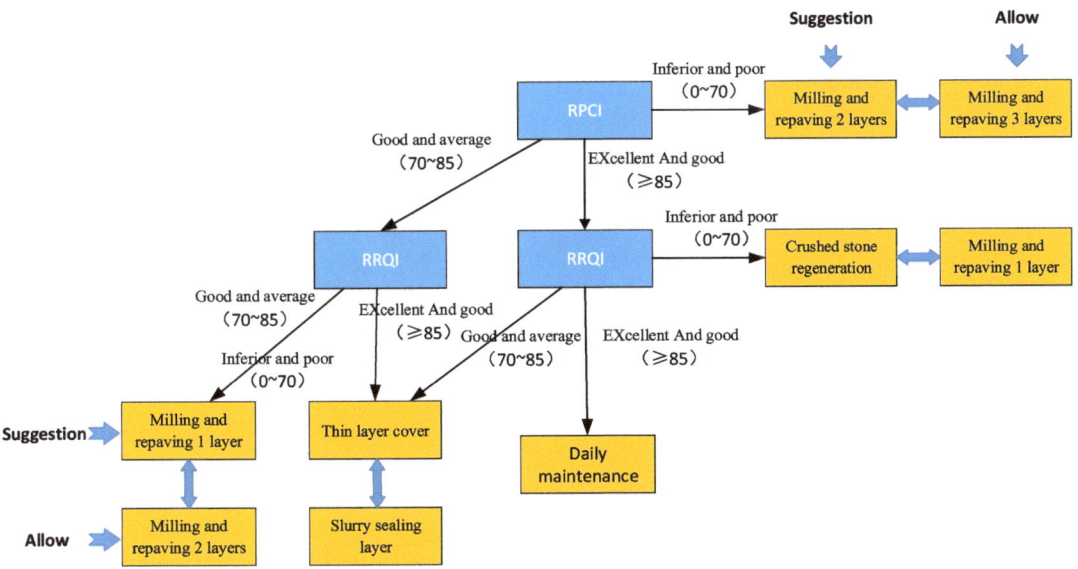

Figure 2. Decision tree for cement pavement maintenance of rural roads.

2.2. Analysis of Pavement Performance Development Law

2.2.1. Performance Decay Analysis

According to statistical analysis of performance testing data during the life cycle of rural roads in China and relevant literature surveys, road performance shows different attenuation trends when different maintenance opportunities and measures are selected (Yu.J [17] et al. 2015, Stein [18] et al. 2018). Figure 3 summarizes and presents decay curves of road performance under three different treatment strategies: preventive maintenance, functional repair priority, and structural repair priority. The bold curve (a) represents the early use of preventive maintenance techniques such as slurry sealing layer when small pavement damage occurs, resulting in slow performance decay to t1 and corresponding repairs to maintain high road conditions. However, as road age increases, overall pavement performance continues to decline in later stages until the road loses its intended service function. The bold curve (b) represents regular maintenance using techniques like crushed stone regeneration, milling, and repaving one or two layers when the pavement structure is damaged to a certain ex-tent and performance decays to t2 after the early adoption of preventive maintenance strategies to restore it to original technical condition. The bold curve (c) only starts selecting the necessary structural repair measures like milling and repaving three layers for maintenance when pavement performance continues to decline until the severe loss of use function at t3, restoring pavement performance quickly to its original level. This curve has a relatively long degradation period with average overall road performance.

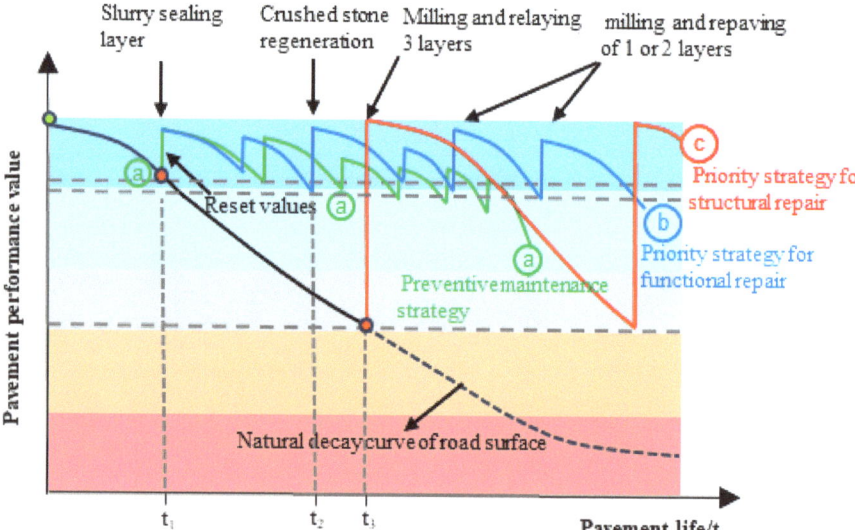

Figure 3. Performance decay curve of rural road pavement.

Based on the above analysis, to address the characteristics of road condition degradation during the life cycle of rural roads, selecting a suitable functional repair priority strategy for curve (b) can maintain the overall performance degradation of road conditions within a reasonable range and achieve long-term stability and preservation of rural road pavement structure.

2.2.2. Selection of Typical Road Sections

Considering differences in pavement structure, maintenance history, and traffic volume, rural roads in different regions often exhibit varying decay patterns. Therefore, before analyzing the degradation of rural road pavement performance, typical road sections should be selected based on these differences (Pantuso [19] et al. 2019). This paper selects typical rural road networks in Haimen, Guannan, and Yangzhou in Jiangsu province, China through extensive investigations and divides them into asphalt and cement pavement sections based on structural types. Then, typical road sections are chosen for pavement performance analysis according to the maintenance history of various treatment measures, such as slurry sealing layer, thin layer cover, and crushed stone regeneration. The specific selection of typical road sections is shown in Table 3.

Table 3. Selection of typical sections of rural roads in the Jiangsu province.

Pavement Structure	Maintenance History	Road Section Location (Region and Year)	Thickness (cm)	Traffic Level	RIPCI
Asphalt pavement	Original pavement	K003 + 200-K005 + 300 (Haimen City, 2008)	30	Medium	Excellent (94.69)
	Slurry sealing layer	K009 + 100-K010 + 000 (Haimen City, 2020)			
	Thin layer cover	K006 + 700-K007 + 200 (Haimen City, 2015)			
	Crushed stone regeneration	K015 + 700-K017 + 200 (Haimen City, 2015)			
	Milling and repaving one layer	K034 + 900-K036 + 600 (Haimen City, 2015)			
	Milling and repaving two layers	K049 + 100-K053 + 200 (Haimen City, 2015)			
Cement pavement	Original pavement	K012 + 000-K016 + 2000 (Guannan County, 2008)	22	Medium	Excellent (92.02)
	Slurry sealing layer	K007 + 500-K009 + 000 (Guannan County, 2019)			
	Thin layer cover	K010 + 500-K013 + 000 (Guannan County, 2019)			
	Crushed stone regeneration	K016 + 000-K016 + 600 (Guannan County, 2019)			
	Milling and repaving one layer	K027 + 200-K028 + 400 (Yangzhou City, 2018)			
	Milling and repaving two layers	K024 + 100-K026 + 500 (Yangzhou City, 2015)			

2.2.3. Determination of Prediction Model

In this section, we aim to establish a reasonable prediction model based on the influence of different treatment measures to evaluate the decay law of pavement conditions with time. In this paper, a large number of detection data of the above-mentioned selected typical sections are analyzed, and combined with the degradation law of rural highway pavement performance, the pavement performance prediction models of rural road RPCI and RRQI based on different treatment measures are established.

(1) Prediction model for RPCI

Based on the regular inspection data of rural roads in Jiangsu province from 2016 to 2021, the RPCI data of typical sections of rural asphalt pavement and cement pavement were fitted and analyzed. The main steps include: (1) grouping the inspection data and determining the corresponding initial decay year; (2) determining the basic parameters through data fitting analysis; (3) considering the impact of the internal health condition index RIPCI on the decay pattern of rural road pavement (RIPCI > 90, the decay coefficient is 1, 80 < RIPCI < 90, the decay coefficient is 0.8, 70 < RIPCI < 80, the decay coefficient is 0.6, RIPCI < 70 decay coefficient is 0); (4) according to the verification of other groups of data, optimize and determine the best parameters when the fitting accuracy requirements are met. Finally, RPCI decay models of five different treatment measures, such as slurry sealing layer, thin layer cover, crushed stone regeneration, milling and repaving one layer, and milling and repaving two layers, are established, respectively, as shown in Figures 4 and 5 below.

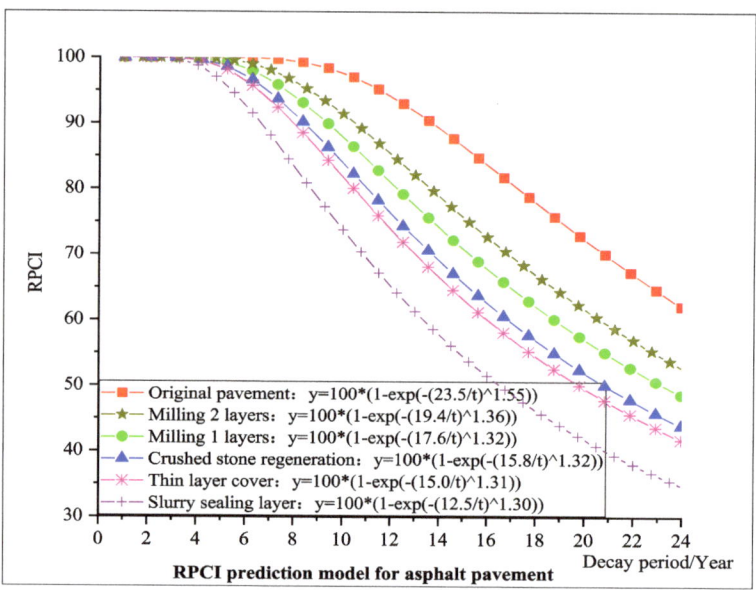

Figure 4. RPCI decay curve of asphalt pavement in rural roads over time.

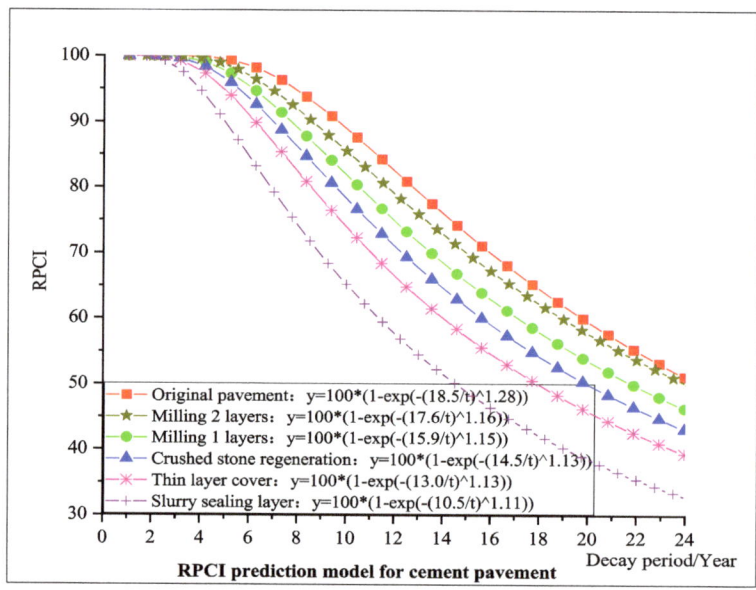

Figure 5. RPCI decay curve of cement pavement damage in rural roads over time.

(2) Prediction model for RRQI

Based on the road condition inspection data from 2016 to 2021, the RRQI data of typical sections of asphalt pavement and cement pavement on rural roads in Jiangsu province were fitted and analyzed. The RRQI decay curves of five different treatment levels were established, including slurry seal layer, thin layer cover layer, crushed stone regeneration, milling and resurfacing one layer, and milling and resurfacing two layers, as shown in Figures 6 and 7 below.

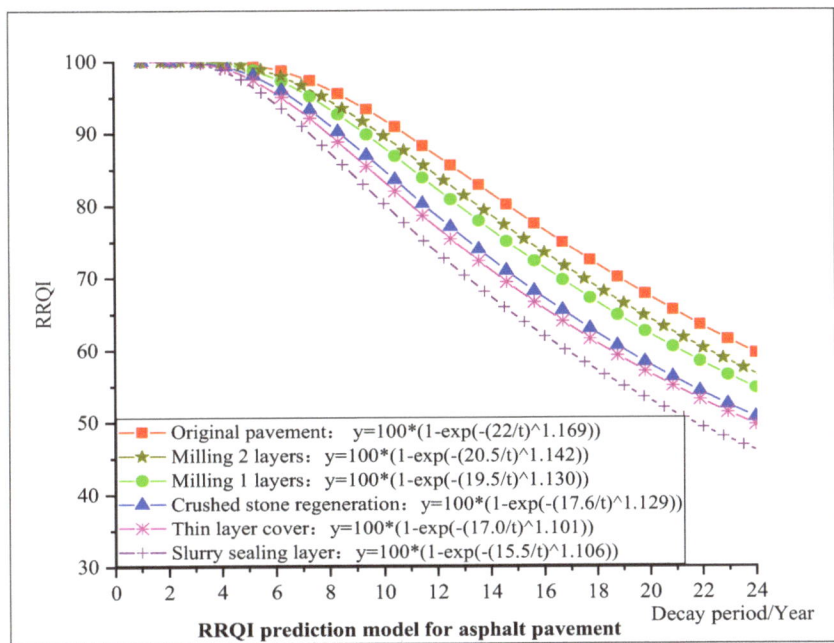

Figure 6. RRQI decay curve of asphalt pavement in rural roads over time.

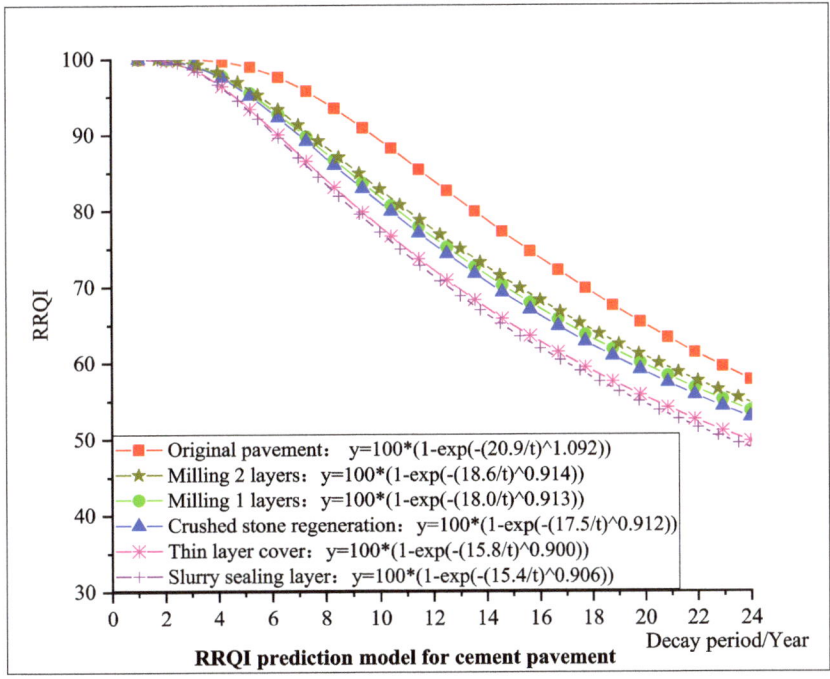

Figure 7. RRQI decay curve of cement pavement in rural roads over time.

2.3. Optimization Methods

2.3.1. Decision Optimization Method

In the rural road network maintenance decision-making process, limited budget, complexity, insufficient program efficiency, and low optimization efficiency are common problems (Chen, W [20] et al. 2021). This paper introduces an improved heuristic optimization algorithm to solve these issues. The method is based on changes in pavement performance after maintenance measures are implemented, aiming to ensure optimal decision-making benefits throughout the life cycle (Chu, J. C [21] et al. 2018). By using a set decision-making model and benefit model, this approach determines the combination of maintenance measures that provides the most long-term benefits for each road section, optimizing a decision-making scheme strategy with the best benefits quickly, as shown in Figure 8. The solution process involves (1) determining the maintenance decision plan for each individual maintenance section within the road network one by one, (2)–(3) combining all maintenance road section decision plans to achieve all possible combinations of programs for the entire road network. (4) The optimization process is based on annual budget cost and a pavement performance-based benefit model as the main optimization link. (5) It calculates and determines the benefits and costs of each maintenance measure based on the benefits model, and (6) conducts a comparative analysis of the cumulative benefits of all strategy schemes through optimization algorithms to determine the best maintenance strategy.

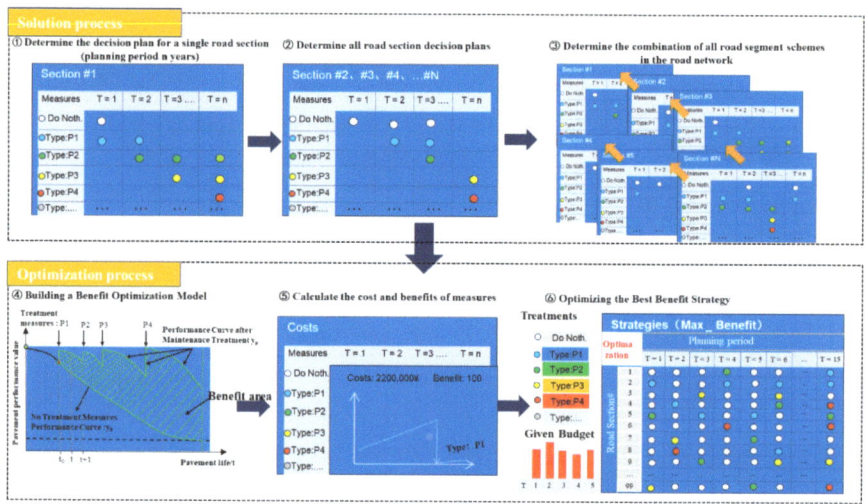

Figure 8. Decision steps for an improved heuristic optimization method.

2.3.2. Benefit Optimization Calculation

Based on the combination of all road section schemes, the maintenance decision-making optimization work is carried out to determine the best maintenance benefit scheme. The research results define the maintenance benefit area as the area enclosed by the pavement performance curve y_p after treatment measures and the natural attenuation curve $y0$ of pavement performance without measures, as shown in Figure 9. The Bene_cost ratio of benefit area to its cost is then taken as the final benefit evaluation value of rural road maintenance.

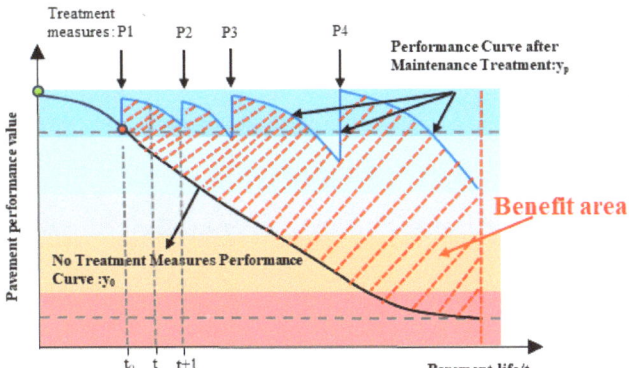

Figure 9. Schematic diagram of maintenance benefit area.

Considering the performance decay characteristics and benefit influencing factors of rural road pavement, the *Bene_cost* generated by RPCI and RRQI key performance indicators was calculated, respectively. According to the actual impact degree of each index, it is weighted and summed according to the given weights of 0.65 and 0.35, and the calculation formula of the comprehensive *Bene_cost* based on moment t is constructed, as shown in Equations (4)–(6) below.

$$COST = L * W * UC \tag{4}$$

$$Bene\_cost_t^i = \begin{cases} \sum_{l=1}^{n_l} (\int_{t_0}^{t} y_p^l - y_0^l) / \sum_{l=1}^{n_l} cost_l & \sum_{l=1}^{n_l} cost_l \neq 0 \\ 0 & \sum_{l=1}^{n_l} cost_l = 0 \end{cases} \tag{5}$$

$$Bene\_cost_t = 0.65 * Bene_{cost\,t}(RPCI) + 0.35 * Bene_{cost\,t}(PRQI) \tag{6}$$

where $COST$ is the cost of maintenance; L and W are length and width, respectively; UC is the unit area cost (¥/m^2); *Bene_cost* is the maintenance benefit calculated based on performance index i for the T year; l is the lane number; n_l is the number of lanes; y_p^l and y_0^l are the performance curves corresponding to the l lane with or without treatment measures taken, respectively.

To improve the calculation efficiency in the process of solution optimization, the improved heuristic optimization method proposed in this paper introduces the allowable deviation variable parameter D based on a given budget, and appropriately "relaxes" the cost constraints, as shown in the following formulas (7) and (8), to quickly realize the scheme combination with the best benefit in the whole life cycle.

$$B_t - D_t \leq Cost_t = \sum_{i'=1}^{m} Cost_{i't} \leq B_t + D_t, \quad t = 1, \ldots, T \tag{7}$$

$$Bene\_cost = \sum_{i'=1}^{m} \sum_{t=1}^{T} Bene\_cost_{i't} \tag{8}$$

where m is the number of road sections; B_t is the budget for each planning year; D_t is the maximum allowable deviation from the budget for each planning year.

2.4. Data Preparation of Case Studies

Based on the above research results, this paper takes the typical rural road network in Haimen City, China as an example, and carries out medium and long-term (2023–2036) maintenance planning analysis and research. The road network in this case mainly includes

10 routes, including Rui Min Line, Huo Si Line, Guo Xin Line, S336 San He Duan, Yang Hai Line, Hai Tian Line, S336 San Chang Duan, De Hai Line, Dong Tong Line and Shu Gang Line, with a total length of 280 km and two lanes in both directions (the width of one lane is 3.75 m). The original road condition data for this case comes from the actual test data of the rural road network RPCI, RRQI, and the Rural Road Inner Pavement Condition Index (RIPCI) in Haimen City in March 2022. As shown in Table 4, the pavement performance data of some sections are given.

Table 4. Performance data of typical sections of Haimen rural road.

Route	Lane	Starting Station	Ending Station	RPCI	RRQI	RIPCI	Pavement Type
Rui Min Line	R (1)	K0 + 000	K1 + 000	96.99	95.89	98.32	Asphalt
Rui Min Line	R (1)	K1 + 000	K2 + 000	96.75	96.21	95.15	Asphalt
Rui Min Line	R (1)	K2 + 000	K3 + 000	89.22	91.28	93.65	Asphalt
……	……	……	……	……	……	……	……
Rui Min Line	R (1)	K19 + 000	K19 + 950	90.34	91.12	93.80	Asphalt
Huo Si Line	L (1)	K0 + 000	K1 + 000	91.60	89.93	92.85	Cement
Huo Si Line	L (1)	K1 + 000	K2 + 000	94.64	95.20	93.46	Cement
Huo Si Line	L (1)	K2 + 000	K3 + 000	95.13	96.40	95.21	Asphalt
……	……	……	……	……	……	……	……
Guo Xin Line	R (1)	K0 + 000	K1 + 000	92.89	93.71	95.78	Asphalt
Guo Xin Line	R (1)	K1 + 000	K2 + 000	84.26	89.79	95.85	Asphalt
Guo Xin Line	R (1)	K2 + 000	K3 + 000	96.39	93.74	98.45	Asphalt
……	……	……	……	……	……	……	……
YangHai Line	R (1)	K0 + 000	K1 + 000	89.41	90.76	95.32	Asphalt
YangHai Line	R (1)	K1 + 000	K2 + 000	91.93	93.34	94.00	Asphalt
……	……	……	……	……	……	……	……
YangHai Line	R (1)	K32 + 000	K32 + 160	91.92	92.19	96.26	Asphalt

At the same time, the road performance data are divided into several standard treatment sections with a length of no more than 1000 m according to the above-mentioned rural road performance evaluation grades, as shown in Figure 10.

Figure 10. Planning section of the rural road network in Haimen City.

3. Results and Discussion

Based on the above case data, the budget for different years is calculated by the developed calculation program (the algorithm is realized by system programming), and the results are compared and analyzed to determine the functional maintenance strategy with a reasonable budget and best benefit.

3.1. Road Condition Prediction Analysis

According to the existing rural road conditions in Haimen City, the performance requirements in the planning period (the overall average value is not less than 85), and the input costs in previous years. This paper preliminarily selects five annual budget options for decision-making calculation, mainly including plan 1: no budget; plan 2: 5 million (¥); plan 3: 10 million (¥); plan 4: 15 million (¥); plan 5: 5 million (¥); (previous four years: 2023–2026), 10 million (¥) (medium-term five years: 2027–2031), 15 million (¥) (later five years: 2032–2036). As shown in Figures 11 and 12 below, the results of the RPCI grade frequency distribution and predicted value of road surface performance under the optimal strategy of different budget schemes are generated.

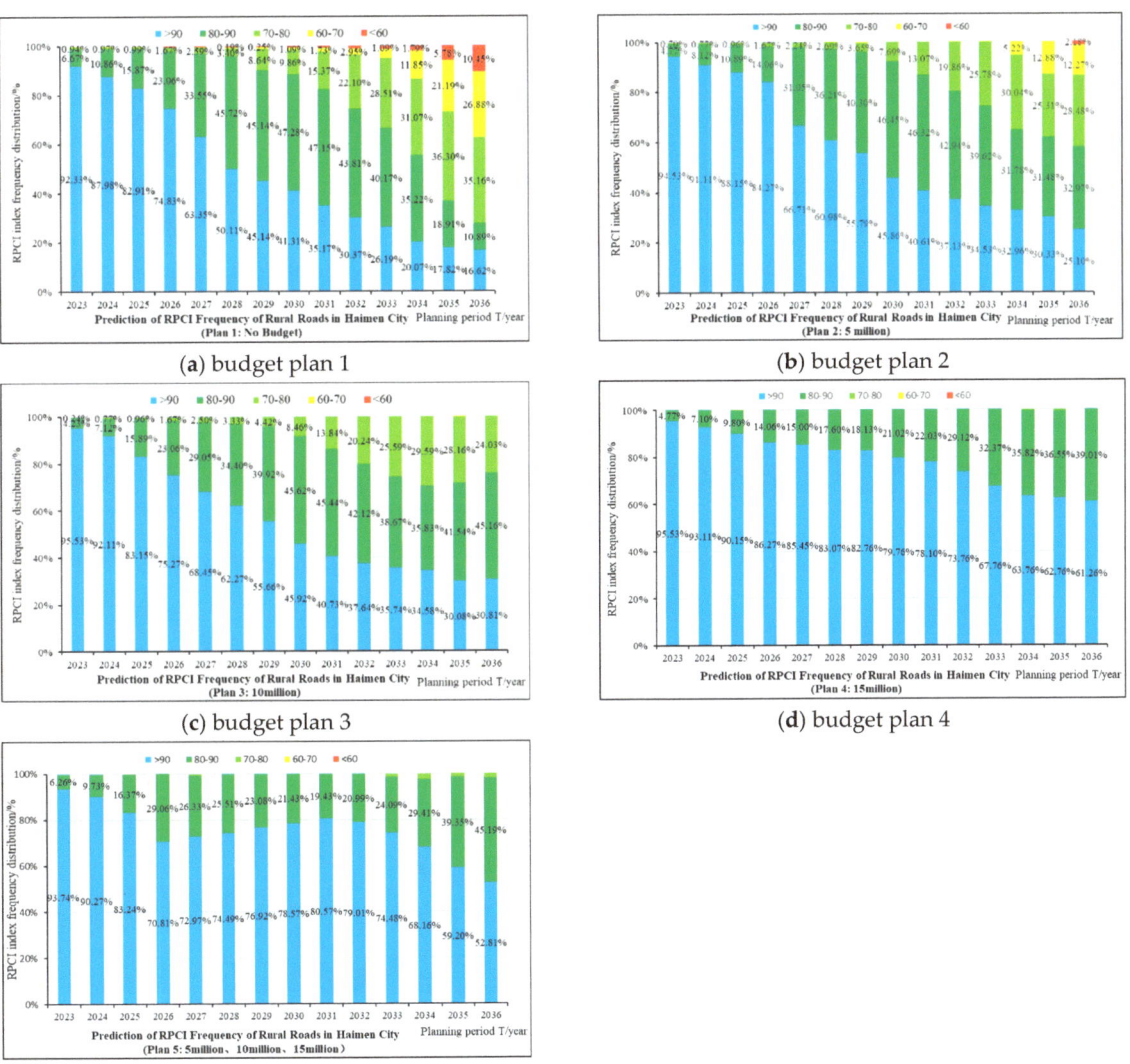

Figure 11. Frequency distribution of RPCI on rural roads in Haimen City under different budget plans.

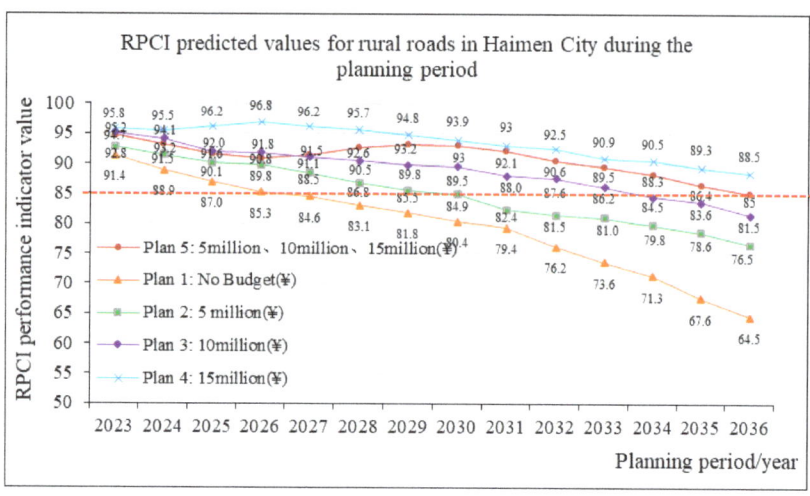

Figure 12. Predicted RPCI of rural roads in Haimen City under different budget plans.

At the same time, this paper further predicts and analyzes the pavement RRQI index under different given annual budget plans. Figures 13 and 14 below show the statistical results of RRQI level frequency distribution and performance value in the next 14 years.

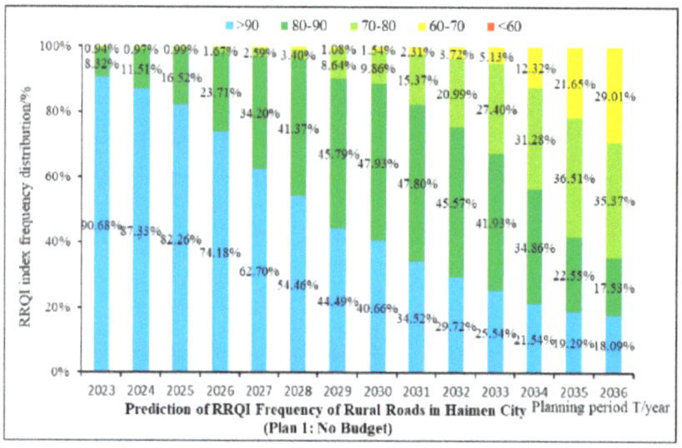

(**a**) budget plan 1

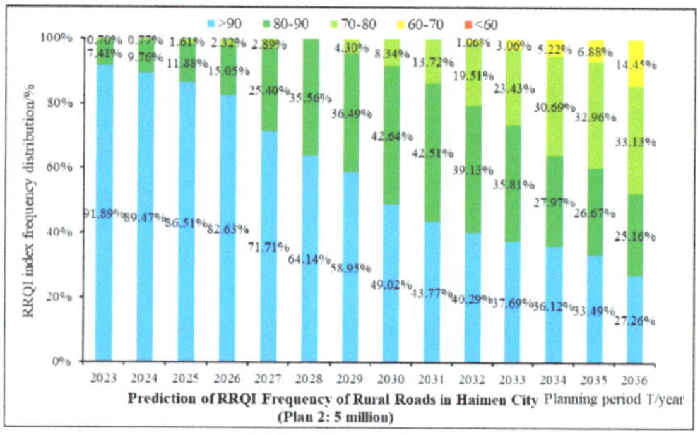

(**b**) budget plan 2

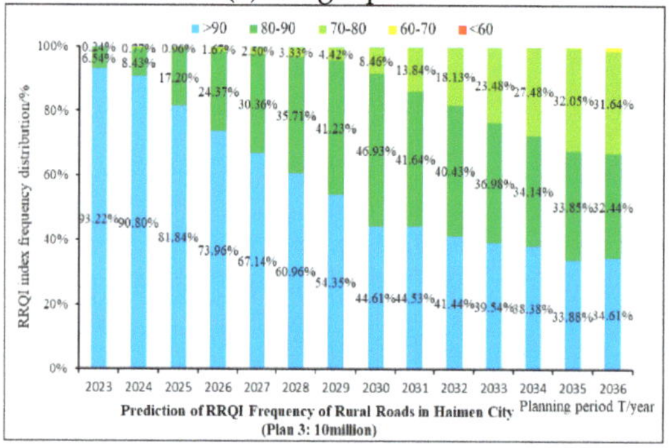

(**c**) budget plan 3

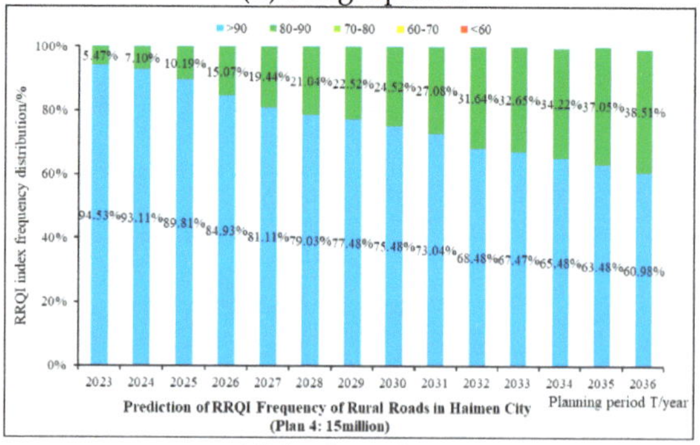

(**d**) budget plan 4

Figure 13. *Cont.*

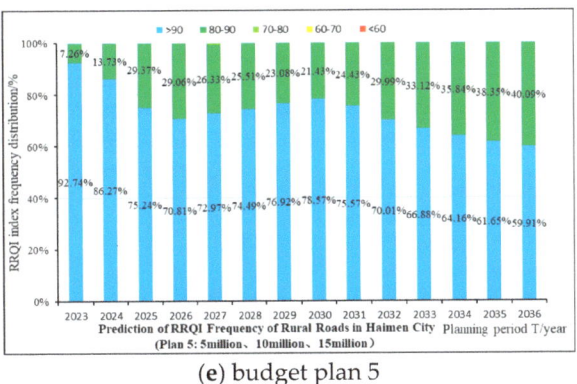

(e) budget plan 5

Figure 13. Frequency distribution of RRQI on rural roads in Haimen City under different budget plans.

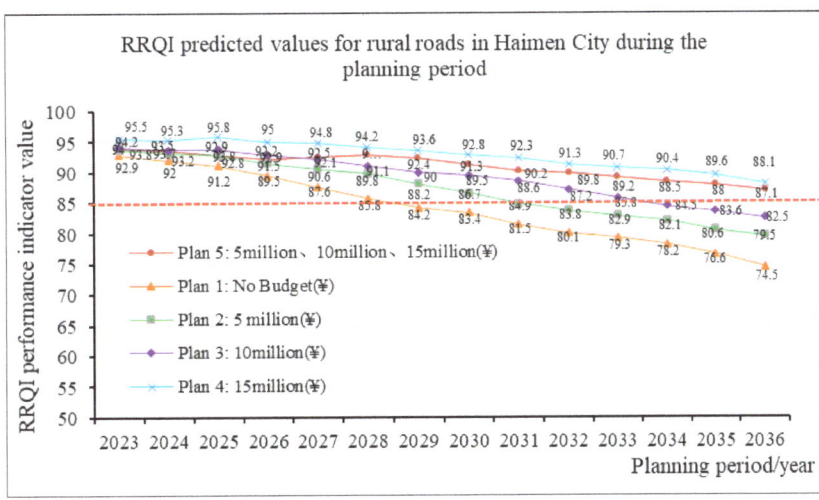

Figure 14. Predicted RRQI of rural roads in Haimen City under different budget plans.

According to the above figure, the RPCI and RRQI values of rural road network performance in Haimen City are in a decreasing trend with the increase in the service life of the pavement. By comparing different plans, it is found that with the increase in annual budget investment, the overall performance of the road network gradually improves, and the improvement effect of road surface RPCI compared with RRQI during the planning period is more obvious. When the annual budget reached more than 10 million, the excellent, good, and average grade rate of RPCI and RRQI indicators reached 95%, and the predicted average reached more than 80 points. After adopting the budget investment of plan 5 phased maintenance, its overall road condition performance is at excellent and good levels, and the predicted value is above 85 points.

Therefore, the phased increase in annual budget input according to budget plan 5 is more effective and reasonable than the above-mentioned conservation budget plan. Moreover, the functional priority maintenance strategy has played a significant role in improving the performance of the pavement, which can meet the service level requirements of the municipal road management department for the road network under its jurisdiction during the planning period.

3.2. Optimization Scheme Determination

Based on the analysis results of the prediction effect of different budget plans, this paper selects the limited budget plan 5 as the minimum cost required to meet the maintenance performance requirements of the road network in Haimen City and determines the treatment plan that meets the most benefits in the next 14-year life cycle of the planned road section. As shown in Table 5 below, 171 maintenance sections require maintenance measures during the entire road network planning period (treatment schemes for some sections are given).

Table 5. Treatment scheme for some sections of maintenance planning in Haimen City.

Year	Route	Lane	Starting Station	Ending Station	Treatment Measures	Cost (China RMB)/¥	Bene_Cost
2023	Guo Xin Line	L (1)	K1 + 000	K2 + 000	Milling and repaving 1 layer	502,500	2.82
2023	Dong Tong	L (1)	K3 + 000	K4 + 000	Crushed stone regeneration	270,000	3.77
2023	Yang Hai Line	R (1)	K17 + 000	K18 + 000	Slurry sealing layer	131,250	9.14
2023	Guo Xin Line	R (1)	K1 + 000	K2 + 000	Milling and repaving 1 layer	502,500	2.82
2023	Rui Min Line	R (1)	K7 + 000	K8 + 000	Milling and repaving 1 layer	502,500	2.86
2023	Yang Hai Line	R (1)	K5 + 000	K6 + 000	Milling and repaving 1 layer	502,500	2.90
2023	Rui Min Line	L (1)	K2 + 000	K3 + 000	Milling and repaving 1 layer	502,500	2.92
2023	Rui Min Line	R (1)	K8 + 000	K9 + 000	Milling and repaving 1 layer	502,500	2.86
2024	Rui Min Line	L (1)	K4 + 000	K5 + 000	Milling and repaving 1 layer	502,500	3.36
2024	Yang Hai Line	R (1)	K20 + 000	K21 + 000	Crushed stone regeneration	270,000	4.44
2024	Yang Hai Line	L (1)	K13 + 000	K14 + 000	Crushed stone regeneration	270,000	4.44
2025	Yang Hai Line	R (1)	K8 + 000	K9 + 000	Milling and repaving 2 layer	502,500	3.54
2025	Rui Min Line	L (1)	K15 + 000	K16 + 000	Milling and repaving 2 layer	502,500	3.74
2025	Guo Xin Line	L (1)	K0 + 000	K1 + 000	Milling and repaving 2 layer	502,500	3.54
……	……	……	……	……	……	……	……
2036	Rui Min Line	L (1)	K5 + 000	K6 + 000	Milling and repaving 2 layer	1,117,500	0.22
2036	Rui Min Line	R (1)	K2 + 000	K3 + 000	Milling and repaving 2 layer	1,117,500	0.23

Through the statistics of the above-mentioned maintenance planning results of Haimen City, Figures 15 and 16 give the area and maintenance cost, respectively, of the types of treatment measures taken each year in the whole road network planning period.

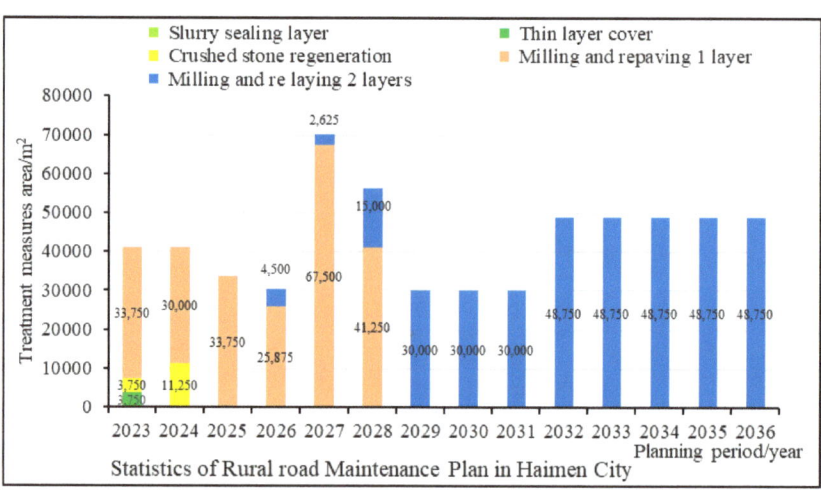

Figure 15. Area statistics of treatment measures in the Haimen rural road planning period.

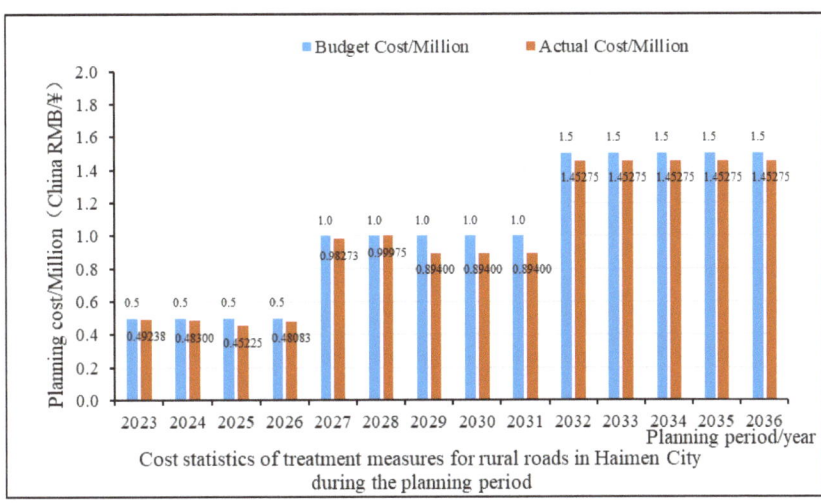

Figure 16. Statistics of treatment measures during the planning period of a rural road in Haimen City.

According to the planning scheme and forecast results determined in the above figure, it can be seen that the overall road condition of the Haimen rural road network is good. In the next two years, the maintenance plan will mainly adopt various treatment measures such as a slurry sealing layer, crushed stone regeneration, and milling and repaving one layer. With the increase in pavement service life, pavement performance will be degraded to a certain extent. In view of the possible local typical diseased sections of the pavement, the planning and decision-making results for 2025–2028 mainly adopt milling and repaving one layer to improve pavement performance. Finally, in the middle and late stages of the planning (2029–2036), pavement performance will be greatly reduced, and the decision-making result is that milling and repaving two layers of strong maintenance measures are adopted to maintain the pavement's service level.

4. Conclusions

This paper analyzes the current situation of complex rural road networks, large maintenance scales, and limited budgets in China. It explores how to conduct medium and long-term scientific maintenance planning to achieve the best maintenance strategy within the service life cycle. The study concludes:

(1) Based on the maintenance characteristics of rural roads in China, typical maintenance technologies suitable for different strength grades are analyzed and selected. RPCI and RRQI decision tree models for asphalt and cement pavements are established, proposing maintenance countermeasure sets under different performance combinations.

(2) Considering the impact of pavement structure, maintenance history, and traffic volume on performance degradation, typical rural road sections in cities and counties like Haimen, Guannan, and Yangzhou in Jiangsu province were selected. By fitting and analyzing a large amount of detection data, RPCI and RRQI pavement performance prediction models based on five treatment grades are established.

(3) To address the complex solution process of rural road maintenance decision-making, an improved heuristic optimization method is proposed, establishing a model based on pavement performance benefit. Through optimization calculations, a maintenance strategy with the best benefits in the life cycle is quickly generated.

(4) A case study of ten typical rural road sections in Haimen City, Jiangsu province was conducted to apply long-term maintenance planning from 2023 to 2036. By comparing and analyzing the prediction effects of pavement performance (RPCI and RRQI) under different budget plans, a maintenance strategy with a reasonable budget

and maximum benefit for the planned road section in the next 14 years life cycle is determined, verifying the feasibility and effectiveness of the research model.

Author Contributions: Conceptualization, C.H.; methodology, C.H.; software, J.H.; validation, X.Y.; investigation, C.H.; data curation, L.C. and T.C.; writing—original draft preparation, C.H. and J.H; writing—review and editing, C.H.; visualization, C.H.; funding acquisition, C.H. All authors have read and agreed to the published version of the manuscript.

Funding: This work was supported by the Jiangsu Science and Technology Innovation Support Program of China (No.BZ2022019), Nanjing Science and Technology Program (No.2021-12004), and the National Key Research and Development Program of China (No.2020YFAO714302).

Institutional Review Board Statement: Not applicable.

Informed Consent Statement: Not applicable.

Data Availability Statement: The data presented in this study are available on request from the corresponding author. (Some data are related to research projects, and are not provided for the time being).

Conflicts of Interest: The authors declare no potential conflict of interest.

References

1. Pantha, B.R.; Yatabe, R.; Bhandary, N.P. GIS-based highway maintenance prioritization model: An integrated approach for highway maintenance in Nepal mountains. *J. Transp. Geogr.* **2010**, *18*, 426–433. [CrossRef]
2. Mergi, K.M.; Mohamed, E. Application of Pavement Condition Index (PCI) Methodology in PavementDistress Evaluation and Maintenance Prioritization. *J. Basic Eng. Stud. Board* **2012**, *1*, 4–6.
3. Mathew, B.S.; Isaac, K.P. Optimization of maintenance strategy for rural road. *Adv. Mater. Res.* **2015**, *40*, 2915–2918.
4. Torres-Machi, C.; Pellicer, E.; Yepes, V.; Chamorro, A. Towards a sustainable optimization of pavement maintenance programs under budgetary restrictions. *J. Clean. Prod.* **2017**, *148*, 90–102. [CrossRef]
5. Agarwal, P.K.; Khan, A.B.; Choudhary, S. A Rational Strategy for Resource Allocation for Rural Road Maintenance. *Transp. Res. Procedia* **2017**, *25*, 2195–2207. [CrossRef]
6. Pasindu, H.; Gamage, D.; Bandara, J. Framework for selecting pavement type for low volume roads. *Transp. Res. Procedia* **2020**, *48*, 3924–3938. [CrossRef]
7. Yogesh, J.; Sanjeev, S. Planning of rural road network using sustainable practices to maximize the accessibility to health and education facilities using ant colony optimization. *J. Books* **2023**, *35*, 324–338.
8. Kabir, G.; Sadiq, R.; Tesfamariam, S. A review of multi-criteria decision-making methods for infrastructure management. *Struct. Infrastruct. Eng.* **2013**, *10*, 1176–1210. [CrossRef]
9. Choi, J.-H. Significance ranking of quality characteristics on pavement performance based on neural network analysis. *KSCE J. Civ. Eng.* **2005**, *9*, 171–178. [CrossRef]
10. Abu Dabous, S.; Zeiada, W.; Zayed, T.; Al-Ruzouq, R. Sustainability-informed multi-criteria decision support framework for ranking and prioritization of pavement sections. *J. Clean. Prod.* **2019**, *244*, 118755. [CrossRef]
11. Fecarotti, C.; Andrews, J.; Pesenti, R. A mathematical programming model to select maintenance strategies in railway networks. *Reliab. Eng. Syst. Saf.* **2021**, *216*, 107940. [CrossRef]
12. Han, C.; Ma, T.; Chen, S. Asphalt pavement maintenance plans an intelligent decision model based on a reinforcement learning algorithm. *Constr. Build. Mater.* **2021**, *299*, 124278. [CrossRef]
13. Hanandeh, S.M. Introducing mathematical modeling to estimate pavement quality index of flexible pavements based on genetic algorithm and artificial neural networks. *Case Stud. Constr. Mater.* **2022**, *16*, e00991. [CrossRef]
14. Kabir, M.; Mobin, J.; Nayeem, M.A.; Habib, M.A.; Rahman, M.S. Multi-objective optimization and heuristic based solutions for evacuation modeling. *Transp. Res. Interdiscip. Perspect.* **2023**, *18*, 100798. [CrossRef]
15. Tang, X.Y.; Xiao, J.Z. Natural gravel-recycled aggregate concrete applied in rural highway pavement: Material properties and life cycle assessment. *J. Clean. Prod.* **2022**, *334*, 130219. [CrossRef]
16. Shtayat, A.; Moridpour, S.; Best, B.; Shroff, A.; Raol, D. A review of monitoring systems of pavement condition in paved and unpaved roads. *J. Traffic Transp. Eng.* **2020**, *7*, 629–638. [CrossRef]
17. Yu, J.; Jahren, C.T.; Williams, R.C. Development of holding strategies for deteriorated low-volume roads: Introduction to test sections in Iowa. *Transp. Res. Rec.* **2015**, *2474*, 217–224. [CrossRef]
18. Stein, N.; Weisbrod, G.; Sieber, M. *Transportation Research Board. Investment Prioritization Methods for Low-Volume Roads*; The National Academies Press: Washington, DC, USA, 2018; 73p, ISBN 9780309390286.
19. Pantuso, A.; Loprencipe, G.; Bonin, G.; Teltayev, B.B. Analysis of Pavement Condition Survey Data for Effective Implementation of a Network Level Pavement Management Program for Kazakhstan. *Sustainability* **2019**, *11*, 901. [CrossRef]

20. Chen, W.; Zheng, M. Multi-objective optimization for pavement maintenance and rehabilitation decision-making: A critical review and future directions. *Autom. Constr.* **2021**, *130*, 103840. [CrossRef]
21. Chu, J.C.; Huang, K.-H. Mathematical programming framework for modeling and comparing network-level pavement maintenance strategies. *Transp. Res. Part B Methodol.* **2018**, *109*, 1–25. [CrossRef]

Disclaimer/Publisher's Note: The statements, opinions and data contained in all publications are solely those of the individual author(s) and contributor(s) and not of MDPI and/or the editor(s). MDPI and/or the editor(s) disclaim responsibility for any injury to people or property resulting from any ideas, methods, instructions or products referred to in the content.

Review

State-of-the-Art Review of Utilization of Microbial-Induced Calcite Precipitation for Improving Moisture-Dependent Properties of Unsaturated Soils

Jue Li [1,2], Wenwei Bi [3], Yongsheng Yao [1,*] and Zhengnan Liu [4]

1. College of Traffic & Transportation, Chongqing Jiaotong University, Chongqing 400074, China
2. Key Laboratory of Special Environment Road Engineering of Hunan Province, Changsha University of Science & Technology, Changsha 410114, China
3. School of Civil Engineering, Chongqing Jiaotong University, Chongqing 400074, China
4. Hunan Communications Research Institute Co., Ltd., Changsha 410075, China
* Correspondence: yaoyongsheng23@cqjtu.edu.cn

Abstract: Unsaturated soil is a form of natural soil whose pores are filled by air and water. Different from saturated soil, the microstructure of unsaturated soil consists of three phases, namely, the solid phase (soil particle), vapor phase, and liquid phase. Due to the matric suction of soil pores, the hydraulic and mechanical behaviors of unsaturated soils present a significant dependence on the moisture condition, which usually results in a series of unpredictable risks, including foundation settlement, landslide, and dam collapse. Microbial-induced calcite precipitation (MICP) is a novel and environmentally friendly technology that can improve the water stability of unsaturated soft or expansive soils. This paper reviews the microscopic mechanisms of MICP and its effect on the mechanical properties of unsaturated soils. The MICP process is mainly affected by the concentration of calcium ions and urea, apart from the concentration of bacteria. The moisture-dependent properties were comparatively analyzed through mechanical models and influence factors on the experimental data among various unsaturated soils. It suggests that the variations in resilient modulus and permanent deformation are strongly related to the extent of MICP applied on unsaturated soils. Finally, the problems in the MICP application, environmental challenges, and further research directions are suggested.

Keywords: microbial-induced calcite precipitation; unsaturated soils; water retention curve; resilient modulus; permanent deformation

Citation: Li, J.; Bi, W.; Yao, Y.; Liu, Z. State-of-the-Art Review of Utilization of Microbial-Induced Calcite Precipitation for Improving Moisture-Dependent Properties of Unsaturated Soils. *Appl. Sci.* **2023**, *13*, 2502. https://doi.org/10.3390/app13042502

Academic Editor: Angeles Sanroman Braga

Received: 13 January 2023
Revised: 8 February 2023
Accepted: 13 February 2023
Published: 15 February 2023

Copyright: © 2023 by the authors. Licensee MDPI, Basel, Switzerland. This article is an open access article distributed under the terms and conditions of the Creative Commons Attribution (CC BY) license (https://creativecommons.org/licenses/by/4.0/).

1. Introduction

Unsaturated soil is a type of soil consisting mainly of solid particles, a liquid matrix, and pore air. Due to the shrinkage interface between liquid and air, the matrix suction becomes an important structural stress within saturated soil [1]. The mechanical properties of unsaturated soil closely depend on the humidity characteristics [2,3]. The dependence of mechanical behaviors on matric suction or moisture involved in many engineering problems has been reported on in studies of foundation engineering, subgrade engineering, and slope engineering [4–8]. For example, after the soft soil humidifying, the stiffness of the soil subgrades decreased evidently, resulting in the settlement and collapse of the pavement structure. Thus, unsaturated soils should be improved in practice by physical and chemical methods.

The existing soil treatments mainly include dynamic compaction methods and the cement grouting method, but these methods all have certain shortcomings [9,10]. Yao et al. [11] strengthened the collapsible dam foundation by means of the dynamic compaction method, and found that its availability of treatment is limited by construction and geological conditions. The grouting method is often used for soft foundation treatment, but it uses a large amount of cement and its production would increase the quantity of CO_2 emissions [12]. More and more attention has been placed on reducing CO_2 emissions in the life cycle of engineering practices, with the increasing awareness of people concerned about the environment [13]. These green and low-carbon practices require a novel technology to decouple the dependence of the soil's treatment by cement. Therefore, the microbial-induced calcite precipitation (MICP) technology has become one of the interest points in geotechnical and geological engineering fields in recent years, since it is an environmentally friendly, noiseless, and low-cost approach for improving the engineering properties of unsaturated soil [14,15].

At present, the cement process of MICP could mainly be classified into four types of bio-mineralization reactions [16], including the urea hydrolysis type [17], ferric reduction type [18], sulfate reduction type [19] and denitrification type [20]. Urea hydrolysis is the most efficient and advantageous way to conduct MICP technology, since it has the advantages of simple operation and is easily controllable [21]. In addition, it can quickly produce calcium carbonate precipitates and has a high microbial survival rate without a special nutrient solution [22]. Studies have been conducted to investigate the improvement of soil mechanical behaviors by urea hydrolysis through macroscopic and microcosmic experiments [23,24]. Martinez et al. [25] applied the MICP grouting method on expansive soil columns and found that the swelling potential and hydrophilicity of expansive soil decreased after the treatment of MICP. Salifu et al. [26] demonstrated that the penetration grouting approach of MICP-solidified fluid can improve the stability of soil slopes, since the generated $CaCO_3$ can fill the volume of the micro-pore structures within soil by 9.9%. Sharma and R. [27] found that the compressive strength of MICP-treated soil was 1.45 to 2.26 times of that of the untreated soil by laboratory tests. Some researchers have reported the effectiveness of MICP treatment on soil mechanical properties, while less considerations and comparisons have been made on the changes of the soil hydraulic properties induced by MICP treatment [28–30]. Specially, it is important to investigate the moisture dependence on the stiffness and deformation of unsaturated soil in subgrade construction.

In this paper, the reaction mechanism of microbial-induced calcite precipitation and its influence on the physical and mechanical properties of unsaturated soil are reviewed. Firstly, the reaction mechanism of urea hydrolysis type MICP technology was introduced, considering different influencing factors, including temperature, PH value, nutrient solution concentration, and calcium ion concentration. Secondly, the structural characteristic and the soil water characteristic curve (SWCC) of unsaturated soil and their influence on the physical and mechanical properties of unsaturated soil are introduced in detail. Thirdly, the changes of the soil microstructure before and after mineralization by MICP technology are analyzed and compared from the macro and micro levels. The influence of MICP technology on the permeability of unsaturated soil and SWCC is also discussed. Furthermore, the relationship between the hydraulic and mechanical properties of unsaturated soil is briefly introduced. Finally, it provides the existing problems, environmental challenges, and further research aspects in the application of MICP.

2. Mechanism of Microbial-Induced Calcite Precipitation (MICP)

2.1. Reaction Mechanism of MICP

The MICP is a widely existing bio-mineralization reaction in nature, accompanied by different microbial activities and chemical processes [31]. Different from the mineralization on the geological surface of earth, bio-mineralization refers to the process in which inorganic elements selectively precipitate from the environment to form minerals on a specific organic matrix with the participation of biological cells. This bio driven mineralization reaction mainly occurs in four ways: urea hydrolysis, denitrification, sulfate reduction, and ferric iron reduction [32]. The method of using microorganism-induced denitrification to precipitate calcium carbonate not only has high cultivation cost, but also has low efficiency of generating calcium carbonate [33]. However, it is undeniable that denitrifying bacteria can grow in situ and play a role under anoxic conditions [34]. In the process of microbial-induced sulfate, the sulfate reduction will produce the hydrogen sulfide gas, which is harmful to the environment and human body [35]. In addition, hydrogen sulfide gas also results in accelerating the corrosion of steel bars in structures. For the ferric iron reduction method, the requirements for the oxidation substrate are very high, meaning that it only works when the solubility of the oxidation substrate is low [36]. The urea hydrolysis method is simple and efficient, given that there is no additional reaction condition and no environmental pollution [37]. Because matrixes (urea and $CaCl_2$) have a high solubility in water solution, the MICP process can generate a lot of $CaCO_3$ in a short time [38]. Scholars generally believe that MICP using urea hydrolysis has an enormous potential in soil treatment [39]. In addition, among all biochemical reactions, the reaction of urea hydrolysis is a main technological path to produce ammonium ions and carbonate ions, and its reaction process is relatively simple. Therefore, the reaction mechanism of urea hydrolysis MICP was taken as an example in the following section.

2.2. Reaction Mechanism of Urea Hydrolysis MICP

Chuo et al. [40] found that 17–30% of bacteria collected from Australia can hydrolyze urea rapidly. The Bacillus pasteurii (BP) has a high urease activity within soil and has been widely used in the MICP treatment [41]. During its metabolism, its cell secretes a large amount of urease to produce adenosine triphosphate (ATP), which promotes the catalytic hydrolysis of urea to produce ammonium and carbonate ions. Meanwhile, the PH value in the system increases in this process. Due to the presence of calcium ions, carbonate ions and calcium ions gradually modulate to form $CaCO_3$ precipitation. The reaction equation of urea hydrolysis is shown in Equations (1)–(5) [42].

$$CO(NH_2)_2 + H_2O \xrightarrow{urease} NH_2COOH + NH_3 \tag{1}$$

$$NH_2COOH + H_2O \rightarrow NH_3 + H_2CO_3 \tag{2}$$

$$H_2CO_3 \rightarrow 2H^+ + CO_3^{2-} \tag{3}$$

$$NH_3 + H_2O \rightarrow NH_4^+ + OH^- \tag{4}$$

$$Ca^{2+} + CO_3^{2-} \rightarrow CaCO_3 \downarrow \tag{5}$$

The details of the urea hydrolysis of $CaCO_3$ precipitated by BP are shown in Figure 1. When BP metabolizes to produce urease, it will secrete a metabolite called bail polymer. Due to the existence of the double electric layer structure of the extracellular polymer and its microorganism, the microorganism tends to adsorb on the surface of the sand particles. Because of the negatively charged functional groups such as hydroxyl, amino, amido, and carboxyl, the surface of the microbial cell wall is also negatively charged and constantly attracts calcium ions in the environment, meaning that a large number of calcium ions gather on the cell surface. The carbonate formed after hydrolysis of urea will form $CaCO_3$ precipitation with these calcium ions and envelop the bacteria [43]. From the whole reaction process, it can be found that bacteria mainly play two roles: the core of which is to provide urease, and the other is to provide crystal nuclei for the formation of CaCO3 crystals [44]. The reaction equation of urease bacteria is displayed in Equations (6)–(10) [45].

$$CO(NH_2)_2 + 2H_2O \rightarrow H_2CO_3 + 2NH_3(g) \tag{6}$$

$$H_2CO_3 + 2NH_3 \leftrightarrow 2NH_4^+ + 2OH^- \tag{7}$$

$$H_2CO_3 \rightarrow H^+ + HCO_3^- \tag{8}$$

$$HCO_3^- + H^+ + 2OH^- \leftrightarrow CO_3^{2-} + 2H_2O \tag{9}$$

$$Ca^{2+} + CO_3^{2-} \leftrightarrow CaCO_3(s) \tag{10}$$

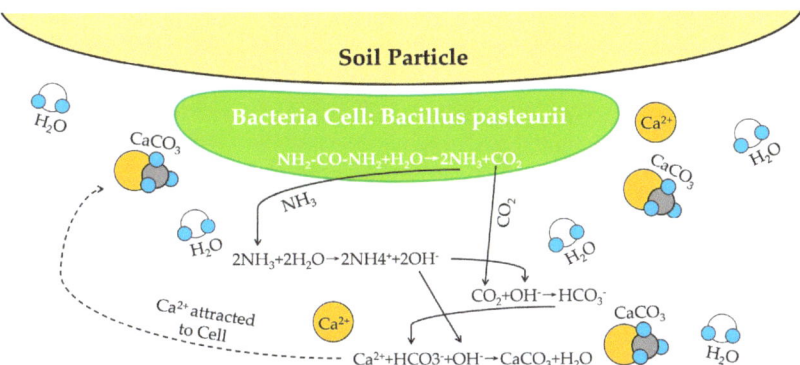

Figure 1. Sketch map of microbial-induced carbonate deposition process on particle surface.

2.3. Influencing Factors of MICP Reaction

The essence of MICP technology is to induce microorganisms to generate $CaCO_3$ precipitation between the gaps within soil to achieve the role of bio-cementation and treatment of soil. However, MICP technology will be limited and constrained by many factors in actual operation [46]. The factors that influence the treatment effect of MICP technology contain temperature, PH value, bio-cement concentration, calcium ion concentration, nutrient solution (urea) concentration, and soil particle size [47]. Mortensen et al. [48] showed that the influencing factors were in the order from large to small as temperature, concentration of bio-cementing fluid, nutrient solution concentration, PH value, and calcium ion concentration, respectively, through single factor and orthogonal tests. Sotoudehfar et al. [49] used the optimized orthogonal test method to explore the influence of various parameters in the process of MICP on the curing effect. The results showed that the curing time had the greatest influence on the curing effect, and the bacterial cell concentration, molar concentration ratio of nutrient solution, and the liquid injection flow rate had similar influences on the curing effect.

2.3.1. Temperature and PH Value

Temperature is the key factor in the success of MICP technology on soil treatment [50]. A change in temperature will affect the growth of bacteria, the activity of microbial enzymes, the biodegradation of bacteria, and the process of binding precipitation, thus affecting the final curing effect. Figure 2a shows the changes of urease and growth activities of BP at different temperatures. An absorbance index at the 600 nm wavelength (OD600) was wildly applied to evaluate the density and growth activity of the BP solution. It found that the growth curve of BP was different when the temperature varied from low to high [51]. It is generally believed that the growth of BP is inhibited at low temperatures, while the urease activity of BP decreases at high temperatures [52,53]. Therefore, the BP should be cultivated under a suitable growth environment (temperature).

In addition to the temperature, urease activity of BP is an important factor. The decrease in enzyme activity will lead to an insufficient precipitation of $CaCO_3$. Kim et al. [54] found that the suitable temperature for the growth of BP Sarcina was 30 °C, at which the strain propagated rapidly and produced high urease activity. When the temperature was less than 10 °C, the urease activity was almost lost. Furthermore, since the urease activity is affected by temperature, Xiao et al. [55] demonstrated that $CaCO_3$ crystals generated in soil samples had a good homogeneity by grouting at low temperature.

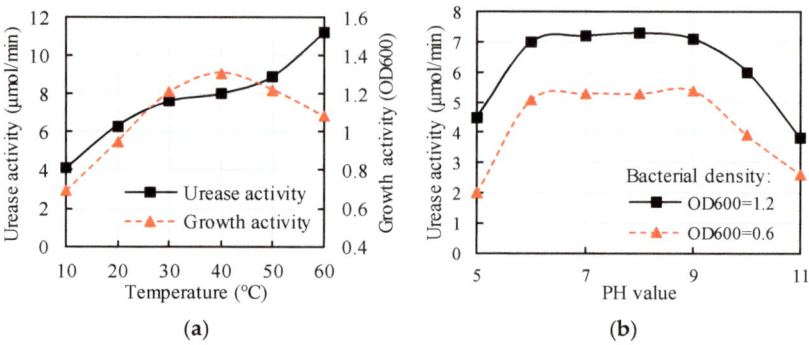

Figure 2. Changes of urease activity influenced by (**a**) Temperature (**b**) PH value.

PH value is one of the important influencing factors on microbial life activities. Its influence is mainly reflected in three aspects: First, it affects the biological activity of macromolecular substances (such as proteins and nucleic acids) by changing their charge. Second, it reduces the absorption and utilization of nutrients by microorganisms by changing the charge of cell membrane. Third, it also reduces the utilization effectiveness of nutrients in the living environment of microorganisms and enhances the toxicity of harmful substances [56]. Figure 2b shows the changes of urease activity with the increasing PH value.

2.3.2. Bio-Cementing Liquid Nutrient Solution Concentration

Bio-cementitious fluid plays an important role in microbial soil treatment. Bio-cementing liquid shall be used in the reaction of microbial-induced $CaCO_3$ deposition, which has a direct impact on the treatment effect [57]. From the MICP principle, the increase in calcium ions and urea in the bio-cementing solution will precipitate more $CaCO_3$. In the current research, the bio-cementing fluid generally includes urea and calcium chloride, but the selection of parameters such as bio-concentration, number of rounds, and ratio are different [58]. Cui et al. [59] believed that the bio-concentration of bio-cementing fluid had a significant impact on the treatment effect. Meanwhile, the low bio-concentration was helpful to obtain higher treatment strength, and the size of generated $CaCO_3$ crystal was also large [46]. Cheng and Cord-Ruwisch [60] found that a too low bio-concentration of bio-cement solution will lead to insufficient $CaCO_3$ and will affect the treatment effect.

2.3.3. Nutrient Solution Concentration

Mujah et al. [61] found that changing the nutrient solution can affect the nucleation rate and the size of $CaCO_3$ crystals. Meanwhile, the effect of nutrient solution on different environments was also different. Wong [62] added urea to the culture medium to increase the precipitation rate of $CaCO_3$, which can overcome the inhibition of solidification under low temperature environments. The adding urea does not only increase the urease activity, but also will cause the soil to become alkaline, thus inhibiting the growth of microorganisms [63]. The high urea content causes the uneven distribution of overall precipitation crystals, resulting in the low strength of soil. Zhao [64] found that the concentration of the nutrient solution has an important impact on the shear strength of solidified muddy soil. With the increasing concentration of the nutrient solution, the internal friction angle first increases and then decreases, and the optimal concentration of the corresponding optimal nutrient solution is 1.60 mol/L. Soon et al. [65] found that the bio-cementation effect will reach a peak value with the change in nutrient concentration, according to which the most appropriate nutrient concentration can be obtained. In addition, cells will shrink due to water loss under a high salt environment, thus affecting the physiological and biochemical reaction process of microorganisms. Therefore, the concentration of nutrient solution is very important in the study of microbial solidification of soil. Whiffin et al. [66] found that the activity of bacterial urease decreased significantly, almost linearly, with the increase in calcium ion concentration, indicating that a high concentration of calcium ions have an evident inhibition on urease under this condition.

In conclusion, the output of $CaCO_3$ is positively related to the concentration of nutrient solution within a certain range, but high concentration inhibits the microbial induced $CaCO_3$ generation. At low concentration, the microbial induced $CaCO_3$ is smaller and more evenly distributed in the soil.

2.3.4. Calcium Source and Its Concentration

The BP cells can be regarded as a formation site to produce $CaCO_3$ precipitation [67]. The MICP reaction process in Figure 1 indicated that the carbonate ions generated by the urea decomposition of BP will be continuously transported from the intracellular to the extracellular and meet with calcium ions in the environment. Therefore, the PH value of calcium sources and the concentration of calcium ions affect the rate, quality, and output of $CaCO_3$ crystals produced in the MICP process. Achal and Pan [68] compared the effects of four calcium sources on BP-induced $CaCO_3$ precipitation, and proposed that calcium chloride is a better calcium source in the MICP process, followed by calcium nitrate. Cheng et al. [69] took seawater as the bio-cementing fluid to conduct MICP process, and the results showed that the strength of samples maximized after 200 grouting times, since calcium ion concentration was low in seawater. The Ca^{2+} concentration is very important for the precipitation and precipitation efficiency of $CaCO_3$ crystals. Okwadha and Li [70] found that high concentrations of urea and $CaCl_2$ (more than 0.5 mol/L) reduces the deposition efficiency of calcium carbonate, and urea and $CaCl_2$ can improve the deposition efficiency of calcium carbonate at low concentrations (0.05–0.25 mol/L). From the current test results, a too low or too high calcium ion concentration cannot have the corresponding calcite yield. The calcium ion concentration should be optimized by laboratory tests to effectively bio-cement the test medium together by MICP calcite.

Based on the above reviews, the MICP technology results from the metabolic processes of bacteria including urease-producing bacteria, sulfate-reducing bacteria, denitrifying bacteria, and oxidizing bacteria. Although the type of bacteria and the reaction mechanism may be different in the MICP application, both the nutrient solution and the calcium source are necessary to generate $CaCO_3$ (calcite). Therefore, the MICP is mainly affected by the concentration of calcium ions and urea.

2.4. Application of MICP in Engineering

The MICP technology comes from the development of microbiology and geotechnical engineering, and is a novel technology with ecologically friendly and sustainable advantages [23]. Now, the technology has achieved good results in engineering applications, including soil treatment, seepage prevention, and cracking repair.

Many scholars have proved that MICP plays a significant role in soil treatment through experimental tests [71–73]. For example, compared with untreated expansive soil samples, it found that the swelling rate of soil samples after MICP mixing treatment was significantly reduced [25]. Sharaky et al. [74] found that the unconfined compression resistance of treated clay samples increased nearly three times through the MICP pressure grouting treatment test of clay. Yasuhara et al. [75] used MICP technology to strengthen the sand and premixed method. The so-called premixing method refers to the use of the mixing method and unconfined compressive strength test to make the reaction liquid better contact with the soil. Compared with other methods, the advantage of this method is that it can make $CaCO_3$ uniformly distributed in the soil.

The $CaCO_3$ generated by MICP technology can also fill the pores of the solidified soil and further reduce permeability to achieve the purpose of plugging [76]. A plugging test of MICP was conducted on fly ash modified concrete using giant bacillus [28]. The results suggested that the calcite precipitation between the aggregate and the bio-cement mortar was a primary reason for reducing the permeability of samples.

Liu et al. [77] also demonstrated that as the $CaCO_3$ precipitate is induced by MICP, it plays a role in bio-cementing soil samples, since it fills cracks among soil particles. Wiktor and Jonkers [78] used an energy dispersive spectrometer to observe the status of concrete cracks repaired by MICP, and their results showed that a crack of the width of 0.46 mm was completely healed after 100 days of repair, which was much larger than that of 0.18 mm in the control group. Algaifi et al. [79] found that the MICP has an advantage in the self-healing of cracks in bio-cement slurry by the theoretical model and microscopic test.

In general, the usage of MICP technology can effectively repair cracks, but it is undeniable that the time period for treatment and repair is long. Subsequent research should be carried out to develop a more efficient and faster MICP technology in the material source and reaction processes.

3. Unsaturated Soil

3.1. Characteristic of Unsaturated Soil

The unsaturated soil exists widely in nature since most of the soil above the groundwater level is in an unsaturated state. Due to the differences in the medium and molding method, the soil has special structure and stress state. There are two types of theory frames to describe mediums in unsaturated soil. Figure 3a considers the unsaturated soil as a three-phase soil, including a solid phase (soil particles and some bio-cementitious substances), a liquid phase (water and aqueous solution), and a gas phase (air and water vapor, etc.). However, with the further study of unsaturated soil mechanics, unsaturated soil is considered as a four phase structure [80]. In addition to the solid, liquid, and gas three-phases, the liquid gas interface is also added as an independent phase. This independent phase can also be called the bound water membrane, as shown in Figure 3b. The nature of the liquid gas interface is not only different from that of water, but also different from that of gas. It is an independent phase. This phase is called the shrink film in surface chemistry. The morphology of the water pores and gas pores of unsaturated soil is closely related to the water content (saturation) of unsaturated soil [81].

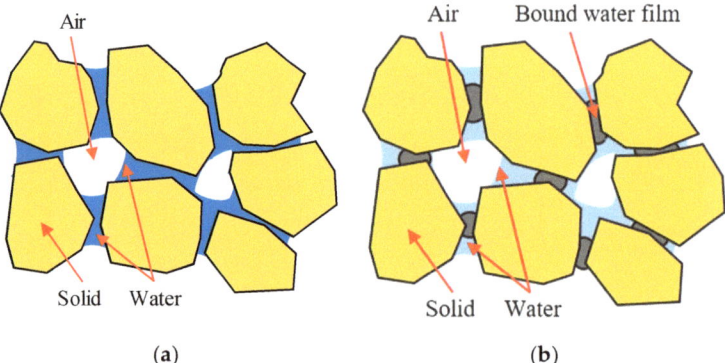

Figure 3. Schematic diagram of mediums in unsaturated soil: (**a**) solid liquid gas three phase system; (**b**) four phase diagram.

The unsaturated soil can be divided into four types: fully connected gas phase, partially connected gas phase, internally connected gas phase, and completely closed gas phase. When the gas phase in the pores exists in a fully connected way, the gas permeability has nothing to do with the water content. With the increase in the water content, the effective stress of the soil mass gradually reduces the volume of gas in the pores. A semi closed or closed bubble is formed, and the pore gas exists in a partially connected or internally connected state. At this time, the suction of soil decreases gradually, and the effective stress of soil should consider the influence of pore air pressure and pore bearing pressure, respectively. When the water content in the soil is very high, the gas phase is completely surrounded by liquid, small in volume, and can only flow with the liquid, which can be regarded as a two-phase system with air and water. At this time, the soil mass is basically saturated, the air permeability of the soil is very small, the suction is basically zero, and the effective stress of the soil mass is the same as that of the saturated soil.

Duan et al. [82] pointed out that the shape of unsaturated soil is more complex than that of saturated soil, and this complex medium composition has an important impact on the strength, deformation, and seepage of soil. Given that the structure of water pores and gas pores in unsaturated soil plays a key role in its engineering properties, the effect of the matrix suction and water content on the properties of unsaturated soil should be further studied.

3.2. Soil Water Characteristics of Unsaturated Soil

Matrix suction is the main reason why unsaturated soil is different from saturated soil, and it is also a key factor to reflect the mechanical properties of unsaturated soil [83]. The SWCC is a conceptual and interpretative tool to describe the soil water holding capacity when water content changes with suction [84]. SWCC defines the relationship between suction (matric suction), volume water content (θ) or saturation (Sr) of unsaturated soil. A typical SWCC is shown in Figure 4 (determined by the change in water content). The suction state (abscissa of the SWCC) can be expressed by the total suction of the soil water potential. In the high humidity state, the matrix suction ($u_a - u_w$) is used, and in the low humidity state, the total suction is used. Since there is little difference between the total suction value and the matrix suction in the low humidity state, the entire SWCC is often expressed by the matrix suction.

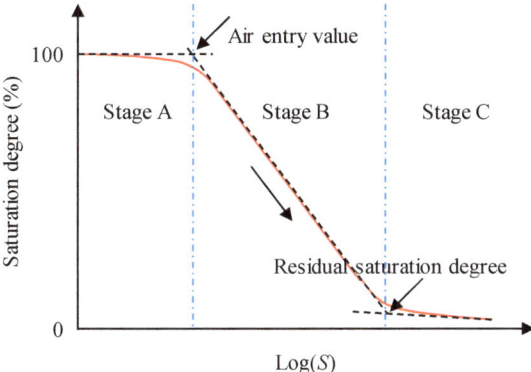

Figure 4. Typical water retention curve.

When the soil changes from a saturated state to a dry state, the distribution of solid, liquid, and gas phases in the soil will also change with the change in stress state. The relationship between these phases has different forms and affects the engineering properties of unsaturated soil. In some cases, the properties may be mainly related to the volume of the separated phase (such as water content), or to the continuity and curvature of the liquid phase (such as permeability coefficient, molecular diffusion), or to the gas phase (such as evaporation coefficient or diffusion coefficient). In other cases, the properties of interphase contact areas that control stress transmission (such as shear strength and volume change) or interphase mass transfer (such as chemical adsorption and volatilization) determine soil properties. The relationship between these phases can be derived from the data of the SWCC, which can then be used to estimate the parameters of unsaturated soil [85].

In the SWCC measure, the saturated water content A can be obtained by tests, while the residual water content B is often difficult to determine, influenced by the instrument precision and soil properties. Therefore, some SWCC models have been proposed to predict the result of the SWCC. The widely used expressions of SWCCs are displayed in Equations (11)–(13).

$$\ln \psi = a + b \ln \theta \tag{11}$$

$$\theta = \left[\frac{1}{1+q\psi^n}\right] \tag{12}$$

$$\theta = \left[\frac{1}{1+(a\psi)^n}\right]^m \tag{13}$$

where ψ is suction; θ is the volume water content; and a, b, q, n, and m are fitting parameters.

3.3. Mechanical Properties of Unsaturated Soil

SWCC is closely related to the strength of unsaturated soil and is an important tool to study the mechanical properties of unsaturated soil. More specifically, SWCC describes the relationship between the thermodynamic potential energy of pore water in soil and the amount of water absorbed by soil system. The SWCC shape of various soils is mainly affected by the properties of soil materials. Fredlund and Xing [86] carried out a large number of tests on different types of unsaturated soils, and showed that the main factors affecting SWCC are mineral composition, pore structure, stress state of soil particles, property of liquid, pore gas, etc.

Many researches have been performed to explore the relationship between water content and mechanical properties of unsaturated soil [87]. The shear strength formula of unsaturated soil can be proposed by Bishop effective stress. It is related to saturation S, which is closely related to SWCC. φ^b is also closely connected with different sections of SWCC, thus it can χ horn φ^b to simplify the test measurement and facilitate the engineering application.

Lamborn [88], based on the expanded micromechanical model, proposed the shear strength formula of unsaturated soil as follows:

$$\tau_f = c' + (\sigma - u_a)\tan(\varphi') + (u_a - u_w)\theta_w \tan(\varphi') \tag{14}$$

$$c_s = (u_a - u_w)\theta_w \tan(\varphi') \tag{15}$$

where τ_f is the shear strength of unsaturated soil; c' and φ' are effective cohesion and effective internal friction angle of saturated soil; $(u_a - u_w)$ is the matrix suction; $(\sigma - u_a)$ is the net normal stress; and θ_w is the volume water content.

Vanapalli et al. [89] developed a comment model for predicting the shear strength by SWCC, as shown in Equations (16) and (17).

$$\tau_f = c' + (\sigma - u_a)\tan(\varphi') + (u_a - u_w)\Theta^\kappa \tan(\varphi') \tag{16}$$

$$c_s = (u_a - u_w)\Theta^\kappa \tan(\varphi') \tag{17}$$

where Θ is the relative volume water content, $\Theta = \theta_w/\theta_s$; θ_s is the saturated volume water content; and κ is a fitting parameter.

Garven and Vanapalli [90] introduced the plasticity index I_p into the fitting model of the parameters κ, as follows:

$$\kappa = -0.0016 I_p^2 + 0.0975 I_p + 1 \tag{18}$$

Furthermore, the numerical simulation provides new insights into moisture and stress of unsaturated soil [91]. Liu et al. [92] analyzed the changes of the yield stress with the capillary cohesion between particles by simulating isotropic compression and biaxial shear tests. Jiang et al. [93] proposed two shear strength functions to reflect both the nonlinear characteristics of unsaturated soil and the influence of grain size distribution. Richefeu et al. [94] found that the density of the liquid bond is a decisive parameter for the overall cohesion of wet granular materials. Within the distance of the liquid bridge fracture, even at low water content, the uniform distribution of liquid will lead to the highest cohesion. Scholtès et al. [95] introduced the micromechanics study of unsaturated granular media in the state of the pendulum liquid bridge.

The resilient modulus (MR) of the subgrade is a key parameter to design pavement structures. The MR of unsaturated soil is dependent on the humidity state of subgrades [96]. In the range of low matric suction, the MR increases nonlinearly with the increase in matric suction; however, this trend cannot continue to a higher matric suction range [97]. Ceratti et al. [98] found that the dynamic resilient modulus of red clay increases with the increase in matrix suction when the matrix suction is less than 1 MPa, and the increase in dynamic resilient modulus is not evident when it exceeds this value. This phenomenon may be due to the larger wetted contact area between soil particles and the more significant contribution of matrix suction to soil strength and stiffness when it is in the low matrix suction range. In the higher matrix suction range, the water content is evidently less, and the wetted contact area of soil particles is limited, which limits the effect of matrix suction on the MR.

4. Influence of MICP on Properties of Unsaturated Soil

4.1. Microstructure of MICP Unsaturated Soil

The micro bonding form determines the mechanical properties such as macro strength, to a certain extent. At present, the main ways to study the microstructure of soil are X-ray diffraction analysis and scanning electron microscope (SEM) observation [99]. Xiao et al. [100] carried out SEM analysis to observe the changes in the product morphology and microstructure of MICP soil. Figure 5 presents the microscopic morphology of untreated sand soil using SEM. It shows that there are a few clay minerals attached to the surface of soil particles in the untreated soil, and no evident $CaCO_3$ crystals are found. The SEM results of MICP-treated sand soil are shown in Figure 6. It is evident that a large number of $CaCO_3$ crystals are generated in the shape of parallelepiped calcite, and the size of crystals is 1–10 μm. Cheng et al. [101] explored the relationship between the concentration of the bacteria solution and the concentration of the bio-cement solution in the MICP process from a microscopic perspective. Some of the $CaCO_3$ crystals were dispersed in the soil pores and played the role of filling pores among soil particles. It was proved that the $CaCO_3$ crystal played a role in bio-cementing soil particles.

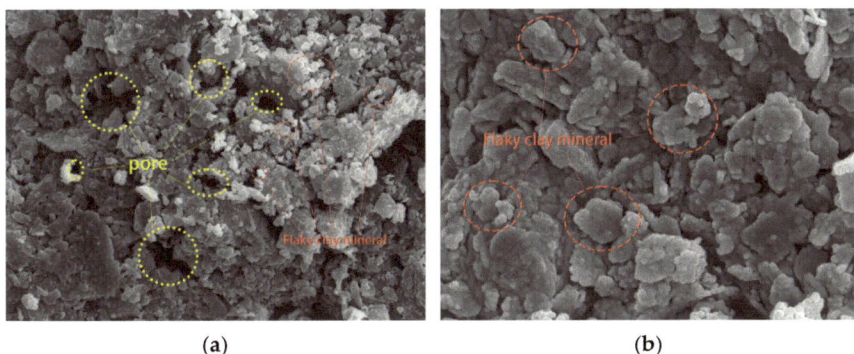

Figure 5. Micromorphology of untreated sand soil: (**a**) pore; (**b**) flaky clay mineral.

Elmaloglou et al. [102] observed the microscopic morphology of the MICP of the experimental device under different solid particle compositions. It was found that the $CaCO_3$ crystals mainly play the role of encapsulation and can evenly fill the internal pores of soil samples. The permeability of ordinary sand can be reduced by three orders of magnitude due to the $CaCO_3$ in the pores after treatment. Porter et al. [103] investigated the morphology of the sand column after curing with BP and found that $CaCO_3$ played a bio-cementing role in greatly improving the connection strength between sand grains. SEM results show that a layer of white and dense hardened shell formed on the surface of the modified soil sample, and the generated $CaCO_3$ presented a lamellar cleavage [104]. In addition, given that the solubility of $CaCO_3$ is small, the MICP process is very helpful to improve the water stability of soil.

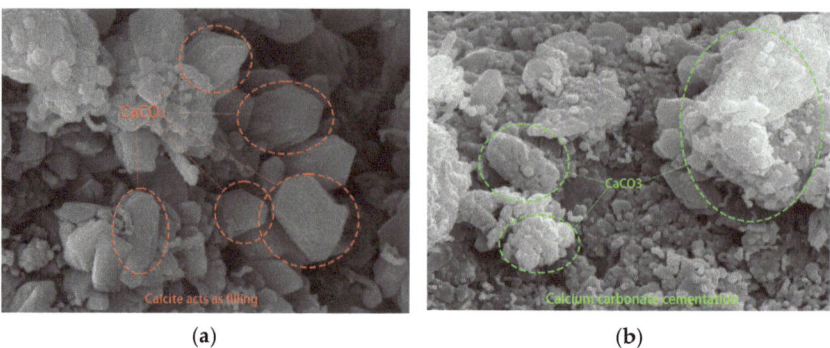

Figure 6. Micromorphology of sand soil after treatment: (**a**) filling pore; (**b**) cementation.

4.2. Permeability of MICP Unsaturated Soil

The $CaCO_3$ crystals deposited in the soil reduced the porosity (or porosity) of the soil. Phillips et al. [105] showed that the permeability of the rock cracks filled with biocementation decreased by about four orders of magnitude. The water pressure of the repaired rock cracks was about three times higher than that of original rock cracks. In addition, the field results showed that the permeability of the rock fractures decreased significantly within a few square meters around the injection well [106]. Wang et al. [107] suggested that the $CaCO_3$ precipitation generated divides the large voids in the soil sample into many small voids, which makes the internal distribution of the sample more uniform and reduces the seepage channel in the soil sample. Ferris et al. [108] found that the permeability of the surface decreased by 50% after 45 h, while the soil pores were almost completely blocked after 120 h. They concluded that the permeability coefficient of the soil sample was determined by the content of $CaCO_3$ in the soil sample. Figure 7 shows the schematic diagram of the MICP soil structure during water infiltration. There were three aspects resulting in the permeability decrease in soil: (1) the generated $CaCO_3$ crystals occupied the void space, which was caused by the reduction in porosity; (2) the interspace or pore throat was blocked by crystals; (3) the bioblockage caused by the production amount or related metabolites. Ivanov and Chu [15] found that some $CaCO_3$ precipitations do not contribute to contact bio-cementation, since these carbonates were either randomly crystallized on the soil particles or precipitated on the formed carbonate bridges. In conclusion, the permeability of soil samples was improved by MICP, since pores within soil were blocked by the formation of $CaCO_3$ crystals and the metabolism of microorganisms.

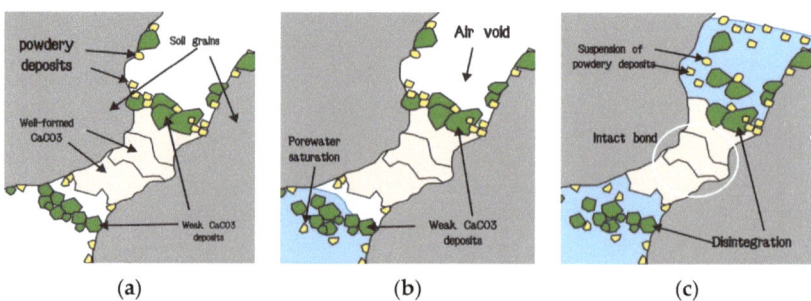

Figure 7. MICP soil infiltration diagram: (**a**) MICP soil diagram before wetting, (**b**) water infiltration into the pores, (**c**) saturated state.

4.3. Water Holding Capacity of MICP Unsaturated Soil

MICP technology mainly changes the water holding capacity of unsaturated soil by generating $CaCO_3$ precipitation to bio-cement soil particle pores [109]. Bo et al. [110] compared the water absorption of soil samples before and after treatment with MICP technology and found that the water absorption of soil samples after treatment is far greater than that of untreated soil. MICP treatment significantly improved the soil water holding capacity and anti-cracking capacity. Figure 8 shows the SWCCs of plain soil, and improved expansive soil are compared under the conditions of compactness of 90% and 95%, respectively. Results show that the pore will become smaller with the increase in compaction degree, thus changing the water holding capacity of soil samples. The SWCC of soil improved by MICP technology changes greatly compared with that of expansive soil before treatment, and the saturated water content of soil improved by MICP technology is higher than that of plain soil. It indicated that the volume of water content of the improved expansive soil changes less under the same matrix suction change, the water holding capacity was stronger, and the water stability was better.

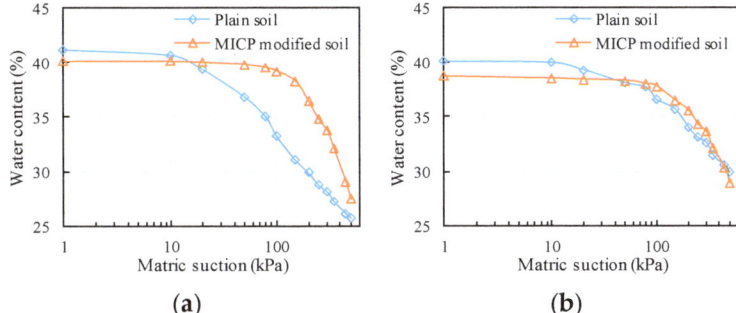

Figure 8. Comparison of SWCCs between plain soil and MICP improved soil with compactness of (**a**) 90% and (**b**) 95%.

4.4. Static Mechanical Behavior of MICP Unsaturated Soil

In the existing research, many scholars have studied the change in soil properties after improvements from various aspects. Wani and Mir [111] investigated the mechanical property of soft soil treated by MICP through unconfined compression tests and found that the strength of MICP soil increased by 3–3.5 times more than that before MICP process. Van Paassen [112] found that the compressive strength of MICP sand was exponential with the amount of $CaCO_3$. Khaleghi and Rowshanzamir [113] finally found that the compressive strength increased by 300 KPa and the permeability decreased significantly after the sand was solidified by MICP. Lian et al. [114] strengthened the sand column by biological grouting. Its unconfined compressive strength reached 1.91 MPa, and the permeability coefficient decreased by three orders of magnitude. Putra et al. [115] added magnesium to optimize the precipitation rate and generation content of $CaCO_3$ precipitation, and the test results showed that the maximum uniaxial compressive strength obtained from the treated sample was 0.6 MPa. Yang et al. [116] found that the improvement of hardness and expansibility of remolded biological treated sand was caused by the particle roughness of $CaCO_3$ coating. Compared with untreated sand, the shear strength was improved. Pakbaz et al. [117] concluded that the shear strength of the samples after MICP treatment increased by 44–86%, since the $CaCO_3$ coating improves the compactness and internal friction angle of the samples.

Chittoori et al. [118] demonstrated that the shear strength and unconfined compressive strength of expansive soil had been significantly improved after improvement by the MICP method; the plastic limit water content of expansive soil had increased; the liquid limit water content, plastic index, and expansion rate had decreased; and the microstructure had changed significantly. Therefore, MICP technology is an effective technical means to improve the compressive strength, shear strength, and free expansion rate of unsaturated soil through laboratory tests. Figure 9a is the change in shear stress with the normal stress of soil samples before and after MICP treatment. It shows that the shear strength of expansive soil after MICP treatment has been significantly improved, and the increase in cohesive force of expansive soil samples before and after treatment is far greater than the increase in the internal friction angle. Figure 9b presents the change in shear strength with the curing days of MICP. It can be seen that MICP technology will significantly improve the shear strength of soft soil, and its shear strength will gradually increase with the increase in curing days (3d–21d).

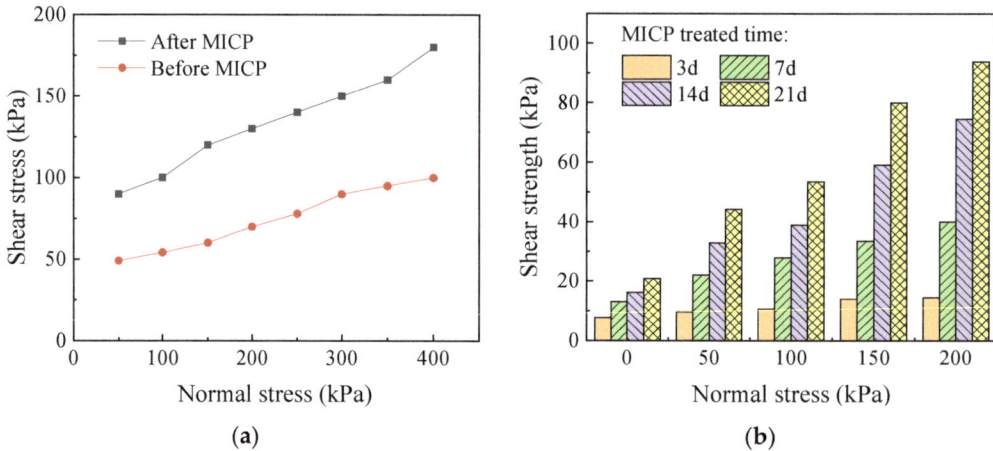

Figure 9. Curves of shear strength for (**a**) comparison between MICP-treated and untreated expansive soils; (**b**) different MICP-treated days.

4.5. Resilient Modulus of MICP Unsaturated Soil

The MR of soil describes the resilient deformation characteristics of soil subgrades under dynamic traffic loads [119]. In the MICP process, $CaCO_3$ precipitation bio-cemented the soil particles and filled the pores between soil particles, leading to the increase in coarse particle content and the decrease in fine particle content in soil. Therefore, with the decrease in fine particle content, the dynamic resilient modulus of improved soil increases. In order to achieve biological stability, Moradi et al. [120] adopted the microbial-induced calcite precipitation (MICP) method. The result shows that the elastic behavior of the treated fine-grained soil was similar to that of coarse grained soil, and the MR of treated soil evidently increased. Bing et al. [121] found that the sensitivity of the MR of the stabilized fine sand to confining pressure decreases when the content of $CaCO_3$ increases. The increase rate of the MR of the saturated stabilized soil is greater than that of the unsaturated stabilized soil. The reason for this structure is due to the improvement of MICP technology. The generated $CaCO_3$ crystals will block and bio-cement the soil particle pores, and the pore volume will decrease with the increase in $CaCO_3$ content. Soil particles can contact closely through $CaCO_3$ crystals, and the MR increases accordingly. Figure 10 shows the relationship between dynamic MR and $CaCO_3$ output. It can be seen from the figure that the output of $CaCO_3$ is closely related to the dynamic MR. The minimum value of dynamic MR increases by about 50% at most, and the maximum value increases by about 66.8%.

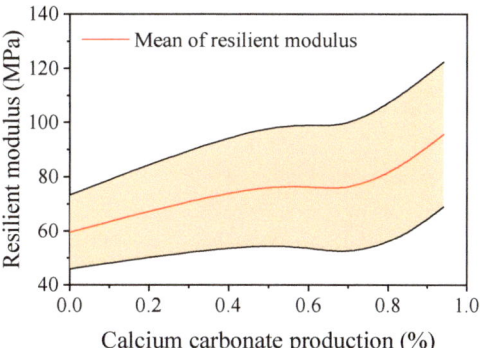

Figure 10. Dynamic resilient modulus with different CaCO$_3$ production.

After microbial improvement, it can be found that there is evident CaCO$_3$ precipitation between soil particles. CaCO$_3$ deposits on the surface of soil particles, forming bio-cement points and connecting soil particles. These bio-cements can be bio-cemented into larger aggregates, which enhances the connection ability between soil particles and improves the stability of soil particles. Therefore, the structural strength of the soil sample is improved, and the physical and mechanical properties of the soil sample are improved.

The comment model for predicting MR is shown in Equation (19) [122]. The dynamic resilient modulus of subgrade soil is affected by factors such as soil type, soil physical properties, stress state, and humidity state.

$$M_R = k_1 Pa \left(\frac{\theta}{P_a}\right)^{k_2} \left(\frac{\tau_{oct}}{P_a} + 1\right)^{k_3} \tag{19}$$

where M_R is the dynamic resilient modulus (MPa); Pa is the atmospheric pressure, and the reference value is 101.3 kPa; τ_{oct} is octahedral shear stress; and k_1, k_2, and k_3 are all model parameters, which meets $k_1 \geq 0$, $k_2 \geq 0$, $k_3 \leq 0$.

Combined with the research on the mechanical properties of MICP improved soil [123], the influence of soil type, water content, thousand density, and plasticity index on the dynamic resilient modulus of improved soil was analyzed. Previous studies found that the model parameters (k_1, k_2, k_3) decreased with the increase in water content. With the decrease in plasticity index, model parameter k_1 decreases and k_2 and k_3 increase. Similarly, $k_3 \leq 0$, and the influence of the plasticity index on k_1 and k_3 is different from that on k_2 [123]. Therefore, after improving by MICP method, the hydrophilicity of soil is weakened, and the variation range of water content is reduced. The plasticity index of soil is significantly reduced after improvement by the MICP method. Evidently, compared with the unmodified soil, the dynamic resilient modulus of the improved soil increases.

5. Conclusions and Suggestions

Microbial-induced calcite precipitation (MICP) is an emerging technology in recent years, which is widely applied in geotechnical and environmental engineering. This study reviews the microcosmic mechanism of MICP technology including the metabolic reactions of bacteria and changes of soil microstructures. Compared with temperatures and PH values, the nutrient solution concentrations and calcium ion concentrations are the main factors influencing the MICP process, since they are necessary for the survival of bacteria and CaCO$_3$ formation. MICP technology can improve the water stability of soft soil, since the soil particles will be covered by a layer of white and dense hardened shell of CaCO$_3$ after treatment, and the water solubility of CaCO$_3$ is very small. Meanwhile, the permeability of soil samples decreases after the MICP process, given that pores within soil are also filled by CaCO3 crystals. These phenomena result in the improvement of the mechanical properties of unsaturated soils. The shear strength of soft soil increases with the MICP curing times. Due to the bio-cementation process of soil particles, the structural strength of the soil sample is improved. Based on the prediction model of resilient modulus, since the fitting parameters increase when the water content decreases, the dynamic resilient modulus of the MICP-treated soil is larger than that of the untreated soil.

As far as the progress of MICP technology mentioned above, there are still some problems that need to be solved urgently.

(1) The current research focuses on the improvement in mechanical properties of sand soil treated by MICP, but long-term water stability is lacking attention. In addition, the effect of the MICP process on the acid resistance, frost resistance, erosion resistance, and the other durability's of unsaturated soil should be further studied.

(2) The diversity and complexities of actual environmental conditions requires the MICP technology to have a corresponding adaptability. Therefore, an environmental adaptability study should be performed for the application of MICP technology.

(3) Although MICP is more environmentally friendly than other treatment approaches of soil, there are still some harmful products emitted to the environment, for example, the ammonia produced by urea hydrolysis. Thus, subsequent research should be conducted in a more environmentally friendly direction or to find suitable methods to reduce the impact of the generated waste on the environment.

(4) In the existing literature, the methods of using MICP technology mainly include mixing, grouting, and soaking. However, both mixing and soaking are limited by construction conditions in engineering practice. Thus, further research work can be attempted in the field test section to find a better way to apply the MICP technology.

Author Contributions: Conceptualization, J.L.; methodology, W.B.; software, W.B.; validation, Z.L.; formal analysis, Y.Y.; investigation, W.B. and Z.L.; resources, J.L.; data curation, W.B. and Y.Y.; writing—original draft preparation, J.L., W.B., and Z.L.; writing—review and editing, J.L. and Y.Y.; visualization, Z.L.; supervision, J.L.; project administration, J.L.; funding acquisition, Y.Y. and J.L. All authors have read and agreed to the published version of the manuscript.

Funding: This research was funded by the National Natural Science Foundation of China, grant number 52208426; Special Financial Aid to the Post-Doctorate Research Project of Chongqing, grant number 2021XM1012; Open Fund of Key Laboratory of Special Environment Road Engineering of Hunan Province (Changsha University of Science and Technology), grant number kfj210501; the Key Research and Development Program of Hunan Province, grant number 2021SK2050; the Science and Technology Project of the Department of Transportation of Jiangxi Province, grant number 2022H0024.

Data Availability Statement: Not applicable.

Conflicts of Interest: The authors declare no conflict of interest.

References

1. Rao, S.M.; Revanasiddappa, K. Role of microfabric in matrix suction of residual soils. *Eng. Geol.* **2005**, *80*, 60–70.
2. Lu, N.; Likos, W.J. Suction Stress Characteristic Curve for Unsaturated Soil. *J. Geotech. Geoenviron. Eng.* **2006**, *132*, 131–142.
3. Zhang, Q.; Cui, Y.; Cao, Z.; Cai, Y.; Gu, C.; Wang, J. Experimental investigation into the shakedown state of unsaturated road base aggregate at various fine contents and matric suctions. *Eng. Geol.* **2022**, *306*, 106744.
4. Rahardjo, H.; Kim, Y.; Satyanaga, A. Role of unsaturated soil mechanics in geotechnical engineering. *Int. J. Geo-Eng.* **2019**, *10*, 8. [CrossRef]
5. Li, S.; Qin, C.; Chian, S.C.; Zhang, W. Another look at the stability of unsaturated soil slopes considering nonuniformity and nonlinearity. *Comput. Geotech.* **2022**, *148*, 104743.
6. Wu, L.; Cheng, P.; Zhou, J.; Li, S. Analytical solution of rainfall infiltration for vegetated slope in unsaturated soils considering hydro-mechanical effects. *Catena* **2022**, *217*, 106472.
7. Feng, R.; Fourtakas, G.; Rogers, B.D.; Lombardi, D. Two-phase fully-coupled smoothed particle hydrodynamics (SPH) model for unsaturated soils and its application to rainfall-induced slope collapse. *Comput. Geotech.* **2022**, *151*, 104964.
8. Chen, J.; Alonso, E.E.; Gu, C.; Cao, Z.; Cai, Y. Long term cyclic behavior of unsaturated granular soils. *Transp. Geotech.* **2018**, *17*, 48–55.
9. Green, R.A.; Mitchell, J.K. Energy-based evaluation and remediation of liquefiable soils. In *Geotechnical Engineering for Transportation Projects*; American Society of Civil Engineers: Los Angeles, CA, USA, 2004; pp. 1961–1970.

10. Li, J.; Qian, J.; He, C. Experimental analysis of cement-treated red sandstone coarse-grained soil and its microstructural evolution. *Case Stud. Constr. Mater.* **2022**, *17*, e01535.
11. Yao, Z.; Zhou, C.; Lin, Q.; Yao, K.; Satchithananthan, U.; Lee, F.H.; Tang, A.M.; Jiang, H.; Pan, Y.; Wang, S. Effect of dynamic compaction by multi-point tamping on the densification of sandy soil. *Comput. Geotech.* **2022**, *151*, 104949.
12. Jiang, H.; Qiu, X. Performance assessment of a newly developed and highly stable grouting material for a completely weathered granite dam foundation. *Constr. Build. Mater.* **2021**, *299*, 123956.
13. Alaloul, W.S.; Altaf, M.; Musarat, M.A.; Faisal Javed, M.; Mosavi, A. Systematic review of life cycle assessment and life cycle cost analysis for pavement and a case study. *Sustainability* **2021**, *13*, 4377.
14. Mitchell, J.K.; Santamarina, J.C. Biological considerations in geotechnical engineering. *J. Geotech. Geoenviron. Eng.* **2005**, *131*, 1222–1233.
15. Ivanov, V.; Chu, J. Applications of microorganisms to geotechnical engineering for bioclogging and biocementation of soil in situ. *Rev. Environ. Sci. Bio/Technol.* **2008**, *7*, 139–153.
16. Qian, X.; Fang, C.; Huang, M.; Achal, V. Characterization of fungal-mediated carbonate precipitation in the biomineralization of chromate and lead from an aqueous solution and soil. *J. Clean. Prod.* **2017**, *164*, 198–208.
17. Liu, B.; Zhu, C.; Tang, C.-S.; Xie, Y.-H.; Yin, L.-Y.; Cheng, Q.; Shi, B. Bio-remediation of desiccation cracking in clayey soils through microbially induced calcite precipitation (MICP). *Eng. Geol.* **2020**, *264*, 105389.
18. Achal, V.; Mukherjee, A.; Goyal, S.; Reddy, M. Corrosion prevention of reinforced concrete with microbial calcite precipitation. *ACI Mater. J.* **2012**, *109*, 157–164.
19. Warthmann, R.; van Lith, Y.; Vasconcelos, C.; McKenzie, J.A.; Karpoff, A.M. Bacterially induced dolomite precipitation in anoxic culture experiments. *Geology* **2000**, *28*, 1091–1094.
20. Van Paassen, L.A.; Daza, C.M.; Staal, M.; Sorokin, D.Y.; van der Zon, W.; van Loosdrecht, M.C. Potential soil reinforcement by biological denitrification. *Ecol. Eng.* **2010**, *36*, 168–175.
21. Bhutange, S.P.; Latkar, M. Microbially induced calcium carbonate precipitation in construction materials. *J. Mater. Civ. Eng.* **2020**, *32*, 03120001.
22. Carmona, J.P.S.F.; Oliveira, P.J.V.; Lemos, L.J.L. Biostabilization of a Sandy Soil Using Enzymatic Calcium Carbonate Precipitation. *Procedia Eng.* **2016**, *143*, 1301–1308.
23. Mujah, D.; Shahin, M.A.; Cheng, L. State-of-the-Art Review of Biocementation by Microbially Induced Calcite Precipitation (MICP) for Soil Stabilization. *Geomicrobiol. J.* **2017**, *34*, 524–537.
24. Chen, F.; Deng, C.; Song, W.; Zhang, D.; Misned, F.A.A.; Mortuza, M.G.; Gadd, G.M.; Pan, X. Biostabilization of Desert Sands Using Bacterially Induced Calcite Precipitation. *Geomicrobiol. J.* **2016**, *33*, 243–249.
25. Martinez, B.C.; DeJong, J.T.; Ginn, T.R.; Montoya, B.M.; Barkouki, T.H.; Hunt, C.; Tanyu, B.; Major, D. Experimental Optimization of Microbial-Induced Carbonate Precipitation for Soil Improvement. *J. Geotech. Geoenviron. Eng.* **2013**, *139*, 587–598.
26. Salifu, E.; MacLachlan, E.; Iyer, K.R.; Knapp, C.W.; Tarantino, A. Application of microbially induced calcite precipitation in erosion mitigation and stabilisation of sandy soil foreshore slopes: A preliminary investigation. *Eng. Geol.* **2016**, *201*, 96–105.
27. Sharma, A.; Ramkrishnan, R. Study on effect of Microbial Induced Calcite Precipitates on strength of fine grained soils. *Perspect. Sci.* **2016**, *8*, 198–202.
28. Achal, V.; Pan, X.; Özyurt, N. Improved strength and durability of fly ash-amended concrete by microbial calcite precipitation. *Ecol. Eng.* **2011**, *37*, 554–559.
29. Fang, C.; Kumari, D.; Zhu, X.; Achal, V. Role of fungal-mediated mineralization in biocementation of sand and its improved compressive strength. *Int. Biodeterior. Biodegrad.* **2018**, *133*, 216–220.
30. Mitchell, A.C.; Dideriksen, K.; Spangler, L.H.; Cunningham, A.B.; Gerlach, R. Microbially enhanced carbon capture and storage by mineral-trapping and solubility-trapping. *Environ. Sci. Technol.* **2010**, *44*, 5270–5276.
31. Umar, M.; Kassim, K.A.; Chiet, K.T.P. Biological process of soil improvement in civil engineering: A review. *J. Rock Mech. Geotech. Eng.* **2016**, *8*, 767–774.
32. Patil, M.; Dalal, P.H.; Shreedhar, S.; Dave, T.N.; Iyer, K.K.R. Biostabilization techniques and applications in Civil Engineering: State-of-the-Art. *Constr. Build. Mater.* **2021**, *309*, 125098.
33. Erşan, Y.Ç.; De Belie, N.; Boon, N. Microbially induced CaCO3 precipitation through denitrification: An optimization study in minimal nutrient environment. *Biochem. Eng. J.* **2015**, *101*, 108–118.
34. Pham, V.P.; Nakano, A.; Van Der Star, W.R.; Heimovaara, T.J.; Van Paassen, L.A. Applying MICP by denitrification in soils: A process analysis. *Environ. Geotech.* **2016**, *5*, 79–93.
35. Hamed Khodadadi, T.; Kavazanjian, E.; van Paassen, L.; DeJong, J. Bio-grout materials: A review. *Grouting* **2017**, *2017*, 1–12.
36. Tsai, C.-P.; Ye, J.-H.; Ko, C.-H.; Lin, Y.-R. An Experimental Investigation of Microbial-Induced Carbonate Precipitation on Mitigating Beach Erosion. *Sustainability* **2022**, *14*, 2513.
37. Hammes, F. Key roles of pH and calcium metabolism in microbial carbonate precipitation. *Rev. Environ. Sci. Biotechnol.* **2002**, *1*, 3–7.
38. Achal, V.; Mukherjee, A.; Sudhakara Reddy, M. Microbial Concrete way to enhance the durability of building structures. *Cell* **2011**, *2*, 2.
39. Naveed, M.; Duan, J.; Uddin, S.; Suleman, M.; Hui, Y.; Li, H. Application of microbially induced calcium carbonate precipitation with urea hydrolysis to improve the mechanical properties of soil. *Ecol. Eng.* **2020**, *153*, 105885.

40. Chuo, S.C.; Mohamed, S.F.; Mohd Setapar, S.H.; Ahmad, A.; Jawaid, M.; Wani, W.A.; Yaqoob, A.A.; Mohamad Ibrahim, M.N. Insights into the current trends in the utilization of bacteria for microbially induced calcium carbonate precipitation. *Materials* **2020**, *13*, 4993.
41. DeJong, J.T.; Mortensen, B.M.; Martinez, B.C.; Nelson, D.C. Bio-mediated soil improvement. *Ecol. Eng.* **2008**, *36*, 197–210.
42. Cheng, L.; Cord-Ruwisch, R.; Shahin, M.A. Cementation of sand soil by microbially induced calcite precipitation at various degrees of saturation. *Can. Geotech. J.* **2013**, *50*, 81–90.
43. Konhauser, K.O. *Introduction to Geomicrobiology*; Blackwell Publishing Company: Malden, MA, USA, 2009.
44. Achal, V.; Pan, X.; Zhang, D. Remediation of copper-contaminated soil by Kocuria flava CR1, based on microbially induced calcite precipitation. *Ecol. Eng.* **2011**, *37*, 1601–1605.
45. Meng, C.; Huihui, X.; Suying, L. Review on Research Progress of MICP Technology. *J. Phys. Conf. Ser.* **2022**, *2185*, 012054.
46. Qabany, A.A.; Soga, K.; Santamarina, C. Factors Affecting Efficiency of Microbially Induced Calcite Precipitation. *J. Geotech. Geoenviron. Eng.* **2012**, *138*, 992–1001.
47. DeJong, J.T.; Soga, K.; Banwart, S.A.; Whalley, W.R.; Ginn, T.R.; Nelson, D.C.; Mortensen, B.M.; Martinez, B.C.; Barkouki, T. Soil engineering in vivo: Harnessing natural biogeochemical systems for sustainable, multi-functional engineering solutions. *J. R. Soc. Interface* **2011**, *8*, 1–15.
48. Mortensen, B.; Haber, M.; DeJong, J.; Caslake, L.; Nelson, D. Effects of environmental factors on microbial induced calcium carbonate precipitation. *J. Appl. Microbiol.* **2011**, *111*, 338–349.
49. Sotoudehfar, A.R.; Sadeghi, M.M.; Mokhtari, E.; Shafiei, F. Assessment of the Parameters Influencing Microbial Calcite Precipitation in Injection Experiments Using Taguchi Methodology. *Geomicrobiol. J.* **2016**, *33*, 163–172.
50. Mitchell, A.C.; Ferris, F.G. The coprecipitation of Sr into calcite precipitates induced by bacterial ureolysis in artificial groundwater: Temperature and kinetic dependence. *Geochim. Cosmochim. Acta* **2005**, *69*, 4199–4210.
51. Sun, X.; Miao, L.; Tong, T.; Wang, C. Study of the effect of temperature on microbially induced carbonate precipitation. *Acta Geotech.* **2019**, *14*, 627–638.
52. Yang, Y.; Chu, J.; Xiao, Y.; Liu, H.; Cheng, L. Seepage control in sand using bioslurry. *Constr. Build. Mater.* **2019**, *212*, 342–349.
53. Martinez, B.; Barkouki, T.; DeJong, J.; Ginn, T. Upscaling microbial induced calcite precipitation in 0.5 m columns: Experimental and modeling results. In *Geo-Frontiers 2011: Advances in Geotechnical Engineering*; American Society of Civil Engineers: Los Angeles, CA, USA, 2011; pp. 4049–4059.
54. Kim, G.; Kim, J.; Youn, H. Effect of Temperature, pH, and Reaction Duration on Microbially Induced Calcite Precipitation. *Appl. Sci.* **2018**, *8*, 1277.
55. Xiao, Y.; Wang, Y.; Wang, S.; Evans, T.M.; Stuedlein, A.W.; Chu, J.; Zhao, C.; Wu, H.; Liu, H. Homogeneity and mechanical behaviors of sands improved by a temperature-controlled one-phase MICP method. *Acta Geotech.* **2021**, *16*, 1417–1427.
56. Brock, T.D.; Madigan, M.T.; Martinko, J.M.; Parker, J. *Brock Biology of Microorganisms*; Prentice-Hall: Upper Saddle River, NJ, USA, 2003.
57. Gomez, M.G.; Martinez, B.C.; DeJong, J.T.; Hunt, C.E.; deVlaming, L.A.; Major, D.W.; Dworatzek, S.M. Field-scale bio-cementation tests to improve sands. *Proc. Inst. Civ. Eng.-Ground Improv.* **2015**, *168*, 206–216.
58. Nemati, M.; Voordouw, G. Modification of porous media permeability, using calcium carbonate produced enzymatically in situ. *Enzym. Microb. Technol.* **2003**, *33*, 635–642.
59. Cui, M.-J.; Zheng, J.-J.; Zhang, R.-J.; Lai, H.-J.; Zhang, J. Influence of cementation level on the strength behaviour of bio-cemented sand. *Acta Geotech.* **2017**, *12*, 971–986.
60. Cheng, L.; Cord-Ruwisch, R. In situ soil cementation with ureolytic bacteria by surface percolation. *Ecol. Eng.* **2012**, *42*, 64–72.
61. Mujah, D.; Cheng, L.; Shahin, M.A. Microstructural and Geomechanical Study on Biocemented Sand for Optimization of MICP Process. *J. Mater. Civ. Eng.* **2019**, *31*, 04019025.
62. Wong, L.S. Microbial cementation of ureolytic bacteria from the genus Bacillus: A review of the bacterial application on cement-based materials for cleaner production. *J. Clean. Prod.* **2015**, *93*, 5–17.
63. Wen, K.; Li, Y.; Liu, S.; Bu, C.; Li, L. Evaluation of MICP treatment through EC and pH tests in urea hydrolysis process. *Environ. Geotech.* **2019**, *8*, 274–281.
64. Zhao, Q. Experimental Study on Soil Improvement Using Microbial Induced Calcite Precipitation (MICP). Ph.D. Thesis, China University of Geosciences, Wuhan, China, 2014.
65. Soon, N.W.; Lee, L.M.; Khun, T.C.; Ling, H.S. Factors affecting improvement in engineering properties of residual soil through microbial-induced calcite precipitation. *J. Geotech. Geoenviron. Eng.* **2014**, *140*, 04014006.
66. Whiffin, V.S.; Paassen, L.A.v.; Harkes, M.P. Microbial Carbonate Precipitation as a Soil Improvement Technique. *Geomicrobiol. J.* **2007**, *24*, 417–423.
67. Ferris, F.; Fyfe, W.; Beveridge, T. Bacteria as nucleation sites for authigenic minerals in a metal-contaminated lake sediment. *Chem. Geol.* **1987**, *63*, 225–232.
68. Achal, V.; Pan, X. Influence of calcium sources on microbially induced calcium carbonate precipitation by Bacillus sp. CR2. *Appl. Biochem. Biotechnol.* **2014**, *173*, 307–317.
69. Cheng, L.; Shahin, M.; Cord-Ruwisch, R. Bio-cementation of sandy soil using microbially induced carbonate precipitation for marine environments. *Géotechnique* **2014**, *64*, 1010–1013.
70. Okwadha, G.D.O.; Li, J. Optimum conditions for microbial carbonate precipitation. *Chemosphere* **2010**, *81*, 1143–1148.

71. Chahal, N.; Rajor, A.; Siddique, R. Calcium carbonate precipitation by different bacterial strains. *Afr. J. Biotechnol.* **2011**, *10*, 8359–8372.
72. Shanahan, C.; Montoya, B. Strengthening coastal sand dunes using microbial-induced calcite precipitation. In Proceedings of the Geo-Congress 2014: Geo-Characterization and Modeling for Sustainability, Atlanta, GA, USA, 23–26 February 2014; pp. 1683–1692.
73. Montoya, B.M.; DeJong, J.T. Stress-Strain Behavior of Sands Cemented by Microbially Induced Calcite Precipitation. *J. Geotech. Geoenviron. Eng.* **2015**, *141*, 04015019.
74. Sharaky, A.M.; Mohamed, N.S.; Elmashad, M.E.; Shredah, N.M. Application of microbial biocementation to improve the physico-mechanical properties of sandy soil. *Constr. Build. Mater.* **2018**, *190*, 861–869.
75. Yasuhara, H.; Neupane, D.; Hayashi, K.; Okamura, M. Experiments and predictions of physical properties of sand cemented by enzymatically-induced carbonate precipitation. *Soils Found.* **2012**, *52*, 539–549.
76. Sun, X.; Miao, L.; Wang, C. Experimental study on calcium carbonate precipitates induced by Bacillus megaterium. In Proceedings of the China-Europe conference on Geotechnical Engineering, Vienna, Austria, 13–16 August 2016; pp. 834–837.
77. Liu, S.; Wen, K.; Armwood, C.; Bu, C.; Li, C.; Amini, F.; Li, L. Enhancement of MICP-treated sandy soils against environmental deterioration. *J. Mater. Civ. Eng.* **2019**, *31*, 04019294.
78. Wiktor, V.; Jonkers, H.M. Quantification of crack-healing in novel bacteria-based self-healing concrete. *Cem. Concr. Compos.* **2011**, *33*, 763–770.
79. Algaifi, H.A.; Bakar, S.A.; Sam, A.R.M.; Abidin, A.R.Z.; Shahir, S.; AL-Towayti, W.A.H. Numerical modeling for crack self-healing concrete by microbial calcium carbonate. *Constr. Build. Mater.* **2018**, *189*, 816–824.
80. Seltacho, S.; Sriboonlue, V.; Suwanang, N.; Wiriyakitnateekul, W.; Hammecker, C. *Quantification and Modeling of Water Flow in Sandy Soils in Northeast Thailand*; CRC Press: London, UK, 2013.
81. Karube, D.; Kawai, K. The role of pore water in the mechanical behavior of unsaturated soils. *Geotech. Geol. Eng.* **2001**, *19*, 211–241.
82. Duan, X.; Zeng, L.; Sun, X. Generalized stress framework for unsaturated soil: Demonstration and discussion. *Acta Geotech.* **2019**, *14*, 1459–1481.
83. Yao, Y.; Li, J.; Xiao, Z.; Xiao, H. Soil-Water characteristics and creep deformation of unsaturated expansive subgrade soil: Experimental test and simulation. *Front. Earth Sci.* **2021**, *9*, 1141.
84. Vanapalli, S.; Fredlund, D.; Pufahl, D. Influence of soil structure and stress history on the soil-water characteristics of a compacted till. *Géotechnique* **2001**, *51*, 573–576.
85. Yao, Y.; Ni, J.; Li, J. Stress-dependent water retention of granite residual soil and its implications for ground settlement. *Comput. Geotech.* **2021**, *129*, 103835.
86. Fredlund, D.G.; Xing, A. Equations for the soil-water characteristic curve. *Can. Geotech. J.* **1994**, *31*, 521–532.
87. Yao, Y.; Li, J.; Ni, J.; Liang, C.; Zhang, A. Effects of gravel content and shape on shear behaviour of soil-rock mixture: Experiment and DEM modelling. *Comput. Geotech.* **2022**, *141*, 104476.
88. Lamborn, M.J. *A Micromechanical Approach to Modeling Partly Saturated Soils*; Texas A&M University: College Station, TX, USA, 1986.
89. Vanapalli, S.; Fredlund, D.; Pufahl, D.; Clifton, A. Model for the prediction of shear strength with respect to soil suction. *Can. Geotech. J.* **1996**, *33*, 379–392.
90. Garven, E.; Vanapalli, S. Evaluation of empirical procedures for predicting the shear strength of unsaturated soils. In Proceedings of the Fourth International Conference on Unsaturated Soils, Carefree, AZ, USA, 2–6 April 2006; pp. 2570–2592.
91. Li, J.; Zhang, J.; Yang, X.; Zhang, A.; Yu, M. Monte Carlo simulations of deformation behaviour of unbound granular materials based on a real aggregate library. *Int. J. Pavement Eng.* **2023**, *24*, 2165650. [CrossRef]
92. Liu, S.H.; Sun, D.A.; Wang, Y. Numerical study of soil collapse behavior by discrete element modelling. *Comput. Geotech.* **2003**, *30*, 399–408.
93. Jiang, M.; Leroueil, S.; Konrad, J. Insight into shear strength functions of unsaturated granulates by DEM analyses. *Comput. Geotech.* **2004**, *31*, 473–489.
94. Richefeu, V.; Youssoufi, M.S.E.; Peyroux, R.; Radjaï, F. A model of capillary cohesion for numerical simulations of 3D polydisperse granular media. *Int. J. Numer. Anal. Methods Geomech.* **2008**, *32*, 1365–1383.
95. Scholtès, L.; Hicher, P.Y.; Nicot, F.; Chareyre, B.; Darve, F. On the capillary stress tensor in wet granular materials. *Int. J. Numer. Anal. Methods Geomech.* **2009**, *33*, 1289–1313.
96. Peng, J.; Zhang, J.; Li, J.; Yao, Y.; Zhang, A. Modeling humidity and stress-dependent subgrade soils in flexible pavements. *Comput. Geotech.* **2020**, *120*, 103413.
97. Yao, Y.; Zheng, J.; Zhang, J.; Peng, J.; Li, J. Model for predicting resilient modulus of unsaturated subgrade soils in south China. *KSCE J. Civ. Eng.* **2018**, *22*, 2089–2098.
98. Ceratti, A.J.; Gehling, W.Y.Y.; Núñez, W.P. Seasonal Variations of a Subgrade Soil Resilient Modulus in Southern Brazil. *Transp. Res. Rec.* **2004**, *1874*, 165–173.
99. Martínez-Nistal, A.; Veniale, F.; Setti, M.; Cotecchia, F. A scanning electron microscopy image processing method for quantifying fabric orientation of clay geomaterials. *Appl. Clay Sci.* **1999**, *14*, 235–243.
100. Xiao, Y.; Zhao, C.; Sun, Y.; Wang, S.; Wu, H.; Chen, H.; Liu, H. Compression behavior of MICP-treated sand with various gradations. *Acta Geotech.* **2021**, *16*, 1391–1400.

101. Cheng, L.; Qian, C.; Wang, R.; Wang, J. Study on the mechanism of calcium carbonate formation induced by carbonate-mineralization microbe. *Acta Chim. Sin.* **2007**, *65*, 2133–2138.
102. Elmaloglou, A.; Terzis, D.; De Anna, P.; Laloui, L. Microfluidic study in a meter-long reactive path reveals how the medium's structural heterogeneity shapes MICP-induced biocementation. *Sci. Rep.* **2022**, *12*, 1–16.
103. Porter, H.; Dhami, N.K.; Mukherjee, A. Synergistic chemical and microbial cementation for stabilization of aggregates. *Cem. Concr. Compos.* **2017**, *83*, 160–170.
104. De Muynck, W.; Debrouwer, D.; De Belie, N.; Verstraete, W. Bacterial carbonate precipitation improves the durability of cementitious materials. *Cem. Concr. Res.* **2008**, *38*, 1005–1014.
105. Phillips, A.J.; Lauchnor, E.G.; Eldring, J.; Esposito, R.A.; Mitchell, A.C.; Gerlach, R.; Cunningham, A.B.; Spangler, L.H. Potential CO_2 leakage reduction through biofilm-induced calcium carbonate precipitation. *Environ. Sci. Technol.* **2013**, *47*, 142–149.
106. Cuthbert, M.O.; McMillan, L.A.; Handley-Sidhu, S.; Riley, M.S.; Tobler, D.J.; Phoenix, V.R. A field and modeling study of fractured rock permeability reduction using microbially induced calcite precipitation. *Environ. Sci. Technol.* **2013**, *47*, 13637–13643.
107. Wang, J.; Long, Y.; Zhao, Y.; Pan, W.; Qu, J.; Yang, T.; Huang, X.; Liu, X.; Xu, N. Laboratory Experiment on Formation of MICP Horizontal Seepage-Reducing Body in Confined Aquifer for Deep Excavation. *Appl. Sci.* **2023**, *13*, 104.
108. Ferris, F.; Stehmeier, L.; Kantzas, A.; Mourits, F. Bacteriogenic mineral plugging. *J. Can. Pet. Technol.* **1997**, *36*, PETSOC-97-09-07.
109. Gowthaman, S.; Nakashima, K.; Kawasaki, S. Effect of wetting and drying cycles on the durability of bio-cemented soil of expressway slope. *Int. J. Environ. Sci. Technol.* **2022**, *19*, 2309–2322.
110. Bo, L.; ChaoSheng, T.; XiaoHua, P.; Cheng, Z.; YaoJia, C.; JinJian, X.; Bin, S. Potential Drought Mitigation Through Microbial Induced Calcite Precipitation-MICP. *Water Resour. Res.* **2021**, *57*, e2020WR029434.
111. Wani, K.M.N.S.; Mir, B.A. Effect of Microbial Stabilization on the Unconfined Compressive Strength and Bearing Capacity of Weak Soils. *Transp. Infrastruct. Geotechnol.* **2021**, *8*, 59–87.
112. Van Paassen, L.A. *Biogrout, Ground Improvement by Microbial Induced Carbonate Precipitation*; Delft University of Technology: Delft, The Netherlands, 2009.
113. Khaleghi, M.; Rowshanzamir, M.A. Biologic improvement of a sandy soil using single and mixed cultures: A comparison study. *Soil Tillage Res.* **2019**, *186*, 112–119.
114. Lian, J.; Xu, H.; He, X.; Yan, Y.; Fu, D.; Yan, S.; Qi, H. Biogrouting of hydraulic fill fine sands for reclamation projects. *Mar. Georesources Geotechnol.* **2018**, *37*, 212–222.
115. Putra, H.; Yasuhara, H.; Kinoshita, N.; Neupane, D.; Lu, C.-W. Effect of Magnesium as Substitute Material in Enzyme-Mediated Calcite Precipitation for Soil-Improvement Technique. *Front. Bioeng. Biotechnol.* **2016**, *4*, 37.
116. Yang, X.; Xiang, H.; Musharraf, Z.; Guoliang, M.; Chang, Z. Review of Strength Improvements of Biocemented Soils. *Int. J. Geomech.* **2022**, *22*, 03122001.
117. Pakbaz, M.S.; Behzadipour, H.; Ghezelbash, G.R. Evaluation of Shear Strength Parameters of Sandy Soils upon Microbial Treatment. *Geomicrobiol. J.* **2018**, *35*, 721–726.
118. Chittoori, B.C.; Burbank, M.; Islam, M.T. Evaluating the effectiveness of soil-native bacteria in precipitating calcite to stabilize expansive soils. In *IFCEE 2018*; American Society of Civil Engineers: Los Angeles, CA, USA, 2018; pp. 59–68.
119. Li, J.; Zhang, J.; Zhang, A.; Peng, J. Evaluation on deformation behavior of granular base material during repeated load triaxial testing by discrete-element method. *Int. J. Geomech.* **2022**, *22*, 04022210.
120. Moradi, G.; Shafaghatian, S.; Katebi, H. Effect of Chemical and Biological Stabilization on the Resilient Modulus of Clay Subgrade Soil. *Int. J. Pavement Res. Technol.* **2022**, *15*, 415–432.
121. Bing, Y.; Hui, L.; Haozhen, L.; Nailing, L.; Guibao, M.; Hengji, Z. Experimental investigation on the mechanical and hydraulic properties of urease stabilized fine sand for fully permeable pavement. *Int. J. Transp. Sci. Technol.* **2020**, *11*, 60–71.
122. Program, N.C.H.R. Guide for mechanistic-empirical design of new and rehabilitated pavement structures. In Proceedings of the 2004 Annual Conference of the Transportation Association of Canada, Quebec City, QC, Canada, 19–22 September 2004.
123. Zhang, J.; Peng, J.; Zeng, L.; Li, J.; Li, F. Rapid estimation of resilient modulus of subgrade soils using performance-related soil properties. *Int. J. Pavement Eng.* **2021**, *22*, 732–739.

Disclaimer/Publisher's Note: The statements, opinions and data contained in all publications are solely those of the individual author(s) and contributor(s) and not of MDPI and/or the editor(s). MDPI and/or the editor(s) disclaim responsibility for any injury to people or property resulting from any ideas, methods, instructions or products referred to in the content.

MDPI AG
Grosspeteranlage 5
4052 Basel
Switzerland
Tel.: +41 61 683 77 34

Applied Sciences Editorial Office
E-mail: applsci@mdpi.com
www.mdpi.com/journal/applsci

Disclaimer/Publisher's Note: The title and front matter of this reprint are at the discretion of the Guest Editors. The publisher is not responsible for their content or any associated concerns. The statements, opinions and data contained in all individual articles are solely those of the individual Editors and contributors and not of MDPI. MDPI disclaims responsibility for any injury to people or property resulting from any ideas, methods, instructions or products referred to in the content.

www.ingramcontent.com/pod-product-compliance
Lightning Source LLC
LaVergne TN
LVHW072314090526
838202LV00019B/2280